iOS 6 Recipes

A Problem-Solution Approach

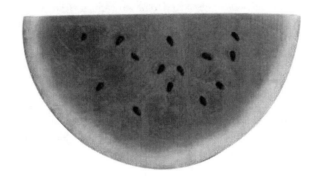

Hans-Eric Grönlund
Colin Francis
Shawn Grimes

Apress

iOS 6 Recipes

ISBN-13 (pbk): 978-1-4302-4599-5

ISBN-13 (electronic): 978-1-4302-4600-8

President and Publisher: Paul Manning
Lead Editor: Steve Anglin
Developmental Editor: Douglas Pundick
Technical Reviewer: Anselm Bradford
Editorial Board: Steve Anglin, Ewan Buckingham, Gary Cornell, Louise Corrigan, Morgan Ertel, Jonathan Gennick, Jonathan Hassell, Robert Hutchinson, Michelle Lowman, James Markham, Matthew Moodie, Jeff Olson, Jeffrey Pepper, Douglas Pundick, Ben Renow-Clarke, Dominic Shakeshaft, Gwenan Spearing, Matt Wade, Tom Welsh
Coordinating Editor: Anamika Panchoo
Copy Editor: Linda Seifert
Compositor: SPi Global
Indexer: SPi Global
Artist: SPi Global
Cover Designer: Anna Ishchenko

Distributed to the book trade worldwide by Springer Science+Business Media New York, 233 Spring Street, 6th Floor, New York, NY 10013. Phone 1-800-SPRINGER, fax (201) 348-4505, e-mail orders-ny@springer-sbm.com, or visit www.springeronline.com.

For information on translations, please e-mail rights@apress.com, or visit www.apress.com.

Apress and friends of ED books may be purchased in bulk for academic, corporate, or promotional use. eBook versions and licenses are also available for most titles. For more information, reference our Special Bulk Sales–eBook Licensing web page at www.apress.com/bulk-sales.

Any source code or other supplementary materials referenced by the author in this text is available to readers at www.apress.com. For detailed information about how to locate your book's source code, go to www.apress.com/source-code.

I dedicate this book to my wife, Esra, who supports my whimsical endeavors.

—Hans-Eric Grönlund

Contents at a Glance

Contents

About the Authors

Hans-Eric Grönlund has developed software professionally since 1990. He's currently an employee at Knowit, a leading Scandinavian IT Consultancy company, where he helps teams develop software with agile methods.

Software development is not only Hans-Eric's profession; it's also his hobby. In his spare time, he has taught himself how to write programs in many different languages on various platforms. His latest passion, obviously, is Objective-C on iOS. Hans-Eric's Twitter ID is @hansEricG.

Colin Francis is an iOS developer originally from Maryland. After studying iOS development with the assistance of Shawn Grimes, the two of them authored iOS 5 Recipes (Apress). He currently lives in Miami, where he works primarily on music-based applications for iOS.

Shawn Grimes and his wife, Stephanie, run Campfire Apps, LLC, a mobile app development company focused on apps for children and families. Together, they have started the APPlied Club program which teaches mobile app development to high school students. Shawn is active in the Baltimore, Maryland development scene and co-runs the Baltimore Mobile Developers group with Chris Stone.

About the Technical Reviewer

Anselm Bradford lectures in digital media at AUT University in New Zealand. In 2013 he will be joining Code for America as a 2013 fellow.

Additionally, he has worked with Apress/friends of ED, O'Reilly Media, Peachpit Press, and Lonely Planet on books in the areas of visual communication, web, and interactive media. He has authorship credit on HTML5 Mastery and CSS3 Solutions (Apress). He may be found on Twitter @anselmbradford, and he occasionally blogs at AnselmBradford.com.

Acknowledgments

I'd like to start by thanking Shawn Grimes and Colin Francis, who wrote the iOS 5 version of this book. Without their great effort, I'd still be struggling with it.

I also must thank Matthew Campbell, who helped me get over the Xcode threshold and get rid of the initial confusion; anyone who has made the transition from other IDEs knows that this can be, well, tricky.

Additionally, I'd like to send a big thank you to the Apress team without whose help this book would not have been possible. Anamika Panchoo for keeping me on track at all times, Douglas Pundick and Anselm Bradford for their extremely helpful technical reviews, and last but not least, Linda Seifert, for correcting my language.

Finally, I'm inclined to thank my wife, Esra, my son, Måns, and my daughter, Aylin, to whom I've been more or less inaccessible during the last few months. I promise I'll make it up to you (and hopefully already have when you read this).

—Hans-Eric Grönlund

Introduction

The easy part of software development is knowing how to write code in the programming language at hand. The tougher part is mastering the programming interfaces of the platform and getting to the level where you can effectively turn ideas into working features with real values.

iOS 6, although extremely powerful and easy to use, is no exception to this. Objective-C, by many considered a rather "funky" programming language, is something you'll get your head around rather quickly, even learn to appreciate. However, you're likely to spend a lot of time learning the various APIs and frameworks.

We believe the best way to acquire the necessary knowledge and reach that plateau of high productivity, is through hands-on experience. We think the best way to learn is to code along, creating small projects in which you can test and tweak the features, get a feeling for them before you implement them in your real projects.

With this idea in mind, we created *iOS 6 Recipes*. It contains over 600 pages of sample code accompanied by instructions on how to create small test apps that allow you to run the code on your iOS 6 device or in the iOS Simulator.

We have tried to cover as many topics as possible using the features of iOS 6. We hope it provides the basic fundament you need to start converting your great ideas into fantastic apps.

Who This Book Is For

When you read this book, it will help if you have a basic knowledge of Objective-C, have taken your first steps in Xcode, and written a couple of Hello World apps. If you haven't, don't worry; just pay extra attention to the first eight recipes of Chapter 1. They should provide most of the basics you need to follow along.

How This Book Is Structured

The example-based chapters of this book do not particularly build off of one another, in the hope that you can simply open up to any chapter of specific interest and start building a certain type of application. It is recommended that you at least skim Chapter 1, "Application Recipes," and then Chapter 2, "Autolayout Recipes," before moving on. The first chapter contains recipes for common tasks, such as creating outlets and actions, which are referenced throughout the text and should be fully understood. The second chapter provides basic knowledge of the new layout scheme of iOS 6. Reading that chapter might prove helpful when you create the user interfaces of the recipes later on.

Throughout this book, it is assumed that you are developing in the latest versions of iOS (6.0) and Xcode (4.5) at the time of writing. This means that every recipe in this text assumes that you will be using Automatic Reference Counting (ARC), and as such does not include significant memory management. This also means that depending on when you are reading this, your results may look slightly different, although the basic functionality should remain similar.

Many of the recipes in this book cannot be fully tested on the iOS simulator, and as such will require both an iOS device and a provisioning profile, which can be acquired when you subscribe to the iOS Developer Program. We've pointed out each recipe that cannot be tested in the iOS Simulator.

> **Note**   With the introduction of iPhone 5, Apple has added a new screen size to the iPhone family. The new 4 inch screen has the same width but is slightly taller than the old 3.5 inch screen. The recipes in this book use the Retina 3.5 Full Screen size metric for their user interfaces. However, thanks to the new Autolayout feature of iOS 6, they will work just as well with the new Retina 4 Full Screen size metric. You can freely choose whichever metric works for you.

Downloading the Code

The code for the examples shown in this book is available on the Apress web site, www.apress.com. A link can be found on the book's information page under the Source Code/Downloads tab. This tab is located underneath the Related Titles section of the page.

Contacting the Author

If you have any questions or comments regarding this book, I'd be happy to hear them. Contact me at hasse42g@gmail.com, or write a comment at my blog, http://www.hans-eric.com.

Application Recipes

We're going to start this book with a set of recipes dealing with the iOS application, its project, and various basic Xcode tasks. The first eight recipes are fundamental, showing things like how to setup an application, how to connect and reference user interface elements to your code, and how to add images and sound files to your project. If you're new to iOS development we suggest you go through those first before moving on.

We also recommend that you take a closer look at Recipe 1-9 to see whether Storyboards is something for you. Storyboards is the new way of designing user interface in iOS, allowing you to gather several views in one file. Although the examples in this book are based on the old way of creating user interfaces, having one `.xib` file per view controller, you could just as easily do them the storyboards way.

The last four recipes in this chapter deal with miscellaneous topics like how to set up simple APIs for default error and exception handling; how to include a Lite version of your app in your projects, and how to make the app launch seem shorter in the eyes of the user.

Recipe 1-1: Setting Up a Single-View Application

Many of the recipes in this book are implemented in a test application with a single view. Such a project is easy to setup in Xcode using the Single View Application template.

To create a new single-view application project in Xcode, go to the main menu and select File ➤ New ➤ Project. This brings up the dialog with available project templates (see Figure 1-1). The template you're looking for is located in the Application page under the iOS section.

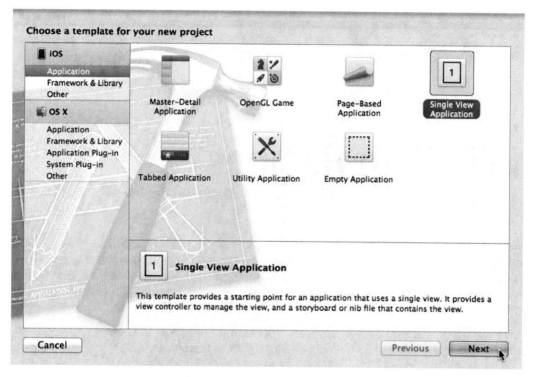

Figure 1-1. *The single view application template in the iOS application section*

After you've selected the Single View Application template and clicked Next, you need to enter a few properties for your application:

- A *Product Name*, for example **My Test App**
- An *Organization Name*, which unless you have one can be your name
- A *Company Identifier*, preferably your Internet domain if you have one

If you like, you can also enter a class prefix that will be applied to all classes you create using the Objective-C file template. This can be a good idea if you want to avoid future name conflicts with third party code, but if this app is only meant for testing a feature, you can leave it blank.

You also need to say which device type your application is for: iPad, iPhone, or both (Universal). Pick iPhone or iPad if you're testing. You can also pick Universal, but then the template will generate more code, which you probably don't need if your only purpose is trying a new feature.

All the code examples in this book assume you're using ARC (Automatic Reference Counting) so make sure that Use Automatic Reference Counting is checked. Also, if you're not planning on using Storyboards (see Recipe 1-9) or unit tests, be sure that the corresponding options are unchecked. Figure 1-2 shows an example of this configuration.

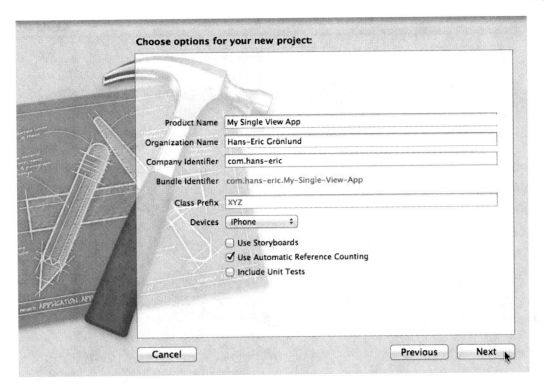

Figure 1-2. Configuring the project

Finally, click the Next button and then select a folder where the project is stored. Bear in mind that Xcode creates a new folder for the project within the folder you picked, so select the root folder for your projects.

There's often a good reason to place the project under version control. It allows you to check changes to the code so that you can go back to a previous version if something goes wrong or you just want to see what's been done. Xcode comes with Git, a well-spread open-source version control system. To initialize it for your project, check the Create local git repository for this project checkbox, as in Figure 1-3.

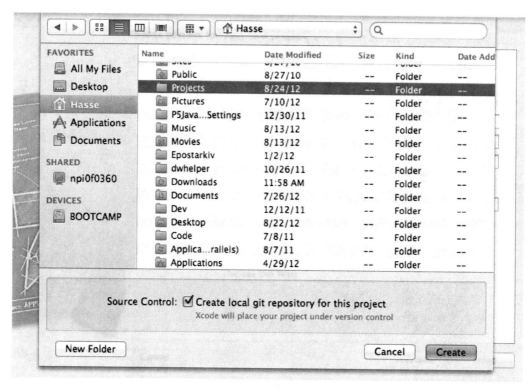

Figure 1-3. Selecting the parent folder for the project

Now when you click the Create button, an application with an app delegate and a view controller will be generated for you (see Figure 1-4). The setup is complete and you can build and run the application (which of course at this point only shows a blank screen).

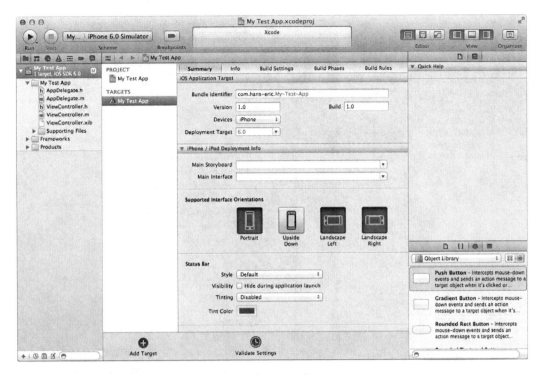

Figure 1-4. A basic application with an app delegate and a view controller

Recipe 1-2: Linking a Framework

The iOS operating system is divided into so called frameworks. To use the functionalities of a framework you need to link the corresponding binary to your project. For the UIKit, Foundation and CoreGraphics frameworks Xcode does this automatically when you create a new project. However, many important features and functions reside in frameworks like CoreMotion, CoreData, MapKit, and so on. For those other frameworks you need to follow these steps to add them.

1. Select the project node (the root node) in the Project navigator panel on the left-side of the Xcode project window. This brings up the Project editor panel.

2. Select the target in the Targets dock. If you have more than one target, for example, a unit test target, you need to perform these steps for all of them.

3. Navigate to the Build Phases tab and expand the section called Link Binary With Libraries. There you see a list of the currently linked frameworks.

4. Click on the Add items (+) button at the bottom of the list. This brings up a list of available frameworks.

5. Select the framework you want to link and use the Add button to include it (see Figure 1-5).

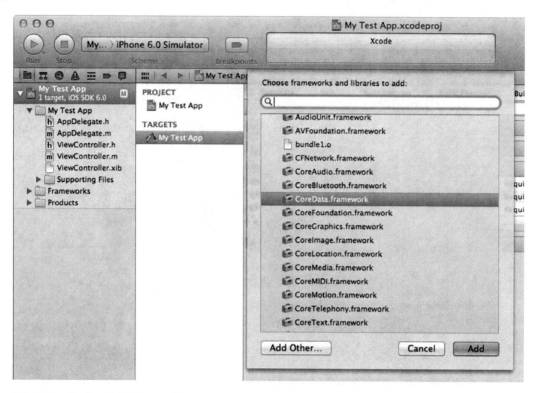

Figure 1-5. Adding the Core Data framework

Tip   To make it easier to find a particular framework you can use the search field to filter the list.

When you add a framework to your project, a corresponding framework reference node is placed in your project tree (see Figure 1-6). What you may want to do is to drag and drop the node to the Frameworks folder where the other framework references reside. It's not strictly necessary but helps your project tree stay organized.

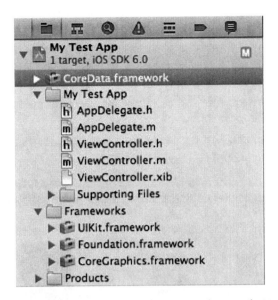

Figure 1-6. When adding a framework, a reference node is created at the top of your project tree

Now, to use the functions and classes from within your code you only need to import the framework API (Application Programming Interface.) This is normally done in a header file (.h) within your project, as in this example where we import the CoreData API in the ViewController.h file.

```
//
//  ViewController.h
//  My Test App
//

#import <UIKit/UIKit.h>
#import <CoreData/CoreData.h>

@interface ViewController : UIViewController

@end
```

> **Note** If you don't know the header file for a framework, don't worry, all framework APIs follow the same pattern, namely #import <FrameworkName/FrameworkName.h>.

With the framework binary linked, and the API imported, you can start using its functions and classes in your code.

Recipe 1-3: Adding a User Interface Control View

iOS provides a number of built-in control views, things such as buttons, labels, text fields, and so on, with which you can compose your user interface. Xcode makes designing user interfaces easy with a built-in editor, Interface Builder. All you need to do is to drag the controls you want from the Object Library and position them the way you want in your view. The editor helps you make a pleasing user interface by snapping to standard spaces.

In this recipe we'll show you how to add a Round Rect Button to your view. We'll assume you've already created a single-view application in which to try this.

Start by selecting the ViewController.xib file to bring up Interface Builder. Be sure the Utilities View (the panel on the right) is visible. If it isn't, select the corresponding button in the toolbar (see Figure 1-7).

Figure 1-7. The button to hide or show the Utilities View is located in the upper-right corner of Xcode

Now be sure the Object Library shows in the Utilities View (lower-right corner of Xcode.) Click the Show the Object Library button (see Figure 1-8) if it isn't.

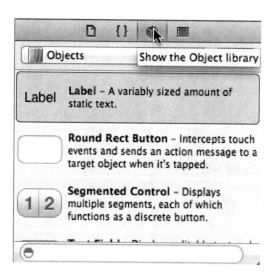

Figure 1-8. The Object Library contains the built-in user interface controls

Locate Round Rect Button in the Object library and drag it onto the view, as in Figure 1-9.

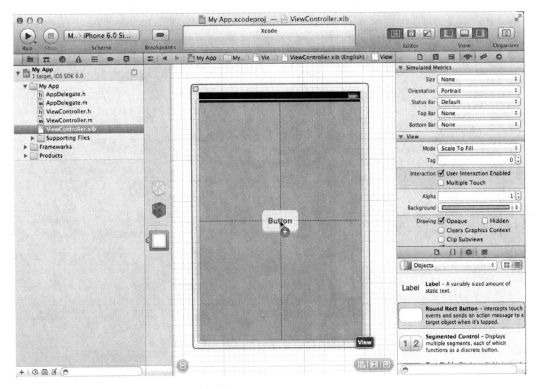

Figure 1-9. Dragging a Round Rect Button from the Object library

You can change the text either by double-clicking the button or by setting the corresponding attribute in the Attribute inspector as shown in Figure 1-10. In the Attribute inspector you can also change other attributes, such as color or font.

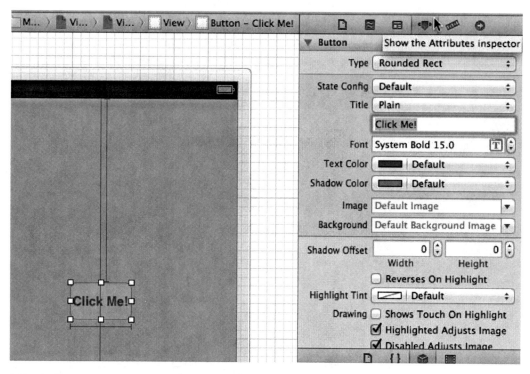

Figure 1-10. Setting the button text in the Attribute inspector

You can now build and run your application. Your button shows but it won't respond to you tapping it. For this you need to connect it to your code via outlets and actions, which is the topic of the next two recipes.

Recipe 1-4: Creating an Outlet

iOS is built on the Model-View-Controller design pattern. One effect of this is that the views are completely separated from code that operates on the views (the so-called controllers). To reference a view from a view controller you need to create an outlet in your controller and hook it up with the view. This can be accomplished in many different ways but the simplest is to use Xcode's Assistant editor.

We'll build on what you did in Recipe 1-3 and create an outlet for the button. Although the referenced view in this example is a button, the steps are the same for any other type of view, be it labels, text fields, table views, and so on.

With Interface Builder active showing your button, click on the Assistant editor button in the upper-right corner of Xcode (see Figure 1-11).

Figure 1-11. The center button in the Editor group activates the Assistant editor

With the Assistant editor active, the edit area is split in two showing Interface Builder on the left and the view controller's header file on the right. Press and hold the Ctrl while dragging a blue line from the button to the code window. A hint with the text `Insert Outlet, Action, or Outlet Collection` should appear as in Figure 1-12.

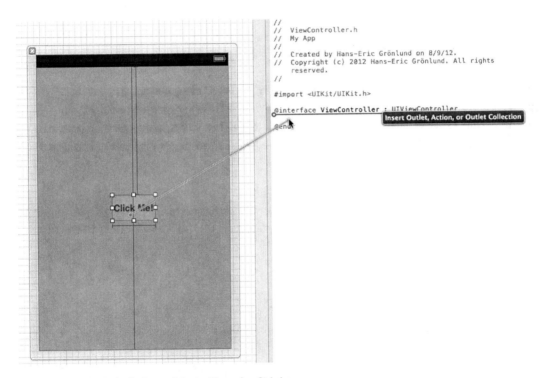

Figure 1-12. Creating an outlet in the assistant editor using Ctrl-drag

Note   Because an outlet is really only a special kind of an Objective-C property, you need to drag the blue line to somewhere it can be declared in code, that is, somewhere between the `@interface` and `@end` declarations.

In the dialog that appears (shown in Figure 1-13,) give the outlet a name. This will be the name of the property that you'll use to reference the button later from your code, so name it accordingly. Be sure that Connection is set to Outlet and that the type is correct (should be UIButton for Round Rect Buttons). Also, because you are using ARC, outlets should always use the Weak storage type.

Figure 1-13. Configuring an outlet

> **Note** Although Objective-C properties generally should use the Strong storage type, outlets are an exception. The details are beyond the scope of this book, but briefly the reason has to do with internal memory management and that using Weak spares you from writing certain cleanup code that you otherwise had to write. Throughout this book, we assume that you're creating your outlets using Weak storage.

When you click the Connect button, Xcode creates a property and hooks it up with the button. Your view controller's header file should now look like in Figure 1-14; the little dot next to the property indicates that it is connected to a view in the .xib file.

```
//
//  ViewController.h
//  My App
//
//  Created by Hans-Eric Grönlund on 8/9/12.
//  Copyright (c) 2012 Hans-Eric Grönlund. All rights
      reserved.
//

#import <UIKit/UIKit.h>

@interface ViewController : UIViewController

@property (weak, nonatomic) IBOutlet UIButton *myButton;

@end
```

Figure 1-14. An outlet property connected to a button in the .xib file

The outlet is now ready and you can reference the button from your code using the property. To demonstrate that, add the following code to the viewDidLoad method in the ViewController.m file:

```
- (void)viewDidLoad
{
    [super viewDidLoad];
    // Do any additional setup after loading the view, typically from a nib.
    [self.myButton setTitle:@"Outlet!" forState:UIControlStateNormal];
}
```

If you build and run your application, as Figure 1-15 shows, the button's title should now read "Outlet!" instead of "Click Me!"

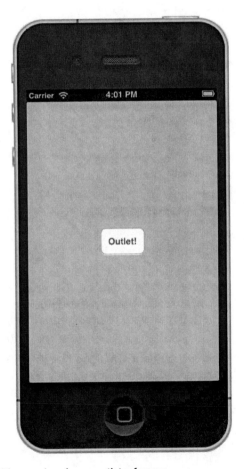

Figure 1-15. The button title changed from code using an outlet reference

The next step is to make something happen when the button is tapped. This is what actions are for, the topic of the next recipe.

Recipe 1-5: Creating an Action

Actions is the way in which user interface controls notifies your code (usually the view controller) that a user event has occurred; for example when a button has been tapped or a value has been changed. The control responds to such an event by calling the action method you've provided.

You will continue to build on what you've done in Recipes 1-3 and 1-4. In this recipe you create and connect an action method to receive Touch Up Inside events from the button. You then add code that displays an alert when the user taps the button.

Your Xcode should still be in Assistant editor mode with both the user interface and the header file showing. If not, follow the steps from Recipe 1-4 to make it show.

Now, Ctrl-click and drag the line from the button to the view controller's @interface section, exactly like as you did when you created the outlet earlier. Only this time, change the connection type to Action as in Figure 1-16.

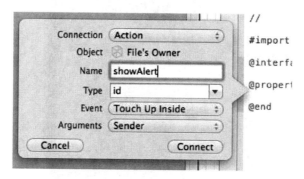

Figure 1-16. Configuring an action method

When you set the connection type to Action, you'll notice that the dialog changes to show a different set of attributes than for connection type Outlet. (Compare Figure 1-16 to Figure 1-13.) New attributes are Type, Event, and Arguments. Usually, the default values provided by Xcode are fine but there may be situations where you'd want to change them. Here's a short description of the three attributes:

- Type: The type of the sender argument. This can be either the generic type id or the specific type, UIButton in this case. It's usually a good idea to use the generic type so that you can invoke the action method in other situations and not be forced to provide a UIButton (in this case).

- Event: This is the event type you want the action method to respond to. The most common events are touch events of various kinds and events that indicate that a value has changed.

- Arguments: This attribute dictates what arguments the action method shall have. Possible values are

  - None, no argument

  - Sender, which has the type you entered in the Type attribute

■ Sender and Event, which is an object holding additional information about the event that occurred

For the sake of this recipe, leave the attributes at id, Touch Up Inside and Sender, respectively, but enter showAlert as the name.

> **Note** The convention in iOS is to name actions after what will happen when an event triggers it rather than a name that conveys the event type. So, pick names such as showAlert, playCurrentTrack and shareImage over names like buttonClicked or textChanged.

You finalize the creation of the action by clicking Connect button in the dialog. Xcode then creates an action method in the view controller's class and hooks it up with the button. Your ViewController.h file should now look like Figure 1-17.

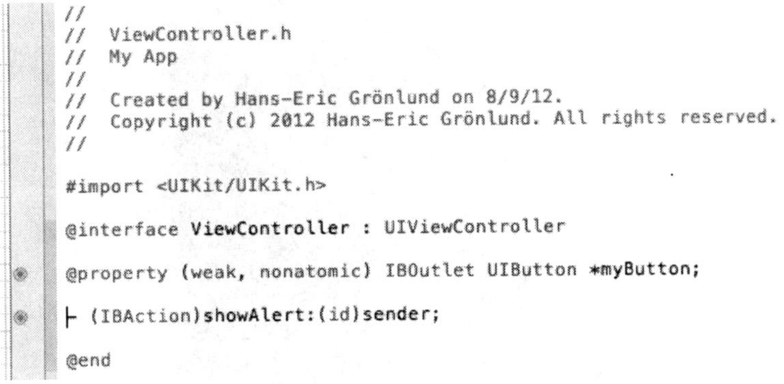

```
//
// ViewController.h
// My App
//
// Created by Hans-Eric Grönlund on 8/9/12.
// Copyright (c) 2012 Hans-Eric Grönlund. All rights reserved.
//

#import <UIKit/UIKit.h>

@interface ViewController : UIViewController

@property (weak, nonatomic) IBOutlet UIButton *myButton;

├ (IBAction)showAlert:(id)sender;

@end
```

Figure 1-17. An outlet and an action connected to an object in the .xib file

Now you're ready to implement the behavior you want when the user taps the button. In this case you show an alert view that says hello.

```
@implementation ViewController

// ...

- (IBAction)showAlert:(id)sender
{
    UIAlertView *alert = [[UIAlertView alloc] initWithTitle:@"Testing Actions"
                                                    message:@"Hello Brother!"
                                                   delegate:nil
                                          cancelButtonTitle:@"Dismiss"
                                          otherButtonTitles:nil];

    [alert show];
}

@end
```

You can now build and run the application. When you tap the button, you should see your greeting alert as in Figure 1-18.

Figure 1-18. An action method showing an alert when the button is tapped

Sometimes it happens that the code and the .xib files get out of sync with connected outlets and actions. Usually this happens when you remove an action method or an outlet property in your code and replace them with new ones. In those cases you get a runtime error and what you need to do is to remove the connection from Interface Builder. You do this in the Connections inspector. Figure 1-19 shows an example where you've ended up with two connected action methods for the same event. You remove the lingering action method by clicking the × icon next to it.

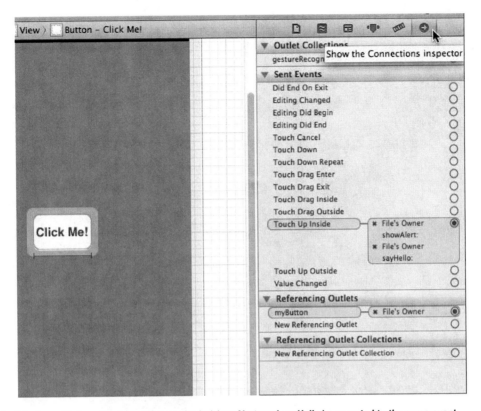

Figure 1-19. A button with two different action methods (showAlert: and sayHello:) connected to the same event

Recipe 1-6: Creating a Class

A common task in iOS programming is to create new classes. Whether your aim is to subclass an existing class, or create a new domain model class to hold your data, you can use the Objective-C class template to generate the necessary files.

In this recipe we'll show you how to create and add a new class to your project. If you don't have a suitable project to try this in, create a new single-view application.

In the Project Navigator, select the group folder in which you want the files for your new class. Normally this is the group folder with the same name as your project, but as your application grows you may want to organize your files into sub folders.

Go to the main menu and select **File ➤ New ➤ File** ... (or simply use the keyboard shortcut Command (⌘) + N). Then select the Objective-C class template in the iOS Cocoa Touch section (see Figure 1-20).

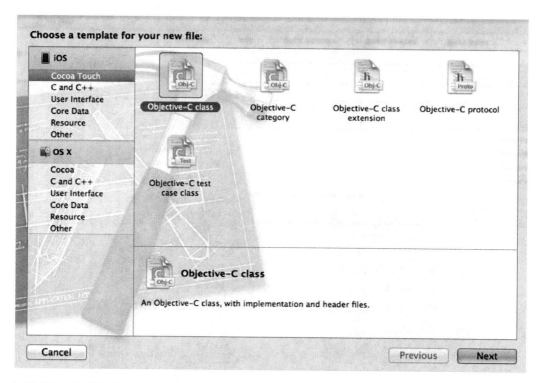

Figure 1-20. Using the Objective-C class template to create a new class

Then on the following page, name the class. The convention in Objective-C is to name classes using the PascalCase style. You'll also need to declare the parent class. If you just want a basic class, for example an internal domain class, you should subclass the NSObject class. It is the base class for all objects in Objective-C.

For the sake of this recipe, enter **MyClass** and **NSObject** (Figure 1-21).

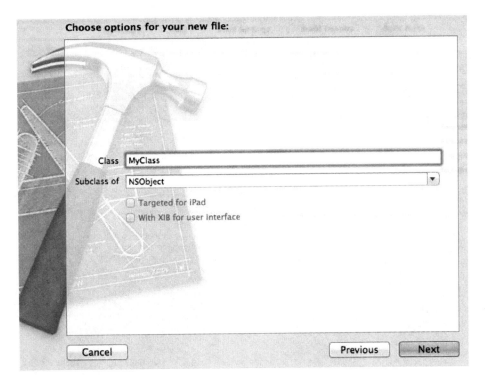

Figure 1-21. Configuring a new class

Note   Depending on which class you select as parent, you may or may not set additional settings such as Targeted for iPad, or With XIB for user interface. These options are active if you subclass a view controller of some kind.

The next step is to select a physical location on the hard disk and a logical location within your project for your new class. That is, the file folder and the group folder. In this step (see Figure 1-22), you can also decide whether your class should be included in the target (that is, the executable file). This is usually what you want, but there may be situations when you want to exclude files. For example, when you have more than one target (maybe a unit test target).

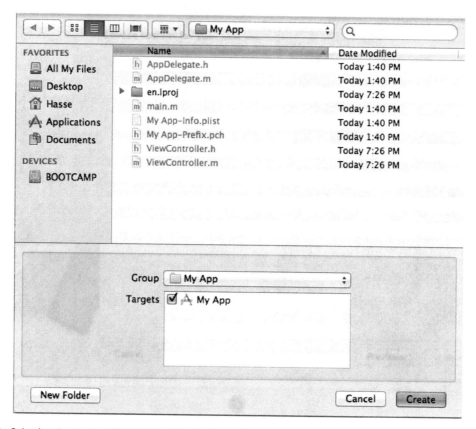

Figure 1-22. Selecting the physical (file folder) and logical (group folder) places for a class

Most of the time you can just accept the default values for the locations, so go ahead and click Create. Xcode then generates two new files to your project: `MyClass.h` and `MyClass.m`. They contain the code of an empty class, as in this header file:

```
//
//  MyClass.h
//  My App
//

#import <Foundation/Foundation.h>

@interface MyClass : NSObject

@end
```

And this implementation file:

```
//
//  MyClass.m
//  My App
//
```

```
#import "MyClass.h"

@implementation MyClass

@end
```

Recipe 1-7: Adding an Info.plist Property

The iOS platform uses a special file called `Info.plist` to store application-wide properties. The file resides in the *Supporting File* folder of your project and is named after your project with `-Info.plist` as suffix. The format of the file is XML (eXtensible Markup Language) but you can more conveniently edit the values in Xcode's property list editor, shown in Figure 1-23.

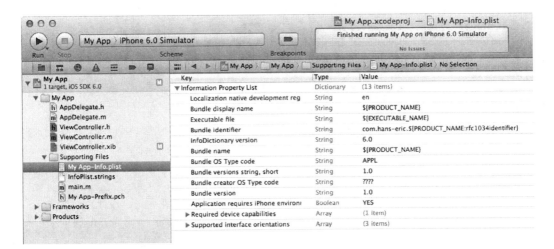

Figure 1-23. The .plist editor in Xcode

The structure of a property list file is that the root element is a dictionary that contains values identified by string keys. The values are often a string but can be other types, such as Booleans, dates, arrays of values, or even dictionaries.

If you select the `Info.plist` in the Project navigator, you see that it already contains several items. These are the most commonly used keys. However, sometimes you need to add a value that isn't contained by default. For example, if your app is using location services and you want to set the `NSLocationUsageDescription` property.

Follow these steps to add a new application property key and value:

1. Expand the Supporting Files folder in the Project navigator.

2. Select the file `<Application Name>-Info.plist`. This brings up the property list editor.

3. Select the root item, called Information Property List.

4. Press the Return key. Xcode adds a new row to the dictionary.

5. Type the property's key identifier or select one from the list that is presented to you. Note that if you enter an identifier and Xcode recognizes it as a standard property, it displays a more descriptive key. For example, NSLocationUsageDescription changes into Privacy - Location Usage Description after pressing Return. Behind the scenes, though, it's the identifier you typed in that's stored.

6. If the property key isn't defined within iOS, that is, it is your own custom key, you are allowed to change the property type. You do this by simply clicking on the type in the Type column and a list of possible values is presented to you.

7. Enter a value for the key by double-clicking the value column of the new row and typing the new value.

Recipe 1-8: Adding a Resource File

Most apps need to access resource files such as images or sound files. You do that by adding them to your project and then referencing them through their names. In this recipe you add an image file to your project and then use it to populate an image view. Although you use an image file in this example, the process is the same for any other type of file.

As usual, you need a single-view project to try this in, so go ahead and create one if you don't have a suitable one already.

The best way to import a file is to simply drag it from Finder, or iPhoto, or any other application that supports the dragging of files. Drag an image file of your liking into the Project Navigator in Xcode. A good place to put resource files is in the Supporting Files group folder, but you can add it to any group folder within your project.

Note   You can also use the File ➤ Add Files to My App menu item to add resource files to your project.

In the dialog that appears, be sure to check the box Copy items into destination group's folder (if needed), as Figure 1-24 shows. This ensures that your image stays with the project even if you move it to a different location.

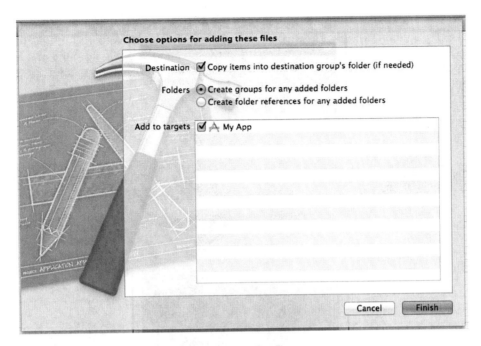

Figure 1-24. Making sure the Copy items box is checked when adding files

Your image, as Figure 1-25 shows, is now part of your project and can be referenced through its filename.

Figure 1-25. An application with an embedded image file

To see how you can reference the image within your application, add to your user interface an Image View and make it fill the entire view. Be sure the image view is selected and go to the Attributes inspector to connect it to your image file. You do that by selecting your file from the Image attribute's drop-down menu. You probably also want to change the Mode attribute to Aspect Fill, or your image may look stretched.

Your app should now resemble the one in Figure 1-26.

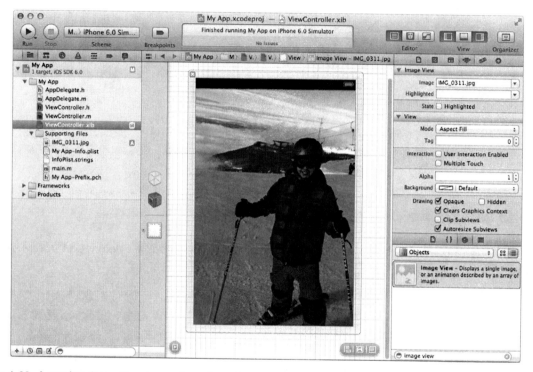

Figure 1-26. A user interface with an image view referencing an embedded image file

Recipe 1-9: Using Storyboards

Remember the days when you had to use paper and pen to sketch out design flows for your apps? Then came flowcharting software, in which you could digitally record your workflows and processes. But it was a manual process to convert those workflows into source code. Apple provides a tool called Storyboards that offers a visual representation of an app's workflow, which can produce a working framework for your app.

In this recipe you'll use Storyboards to build a simple multipage application that contains information about a made-up app-making company. We'll also show you how you can embed the storyboard to an existing application, making it show when you tap an About button.

So What's in a Story(board)?

A storyboard is a collection of .xib files packaged together along with some metadata about the views and their relationships to each other. It is the ultimate separation of views from models and controllers that you have been hearing about since the early days of MVC (Model-View-Controller) programming. The storyboard has two main components: scenes and segues.

Scenes

Scenes are any view that fills the screen of the device. They contain UI objects and are controlled by view controllers. This is almost exactly like the .xib files that you are familiar with editing in Interface Builder. Figure 1-27 displays five different scenes in the storyboard that you will soon build.

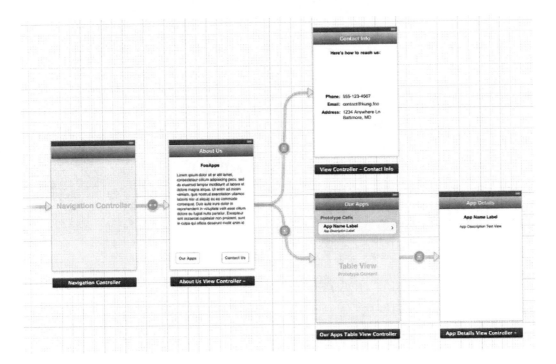

Figure 1-27. A storyboard with five scenes

Segues

Segues are the transitions that present subsequent views in a storyboard. The segue can present a view with a push, as a modal view, as a pop-over, or with a custom transition. A segue is of the class UIStoryboardSegue and contains three properties: sourceViewController, destinationViewController, and identifier. The identifier is an NSString that can be used to identify specific segues from your code.

You would normally initiate a segue based on an action from the user. This can be the touching of a button or tableview cell, or it could be the result of a gesture recognizer. Segues are represented on the storyboard by a line connecting two scenes, as shown in Figure 1-28.

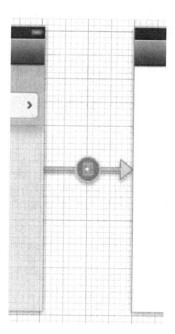

Figure 1-28. A segue connecting two scenes

Setting Up the Application with a Storyboard

Storyboards are available in all the application templates in Xcode except the empty project template. For this recipe you'll use the Single View Application template. Name the project **About Us** and be sure to the Use Storyboards option is checked, as demonstrated in Figure 1-29.

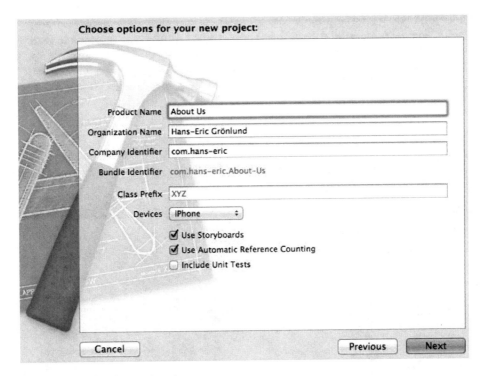

Figure 1-29. Configuring a project for storyboard use

After you've created your project, you'll see in the Project Navigator, as Figure 1-30 demonstrates, that your project contains a file named `MainStoryboard.storyboard`. Click on this file to load it into Interface Builder and start building your storyboard.

Figure 1-30. A project with a storyboard file

In this example you build a simple project that displays information about your company. It uses a navigation bar to display the title of the current page so the first thing you're going to do is to embed the main view in a navigation controller. You do this by selecting the view and then selecting **Editor ➤ Embed In ➤ Navigation Controller** in the main menu. This creates a navigation controller and adds it to your storyboard, connected to your main view through a segue. Figure 1-31 shows an example.

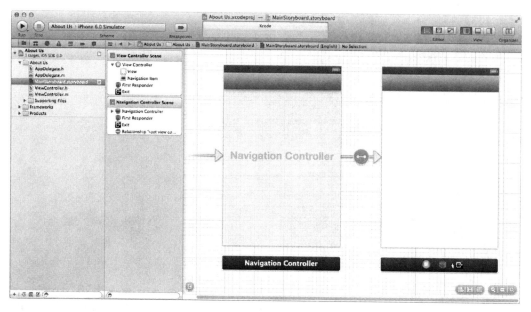

Figure 1-31. The main view in a storyboard, embedded in a view controller

Now create the user interface of the main view. Add a label, a text view, and two buttons to it and make it resemble Figure 1-32.

Figure 1-32. A simple user interface to display company information

Adding a New Scene to the Storyboard

The next step is to add a new scene that displays the company contact information when the Contact Us button is tapped. You do this by dragging a View Controller from the Object library onto the storyboard.

Set up the user interface of the new scene so that it resembles the view on the right in Figure 1-33.

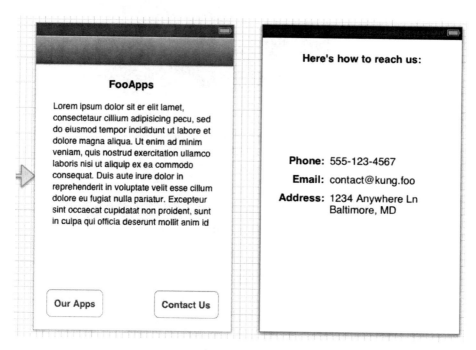

Figure 1-33. The storyboard with a new scene for contact information

To connect the new contact information view to the About Us view, you are going to Ctrl-click the Contact Us button and drag a line to the Contact Info view, as in Figure 1-34. This is the same action used to connect outlets, only this time you're using it to create a transition between two scenes.

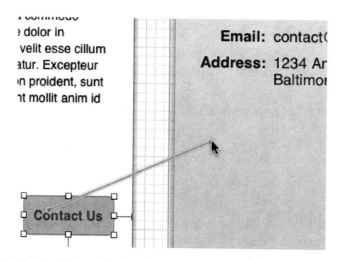

Figure 1-34. Pressing and holding the Ctrl key while dragging a line between the button and the scene creates a transition

When you release the mouse button, a pop-up will display, asking how you want the transition to be performed. You can choose between push, modal and custom. Because you are using a Navigation Controller, select push (as in Figure 1-35) so that a back button is be automatically setup for you in the navigation bar.

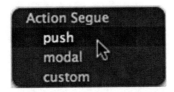

Figure 1-35. Selecting push action segue

After the connection is made, you'll notice that the navigation bar is automatically added to the new view. Now, let's make the navigation bar display the title of the current scene. One way to do that is to select the Navigation Item in the View Controller navigator (see Figure 1-36). (Another way is to simply click on the navigation bar.)

Figure 1-36. Selecting the Navigation Item of a Storyboard View Controller

You can then set the Title attribute in the Attribute inspector, as shown in Figure 1-37. Set the title of the main view controller to **About Us**. Then select the view containing the contact information and set its Navigation item's title to **Contact Info**.

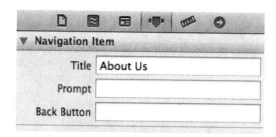

Figure 1-37. Setting the title of a navigation item

One habit to get into is providing your segues with an identifier. This helps future-proof your apps if you end up connecting multiple segues to one view. You can to check the identifier of the calling segue to see the path the user took to reach that view and respond accordingly. You can set the identifier of a segue by selecting it in the storyboard and viewing its properties in the Attributes inspector, as shown in Figure 1-38.

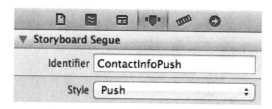

Figure 1-38. Setting a segue identifier in the Attributes inspector

If you run this app now, as shown by Figures 1-39 and 1-40, the Contact Us button will work and will display the Contact Info view. Note that this works without having to write one single line of code!

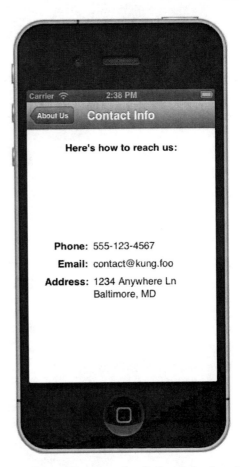

Figure 1-39. *Main simulated view*

Figure 1-40. *The resulting view when Contact Us has been tapped*

Adding a Table View Scene

Now let's shift focus to the Our Apps button. What you want to do is to display a view that lists the company's other apps so they can get some cross promotion. The first thing that should come to mind when talking about lists in iOS is `UITableViewController`. And storyboarding takes `UITableViewController` to a whole new level of convenience.

You're going to drag a `UITableViewController` to the storyboard, creating an Apps Table view. The first thing that you may notice is that this looks a little different than the regular `UITableViewController` available in Interface Builder. (Refer to Chapter 3 for an extensive introduction to table views as they are used outside Storyboards.)

In a table view scene there is a section called Prototype Cells at the top (see Figure 1-41). With storyboards, you can customize the layout and objects of a `UITableViewCell` with something called a prototype. We'll go into this further later on.

Figure 1-41. *A Table View Controller scene*

Select the Table View, and in the Attributes inspector, change the table view's Content attribute from Dynamic Prototypes to Static Cells. Also, change the Style attribute to Grouped, which gives the cell group nice rounded edges. Figure 1-42 shows these settings and the resulting table view.

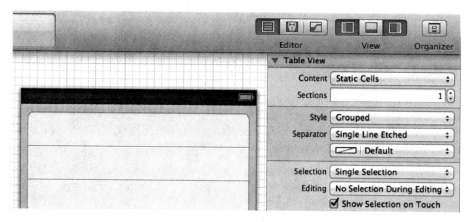

Figure 1-42. *A table view scene with Content set to Static Cells and Style to Grouped*

Because every cell is going to have the same layout, delete the bottom two cells so that you can customize and then quickly duplicate the top cell. You can customize the cell like any other container view, by dragging objects from the Object library. We're going to make a simple customization using only two labels, a bold text label for the title and a smaller one for the subtitle. If you feel up to it, go ahead and add additional components, for example, an image view for an app icon. This example stops at the two labels, as shown in Figure 1-43.

Figure 1-43. A customized table view cell

Now you'll duplicate the cell to create three instances of it. Do that by clicking and holding the Alt key (⌥), while dragging the cell downward to duplicate it. Repeat again to add a third row to the table view. Now you can customize the two new cells to contain unique information, resembling Figure 1-44.

Figure 1-44. A table view with three custom cells

All that is left is to connect the Our Apps button to this new view. Select the button in the About Us view, and Ctrl-click-drag to the table view scene you just created to set up a push segue between the Our Apps button and the table view scene. Your storyboard now looks something like that shown in Figure 1-45.

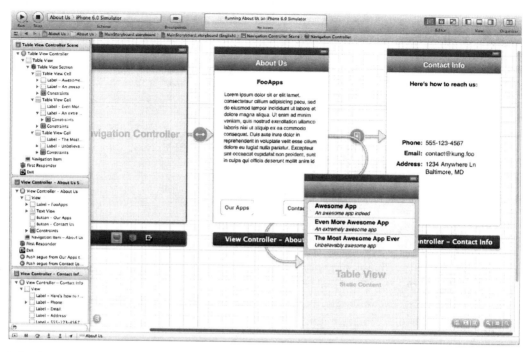

Figure 1-45. A storyboard with three scenes

Note What you may discern from Figure 1-45 is that Storyboards require a lot of screen space. As your app grows it can get quite difficult to work effectively with the user interface, especially so for iPad apps. This is one of the reasons why some developers, despite all the advantages that come with Storyboards, prefer to stick with .xib files to keep designing the user interfaces individually.

Now when you run the application, you can tap the Our Apps button and the table view scene will show as in Figure 1-46—still without having written any code. Amazing!

Figure 1-46. The table view scene showing a list of "awesome" apps

Adding a Detail View

The previous app segment works well enough without any code, but just by adding a little bit of code behind the scenes you can create an even more powerful interface, in a very short period of time.

When you see a table view, you instinctively know that there is likely to be a detailed view waiting for you when you touch one of the cells. Let's add that detail view now. Drag and drop a new view controller onto the storyboard. Make it look like Figure 1-47 by adding a label for the title and a text view for the description text. In a real scenario, this page would likely contain additional information like a link to a web page from where you can purchase the app in question. However, we're going to keep this example as simple as possible and just show the name and the description.

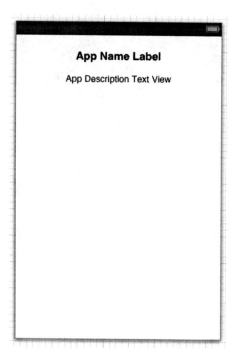

Figure 1-47. A detail view user interface

You want each of the table view cells to segue to this view when touched, so Ctrl-drag the line from each of the three cells to the detail view. This time when you release the mouse button, you'll notice that you can choose between setting up a Selection Segue or an Accessory Action. (See Figure 1-48.) For the purpose of this recipe, though, create push selection segues that will trigger a transition when the cell is selected (as opposed to when its accessory button is tapped).

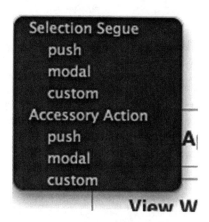

Figure 1-48. A pop-up with options to create either a Selection Segue or an Accessory Button Action for a table view cell

Again, once you've connected the cells to the detail view using the push method, the view will display the navigator bar. In the same way you did before, set the title in the corresponding Navigator Item to App Details.

As Figure 1-49 shows, there should now be three segues connecting the table view to the app details scene.

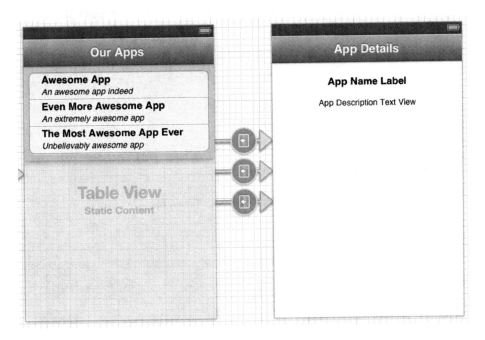

Figure 1-49. Multiple segues connecting a table view to a detail view

Select the first segue and enter an identifier for it in the Attributes inspector. Set it to **PushAppDetailsFromCell1** as shown in Figure 1-50.

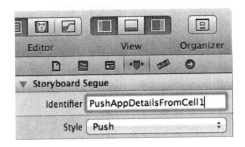

Figure 1-50. Setting an identifier for a segue that's pushing a detail view

Repeat the process for the other two segues, and set their identifier to **PushAppDetailsFromCell2** and **PushAppDetailsFromCell3**, respectively. You'll use these identifiers later to identify which segue triggered a transition to the App Details scene.

You've gotten this far without using any code, but that convenience is about to end. You need to start generating some dynamic content on the App Details view controller, and you are going to need to dive into some code for that.

First, you are going to create a model class to hold information about your apps. Create a new class, a subclass of NSObject, with the name AppDetails. (Refer to Recipe 1-6 on how to create a new class.)

Add the following properties and init method declarations to the header file of the new class:

```
//
//  AppDetails.h
//  About Us
//

#import <Foundation/Foundation.h>
@interface AppDetails : NSObject

@property(strong, nonatomic) NSString *name;
@property(strong, nonatomic) NSString *description;

-(id)initWithName:(NSString *)name description:(NSString *)descr;

@end
```

The implementation of the initWithName:description: method goes into the AppDetails.m file, like so:

```
//
//  AppDetails.m
//  About Us
//

#import "AppDetails.h"

@implementation AppDetails

-(id)initWithName:(NSString *)name description:(NSString *)descr
{
    self = [super init];
    if (self)
    {
        self.name = name;
        self.description = descr;
    }
    return self;
}

@end
```

Setting Up a Custom View Controller

With the data object in place, you can make the detail view controller display the attributes of an
AppDetails object. For that, you need to attach a custom view controller class to the detail view.

To set up the custom view controller, create a new Objective-C class with the name
AppDetailsViewController and make it a subclass of UIViewController. Be sure to uncheck the
With XIB for user interface option because this class is used to control a storyboard view, you don't
need a .xib file to go with it.

The next step is to attach the new view controller class to the App Details scene. Go back to the
storyboard editor and select the view controller object at the bottom of the App Details scene (see
Figure 1-51).

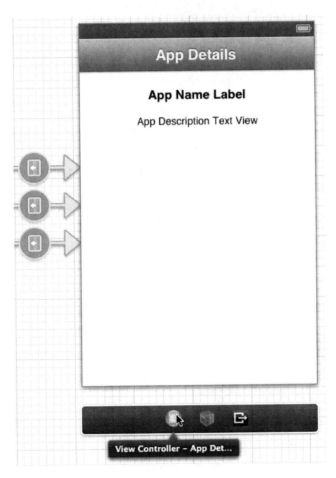

Figure 1-51. Selecting the view controller object of a scene

With the view controller object selected, go to the Identity inspector and set the Class attribute to AppDetailsViewController, as Figure 1-52 demonstrates.

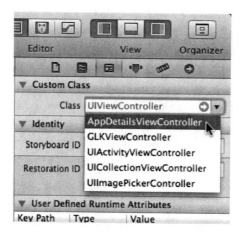

Figure 1-52. *Attaching a custom view controller class to a scene*

The next step is to create outlets for the name label and the description text view. You do this the same way as with .xib files, using the Assistant Editor (see Recipe 1-4.) Name the outlets nameLabel and descriptionTextView, respectively.

You also need a property to hold the current app details object. Add the following code to your AppDetailsViewController.h file:

```
//
//  AppDetailsViewController.h
//  About Us
//

#import <UIKit/UIKit.h>
#import "AppDetails.h"

@interface AppDetailsViewController : UIViewController

@property (weak, nonatomic) IBOutlet UILabel *nameLabel;
@property (weak, nonatomic) IBOutlet UITextView *descriptionTextView;
@property (strong, nonatomic) AppDetails *appDetails;

@end
```

And in AppDetailsViewController.m, add the following code to the viewDidLoad method:

```
- (void)viewDidLoad
{
    [super viewDidLoad];
    // Do any additional setup after loading the view.
    self.nameLabel.text = self.appDetails.name;
    self.descriptionTextView.text = self.appDetails.description;
}
```

The App Details scene is now ready to accept an AppDetails object and populate its label and text view with data from it. What's left is to provide the scene with an appropriate object. For this you need to create yet another custom view controller class, this time for the table view scene.

So, as you did before with the App Details scene, create a new Objective-C class. This time make it a subclass of UITableViewController and name it OurAppsTableViewController. Attach the new class to the Our Apps scene by selecting its view controller object and in the Identity inspector set OurAppsTableViewController as its class.

Open the new OurAppsTableViewController.m file. The first thing you're going to do is to get rid of the existing table view datasource and delegate methods that are there by default. This is because you're using a static table view content defined in your storyboard. So delete or comment out the following methods:

- numberOfSectionsInTableView:

- tableView:numberOfRowsInSection:

- tableView:cellForRowAtIndexPath:

- tableView:didSelectRowAtIndexPath:

Now what you want to do is to intersect when one of the three segues are triggered to perform a transition to the App Details scene. This can be done by overriding the prepareForSegue:sender: method.

Add the following code to OurAppsTableViewController.m:

```objc
//
//  OurAppsTableViewController.m
//  About Us
//

#import "OurAppsTableViewController.h"
#import "AppDetailsViewController.h"
#import "AppDetails.h"

@implementation OurAppsTableViewController

- (void)prepareForSegue:(UIStoryboardSegue *)segue sender:(id)sender
{
    NSString *name;
    NSString *description;
    if ([segue.identifier isEqualToString:@"PushAppDetailsFromCell1"])
    {
        name = @"Awesome App";
        description = @"Long description of the awesome app...";
    }
    else if ([segue.identifier isEqualToString:@"PushAppDetailsFromCell2"])
    {
        name = @"Even More Awesome App";
        description = @"Long description of the even more awesome app...";
    }
```

```
else if ([segue.identifier isEqualToString:@"PushAppDetailsFromCell3"])
{
    name = @"The Most Awesome App Ever";
    description = @"Long description of the most awesome app ever seen...";
}
else
{
    return;
}

AppDetailsViewController *appDetailsViewController = segue.destinationViewController;
appDetailsViewController.appDetails =
    [[AppDetails alloc] initWithName:name description:description];
}

// ...

@end
```

As you can see from the code, you are identifying the segue by its identifier and creating an `AppDetails` object with information about the corresponding app. You then hand over the object to the view controller for the App Details scene.

If you run your app now, you'll see that each of the table view cells will show different information in the App Details scene. Figure 1-53 demonstrates a simulated result of this application.

Figure 1-53. Three App Details scenes with information about three apps

Using Cell Prototypes

The app is working as intended up to this point, but what if you add new apps to your inventory? With the current implementation, you would have to update the table view with new cells for each new app item. In this section we show you how you can update the table view dynamically instead, using cell prototypes instead of static cell instances.

You start by changing the table view from static to dynamic. Go back to the Our Apps scene and delete the three rows. This removes the three connected segues as well. Now, select the table view and then in the Attributes inspector, change the Content attribute from Static Cells to Dynamic Prototypes, as shown in Figure 1-54.

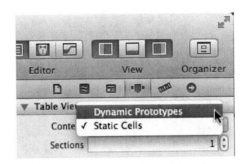

Figure 1-54. Changing table view content from Static Cells to Dynamic Prototypes

Next you need a prototype cell that will be the template for the cells you'll add dynamically later, so go ahead and drag a new table view cell from the Object library onto the table view. You can design the cell the same way you did with the static cells earlier, however you'll make one change by adding a Disclosure Indicator icon to it. (You do this with the Accessory attribute for the cell.) Figure 1-55 shows the prototype cell.

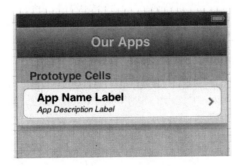

Figure 1-55. A table view cell prototype with two labels and a disclosure indicator

What you need to do now is to create a custom table view cell class and connect it to the prototype. Create a new Objective-C class, name it AppTableViewCell and make it a subclass of UITableViewCell. Then in the Identity inspector for the prototype cell, change the Class attribute to AppTableViewCell (as shown in Figure 1-56).

Figure 1-56. Attaching a custom class to a prototype cell

You also need to set a Reuse Identifier that will be used later to get instances based on the prototype cell. Go to the Attributes inspector and enter **AppCell** for the Identifier attribute, as shown by Figure 1-57.

Figure 1-57. Setting a reuse identifier for a cell prototype

Next, create outlets for the name label and the description label in AppTableViewCell.h. Name the outlets nameLabel and descriptionLabel, respectively.

You also need to create a segue for the transition to the App Details scene. Ctrl-drag a line from the prototype cell to the App Details scene. As you did before with the static cells, use the push selection segue type.

Select the segue you just created and set its Identifier attribute to PushAppDetails.

You are now finished with the setup of the prototype cell, what's left is to write the code for the dynamic displaying of the table view content. Switch to OurAppsTableViewController.h and import the prototype cell class:

```
#import "AppTableViewCell.h"
```

Then go to OurAppsTableViewController.m and add the following code:

```
- (NSInteger)numberOfSectionsInTableView:(UITableView *)tableView
{
    return 1;
}


- (NSInteger)tableView:(UITableView *)tableView numberOfRowsInSection:(NSInteger)section
```

```
{
    return 3;
}

- (UITableViewCell *)tableView:(UITableView *)tableView cellForRowAtIndexPath:(NSIndexPath *)
indexPath
{
    //Set the CellIdentifier that you set in the storyboard
    static NSString *CellIdentifier = @"AppCell";

    AppTableViewCell *cell = [tableView dequeueReusableCellWithIdentifier:CellIdentifier];

    switch (indexPath.row)
    {
        case 0:
            cell.nameLabel.text = @"Awesome App";
            cell.descriptionLabel.text = @"Long description of the awesome app...";
            break;
        case 1:
            cell.nameLabel.text = @"Even More Awesome App";
            cell.descriptionLabel.text = @"Long description of the even more awesome app...";
            break;
        case 2:
            cell.nameLabel.text = @"The Most Awesome App Ever";
            cell.descriptionLabel.text =
                @"Long description of the most awesome app ever seen...";
            break;

        default:
            cell.nameLabel.text = @"Unkown";
            cell.descriptionLabel.text = @"Unknown";
            break;
    }

    return cell;
}
```

You can now make the prepareForSegue:sender: method a lot simpler by utilizing the information stored in the cells.

Then change the prepareForSegue:sender: method's implementation into this:

```
- (void)prepareForSegue:(UIStoryboardSegue *)segue sender:(id)sender
{
    if ([segue.identifier isEqualToString:@"PushAppDetails"])
    {
        AppDetailsViewController *appDetailsViewController = segue.destinationViewController;
        AppTableViewCell *cell = sender;
        appDetailsViewController.appDetails =
            [[AppDetails alloc] initWithName:cell.nameLabel.text
                                 description:cell.descriptionLabel.text];
    }
}
```

Now when you run the app, the table view loads as before using the one prototype cell and the datasource. Figure 1-58 shows the simulated result of your newest updates to your application. In this example you are still using static data for the AppDetails class, but this app could easily be extended to use a core data object model or even pull a list of apps from a remote file on your server. Those features will be covered more in Chapter 12.

Figure 1-58. The same table view loading its content through its view controller using a prototype cell

Recipe 1-10: Handling Errors

How well your application is handling errors may very well be the difference between success and failure in terms of user experience. Nevertheless error handling is an often neglected part of software development, and iOS developers are no exception. Apps that crash without explanation or fail silently with all sorts of weird behavior are not uncommon.

Handling errors is something you should spend a little extra effort on to get right, and like all things boring you're better off dealing with them straight away. One thing you can do to make the effort easier is to create a default error handler, a single piece of code that can handle most of your errors.

This recipe shows you how to set up a simple error handler that, based on the error object you provide, alerts the user and even provides him or her with recovery options when available.

Setting Up a Framework for Error Handling

By convention in iOS, fatal, non-recoverable errors are implemented using exceptions. For potentially recoverable errors, however, the idiom is to use a more traditional method with a Boolean return value and an out parameter containing the error details. Here's an example of this pattern, with Core Data's NSManagedObjectContext:save: method:

```
NSError *error = nil;
if ([managedObjectContext save:&error] == NO)
{
    NSLog(@"Unhandled error:\n%@, %@", error, [error userInfo]);
}
```

The error handling in the preceding example dumps the error details to the standard output and then silently carries on as if nothing happened; Obviously, this approach is rather poor and is not the best strategy from a usability perspective.

What you do in this recipe, is build a small framework that helps you handle errors with the same ease as here, but with a much better user experience. Specifically, you'll write code like this:

```
NSError *error = nil;
if ([managedObjectContext save:&error] == NO)
{
    [ErrorHandler handleError:error fatal:NO];
}
```

Let's set up the scaffolding for the internal error handling framework. Start by creating a new single-view application project. In this new project, create a new NSObject subclass with the name ErrorHandler. Open ErrorHandler.h and add the following declaration:

```
//
//  ErrorHandler.h
//  Recipe 1-10: Default Error Handling
//

#import <Foundation/Foundation.h>

@interface ErrorHandler : NSObject

+(void)handleError:(NSError *)error fatal:(BOOL)fatalError;

@end
```

For now, just add an empty stub of this class method in the ErrorHandler.m file, like so:

```
//
//  ErrorHandler.m
//  Recipe 1-10: Default Error Handling
//

#import "ErrorHandler.h"
```

```
@implementation ErrorHandler
```

```
+(void)handleError:(NSError *)error fatal:(BOOL)fatalError
{
    // TODO: Handle the error
}
```

```
@end
```

You'll start implementing this method in a minute, but first you're going to set up code that will test it. You're going to create a simple user interface with two buttons that fake a non-fatal and a fatal error, respectively.

Open ViewController.xib and drag out two buttons from the Object library and make them resemble the ones in Figure 1-59.

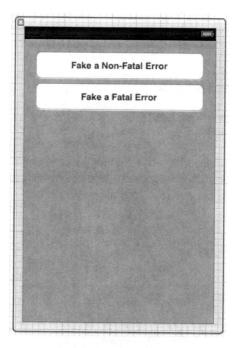

Figure 1-59. *Buttons that fake an error and invoke the error handling method*

Create actions named fakeNonFatalError and fakeFatalError for the respective buttons. Also, import ErrorHandler.h in the view controller's header file. ViewController.h should now resemble this code:

```
//
//  ViewController.h
//  Recipe 1-10: Default Error Handling
//
```

```
#import <UIKit/UIKit.h>
#import "ErrorHandler.h"

@interface ViewController : UIViewController

- (IBAction)fakeNonFatalError:(id)sender;
- (IBAction)fakeFatalError:(id)sender;

@end
```

Now, switch to ViewController.m and add the following implementation for the fakeNonFatalError: action method. It simply creates a fake NSError object with a single recovery option (Retry). The error object is then handed over to the error handler class, with a flag saying it's not a fatal error (meaning it shouldn't cause the app to shut itself down):

```
- (IBAction)fakeNonFatalError:(id)sender
{
    NSString *description = @"Connection Error";
    NSString *failureReason = @"Can't seem to get a connection.";
    NSArray *recoveryOptions = @[@"Retry"];
    NSString *recoverySuggestion = @"Check your wifi settings and retry.";

    NSDictionary *userInfo =
        [NSDictionary dictionaryWithObjects:
            @[description, failureReason, recoveryOptions, recoverySuggestion, self]
        forKeys:
            @[NSLocalizedDescriptionKey,NSLocalizedFailureReasonErrorKey,
                NSLocalizedRecoveryOptionsErrorKey, NSLocalizedRecoverySuggestionErrorKey,
                NSRecoveryAttempterErrorKey]];

    NSError *error = [[NSError alloc] initWithDomain:@"com.hans-eric.ios6recipesbook" code:42
        userInfo:userInfo];

    [ErrorHandler handleError:error fatal:NO];
}
```

For now, you don't need to know the details of the preceding method, but the userInfo dictionary that you've built for this fake error contains the key NSRecoveryAttempterErrorKey with the value set to self. What this means, is that the view controller acts as the Recovery attempter object for this error. For reasons that will become clear later, you need to implement one method from the NSRecoveryAttempting protocol, namely attemptRecoveryFromError:optionIndex:. This method is invoked on the recovery attempts that you implement later. For the purpose of this recipe, you simply fake a failed recovery attempt by returning NO, as shown here:

```
- (BOOL)attemptRecoveryFromError:(NSError *)error optionIndex:(NSUInteger)recoveryOptionIndex
{
    return NO;
}
```

Next, you implement the fakeFatalError: action method. It creates a simpler error, without recovery options, but flags the error as fatal in the error handling method. Here's the implementation:

```
- (IBAction)fakeFatalError:(id)sender
{
    NSString *description = @"Data Error";
    NSString *failureReason = @"Data is corrupt. The app must shut down.";
    NSString *recoverySuggestion = @"Contact support!";

    NSDictionary *userInfo = [NSDictionary dictionaryWithObjects:
            @[description, failureReason]
        forKeys:
            @[NSLocalizedDescriptionKey, NSLocalizedFailureReasonErrorKey]];

    NSError *error = [[NSError alloc] initWithDomain:@"com.hans-eric.ios6recipesbook"
                                                code:22 userInfo:userInfo];

    [ErrorHandler handleError:error fatal:YES];
}
```

Now that you have the interface of the default error handling API set up and the ways to test it, you can start implementing the actual error handling.

Notifying the User

The very least a decent default error handling method should do, is to notify the user that an error has occurred. Switch back to the ErrorHandler.m file and add the following code to the handleError:fatal: method:

```
+(void)handleError:(NSError *)error fatal:(BOOL)fatalError
{
    NSString *localizedCancelTitle = NSLocalizedString(@"Dismiss", nil);
    if (fatalError)
        localizedCancelTitle = NSLocalizedString(@"Shut Down", nil);

    // Notify the user
    UIAlertView *alert = [[UIAlertView alloc] initWithTitle:[error localizedDescription]
                                                    message:[error localizedFailureReason]
                                                   delegate:nil
                                          cancelButtonTitle:localizedCancelTitle
                                          otherButtonTitles:nil];

    [alert show];
    // Log to standard out
    NSLog(@"Unhandled error:\n%@, %@", error, [error userInfo]);
}
```

You can now build and run the application to see how this will look. Try tapping the non-fatal error button first, which should display an alert like the one in Figure 1-60.

Figure 1-60. An error alert with a fake error

If you tap the button that fakes a fatal error, you'll get a similar alert. However, what you want for errors flagged as fatal, is that the app is shut down automatically after the user has been notified. Let's implement that now.

What you're going to do is to provide the alert view with a delegate. That way you can intercept when the user dismisses the alert view, so that you can abort the execution there. Add the following code to the handleError:fatal: method. At this point it does not compile, but don't worry, you sort it out in a minute:

```
+(void)handleError:(NSError *)error fatal:(BOOL)fatalError
{
    NSString *localizedCancelTitle = NSLocalizedString(@"Dismiss", nil);
    if (fatalError)
        localizedCancelTitle = NSLocalizedString(@"Shut Down", nil);

    // Notify the user
    ErrorHandler *delegate = [[ErrorHandler alloc] initWithError:error fatal:fatalError];
    if (!retainedDelegates) {
```

```
            retainedDelegates = [[NSMutableArray alloc] init];
        }
        [retainedDelegates addObject:delegate];

        UIAlertView *alert = [[UIAlertView alloc] initWithTitle:[error localizedDescription]
                                              message:[error localizedFailureReason]
                                              delegate:delegate
                                     cancelButtonTitle:localizedCancelTitle
                                     otherButtonTitles:nil];

        [alert show];
        // Log to standard out
        NSLog(@"Unhandled error:\n%@, %@", error, [error userInfo]);
}
```

The `retainedDelegates` hack deserves some explanation. The delegate property of an alert view is a so-called weak reference. What this means is that it will not keep the delegate from deallocating if all other references to it are released.

To keep the delegate from being prematurely deallocated (by ARC) you'll use a static array. As long as a delegate is a member of the `retainedDelegates` array, a strong reference is kept that will keep the delegate alive. As you'll see later, once the delegate's job is finished it will remove itself from the array and allow it to become deallocated.

Add the actual declaration at the top of the `@implementation` block of the `ErrorHandler` class, like so

```
//
//  ErrorHandler.m
//  Recipe 1-10: Default Error Handling
//

#import "ErrorHandler.h"

@implementation ErrorHandler

static NSMutableArray *retainedDelegates = nil;

// ...

@end
```

Now, go to the `ErrorHandler.h` file again, and add the following code

```
//
//  ErrorHandler.h
//  Recipe 1-10: Default Error Handling
//

#import <Foundation/Foundation.h>

@interface ErrorHandler : NSObject<UIAlertViewDelegate>
```

```
@property (strong, nonatomic)NSError *error;
@property (nonatomic)BOOL fatalError;

-(id)initWithError:(NSError *)error fatal:(BOOL)fatalError;

+(void)handleError:(NSError *)error fatal:(BOOL)fatalError;

@end
```

What you've done now is to turn the ErrorHandler class into an alert view delegate. You could of course have created a new class for this purpose, but this is a bit easier. Now, switch to ErrorHandler.m and implement the initWithError: method:

```
-(id)initWithError:(NSError *)error fatal:(BOOL)fatalError
{
    self = [super init];
    if (self) {
        self.error = error;
        self.fatalError = fatalError;
    }
    return self;
}
```

Finally, implement the clickedButtonAtIndex: delegate method to abort in case of a fatal error. As you can see from the code that follows, you also release the delegate by removing it from the retainedDelegates array:

```
-(void)alertView:(UIAlertView *)alertView clickedButtonAtIndex:(NSInteger)buttonIndex
{
    if (self.fatalError) {
        // In case of a fatal error, abort execution
        abort();
    }
    // Job is finished, release this delegate
    [retainedDelegates removeObject:self];
}
```

If you re-run the app now and tap the Fake a Fatal Error button, the app will abort execution right after you've dismissed the error message by tapping the Shut Down button (see Figure 1-61).

Figure 1-61. An alert view displaying a fake fatal error

Notifying the user and logging the error is the least we should do when handling an unexpected error so the code you've implemented so far is a good candidate for a default error handling method. However, there is one more feature of the NSError class that you'd want to support: Recovery options.

Implementing Recovery Options

NSError offers a way for the notifying method to provide custom recovery options. For example, a method that is called to establish a connection of some kind may provide a "Retry" option in case of a timeout failure.

The localizedRecoveryOptions array of an NSObject holds the titles of available recovery options defined by the callee method. Additionally, the localizedRecoverySuggestion property can be used to give the user an idea of how to handle the error. The option titles as well as the recovery suggestion are suitable for communicating directly with the user, for example in an alert view.

The last piece of the NSError recovery functionality is the recoveryAttempter property. It references an object that conforms to the NSErrorRecoveryAttempting informal protocol, which is what you will use to invoke a particular recovery action.

Let's integrate this information in the handleError:fatalError: method:

```
+(void)handleError:(NSError *)error fatal:(BOOL)fatalError
{
    NSString *localizedCancelTitle = NSLocalizedString(@"Dismiss", nil);
    if (fatalError)
        localizedCancelTitle = NSLocalizedString(@"Shut Down", nil);

    // Notify the user
    ErrorHandler *delegate = [[ErrorHandler alloc] initWithError:error fatal:fatalError];
    if (!retainedDelegates) {
        retainedDelegates = [[NSMutableArray alloc] init];
    }
    [retainedDelegates addObject:delegate];

    UIAlertView *alert = [[UIAlertView alloc] initWithTitle:[error localizedDescription]
                                        message:[error localizedFailureReason]
                                        delegate:delegate
                                  cancelButtonTitle:localizedCancelTitle
                                  otherButtonTitles:nil];

    if ([error recoveryAttempter])
    {
        // Append the recovery suggestion to the error message
        alert.message = [NSString stringWithFormat:@"%@\n%@", alert.message,
            error.localizedRecoverySuggestion];
        // Add buttons for the recovery options
        for (NSString * option in error.localizedRecoveryOptions)
        {
            [alert addButtonWithTitle:option];
        }
    }

    [alert show];
    // Log to standard out
    NSLog(@"Unhandled error:\n%@, %@", error, [error userInfo]);
}
```

You implement the actual recovery attempts in the alertView:clickedButtonAtIndex: method, by making the following changes to it:

```
-(void)alertView:(UIAlertView *)alertView clickedButtonAtIndex:(NSInteger)buttonIndex
{
    if (buttonIndex != [alertView cancelButtonIndex])
    {
        NSString *buttonTitle = [alertView buttonTitleAtIndex:buttonIndex];
        NSInteger recoveryIndex = [[self.error localizedRecoveryOptions]
                        indexOfObject:buttonTitle];
```

```
        if (recoveryIndex != NSNotFound)
        {
            if ([[self.error recoveryAttempter] attemptRecoveryFromError:self.error
                                                    optionIndex:recoveryIndex] == NO)
            {
                // Redisplay alert since recovery attempt failed
                [ErrorHandler handleError:self.error fatal:self.fatalError];
            }
        }
    }
    else
    {
        // Cancel button clicked

        if (self.fatalError)
        {
            // In case of a fatal error, abort execution
            abort();
        }
    }

    // Job is finished, release this delegate
    [retainedDelegates removeObject:self];
}
```

You're now finished with the default error handling method. To test this last feature, build and run the app and tap the Non-Fatal Error button again. This time the error alert resembles the one in Figure 1-62.

Figure 1-62. An error alert with a Retry option

Now you have a convenient default error handling method that extracts information from an NSError object and does the following:

1. Alerts the user.

2. If available, provides the user with recovery options.

3. Logs the error to the standard error output.

In the next recipe we show you how you can handle exceptions with the same ease.

Recipe 1-11: Handling Exceptions

Exceptions in iOS are by convention reserved for unrecoverable errors. When an exception is raised, it should ultimately result in program termination. For that reason iOS apps rarely catch exceptions internally but let the default exception handling method deal with them.

The default exception handling method catches any uncaught exceptions, writes some debug information to the console and then terminates the program. Although this is the safe way to deal with iOS exceptions, there is a severe usability problem attached to this approach. Because the console can't be seen from a real device, the app just disappears at the hands of the user—with no explanation whatsoever.

This recipe shows you how you can make the user experience a little better while keeping a reasonably safe exception handling approach that will work in most situations.

A Strategy for Handling Exceptions

As a general solution, terminating the app on uncaught exceptions is a good strategy since it's safe and will prevent bad things like data corruption from happening. However, we'd like to make a couple of improvements to the default exception handling of iOS.

The first thing we want to do is to notify the user about the uncaught exception. From a user's point of view this is best done at the time of the exception, just before the program terminates. However, the program may then be operating in a hostile environment due to fatal errors like out-of-memory or pointer errors. In those situations, complex things like user interface programming should be avoided.

A good compromise is therefore to log the error and alert the user on the next app launch. To accomplish this you need to intercept uncaught exceptions and set a flag that persists between the two sessions.

Setting Up a Test Application

Like you did in the previous recipe you're going to setup a test application to try this out. Start by creating a new single-view application. Then add a button to the main view, make it look something like Figure 1-63.

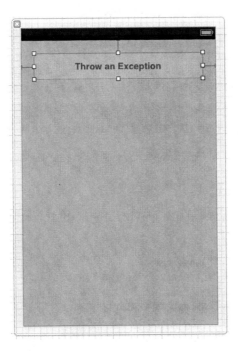

Figure 1-63. A button to throw a fake exception

Add an action for the button called throwFakeException and add the following implementation to it:

```
- (IBAction)throwFakeException:(id)sender
{
    NSException *e = [[NSException alloc] initWithName:@"FakeException"
        reason:@"The developer sucks!" userInfo:[NSDictionary dictionaryWithObject:@"Extra info"
        forKey:@"Key"]];
    [e raise];
}
```

With the test code in place, you can move on to the implementation of the handling of exceptions.

Intercepting Uncaught Exceptions

The way to intercept uncaught exceptions in iOS is to register a handler with the NSSetUncaughtException function. The handler is a void function with an NSException reference as the only parameter, like this one:

```
void myExceptionHandler(NSException *exception)
{
    // Handle Exceptions
}
```

The exception handler you're going to implement should set a flag that informs the app that an exception occurred on the last run. For that you'll use NSUserDefaults, which is designed for persisting settings between sessions. Now, in the AppDelegate.m file, add the following method:

```
void exceptionHandler(NSException *exception)
{
    //Set flag
    NSUserDefaults *settings = [NSUserDefaults standardUserDefaults];

    [settings setBool:YES forKey:@"ExceptionOccurredOnLastRun"];
    [settings synchronize];
}
```

Next, register the exception handler in the application:didFinishLaunchingWithOptions: method, like so:

```
-(BOOL)application:(UIApplication *)application
didFinishLaunchingWithOptions:(NSDictionary *)launchOptions
{

    NSSetUncaughtExceptionHandler(&exceptionHandler);

    // Normal Setup Code
    // ...
}
```

The next thing you'll do is to add a check in application:didFinishLaunchingWithOptions: to see if the last session ended in an exception. If that's the case you'll reset the flag and notify the user with an alert view. Add this code before the line where you register the exception handler, like so

```
- (BOOL)application:(UIApplication *)application didFinishLaunchingWithOptions:(NSDictionary *)
launchOptions
{
    // Default exception handling code
    NSUserDefaults *settings = [NSUserDefaults standardUserDefaults];

    if ([settings boolForKey:@"ExceptionOccurredOnLastRun"])
    {
        // Reset exception occurred flag
        [settings setBool:NO forKey:@"ExceptionOccurredOnLastRunKey"];
        [settings synchronize];

        // Notify the user
        UIAlertView *alert = [[UIAlertView alloc] initWithTitle:@"We're sorry"
            message:@"An error occurred on the previous run." delegate:nil
            cancelButtonTitle:@"Dismiss" otherButtonTitles:nil];
        [alert show];
    }
```

```
NSSetUncaughtExceptionHandler(&exceptionHandler);

    // ...
}
```

Now you have the basic structure of your improved default handling method in place. If you run the app now and tap the button to raise the fake exception, your app will terminate. However, if you start it up again you'll get an alert like the one in Figure 1-64, notifying you of the error that occurred earlier.

Figure 1-64. An error message notifying the user of an error that caused the app to close down on the last run

That's great, but let's make this feature a bit more useful.

Reporting Errors

Many uncaught exceptions in iOS apps are pure programming errors, bugs that you can fix if you only get proper information about them. For this reason iOS creates a crash report when an app has terminated due to an uncaught exception.

However, even though a developer can extract the information about crashes, he or she needs to connect the device to a computer to do so. If your app is out there in the hands of real users, retrieving the crash report may be impossible or inconvenient at best.

As an alternative we'd like users to be able to send these error reports directly to us. You can do so by adding an Email Report button to the error alert.

First, you need to store information about the exception so that you can retrieve it on the next run if the user decides to send the error report. A good way to do this is to use the natural source of error logging, the stderr stream.

The stderr stream is the channel to which NSLog sends the log messages. By default this is the console but it's possible to redirect the stderr stream to a file by using the freopen function. To do that, add the following code to the application:didFinishLaunchingWithOptions: method:

```
- (BOOL)application:(UIApplication *)application didFinishLaunchingWithOptions:(NSDictionary *)
launchOptions
{
    // Default exception handling code
    NSUserDefaults *settings = [NSUserDefaults standardUserDefaults];

    if ([settings boolForKey:@"ExceptionOccurredOnLastRun"])
    {
        // Reset exception occurred flag
        [settings setBool:NO forKey:@"ExceptionOccurredOnLastRunKey"];
        [settings synchronize];

        // Notify the user
        UIAlertView *alert = [[UIAlertView alloc] initWithTitle:@"We're sorry" message:@"An error
occurred on the previous run." delegate:nil cancelButtonTitle:@"Dismiss" otherButtonTitles:nil];
        [alert show];
    }


    NSSetUncaughtExceptionHandler(&exceptionHandler);

    // Redirect stderr output stream to file
    NSArray *paths = NSSearchPathForDirectoriesInDomains(NSDocumentDirectory,
                                                NSUserDomainMask, YES);
    NSString *documentsPath = [paths objectAtIndex:0];
    NSString *stderrPath = [documentsPath stringByAppendingPathComponent:@"stderr.log"];

    freopen([stderrPath cStringUsingEncoding:NSASCIIStringEncoding], "w", stderr);

    // ...
}
```

This makes it so that all entries to NSLog are written to a file named stderr.log in the app's documents directory on the device. The file is re-created (thanks to the **"w"** argument) for each new session so the file only contains information and error logs from the last run, which is what you want for the error report.

On uncaught exceptions, iOS writes some basic information about the crash to stderr (and thus your file). However, two important pieces of information are not logged, namely the exception's userInfo dictionary and a symbolized (that is, readable) call stack. Fortunately you can add that information from your exception handling function:

```
void exceptionHandler(NSException *exception)
{
    NSLog(@"Uncaught exception: %@\nReason: %@\nUser Info: %@\nCall Stack: %@",
          exception.name, exception.reason, exception.userInfo, exception.callStackSymbols);
    //Set flag
    NSUserDefaults *settings = [NSUserDefaults standardUserDefaults];

    [settings setBool:YES forKey:@"ExceptionOccurredOnLastRun"];
    [settings synchronize];
}
```

Now that you have the exception data persisted, you can move on to add the button with which the user can send the information to you.

Adding the Button

To add an Email Report button, you make two small changes to the code that creates the alert view:

```
UIAlertView *alert = [[UIAlertView alloc] initWithTitle:@"We're sorry"
    message:@"An error occurred on the previous run." delegate:self
    cancelButtonTitle:@"Dismiss" otherButtonTitles:nil];
[alert addButtonWithTitle:@"Email a Report"];
[alert show];
```

You added a button to the alert view and told it to send all events to the AppDelegate object (by declaring self as the delegate). To avoid the compiler warning, you also need to make the AppDelegate an alert view delegate by declaring the UIAlertViewDelegate protocol. To do that, open AppDelegate.h and make the following change:

```
@interface AppDelegate : UIResponder <UIApplicationDelegate, UIAlertViewDelegate>
//...

@end
```

Now you can add the `alertView:didDismissWithButtonIndex:` alert view delegate method to intercept when a user taps the Email Report button. Go back to AppDelegate.m and add the following code:

```
-(void)alertView:(UIAlertView *)alertView didDismissWithButtonIndex:(NSInteger)buttonIndex
{
    if (buttonIndex == 1)
    {
        //todo: Email a Report here
    }
}
```

Before you go on and write the code for the email report, you need to fix a problem with the current code. Because alert views in iOS are displayed asynchronously, the code for redirecting the `stderr` output is run before `application:didDismissWithButtonIndex:` is invoked. This erases the content of the file prematurely.

To fix this you have to make two changes.

First, in `application:didFinishLaunchingWithOptions:` be sure that the exception handling setup code is only run if there has been no exception, by adding the following code:

```
- (BOOL)application:(UIApplication *)application didFinishLaunchingWithOptions:(NSDictionary *)
launchOptions
{
    // Default exception handling code
    NSUserDefaults *settings = [NSUserDefaults standardUserDefaults];

    if ([settings boolForKey:@"ExceptionOccurredOnLastRun"])
    {
        // Reset exception occurred flag
        [settings setBool:NO forKey:@"ExceptionOccurredOnLastRunKey"];
        [settings synchronize];

        // Notify the user
        UIAlertView *alert = [[UIAlertView alloc] initWithTitle:@"We're sorry" message:@"An error
occurred on the previous run." delegate:self cancelButtonTitle:@"Dismiss" otherButtonTitles:nil];
        [alert addButtonWithTitle:@"Email a Report"];
        [alert show];
    }
    else
    {

        NSSetUncaughtExceptionHandler(&exceptionHandler);

        // Redirect stderr output stream to file
        NSArray *paths = NSSearchPathForDirectoriesInDomains(NSDocumentDirectory,
                                                    NSUserDomainMask, YES);
        NSString *documentsPath = [paths objectAtIndex:0];
        NSString *stderrPath = [documentsPath stringByAppendingPathComponent:@"stderr.log"];
```

```
        freopen([stderrPath cStringUsingEncoding:NSASCIIStringEncoding], "w", stderr);
    }

    // ...
}
```

The second thing you need to do is to add the setup code to the `alertView:didDismissWithButtonIndex:` so that it sets up the exception handling for the other case too, when there has been an exception. Here are the necessary changes:

```
-(void)alertView:(UIAlertView *)alertView didDismissWithButtonIndex:(NSInteger)buttonIndex
{
    NSArray *paths = NSSearchPathForDirectoriesInDomains(NSDocumentDirectory,
                                            NSUserDomainMask, YES);
    NSString *documentsPath = [paths objectAtIndex:0];
    NSString *stderrPath = [documentsPath stringByAppendingPathComponent:@"stderr.log"];

    if (buttonIndex == 1)
    {
        //todo: Email a Report here
    }

    NSSetUncaughtExceptionHandler(&exceptionHandler);

    // Redirect stderr output stream to file
    freopen([stderrPath cStringUsingEncoding:NSASCIIStringEncoding], "w", stderr);
}
```

Now you're ready for the final step: composing an error report email.

Emailing the Report

When the user presses the Email Report button, you'll use the `MFMailComposeViewController` class to handle the email. This class is part of the `MessageUI` framework so go ahead and link it to the project. (Details about how to link framework binaries can be found in Recipe 1-2).

Then you need to import `MessageUI.h` and `MFMailComposeViewController.h` to your `AppDelegate.h` file. Also, because you'll need to respond to events from the mail view controller, add `MFMailComposeViewControllerDelegate` to the list of supported protocols. The `AppDelegate.h` file should now look like this code:

```
#import <UIKit/UIKit.h>
#import <MessageUI/MessageUI.h>
#import <MessageUI/MFMailComposeViewController.h>

@class ViewController;
```

```
@interface AppDelegate : UIResponder <UIApplicationDelegate, UIAlertViewDelegate,
MFMailComposeViewControllerDelegate>

// ...

@end
```

Now you can create and present a `MFMailComposeViewController` with the error report. Add the following code to the `alertView:didDismissWithButtonIndex:` method:

```
-(void)alertView:(UIAlertView *)alertView didDismissWithButtonIndex:(NSInteger)buttonIndex
{
    NSArray *paths = NSSearchPathForDirectoriesInDomains(NSDocumentDirectory,
                                                NSUserDomainMask, YES);
    NSString *documentsPath = [paths objectAtIndex:0];
    NSString *stderrPath = [documentsPath stringByAppendingPathComponent:@"stderr.log"];

    if (buttonIndex == 1)
    {
        // Email a Report
        MFMailComposeViewController *mailComposer = [[MFMailComposeViewController alloc] init];
        mailComposer.mailComposeDelegate = self;
        [mailComposer setSubject:@"Error Report"];
        [mailComposer setToRecipients:[NSArray arrayWithObject:@"support@mycompany.com"]];
        // Attach log file
        NSArray *paths = NSSearchPathForDirectoriesInDomains(NSDocumentDirectory,
                                                    NSUserDomainMask, YES);
        NSString *documentsPath = [paths objectAtIndex:0];
        NSString *stderrPath = [documentsPath stringByAppendingPathComponent:@"stderr.log"];
        NSData *data = [NSData dataWithContentsOfFile:stderrPath];
        [mailComposer addAttachmentData:data mimeType:@"Text/XML" fileName:@"stderr.log"];
        UIDevice *device = [UIDevice currentDevice];
        NSString *emailBody =
            [NSString stringWithFormat:@"My Model: %@\nMy OS: %@\nMy Version: %@",
                [device model], [device systemName], [device systemVersion]];
        [mailComposer setMessageBody:emailBody isHTML:NO];
        [self.window.rootViewController presentViewController:mailComposer animated:YES
                                                completion:nil];
    }

    NSSetUncaughtExceptionHandler(&exceptionHandler);

    // Redirect stderr output stream to file
    freopen([stderrPath cStringUsingEncoding:NSASCIIStringEncoding], "w", stderr);
}
```

To dismiss the mail compose controller you also need to respond to the
`mailComposeController:didFinishWithResult:error:` message, sent by the controller upon send or
cancel events:

```
-(void)mailComposeController:(MFMailComposeViewController *)controller didFinishWithResult:(MFMailCo
mposeResult)result error:(NSError *)error
{
    [self.window.rootViewController dismissViewControllerAnimated:YES completion:nil];
}
```

Your app now has a good default exception handling that is both user friendly, useful, and safe.
When you test it now, you'll see that the alert view has an additional button that allows you to send
the report through mail. Figure 1-65 shows you an example of this.

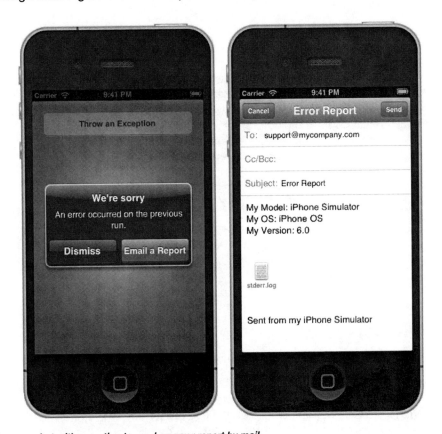

Figure 1-65. An error alert with an option to send an error report by mail

A Final Touch

There is one more thing you may want to consider when implementing this recipe. Because you
redirect `stderr` to a file, no error logging is displayed in the output console. This may be a problem
during development when you conduct most of your testing in the simulator. During that time, you
probably want the error messages to show in the console rather than being stored in a file.

Fortunately, there is a simple solution. You can use the predefined conditional TARGET_IPHONE_SIMULATOR to set up our exception handling code only when the app is run on a real device. Here's how you do it:

```
- (BOOL)application:(UIApplication *)application didFinishLaunchingWithOptions:(NSDictionary *)
launchOptions
{
    #if !TARGET_IPHONE_SIMULATOR
    // Default exception handling code

    // ...

    #endif

    // Other Setup Code

    // ...
}
```

This concludes our default exception handling recipe. By having a well thought-through strategy for handling errors you not only save time for yourself, you also pay the users the respect they deserve. We hope that with the help of these two recipes you have seen the value of good exception handling, and that it's really not that difficult to achieve. You've probably already seen ways in which these simple examples can be improved. Why not venture into that? After all, the sooner you build these features into your app, the more use you'll have for them.

Recipe 1-12: Adding a Lite Version

Offering a lite version of your app is a great way to give customers a chance to try your app before buying it. Maintaining two code bases however can be quite tiresome and get out of hand as you implement new features into your app. This recipe shows you how you can set up the project to include both versions in one code base.

Adding a Build Target

For this recipe we have created a new Single View Application with the name SampleProject.

Select your project file in the Navigator area, and then select the build target for your project. Now press ⌘+D to duplicate the target. You are prompted to Duplicate Only or Duplicate and Transition to iPad, as shown in Figure 1-66. Click Duplicate Only to create a new target to use for your Lite build. This results in a separate build target with which you can implement a second version.

Figure 1-66. Project duplication options

Rename the new target with an appending "Lite" text by double-clicking the target name. You also want to change the new target's Product Name attribute to signal that it's a Lite version. You find the Product Name attribute in the Build Settings tab under the Packaging heading (see Figure 1-67).

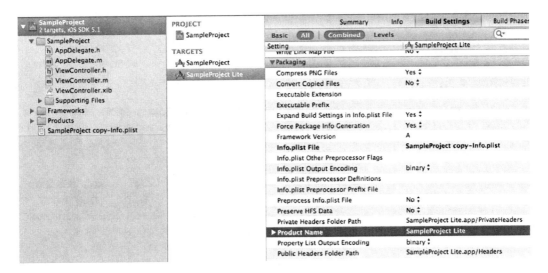

Figure 1-67. Appending "Lite" to the target's name and the Product Name build setting

> **Tip**   The easiest way to find a particular build attribute is to use the search field in the upper-left corner of the Build Settings tab. Just type **Product Name** and the attributes are filtered out as you type.

You can now build and run the lite version. To do that you need to change the active scheme. When you duplicated the regular target earlier, Xcode created a new build scheme for you. This new scheme is named the same as the initial name of the duplicated target, namely SampleProject copy. Even though you have changed the name of the target to SampleProject Lite, Xcode doesn't change the scheme name accordingly. If this bothers you, you can rename it in the Manage Schemes window, which you can reach from the Active Scheme button (see Figure 1-68).

Figure 1-68. *Go to Manage Schemes if you want to change the name of the Lite build scheme*

Note   Keep in mind that the two targets must have separate bundle identifiers to show up as separate apps when you install and run them on your device (or simulator). Xcode sets up different bundle identifiers by default, but be careful when making changes.

Coding for a Specific Version

Now you need a way to differentiate between the two builds in your source code. For instance, you may want to limit some features in the Lite version, or show ads to the non-paying users. Some code in the Lite version should not be compiled into the full version and vice versa. This is where Preprocessor Macros come in handy.

What you want to do is to add a preprocessing macro named LITE_VERSION. Again this is done in the Build Settings tab, under the compiler's preprocessing header. Hover over the Debug macro, click on its add icon (+) that appears next to it and enter **LITE_VERSION** in the edit field. Be sure to do the same for the Release macro as well. Figure 1-69 shows an example of these changes.

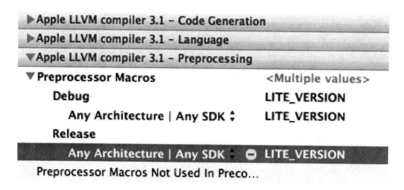

Figure 1-69. *Defining the LITE_VERSION conditional in the preprocessor macros*

To build different features into your app, you will need to use that preprocessor macro you created. Anywhere in your code that you want to specify different code for your lite version versus the full version, use the following `#ifdef` directive:

```
#ifdef LITE_VERSION
// Stuff for Lite version
#else
// Stuff for Full version
#endif
```

Alternatively, you can use the negated form if that's more convenient.

```
#ifndef LITE_VERSION
// Code exclusively for Full version
#endif
```

> **Note** You can also control what files are included in each build. For instance, you may not need to include the full version artwork in the lite version. Click your Lite project target and go to the Build Phases tab. Expand the Copy Bundle Resources ribbon, and remove or add any files that are specific to the lite version.

Recipe 1-13: Adding Launch Images

For the sake of user experience it is generally considered bad practice to show a so-called "splash screen" at application startup. The user is normally eager to start playing with your app and not interested in your branding information. Nor are they particularly eager to watch your cool video, regardless of how much time and money you spent on it.

The extra few seconds it takes for the user to view and/or dismiss the splash screen can be quite annoying and may be unfavorable to the overall experience.

However, there is an exception to the rule. Many apps take a little while to load, a few seconds during which it remains unresponsive and uninteresting. Because this may be as bad a splash screen in terms of user experience, your app should do what it can to mitigate the effect. One way of doing this is to display an image that is removed as soon as the launch is finished and the app is ready to take on user actions.

These images are called "launch images" and are really easy to implement in iOS. The function of displaying an image while the app is loading is already built-in. All you have to do is to provide the appropriate images.

Launch Image Files

Depending on the nature of your app and which devices it supports, you'll need to create one or more launch images. To include a launch image in your app is just a matter of adding it to the project. A simple naming convention then tells iOS if it's a launch image and of what kind.

Launch images are required to be of the PNG file format, and their filenames begin with the identifier Default (with a capital D) and then optionally followed by orientation, scale, and device specifiers in the following form:

```
Default [-<orientation>] [@<scale>] [~<device>] .png
```

Table 1-1 lists some common Launch image types and their filenames.

Table 1-1. Common Launch Image Types

Filename	Image Dimension	Comment
Default.png	320 x 480 (iPhone) 768 x 1004 (iPad)	This is the fallback file. If no other suitable launch image were found, iOS will use this.
Default~iphone.png	320 x 480	iPhone apps are always launched in portrait mode
Default@2x~iphone.png	640 x 960	Retina (iPhone 4 & 4S)
Default-568h@2x.png	640 x 1136	iPhone 5
Default-Portrait~ipad.png	768 x 1004	
Default-Portrait@2x~ipad.png	1536 x 2008	Retina (iPad 3)
Default-Landscape~ipad.png	1024 x 748	
Default-Landscape@2x~ipad.png	2048 x 1496	Retina (iPad 3)

There is a difference between iPhone and iPad launch images that you should be aware of when designing your launch images. iPhone app launch images covers the entire screen while iPad launch images don't include the space for the status bar. This is why iPad launch images are 20 pixels shorter (40 pixels for retina displays) in one dimension.

> **Note**   The filesystem of iOS is case sensitive. Therefore it's important that you pay attention to the casing when you name your launch files. Otherwise your app will not recognize them and show them at startup.

There are more options than we've put in the table, like upside-down portrait and left- or right-oriented landscape. However, it is recommended that you keep the number of launch images to a minimum as they add to the total size of your app.

> **Note**   Because iPhone apps, regardless of actual orientation, always launch in a portrait mode you only need one launch image for those. However, iPad apps usually need two images: one for portrait orientation and one for landscape. Universal apps therefore normally need three launch images: portrait for iPhone, and portrait and landscape for iPad.

After you've created the launch images, you can add them to your project. This is done by Ctrl-clicking the Supporting Files folder of your project and choosing Add Files to <your project> from the context menu (see Figure 1-70).

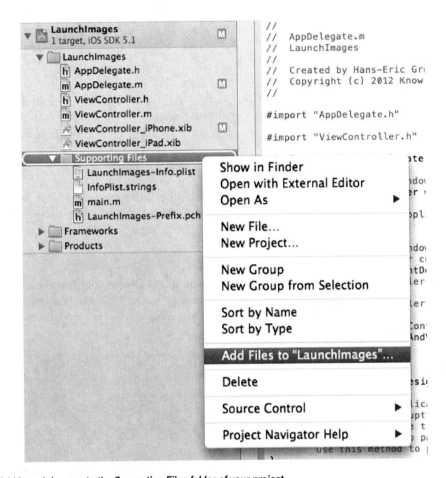

Figure 1-70. Add launch images to the Supporting Files folder of your project

Be sure to check the Copy items into destination group's folder (if needed) option as in Figure 1-71, so that the images are copied into the app's bundle.

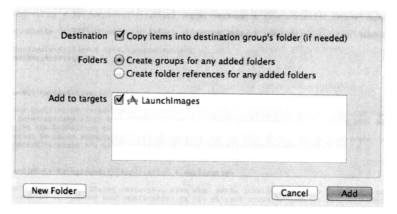

Figure 1-71. *Make sure Copy items into destination group's folder (if needed) is checked*

Now, provided that you named your launch image(s) correctly, it/they will be shown during application launch and replaced with the main view once the app is ready for user interaction.

Designing Launch Images

Apple's philosophy regarding launch images is that they should resemble the main view of the app as much as possible. This makes the loading time seem a little bit quicker and therefore more responsive than if the launch image has a more splash-like design, which contains, say, branding information.

So, for instance, if your app's main view consists of a table view, your launch image could look something like Figure 1-72.

Figure 1-72. *A launch image should resemble the main view of your app*

Also, it's recommended that launch images don't contain elements that may need to be translated or changed during localization. For example, the launch image in Figure 1-67 doesn't contain any navigation bar buttons. These have been edited out as well as the elements in the status bar.

Even though there is support for language specific versions of the launch images, it's suggested you don't use it due to the increased amount of space the additional launch images will require.

Summary

In this chapter you've acquired (or refreshed) some fundamental knowledge you need to follow the remaining recipes of this book. You've seen how to set up a basic application, how to build user interfaces, and how to control them from your code. You've also seen an extensive example of how to use Storyboards, the new way in which Apple wants you to build and structure user interfaces. Additionally, you've learned the difference between errors and exceptions in iOS, and seen how you can implement a strategy to handle them.

By now you should be more than ready to take on the rest of this book.

Chapter 2

Layout Recipes

The user interface and its layout is essential to most applications; especially so in iOS with its orientation-sensitive devices. Users pretty much expect apps of today to support both portrait and landscape orientation. They also expect apps to run on both iPhone and iPad. In other words, they expect your apps to have dynamic layouts.

This chapter shows you how to use Autolayout, a great new way to build dynamic user interfaces in iOS 6.

Recipe 2-1: Using Autolayout

Autolayout is a new feature in iOS 6 that provides a way to handle view layouts in iOS apps. It supersedes the old "springs and struts" layout system, which is still present but now more or less obsolete; all you could do with "springs and struts" can now be done using Autolayout. In addition, Autolayout offers a much more powerful model with which you can build layouts that scale and adapt to screen rotations in a way that was not possible without reverting to code. In this recipe we show you how Autolayout works and how you can start taking advantage of it.

Autolayout Constraints

Autolayout, in its essence, consists of "constraints" dictating the relationship between user interface elements, and a layout engine that enforces the constraints. If you have created a new project in Xcode 4.5, you've probably already been using Autolayout and constraints. The feature, which is turned on by default, makes Interface Builder set up constraints automatically for you when you build the user interface. To see how this is done you're going to create an application with a simple user interface that automatically adapts to both portrait and landscape orientations.

Start by creating a new single-view application. Next build a user interface such as the one in Figure 2-1, using labels, a text field, and a text view.

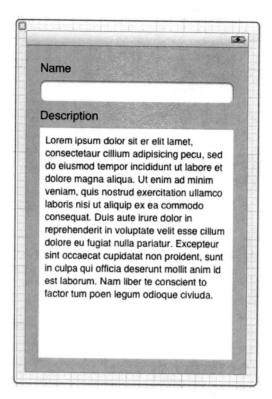

Figure 2-1. The user interface in portrait orientation

When you position and size the elements, be sure to use the default spacing to the main view's boundaries as well as between the subviews, i.e., where Interface Builder snaps during drag, as shown in Figure 2-2.

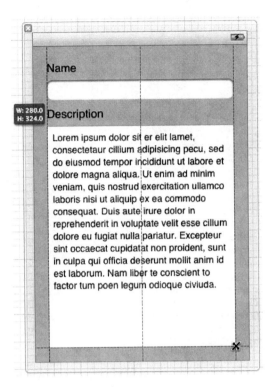

Figure 2-2. The dashed lines in Interface Builder indicate default spacing

While you were building the user interface by positioning and sizing the elements, Interface Builder automatically created the corresponding constraints for you. You can see evidence of these constraints directly in the editor by selecting a view. For example if you select the text field, as in Figure 2-3, you can see that Interface Builder has created four constraints; one for aligning the left edge to the default distance to the main view's bound, one for aligning to the right, one for aligning the top edge to the bottom edge of the Name label, and one for aligning to the Description label below.

Figure 2-3. A text field with constraints for its left, right, top, and bottom edges

Let's take a closer look at these constraints. With the text field still selected, go to the Size inspector (in the Utilities View to the right). As shown in Figure 2-4, there's a section called Constraints that contains the four constraints of the text field. As you can see, there is the constraint for leading space to Superview, trailing space to Superview, top space to the Name label, and bottom space to the Description label; all with default sized spacing.

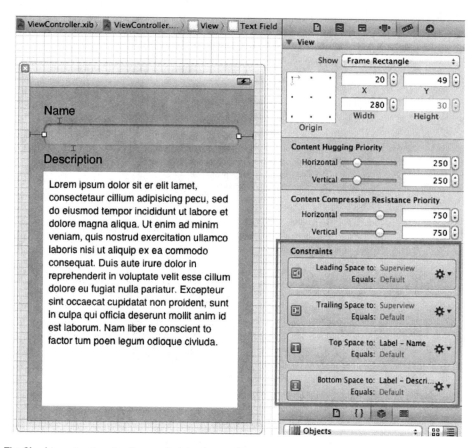

Figure 2-4. The Size inspector showing the constraints of a text field

Now, open the Attribute inspector for the Leading Space to: constraint by selecting Select and Edit from the Options menu, as shown in Figure 2-5.

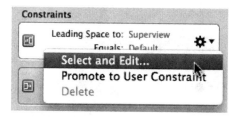

Figure 2-5. The Options menu of a constraint

As you can see in Figure 2-6, this constraint is a Horizontal Space Constraint. We'll talk more about the properties of the constraints later, but for now it's sufficient to know that the constant (in this case the distance between the left edge of the main view and the left edge of the text field) is set to the Standard spacing.

Figure 2-6. The properties of a Horizontal Space Constraint

Go ahead and explore the rest of the constraints, of the text field and of the other views, so that you get a feeling of how the system sets them up. Be sure not to change any values at this point, as it will most likely confuse you. Later, however, you'll learn how to customize the constraints to suit your needs.

Now let's see what the Autolayout system does with these constraints. Build and run your application in the iOS Simulator. When the app has launched, press cmd (⌘)+**right arrow keys** to rotate the device to landscape orientation. As you can see from Figure 2-7, the user interface adapts nicely to the new orientation. This is the work of Autolayout. And you didn't have to do anything to make it work, only lay out your views in Interface Builder as you always do.

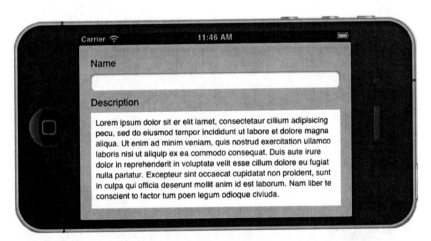

Figure 2-7. Autolayout automatically adapts the user interface to landscape and portrait orientations

In contrast, let's look at how the app behaves with Autolayout turned off. Go to the File Inspector (again located in Xcode's right Utilities View panel.) and in the Interface Builder Document section (see Figure 2-8) uncheck Use Autolayout.

Figure 2-8. *Autolayout is turned on by default for new projects*

After unchecking Use Autolayout, build and run the app again. As you can see in Figure 2-9, rotating the device results in a significantly worse user experience.

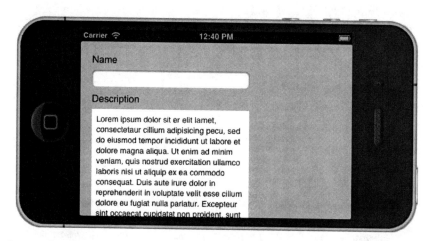

Figure 2-9. *A landscape orientation user interface without Autolayout enabled*

Now before moving on, don't forget to reactivate the Use Autolayout setting by returning to the File Inspector and re-checking Use Autolayout.

Constraint Priorities

You're probably not overly impressed with the previous Autolayout example; indeed, all that we've shown so far can be done using the old layout system. However, what if you wanted a slightly different layout behavior of, for example, the Name text field. What if you didn't want it to grow beyond a certain width when switching between device orientations. (It's a common principle in human computer interaction that the size of input fields should reflect the size of expected content.) Let's say that you want the Name text field to grow when the screen rotates, but only up to 350 pixels. This is where Autolayout starts to shine.

Translated into the language of constraints, you want to add a constraint that states that the text field's width must be of no more than 350 pixels. But adding this constraint yields a logical problem. When the screen rotates, the system can't satisfy both the constraint that pins the right edge of the text field, and the one that dictates its maximum width.

What can you do about that? One thought would be to remove the constraint inserted by Interface Builder. However, it doesn't take much thought to realize that that would leave you with a constraint that's true for many values, but not decisive enough to settle for one value. No, you need both constraints: you want the right edge of the text field to pin to the right edge of the screen *unless that makes the width larger than 350 pixels*. The solution is Constraint Priorities.

Autolayout offers the possibility to set a priority value between 0 and 1000 on individual constraints. A value of 1000 means that the constraint is required, but for any other value the constraint with the higher priority takes precedence. In this case, this means that you can make the width constraint required but set a lower priority of the pin to right edge constraint. Then, when the screen rotates, the width constraint will "win" over the other and you will get the effect you seek.

Start by adding the width constraint. You do this by selecting the text field and clicking the Pin button in the Autolayout bar located in the lower-right corner of the interface editor. The Pin button is the one in the middle. Then select the Width constraint, as shown in Figure 2-10.

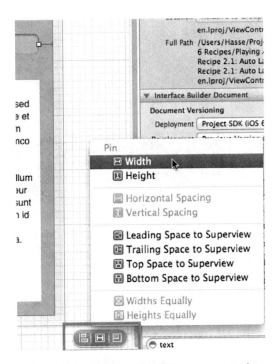

Figure 2-10. The Autolayout bar in Interface Builder allows you to add your own constraints

Now, in the Attributes Inspector for the new Width Constraint, set the relation to Less Than or Equal and the constant to **350**. Leave the priority at 1,000 (required).

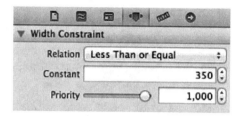

Figure 2-11. Setting a Width Constraint to Less Than or Equal to 350

What's left now is to lower the priority of the trailing space to Superview constraint. Make sure the text field is selected. Then in the Size Inspector, click the Trailing Space to: Superview constraint and choose Select and Edit from the options menu for that constraint. Change the value of the Priority property to **500**, as in Figure 2-12.

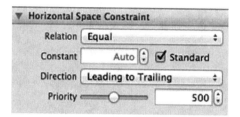

Figure 2-12. Lowering priority of a constraint to 500

If you build and run your application now, you will see that when you rotate the device, the text field, as in Figure 2-13, grows but stays at the maximum width of 350.

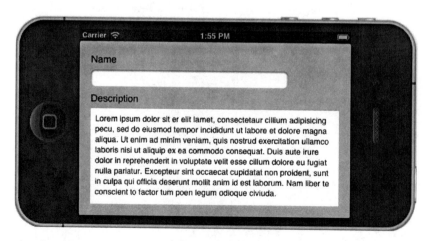

Figure 2-13. A user interface with a text field that has a Width Constraint of 350 pixels

Adding a Trailing Button

Let's make things a little more complicated. What if you want to add a Pick a name button on the right side of the text field and still keep the current width constraint? You can accomplish this using Autolayout.

Before jumping in and adding constraints, it's a good idea to stop and think about the layout in terms of constraints. You want to:

1. Allow the width of the text field to be less or equal to 350.

2. Pin the trailing edge of the text field to the leading edge of the button.

3. Pin the trailing edge of the button to the trailing edge of the screen unless the first constraint is violated.

> **Note**   The reason we're using the terms Leading and Trailing instead of Left and Right (which are also valid attributes) is that trailing and leading is adapting to changes of text directions in, for example, the Hebrew language. On such a locale, leading becomes right and trailing becomes left, and the user interface adapts accordingly. Yet another reason to use Autolayout.

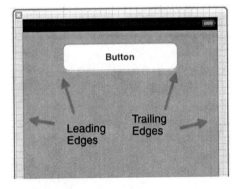

Figure 2-14. Leading and trailing edges in a left-to-right language locale

Before you add the button to the user interface, it's important that you reset the priority of the Trailing Space to: Superview constraint and make it make it a required. Otherwise Interface Builder will be confused and set up constraints that you don't want. So go ahead and select the Trailing Space to: Superview constraint and set its Priority attribute back to **1,000**.

Now add a button with the text **Pick** and position it as in Figure 2-15. Be sure to snap against the standard positions so that the correct constraints are created (according to preceding points 2 and 3.)

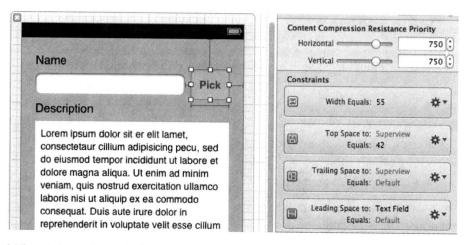

Figure 2-15. Adding a button and snapping it against the trailing edges of the text field and the Superview

You should now have constraints corresponding to points 1, 2 and 3. Verify that your text field has the following constraints (order may differ):

- Width <= 350
- Top Space to: Label – Name
- Leading Space to: Superview
- Bottom Space to: Label – Description
- Trailing Space to: Button - Pick

And, the button's constraints:

- Width Equals: 55
- Top Space to: Superview
- Trailing Space to: Superview
- Align Baseline to: Text Field
- Leading Space to: Text Field

Caution   If your list of constraints differ from the preceding list, delete the constraints (that are allowed by the system to be removed) and reposition the controls. Interface Builder then re-creates the constraints you want.

What's missing now is to lose the constraint of the button's trailing edge. In the same way as previously, select the button and the Trailing Space to: Superview constraint. Change its Priority attribute to **500**.

Build and run. When rotated, the user interface should adapt nicely and keep the text field at the maximum width, while the button stays pinned to its right, as shown in Figure 2-16.

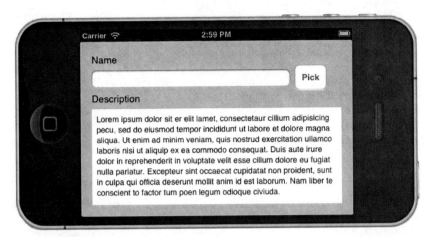

Figure 2-16. A user interface with a text field that has a Width Constraint of 350 pixels and a button trailing to its right

Although simple, we hope that the example here has opened your eyes to the possibilities of Autolayout. The next recipe takes it to the next level, where you'll create constraints from code, constructing a truly dynamic layout.

Recipe 2-2: Programming Autolayout

The preferred way to setup Autolayout constraints is to use Interface Builder (as shown in Recipe 2.1.) The main reason being that Interface Builder won't let you setup constraints that are unsatisfiable or ambiguous. For example, you can't remove or change existing constraints in such a way that violates correctness. This can be a frustrating experience, but it forces you to learn Autolayout up front and not in time-consuming debug sessions (which is worse).

However, there are situations where you can't define your Autolayout constraints in Interface Builder, for example if you create the user interface components dynamically in code. For these situations you need to revert to code for setting up the constraints. In this recipe we'll show you how.

Setting Up the Application

You're going to build a simple app that has three buttons; one for adding a new image view to the screen, one for removing the last image view added, and one for removing all added image views. You're going to use Autolayout to position the buttons in a row at the top of your screen. You also use Autolayout to position the image views so that they overlap each other with the last added image view on top, and each image view has a ten percent increase in size compared to the previous.

Start by creating a new single-view application and then add the following properties to its view controller:

```
//
// ViewController.h
// Recipe 2.2: Coding Autolayout
//
```

```
#import <UIKit/UIKit.h>

@interface ViewController : UIViewController

@property (strong, nonatomic) UIButton *addButton;
@property (strong, nonatomic) UIButton *removeButton;
@property (strong, nonatomic) UIButton *clearButton;
@property (strong, nonatomic) NSMutableArray *imageViews;
@property (strong, nonatomic) NSMutableArray *imageViewConstraints;

@end
```

You're going to create the three buttons directly in code using a `helper` method to reduce code duplication. Switch to ViewController.m and add the following code:

```
- (UIButton *)addButtonWithTitle:(NSString *)title action:(SEL)selector
{
    UIButton *button = [UIButton buttonWithType:UIButtonTypeRoundedRect];
    [button setTitle:title forState:UIControlStateNormal];
    [button addTarget:self action:selector forControlEvents:UIControlEventTouchUpInside];
    button.translatesAutoresizingMaskIntoConstraints = NO;
    [self.view addSubview:button];
    return button;
}
```

The method creates a new Round Rect Button with the provided title and action method. What's notable here is the setting of the `translatesAutoresizingMaskIntoConstraints` property of the button to NO. This is important to do if you're defining your own Autolayout constraints, otherwise you're likely to end up with conflicting constraints. Recipe 2-3 has more to say on this subject.

> **Note**   You don't explicitly set view frames when using Autolayout. Instead, a view's position and size are dictated by the constraints you define.

With the `helper` method in place you can turn to the `viewDidLoad` method and add code to create the buttons:

```
- (void)viewDidLoad
{
    [super viewDidLoad];
    self.addButton = [self addButtonWithTitle:@"Add" action:@selector(addImageView)];
    self.removeButton = [self addButtonWithTitle:@"Remove" action:@selector(removeImageView)];
    self.clearButton = [self addButtonWithTitle:@"Clear" action:@selector(clearImageViews)];
}
```

Next, add stubs for the three action methods now connected to the respective button. You'll implement these methods later, but leave them empty for now:

```
- (void)addImageView
{
}

- (void)removeImageView
{
}

- (void)clearImageViews
{
}
```

If you run your application now, you would see nothing but a gray screen. The buttons wouldn't show because you haven't yet defined any Autolayout constraints to dictate their positions and sizes. So let's go ahead and do that.

There are two principle ways to create constraints from code. You can either use the so called Visual Format Language, or you can use the `constraintWithItem:attribute:relatedBy:toItem:attribute :multiplier:constant:` method. The former has the advantage that it provides better visualization of the constraints created; the latter, on the other hand, provides completeness (not all constraints can be expressed using the Visual Format Language).

Often you'll mix the two ways to create your constraints. In this case you use the format language for positioning the buttons, and a mix of the two for placing the image views.

The Visual Format Language

Before moving on and starting to create the constraints, let's take a quick look at the Visual Format Language. For example, this string defines constraints that position `button2` right next to `button1` with a spacing of 20 pixels between the two:

```
[button1]-20-[button2]
```

A single hyphen indicates default spacing:

```
[button1]-[button2]
```

Here are same constraints but for vertical layout:

```
V:[button1]-[button2]
```

Although horizontal is the default, you can explicitly state it:

```
H:[button1]-[button2]
```

The spacing toward the Superview is indicated with a | character. The following example states that `textField` should be pinned to both leading and trailing ends of the Superview, with a default spacing:

```
|-[textField]-|
```

You can also define a component size. This example says that `button1` shall be 50 pixels wide and that `button2` has the same width as `button1`:

```
[button1(50)]-[button2(==button1)]
```

You also can have inequalities, as in the following example, which states that `button1` shall be at least 50 pixels wide:

```
[button1(>=50)]
```

You can set both a minimum and a maximum width at the same time:

```
[button1(>=50, <=100)]
```

You also can set priorities on the size constraints, for example that `button1` shall be at least 50 pixels wide, but with a priority at 500, which makes it non-required but desirable:

```
[button1(>=50@500)
```

Table 2-1 shows the syntax elements and some additional examples of the Visual Format Language.

Table 2-1. Visual Format Language Syntax Elements

Syntax Elements	Examples	Description
H:, V:	H:|-[statusLabel]-| V:|[textView]|	Horizontal or vertical orientation. Default orientation is horizontal so the H: can therefore be omitted.
|	|[textView]|	Indicates the Superview; its leading end if on the left side and trailing on the right
-	[button1]-[button2]	Standard space
-N-	|-20-[view]	An N-sized spacing
[view]		Indicates a subview
==, >=, <=	[view1(==view2)] [view(>=30, <=100)]	Relation operators. Can only be used in size constraints
@N	[view(==50@500)] [view1(==view2@500, >=30)]	Constraint priority. Can only be used in size constraints. Default priority is 1000 (i.e., a required constraint)

Now, let's add constraints that position the three buttons in a row at the top of the screen. Because these constraints are always the same, you add them directly in the viewDidLoad method. You start by creating a dictionary containing the buttons with identifying keys. Autolayout uses the dictionary to map identifiers in the format language strings to the corresponding views (buttons in this case):

```
NSDictionary *viewsDictionary =
    [[NSDictionary alloc] initWithObjectsAndKeys:
        self.addButton, @"addButton",
        self.removeButton, @"removeButton",
        self.clearButton, @"clearButton", nil];
```

Then you add the constraints that pin the buttons to each other in a row. You do this by calling addConstraints:constraintsWithVisualFormat:options:metrics:views: method of the main view, providing the visual format string (marked in bold here):

```
[self.view addConstraints:[NSLayoutConstraint
    constraintsWithVisualFormat:@"H:|-[addButton]-[removeButton]-[clearButton]"
    options:0 metrics:nil views:viewsDictionary]];
```

Next, you pin the buttons to the top of the screen:

```
[self.view addConstraints:[NSLayoutConstraint
    constraintsWithVisualFormat:@"V:|-[addButton]"
    options:0 metrics:nil views:viewsDictionary]];
[self.view addConstraints:[NSLayoutConstraint
    constraintsWithVisualFormat:@"V:|-[removeButton]"
    options:0 metrics:nil views:viewsDictionary]];
[self.view addConstraints:[NSLayoutConstraint
    constraintsWithVisualFormat:@"V:|-[clearButton]"
    options:0 metrics:nil views:viewsDictionary]];
```

Here's what the viewDidLoad looks like at this point:

```
- (void)viewDidLoad
{
    [super viewDidLoad];
    self.addButton = [self addButtonWithTitle:@"Add" action:@selector(addImageView)];
    self.removeButton = [self addButtonWithTitle:@"Remove" action:@selector(removeImageView)];
    self.clearButton = [self addButtonWithTitle:@"Clear" action:@selector(clearImageViews)];

    NSDictionary *viewsDictionary =
        [[NSDictionary alloc] initWithObjectsAndKeys:
            self.addButton, @"addButton",
            self.removeButton, @"removeButton",
            self.clearButton, @"clearButton", nil];

    [self.view addConstraints:[NSLayoutConstraint
        constraintsWithVisualFormat:@"H:|-[addButton]-[removeButton]-[clearButton]"
        options:0 metrics:nil views:viewsDictionary]];
```

```
    [self.view addConstraints:[NSLayoutConstraint
        constraintsWithVisualFormat:@"V:|-[addButton]"
        options:0 metrics:nil views:viewsDictionary]];
    [self.view addConstraints:[NSLayoutConstraint
        constraintsWithVisualFormat:@"V:|-[removeButton]"
        options:0 metrics:nil views:viewsDictionary]];
    [self.view addConstraints:[NSLayoutConstraint
        constraintsWithVisualFormat:@"V:|-[clearButton]"
        options:0 metrics:nil views:viewsDictionary]];
}
```

You now can build and run your application. Your screen should look like the one in Figure 2-17.

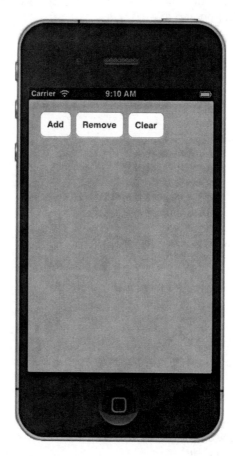

Figure 2-17. *A row of buttons positioned using Autolayout*

Now that you've verified that the layout is as expected, it's time to implement the respective button's action method. We'll start with the adding of image views.

Adding Image Views

Before you move on and start implementing the `addImageView` action method, you need to do a little more setup and initialization. First, you need an image that you're going to populate the image views with. (For simplicity we use the same image for all image views.) Therefore, using a Finder window, drag an image of your liking (and which is in the PNG format) to your Supporting Files folder of your project. (Chapter 1 contains a detailed description on how to add resource files, such as images, to an Xcode project.) In the following code, be sure to replace the name `"sweflag"` which is the name of the image we chose, to the name of your image file.

Next, initialize the two array properties that you added to the view controller's header file in the beginning of this recipe. Add the following code to the `viewDidLoad` method. The code for creating the three buttons and their constraints has been removed for brevity:

```
- (void)viewDidLoad
{
    [super viewDidLoad];

    // ...

    self.imageViews = [[NSMutableArray alloc]initWithCapacity:10];
    self.imageViewConstraints = [[NSMutableArray alloc]initWithCapacity:10];
}
```

Now implement the `addImageView` action method:

```
- (void)addImageView
{
    UIImage *image = [UIImage imageNamed:@"sweflag"];
    UIImageView *imageView = [[UIImageView alloc] initWithImage:image];
    [self.view addSubview:imageView];
    imageView.translatesAutoresizingMaskIntoConstraints = NO;
    [self.imageViews addObject:imageView];

    [self rebuildImageViewsConstraints];
}
```

The implementation is straightforward. It creates and adds an image view to the main view, sets its `translatesAutoresizingMaskIntoConstraints` to NO, so as to not conflict with the custom constraints you'll set up in a minute, adds itself to the `imageViews` array for later reference, and finally orders a rebuild of all the image views' constraints.

Defining the Image Views' Constraints

The `rebuildImageViewsConstraints` helper method removes all previous image view constraints and re-creates them. Here's the basic structure without the actual creating of the constraints:

```
- (void)rebuildImageViewsConstraints
{
    [self.view removeConstraints:self.imageViewConstraints];
    [self.imageViewConstraints removeAllObjects];

    if (self.imageViews.count == 0)
        return;

    // TODO: Build the imageViewConstraints array

    [self.view addConstraints:self.imageViewConstraints];
}
```

To build the imageViewConstraints array (beginning at the code comment in the prior code block) you start with the constraints that pin the first image view to the left side of the screen and right below the row of buttons. At the same time you set the first image view's size to 50 by 50 pixels. Here's the code:

```
UIImageView *firstImageView = [self.imageViews objectAtIndex:0];

NSDictionary *viewsDictionary = [[NSDictionary alloc]
    initWithObjectsAndKeys:self.addButton, @"firstButton", firstImageView, @"firstImageView", nil];

// Pin first view to the top left corner
[self.imageViewConstraints addObjectsFromArray:[NSLayoutConstraint
    constraintsWithVisualFormat:@"H:|-[firstImageView(50)]"
    options:0 metrics:nil views:viewsDictionary]];

[self.imageViewConstraints addObjectsFromArray:[NSLayoutConstraint
    constraintsWithVisualFormat:@"V:[firstButton]-[firstImageView(50)]"
    options:0 metrics:nil views:viewsDictionary]];
```

Each of the remaining image views (if any) overlap the previous one with an offset of 10 pixels to the right and down. Additionally, for effects, each image is ten percent bigger than the previous. *In pseudo code*, what you want to do is something like this:

```
imageView(N).X = imageView(N-1).X + 10;
imageView(N).Y = imagView(N-1).Y + 10;
imageView(N).Width = imageView(N-1).Width * 1.1;
imageView(N).Height = imageView(N-1).Height * 1.1;
```

Unfortunately, this is nothing you can translate to Autolayout constraints using the visual format notation. Instead you create the corresponding constraints explicitly, like so:

```
if (self.imageViews.count > 1)
{
    UIImageView *previousImageView = firstImageView;

    for (int i=1; i < self.imageViews.count; i++)
    {
        UIImageView *imageView = [self.imageViews objectAtIndex:i];
```

```
[self.imageViewConstraints addObject:[NSLayoutConstraint
    constraintWithItem:imageView attribute:NSLayoutAttributeLeading
    relatedBy:NSLayoutRelationEqual
    toItem:previousImageView attribute:NSLayoutAttributeLeading
    multiplier:1 constant:10]];

[self.imageViewConstraints addObject:[NSLayoutConstraint
    constraintWithItem:imageView attribute:NSLayoutAttributeTop
    relatedBy:NSLayoutRelationEqual
    toItem:previousImageView attribute:NSLayoutAttributeTop
    multiplier:1 constant:10]];

[self.imageViewConstraints addObject:[NSLayoutConstraint
    constraintWithItem:imageView attribute:NSLayoutAttributeWidth
    relatedBy:NSLayoutRelationEqual
    toItem:previousImageView attribute:NSLayoutAttributeWidth
    multiplier:1.1 constant:0]];

[self.imageViewConstraints addObject:[NSLayoutConstraint
    constraintWithItem:imageView attribute:NSLayoutAttributeHeight
    relatedBy:NSLayoutRelationEqual
    toItem:previousImageView attribute:NSLayoutAttributeHeight
    multiplier:1.1 constant:0]];

    previousImageView = imageView;
    }
}
```

Note   The Visual Format Language of Autolayout was designed for readability over completeness.
Therefore you cannot use it to express special cases like overlaps and multiplied property references.
For these cases you have to create the constraints explicitly using the `constraintWithItem:`
`attribute:relatedBy:toItem:attribute:multiplier:constant:` method.

Here's the complete `rebuildImageViewsConstraints` method:

```
- (void)rebuildImageViewsConstraints
{
    [self.view removeConstraints:self.imageViewConstraints];
    [self.imageViewConstraints removeAllObjects];

    if (self.imageViews.count == 0)
        return;

    UIImageView *firstImageView = [self.imageViews objectAtIndex:0];

    // Pin first view to the top left corner
    NSDictionary *viewsDictionary =
        [[NSDictionary alloc] initWithObjectsAndKeys:
```

```objc
            self.addButton, @"firstButton",
            firstImageView, @"firstImageView", nil];

    [self.imageViewConstraints addObjectsFromArray:[NSLayoutConstraint
        constraintsWithVisualFormat:@"H:|-[firstImageView(50)]"
        options:0 metrics:nil views:viewsDictionary]];

    [self.imageViewConstraints addObjectsFromArray:[NSLayoutConstraint
        constraintsWithVisualFormat:@"V:[firstButton]-[firstImageView(50)]"
        options:0 metrics:nil views:viewsDictionary]];

    if (self.imageViews.count > 1)
    {
        UIImageView *previousImageView = firstImageView;

        for (int i=1; i < self.imageViews.count; i++)
        {
            UIImageView *imageView = [self.imageViews objectAtIndex:i];

            [self.imageViewConstraints addObject:[NSLayoutConstraint
                constraintWithItem:imageView attribute:NSLayoutAttributeLeading
                relatedBy:NSLayoutRelationEqual
                toItem:previousImageView attribute:NSLayoutAttributeLeading
                multiplier:1 constant:10]];

            [self.imageViewConstraints addObject:[NSLayoutConstraint
                constraintWithItem:imageView attribute:NSLayoutAttributeTop
                relatedBy:NSLayoutRelationEqual
                toItem:previousImageView attribute:NSLayoutAttributeTop
                multiplier:1 constant:10]];

            [self.imageViewConstraints addObject:[NSLayoutConstraint
                constraintWithItem:imageView attribute:NSLayoutAttributeWidth
                relatedBy:NSLayoutRelationEqual
                toItem:previousImageView attribute:NSLayoutAttributeWidth
                multiplier:1.1 constant:0]];

            [self.imageViewConstraints addObject:[NSLayoutConstraint
                constraintWithItem:imageView attribute:NSLayoutAttributeHeight
                relatedBy:NSLayoutRelationEqual
                toItem:previousImageView attribute:NSLayoutAttributeHeight
                multiplier:1.1 constant:0]];

            previousImageView = imageView;
        }

    }

    [self.view addConstraints:self.imageViewConstraints];
}
```

The only thing remaining now is to implement the action methods for removing the last image view and removing all image views:

```
- (void)removeImageView
{
    if (self.imageViews.count > 0)
    {
        [self.imageViews.lastObject removeFromSuperview];
        [self.imageViews removeLastObject];
        [self rebuildImageViewsConstraints];
    }
}

- (void)clearImageViews
{
    if (self.imageViews.count > 0)
    {
        for (int i = self.imageViews.count - 1; i >= 0; i--)
        {
            UIImageView *imageView = [self.imageViews objectAtIndex:i];
            [imageView removeFromSuperview];
            [self.imageViews removeObjectAtIndex:i];
        }

        [self rebuildImageViewsConstraints];
    }
}
```

Your app is now finished and if you build and run it, you should be able to repeatedly add and remove image views using the three buttons. Figure 2-18 shows an example in which we've added several image views.

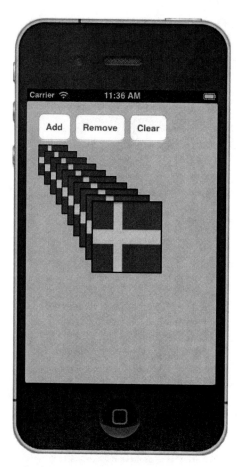

Figure 2-18. Overlapping image views positioned using Autolayout

As Figure 2-19 shows, thanks to Autolayout the app works equally well in landscape orientation.

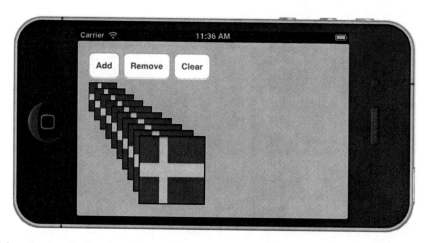

Figure 2-19. Autolayout automatically adjusts the layout when rotated into landscape orientation

Recipe 2-3: Debugging Autolayout

Dealing with Autolayout can be quite difficult, especially when you're new to it. The general advice here is to think carefully about the constraints before you start coding them. However, to minimize the time spent in trial-and-error mode it's important to know what's actually wrong with a problematic layout; i.e., you need to know how to debug it.

Besides syntax errors in Visual Format strings there are two major ways in which an Autolayout may fail. The first is *unsatisfiability*, that is, two or more constraints conflicting with each other in such a way that the layout engine can't simultaneously satisfy them. The second way is caused by *ambiguity*. That happens when the defined constraints aren't specific enough, leaving the layout engine with several possible values for a property.

In this recipe we show you examples of both ambiguous and unsatisfiable constraints. We'll show you how to identify them and how to tackle them.

Dealing with Ambiguous Layouts

To get started you need a new project, so go ahead and create one using the single-view template. Start with a simple case of an ambiguous layout. Let's say you want to programmatically add three buttons of equal size to the top of the screen. In the view controller's `viewDidLoad` method, add the following code to create the buttons and add them to the main view:

```
- (void)viewDidLoad
{
    [super viewDidLoad];

    UIButton *button1 = [UIButton buttonWithType:UIButtonTypeRoundedRect];
    [button1 setTitle:@"Button 1" forState:UIControlStateNormal];
    button1.translatesAutoresizingMaskIntoConstraints = NO;
    [self.view addSubview:button1];

    UIButton *button2 = [UIButton buttonWithType:UIButtonTypeRoundedRect];
    [button2 setTitle:@"Button 2" forState:UIControlStateNormal];
    button2.translatesAutoresizingMaskIntoConstraints = NO;
    [self.view addSubview:button2];

    UIButton *button3 = [UIButton buttonWithType:UIButtonTypeRoundedRect];
    [button3 setTitle:@"Button 3" forState:UIControlStateNormal];
    button3.translatesAutoresizingMaskIntoConstraints = NO;
    [self.view addSubview:button3];
}
```

Then add constraints to pin the buttons to the top of the screen:

```
- (void)viewDidLoad
{
    [super viewDidLoad];

    // ...
```

```
    NSDictionary *viewsDictionary = NSDictionaryOfVariableBindings(button1, button2, button3);

    [self.view addConstraints:[NSLayoutConstraint constraintsWithVisualFormat:@"V:|-[button1]"
        options:0 metrics:nil views:viewsDictionary]];
    [self.view addConstraints:[NSLayoutConstraint constraintsWithVisualFormat:@"V:|-[button2]"
        options:0 metrics:nil views:viewsDictionary]];
    [self.view addConstraints:[NSLayoutConstraint constraintsWithVisualFormat:@"V:|-[button3]"
        options:0 metrics:nil views:viewsDictionary]];
}
```

> **Note** NSDictionaryOfVariableBindings() is a convenience function for creating the dictionary
> needed by NSLayoutConstraint to map identifiers in your visual format strings to the views. It
> creates entries for the provided views using the variable names as keys.

Finally, add constraints for the horizontal layout, pinning the buttons to each other and to the bounds of the screen:

```
- (void)viewDidLoad
{
    [super viewDidLoad];

    // ...

    NSDictionary *viewsDictionary = NSDictionaryOfVariableBindings(button1, button2, button3);

    [self.view addConstraints:[NSLayoutConstraint constraintsWithVisualFormat:@"V:|-[button1]"
        options:0 metrics:nil views:viewsDictionary]];
    [self.view addConstraints:[NSLayoutConstraint constraintsWithVisualFormat:@"V:|-[button2]"
        options:0 metrics:nil views:viewsDictionary]];
    [self.view addConstraints:[NSLayoutConstraint constraintsWithVisualFormat:@"V:|-[button3]"
        options:0 metrics:nil views:viewsDictionary]];

    [self.view addConstraints:[NSLayoutConstraint
        constraintsWithVisualFormat:@"|-[button1]-[button2]-[button3]-|"
        options:0 metrics:nil views:viewsDictionary]];
}
```

Build and run the app, expecting to see your buttons in a nice row at the top of the screen. The buttons show up, but when you rotate the screen, as shown in Figure 2-20, one of the buttons gets significantly wider than the other two.

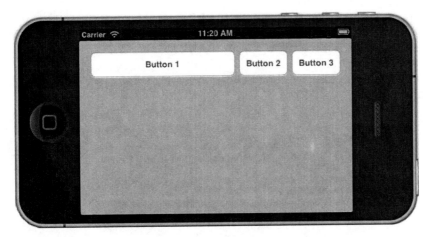

Figure 2-20. Due to ambiguous constraints, one of the buttons is wider than the other two

What's going on here? Your first thought when something like this happens is that you might have ambiguous constraints. To verify that that's the case, leave the app running but go back to Xcode and press the Pause Program Execution button (see Figure 2-21) in the Debug Area toolbar.

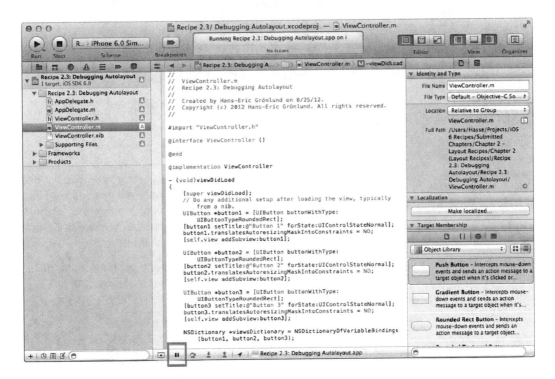

Figure 2-21. The Pause Program Execution button in Xcode

With the program paused, you can then use the (lldb) prompt to enter the following command:

```
po [[UIWindow keyWindow] _autolayoutTrace]
```

You then get a trace showing that the three buttons indeed have ambiguous layouts (see Figure 2-22).

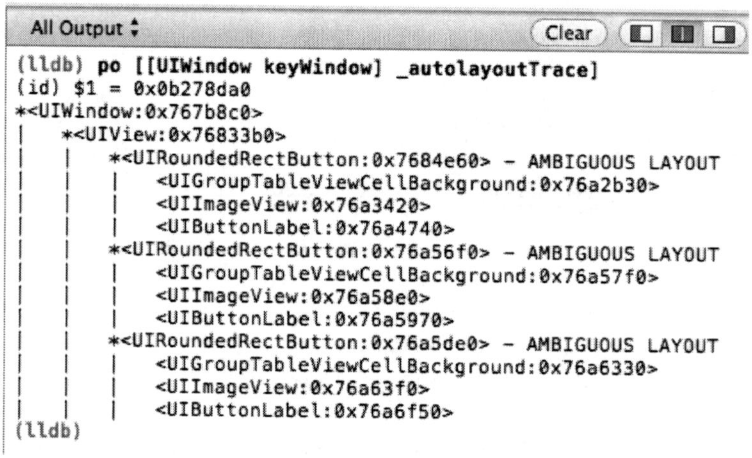

```
All Output ⬍                                              Clear  ⬜ ⬛ ⬜
(lldb) po [[UIWindow keyWindow] _autolayoutTrace]
(id) $1 = 0x0b278da0
*<UIWindow:0x767b8c0>
|   *<UIView:0x76833b0>
|   |   *<UIRoundedRectButton:0x7684e60> - AMBIGUOUS LAYOUT
|   |   |   <UIGroupTableViewCellBackground:0x76a2b30>
|   |   |   <UIImageView:0x76a3420>
|   |   |   <UIButtonLabel:0x76a4740>
|   |   *<UIRoundedRectButton:0x76a56f0> - AMBIGUOUS LAYOUT
|   |   |   <UIGroupTableViewCellBackground:0x76a57f0>
|   |   |   <UIImageView:0x76a58e0>
|   |   |   <UIButtonLabel:0x76a5970>
|   |   *<UIRoundedRectButton:0x76a5de0> - AMBIGUOUS LAYOUT
|   |   |   <UIGroupTableViewCellBackground:0x76a6330>
|   |   |   <UIImageView:0x76a63f0>
|   |   |   <UIButtonLabel:0x76a6f50>
(lldb)
```

Figure 2-22. An Autolayout trace indicating ambiguous layouts

> **Note** po (or `print-object`) is a debugger command that prints out the description text of an object. It can be a very useful tool when debugging your application.

So what's the problem? Usually when it comes to ambiguous layouts it's a sign that you're missing one or more constraints. The problem in this case is that you haven't specified the widths of the buttons enough. All you've said is that the buttons should be pinned to each other and to the edges of the screen, so when the size of the screen increases, the layout engine has several options: It can increase the width of the first button, or it can increase the width of the second button, and so on.

What you want, though, is to have buttons of equal widths. So to solve the problem. just add constraints saying that button2 and button3 are of the same width as button1, like so:

```
- (void)viewDidLoad
{
    [super viewDidLoad];

    // ...

    NSDictionary *viewsDictionary = NSDictionaryOfVariableBindings(button1, button2, button3);

    [self.view addConstraints:[NSLayoutConstraint constraintsWithVisualFormat:@"V:|-[button1]"
        options:0 metrics:nil views:viewsDictionary]];
```

```
[self.view addConstraints:[NSLayoutConstraint constraintsWithVisualFormat:@"V:|-[button2]"
    options:0 metrics:nil views:viewsDictionary]];
[self.view addConstraints:[NSLayoutConstraint constraintsWithVisualFormat:@"V:|-[button3]"
    options:0 metrics:nil views:viewsDictionary]];

[self.view addConstraints:[NSLayoutConstraint
    constraintsWithVisualFormat:@"|-[button1]-[button2(==button1)]-[button3(==button1)]-|"
    options:0 metrics:nil views:viewsDictionary]];
}
```

This leaves the layout engine with only one option: to increase the widths equally for all three buttons. So now when you build and run you'll get the expected result as in Figure 2-23.

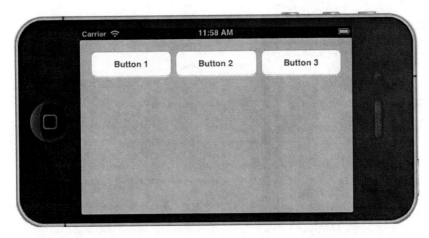

Figure 2-23. A user interface with constraints specifying the buttons to be of equal width

Handling Unsatisfiability

The opposite of ambiguous constraints is unsatisfiable constraints. In those cases, the probable cause is not too few, but too many constraints. This can be a little more tricky to solve because you've added those constraints for a purpose. Therefore the unsatisfiability might be a sign that you've made logical errors and need to rethink the whole layout.

However, let's start with a simple yet common mistake that occurs in unsatisfiable constraints. Let's say you forgot to set the translatesAutoresizingMaskIntoConstraints to NO for one of your buttons. That usually ends up in conflicting constraints between the ones the framework adds (for the autoresizing mask) and your own.

To see what happens, comment out the following row that sets the translatesAutoresizingMaskIntoConstraints property of your third button:

```
- (void)viewDidLoad
{
    [super viewDidLoad];

    // ...
```

```
    UIButton *button3 = [UIButton buttonWithType:UIButtonTypeRoundedRect];
    [button3 setTitle:@"Button 3" forState:UIControlStateNormal];
    // button3.translatesAutoresizingMaskIntoConstraints = NO;
    [self.view addSubview:button3];

    // ...
}
```

If you build and run now, you'll see that the buttons seem to have disappeared from the screen, as in Figure 2-24.

Figure 2-24. *Forgetting to turn off the automatic creation of autoresizing mask constraints can end up in unsatisfiable constraints errors like this*

If you look in the error log, you'll see a long error text starting with the reason for the failure:

2012-08-07 12:49:34.504 Testing Debugging Constraints[17898:11303] **Unable to simultaneously satisfy constraints.**

Further down the log message you'll find a list of the constraints involved, and also a hint about what may be going on:

(Note: **If you're seeing NSAutoresizingMaskLayoutConstraints that you don't understand, refer to the documentation for the UIView property translatesAutoresizingMaskIntoConstraints**)
```
(
    "<NSAutoresizingMaskLayoutConstraint:0x7528980 h=--& v=--& UIRoundedRectButton:0x71327f0.midX
==>",
    "<NSLayoutConstraint:0x7134d60 H:[UIRoundedRectButton:0x7132100]-(NSSpace(8))-
[UIRoundedRectButton:0x71327f0]>",
    "<NSLayoutConstraint:0x7134da0 UIRoundedRectButton:0x71327f0.width ==
UIRoundedRectButton:0x712e150.width>",
    "<NSLayoutConstraint:0x7134ce0 UIRoundedRectButton:0x7132100.width ==
UIRoundedRectButton:0x712e150.width>",
    "<NSLayoutConstraint:0x7134c10 H:[UIRoundedRectButton:0x712e150]-(NSSpace(8))-
[UIRoundedRectButton:0x7132100]>",
    "<NSLayoutConstraint:0x7134bb0 H:|-(NSSpace(20))-[UIRoundedRectButton:0x712e150]    (Names:
'|':UIView:0x712e760 )>"
)
```

Indeed, you seem to have NSAutoresizingMaskLayoutConstraints associated with one of your buttons. So there's your problem. Uncomment the row you previously commented out and re-run your application. It should now work as previously.

Now, let's create another example of an unsatisfiable layout. Let's say you want to change the layout from the previous section (the one with three buttons) so that the button widths don't grow beyond 100 pixels wide when the screen rotates. Add the following width constraint:

```
[self.view addConstraints:[NSLayoutConstraint
    constraintsWithVisualFormat:@"|-[button1(<=100)]-[button2(==button1)]-[button3(==button1)]-|"
    options:0 metrics:nil views:viewsDictionary]];
```

You build and run and all looks great in portrait mode, but when you rotate the screen, a strange thing happens. As Figure 2-25 shows, the first two buttons get aligned to the left, while the third button is pinned to the right side of the screen.

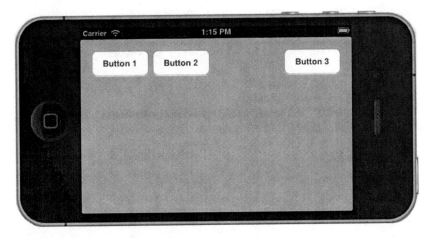

Figure 2-25. Casually adding a width constraint can have unexpected results

Again, the error log indicates that you are dealing with unsatisfiable constraints. Let's take a closer look at the involved constraints:

```
(
    "<NSLayoutConstraint:0xff4eb60 H:[UIRoundedRectButton:0xff4c510]-(NSSpace(20))-|    (Names:
'|':UIView:0xff48470 )>",
    "<NSLayoutConstraint:0xff4eae0 H:[UIRoundedRectButton:0xff4be20]-(NSSpace(8))-
[UIRoundedRectButton:0xff4c510]>",
    "<NSLayoutConstraint:0xff4eb20 UIRoundedRectButton:0xff4c510.width ==
UIRoundedRectButton:0xff47e40.width>",
    "<NSLayoutConstraint:0xff4ea70 UIRoundedRectButton:0xff4be20.width ==
UIRoundedRectButton:0xff47e40.width>",
    "<NSLayoutConstraint:0xff4ea30 H:[UIRoundedRectButton:0xff47e40]-(NSSpace(8))-
[UIRoundedRectButton:0xff4be20]>",
    "<NSLayoutConstraint:0xff4e9e0 H:[UIRoundedRectButton:0xff47e40(<=100)]>",
    "<NSLayoutConstraint:0xff4e8f0 H:|-(NSSpace(20))-[UIRoundedRectButton:0xff47e40]    (Names:
'|':UIView:0xff48470 )>",
    "<NSAutoresizingMaskLayoutConstraint:0x7552280 h=--- v=--- V:[UIWindow:0x71a5060(480)]>",
    "<NSAutoresizingMaskLayoutConstraint:0x71a8870 h=-&- v=-&- UIView:0xff48470.height ==
UIWindow:0x71a5060.height>"
)
```

The two `NSAutoresizingMaskLayoutConstraint` entries are associated with the main view and are okay (you shouldn't turn the `translatesAutoresizingMaskIntoConstraints` for root views). But the others give clues of what's going on. The problem here is that you have pinned the group of buttons to the screen edges. So when the screen rotates, the button widths will grow beyond 100 pixels and the layout engine can't satisfy the width constraint you added.

What you need to do here is to rethink the layout. What do you want?

1. Buttons of equal widths

2. Buttons positioned next to each other, with the default spacing.

3. The left and right buttons pinned to the respective screen edge, unless that causes the button widths to grow beyond 100 pixels. In that case, you want the group of buttons to stay centered in the screen.

The key here is in the third point where "unless" indicates that you should use non-required constraints. But start with the first two points. They can be expressed in the same visual format string:

```
[self.view addConstraints:[NSLayoutConstraint
    constraintsWithVisualFormat:@"[button1(<=100)]-[button2(==button1)]-[button3(==button1)]"
    options:0 metrics:nil views:viewsDictionary]];
```

> **Note**   You may be wondering why we, in the above format string, don't also pin `button1` to the left edge of the screen, and `button3` to the right. The reason is that those constraints should be non-required, but in the visual format language you can only set priorities (for example, making them non-required) for size constraints. It's not possible to set priorities for constraints that operate on properties like leading and trailing edges.

Next, you want to loosely pin the group of buttons to the screen edges (with a 20-pixel spacing):

```
NSLayoutConstraint *pinToLeft =
    [NSLayoutConstraint
        constraintWithItem:button1 attribute:NSLayoutAttributeLeading
        relatedBy:NSLayoutRelationEqual
        toItem:self.view attribute:NSLayoutAttributeLeading
        multiplier:1 constant:20];
pinToLeft.priority = 500;
[self.view addConstraint:pinToLeft];

NSLayoutConstraint *pinToRight =
    [NSLayoutConstraint
        constraintWithItem:button3 attribute:NSLayoutAttributeTrailing
        relatedBy:NSLayoutRelationEqual
        toItem:self.view attribute:NSLayoutAttributeTrailing
        multiplier:1 constant:20];
pinToRight.priority = 500;
[self.view addConstraint:pinToRight];
```

Finally, you need the rule that tells the group to center in the screen. This can be a required constraint because it is true even if the group is pinned to the screen edges:

```
NSLayoutConstraint *center =
    [NSLayoutConstraint
        constraintWithItem:button2 attribute:NSLayoutAttributeCenterX
        relatedBy:NSLayoutRelationEqual toItem:self.view attribute:NSLayoutAttributeCenterX
         multiplier:1 constant:0];
[self.view addConstraint:center];
```

Here's the resulting `viewDidLoad` method, changes marked in bold:

```
- (void)viewDidLoad
{
    [super viewDidLoad];

    UIButton *button1 = [UIButton buttonWithType:UIButtonTypeRoundedRect];
    [button1 setTitle:@"Button 1" forState:UIControlStateNormal];
    button1.translatesAutoresizingMaskIntoConstraints = NO;
    [self.view addSubview:button1];
```

```objc
    UIButton *button2 = [UIButton buttonWithType:UIButtonTypeRoundedRect];
    [button2 setTitle:@"Button 2" forState:UIControlStateNormal];
    button2.translatesAutoresizingMaskIntoConstraints = NO;
    [self.view addSubview:button2];

    UIButton *button3 = [UIButton buttonWithType:UIButtonTypeRoundedRect];
    [button3 setTitle:@"Button 3" forState:UIControlStateNormal];
    button3.translatesAutoresizingMaskIntoConstraints = NO;
    [self.view addSubview:button3];

    NSDictionary *viewsDictionary = NSDictionaryOfVariableBindings(button1, button2, button3);

    [self.view addConstraints:
     [NSLayoutConstraint constraintsWithVisualFormat:@"V:|-[button1]" options:0 metrics:nil
views:viewsDictionary]];
    [self.view addConstraints:
     [NSLayoutConstraint constraintsWithVisualFormat:@"V:|-[button2]" options:0 metrics:nil
views:viewsDictionary]];
    [self.view addConstraints:
     [NSLayoutConstraint constraintsWithVisualFormat:@"V:|-[button3]" options:0 metrics:nil
views:viewsDictionary]];

    [self.view addConstraints:[NSLayoutConstraint
        constraintsWithVisualFormat:@"[button1(<=100)]-[button2(==button1)]-[button3(==button1)]"
        options:0 metrics:nil views:viewsDictionary]];

    NSLayoutConstraint *pinToLeft = [NSLayoutConstraint
        constraintWithItem:button1 attribute:NSLayoutAttributeLeading
        relatedBy:NSLayoutRelationEqual
        toItem:self.view attribute:NSLayoutAttributeLeading
        multiplier:1 constant:20];
    pinToLeft.priority = 500;
    [self.view addConstraint:pinToLeft];

    NSLayoutConstraint *pinToRight = [NSLayoutConstraint
        constraintWithItem:button3 attribute:NSLayoutAttributeTrailing
        relatedBy:NSLayoutRelationEqual
        toItem:self.view attribute:NSLayoutAttributeTrailing
        multiplier:1 constant:20];
    pinToRight.priority = 500;
    [self.view addConstraint:pinToRight];

    NSLayoutConstraint *center = [NSLayoutConstraint
        constraintWithItem:button2 attribute:NSLayoutAttributeCenterX
        relatedBy:NSLayoutRelationEqual
        toItem:self.view attribute:NSLayoutAttributeCenterX
        multiplier:1 constant:0];
    [self.view addConstraint:center];
}
```

Now you can build and run your application again. It should look as before in portrait orientation, but when rotated to landscape there should be no errors showing up in the error log, and the user interface should look like you wanted it, as in Figure 2-26.

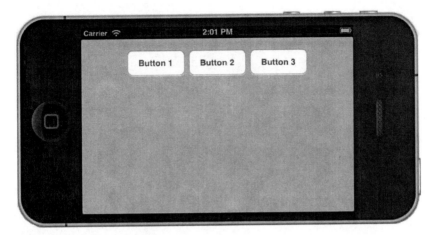

Figure 2-26. A layout with maximum button widths correctly set

Summary

In this chapter you learned the basics of Autolayout and how to use it to build dynamic user interfaces that adapt to changes in screen size and orientation. You set up constraints in Interface Builder, as well as in code. You also looked at the two error states, ambiguous constraints and unsatisfiable constraints, and how to debug them.

Chapter 3

Table and Collection View Recipes

All day, every single day, we receive information. Whether in the form of video, radio, music, e-mails, 140-character messages, or even sights and sounds, there is always new data to acquire and process. As developers, we work to create and manage the medium between this information and the end-users through data organization and display. We must be able to take the immense stream of information available and process it down to simple, concise pieces that our specific audience will be interested in. On top of this, we also have to make our data look visually appealing, while still maintaining efficiency and organization.

In iOS development there are two great tools for achieving these goals: UITableView with its well-known user interface that has pretty much become what users expect from data-based apps, and the brand new UICollectionView, which brings multi-column support to the table. Throughout this chapter, we focus on the step-by-step methodology for creating, implementing, and customizing these useful tools.

Recipe 3-1: Creating an Ungrouped Table

You can use two kinds of UITableViews in iOS: the grouped table and the ungrouped table. Your use of one or the other will depend on the requirements of your application, but we start here by focusing on an ungrouped table due to its ease of implementation.

Setting Up the Application

To build a fully functional and customizable UITableView-based application, you start from the ground up with an empty application and end up with a useful table to display information about various countries. In Xcode, make a new project, and select the Empty Application template. This gives you only an application delegate, from which you can build all your view controllers.

You will be using a single project throughout this entire chapter, so rather than naming projects by recipe name, give your project whichever name you prefer. (We chose "Countries" because the application displays information about different countries.) Also, be sure to uncheck the Use Core Data option because we won't be using it in this chapter. However, and as always in this book, leave the Use Automatic Reference Counting option checked. Figure 3-1 shows these options.

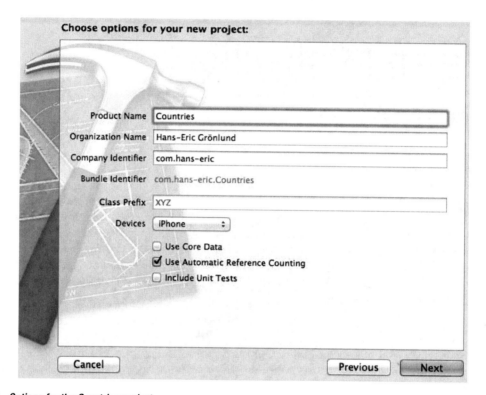

Figure 3-1. *Options for the Countries project*

Because you started with an empty application, you begin by making your main view controller, which contains your table view.

Create a new file using the Objective-C class template. On the next screen, enter MainTableViewController as the class name and select UIViewController as the subclass. It's important that you also check the With XIB for user interface option so that Xcode creates a user interface file for your view controller.

> **Note**   Some may find it more convenient to create a subclass of UITableViewController, as you are immediately given a UITableView, as well as some of the methods required to use it. The downside of this method is that the UITableView given in the controller's .xib file is more difficult to configure and reframe. For this reason, you are using a UIViewController subclass, and you will simply add in your UITableView, and its methods, yourself.

Now, select the `MainTableViewController.xib` file to bring up Interface Builder. Continue by dragging a table view from the Object library into your view. Rather than making the table take up the entire view, shrink it down a bit and have a 20-point padding around it. Select the main view, and change the background color to a light gray so that you can differentiate it from your `UITableView`. This results in the display shown in Figure 3-2.

Figure 3-2. A table view with a 20-point padding around it

Now switch to the `MainViewController.m` file and set the title in the `viewDidLoad` method, as follows:

```
- (void)viewDidLoad
{
    [super viewDidLoad];
    // Do any additional setup after loading the view from its nib.
    self.title = @"Countries";
}
```

The title appears in the navigation bar that you set up next. This is done in the application delegate, so switch to your `AppDelegate.h` file and add the following code:

```
//
//  AppDelegate.h
//  Countries
//
```

```
#import <UIKit/UIKit.h>
#import "MainTableViewController.h"

@interface AppDelegate : UIResponder <UIApplicationDelegate>

@property (strong, nonatomic) UIWindow *window;
@property (nonatomic, strong) UINavigationController *navigationController;
@property (nonatomic, strong) MainTableViewController *tableViewController;

@end
```

> **Note**   Since iOS 6 you no longer need to @synthesize your properties. The new compiler creates getters and setters automatically if they haven't been declared explicitly. Also, in iOS 6 there's no need for setting your properties to nil in the viewDidUnload method; yet another scaffolding responsibility has been lifted off our shoulders, freeing up more time to spend on more important creative coding endeavors. Cheers to that!

Now switch to AppDelegate.m and add the following code to the application:didFinishLaunchingWithOptions: method:

```
- (BOOL)application:(UIApplication *)application
didFinishLaunchingWithOptions:(NSDictionary *)launchOptions
{
    self.window = [[UIWindow alloc] initWithFrame:[[UIScreen mainScreen] bounds]];
    // Override point for customization after application launch.
    self.window.backgroundColor = [UIColor whiteColor];

    self.tableViewController = [[MainTableViewController alloc] init];
    self.navigationController = [[UINavigationController alloc]

    initWithRootViewController:self.tableViewController];
    self.window.rootViewController = self.navigationController;
    [self.window makeKeyAndVisible];
    return YES;
}
```

The application skeleton is now complete. It has a navigation controller with your MainTableViewController as the root view controller. When running the project in the simulator, you should see a screen like the one in Figure 3-3.

Figure 3-3. *Basic application with an empty UITableView*

Adding a Model for Countries

You use an array to store the information used to display your table's information. Declare it a property of your view controller, with the type NSMutableArray and the name countries, as shown in the following code.

```
//
//  MainTableViewController.h
//  Countries
//

#import <UIKit/UIKit.h>

@interface MainTableViewController : UIViewController

@property (strong, nonatomic) NSMutableArray *countries;

@end
```

In the array you will store objects representing countries, so let's create a model for that. Create a new file as before, using the Objective-C class template. Name your new class Country, and make sure that it is a subclass of NSObject.

You'll store four pieces of information in your Country class: name, capital city, motto, and a UIImage that contains the country's flag. Define these properties in your Country.h, as follows:

```
//
//  Country.h
//  Countries
//

#import <Foundation/Foundation.h>

@interface Country : NSObject

@property (nonatomic, strong) NSString *name;
@property (nonatomic, strong) NSString *capital;
@property (nonatomic, strong) NSString *motto;
@property (nonatomic, strong) UIImage *flag;

@end
```

Now that your model is set up, you can return to your view controller. The compiler needs to access the methods of the new Country class that you have just set up, so add the following import statement to MainTableViewController.h.

```
#import "Country.h"
```

Now before you can proceed to create the test data, make sure you have downloaded the image files for the flags that you will be using for the countries you add. In this recipe you use flags of the United States, England (as opposed to the UK), Scotland, France, and Spain. We downloaded some public domain flag images from Wikipedia; United States, France, and Spain from http://en.wikipedia.org/wiki/Gallery_of_sovereign-state_flags, and England and Scotland from http://commons.wikimedia.org/wiki/Flags_of_formerly_independent_states. An image size of around 200 pixels is good enough for your purposes.

> **Caution**   Whenever you are working with images, watch carefully for any and all copyright issues.
> Public domain images, such as those used here from Wikipedia, are free to use and fairly easy to find.

After you have the files all downloaded and visible in the Finder, select and drag them into your project in Xcode under Supporting Files. A dialog appears with options for adding the files to your project. Make sure that the option labeled Copy items into destination group's folder (if needed) is checked, as in Figure 3-4.

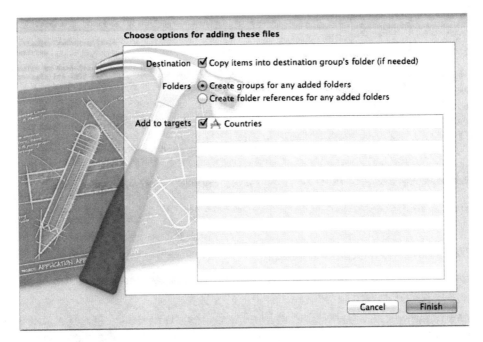

Figure 3-4. Dialog for adding files; make sure the first option is checked

Set up your test data, the five countries mentioned earlier, in your viewDidLoad method, as follows:

```
- (void)viewDidLoad
{
    [super viewDidLoad];
    // Do any additional setup after loading the view from its nib.
    self.title = @"Countries";
    Country *usa = [[Country alloc] init];
    usa.name = @"United States of America";
    usa.motto = @"E Pluribus Unum";
    usa.capital = @"Washington, D.C.";
    usa.flag = [UIImage imageNamed:@"usa.png"];

    Country *france = [[Country alloc] init];
    france.name = @"French Republic";
    france.motto = @"Liberté, Égalité, Fraternité";
    france.capital = @"Paris";
    france.flag = [UIImage imageNamed:@"france.png"];

    Country *england = [[Country alloc] init];
    england.name = @"England";
    england.motto = @"Dieu et mon droit";
    england.capital = @"London";
    england.flag = [UIImage imageNamed:@"england.png"];

    Country *scotland = [[Country alloc] init];
    scotland.name = @"Scotland";
```

```
    scotland.motto = @"In My Defens God Me Defend";
    scotland.capital = @"Edinburgh";
    scotland.flag = [UIImage imageNamed:@"scotland.png"];

    Country *spain = [[Country alloc] init];
    spain.name = @"Kingdom of Spain";
    spain.motto = @"Plus Ultra";
    spain.capital = @"Madrid";
    spain.flag = [UIImage imageNamed:@"spain.png"];

    self.countries =
        [NSMutableArray arrayWithObjects:usa, france, england, scotland, spain, nil];

}
```

Displaying Data in a Table View

To display your test data in your table view you need a way to reference it from your code. So go ahead and create an outlet named countriesTableView.

Your table view communicates with your program through two protocols: UITableViewDelegate and UITableViewDataSource. Make your view controller the delegate for both these protocols, so add them to its header, as follows:

```
//
//  MainTableViewController.h
//  Countries
//

#import <UIKit/UIKit.h>
#import "Country.h"

@interface MainTableViewController : UIViewController<UITableViewDelegate,
                                                      UITableViewDataSource>

@property (weak, nonatomic) IBOutlet UITableView *countriesTableView;
@property (strong, nonatomic) NSMutableArray *countries;

@end
```

The next step is to connect your view controller to the table view. Switch to MainTableViewController.m and set the table view's delegate and dataSource properties in the viewDidLoad method, as follows:

```
- (void)viewDidLoad
{
    [super viewDidLoad];
    // Do any additional setup after loading the view from its nib.
    self.title = @"Countries";
    self.countriesTableView.delegate = self;
    self.countriesTableView.dataSource = self;
```

```
Country *usa = [[Country alloc] init];
usa.name = @"United States of America";
usa.motto = @"E Pluribus Unum";
usa.capital = @"Washington, D.C.";
usa.flag = [UIImage imageNamed:@"usa.png"];

// ...
}
```

For the sake of organization, all the methods that a UITableView can call are split into two groups: delegate methods and data source methods. Delegate methods are used to handle any kind of visual elements of the UITableView, such as the row height of cells. Data source methods, on the other hand, deal with the information displayed in the UITableView, such as the configuration of any given cell's information.

To create an ungrouped UITableView, you must correctly implement two main methods.

First, you need to specify how many rows will be displayed in the table view. This is done via the tableView:numberOfRowsInSection: method. Your table view has only one section, because it's ungrouped, so there is no need to consult the section parameter. All you need to do is to return the number of countries in your array:

```
-(NSInteger)tableView:(UITableView *)tableView numberOfRowsInSection:(NSInteger)section
{
    return [self.countries count];
}
```

Second, you must create a method to specify how the UITableView's cells are configured using the tableView:cellForRowAtIndexPath: method. Following is a generic implementation of this method, which you modify for your data:

```
- (UITableViewCell *)tableView:(UITableView *)tableView
cellForRowAtIndexPath:(NSIndexPath *)indexPath
{
    static NSString *CellIdentifier = @"Cell";

    UITableViewCell *cell =
        [tableView dequeueReusableCellWithIdentifier:CellIdentifier];
    if (cell == nil)
    {
        cell = [[UITableViewCell alloc] initWithStyle:UITableViewCellStyleDefault
                    reuseIdentifier:CellIdentifier];
        cell.accessoryType = UITableViewCellAccessoryDisclosureIndicator;
        cell.textLabel.font = [UIFont systemFontOfSize:19.0];
        cell.detailTextLabel.font = [UIFont systemFontOfSize:12];
    }

    cell.textLabel.text = [NSString stringWithFormat:@"Cell %i", indexPath.row];

    return cell;
}
```

If you run your application now, you will see that your table view has five cells, one for each entry in your countries array. Each cell, as Figure 3-5 shows, has a generic title (Cell 0, Cell 1, Cell 2, etc.) and a disclosure accessory indicator.

Figure 3-5. Your app displaying five cells with a generic text and a disclosure accessory indicator

Because you haven't implemented any functionality for the accessory views yet, nothing happens when you tap the cells. You take care of that, as well as customizing the look and content of the cells in a minute, but first here's a note on cell reuse.

A Note on Cached Cells

The previous code deserves some explanation. A table view in iOS tries to save up on memory and time by reusing cells that are currently not in view of the user. It takes a cell that has been scrolled out of sight and reuses it to display another cell that has become visible.

However, it's up to you to make the reuse scheme work. First you must define the different types of cells your table view supports (that is, cells that share the same look and components). Each such cell type is identified by a reuse identifier of your choice.

The second thing your app must do is to call dequeueReusableCellWithIdentifier: method to see whether there is a free cell to reuse before you allocate a new one. In the previous sample, you can see that you first attempt to dequeue a reusable cell. If none are available (that is, if cell is nil), then you create a new cell and give it a generic setup that can be reused for all your cells. Then, no matter whether the cell was dequeued or created, you update the text to the appropriate value.

Configuring the Cells

Now that your application is up, running, and displaying some kind of information, you can work on your specific implementation.

To configure your cells to properly fit your data, the first thing you have to do is change the display style of your rows. Change the allocation/initialization line in your tableView:cellForRowAtIndexPath: method to the following:

```
cell = [[UITableViewCell alloc] initWithStyle:UITableViewCellStyleSubtitle
reuseIdentifier:CellIdentifier];
```

There are four different UITableViewCell styles that you can use, each with a slightly different display:

- UITableViewCellStyleDefault: Only one label, as shown in Figure 3-5.
- UITableViewCellStyleSubtitle: Just like the Default style, but with a subtitle line underneath the main text.
- UITableViewCellStyleValue1: Two text lines, with the primary line on the left side of the cell and the secondary detail text label on the right.
- UITableViewCellStyleValue2: Two text lines with the focus on the detail text label.

Next, you can actually set the cell's text label to be the name of the country, rather than simply the count of the cell. Adjust the setting of the cell.textLabel.text property to the following:

```
Country *item = [self.countries objectAtIndex:indexPath.row];
cell.textLabel.text = item.name;
```

You can set the subtitle of the text very similarly using the detailTextLabel property of the cell. Set it to the capital of the country.

```
cell.detailTextLabel.text = item.capital;
```

The UITableViewCell class also has a property called imageView, which, when given an image, places it to the left of the title label. Implement this action by adding the following line to your cell configuration:

```
cell.imageView.image = item.flag;
```

You'll probably notice that if you run your program now, all your flags will appear, but with varying aspect ratios, making your view look less professional. Setting the frame of the cell's imageView will not fix this problem, so here is a quick solution.

First, in your view controller implementation file, define a class method that draws a UIImage in a given size, as follows:

```
+ (UIImage *)scale:(UIImage *)image toSize:(CGSize)size
{
    UIGraphicsBeginImageContext(size);
    [image drawInRect:CGRectMake(0, 0, size.width, size.height)];
    UIImage *scaledImage = UIGraphicsGetImageFromCurrentImageContext();
    UIGraphicsEndImageContext();
    return scaledImage;
}
```

Place this method's handler in your view controller's private @interface declaration to avoid any potential compiler problems. The private @interface declaration is where you put your private method declarations; it resides at the top of your view controller's implementation file, as shown in the following code:

```
//
//  MainTableViewController.m
//  Countries
//

#import "MainTableViewController.h"

@interface MainTableViewController ()

+ (UIImage *)scale:(UIImage *)image toSize:(CGSize)size;

@end

@implementation MainTableViewController

// ...

// Implementation of the scale method goes here
+ (UIImage *)scale:(UIImage *)image toSize:(CGSize)size
{
    // ...
}

@end
```

Then, you can adjust the image setting lines of code to utilize this method.

```
cell.imageView.image =
    [MainTableViewController scale: item.flag toSize:CGSizeMake(115, 75)];
```

After all these configurations, the resulting `tableView:cellForRowAtIndexPath:` method looks like the following:

```
- (UITableViewCell *)tableView:(UITableView *)tableView
cellForRowAtIndexPath:(NSIndexPath *)indexPath
{
    static NSString *CellIdentifier = @"Cell";

    UITableViewCell *cell = [tableView dequeueReusableCellWithIdentifier:CellIdentifier];
    if (cell == nil)
    {
        cell = [[UITableViewCell alloc]
initWithStyle:UITableViewCellStyleSubtitle reuseIdentifier:CellIdentifier];
        cell.accessoryType = UITableViewCellAccessoryDisclosureIndicator;
        cell.textLabel.font = [UIFont systemFontOfSize:19.0];
        cell.detailTextLabel.font = [UIFont systemFontOfSize:12];
    }

    Country *item = [self.countries objectAtIndex:indexPath.row];
    cell.textLabel.text = item.name;
    cell.detailTextLabel.text = item.capital;
    cell.imageView.image =
        [MainTableViewController scale: item.flag toSize:CGSizeMake(115, 75)];

    return cell;
}
```

Build and run your application; it should resemble Figure 3-6, complete with country information and flag images.

Figure 3-6. Your table populated with country information

A Note on Rounded Corners

Whenever you look at any well-made iOS application, you will probably notice that almost every single element has its corners rounded. This is one of those small details that most people don't notice but that dramatically improves the visual quality of an application. Fortunately, it's actually fairly simple to implement with just two steps.

First, import the Quartz Core API to your view controller's header file:

```
#import <QuartzCore/QuartzCore.h>
```

Once you've done that, you can access the `layer` property of any class that inherits from `UIView`, which has a `cornerRadius` property that can be set. Here you'll go ahead and round the corners on your `UITableView` by adding the following line to your `viewDidLoad` method:

```
- (void)viewDidLoad
{
    [super viewDidLoad];
```

```
    // Do any additional setup after loading the view from its nib.
    self.title = @"Countries";
    self.countriesTableView.delegate = self;
    self.countriesTableView.dataSource = self;
    self.countriesTableView.layer.cornerRadius = 8.0;

    // ...

}
```

When you run your app now, it resembles Figure 3-7.

Figure 3-7. Your table view with rounded corners

Implementing the Accessory Views

So now that you have a nice looking table with your five countries, you can work on extending beyond the basic functionality of the table view. First, you'll focus on the most straightforward ability, to act upon the selection of a specific row.

For the purpose of this recipe, you will build your application in such a way that upon the selection of a row, a separate view controller presents that will display all the known information about the selected country.

Start by creating a new view controller like the one you did in the beginning of this recipe, by using the Objective-C class template and UIViewController as parent class. Name the new class CountryDetailsViewController and make sure the With XIB for user interface option is checked.

Construct this controller's view in its .xib file to resemble the one shown in Figure 3-8 by using a combination of labels, text fields, and an image view. To enhance the look a little, we added a slight shadow to the "Country Name" label using the Attribute inspector.

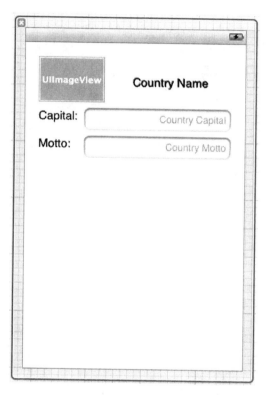

Figure 3-8. CountryDetailsViewController's .xib file and configuration

Create outlets for the components that you'll be changing dynamically (that is, the country label, the image view, and the two text fields). Use the following respective property names:

- nameLabel
- capitalTextField
- mottoTextField
- flagImageView

You need to be able to manipulate the behavior of the two text fields. To allow your view controller to respond to events from these text fields, add the UITextFieldDelegate protocol to its header.

```
@interface CountryDetailsViewController : UIViewController <UITextFieldDelegate>
```

To make your view controller as generic as possible, give it a property of your Country class to hold the currently displayed data. This way, you simply populate your view with the necessary data, and if desired, you could even make it possible to easily repopulate with different data without changing views. Add an import statement for the Country class.

```
#import "Country.h"
```

Declare the property as follows:

```
@property (strong, nonatomic) Country *currentCountry;
```

Your detailed view controller needs a way to tell whoever invoked it that it's finished and should be removed from view. The convention in iOS is to set up a custom protocol and a delegate property for that purpose. So make the following additions to your CountryDetailsViewController.h file:

```
//
//  CountryDetailsViewController.h
//  Countries
//

#import <UIKit/UIKit.h>
#import "Country.h"

// Forward declaration needed for the protocol to use
// the CountryDetailsViewController type
@class CountryDetailsViewController;

@protocol CountryDetailsViewControllerDelegate <NSObject>
-(void)countryDetailsViewControllerDidFinish:(CountryDetailsViewController *)sender;
@end

@interface CountryDetailsViewController : UIViewController <UITextFieldDelegate>

@property (weak, nonatomic) IBOutlet UILabel *nameLabel;
@property (weak, nonatomic) IBOutlet UIImageView *flagImageView;
@property (weak, nonatomic) IBOutlet UITextField *capitalTextField;
@property (weak, nonatomic) IBOutlet UITextField *mottoTextField;

@property (strong, nonatomic) Country *currentCountry;
@property (strong, nonatomic) id<CountryDetailsViewControllerDelegate> delegate;

@end
```

Now, switch your focus to the implementation file of your details view controller. There's plenty to be done there as well, so let's start by adding a method to populate the view.

```
-(void)populateViewWithCountry:(Country *)country
{
    self.currentCountry = country;
```

```
    self.flagImageView.image = country.flag;
    self.nameLabel.text = country.name;
    self.capitalTextField.text = country.capital;
    self.mottoTextField.text = country.motto;
}
```

You will want this method to be called after your view is loaded, but right before your view is displayed, which is when `viewWillAppear:animated:` is invoked. So add that delegate method to your detailed view controller, as follows:

```
-(void)viewWillAppear:(BOOL)animated
{
    [self populateViewWithCountry:self.currentCountry];
}
```

Next, let's consider the text fields. You want to dismiss the keyboard when the user is done editing, so you should implement the `textFieldShouldReturn:` delegate method.

```
-(BOOL)textFieldShouldReturn:(UITextField *)textField
{
    [textField resignFirstResponder];
    return NO;
}
```

For the foregoing delegate method to be called, you need to connect your view controller to the delegate properties of the text fields. Do this in the `viewDidLoad` method.

```
self.mottoTextField.delegate = self;
self.capitalTextField.delegate = self;
```

Because you are allowing the user to make changes to your data, you should include a button to revert to the original data to cancel edits. Add this to the right side of your navigation bar by adding the following code to the `viewDidLoad` method:

```
- (void)viewDidLoad
{
    [super viewDidLoad];
    // Do any additional setup after loading the view from its nib.
    self.mottoTextField.delegate = self;
    self.capitalTextField.delegate = self;

    UIBarButtonItem *revertButton =
        [[UIBarButtonItem alloc] initWithTitle:@"Revert"
                                         style:UIBarButtonItemStyleBordered
                                        target:self
                                        action:@selector(revert)];
    self.navigationItem.rightBarButtonItems =
        [NSArray arrayWithObject:revertButton];
}
```

The revert selector that you specified as your revertButton's action is easily implemented. It should merely repopulate the view with the data from the currentCountry property:

```
-(void)revert
{
    [self populateViewWithCountry:self.currentCountry];
}
```

The last thing you need to do is implement functionality to save any changes to the given Country upon returning to your MainTableViewController. You implement the method viewWillDisappear:animated: to do this.

```
-(void)viewWillDisappear:(BOOL)animated
{
    // End any editing that may be in progress at this point
    [self.view.window endEditing: YES];

    // Update the country object with the new values
    self.currentCountry.capital = self.capitalTextField.text;
    self.currentCountry.motto = self.mottoTextField.text;
    [self.delegate countryDetailsViewControllerDidFinish:self];
}
```

The detailed view controller is finished for now; switch back to the header file of your MainTableViewController and add the CountryDetailsDelegate protocol that you created to the header. You need to import the class you created first.

```
#import "CountryDetailsViewController.h"
```

To make your implementation of the CountryDetailsViewController delegate method easier, you want to create an instance variable that refers to the index path of whichever row was selected, so that you can save processing power by refreshing only that row. After you add the variable of type NSIndexPath, called selectedIndexPath, your header file should now look as follows, with recent changes marked in bold:

```
//
//  MainTableViewController.h
//  Countries
//

#import <UIKit/UIKit.h>
#import <QuartzCore/QuartzCore.h>
#import "Country.h"
#import "CountryDetailsViewController.h"

@interface MainTableViewController : UIViewController <UITableViewDelegate,
    UITableViewDataSource, CountryDetailsViewControllerDelegate>
{
    NSIndexPath *selectedIndexPath;
}
```

```
@property (weak, nonatomic) IBOutlet UITableView *countriesTableView;
@property (strong, nonatomic) NSMutableArray *countries;

@end
```

You can now implement the CountryDetailsViewController's delegate. Switch to
MainTableViewController.m and add the delegate method as follows:

```
-(void)countryDetailsViewControllerDidFinish:(CountryDetailsViewController *)sender
{
    if (selectedIndexPath)
    {
        [self.countriesTableView beginUpdates];
        [self.countriesTableView reloadRowsAtIndexPaths:
                [NSArray arrayWithObject:selectedIndexPath]
                withRowAnimation:UITableViewRowAnimationNone];
        [self.countriesTableView endUpdates];
    }
    selectedIndexPath = nil;
}
```

The beginUpdates and endUpdates methods, though somewhat unnecessary here, are very useful
for reloading data in a table view. They specify that any calls to reload data in between those calls
should be animated. Because all your reloading of data occurs while the UITableView is offscreen, it
is not quite necessary, but it does not harm your application.

Finally, to actually act on the selection of a given row in a UITableView, all you need to do is
implement the UITableView's delegate method tableView:didSelectRowAtIndexPath:

```
-(void)tableView:(UITableView *)tableView
didSelectRowAtIndexPath:(NSIndexPath *)indexPath
{
    [tableView deselectRowAtIndexPath:indexPath animated:YES];

    selectedIndexPath = indexPath;

    Country *chosenCountry = [self.countries objectAtIndex:indexPath.row];
    CountryDetailsViewController *detailedViewController =
        [[CountryDetailsViewController alloc] init];
    detailedViewController.delegate = self;
    detailedViewController.currentCountry = chosenCountry;

    [self.navigationController pushViewController:detailedViewController animated:YES];
}
```

The UITableView class also has multiple other methods for dealing with the selection or deselection
of a row, including tableView:willSelectRowAtIndexPath: (which is called before its
-tableView:didSelectRowAtIndexPath counterpart), as well as
tableView:willDeselectRowAtIndexPath: and tableView:didDeselectRowAtIndexPath:.
Using these four delegate methods, you can fully customize the behavior of a UITableView
to fit any application.

When running this project now, you can view and edit country information, as in Figure 3-9.

Figure 3-9. The resulting display of your CountryDetailsViewController

Enhanced User Interaction

When you're dealing with applications that focus on UITableViews, you often want to allow the user to access multiple views from the same table. For example, the Phone application on an iPhone has a voicemail tab, which displays a UITableView containing the various voicemails left on the phone. The user can then either play the voicemail by selecting a row from the table or view the contact information of the original caller by selecting a smaller blue button on the right side of the row. You can implement a similar behavior by implementing another UITableView delegate method.

First, you must change the type of "accessory" of the cells in your UITableView. This refers to the icon displayed on the far right side of any given row. In your tableView:cellForRowAtIndexPath: method, find the following line:

```
cell.accessoryType = UITableViewCellAccessoryDisclosureIndicator;
```

Change this value to UITableViewCellAccessoryDetailDisclosureButton. This gives you the blue button that can respond to touches. The four possible values for this property are as follows:

- UITableViewCellAccessoryNone: Specifies a lack of accessory.
- UITableViewCellAccessoryDisclosureIndicator: Adds a gray arrow on the right side of a row, as you have been using until now.
- UITableViewCellAccessoryDetailDisclosureButton: Your most recent choice, which specifies an interaction-enabled button.
- UITableViewCellAccessoryCheckmark: Adds a checkmark to a given row; this is especially useful in conjunction with the tableView:didSelectRowAtIndexPath: method to add and remove check marks from a list as you find necessary.

> **Note** Whereas these four available accessory types are pretty useful and cover almost any generic use, it's certainly easy to think of a reason to want something entirely different over on the right side of your row. You can easily customize a UITableViewCell's accessory through the accessoryView property to be any other UIView subclass.

Now that you turned your accessory into a button, it is actually incredibly easy to implement an action to handle this interaction. You implement another UITableView delegate method, tableView: accessoryButtonTappedForRowWithIndexPath:. For your testing purposes, make this action exactly the same as that of a row selection, with an extra NSLog(), although it should be very easy to see how you could implement different behavior.

```
-(void)tableView:(UITableView *)tableView
accessoryButtonTappedForRowWithIndexPath:(NSIndexPath *)indexPath
{
    [tableView deselectRowAtIndexPath:indexPath animated:YES];

    selectedIndexPath = indexPath;

    Country *chosenCountry = [self.countries objectAtIndex:indexPath.row];
    CountryDetailsViewController *detailedViewController =
        [[CountryDetailsViewController alloc] init];
    detailedViewController.delegate = self;
    detailedViewController.currentCountry = chosenCountry;

    NSLog(@"Accessory Button Tapped");
    [self.navigationController pushViewController:detailedViewController animated:YES];
}
```

When you run this app, tapping the accessory buttons should run your newest functionalities, as shown in Figure 3-10.

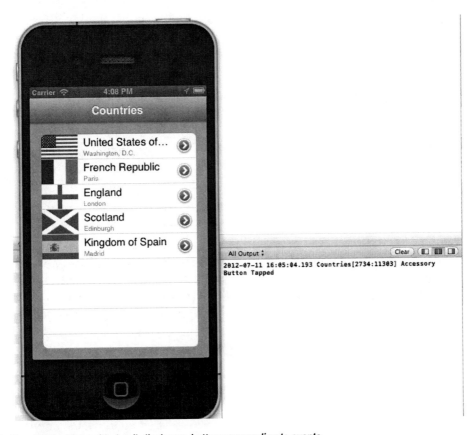

Figure 3-10. Your UITableView with detail-disclosure buttons responding to events

A Note on Cell View Customization

Just as with the accessory view, several other parts of a UITableViewCell are customizable by way of their views. The UITableViewCell class includes several properties for other views that you can edit, including the following:

- imageView: The UIImageView to the left of the textLabel in a cell, as shown by your flags in the previous example; if no image is given to this view, then the cell will appear as if the UIImageView did not exist (as opposed to a blank UIImageView taking up space).

- contentView: The main UIView of the UITableViewCell, which includes all the text; you may want to customize this to implement a more powerful or versatile UITableViewCell.

- backgroundView: A UIView set to nil in plain-style tables (like you have used so far), and otherwise for grouped tables; this view appears behind all other views in the table, so it is great for specifically customizing the visual display of the cell.

- selectedBackgroundView: This UIView is inserted above the backgroundView but behind all other views when a cell is selected. It can also be easily given an alpha animation (fading opacity in or out) by use of the -setSelected:animated: action.

- multipleSelectionBackgroundView: This UIView acts just like the selectedBackgroundView but is used for when a UITableView is enabled to allow the selection of multiple rows.

- accessoryView: As discussed earlier, this allows you to create entirely different views for a row's accessory, so you could implement your own custom display and behavior beyond the preset values.

- editingAccessoryView: This is similar to the accessoryView property but specifically for when a UITableView is in "editing" mode, which you will see in detail soon.

Although most developers stick to the pretty generic UITableView, because it fits well with the iOS design theme, if you look around you can find some pretty creative implementations using custom views. All this extra customization may add a lot of development time to your project, but a high-quality, custom UITableView certainly stands out in an application for its uniqueness.

Recipe 3-2: Editing a UITableView

If you look at almost any UITableView in an application you commonly use, such as your device's music player, you'll probably notice that you can edit the table in some way. In your Music application, you can swipe across a row to reveal a Delete button, which when tapped will remove the item in question; in your Mail application, you can press the Edit button in the upper-rightcorner to allow the selection of multiple messages for deletion, movement, and other functions. Both of these functionalities are based on the concept of editing a UITableView.

The first thing you can look at is the idea of putting your UITableView into editing mode, because for your users to use your editing functionality, they need to access it. Do this by adding an Edit button to the top-right corner of your view. This is surprisingly easy to do by adding the following line to the viewDidLoad method of your main table view controller:

```
- (void)viewDidLoad
{
    [super viewDidLoad];
    // Do any additional setup after loading the view from its nib.
    self.title = @"Countries";
    self.countriesTableView.delegate = self;
    self.countriesTableView.dataSource = self;
    self.countriesTableView.layer.cornerRadius = 8.0;
    self.navigationItem.rightBarButtonItem = self.editButtonItem;

    // ...
}
```

This editButtonItem property is not actually a property that you need to define, as it is preset for all UIViewController subclasses. The great thing about this button is that it is programmed not only to call a specific method already but also to toggle its text between Edit and Done.

The editButtonItem by default is set to call the method setEditing:animated: for which you create a simple implementation.

```
-(void)setEditing:(BOOL)editing animated:(BOOL)animated
{
    [super setEditing:editing animated:animated];
    [self.countriesTableView setEditing:editing animated:animated];
}
```

The main ideas of this method are simple: first you call the super method, which handles the toggling of the button's text, and then you set the editing mode of your UITableView according to the parameters given.

At this point, your application's Edit button triggers the editing mode of the UITableView, allowing you to reveal Delete buttons for any given row. However, because you haven't actually implemented any behavior for these buttons, you can't actually delete any rows from your table yet. To do this, you must first implement one more delegate method, tableView:commitEditingStyle: forRowAtIndexPath:.

Following is a pretty basic implementation of the method that you'll start with:

```
-(void)tableView:(UITableView *)tableView
commitEditingStyle:(UITableViewCellEditingStyle)editingStyle
forRowAtIndexPath:(NSIndexPath *)indexPath
{
    if (editingStyle == UITableViewCellEditingStyleDelete)
    {
        Country *deletedCountry = [self.countries objectAtIndex:indexPath.row];
        [self.countries removeObject:deletedCountry];

        [countriesTableView
            deleteRowsAtIndexPaths:[NSArray arrayWithObject:indexPath]
            withRowAnimation:UITableViewRowAnimationAutomatic];
    }
}
```

It is important that you make sure to delete the actual piece of data from your model before removing the row(s) from your UITableView, like in the previous recipe, when you first deleted a country from the array and then removed its table view row. If you don't do it in that order, your application may throw an exception.

Now, when you run your app, you can tap the Edit button to put your UITableView into editing mode, resembling Figure 3-11.

Figure 3-11. Your UITableView in editing mode, with functionality for removing rows

UITableView Row Animations

In the method you just added, you specified a specific animation type to be performed on the deletion of a row, called UITableViewRowAnimationAutomatic. The parameter that accepts this value has various other preset values with which you can customize the visual behavior of your rows, including the following:

- UITableViewRowAnimationBottom
- UITableViewRowAnimationFade
- UITableViewRowAnimationLeft
- UITableViewRowAnimationMiddle
- UITableViewRowAnimationNone
- UITableViewRowAnimationRight
- UITableViewRowAnimationTop

The animation type that you choose won't make any significant difference in how your application performs, but it can certainly change how an application looks and feels to the user. It's best to play around with these and see which animation looks best in your application.

At this point, your method should now be able to handle the deletion of rows from your table. Because you wrote your program to re-create your data every time the application runs, it should be pretty easy to test this. When you are about to delete a row from a table, your table resembles Figure 3-12.

Figure 3-12. Deleting a row from a table

But Wait, There's More!

Deletion is not the only kind of editing that can occur in a UITableView. Although not used quite as often, iOS includes functionality to allow rows to be created and inserted with the same method with which they were deleted.

The default editing style for any row in a UITableView is UITableViewCellEditingStyleDelete, so to implement row insertion, you need to change this. For fun, you will give every other row an "insertion" editing style by implementing the tableView:editingStyleForRowAtIndexPath: method.

```
-(UITableViewCellEditingStyle)tableView:(UITableView *)tableView
editingStyleForRowAtIndexPath:(NSIndexPath *)indexPath
{
    if ((indexPath.row % 2) == 1)
    {
        return UITableViewCellEditingStyleInsert;
    }
    return UITableViewCellEditingStyleDelete;
}
```

Just as before, you need to specify the behavior to be followed upon the selection of an Insertion button. You add a case to your tableView:commitEditingStyle:forRowAtIndexPath: so the method now looks as follows:

```
-(void)tableView:(UITableView *)tableView
commitEditingStyle:(UITableViewCellEditingStyle)editingStyle
forRowAtIndexPath:(NSIndexPath *)indexPath
{
    if (editingStyle == UITableViewCellEditingStyleDelete)
    {
        Country *deletedCountry = [self.countries objectAtIndex:indexPath.row];
        [self.countries removeObject:deletedCountry];

        [countriesTableView
            deleteRowsAtIndexPaths:[NSArray arrayWithObject:indexPath]
            withRowAnimation:UITableViewRowAnimationAutomatic];
    }
    else if (editingStyle == UITableViewCellEditingStyleInsert)
    {
        Country *copiedCountry = [self.countries objectAtIndex:indexPath.row];
        Country *newCountry = [[Country alloc] init];
        newCountry.name = copiedCountry.name;
        newCountry.flag = copiedCountry.flag;
        newCountry.capital = copiedCountry.capital;
        newCountry.motto = copiedCountry.motto;

        [self.countries insertObject:newCountry atIndex:indexPath.row+1];

        [self.countriesTableView insertRowsAtIndexPaths:
                [NSArray arrayWithObject:[NSIndexPath indexPathForRow:indexPath.row+1
                                            inSection:indexPath.section]]
                withRowAnimation:UITableViewRowAnimationRight];
    }
}
```

You can see that you have chosen a pretty easy implementation for insertion. All you have done is to insert a copy of the selected row. You should note that by changing the index values in this method, you could easily insert objects into nearly any row in the table; it is not necessary to insert into only the following row.

As with the deletion, you must make sure that your data model is updated before your table view, so you add the new Country to your array before you insert the new row into your UITableView.

When running your app and editing your table, you can see both deletion and insertion buttons, as in Figure 3-13.

Figure 3-13. *Editing a UITableView with insertion or deletion*

You can use two other UITableView delegate methods in combination with editing to further customize your application's behavior. We'll just mention them quickly here before closing this recipe and going on with reordering of table views.

- The tableView:willBeginEditingRowAtIndexPath: method allows you to get a kind of "first look" at whichever row was selected for editing, and act accordingly.

- The tableView:didEndEditingRowAtIndexPath: method can be used as a completion block, in that you can specify any actions you deem necessary to be performed with a row, but only after you have completed a row's editing.

Recipe 3-3: Reordering a UITableView

Now that we have covered deletion and insertion of rows, the next logical step in terms of functionality of a table would be to make it so that you can move around your rows. This is actually pretty simple to incorporate given how you have set up your application.

First you have to specify which of your rows are allowed to move. You do this in the `tableView:canMoveRowAtIndexPath:` delegate method:

```
-(BOOL)tableView:(UITableView *)tableView
canMoveRowAtIndexPath:(NSIndexPath *)indexPath
{
    return YES;
}
```

We took the easy way out of this by simply making all the rows editable, but you can of course change this depending on your application.

Now you simply need to implement a delegate to update your data model on the successful movement of a row:

```
-(void)tableView:(UITableView *)tableView moveRowAtIndexPath:
(NSIndexPath *)sourceIndexPath toIndexPath:(NSIndexPath *)destinationIndexPath
{
    [self.countries exchangeObjectAtIndex:sourceIndexPath.row
        withObjectAtIndex:destinationIndexPath.row];
    [self.countriesTableView reloadData];
}
```

Just as with insertion, you must make sure to correct your array to match the reordering, but the UITableView handles the actual swapping of rows automatically.

For extra control over the reordering of the table, you can implement an extra method called `tableView:targetIndexPathForMoveFromRowAtIndexPath:`. This delegate method is called every time a cell is dragged over another cell as a possible movement, and its normal use is for "retargeting" a destination row. In this way, you can check the proposed destination and either confirm the proposed move or reject it and return a different destination.

Although you haven't implemented functionality to confirm or reject your proposed movements, your application can now successfully move and reorder your rows in addition to your previous deletion and copying functionalities, as in Figure 3-14.

Figure 3-14. Your table with a reordering of cells feature

Recipe 3-4: Creating a Grouped UITableView

Now that you have nearly completely gone through all the basics of using an ungrouped UITableView, you can adjust your application to consider a "grouped" approach. All the functionalities you implemented with an ungrouped table also apply to a grouped one, so you will not have to make a great deal of changes.

The absolute first thing you need to do to use a grouped table is to switch the "style" of the UITableView from "plain" to "grouped." The easiest way to do this is in your view controller's .xib file by selecting your UITableView and changing the style in the Attribute inspector, resulting in a display similar to the one in Figure 3-15.

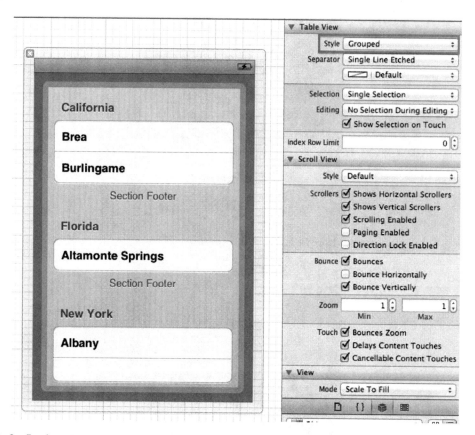

Figure 3-15. Configuring a "grouped" UITableView

While this is the only thing necessary to change the style of your table, the problem is that until now, your data model has been formatted for an ungrouped style. You don't have your data grouped at all. To remedy this problem, you will change the organization with which your data are stored.

Rather than having one array containing all five of your countries, you will separate your countries into their groups, with each group being an NSMutableArray, and then put these arrays into a larger NSMutableArray. (Although a better practice would be to make these immutable, we have chosen a mutable version to make editing your data model from the table a simpler process.)

For your application, divide your five Country objects into two categories: one of countries in the United Kingdom and one of all the others.

First, you need to create two more NSMutableArrays to be your subarrays, so add these two properties to MainTableViewController.h. You will end up with a total of three NSMutableArray properties.

```
@property (strong, nonatomic) NSMutableArray *countries;
@property (strong, nonatomic) NSMutableArray *unitedKingdomCountries;
@property (strong, nonatomic) NSMutableArray *nonUKCountries;
```

Now change your `viewDidLoad` method to accommodate this change. Delete the following line from this method:

```
self.countries =
    [NSMutableArray arrayWithObjects:usa, france, england, scotland, spain, nil];
```

Now replace that line with the following to properly organize your countries:

```
    self.unitedKingdomCountries = [NSMutableArray arrayWithObjects:england, scotland, nil];
    self.nonUKCountries = [NSMutableArray arrayWithObjects:usa, france, spain, nil];
    self.countries = [NSMutableArray arrayWithObjects:self.unitedKingdomCountries,
self.nonUKCountries, nil];
```

Now comes the slightly tricky part where you have to make sure all your data source and delegate methods are adjusted to your new format. First, you have to include a retrieval of the group's array, and then you have to retrieve a specific country from there in each method. First, change your `tableView:cellForRowAtIndexPath:`

```
- (UITableViewCell *)tableView:(UITableView *)tableView
cellForRowAtIndexPath:(NSIndexPath *)indexPath
{
    static NSString *CellIdentifier = @"Cell";

    UITableViewCell *cell = [tableView dequeueReusableCellWithIdentifier:CellIdentifier];
    if (cell == nil)
    {
        cell = [[UITableViewCell alloc] initWithStyle:UITableViewCellStyleSubtitle
                reuseIdentifier:CellIdentifier];
        cell.accessoryType = UITableViewCellAccessoryDetailDisclosureButton;
        cell.textLabel.font = [UIFont systemFontOfSize:19.0];
        cell.detailTextLabel.font = [UIFont systemFontOfSize:12];
    }

    NSArray *group = [self.countries objectAtIndex:indexPath.section];
    Country *item = [group objectAtIndex:indexPath.row];
    cell.textLabel.text = item.name;
    cell.detailTextLabel.text = item.capital;
    cell.imageView.image =
        [MainTableViewController scale: item.flag toSize:CGSizeMake(115, 75)];

    return cell;
}
```

Up next is `tableView:numberOfRowsInSection:`.

```
-(NSInteger)tableView:(UITableView *)tableView numberOfRowsInSection:(NSInteger)section
{
    NSArray *group = [self.countries objectAtIndex:section];
    return [group count];
}
```

Here is tableView:didSelectRowAtIndexPath:.

```
-(void)tableView:(UITableView *)tableView didSelectRowAtIndexPath:(NSIndexPath *)indexPath
{
    [tableView deselectRowAtIndexPath:indexPath animated:YES];

    selectedIndexPath = indexPath;

    NSArray *group = [self.countries objectAtIndex:indexPath.section];
    Country *chosenCountry = [group objectAtIndex:indexPath.row];
    CountryDetailsViewController *detailedViewController =
        [[CountryDetailsViewController alloc] init];
    detailedViewController.delegate = self;
    detailedViewController.currentCountry = chosenCountry;

    [self.navigationController pushViewController:detailedViewController animated:YES];
}
```

And the same change in tableView:accessoryButtonTappedForRowWithIndexPath:.

```
-(void)tableView:(UITableView *)tableView
accessoryButtonTappedForRowWithIndexPath:(NSIndexPath *)indexPath
{
    [tableView deselectRowAtIndexPath:indexPath animated:YES];

    selectedIndexPath = indexPath;

    NSArray *group = [self.countries objectAtIndex:indexPath.section];
    Country *chosenCountry = [group objectAtIndex:indexPath.row];
    CountryDetailsViewController *detailedViewController =
        [[CountryDetailsViewController alloc] init];
    detailedViewController.delegate = self;
    detailedViewController.currentCountry = chosenCountry;

    NSLog(@"Accessory Button Tapped");
    [self.navigationController pushViewController:detailedViewController animated:YES];
}
```

For the tableView:moveRowAtIndexPath:toIndexPath: method, you will make a quick assumption that you are moving only rows that are in the same section to make your coding easier. Notice when you run the application later that this actually works well. As with your current implementation, the UITableView does not allow a Country to switch groups, just as expected in this particular application. For an application where it may be reasonable to have objects change groups, include code to do so accordingly.

```
-(void)tableView:(UITableView *)tableView moveRowAtIndexPath:
(NSIndexPath *)sourceIndexPath toIndexPath:(NSIndexPath *)destinationIndexPath
{
    //Assume same Section
    NSMutableArray *group = [self.countries objectAtIndex:sourceIndexPath.section];
```

```
    if (destinationIndexPath.row < [group count])
    {
        [group exchangeObjectAtIndex:sourceIndexPath.row
            withObjectAtIndex:destinationIndexPath.row];
    }
    [self.countriesTableView reloadData];
}
```

The last method you must fix is tableView:commitEditingStyle:forRowAtIndexPath:, which looks like so:

```
-(void)tableView:(UITableView *)tableView
commitEditingStyle:(UITableViewCellEditingStyle)editingStyle
forRowAtIndexPath:(NSIndexPath *)indexPath
{
    if (editingStyle == UITableViewCellEditingStyleDelete)
    {
        NSMutableArray *group = [self.countries objectAtIndex:indexPath.section];
        Country *deletedCountry = [group objectAtIndex:indexPath.row];
        [group removeObject:deletedCountry];

        [countriesTableView deleteRowsAtIndexPaths:[NSArray arrayWithObject:indexPath]
withRowAnimation:UITableViewRowAnimationAutomatic];
    }
    else if (editingStyle == UITableViewCellEditingStyleInsert)
    {
        NSMutableArray *group = [self.countries objectAtIndex:indexPath.section];
        Country *copiedCountry = [group objectAtIndex:indexPath.row];
        Country *newCountry = [[Country alloc] init];
        newCountry.name = copiedCountry.name;
        newCountry.flag = copiedCountry.flag;
        newCountry.capital = copiedCountry.capital;
        newCountry.motto = copiedCountry.motto;

        [group insertObject:newCountry atIndex:indexPath.row+1];

        [self.countriesTableView insertRowsAtIndexPaths:
            [NSArray arrayWithObject:[NSIndexPath indexPathForRow:indexPath.row+1
             inSection:indexPath.section]]
             withRowAnimation:UITableViewRowAnimationRight];
    }
}
```

Finally, because you did switch your UITableView over to a grouped style, you need to implement just two extra methods to ensure correct functionality.

First, you need to specify how many sections your UITableView will have with the following method:

```
-(NSInteger)numberOfSectionsInTableView:(UITableView *)tableView
{
    return [self.countries count];
}
```

Second, you should specify headers for each section, which will basically be the titles for your groups. Because you already know how your data is formatted, this is pretty easy to do.

```
-(NSString *)tableView:(UITableView *)tableView titleForHeaderInSection:(NSInteger)section
{
    if (section == 0)
    {
        return @"United Kingdom Countries";
    }
    return @"Non-United Kingdom Countries";
}
```

If your data model was more complicated, you would probably want to have the names of your groups stored somewhere with the groups themselves. Using an NSDictionary would be a particularly good way to use this by making the headers, as strings, the keys for your NSArray group objects.

The UITableViewDelegate protocol also includes a method that allows the developer to customize the text displayed in a Delete button when editing a UITableView. This method is entirely optional and varies in its use based on the needs of any given application.

```
-(NSString *)tableView:(UITableView *)tableView
titleForDeleteConfirmationButtonForRowAtIndexPath:(NSIndexPath *)indexPath
{
    return NSLocalizedString(@"Remove", @"Delete");
}
```

After all these changes, running your app should result in a view similar to the one in Figure 3-16.

Figure 3-16. Your application with grouped items and section headers

As a final embellishment for your table, you can also add footers to your sections. These work just like headers, but, as you might guess, they appear on the bottom of your groups. Here's a quick method to add footers to your UITableView.

```
-(NSString *)tableView:(UITableView *)tableView titleForFooterInSection:(NSInteger)section
{
    if (section == 0)
        return @"United Kingdom Countries";
    return @"Non-United Kingdom Countries";
}
```

In keeping with all the other customizable parts of a UITableView, these headers and footers are also easily customized beyond a simple NSString. If you use the methods tableView:viewForHeaderInSec tion: and tableView:viewForFooterInSection:, you can programmatically create your own subview to be used as a header or footer, allowing for full control over your UITableView's display.

At this point, you now have a fully functional grouped UITableView, complete with all the same abilities as your ungrouped one! Figure 3-17 shows the final result of your setup.

Figure 3-17. Your completed grouped UITableView with both headers and footers

Recipe 3-5: Registering a Custom Cell Class

Let's for a minute return to the method that's responsible for creating and initializing a given table view cell. For reference, here's the implementation from the previous recipes:

```
- (UITableViewCell *)tableView:(UITableView *)tableView
cellForRowAtIndexPath:(NSIndexPath *)indexPath
{
    static NSString *CellIdentifier = @"Cell";

    UITableViewCell *cell =
        [tableView dequeueReusableCellWithIdentifier:CellIdentifier];
    if (cell == nil)
    {
        cell = [[UITableViewCell alloc] initWithStyle:UITableViewCellStyleSubtitle
                                      reuseIdentifier:CellIdentifier];
        cell.accessoryType = UITableViewCellAccessoryDetailDisclosureButton;
        cell.textLabel.font = [UIFont systemFontOfSize:19.0];
        cell.detailTextLabel.font = [UIFont systemFontOfSize:12];
    }
```

```
    NSArray *group = [self.countries objectAtIndex:indexPath.section];
    Country *item = [group objectAtIndex:indexPath.row];
    cell.textLabel.text = item.name;
    cell.detailTextLabel.text = item.capital;
    cell.imageView.image =
        [MainTableViewController scale: item.flag toSize:CGSizeMake(115, 75)];

    return cell;
}
```

The code follows a common implementation pattern of the `tableView:cellForRowAtIndexPath:`
method and it does its job well. However, there are a couple of problems with it. For one thing, it's
quite long and it's not obvious from a quick glance what it does. A more serious problem is that it's
not particularly reusable; if you create another application and want similar-looking table view cells,
your only option is to copy and paste the foregoing code into the other project.

A better solution would be to make a custom table view cell class of your own so that you can reuse
it between projects, or even within one project if it contains several table views. A custom class
could also make the setup code significantly simpler and more self-explanatory. Recipe 3-5 shows
you how to change the Country project's current implementation of the
`tableView:cellForRowAtIndexPath:` method into one that utilizes a custom table view cell class.

Creating a Custom Table View Cell Class

Start by creating a new class using the `Objective-C` class template. Name the new class
`CountryCell` and make it a subclass of `UITableViewCell`. Now, open `CountryCell.h` and add a
country property to the class, like so:

```
//
//  CountryCell.h
//  Countries
//

#import <UIKit/UIKit.h>
#import "Country.h"

@interface CountryCell : UITableViewCell

@property (strong, nonatomic) Country *country;

@end
```

Now, switch to the CountryCell.m file. The designated initializer of table view cells is the
`initWithStyle:reuseIdentifier:` method. Override this method and provide the initialization that is
common for all country cells—that is, cell style, accessory type, and the fonts of the two labels.

```
- (id)initWithStyle:(UITableViewCellStyle)style reuseIdentifier:(NSString *)reuseIdentifier
{
    self = [super initWithStyle:UITableViewCellStyleSubtitle
            reuseIdentifier:reuseIdentifier];
```

```
    if (self)
    {
        // Initialization code
        self.accessoryType = UITableViewCellAccessoryDetailDisclosureButton;
        self.textLabel.font = [UIFont systemFontOfSize:19.0];
        self.detailTextLabel.font = [UIFont systemFontOfSize:12];
    }
    return self;
}
```

Next, we're going to implement a special setter method for the country property that updates the parts of the cell that are different for each country. These are the text label, the detailed text label, and the flag image. You implement the setter as follows:

```
- (void)setCountry:(Country *)country
{
    if (country != _country)
    {
        _country = country;
        self.textLabel.text = _country.name;
        self.detailTextLabel.text = _country.capital;
        self.imageView.image =
            [CountryCell scale: _country.flag toSize:CGSizeMake(115, 75)];
    }
}
```

If you try to compile the code now it will fail because it doesn't recognize the scale:toSize: class method, which is currently declared in MainTableViewController. In a real scenario you'd probably want to move the method to some kind of helper class that is shared throughout your application, but for the purpose of this recipe it's sufficient to move it from MainTableViewController into your CountryCell class.

Your complete implementation file should now resemble the code that follows.

```
//
//  CountryCell.m
//  Countries
//

#import "CountryCell.h"

@implementation CountryCell

@synthesize country = _country;

- (id)initWithStyle:(UITableViewCellStyle)style reuseIdentifier:(NSString *)reuseIdentifier
{
    self = [super initWithStyle:UITableViewCellStyleSubtitle reuseIdentifier:reuseIdentifier];
    if (self)
    {
        // Initialization code
        self.accessoryType = UITableViewCellAccessoryDetailDisclosureButton;
```

```
        self.textLabel.font = [UIFont systemFontOfSize:19.0];
        self.detailTextLabel.font = [UIFont systemFontOfSize:12];
    }
    return self;
}

+ (UIImage *)scale:(UIImage *)image toSize:(CGSize)size
{
    UIGraphicsBeginImageContext(size);
    [image drawInRect:CGRectMake(0, 0, size.width, size.height)];
    UIImage *scaledImage = UIGraphicsGetImageFromCurrentImageContext();
    UIGraphicsEndImageContext();
    return scaledImage;
}

- (void)setCountry:(Country *)country
{
    if (country != _country)
    {
        _country = country;
        self.textLabel.text = _country.name;
        self.detailTextLabel.text = _country.capital;
        self.imageView.image =
            [CountryCell scale: _country.flag toSize:CGSizeMake(115, 75)];
    }
}

@end
```

Your custom table view cell class is now ready to be used from your table view controller.

Registering Your Cell Class

Switch to MainTableViewController.m and add the following line to its viewDidLoad method. To make it compile, you also need to import CountryCell.h.

```
#import "MainTableViewController.h"
#import "CountryCell.h"

@implementation MainTableViewController

// ...

- (void)viewDidLoad
{
    [super viewDidLoad];
    // Do any additional setup after loading the view from its nib.
    self.title = @"Countries";
    self.countriesTableView.delegate = self;
    self.countriesTableView.dataSource = self;
```

```
    self.countriesTableView.layer.cornerRadius = 8.0;
    self.navigationItem.rightBarButtonItem = self.editButtonItem;

    [self.countriesTableView registerClass:CountryCell.class
        forCellReuseIdentifier:@"CountryCell"];

    // ...
}
```

The preceding code registers your `CountryCell` class with the table view. This uses a new feature of iOS 6 that changes the semantics of the `dequeueReusableCellWithIdentifier:` method a little. The new behavior of that method is that if a suitable cached cell object could not be found, a new cell is created if a registered class with the given identifier exists.

It's now time to reap the benefits of your changes and implement the `tableView:` `cellForRowAtIndexPath:` method, which at this point can be shrunk into only four lines of code:

```
- (UITableViewCell *)tableView:(UITableView *)tableView
cellForRowAtIndexPath:(NSIndexPath *)indexPath
{
    CountryCell *cell = [tableView dequeueReusableCellWithIdentifier:@"CountryCell"];
    NSArray *group = [self.countries objectAtIndex:indexPath.section];
    cell.country = [group objectAtIndex:indexPath.row];
    return cell;
}
```

If you build and run your code now, it should work just like before. But your code is a little bit better encapsulated and better prepared for reuse.

Recipe 3-6: Creating a Flag Picker Collection View

One of the great new features of iOS 6 is the Collection View. It has evolved from the good old Table View but not to be its replacement, but rather as a natural complement. Unlike Table Views, which display data in a single column and have a lot of built-in functionality based on that layout, Collection Views provide a total control of how items are laid out but offer less built-in functions. It offers more possibilities but at the price of more work on the behalf of the developer.

The exceptional flexibility of the Collection View comes from a total separation between the view and its layout. What this means is that you can get full control of the layout of items by providing a custom Layout object. However, Apple provides a ready to use Layout class that will work in most situations. It provides a basic multicolumn layout that expands in one direction (that is, either supports horizontal or vertical scrolling).

In this recipe we'll show you how to setup a Collection View with this built-in Layout class, called `UICollectionViewFlowLayout`. You'll use it to create a picker view in which a user can browse a collection of flags and select one of them.

Setting Up the Application

Because this app displays a collection of flags, you should start by gathering some flag images for your test data. Download as many flag images as you like from `http://en.wikipedia.org/wiki/ Gallery_of_sovereign-state_flags`, but to make sense there should be at least 15 of them from several continents. As a reference, we downloaded the following flags:

- African flags: Ghana, Kenya, Morocco, Mozambique, Rwanda, and South Africa

- Asian flags: China, India, Japan, Mongolia, Russia, and Turkey

- Australasian flags: Australia and New Zealand

- European flags: France, Germany, Iceland, Ireland, Italy, Malta, Poland, Spain, Sweden, and United Kingdom

- North American flags: Canada, Mexico, and United States

- South American flags: Argentina, Brazil, and Chile

> **Tip**   To keep the app size down, download the 200-pixel PNG format of the flags. This format and size is found by clicking the flag image on the Wikipedia flag gallery, which takes you to a page with links to the available sizes and formats for the flag image. It's also recommended that you change their file names to contain only the name of the country, for example, France.png.

Now, create a new single-view application and add the flag images to the project. An easy way to do this is to gather the flag images in a folder and drag it onto the Project Navigator. It may be a good idea to create a new group folder to host the files, preferably in the Supporting Files folder as shown in Figure 3-18.

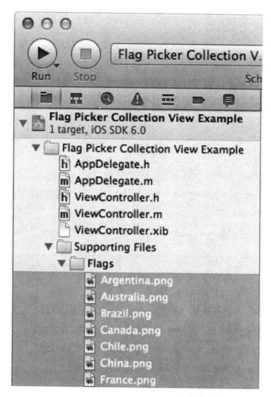

Figure 3-18. An application with flag resource images in a group folder of their own

The next thing you're going to do is to setup a simple user interface that displays a big flag and the name of the country it belongs to. A button below the flag will allow the user to select a different flag using the Flag Picker that you'll soon build. Select the ViewController.xib file to bring up Interface Builder, add a label, an image view and a button to the view in such a way that it resembles Figure 3-19. Initialize the image view with one of your flag images by setting the image view's Image attribute in the Attribute Inspector.

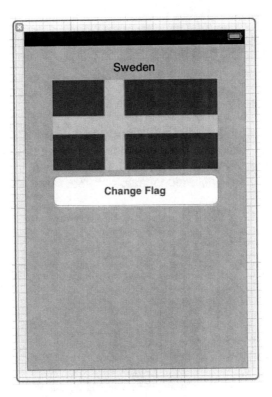

Figure 3-19. A simple user interface that displays a country name and its flag

Now, since you'll change the content of both the label and the image view at runtime, you need outlets to reference them from you code. Create these outlets and name them countryLabel and flagImageView, respectively. Similarly, create an action named pickFlag for when the user taps the button.

Your ViewController.h file should now resemble this code:

```
//
//  ViewController.h
//  Flag Picker Collection View Example
//

#import <UIKit/UIKit.h>

@interface ViewController : UIViewController

@property (weak, nonatomic) IBOutlet UILabel *countryLabel;
@property (weak, nonatomic) IBOutlet UIImageView *flagImageView;

- (IBAction)pickFlag:(id)sender;

@end
```

You're now going to leave the main user interface for a while and instead turn to implement the Flag Picker View Controller that will be displayed from the `pickFlag:` action method. But before you can do that you need to create a simple data model that you can use to transfer data between the picker and the main view.

Creating a Data Model

In this recipe you're going to setup a really simple model to hold the data. You're going to create a class that holds an image of a flag and the name of the country it belongs to. Create a new Objective-C class named `Flag` and with `NSObject` as its parent. Then, in `Flag.h`, add the following code to declare properties and an initialization method for the class:

```
//
//  Flag.h
//  Flag Picker Collection View Example
//

#import <Foundation/Foundation.h>

@interface Flag : NSObject

@property (strong, nonatomic)NSString *name;
@property (strong, nonatomic)UIImage *image;

- (id)initWithName:(NSString *)name imageName:(NSString *)imageName;

@end
```

Now, switch to `Flag.m` for the implementation of the initialization method:

```
//
//  Flag.m
//  Flag Picker Collection View Example
//

#import "Flag.h"

@implementation Flag

- (id)initWithName:(NSString *)name imageName:(NSString *)imageName
{
    self = [super init];
    if (self) {
        self.name = name;
        NSString *imageFile = [[NSBundle mainBundle]
pathForResource:imageName ofType:@"png"];
        self.image = [[UIImage alloc] initWithContentsOfFile:imageFile];
    }
    return self;
}

@end
```

Note that the initWithName:imageName: method loads the image resource file into memory. In a real scenario you'd probably want to use lazy initialization in a custom property getter to defer the loading until the image is actually requested. But for this recipe, loading the flag file on creation is fine.

You're now ready to move on and start implementing the Flag Picker.

Building the Flag Picker

When the user taps the Change Flag button of the user interface, what you're going to do is display a collection of flags for the user to choose between. This is the perfect job for a Collection View so let's set up one.

First you need a new view controller to handle the Collection View so go ahead and create a new subclass of UICollectionViewController. Name the new class FlagPickerViewController. You do not need an .xib file to handle its user interface so make sure the option With XIB for user interface is unchecked.

Now with the new class in place you can go on and set up the delegation pattern to use to notify the main view that a flag has been picked. Go to the header file of the new class and add the following code:

```objectivec
//
//  FlagPickerViewController.h
//  Flag Picker Collection View Example
//

#import <UIKit/UIKit.h>
#import "Flag.h"

@class FlagPickerViewController;

@protocol FlagPickerViewControllerDelegate <NSObject>

-(void)flagPicker:(FlagPickerViewController *)flagPicker didPickFlag:(Flag *)flag;

@end

@interface FlagPickerViewController : UICollectionViewController

- (id)initWithDelegate:(id<FlagPickerViewControllerDelegate>)delegate;

@property (weak, nonatomic)id<FlagPickerViewControllerDelegate> delegate;

@end
```

You also need some instance variables to hold the available flags. Because you are going to group the flags according to which continent they stem from, you need six arrays:

```
//
//  FlagPickerViewController.h
//  Flag Picker Collection View Example
//

// ...

@interface FlagPickerViewController : UICollectionViewController
{
@private
    NSArray *africanFlags;
    NSArray *asianFlags;
    NSArray *australasianFlags;
    NSArray *europeanFlags;
    NSArray *northAmericanFlags;
    NSArray *southAmericanFlags;
}

- (id)initWithDelegate:(id<FlagPickerViewControllerDelegate>)delegate;

@property (weak, nonatomic)id<FlagPickerViewControllerDelegate> delegate;

@end
```

Now, switch to the FlagPickerViewController.m file and add the following implementation for the initialization method:

```
//
//  FlagPickerViewController.m
//  Flag Picker Collection View Example
//

#import "FlagPickerViewController.h"

@implementation FlagPickerViewController

- (id)initWithDelegate:(id<FlagPickerViewControllerDelegate>)delegate
{
    UICollectionViewFlowLayout *layout =
        [[UICollectionViewFlowLayout alloc] init];
    self = [super initWithCollectionViewLayout:layout];
    if (self)
    {
        self.delegate = delegate;
    }
```

```
    return self;
}

// ...

@end
```

As you can see from the preceding code, the method creates a layout object to handle the positioning of the items. We're using the built-in UICollectionViewFlowLayout that provides a simple multicolumn layout that flows in one direction (horizontally by default). The method also sets the delegate property that you will use later to notify the invoker that a selection has been made.

Next create the collection of available flags. Find the viewDidLoad method and add the following code. (Note that you should adjust the code according to which flags you actually downloaded and imported into your project.)

```
- (void)viewDidLoad
{
    [super viewDidLoad];
    // Do any additional setup after loading the view from its nib.

    africanFlags = [NSArray arrayWithObjects:
        [[Flag alloc] initWithName:@"Ghana" imageName:@"Ghana"],
        [[Flag alloc] initWithName:@"Kenya" imageName:@"Kenya"],
        [[Flag alloc] initWithName:@"Morocco" imageName:@"Morocco"],
        [[Flag alloc] initWithName:@"Mozambique" imageName:@"Mozambique"],
        [[Flag alloc] initWithName:@"Rwanda" imageName:@"Rwanda"],
        [[Flag alloc] initWithName:@"South Africa" imageName:@"South_Africa"],
        nil];

    asianFlags = [NSArray arrayWithObjects:
        [[Flag alloc] initWithName:@"China" imageName:@"China"],
        [[Flag alloc] initWithName:@"India" imageName:@"India"],
        [[Flag alloc] initWithName:@"Japan" imageName:@"Japan"],
        [[Flag alloc] initWithName:@"Mongolia" imageName:@"Mongolia"],
        [[Flag alloc] initWithName:@"Russia" imageName:@"Russia"],
        [[Flag alloc] initWithName:@"Turkey" imageName:@"Turkey"],
        nil];

    australasianFlags = [NSArray arrayWithObjects:
        [[Flag alloc] initWithName:@"Australia" imageName:@"Australia"],
        [[Flag alloc] initWithName:@"New Zealand" imageName:@"New_Zealand"],
        nil];

    europeanFlags = [NSArray arrayWithObjects:
        [[Flag alloc] initWithName:@"France" imageName:@"France"],
        [[Flag alloc] initWithName:@"Germany" imageName:@"Germany"],
        [[Flag alloc] initWithName:@"Iceland" imageName:@"Iceland"],
        [[Flag alloc] initWithName:@"Ireland" imageName:@"Ireland"],
        [[Flag alloc] initWithName:@"Italy" imageName:@"Italy"],
        [[Flag alloc] initWithName:@"Poland" imageName:@"Poland"],
```

```
          [[Flag alloc] initWithName:@"Russia" imageName:@"Russia"],
          [[Flag alloc] initWithName:@"Spain" imageName:@"Spain"],
          [[Flag alloc] initWithName:@"Sweden" imageName:@"Sweden"],
          [[Flag alloc] initWithName:@"Turkey" imageName:@"Turkey"],
          [[Flag alloc] initWithName:@"United Kingdom" imageName:@"United_Kingdom"],
          nil];

    northAmericanFlags = [NSArray arrayWithObjects:
          [[Flag alloc] initWithName:@"Canada" imageName:@"Canada"],
          [[Flag alloc] initWithName:@"Mexico" imageName:@"Mexico"],
          [[Flag alloc] initWithName:@"United States" imageName:@"United_States"],
          nil];

    southAmericanFlags = [NSArray arrayWithObjects:
          [[Flag alloc] initWithName:@"Argentina" imageName:@"Argentina"],
          [[Flag alloc] initWithName:@"Brazil" imageName:@"Brazil"],
          [[Flag alloc] initWithName:@"Chile" imageName:@"Chile"],
          nil];
}
```

Collection Views follow the same data pattern as Table Views, meaning that they allow data to be grouped into sections. As you'll see, the delegate methods to notify the Collection View how many sections there are and how many items they contain are very similar to the ones used for Table Views. Add the following two methods to provide that data:

```
//
//  FlagPickerViewController.m
//  Flag Picker Collection View Example
//

// ...


@implementation FlagPickerViewController

// ...


-(NSInteger)numberOfSectionsInCollectionView:(UICollectionView *)collectionView
{
    return 6;
}


-(NSInteger)collectionView:(UICollectionView *)collectionView
numberOfItemsInSection:(NSInteger)section
{
    switch (section) {
        case 0:
            return africanFlags.count;
        case 1:
            return asianFlags.count;
        case 2:
            return australasianFlags.count;
```

```
        case 3:
            return europeanFlags.count;
        case 4:
            return northAmericanFlags.count;
        case 5:
            return southAmericanFlags.count;

        default:
            return 0;
    }
}

@end
```

> **Note** As you may have noticed, we did not explicitly assign a data source delegate for the Collection View. The Collection View Controller class handles this automatically; if you don't provide a specific delegate object it will assign itself to the task. This is true for both the `UICollectionViewDelegate` and the `UICollectionViewDataSource` properties of the Collection View.

Now you have set up the Collection View so that it knows how many sections and how many items it should display. The next step is to let the Collection View know how to display the items. This is done by creating and registering cell views and so called supplementary view.

Defining the Collection View Interface

A Collection View delegates the actual displaying of items and section specific details to views provided by you. These views are called Cell Views and Supplementary Views. Supplementary Views are things like section headers and footers, while Cells are the individual items. It's your job to define these views and register them with the Collection View.

You're going to set up these cells programmatically, and you'll start with the Cell View. It should contain a thumbnail image of a flag and a small label displaying the country name. Start by creating a new `UICollectionViewCell` subclass with the name `FlagCell`. Then add the following property declarations to the header file of the new class:

```
//
//  FlagCell.h
//  Flag Picker Collection View Example
//

#import <UIKit/UIKit.h>

@interface FlagCell : UICollectionViewCell

@property (strong, nonatomic) UILabel *nameLabel;
@property (strong, nonatomic) UIImageView *flagImageView;

@end
```

In the implementation file, add the following initialization code to the `initWithFrame:` method. The code basically does two things: it creates and adds a label and an image view to the content view of the cell, and it change the color of the background view that's displayed when the cell is highlighted:

```
//
//  FlagCell.m
//  Flag Picker Collection View Example
//

#import "FlagCell.h"

@implementation FlagCell

- (id)initWithFrame:(CGRect)frame
{
    self = [super initWithFrame:frame];
    if (self) {
        // Initialization code
        self.nameLabel =
            [[UILabel alloc] initWithFrame:CGRectMake(0, 56, 100, 19)];
        self.nameLabel.textAlignment = NSTextAlignmentCenter;
        self.nameLabel.backgroundColor = [UIColor clearColor];
        self.nameLabel.textColor = [UIColor whiteColor];
        self.nameLabel.font = [UIFont systemFontOfSize:12.0];
        [self.contentView addSubview:self.nameLabel];

        self.flagImageView =
            [[UIImageView alloc] initWithFrame:CGRectMake(6, 6, 88, 49)];
        [self.contentView addSubview:self.flagImageView];

        self.selectedBackgroundView = [[UIView alloc] initWithFrame:frame];
        self.selectedBackgroundView.backgroundColor = [UIColor grayColor];
    }
    return self;
}

@end
```

Now, you're going to repeat the process for the header supplementary view. It'll simply contain a label to display the name of the continent in the header of the respective section. Create a new class, this time as a subclass of UICollectionReusableView and with the name ContinentHeader. Then add the following property declaration to its header file:

```
//
//  ContinentHeader.h
//  Flag Picker Collection View Example
//

#import <UIKit/UIKit.h>
```

```
@interface ContinentHeader : UICollectionReusableView

@property (strong, nonatomic) UILabel *label;

@end
```

Then add the following initialization code to the implementation file:

```
//
//  ContinentHeader.m
//  Flag Picker Collection View Example
//

#import "ContinentHeader.h"

@implementation ContinentHeader

- (id)initWithFrame:(CGRect)frame
{
    self = [super initWithFrame:frame];
    if (self) {
        // Initialization code
        self.label = [[UILabel alloc] initWithFrame:
            CGRectMake(0, 0, frame.size.width, frame.size.height)];
        self.label.font = [UIFont systemFontOfSize:20];
        self.label.textColor = [UIColor whiteColor];
        self.label.backgroundColor = [UIColor clearColor];
        self.label.textAlignment = NSTextAlignmentCenter;
        [self addSubview:self.label];
    }
    return self;
}

@end
```

Now, to be able to use these two views to display the content you need to register them with the Collection View. Go back to the FlagPickerViewController.m file and add the following code to the viewDidLoad method (note that the code to set up the flag data has been removed for brevity):

```
//
//  FlagPickerViewController.m
//  Flag Picker Collection View Example
//

#import "FlagPickerViewController.h"
#import "FlagCell.h"
#import "ContinentHeader.h"

@implementation FlagPickerViewController

// ...
```

```
- (void)viewDidLoad
{
    [super viewDidLoad];
    // Do any additional setup after loading the view from its nib.

    // ...

    [self.collectionView registerClass:FlagCell.class
        forCellWithReuseIdentifier:@"FlagCell"];
    [self.collectionView registerClass:ContinentHeader.class
        forSupplementaryViewOfKind:UICollectionElementKindSectionHeader
        withReuseIdentifier:@"ContinentHeader"];
}

// ...

@end
```

With the cell and supplementary views registered you can go ahead and implement the delegate methods that will create and set them up. Still in the `FlagPickerViewController.m` file, add the following delegate method:

```
-(UICollectionViewCell*)collectionView:(UICollectionView *)collectionView
cellForItemAtIndexPath:(NSIndexPath *)indexPath
{
FlagCell *cell =
        [collectionView dequeueReusableCellWithReuseIdentifier:@ "FlagCell"
        forIndexPath:indexPath];
    Flag *flag = [self flagForIndexPath:indexPath];
    cell.nameLabel.text = flag.name;
    cell.flagImageView.image = flag.image;
    return cell;
}
```

The `dequeueReusableCellWithReuseIdentifier:` method looks to see whether it can reuse an already created cell or create a new one if there's none. No matter what, you can rely on receiving an allocated instance of a cell that you just update with the current data before you return it to the Collection View.

Also, the this method uses a helper method, `flagForIndexPath:` to get the corresponding Flag instance from the data model. The implementation of that helper method is as follows:

```
-(Flag *)flagForIndexPath:(NSIndexPath *)indexPath
{
    switch (indexPath.section) {
        case 0:
            return [africanFlags objectAtIndex:indexPath.row];
        case 1:
            return [asianFlags objectAtIndex:indexPath.row];
        case 2:
            return [australasianFlags objectAtIndex:indexPath.row];
```

```
    case 3:
        return [europeanFlags objectAtIndex:indexPath.row];
    case 4:
        return [northAmericanFlags objectAtIndex:indexPath.row];
    case 5:
        return [southAmericanFlags objectAtIndex:indexPath.row];

    default:
        return nil;
    }
}
```

Now, the corresponding delegate method for the supplementary view (the section header) looks like the code that follows. Add it to the `FlagPickerViewController` class as well:

```
- (UICollectionReusableView *)collectionView:(UICollectionView *)collectionView
viewForSupplementaryElementOfKind:(NSString *)kind atIndexPath:(NSIndexPath *)indexPath
{
    ContinentHeader *headerView = [collectionView
dequeueReusableSupplementaryViewOfKind:UICollectionElementKindSectionHeader
withReuseIdentifier:@"ContinentHeader" forIndexPath:indexPath];

    headerView.label.text = [self nameForSection:indexPath.section];

    return headerView;
}
```

Again, you are using a helper method to get data from your data model. This time you query the name of a section using this implementation:

```
- (NSString *)nameForSection:(NSInteger)index
{
    switch (index)
    {
        case 0:
            return @"African Flags";
        case 1:
            return @"Asian Flags";
        case 2:
            return @"Australasian Flags";
        case 3:
            return @"European Flags";
        case 4:
            return @"North American Flags";
        case 5:
            return @"South American Flags";
        default:
            return @"Unknown";
    }
}
```

Now, what's remaining before the defining of the Collection View user interface is complete, is to set the sizes of the cells and supplementary views. You do that in the `collectionView:collectionViewLayout:sizeForItemAtPath:` and the `collectionView:collectionViewLayout:referenceSizeForHeaderInSection:` delegate methods, respectively:

```
- (CGSize)collectionView:(UICollectionView *)collectionView
layout:(UICollectionViewLayout*)collectionViewLayout
sizeForItemAtIndexPath:(NSIndexPath *)indexPath
{
    return CGSizeMake(100, 75);
}

- (CGSize)collectionView:(UICollectionView *)collectionView
layout:(UICollectionViewLayout*)collectionViewLayout
referenceSizeForHeaderInSection:(NSInteger)section
{
    return CGSizeMake(50, 50);
}
```

> **Note** When you set the size of a header or footer in a Collection View Flow Layout, only one dimension is considered. For example, if the flow is vertical, only the height component of the `CGSize` is used to determine the actual size of the supplementary view. The width is instead inferred by the width of the Collection View. The converse is true for horizontal flows which only considers the width you provide.

The last thing you need to do in the Flag Picker is to add code to notify the main view when a flag has been picked. This is easy now that the infrastructure is in place. Add the following method to `FlagPickerViewController`:

```
-(void)collectionView:(UICollectionView *)collectionView
didSelectItemAtIndexPath:(NSIndexPath *)indexPath
{
    Flag *selectedFlag = [self flagForIndexPath:indexPath];
    [self.delegate flagPicker:self didPickFlag:selectedFlag];
}
```

You're done with the implementation of the Flag Picker. Now it's time to turn your focus back to the main view.

Displaying the Flag Picker

To use the Flag Picker you just built, you first need to prepare the main view controller to be a Flag Picker delegate. Making it conform to the FlagPickerViewControllerDelegate protocol you defined earlier does this. Switch to ViewController.h and add the following code:

```
//
// ViewController.h
// Flag Picker Collection View Example
//

#import <UIKit/UIKit.h>
#import "FlagPickerViewController.h"

@interface ViewController : UIViewController <FlagPickerViewControllerDelegate>

@property (weak, nonatomic) IBOutlet UILabel *countryLabel;
@property (weak, nonatomic) IBOutlet UIImageView *flagImageView;

- (IBAction)pickFlag:(id)sender;

@end
```

Finally, you can now implement the pickFlag: action method. Go to ViewController.m and add the following implementation:

```
- (IBAction)pickFlag:(id)sender
{
    UICollectionViewController *flagPicker =
        [[FlagPickerViewController alloc] initWithDelegate:self];

    [self presentViewController:flagPicker animated:YES completion:NULL];
}
```

Finally, add the method that responds to a selection event from the Flag Picker. It simply dismisses the Flag Picker and updates the image view and the label with the new information:

```
-(void)flagPicker:(FlagPickerViewController *)flagPicker
didPickFlag:(Flag *)flag
{
    self.flagImageView.image = flag.image;
    self.countryLabel.text = flag.name;
    [self dismissViewControllerAnimated:YES completion:NULL];
}
```

You now can build and run your application. When you tap the Change Flag button you should be presented with a view resembling the one in Figure 3-20.

Figure 3-20. A Collection View displaying a set of flags

You can scroll among the flags and select one that will then be used to update the main view, such as in Figure 3-21.

Figure 3-21. An updated main view after a flag has been selected in the Flag Picker

However, there is one small problem that you'll notice if you rotate the device (by pressing ⌘ + →) and activate the Flag Picker. As Figure 3-22 shows, the section headers are no longer centered.

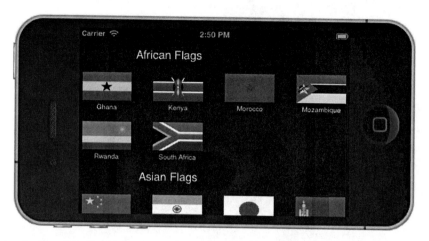

Figure 3-22. *The header files of the Flag Picker don't get properly centered in landscape orientation*

Using Autolayout to Center the Headers

The reason the header labels don't stay centered is that they are created with a fixed size. This works as long as the app stays in portrait mode, but when the screen rotates, the static sized labels don't follow, causing the effect you saw in Figure 3-22.

To fix that problem you can use a little Autolayout magic. Go to ContinentHeader.m and add the following code to the initWithFrame: method:

```
//
// ContinentHeader.m
// Flag Picker Collection View Example
//

#import "ContinentHeader.h"

@implementation ContinentHeader

- (id)initWithFrame:(CGRect)frame
{
    self = [super initWithFrame:frame];
    if (self) {
        // Initialization code
        self.label = [[UILabel alloc] initWithFrame:
            CGRectMake(0, 0, frame.size.width, frame.size.height)];
        self.label.font = [UIFont systemFontOfSize:20];
        self.label.textColor = [UIColor whiteColor];
        self.label.backgroundColor = [UIColor clearColor];
        self.label.textAlignment = NSTextAlignmentCenter;
        [self addSubview:self.label];
```

```
        self.label.translatesAutoresizingMaskIntoConstraints = NO;

        NSDictionary *viewsDictionary =
            [[NSDictionary alloc] initWithObjectsAndKeys:
             self.label, @"label", nil];
        [self addConstraints:
            [NSLayoutConstraint constraintsWithVisualFormat:@"H:|[label]|"
            options:0 metrics:nil views:viewsDictionary]];
    }
    return self;
}

@end
```

What we just did was to add an Autolayout constraint that instructs the label to expand to the width of its parent (the Header View) and stay that way even if the parent's frame changes.

If you run the app now, you'll see that the change has the desired effect on the headers. They are now centered even in landscape orientation as shown in Figure 3-23.

Figure 3-23. The continent labels in this app are centered using Autolayout

Summary

In this chapter we have shown you two of the core components of the iOS 6 platform: the Table View and the new Collection View. We have shown you how to set them up and use them within your app. We have also given you a glimpse of the amount of customization control the developer has over these views, though the full Apple documentation has a great deal more to say on the subject.

However, the key to Table Views and Collection Views is not how they work, but the data they present. It is up to you as a developer to find the information that users want or need and present it to them in the most efficient, flexible way possible. Table Views and Collection Views are fantastic tools, but the purpose they serve is far more important, and this is what will ultimately be the final product that you deliver to your customers.

Chapter 4

Location Recipes

Knowing a device's correct location and heading has enabled developers to take apps to a whole new level. Apps that utilize location services in new ways keep showing up and the potential use cases seem endless. You can build entire apps around these features, such as routing or fitness tracking apps; or you can use location services to enhance the user's experience in more traditional apps. A good example of the latter is the built-in Reminders app, which can remind you of certain tasks when you reach a certain location, such as calling a friend when you get home.

Apple has been paying a lot of attention to this field lately and iOS 6 offers better accuracy and better availability than its predecessor, as well as some new default behaviors that will improve battery life. With iOS 6 you are better equipped than ever to make your apps location aware. This chapter shows you how to get started.

About Core Location

The Core Location framework has everything you need to implement location awareness into your app. In particular, it supports

- Location tracking
- Monitoring significant location changes
- Monitoring entrance or exits of custom regions
- Getting the current heading
- Translating coordinates into addresses (forward geocoding)
- Translating addresses into coordinates (reverse geocoding)

To do its job, Core Location utilizes data from several sources, including cellular masts, nearby Wi-Fi networks, GPS, and the magnetometer. There is some really complex stuff going on inside that we don't have to care about; the framework encapsulates it into an easy-to-use, all-in-one-place API.

Standard and Significant Change Services

There are two primary methods for finding the location of a device: *the standard location service* and *the significant location change service*. Which one you use depends on how accurate you need that information to be and how often you need to be notified that a device's location has changed.

The standard location service provides more accurate location information and invokes the GPS if the requested accuracy requires it. This greater accuracy comes at a cost in terms of a longer time to get a location and an increased drain of the battery. If you are going to use the standard location service, you should use it with precision and only when necessary.

The significant location change service provides some flexibility and is recommended for most applications that don't need highly accurate location information. For instance, if you need to know the town or city where someone is located, the significant location change service is perfectly acceptable. You get a fast response without using a lot of battery power because it uses the cellular signal to determine the device's location. Another benefit of the significant location change service is it runs in the background on the device. Your app does not have to be running in the foreground to receive location updates from this service, unlike the standard location service.

What's New in iOS 6

The biggest change in the Core Location framework in iOS 6 has been on the inside. Still, there are a couple of changes in the API that are worth noting—for example, how to control the new autopause behavior of the location services and the deprecation of the Purpose property.

Autopause

Receiving location updates with high accuracy is a relatively expensive task in terms of battery power. You should therefore minimize the number of updates that are not needed. To help, Apple has implemented a new behavior that pauses updates automatically if the app is in background mode and receives updates that seem unnecessary—for example, if during several updates the device has stopped moving, or desired accuracy can't be provided.

When paused, the `locationManagerDidPauseLocationUpdates:` delegate method notifies the app. When the app is brought back to the foreground again, the location updates are resumed and you'll get a `locationManagerDidResumeLocationUpdates:` message.

This behavior is turned on by default, but your app can turn it off with the `pausesLocationUpdatesAutomatically` property. Most apps, however, don't need to care about autopausing. It probably works just like the user would expect and apps should take great care to minimize location updates anyway.

Activity-Type Property

To help the Core Location framework make better guesses as to what updates may be beneficial to the user, you should set the new property `activityType`. Currently, four values are available:

- `CLActivityTypeFitness`, for movement on foot or by bicycle.
- `CLActivityTypeAutomotiveNavigation`, for movement by car or motorcycle.

- CLActivityTypeOtherNavigation, for other vehicular navigation; e.g. by boat, by train, or by plane.

- CLActivityTypeOther, for any other type of usage.

For example:

```
locationManager.activityType = CLActivityTypeFitness
```

Deprecated Functionality

The locationManager.purpose property has been deprecated in iOS 6. The new way of explaining to the user why your app is requesting location services is to add the NSLocationUsageDescription key in your application's property list and put the purpose string there. (Chapter 1 contains a recipe on how to add keys to the property list.)

Also, the startMonitoringForReqion:desiredAccuracy: method of the location manager has been deprecated. Instead, you should use the locationManager:startMonitoringForRegion: method.

On the location manager delegate, the new locationManager:didUpdateLocations: method supersedes the locationManager:didUpdateToLocation:fromLocation: method, which has also been deprecated.

Requiring Location Service

If your app can't work at all without location services, you should prevent it from being loaded on a device that does not have the proper support. This is done by adding one or more values to the Required device capabilities array in the app's property list. Figure 4-1 shows an example in which we've added general location services to the list of required capabilities.

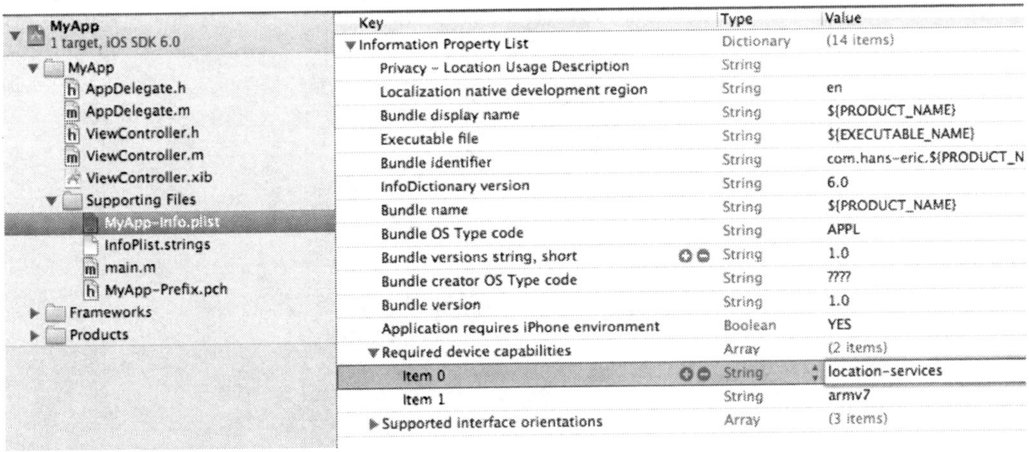

Figure 4-1. Making location services a required capability in the app's Info.plist file

You can add a number of different values to the Required device capabilities array, three of which are used in regard to Core Location: location-services, gps, and magnetometer.

Recipe 4-1: Getting Basic Location Information

This recipe shows you how to use the standard location service to give you some basic information about the device's current location, course, and speed.

Setting Up the Application

Start off by creating a new single-view application and add the Core Location framework to the project. (See Chapter 1 for instructions on how to create the project and link the framework library.)

You are going to use a very simple user interface with a single label to display the location information, and a switch control to let the user turn location updates on and off. So bring up the interface builder by selecting the view controller .xib file in the project navigator. Add the label and the switch to your user interface by dragging them from the object library. Make the label big enough to contain five rows; also be sure to set the label's Lines property to 5 in the Attributes Inspector tab of the utilities pane. Likewise, make sure the initial state of the switch is set to "Off."

Your user interface should now resemble the one in Figure 4-2.

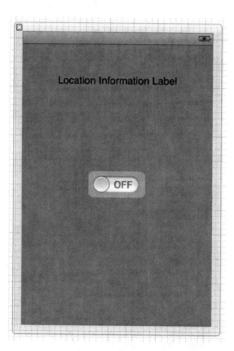

Figure 4-2. *User interface for Recipe 4-1*

Now create outlet properties for the label and the switch. Name them locationInformationLabel and locationUpdatesSwitch. You also need to know when the user taps on the switch control, so go ahead and create an action for the switch. Name it toggleLocationUpdates and set the event type to Value Changed. (If you are uncertain of outlets and actions you can find instructions on how to create them in Chapter 1.)

All interaction with the Core Location framework goes through a location manager. With it you can start and stop the location updates. For convenience, set the view controller to be the location manager's delegate; it is the "hub" of action for dealing with all location-based services. Therefore, add CLLocationManagerDelegate as a supported protocol of the view controller's class.

```
// ...
#import <CoreLocation/CoreLocation.h>

@interface ViewController : UIViewController<CLLocationManagerDelegate>

// ...

@end
```

Now you need an instance variable for your location manager. Add it to the view controller as well, and name it _locationManager (see the following code).

```
// ...

@interface ViewController : UIViewController<CLLocationManagerDelegate>
{
    CLLocationManager *_locationManager;
}

// ...

@end
```

Your view controller's header file should now look something like this:

```
//
//  ViewController.h
//  Recipe 4.1: Basic Location Information
//

#import <UIKit/UIKit.h>
#import <CoreLocation/CoreLocation.h>

@interface ViewController : UIViewController<CLLocationManagerDelegate>
{
    CLLocationManager *_locationManager;
}

@property (strong, nonatomic) IBOutlet UILabel *locationInformationLabel;
@property (strong, nonatomic) IBOutlet UISwitch *locationUpdatesSwitch;

- (IBAction)toggleLocationUpdates:(id)sender;

@end
```

Finally, because you are planning to use the location services, you should provide a purpose description. This is done in the application's Info.plist file. Add the key NSLocationUsageDescription with the value "We're testing standard location services" (without the quotes), as shown in Figure 4-3. When the user is prompted to allow your application access to his or her location, that text is displayed, telling the user what you plan to do with his or her device's location information.

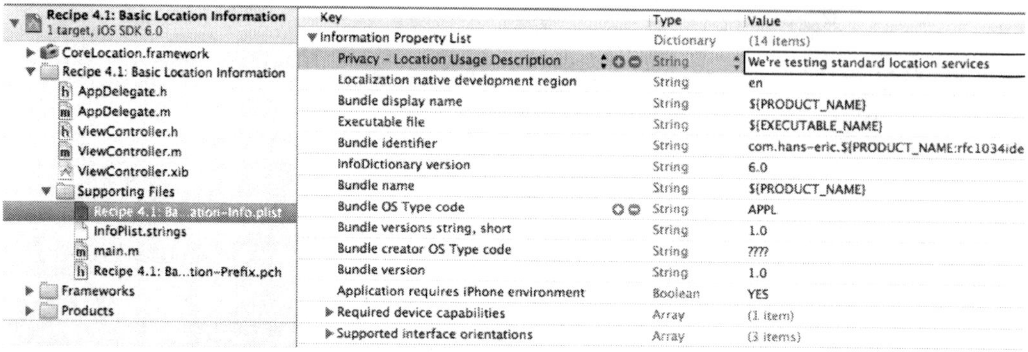

Figure 4-3. *Setting location usage description*

Your application skeleton is ready and now is a good time to build and run it. Nothing interesting will happen though when you interact with its user interface; you have yet to implement the code that starts and stops location services, as well as the one that receives the location updates. Let's get started.

Starting and Stopping Location Updates

Now that the interface has been defined, move to the view controller's implementation file (.m) and start implementing these methods and objects. The first thing you're going to tackle is the toggleLocationUpdates: action which is invoked when the user touches the switch control.

You need to take a different action depending on whether the user turned the updates on or off, obviously. If the switch was turned on, you first want to check whether location services are enabled. If they are not, display an alert and turn the switch back to off.

```
- (IBAction)toggleLocationUpdates:(id)sender
{
    if (self.locationUpdatesSwitch.on == YES)
    {
        if ([CLLocationManager locationServicesEnabled] == NO)
        {
            UIAlertView *locationServicesDisabledAlert =
                [[UIAlertView alloc] initWithTitle:@"Location Services Disabled"
                message:@"This feature requires location services. Enable it in the privacy settings
on your device"
                    delegate:nil
                    cancelButtonTitle:@"Dismiss"
                    otherButtonTitles:nil];
            [locationServicesDisabledAlert show];
            self.locationUpdatesSwitch.on = NO;
            return;
        }
```

```
        // ...

    }
    else
    {
        // Switch was turned Off
    }
}
```

Next, if "location services" is enabled, go on and initialize the location manager if it hasn't been previously initialized. For the standard location service, you should always set the desiredAccuracy and distanceFilter properties of the location manager. Also, it's recommended that you set the activityType.

The desiredAccuracy property tells the Core Location framework how accurate (in meters) you want your location information to be. The accuracy, however, is not guaranteed, and the device will try to use the resources available to it to get information as close to your desired accuracy as possible. Apple recommends that you be as conservative as possible with this setting. If you don't need to know the street address of the current device, use a lower accuracy setting. A number of constants are available to use for your convenience:

- kCLLocationAccuracyBestForNavigation
- kCLLocationAccuracyBest
- kCLLocationAccuracyNearestTenMeters
- kCLLocationAccuracyHundredMeters
- kCLLocationAccuracyKilometer
- kCLLocationAccuracyThreeKilometers

> **Note**   If you are not familiar with the metric system, a meter (m) is slightly longer than a yard (1 yard = 0.9144 m), and a kilometer (km) is just over half a mile (1 mile = 1.609 km).

The distanceFilter property is how far a device has to move (again in meters) before you want to be notified (via your delegate) of its new position. The only constant provided for this property is kCLDistanceFilterNone, which reports all changes in location to your delegate.

The activityType is used by Core Location framework to better figure out when it should autopause location updates. For a list of possible values, refer to the list in the section "Activity-Type Properties."

Once you've set the properties and the delegate in the ViewController.m file, you can start the location services by calling the startUpdatingLocation method on your CLLocationManager.

```
if (self.locationUpdatesSwitch.on == YES)
{
    if ([CLLocationManager locationServicesEnabled] == NO)
    {
        // ...
    }
```

```
    if (_locationManager == nil)
    {
        _locationManager = [[CLLocationManager alloc] init];
        _locationManager.desiredAccuracy = kCLLocationAccuracyBest;
        _locationManager.distanceFilter = 1; // meter
        _locationManager.activityType = CLActivityTypeOther;
        _locationManager.delegate = self;
    }

    [_locationManager startUpdatingLocation];

}
else
  // ...
```

The next step is not strictly necessary, but if you care about compatibility with pre-iOS 6 versions, you should also set the deprecated purpose property of the location manager. Because you have already provided the usage description in Info.plist (which is the new way of doing this), just grab the text from there.

```
if (_locationManager == nil)
{
    _locationManager = [[CLLocationManager alloc] init];
    _locationManager.desiredAccuracy = kCLLocationAccuracyBest;
    _locationManager.distanceFilter = 1; // meter
    _locationManager.activityType = CLActivityTypeOther;
    _locationManager.delegate = self;

    // For backward compatibility, set the deprecated purpose property
    // to the same as NSLocationUsageDescription in the Info.plist
    _locationManager.purpose = [[NSBundle mainBundle]
        objectForInfoDictionaryKey:@"NSLocationUsageDescription"];
}
```

That concludes the code used when the user turns updates on. For the off part, you simply want to stop the updates if they have been started.

```
- (IBAction)toggleLocationUpdates:(id)sender
{
    if (self.locationUpdatesSwitch.on == YES)
    {
        // ...
    }
    else
    {
        // Switch was turned Off
        // Stop updates if they have been started
        if (_locationManager !=nil)
        {
            [_locationManager stopUpdatingLocation];
        }
    }
}
```

Receiving Location Updates

The delegate methods need to be set up next. These methods are called when a location update is received or when there is an error getting the location. Let's start with the error delegate method (i.e., `locationManager:didFailWithError:`).

The most common source of an error occurs when the user is prompted to allow location services for your app and the user declines. If this happens, you can stop the updates by turning the switch back to off. This triggers a Value Changed event and thus invokes the `toggleLocationUpdates:` method, which turns the updates off.

For any other error, log in to the console. Your code should look something like this:

```
- (void)locationManager:(CLLocationManager *)manager didFailWithError:(NSError *)error
{
    if (error.code == kCLErrorDenied)
    {
        // Turning the switch to off will trigger the
        // toggleLocationServices action,
        // which in turn will stop further updates from coming
        self.locationUpdatesSwitch.on = NO;
    }
    else
    {
        NSLog(@"%@", error);
    }
}
```

The delegate method that handles location updates is a little more involved. The method, `locationManager:didUpdateLocations:` delivers an array of locations that have been registered since the last update, the most recent last. For this recipe, you're only interested in the most recent event, so just extract that one.

```
- (void)locationManager:(CLLocationManager *)manager
didUpdateLocations:(NSArray *)locations
{
    CLLocation *lastLocation = [locations lastObject];
    // ...
}
```

The location is represented by a `CLLocation` object which contains a lot of valuable information, including the location coordinate, accuracy information, and the timestamp of the location update.

Before your app processes a location object, you want to check whether the timestamp of the location object is recent. Core Location has a habit of presenting the last known location as the first call to the delegate method before it has a lock on the new location. There is often no need to process a location object that represents the device's location at some point in history when you need to know where it is now. Therefore you filter out location events that are more than 30 seconds old:

```
- (void)locationManager:(CLLocationManager *)manager
didUpdateLocations:(NSArray *)locations
```

```
{
    CLLocation *lastLocation = [locations lastObject];
    // Make sure this is a recent location event
    NSTimeInterval eventInterval = [lastLocation.timestamp timeIntervalSinceNow];
    if(abs(eventInterval) < 30.0)
    {
        // This is a recent event
    }
}
```

The other property you need to check before you process an event is its accuracy. Again, there is no need to process an event if it is not within the accuracy bounds that you are expecting. It might be better to wait for the device to obtain a more accurate reading than to present bad information to the user. The location object contains two accuracy properties: horizontalAccuracy and verticalAccuracy.

The horizontalAccuracy property represents the radius of the circle, in meters, within which the location could be located. You can see this circle in the built-in Maps application when you are showing your location. A negative value indicates that the coordinate is invalid.

The verticalAccuracy property is how far, plus or minus in meters, the altitude of the device could be off. Again, a negative value indicates an invalid altitude reading. If the device does not have a GPS, the verticalAccuracy property will always be negative because a GPS is needed to determine the device's altitude.

Below is the code extended with a check that the received location's horizontal accuracy is not invalid and within 20 meters.

```
- (void)locationManager:(CLLocationManager *)manager
didUpdateLocations:(NSArray *)locations
{
    // Make sure this is a recent location event
    CLLocation *lastLocation = [locations lastObject];
    NSTimeInterval eventInterval = [lastLocation.timestamp timeIntervalSinceNow];
    if(abs(eventInterval) < 30.0)
    {
        // Make sure the event is accurate enough
        if (lastLocation.horizontalAccuracy >= 0 &&
            lastLocation.horizontalAccuracy < 20)
        {
            self.locationInformationLabel.text = lastLocation.description;
        }
    }
}
```

The description property of a location object returns all the information in one dense string. It is a very easy method for seeing what location information is being returned by the device. We don't recommend showing this string to the end user directly, as it contains a great deal of information, but it could be useful for debugging and verifying that location information is being updated and is correct or accurate. For this project, you have set your locationInfomationLabel text to the lastLocation.description value, resulting in the previous completed delegate method.

Your application is now finished and ready for testing.

Testing Location Updates

The iOS simulator contains several convenient ways to test location events. Like Figure 4-4 shows, there are functions for setting a custom location, or simulating different scenarios such as a city run or a freeway drive.

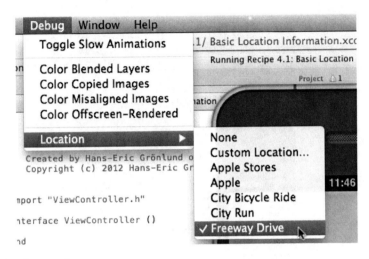

Figure 4-4. *Simulating location events*

Launch the app on the iOS simulator. When you touch the switch and turn it to "On," you will be prompted to allow this application access to your device's location. Notice in Figure 4-5 that the string you set in the application's property list is displayed.

Figure 4-5. *Your application requesting location permissions*

Click OK. Notice that the location information label is not updating even though the switch is on. This is because you haven't started any location simulations yet. In the iOS simulator, go to the menu **Debug ➤ Location ➤ Freeway** Drive, and the label should start to update with information about the prerecorded drive that Apple has provided. Figure 4-6 shows a sample of information delivered by the simulated drive.

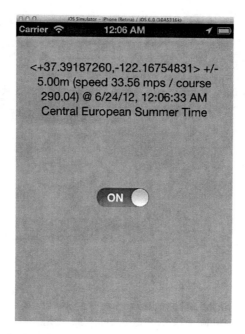

Figure 4-6. *Displaying simulated location information*

And that concludes Recipe 4-1. The next recipe deals with a way to get location changes that require a lot less battery power.

Recipe 4-2: Significant Location Changes

Being a location-aware app doesn't always mean that it needs the high-accuracy location update that the standard location service provides. Many apps do just fine by knowing which town, city, or even country the device is currently in. For those apps, the significant location change service is the preferred way to retrieve locations; it is faster, requires significantly less battery power, and can run in the background.

This recipe shows you how to set up an application to use the significant location change service to get locations.

Setting Up the Application

Programming the significant location changes services is a lot like programming the standard location services, and the setup is virtually identical. You can either duplicate the project from Recipe 4-1 or create a new single-view application and do the following as preparation:

1. Link the application to the Core Location framework.

2. Set a usage description (e.g., "Testing the significant location change service") for the NSLocationUsageDescription Info.plist key ("Privacy–Location Usage Description" in the property list).

3. Add a label and a switch control to the main view (the .xib file), which should look something like Figure 4-2 in Recipe 4-1. The label should contain about five lines and the switch should be initially set to "Off."

4. Create outlets for the label and the switch, name them locationInformationLabel and locationUpdatesSwitch, respectively.

5. Create an action for the switch, name it toggleLocationUpdates, and set the event type to Value Change.

6. Import the Core Location framework API by adding the following declaration in your view controller's header file: #import <CoreLocation/CoreLocation.h>.

7. Make the view controller a location manager delegate by adding the CLLocationManagerDelegate protocol to the ViewController class.

8. Finally, add a CLLocationManager * instance variable to the view controller, name it _locationManager.

Refer to Recipe 4-1 for the details regarding the preceding steps. Your view controller's header class should now look something like this:

```
//
// ViewController.h
// Recipe 4.2: Significant Location Change
//

#import <UIKit/UIKit.h>
#import <CoreLocation/CoreLocation.h>

@interface ViewController : UIViewController<CLLocationManagerDelegate>
{
    CLLocationManager *_locationManager;
}

@property (strong, nonatomic) IBOutlet UILabel *locationInformationLabel;
@property (strong, nonatomic) IBOutlet UISwitch *locationUpdatesSwitch;

- (IBAction)toggleLocationUpdates:(id)sender;

@end
```

Build and run to make sure everything is OK for the next step.

Enabling Background Updates

For this recipe you will enable location updates to come even when your app is residing in the background mode. To do this you need to add another key to the Info.plist file. So go ahead and add the UIBackgroundModes key (or "Required background modes" as Xcode translates it to in the user interface). This is an array value and what you want to do is to add a sub item to it with the value App registers for location updates, as in Figure 4-7.

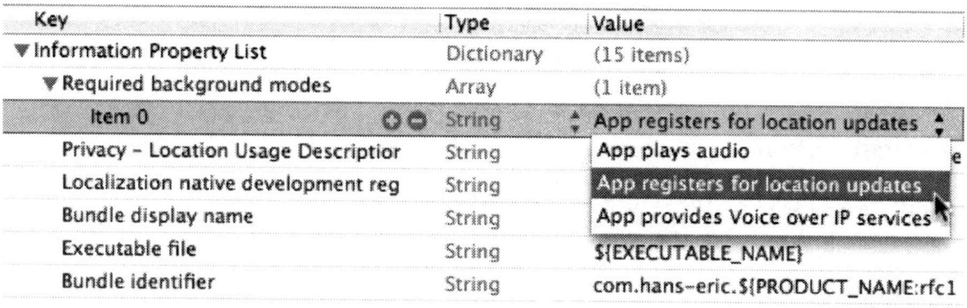

Key	Type	Value
▼ Information Property List	Dictionary	(15 items)
▼ Required background modes	Array	(1 item)
Item 0 ⊕ ⊖ String		⊕ App registers for location updates ⊕
Privacy – Location Usage Descriptior	String	App plays audio
Localization native development reg	String	App registers for location updates
Bundle display name	String	App provides Voice over IP services
Executable file	String	${EXECUTABLE_NAME}
Bundle identifier	String	com.hans-eric.${PRODUCT_NAME:rfc1

Figure 4-7. Specifying location changes as a required background mode

Now switch focus to the implementation file (.m) of the view controller. Start with the toggleLocationUpdates: method. It gets invoked each time the user changes the value of the switch control.

You'll recognize a lot of the code because it's more or less the same as in Recipe 4-1. The only difference is that you use start and stopMonitoringSignificantLocationChanges instead of start and stopUpdatingLocation. Also, significant location change service doesn't care about the desiredAccuracy, distanceFilter, and activityType properties, so you can leave them out.

Below is the new toggleLocationUpdates: method, differences marked in bold. Go ahead and implement it in your project.

```
- (IBAction)toggleLocationUpdates:(id)sender
{
    if (self.locationUpdatesSwitch.on == YES)
    {
        if ([CLLocationManager locationServicesEnabled] == NO)
        {
            UIAlertView *locationServicesDisabledAlert = [[UIAlertView alloc]
                initWithTitle:@"Location Services Disabled"
                message:@"This feature requires location services. Enable it in the privacy settings
on your device"
```

```
                    delegate:nil
                    cancelButtonTitle:@"Dismiss"
                    otherButtonTitles:nil];
                [locationServicesDisabledAlert show];
                self.locationUpdatesSwitch.on = NO;
                return;
            }

        if (_locationManager == nil)
        {
            _locationManager = [[CLLocationManager alloc] init];
            // Significant location change service does not use desiredAccuracy,
            // distanceFilter or activityType properties so no need to set them
            _locationManager.delegate = self;

            // For backward compatibility, set the deprecated purpose property
            // to the same as NSLocationUsageDescription in the Info.plist
            _locationManager.purpose = [[NSBundle mainBundle]
objectForInfoDictionaryKey:@"NSLocationUsageDescription"];
        }
        [_locationManager startMonitoringSignificantLocationChanges];
    }
    else
    {
        // Switch was turned Off
        // Stop updates if they have been started
        if (_locationManager != nil)
        {
            [_locationManager stopMonitoringSignificantLocationChanges];
        }
    }
}
```

Now you have to set up the delegate methods. They are identical to what you did in the previous recipe. Here locationManager:didFailWithError:

```
- (void)locationManager:(CLLocationManager *)manager didFailWithError:(NSError *)error
{
    if (error.code == kCLErrorDenied)
    {
        // Turning the switch to off will trigger the toggleLocationServices action,
        // which in turn will stop further updates from coming
        self.locationUpdatesSwitch.on = NO;
    }
    else
    {
        NSLog(@"%@", error);
    }
}
```

And locationManager:didUpdateLocations:

```
- (void)locationManager:(CLLocationManager *)manager didUpdateLocations:(NSArray *)locations
{
    // Make sure this is a recent location event
    CLLocation *lastLocation = [locations lastObject];
    NSTimeInterval eventInterval = [lastLocation.timestamp timeIntervalSinceNow];
    if(abs(eventInterval) < 30.0)
    {
        // Make sure the event is accurate enough
        if (lastLocation.horizontalAccuracy >= 0 &&
            lastLocation.horizontalAccuracy < 20)
        {
            self.locationInformationLabel.text = lastLocation.description;
        }
    }
}
```

The app is nearly finished so you can build and test it now. Then you'll make it slightly more interesting by presenting notifications to the user when his or her location changes *significantly*.

Adding Local Notifications

Now you are going to make an addition to the locationManager:didUpdateLocations: method. If the application is currently in the background state you'll generate a local notification so that the user can see when a location is updated while the app is not running.

```
- (void)locationManager:(CLLocationManager *)manager
didUpdateLocations:(NSArray *)locations
{
    // Make sure this is a recent location event
    CLLocation *lastLocation = [locations lastObject];
    NSTimeInterval eventInterval = [lastLocation.timestamp timeIntervalSinceNow];
    if(abs(eventInterval) < 30.0)
    {
        // Make sure the event is accurate enough
        if (lastLocation.horizontalAccuracy >= 0 &&
            lastLocation.horizontalAccuracy < 20)
        {
            self.locationInformationLabel.text = lastLocation.description;

            UILocalNotification *notification = [[UILocalNotification alloc] init];
            notification.alertBody =
              [NSString stringWithFormat:@"New Location: %.3f, %.3f",
                lastLocation.coordinate.latitude, lastLocation.coordinate.longitude];
            notification.alertAction = @"Ok";
            notification.soundName = UILocalNotificationDefaultSoundName;
            //Increment the applicationIconBadgeNumber
            notification.applicationIconBadgeNumber =
              [[UIApplication sharedApplication] applicationIconBadgeNumber] + 1;
```

```
        [[UIApplication sharedApplication]
            presentLocalNotificationNow: notification];
    }
  }
}
```

With this new app, you can receive local notifications for each significant location change, even while the application is not in the foreground. These changes are reflected in a notification badge on the app's icon, as well as a normal device notification.

Recipe 4-3: Tracking Magnetic Bearing

Modern iPhones and iPads contain magnetometers, hardware that can be used to determine the direction in which the device is being held. The measurement is based on the device's position in relation to the magnetic north pole of the earth.

The magnetic poles are not the same as the geographic poles of the earth. Magnetic north is located in Northern Canada and moves slowly by approximately 55–60 km per year toward the west as the earth's core changes.

Despite being somewhat inaccurate, the magnetic bearing is good enough for most applications, and it's much less expensive in terms of battery power. This recipe shows you how to implement tracking of the magnetic bearing of the device.

About Heading Tracking

Implementing heading tracking is very similar to implementing any of the location tracking services discussed so far. You will include the Core Location framework in your project, create a location manager object, and define its delegate and delegate methods.

It is assumed that the device heading is measured while in portrait mode with the top pointing away from the user. You can change this by setting the headingOrientation property on the CLLocationManager object.

The options for this property are as follows:

- CLDeviceOrientationPortrait (default)
- CLDeviceOrientationPortraitUpsideDown
- CLDeviceOrientationLandscapeLeft
- CLDeviceOrientationLandscapeRight

Setting Up the Application

Let's start, as usual, by creating a new single-view application project. You are going to build an application very similar to the previous two recipes, so either copy one of those projects or create a new one based on the following steps. In case you've decided to make a copy of a previous project we've marked the differences in bold.

1. Link the application to the Core Location framework.

2. Add a label and a switch control to the main view (the .xib file), which should look something like Figure 4-2 in Recipe 4-1. The switch should be initially set to "Off."

3. Create outlets for the label and the switch, name them headingInformationLabel and headingUpdatesSwitch, respectively.

4. Create an action for the switch, name it toggleHeadingUpdates, and set the event type to Value Change.

5. Import the Core Location framework API by adding the following declaration in your view controller's header file: #import <CoreLocation/CoreLocation.h>

6. Make the view controller a location manager delegate by adding the CLLocationManagerDelegate protocol to the ViewController class.

7. Finally, add a CLLocationManager * instance variable to the view controller, name it _locationManager.

Refer to Recipe 4-1 for the details regarding the preceding steps. Your view controller's header class should now look something like the following:

```
//
//  ViewController.h
//  Recipe 4.3: Determining Magnetic Bearing
//

#import <UIKit/UIKit.h>
#import <CoreLocation/CoreLocation.h>

@interface ViewController : UIViewController<CLLocationManagerDelegate>
{
    CLLocationManager *_locationManager;
}

@property (strong, nonatomic) IBOutlet UILabel *headingInformationLabel;
@property (strong, nonatomic) IBOutlet UISwitch *headingUpdatesSwitch;

- (IBAction)toggleHeadingUpdates:(id)sender;

@end
```

> **Note**   If you've copied the project, you need to change the names of the outlets and the action. Be
> sure to use the Rename Refactoring tool in Xcode to do the renaming for you. This way you don't have
> to reconnect them in interface builder.
>
> To bring up the Rename tool, select the outlet (or action) property name that you want to rename; Ctrl-click
> to bring up the context menu and select Refactor|Rename....

Starting and Stopping Heading Updates

Switch to the view controller's implementation file (ViewController.m), and scroll to the bottom to
start defining the toggleHeadingUpdates method.

Not all iOS devices can deliver heading information. Therefore, when the user has turned the switch
to on, check whether heading is available. If it's not, turn the switch back to off and inform the user
via the label.

```
- (IBAction)toggleHeadingUpdates:(id)sender
{
    if (self.headingUpdatesSwitch.on == YES)
    {
        // Heading data is not available on all devices
        if ([CLLocationManager headingAvailable] == NO)
        {
            self.headingInformationLabel.text = @"Heading services unavailable";
            self.headingUpdatesSwitch.on = NO;
            return;
        }

        // ...
```

Now initialize the location manager, if it hasn't already been instantiated. When creating an instance
of CLLocationManager that is going to track heading changes, you should specify the headingFilter
property. This property specifies how far (in degrees) your heading has to change before your
delegate method is called.

```
if (_locationManager == nil)
{
    _locationManager = [[CLLocationManager alloc] init];
    _locationManager.headingFilter = 5; // degrees
    _locationManager.delegate = self;
}
```

Finally, start and stop heading updates with the startUpdatingHeading and stopUpdatingHeading
methods. The complete toggleHeadingUpdates should look something like this:

```
- (IBAction)toggleHeadingUpdates:(id)sender
{
```

```
if (self.headingUpdatesSwitch.on == YES)
{
    // Heading data is not available on all devices
    if ([CLLocationManager headingAvailable] == NO)
    {
        self.headingInformationLabel.text = @"Heading services unavailable";
        self.headingUpdatesSwitch.on = NO;
        return;
    }

    if (_locationManager == nil)
    {
        _locationManager = [[CLLocationManager alloc] init];
        _locationManager.headingFilter = 5; // degrees
        _locationManager.delegate = self;
    }

    [_locationManager startUpdatingHeading];
    self.headingInformationLabel.text = @"Starting heading tracking...";
}
else
{
    // Switch was turned Off
    self.headingInformationLabel.text = @"Stopped heading tracking";
    // Stop updates if they have been started
    if (_locationManager != nil)
    {
        [_locationManager stopUpdatingHeading];
    }
}
}
```

Implementing Delegate Methods

The delegate methods need to be defined next. With heading tracking services, three delegate methods need to be defined:

- locationManager:didFailWithError:

- locationManager:didUpdateHeading:

- locationManagerShouldDisplayHeadingCalibration:

The first method, didFailWithError, is the same delegate method you have implemented with the location tracking services discussed previously. However, the difference is that the user, unlike location services, cannot deny heading tracking. So if an error occurs, you simply log the error to the console and hope it's temporary. This is adequate for your testing purposes, but in a real-use scenario you probably want to find out what kind of errors might occur and take appropriate action. You may also want to read the recipe on default error handling in Chapter 1 for ideas on how you can generally approach errors.

```
-(void)locationManager:(CLLocationManager *)manager didFailWithError:(NSError *)error
{
    NSLog(@"Error while tracking heading: %@", error);
}
```

The next method, didUpdateHeading, gets invoked when the change in heading of the device exceeds your headingFilter property. As with location updates, first check to see whether the update is a recent reading. Also, make sure that the reading is valid by checking the headingAccuracy property, which will be negative if the heading is invalid. If the reading is both recent and valid, update the label with the value from the magneticHeading property, rounding off to one decimal.

```
-(void)locationManager:(CLLocationManager *)manager
didUpdateHeading:(CLHeading *)newHeading
{
    NSTimeInterval headingInterval = [newHeading.timestamp timeIntervalSinceNow];
    // Check if reading is recent
    if(abs(headingInterval)<30)
    {
        // Check if reading is valid
        if(newHeading.headingAccuracy<0)
            return;

        self.headingInformationLabel.text =
            [NSString stringWithFormat:@"%.1f°", newHeading.magneticHeading];
    }
}
```

> **Tip**   You can use Alt+Shift+8 to insert the degree (°) symbol.

The final delegate method you need to implement is locationManagerShouldDisplayHeadingCalibration. This method determines whether the heading calibration screen should be presented. This is the scene that prompts a user to move his or her device in a figure-eight pattern to calibrate the magnetometer (see Figure 4-8). This is a rather helpful feature, so simply return YES:

```
-(BOOL)locationManagerShouldDisplayHeadingCalibration:(CLLocationManager *)manager
{
    return YES;
}
```

Figure 4-8. *Heading calibration message*

The application is now finished. Unfortunately, the simulator doesn't support heading simulation so you'll need to test it on an actual device. When run, it'll look something like Figure 4-9. It displays the heading relative to the magnetic north pole. A value close to 0 or 360 means north, 90 means east, 180 south, and 240 west.

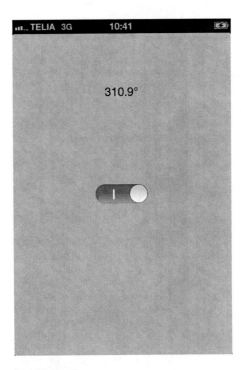

Figure 4-9. The application displaying magnetic bearing

That concludes Recipe 4-3. In the next recipe you'll extend this project to include true bearing tracking alongside the magnetic bearing.

Recipe 4-4: Tracking True Bearing

You have figured out how to get the magnetic north heading, but what about true north? The difference between magnetic north and true north is called *declination*. Declination can vary greatly depending on where you are on the planet, but if you know where you are you can calculate it. Core Location framework does this for you and provides it in the trueHeading property of a CLHeading object. All you need to do is also call the startUpdatingLocation method on your location manager to get the true north heading.

In this recipe you extend the project in Recipe 4-3 to include true heading tracking along with the magnetic bearing. So it may be a good idea to make a backup of that project before you start.

Adding True Bearing

Because you are using the location service again, start by adding the NSLocationUsageDescription key with a usage description, for example "Testing true bearing."

Next, add a second label for displaying the true heading in the main view. Your user interface should now look something like Figure 4-10.

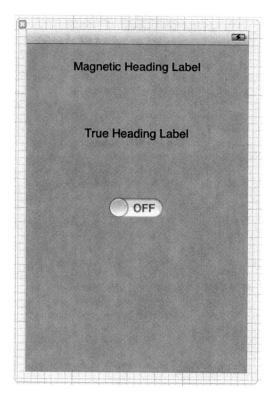

Figure 4-10. New user interface with an added label

Create an outlet named trueHeadingInformationLabel for the new label. Your view controller's interface file (.h) should now look like the following block:

```
//
// ViewController.h
// Recipe 4.4: Determining True Bearing
//

#import <UIKit/UIKit.h>
#import <CoreLocation/CoreLocation.h>

@interface ViewController : UIViewController <CLLocationManagerDelegate>
{
    CLLocationManager *_locationManager;
}

@property (strong, nonatomic) IBOutlet UILabel *headingInformationLabel;
@property (strong, nonatomic) IBOutlet UILabel *trueHeadingInformationLabel;
@property (strong, nonatomic) IBOutlet UISwitch *headingUpdatesSwitch;

- (IBAction)toggleHeadingUpdates:(id)sender;

@end
```

Only a few changes need to be made to your existing code. Let's start with the
toggleHeadingUpdates: method.

Because you will be using location services again, reintroduce the control code from Recipe 4-1 that
makes sure location services are enabled.

```
if (self.headingUpdatesSwitch.on == YES)
{
    // ...

    if ([CLLocationManager locationServicesEnabled] == NO)
    {
        UIAlertView *locationServicesDisabledAlert = [[UIAlertView alloc]
            initWithTitle:@"Location Services Disabled"
            message:@"This feature requires location services. Enable it in the privacy settings on
your device"
            delegate:nil
            cancelButtonTitle:@"Dismiss"
            otherButtonTitles:nil];

        [locationServicesDisabledAlert show];
        self.headingUpdatesSwitch.on = NO;
        return;
    }

    // ...
```

Then, in order to get true heading readings you need to start the location services in addition to
starting heading updates. You may also want to set the deprecated purpose property of the location
manager. Here's the complete toggleHeadingUpdates: method with the changes in bold.

```
- (IBAction)toggleHeadingUpdates:(id)sender
{
    if (self.headingUpdatesSwitch.on == YES)
    {
        // Heading data is not available on all devices
        if ([CLLocationManager headingAvailable] == NO)
        {
            self.headingInformationLabel.text = @"Heading services unavailable";
            self.headingUpdatesSwitch.on = NO;
            return;
        }

        if ([CLLocationManager locationServicesEnabled] == NO)
        {
            UIAlertView *locationServicesDisabledAlert =
                [[UIAlertView alloc] initWithTitle:@"Location Services Disabled"
                message:@"This feature requires location services. Enable it in the privacy settings
on your device"
                delegate:nil
                cancelButtonTitle:@"Dismiss"
                otherButtonTitles:nil];
```

```
            [locationServicesDisabledAlert show];
            self.headingUpdatesSwitch.on = NO;
            return;
        }

        if (_locationManager == nil)
        {
            _locationManager = [[CLLocationManager alloc] init];
            _locationManager.headingFilter = 5; // degrees
            _locationManager.delegate = self;

            // For backward compatibility, set the deprecated purpose property
            // to the same as NSLocationUsageDescription in the Info.plist
            _locationManager.purpose = [[NSBundle mainBundle]
                objectForInfoDictionaryKey:@"NSLocationUsageDescription"];
        }
        [_locationManager startUpdatingHeading];
        // Start location service in order to get true heading
        [_locationManager startUpdatingLocation];
        self.headingInformationLabel.text = @"Starting heading tracking...";
    }
    else
    {
        // Switch was turned Off
        self.headingInformationLabel.text = @"Stopped heading tracking";
        // Stop updates if they have been started
        if (_locationManager != nil)
        {
            [_locationManager stopUpdatingHeading];
            [_locationManager stopUpdatingLocation];
        }
    }
}
```

Also, insert the error handling code to the locationManager:didFailWithError: delegate method.

```
- (void)locationManager:(CLLocationManager *)manager didFailWithError:(NSError *)error
{
    if (error.code == kCLErrorDenied)
    {
        // Turning the switch to off will indirectly stop
        // further updates from coming
        self.headingUpdatesSwitch.on = NO;
    }
    else
    {
        NSLog(@"%@", error);
    }
}
```

Now, in your `didUpdateHeading:` method, add a new statement to check the `trueHeading` value. A negative `trueHeading` value indicates that it's invalid, so you want to use the `trueHeading` property only if it is greater than or equal to 0:

```
-(void)locationManager:(CLLocationManager *)manager
didUpdateHeading:(CLHeading *)newHeading
{
    NSTimeInterval headingInterval = [newHeading.timestamp timeIntervalSinceNow];
    if(abs(headingInterval)<30)
    {
        if (newHeading.headingAccuracy<0)
            return;

        self.headingInformationLabel.text =
            [NSString stringWithFormat:@"Magnetic Heading: %.1f°",
                newHeading.magneticHeading];

        if(newHeading.trueHeading >= 0)
            self.trueHeadingInformationLabel.text =
                [NSString stringWithFormat:@"True Heading: %.1f°",
                    newHeading.trueHeading];
    }
}
```

> **Note**   Like the other recipes in this chapter that make use of the magnetometer, this functionality only works on a physical device, and not in the simulator.

Upon testing this application, you can get a simple readout of your device's true and magnetic headings. As you can see in Figure 4-11, the two values differ somewhat, more or less depending on your current location.

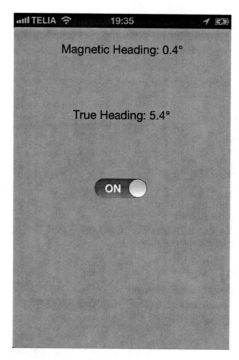

Figure 4-11. Displaying both magnetic and true heading values

Recipe 4-5: Region Monitoring

Core Location provides a method for monitoring when a device enters or exits a circular region. This can be a very useful feature for an application; for example, it can trigger an alert when a device enters the vicinity of a certain location, like triggering an alert to pick up milk when you get near the grocery store. You could also use it to send a notification to your family when you leave work to let them know that you are on your way home. Many possibilities are available if you let your imagination do a little wandering.

A Thing or Two About Regions

Regions are defined by a center coordinate and a radius measured in meters. The monitoring method triggers an event only when you cross a region boundary. It will not trigger an event if the device exists in the region when the monitoring starts. Events are triggered only when a device enters or exits a region.

Once you create a CLLocationManager object, you can register multiple regions for monitoring using the startMonitoringForRegion: method. The regions that you register for monitoring are persistent across multiple launches of your application. If your application is not running when a boundary event occurs, your application is automatically relaunched in the background so that it can process the event. All the regions you set up previously are available in the monitoredRegions property of the CLLocationManager object.

Regions are shared system-wide, and only a limited number of regions can be monitored at a given time. You should always limit the number of defined regions that you are currently monitoring so as not to consume the system resources. You should remove regions for monitoring that are not near the device's current location. For instance, there is no need to monitor for regions in Maryland if the device is on the West Coast. The error `kCLErrorRegionMonitoringFailure` will be presented to the `locationManager:monitoringDidFailForRegion:withError:` delegate method if space is unavailable when you try to register a new region for monitoring.

Welcome to Baltimore!

In this project, you are going to create a region for the city of Baltimore, Maryland, and welcome visitors to the city when they enter it. You start by creating a new single-view application.

You are going to follow the same pattern and build a user interface much like the previous recipes. Follow these steps to set up the application:

1. Link the application to the Core Location framework.

2. Set a usage description (e.g., "`Testing region monitoring`") for the `NSLocationUsageDescription` key in the application's property list

3. Add a label and a switch control to the main view (the `.xib` file), which should look something like Figure 4-2 in Recipe 4-1. The switch should be initially set to "Off."

4. Create outlets for the label and the switch, name them `regionInformationLabel` and `regionMonitoringSwitch`.

5. Create an action for the switch; name it `toggleRegionMonitoring` and make sure the event type is set to `Value Change`.

6. Import the core location framework API by adding the following declaration in your view controller's header file:

   `#import <CoreLocation/CoreLocation.h>`.

7. Make the view controller a location manager delegate by adding the `CLLocationManagerDelegate` protocol to the ViewController class.

8. Finally, add a `CLLocationManager *` instance variable to the view controller, name it `_locationManager`.

Your view controller's header file should now look like the following:

```
//
//  ViewController.h
//  Recipe 4.5: Welcome to Baltimore
//
```

```
#import <UIKit/UIKit.h>
#import <CoreLocation/CoreLocation.h>

@interface ViewController : UIViewController<CLLocationManagerDelegate>
{
    CLLocationManager *_locationManager;
}

@property (strong, nonatomic) IBOutlet UILabel *regionInformationLabel;
@property (strong, nonatomic) IBOutlet UISwitch *regionMonitoringSwitch;

- (IBAction)toggleRegionMonitoring:(id)sender;

@end
```

Switching to the implementation file (.m), you can implement your region tracking methods. Let's start with the `toggleRegionMonitoring:` method. If the switch is turned on, you should check whether region monitoring is available and enabled by the user before you start the monitoring. Note that you check whether monitoring is enabled by using the `authorizationStatus` class method. If the status is `kCLAuthorizationStatusNotDetermined`, the user will be prompted by the operating system and asked for permission to use the location services.

```
- (IBAction)toggleRegionMonitoring:(id)sender
{
    if (regionMonitoringSwitch.on == YES)
    {
        if([CLLocationManager regionMonitoringAvailable])
        {
            CLAuthorizationStatus status = [CLLocationManager authorizationStatus];

            if (status == kCLAuthorizationStatusAuthorized ||
                status == kCLAuthorizationStatusNotDetermined)
            {
                // Start monitoring here
            }
            else
            {
                self.regionInformationLabel.text = @"Region monitoring disabled";
                regionMonitoringSwitch.on = NO;
            }

        }
        else
        {
            self.regionInformationLabel.text = @"Region monitoring not available";
            regionMonitoringSwitch.on = NO;
        }
    }
}
```

In the same method, within the `if` statement that checks the authorization status you will need to instantiate your location manager instance variable if it is not already created. You'll also need to set desiredAccuracy, delegate, and (for backward compatibility with pre-iOS 6 versions) the purpose property.

```
if (status == kCLAuthorizationStatusAuthorized ||
    status == kCLAuthorizationStatusNotDetermined)
{
    if(_locationManager == nil)
    {
        _locationManager=[[CLLocationManager alloc] init];
        _locationManager.desiredAccuracy=kCLLocationAccuracyHundredMeters;
        // For backward compatibility, set the deprecated purpose property
        // to the same as NSLocationUsageDescription in the Info.plist
        _locationManager.purpose=[[NSBundle mainBundle]
            objectForInfoDictionaryKey:@"NSLocationUsageDescription"];
        _locationManager.delegate=self;
    }

    // ...
```

You need to define the center coordinate of the region you want to monitor and the radius of the region. Be careful when specifying the radius because if it is too large, the monitoring will fail. You can check to make sure your radius is within the radius bounds by comparing it to the maximumRegionMonitoringDistance property of the CLLocationManager object.

Once you have the center coordinate and radius, you create the CLRegion object and provide it with an identifier for future reference:

```
CLLocationCoordinate2D baltimoreCoordinate =
    CLLocationCoordinate2DMake(39.2963, -76.613);
int regionRadius = 3000; // meters
if (regionRadius > _locationManager.maximumRegionMonitoringDistance)
{
    regionRadius = _locationManager.maximumRegionMonitoringDistance;
}
CLRegion *baltimoreRegion = [[CLRegion alloc]
                            initCircularRegionWithCenter: baltimoreCoordinate
                            radius: regionRadius
                            identifier: @"baltimoreRegion"];
```

Once the region has been created, you can start monitoring for boundary events of that region by calling the startMonitoringForRegion: method of your location manager.

```
[_locationManager startMonitoringForRegion: baltimoreRegion];
```

One last thing you want to do is turn off region monitoring if the user slides the switch to the "Off" position. To do this, access the monitoredRegions property of your location manager and turn off region monitoring for all the currently monitored regions. You could also choose to selectively turn off specific regions by utilizing the identifier property of the CLRegion.

```
if (regionMonitoringSwitch.on == YES)
{
    // ...
}
else
{
    if (_locationManager != nil)
    {
        for (CLRegion *monitoredRegion in [_locationManager monitoredRegions])
        {
            [_locationManager stopMonitoringForRegion:monitoredRegion];
            self.regionInformationLabel.text =
                [NSString stringWithFormat:@"Turned off region monitoring for: %@",
                    monitoredRegion.identifier];
        }
    }
}
```

The delegate methods need to be defined as well. There are two delegate methods for handling boundary events and one for handling errors:

- locationManager:didEnterRegion:

- locationManager:didExitRegion:

- locationManager:monitoringDidFailForRegion:withError:

There are two main error codes that are related to region monitoring. One is kCLErrorRegionMonitoringDenied, and it is used when the user of the device has specifically denied access to region monitoring. The other is kCLErrorRegionMonitoringFailure, and it is used when monitoring for a specific region has failed, usually because the system has no more region resources available to the application.

```
-(void)locationManager:(CLLocationManager *)manager
monitoringDidFailForRegion:(CLRegion *)region withError:(NSError *)error
{
    switch (error.code)
    {
        case kCLErrorRegionMonitoringDenied:
        {
            self.regionInformationLabel.text =
                @"Region monitoring is denied on this device";
            break;
        }
        case kCLErrorRegionMonitoringFailure:
        {
            self.regionInformationLabel.text =
                [NSString stringWithFormat:@"Region monitoring failed for region: %@",
                    region.identifier];
            break;
        }
```

```
        default:
        {
            self.regionInformationLabel.text =
                [NSString stringWithFormat:@"An unhandled error occured: %@",
                    error.description];
            break;
        }
    }
}
```

`locationManager:didEnterRegion:` and `locationManager:didExitRegion:` can perform any function that you want, and because the application could be in the background when the boundary event occurs, you will use local notifications in addition to updating the label to let the user know the event occurred:

```
-(void)locationManager:(CLLocationManager *)manager didEnterRegion:(CLRegion *)region
{
    self.regionInformationLabel.text = @"Welcome to Baltimore!";

    UILocalNotification *entranceNotification = [[UILocalNotification alloc] init];
    entranceNotification.alertBody = @"Welcome to Baltimore!";
    entranceNotification.alertAction = @"Ok";
    entranceNotification.soundName = UILocalNotificationDefaultSoundName;
    [[UIApplication sharedApplication]
        presentLocalNotificationNow: entranceNotification];
}

-(void)locationManager:(CLLocationManager *)manager didExitRegion:(CLRegion *)region
{
    self.regionInformationLabel.text =
        @"Thanks for visiting Baltimore! Come back soon!";

    UILocalNotification *exitNotification = [[UILocalNotification alloc] init];
    exitNotification.alertBody = @"Thanks for visiting Baltimore! Come back soon!";
    exitNotification.alertAction = @"Ok";
    exitNotification.soundName = UILocalNotificationDefaultSoundName;
    [[UIApplication sharedApplication]
        presentLocalNotificationNow:exitNotification];
}
```

To test this functionality using the iOS simulator, you must be able to feed in custom coordinates to be simulated. Like the freeway simulation in previous recipes, you can enter custom coordinates by navigating to Debug ➤ Location ➤ Custom Location . . ., from which you can enter your own coordinates to test with. As an example, you could try latitude 39.3 and longitude −76.6, which should bring you inside the Baltimore region and make your app respond with the welcoming message. Then change the latitude to 39.0 (same longitude as before) and see your app welcome you back.

Recipe 4-6: Implementing Geocoding

Location coordinates are useful to applications, but they are not very friendly to human beings. When is the last time you wrote your address using latitude and longitude coordinates? It's just not human-friendly. Human locations are expressed in names that reference countries, states, cities, and so on. So when a device's user asks, "Where am I?," the user doesn't want to know the GPS coordinates—the user wants to know what town or city he or she is in.

Fortunately, Apple has provided a method called *reverse geocoding*, that converts location coordinates into a human-readable format. This feature used to be provided by the Map Kit framework, but it has been incorporated into the Core Location framework since iOS 5.

> **Note**   A device must have network access to perform geocoding requests.

Implementing Reverse Geocoding

Geocoding is performed using the CLGeocoder class. You instantiate a CLGeocoder object and then pass it a coordinate and a block of code to perform once it has performed the geocoding. This is a little different than the other location recipes discussed thus far that used delegate methods.

Let's create a new single-view application. To set up the project, take the following steps:

1. Link the application to the Core Location framework.

2. Set a usage description (e.g., "Testing geocoding") for the NSLocationUsageDescription key in the application's property list.

3. Add a label and a button to the main view (the .xib file), which should look something like Figure 4-12. The label should contain about five lines (don't forget to set the Lines property in the attributes inspector).

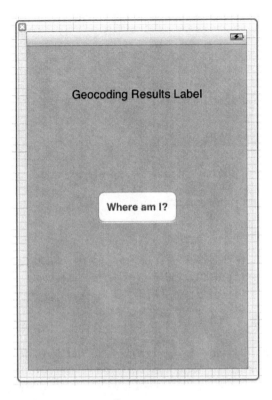

Figure 4-12. *Initial user interface for reverse geocoding*

4. Create outlets for the label and the button, name them geocodingResultsLabel and reverseGeocodingButton.

5. Create an action for the switch, name it findCurrentAddress, and make sure the event type is set to Value Change.

6. Import the Core Location framework API by adding the following declaration in your view controller's header file: #import <CoreLocation/CoreLocation.h>.

7. Make the view controller a location manager delegate by adding the CLLocationManagerDelegate protocol to the ViewController class.

8. Add a CLLocationManager * instance variable to the view controller, name it _locationManager.

9. Add a second instance variable, this time of the CLGeocoder * type and with the name _geocoder.

Your view controller's header file should now look like the following:

```
//
//  ViewController.h
//  Recipe 4.6: Geocoding
//

#import <UIKit/UIKit.h>
#import <CoreLocation/CoreLocation.h>

@interface ViewController : UIViewController<CLLocationManagerDelegate>
{
    CLLocationManager *_locationManager;
    CLGeocoder *_geocoder;
}

@property (strong, nonatomic) IBOutlet UILabel *geocodingResultsLabel;
@property (strong, nonatomic) IBOutlet UIButton *reverseGeocodingButton;
- (IBAction)findCurrentAddress:(id)sender;

@end
```

Switch to the implementation file (ViewController.m), and scroll to the bottom to implement the method findCurrentAddress. Because this has been covered in previous recipes in this chapter, we're not going to go into detail about this, but we will cover some highlights.

You want to follow the best practices of geocoding and not geocode a location that is too near to one you have already geocoded or that is too recent, so you're going to set your distanceFilter property on your CLLocationManager object to 500 meters.

You are also going to set your desired accuracy to the constant kCLLocationAccuracyHundredMeters so that you get a faster response from the location tracking services and limit the drain on the battery.

```
- (IBAction)findCurrentAddress:(id)sender
{
    if([CLLocationManager locationServicesEnabled])
    {
        if(_locationManager == nil)
        {
            _locationManager = [[CLLocationManager alloc] init];
            _locationManager.distanceFilter = 500;
            _locationManager.desiredAccuracy = kCLLocationAccuracyHundredMeters;
            _locationManager.delegate = self;

            // For backward compatibility, set the deprecated purpose property
            // to the same as NSLocationUsageDescription in the Info.plist
            _locationManager.purpose = [[NSBundle mainBundle]
                objectForInfoDictionaryKey: @"NSLocationUsageDescription"];
        }
```

```
        [_locationManager startUpdatingLocation];
        self.geocodingResultsLabel.text = @"Getting location...";
    }
    else
    {
        self.geocodingResultsLabel.text = @"Location services are unavailable";
    }
}
```

Now add your delegate methods for the CLLocationManager object. The first is the locationManager: didFailWithError method:

```
-(void)locationManager:(CLLocationManager *)manager didFailWithError:(NSError *)error
{
    if(error.code == kCLErrorDenied)
    {
        self.geocodingResultsLabel.text = @"Location information denied";
    }
}
```

Next is the locationManager:didUpdateToLocations: delegate method to be defined. Start with the standard checks to make sure the newLocation timestamp property is recent and that it is valid:

```
- (void)locationManager:(CLLocationManager *)manager
didUpdateLocations:(NSArray *)locations
{
    // Make sure this is a recent location event
    CLLocation *newLocation = [locations lastObject];
    NSTimeInterval eventInterval = [newLocation.timestamp timeIntervalSinceNow];
    if(abs(eventInterval) < 30.0)
    {
        // Make sure the event is valid
        if (newLocation.horizontalAccuracy < 0)
            return;

        // ...
    }
}
```

Next check whether the _geocoder instance variable has been instantiated, and if not, create it. Also make sure that you stop any existing geocoding services before performing a new one.

```
- (void)locationManager:(CLLocationManager *)manager
    didUpdateLocations:(NSArray *)locations
{
    // Make sure this is a recent location event
    CLLocation *newLocation = [locations lastObject];
    NSTimeInterval eventInterval = [newLocation.timestamp timeIntervalSinceNow];
    if(abs(eventInterval)<30.0)
```

```
    {
        // Make sure the event is valid
        if (newLocation.horizontalAccuracy < 0)
            return;

        // Instantiate _geoCoder if it has not been already
        if (_geocoder == nil)
            _geocoder = [[CLGeocoder alloc] init];

        //Only one geocoding instance per action
        //so stop any previous geocoding actions before starting this one
        if([_geocoder isGeocoding])
            [_geocoder cancelGeocode];
    }
}
```

Finally, start your reverse geocoding process and define the completion handler. The completion handler receives two objects: an array of placemarks and an error object. If the array contains one or more objects, then the reverse geocoding was successful. If not, then you can check the error code for details.

The resulting location:didUpdateToLocations: method is as follows:

```
- (void)locationManager:(CLLocationManager *)manager didUpdateLocations:(NSArray *)locations
{
    // Make sure this is a recent location event
    CLLocation *newLocation = [locations lastObject];
    NSTimeInterval eventInterval = [newLocation.timestamp timeIntervalSinceNow];
    if(abs(eventInterval)<30.0)
    {
        // Make sure the event is valid
        if (newLocation.horizontalAccuracy < 0)
            return;

        // Instantiate _geoCoder if it has not been already
        if (_geocoder == nil)
            _geocoder = [[CLGeocoder alloc] init];

        //Only one geocoding instance per action
        //so stop any previous geocoding actions before starting this one
        if([_geocoder isGeocoding])
            [_geocoder cancelGeocode];

        [_geocoder reverseGeocodeLocation: newLocation
            completionHandler: ^(NSArray* placemarks, NSError* error)
            {
                if([placemarks count] > 0)
                {
                    CLPlacemark *foundPlacemark = [placemarks objectAtIndex:0];
                    self.geocodingResultsLabel.text =
```

```
                        [NSString stringWithFormat:@"You are in: %@",
                            foundPlacemark.description];
                }
                else if (error.code == kCLErrorGeocodeCanceled)
                {
                    NSLog(@"Geocoding cancelled");
                }
                else if (error.code == kCLErrorGeocodeFoundNoResult)
                {
                    self.geocodingResultsLabel.text = @"No geocode result found";
                }
                else if (error.code == kCLErrorGeocodeFoundPartialResult)
                {
                    self.geocodingResultsLabel.text = @"Partial geocode result";
                }
                else
                {
                    self.geocodingResultsLabel.text =
                        [NSString stringWithFormat:@"Unknown error: %@",
                            error.description];
                }
            }
        ];

        //Stop updating location until they click the button again
        [manager stopUpdatingLocation];
    }
}
```

You now have an application that can do reverse geocoding and find the address of the current location. Build and run it before moving on and extending the application with some forward geocoding.

Implementing Forward Geocoding

In iOS 5, forward geocoding was introduced as well. This means that you can pass an address to a geocoder and receive the coordinates for that address. The more information you can provide about an address, the more accurate the resulting forward geocode will be.

Let's extend the application with a feature that translates a given address into coordinates. Start by adding a text field and another button to the user interface. It should resemble Figure 4-13.

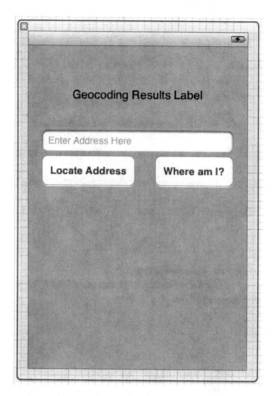

Figure 4-13. The updated user interface with forward geocoding

Now, add an outlet called addressTextField for the text field. Next, add an action for the button and name it findCoordinateOfAddress.

In the findCoordinateOfAddress: action, the plan is to take the text the user has entered into the text field and send it to your geocoder object for translation into coordinates. The geocode process may result in multiple matches of possible coordinates, but the best guess is always first. Here's the implementation of the method.

```
- (IBAction)findCoordinateOfAddress:(id)sender
{
    // Instantiate _geocoder if it has not been already
    if (_geocoder == nil)
        _geocoder = [[CLGeocoder alloc] init];

    NSString *address = self.addressTextField.text;
    [_geocoder geocodeAddressString:address
        completionHandler:^(NSArray *placemarks, NSError *error)
        {
            if ([placemarks count] > 0)
            {
                CLPlacemark *placemark = [placemarks objectAtIndex:0];

                self.geocodingResultsLabel.text = placemark.location.description;
            }
```

```
        else
        {
            self.geocodingResultsLabel.text = error.localizedDescription;
        }
    }
    ];
}
```

In case of an error, the foregoing implementation outputs the error message to the label. There are, however, a couple of errors your code should expect and handle. These include network errors, core location denied by user errors, and errors when no geocoding results are found. Following is an updated implementation that extracts these errors and provides (slightly) better error messages in these cases:

```
- (IBAction)findCoordinateOfAddress:(id)sender
{
    // Instantiate _geocoder if it has not been already
    if (_geocoder == nil)
        _geocoder = [[CLGeocoder alloc] init];

    NSString *address = self.addressTextField.text;
    [_geocoder geocodeAddressString:address
        completionHandler:^(NSArray *placemarks, NSError *error)
        {
            if ([placemarks count] > 0)
            {
                CLPlacemark *placemark = [placemarks objectAtIndex:0];

                self.geocodingResultsLabel.text = placemark.location.description;
            }
            else if (error.domain == kCLErrorDomain)
            {
                switch (error.code)
                {
                    case kCLErrorDenied:
                        self.geocodingResultsLabel.text
                            = @"Location Services Denied by User";
                        break;
                    case kCLErrorNetwork:
                        self.geocodingResultsLabel.text = @"No Network";
                        break;
                    case kCLErrorGeocodeFoundNoResult:
                        self.geocodingResultsLabel.text = @"No Result Found";
                        break;
                    default:
                        self.geocodingResultsLabel.text = error.localizedDescription;
                        break;
                }
            }
```

```
        else
        {
            self.geocodingResultsLabel.text = error.localizedDescription;
        }
    }
    ];
}
```

That concludes Recipe 4-6. Let's end with some best practices advice for geocoding.

Best Practices

Here are some best practices to be aware of when using reverse or forward geocoding:

- You should send only one geocoding request at a time.

- If the user performs an action that will result in the same location being geocoded, the results should be reused rather than requesting the same location multiple times.

- You should not send more than one geocoding request per minute. You should check to see whether the user has moved a significant distance before calling another geocoding request.

- Do not perform a geocoding request if you will not see the results (e.g., if your application is running in the background).

Summary

The Core Location framework is a powerful framework that can be utilized by any number of application features. As demonstrated in this chapter, you can determine where a device is located, which direction a device is facing, and when a device enters or exits a specific region. Beyond those powerful features, you can also perform lookups on geographical coordinates to determine human-readable location information to be presented to your end user as well as provide complementary services to perform the reverse.

Apple has walked a fine line of making powerful features available to developers while also respecting a user's privacy and the battery drain on a device. As developers, we should work to deliver exciting features and functionality in our applications while maintaining the same level of respect for our users.

Chapter 5

Motion Recipes

One of the more impressive features of iOS devices is the built-in motion sensor. With motion sensors, iOS developers can create absolutely amazing apps–applications we could only dream about back in early 2000. Nowadays we can just point our phones to the night sky and instantly learn the names of stars and constellations; we can play virtual marble labyrinth games that are so close to the real experience that it's almost frightening. Motion sensors have truly enriched the field of app development.

Through the Core Motion framework you have easy access to the device's accelerometer, gyroscope, and magnetometer. It is your job to employ these tools to enhance the user's experience and create new cool features. The recipes in this chapter will help you get started.

All but the first recipe in this chapter require a physical device to test the functionality, because there currently is no way to simulate data from the Core Motion framework.

Recipe 5-1: Recognizing Shake Events

Before diving into the Core Motion framework let's first deal with a related topic: the shaking of a device. A large number of applications utilize this functionality in a variety of ways, with results ranging from the shuffling of songs to the refreshing of information. While this implementation does not necessarily rely on the Core Motion framework, its key concept of being able to detect physical changes to your device makes it an important functionality to understand.

Intercepting Shake Events

Although you could use the Core Motion framework to identify shake events you'll use the more convenient `motionEnded:withEvent:` message. When a user shakes the device, this message is being dispatched to the first responder of your application.

So, for example, you could set up your application's main view to receive shake events using code as listed here.

```
@implementation ViewController

// ...

- (BOOL) canBecomeFirstResponder
{
    return YES;
}

- (void) viewWillAppear: (BOOL)animated
{
    [self.view becomeFirstResponder];
    [super viewWillAppear:animated];
}

- (void) viewWillDisappear: (BOOL)animated
{
    [self.view resignFirstResponder];
    [super viewWillDisappear:animated];
}

- (void) motionEnded: (UIEventSubtype)motion withEvent: (UIEvent *)event
{
    if (event.subtype == UIEventSubtypeMotionShake)
    {
        // Device was shaken
    }
}

// ...

@end
```

While the code in Listing 5-1 works for most situations, a slightly more sophisticated solution allows you to recognize shake events from all over your application. The next section shows you how to do it.

Subclassing the Window

If there are no receivers of the `motionEnded:withEvent:` message within the chain of responders, the message is sent to the application's window object. What you want to do is to intercept `motionEnded:withEvent:` on the window object and implement your own notification scheme, letting any interested object in your application know when the device has been shaken.

The first thing you need to do is to subclass the application's window object. To do that, create a new Objective-C class and name it `MainWindow`. Be sure to make it a subclass of `UIWindow` (see Figure 5-1).

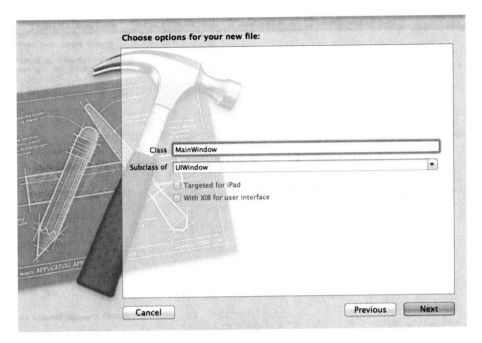

Figure 5-1. Subclassing UIWindow by creating an Objective-C class

Next change the application's setup code to use your custom window class. This is done with a small change in the app delegate's didFinishLaunchingWithOptions: method. Depending on which template you used to create the application project, the surrounding code may be different but the change is the same. Here's how it looks in a single-view application (you'll also need to import the MainWindow.h file in your AppDelegate.h file or the following code won't compile):

```
- (BOOL)application:(UIApplication *)application
didFinishLaunchingWithOptions:(NSDictionary *)launchOptions
{
    self.window = [[MainWindow alloc] initWithFrame:[[UIScreen mainScreen] bounds]];
    // Override point for customization after application launch.
    self.viewController = [[ViewController alloc] initWithNibName:@"ViewController" bundle:nil];
    self.window.rootViewController = self.viewController;
    [self.window makeKeyAndVisible];
    return YES;
}
```

Now you have an architecture that allows you to intercept events sent to the main window. It's time to implement your application-wide shake notifications.

Implementing Shake Notifications

In MainWindow.h, add the following code.

```
@implementation MainWindow

// ...

- (void)motionEnded:(UIEventSubtype)motion withEvent:(UIEvent *)event
{
    if (event.type == UIEventTypeMotion && event.subtype == UIEventSubtypeMotionShake)
    {
        [[NSNotificationCenter defaultCenter] postNotificationName:@"NOTIFICATION_SHAKE"
                                        object:self];
    }
}

// ...

@end
```

This code intercepts a shake event and uses the NSNotificationCenter class to post a notification. NSNotificationCenter implements an Observer pattern for simple notifications reachable from any part of your application. The type of notification is identified by its name; this uses NOTIFICATION_SHAKE but you can pick any name you like.

An object interested in your shake notifications can register an action method with the notification center. As an example, let's say you want to be notified about shakes in the application's main view. You could then do something such as the code here:

```
@implementation ViewController

// ...

- (void) viewWillAppear: (BOOL)animated
{
    [[NSNotificationCenter defaultCenter] addObserver:self
                                        selector:@selector(shakeDetected:)
                                        name:@"NOTIFICATION_SHAKE" object:nil];
    [super viewWillAppear:animated];
}

- (void) viewWillDisappear: (BOOL)animated
{
    [[NSNotificationCenter defaultCenter] removeObserver:self];
    [super viewWillDisappear:animated];
}
```

```
-(void)shakeDetected:(NSNotification *)paramNotification
{
    NSLog(@"Shaken not stirred");
}

// ...

@end
```

As you can see in the preceding code, if the view is removed from sight, you unregister the observer that listens to the shake notifications. This may or may not be what you want. If you want to keep on tracking shake events even though the view has disappeared, don't leave the call to removeObserver: out.

Testing Shake Events

Now you're finished and you can run and test your application.

Although Core Motion features require a real device to be tested, shake events can actually be tested within the simulator. Simply use the Shake Gesture item under the Hardware menu, as shown in Figure 5-2.

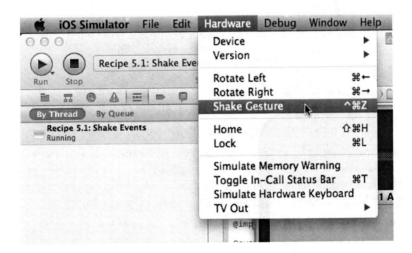

Figure 5-2. Shake events can be simulated

Figure 5-3 shows the test application after it has responded to a shake event.

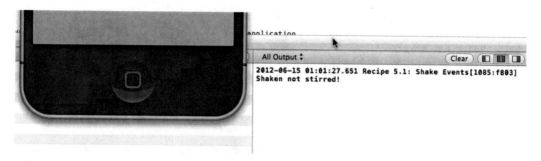

Figure 5-3. Your test app writes to the output console upon shake events

Recipe 5-2: Accessing Raw Core Motion Data

Using this recipe, you'll create a simple application that receives and displays the raw data from the accelerometer, the gyroscope, and the magnetometer sensors. You'll need a real device that has these sensors (e.g., an iPhone 4) to test the app.

The Core Motion Sensors

In Core Motion, you can access three different pieces of hardware on a device, assuming that the device is new enough to be equipped with said hardware (see Table 5-1).

- The *accelerometer* measures acceleration, caused by gravity or user acceleration, of the device. The information can provide insight into the current orientation, as well as the current general movement of the device.

- The *gyroscope* measures rotation of the device along multiple axes.

- The *magnetometer* provides data regarding the magnetic field passing through the device. This is normally the Earth's magnetic field, but it may also be any other magnetic fields nearby. Remember to be careful when testing this feature; placing any kind of powerful magnet near your device could harm it.

Table 5-1 shows the availability of the sensors on various iOS devices.

Table 5-1. Sensor Support on Various Devices

Accelerometer	Available on all iPhones, iPads, and iPods.
Gyroscope	Available on iPhone 4, iPad2, iPod 4, and later.
Magnetometer	Available on iPhone 3GS and later, as well as on all iPads.

For all three sensors, data comes in the form of a three-dimensional vector, with components X, Y, and Z. If you are holding your device facing you with the bottom facing the ground, the x-axis cuts horizontally through your device; the y-axis runs vertically from bottom up, and the z-axis runs through the center of the device toward you.

In the case of the gyroscope, the values are the rotation rate *around* these axes. To find out which direction results in positive rotation rate values you can use the right-hand rule. Imagine that you hold your open right hand in such a way that your thumb points toward the positive end of the axis. Then a positive rotation around the axis is the direction in which your fingers curve when you close your hand.

Rotation around the X, Y, and Z axes are called pitch, roll, and yaw, respectively. Figure 5-4 shows the axes and the positive directions of these rotations.

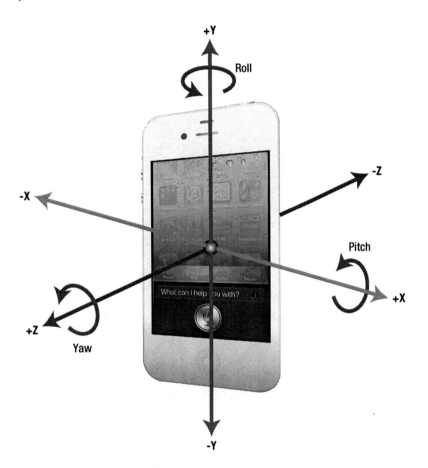

Figure 5-4. Directions and rotations as defined in iOS

Setting Up the Project

You will create a simple app that displays the current data from the three sensors. As you move the device around you can see how the movement affects their output.

Begin by creating a new single-view application and give it a suitable project name, for example "Raw Motion Data Test." Now, because you're going to use the Core Data framework you need to link CoreMotion.framework binary to your project.

Next, add labels to the main view and organize them so that the view resembles Figure 5-5. You will need 21 labels.

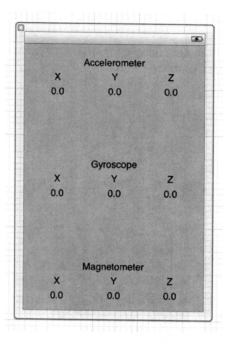

Figure 5-5. Main view interface

Your app is going to update the labels containing values (i.e., the ones with the text 0.0 in Figure 5-4). Therefore, create outlets for those nine labels so that you'll be able to change their text at runtime.

Give the outlets the following names.

- Accelerometer value labels: xAccLabel, yAccLabel, and zAccLabel.
- Gyroscope value labels: xGyroLabel, yGyroLabel, and zGyroLabel.
- Magnetometer value labels: xMagLabel, yMagLabel, and zMagLabel.

For instructions on how to create outlets for view components, see the corresponding recipes in Chapter 1.

When done, your view controller interface declaration should resemble this:

```
@interface ViewController : UIViewController

@property (strong, nonatomic) IBOutlet UILabel *xAccLabel;
@property (strong, nonatomic) IBOutlet UILabel *yAccLabel;
@property (strong, nonatomic) IBOutlet UILabel *zAccLabel;
@property (strong, nonatomic) IBOutlet UILabel *xGyroLabel;
@property (strong, nonatomic) IBOutlet UILabel *yGyroLabel;
@property (strong, nonatomic) IBOutlet UILabel *zGyroLabel;
```

```
@property (strong, nonatomic) IBOutlet UILabel *xMagLabel;
@property (strong, nonatomic) IBOutlet UILabel *yMagLabel;
@property (strong, nonatomic) IBOutlet UILabel *zMagLabel;

@end
```

Now you have the basic structure for the application. It's time to dig out the data from the Core Motion framework.

Accessing Sensor Data

The Core Motion framework relies heavily on a single class called CMMotionManager. This class acts as a hub through which you access the motion sensors. You'll set up a lazy initialization property to access a single instance of that class.

Make the following changes to the view controller's header class. Note that the outlet properties have been removed for the sake of brevity. Don't remove them in your code.

```
#import <UIKit/UIKit.h>
#import <CoreMotion/CoreMotion.h>

@interface ViewController : UIViewController

// ...

@property (strong, nonatomic) CMMotionManager *motionManager;

@end
```

Now switch to ViewController.m and add the following code to the view controller's implementation section. Again, code has been removed for brevity.

```
@implementation ViewController

// ...

-(CMMotionManager *)motionManager
{
    // Lazy initialization
    if (_motionManager == nil)
    {
        _motionManager = [[CMMotionManager alloc] init];
    }
    return _motionManager;
}

// ...

@end
```

Because you'll be moving around the device to get different readings, you should stop the autorotation of the user interface. You do that by setting portrait as the only supported interface orientation for this application. You can do that in the Supported Interface Orientations section on the Project Editor's Summary page (see Figure 5-6).

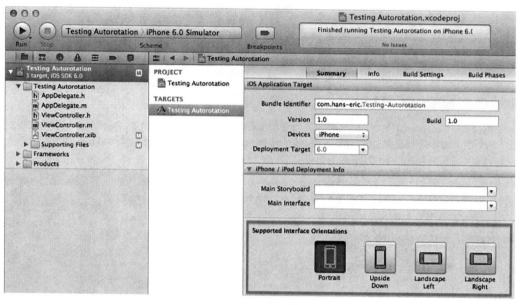

Figure 5-6. *Setting supported interface orientations*

What you want to do is to start receiving data from your sensors and update the respective labels with the information. To do that you need to perform the following steps:

1. Check whether the sensor in question is available.

2. Set an update interval.

3. Start the updating and provide the piece of code that shall be invoked on each interval.

Translated into code this becomes, here for the accelerator, the following:

```
// Start accelerometer if available
if ([self.motionManager isAccelerometerAvailable])
{
    //Update twice per second
    [self.motionManager setAccelerometerUpdateInterval:1.0/2.0];
    [self.motionManager startAccelerometerUpdatesToQueue:[NSOperationQueue mainQueue]
                    withHandler:
        ^(CMAccelerometerData *data, NSError *error)
        {
            // New data arrived, update accelerometer labels
            self.xAccLabel.text = [NSString stringWithFormat:@"%f",
                            data.acceleration.x];
```

```
            self.yAccLabel.text = [NSString stringWithFormat:@"%f",
                                    data.acceleration.y];
            self.zAccLabel.text = [NSString stringWithFormat:@"%f",
                                    data.acceleration.z];
        }
    ];
}
```

The startAcceleratorUpdatesToQueue:withHandler: method retains the code block (the so-called handler) and executes it as a task within the given operation queue repeatedly on the given interval. In our case, it will result in the accelerator labels being updated with the latest values from the accelerometer.

The other sensors have a similar programming interface. The following code shows methods that start and stop all three sensors at once. Add them to your project's view controller.

```
- (void)startUpdates
{
    // Start accelerometer if available
    if ([self.motionManager isAccelerometerAvailable])
    {
        [self.motionManager setAccelerometerUpdateInterval:1.0/2.0];
        [self.motionManager startAccelerometerUpdatesToQueue:
                            [NSOperationQueue mainQueue]
                            withHandler:
        ^(CMAccelerometerData *data, NSError *error)
        {
            self.xAccLabel.text = [NSString stringWithFormat:@"%f",
                                    data.acceleration.x];
            self.yAccLabel.text = [NSString stringWithFormat:@"%f",
                                    data.acceleration.y];
            self.zAccLabel.text = [NSString stringWithFormat:@"%f",
                                    data.acceleration.z];
        }];
    }

    // Start gyroscope if available
    if ([self.motionManager isGyroAvailable])
    {
        [self.motionManager setGyroUpdateInterval:1.0/2.0];
        [self.motionManager startGyroUpdatesToQueue:
                            [NSOperationQueue mainQueue]
                            withHandler:
        ^(CMGyroData *data, NSError *error)
        {
            self.xGyroLabel.text = [NSString stringWithFormat:@"%f",
                                    data.rotationRate.x];
            self.yGyroLabel.text = [NSString stringWithFormat:@"%f",
                                    data.rotationRate.y];
            self.zGyroLabel.text = [NSString stringWithFormat:@"%f",
                                    data.rotationRate.z];
        }];
    }
```

```
    // Start magnetometer if available
    if ([self.motionManager isMagnetometerAvailable])
    {
        [self.motionManager setMagnetometerUpdateInterval:1.0/2.0];
        [self.motionManager startMagnetometerUpdatesToQueue:[NSOperationQueue mainQueue]
                        withHandler:
         ^(CMMagnetometerData *data, NSError *error)
         {
             self.xMagLabel.text = [NSString stringWithFormat:@"%f",
                                    data.magneticField.x];
             self.yMagLabel.text = [NSString stringWithFormat:@"%f",
                                    data.magneticField.y];
             self.zMagLabel.text = [NSString stringWithFormat:@"%f",
                                    data.magneticField.z];
         }];
    }
}


-(void)stopUpdates
{
    if ([self.motionManager isAccelerometerAvailable] &&
        [self.motionManager isAccelerometerActive])
    {
        [self.motionManager stopAccelerometerUpdates];
    }

    if ([self.motionManager isGyroAvailable] &&
        [self.motionManager isGyroActive])
    {
        [self.motionManager stopGyroUpdates];
    }

    if ([self.motionManager isMagnetometerAvailable] &&
        [self.motionManager isMagnetometerActive])
    {
        [self.motionManager stopMagnetometerUpdates];
    }
}
```

Now what's left is to find suitable places to invoke startUpdates and stopUpdates. This time start the updates when the app becomes active and stop them when resigning from active state (i.e., when the app enters the background state). This can be done from your app delegate. For that to work you need to make the startUpdates and stopUpdates methods public. So add the following code to ViewController.h:

```
#import <UIKit/UIKit.h>
#import <CoreMotion/CoreMotion.h>

@interface ViewController : UIViewController
```

```
// ... Outlet properties removed for brevity

@property (nonatomic, strong) CMMotionManager *motionManager;

- (void)startUpdates;
- (void)stopUpdates;

@end
```

Now add the following code to your application delegate (in AppDelegate.m).

```
- (void)applicationWillResignActive:(UIApplication *)application
{
    [self.viewController stopUpdates];
}

- (void)applicationDidBecomeActive:(UIApplication *)application
{
    [self.viewController startUpdates];
}
```

Your app is now finished and ready to run. Remember, the simulator has no support for any of the three sensors so nothing interesting will happen during simulation. You need a real device to test this app. Figure 5-7 shows a screenshot of the app in action.

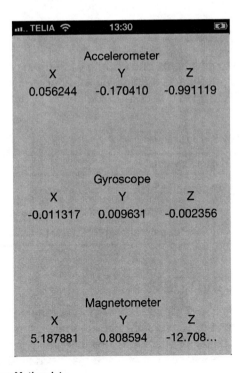

Figure 5-7. An app displaying raw Core Motion data

Pushing or Pulling

There are two ways to access updated data from the sensors. In this recipe you used "pushing." What this means is that the motion manager will invoke your code on the given intervals and provide it with the new values. This system is implemented in the `start<Sensor>UpdatesToQueue:withHandler` methods, where you provide the code in the form of a block.

The other strategy is "pulling," and it's the preferred method if your app has a render loop from which you can query the values yourself on a regular basis. This can be a little more efficient and is generally better suited for game apps.

Pulling is implemented in the `start<Sensor>Updates` method. It keeps the properties `accelerometerData`, `gyroData`, and `magnetometerData` on the motion manager updated with the most recent value. Your app can then, at its own convenience, retrieve the values from those properties, as the following code shows.

```
// Start updates in pull mode
[self.motionManager startAccelerometerUpdates];

// Pull the values from somewhere within an update loop
self.xMagLabel.text = [NSString stringWithFormat:@"%f",
                    self.motionManager.magnetometerData.magneticField.x];
self.yMagLabel.text = [NSString stringWithFormat:@"%f",
                    self.motionManager.magnetometerData.magneticField.y];
self.zMagLabel.text = [NSString stringWithFormat:@"%f",
                    self.motionManager.magnetometerData.magneticField.z];
```

Selecting an Update Interval

You can set the update interval to as little as one update each ten milliseconds (1/100). However, you should strive to the highest possible value that will work for your application because that will improve battery time. Table 5-2 provides a general guideline for update intervals.

Table 5-2. Guideline Values for Update Intervals

Update Interval	Usage Example
10 ms (1/100)	For detecting high-frequency motion.
20 ms (1/50)	Suitable for games that uses real-time user input.
100 ms (1/10)	Suitable for determining the current orientation of the device.

The Nature of Raw Motion Data

When running the app, you may have discovered how incomprehensible the data from the sensors are. This is because the data from the sensors are biased–that is, they are affected by more than one force. The accelerometer, for instance, is affected by Earth's gravity as well as the movement from the user's hand. The magnetometer senses not only the magnetic field of the Earth but also all other magnetic fields in your vicinity.

The biased nature of the raw data makes the data difficult to interpret. You need tricks like high and low pass filters to isolate the various components. Fortunately, Core Motion comes with a way to access unbiased data from the sensors which makes it easy to figure out the devices' real orientation and motion. Recipe 5-3 teaches you how to use this convenient feature.

Recipe 5-3: Accessing Device Motion Data

The previous recipe showed you how to access raw motion data from the three sensors. While easy to access, the raw biased data are not easy to use. They require various filtering techniques to isolate the different forces that affect the sensors to make real use of the data. The good news is that Apple has done the dirty work for you, ready to be utilized via the `deviceMotion` property of the motion manager. This recipe shows you how.

The Device Motion Class

Just like the accelerometer, gyroscope, and magnetometer from the previous recipe, you can access `CMDeviceMotion` by starting and stopping updates using very similar methods: `startDeviceMotionUpdates` and `startDeviceMotionUpdatesToQueue:withHandler:`. However, you also have two extra methods that allow you to specify a "reference frame," `startDeviceMotionUpdatesUsingReferenceFrame:` and `startDeviceMotionUpdatesUsingReferenceFrame:toQueue:WithHandler:`. The reference frame is discussed shortly.

When retrieving data using an instance of `CMDeviceMotion` (through the `deviceMotion` property in your `CMMotionManager`), you can access six different properties.

- The `attitude` property is an instance of the `CMAttitude` class. It gives you a detailed insight into the device's orientation at a given time as compared to a reference frame. Through this class you can access properties such as roll, pitch, and yaw. These values are measured in radians and allow you an accurate measurement of your device's orientation.

- As shown previously in Figure 5-4, `roll` specifies the device's position of rotation around the *y-axis*, pitch the position of rotation around the *x-axis*, and yaw around the *z-axis*.

- The `rotationRate` property is just like the one you saw in the previous recipe, except that it gives a more accurate reading. It does this by reducing device bias that causes a still device to have nonzero rotation values.

- The `gravity` property represents the acceleration caused solely by gravity on the device.

- The `userAcceleration` represents the physical acceleration imparted on a device by the user outside gravitational acceleration.

- The `magneticField` value is similar to the one you saw in Recipe 5-2; however, it removes any device bias, resulting in more accurate readings.

> **Note**   If you are unfamiliar with them, radians are a different way of measuring rotation from the more commonly used degrees. They are based around the value pi (π). A radian value of pi (roughly 3.14) is equivalent to a 180-degree rotation, so any radian value can be converted to degrees by dividing by pi, and then multiplying by 180 like so: $d = r * 180 / \pi$.

Setting Up the Application

You'll create an application similar to the one you built in Recipe 5-2. So go ahead and create a new single-view application project and link in the Core Motion framework.

> **Caution**   Failing to link the Core Motion framework results in a linker error, such as the one that follows, when you try to build your application later on.
>
> ```
> Undefined symbols for architecture armv7:
>
>   "_OBJC_CLASS_$_CMMotionManager", referenced from:
>
>       objc-class-ref in ViewController.o
> ```

Now create a user interface like the one in Figure 5-8. You'll need 35 label objects, 15 of which are displaying values. Because you will update those labels at runtime you'll need to create outlets for them. Use the following names for the outlets:

- Attitude value labels: rollLabel, pitchLabel, and yawLabel.
- Rotation rate value labels: xRotLabel, yRotLabel, and zRotLabel.
- Gravity value labels: xGravLabel, yGravLabel, and zGravLabel.
- User acceleration labels: xAccLabel, yAccLabel, and zAccLabel.
- Magnetic field labels: xMagLabel, yMagLabel, and zMagLabel.

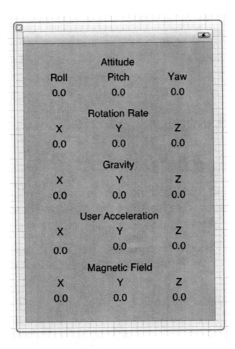

Figure 5-8. User interface of the device motion app

Now, as you did in Recipe 5-2, add a motion manager property to the view controller.

```
#import <UIKit/UIKit.h>
#import <CoreMotion/CoreMotion.h>

@interface ViewController : UIViewController

// ...

@property (strong, nonatimic) CMMotionManager *motionManager;

@end
```

The property should have the same lazy initialization implementation as before:

```
@implementation ViewController

// ...

-(CMMotionManager *)motionManager
{
    // Lazy initialization
    if (_motionManager == nil)
    {
        _motionManager = [[CMMotionManager alloc] init];
    }
```

```
    return _motionManager;
}

// ...

@end
```

Also, as in Recipe 5-2, your app should support only portrait orientation.

Accessing Device Motion Data

Starting and stopping updates and retrieving the data from the device motion property follow the same pattern that you used for accessing the three sensors' raw data. The difference is that you only need one start statement, which allows you to reach all the data at once.

So, add the following methods to your view controller. Be sure to add their declarations to the header file as well because you'll invoke them from the application delegate later.

```objc
- (void)startUpdates
{
    // Start device motion updates
    if ([self.motionManager isDeviceMotionAvailable])
    {
        //Update twice per second
        [self.motionManager setDeviceMotionUpdateInterval:1.0/2.0];
        [self.motionManager startDeviceMotionUpdatesToQueue:[NSOperationQueue mainQueue]
                                                withHandler:
         ^(CMDeviceMotion *deviceMotion, NSError *error)
         {
             // Update attitude labels
             self.rollLabel.text = [NSString stringWithFormat:@"%f",
                                    deviceMotion.attitude.roll];
             self.pitchLabel.text = [NSString stringWithFormat:@"%f",
                                     deviceMotion.attitude.pitch];
             self.yawLabel.text =  [NSString stringWithFormat:@"%f",
                                    deviceMotion.attitude.yaw];

             // Update rotation rate labels
             self.xRotLabel.text = [NSString stringWithFormat:@"%f",
                                    deviceMotion.rotationRate.x];
             self.yRotLabel.text = [NSString stringWithFormat:@"%f",
                                    deviceMotion.rotationRate.y];
             self.zRotLabel.text = [NSString stringWithFormat:@"%f",
                                    deviceMotion.rotationRate.z];

             // Update user acceleration labels
             self.xGravLabel.text = [NSString stringWithFormat:@"%f",
                                     deviceMotion.gravity.x];
             self.yGravLabel.text = [NSString stringWithFormat:@"%f",
                                     deviceMotion.gravity.y];
             self.zGravLabel.text = [NSString stringWithFormat:@"%f",
                                     deviceMotion.gravity.z];
```

```
        // Update user acceleration labels
        self.xAccLabel.text = [NSString stringWithFormat:@"%f",
                                    deviceMotion.userAcceleration.x];
        self.yAccLabel.text = [NSString stringWithFormat:@"%f",
                                    deviceMotion.userAcceleration.y];
        self.zAccLabel.text = [NSString stringWithFormat:@"%f",
                                    deviceMotion.userAcceleration.z];

        // Update magnetic field labels
        self.xMagLabel.text = [NSString stringWithFormat:@"%f",
                                    deviceMotion.magneticField.field.x];
        self.yMagLabel.text = [NSString stringWithFormat:@"%f",
                                    deviceMotion.magneticField.field.y];
        self.zMagLabel.text = [NSString stringWithFormat:@"%f",
                                    deviceMotion.magneticField.field.z];
    }];
    }
}

-(void)stopUpdates
{
    if ([self.motionManager isDeviceMotionAvailable] &&
        [self.motionManager isDeviceMotionActive])
    {
        [self.motionManager stopDeviceMotionUpdates];
    }
}
```

Finally, invoke the start and stop updates methods from the app delegate's
applicationWillResignActive: and applicationDidBecomeActive: methods, respectively.

```
- (void)applicationWillResignActive:(UIApplication *)application
{
    [self.viewController stopUpdates];
}

- (void)applicationDidBecomeActive:(UIApplication *)application
{
    [self.viewController startUpdates];
}
```

So now if you run this application, you will probably notice that most of your values are more
stable than those from the raw sensor data of Recipe 5-2. You may also see all zeros for your
magnetometer readings. Move your device in a figure-eight motion to calibrate your magnetometer
until these values start updating.

Setting a Reference Frame

Though not required, you can specify a reference frame for your attitude data. This is done by using
the startDeviceMotionUpdatesUsingReferenceFram:toQueue:withHandler: method.

One of the following is a possible value for the reference frame parameter:

- CMAttitudeReferenceFrameXArbitraryZVertical, which specifies a reference frame with the z-axis along the vertical and the x-axis along any arbitrary direction; simply put, the device is flat and face-up.

- CMAttitudeReferenceFrameXArbitraryCorrectedZVertical, which is the same as the previous value except the magnetometer is used to provide better accuracy. This option increases CPU (central processing unit) usage and requires the magnetometer to be both available and calibrated.

- CMAttitudeReferenceFrameXMagneticNorthZVertical, which reference a frame that has the z-axis vertical as before, but with the x-axis directed toward "magnetic north." This option requires the magnetometer to be available and calibrated, which means you will probably have to wave your device around a bit before you can get any readings in your application.

- CMAttitudeReferenceFrameXTrueNorthZVertical, which is just like the previous, but the x-axis is directed toward "true north" rather than "magnetic north." The location of the device must be available for the device to be able to calculate the difference between the two.

> **Note**   There's a difference between "magnetic north" and "true north." Magnetic north is the magnetic north pole of the Earth, which is where any compass will point. This point, however, is not constant due to changes in the Earth's core and is moving more than 30 miles per year. True north refers to the direction toward the actual north pole of the Earth, which stays constant.

You will choose the third option, CMAttitudeReferenceFrameXMagneticNorthZVertical, for your application. Change your call to the startDeviceMotionUpdatesToQueue:withHandler: method to the following:

```
[self.motionManager startDeviceMotionUpdatesUsingReferenceFrame:
                CMAttitudeReferenceFrameXMagneticNorthZVertical
                toQueue:[NSOperationQueue mainQueue]
                withHandler:
  ^(CMDeviceMotion *deviceMotion, NSError *error)
  {
    // ... Update value labels here
  }];
```

Now, when you run your application, you may start off seeing "0.0" for all your values. If that's the case, you can move your device around in a figure-eight motion to get your magnetometer calibrated; the values should start updating soon enough.

You should notice now that if you lay your device on a flat surface and then turn the device around the z-axis, at the moment that your x-axis is aligned with the Earth's magnetic field, your yaw value should get close to zero, as in Figure 5-9.

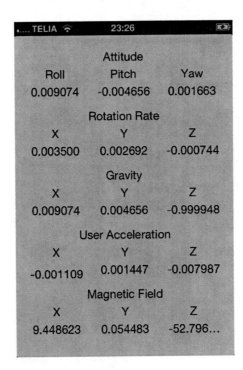

Figure 5-9. Your application receiving calibrated device information

Recipe 5-4: Moving a Label with Gravity

Recipes 5-2 and 5-3 showed you how to access the various Core Motion data. It's time to put that knowledge into use and make it a little more interesting. Using this recipe you'll create an application with a single label that you'll be able to move around by tilting your device.

Setting Up the Application

You'll use the same basic architecture that you built in the previous two recipes. So once again start by creating a new single-view application and linking it to CoreMotion.framework. Then add the following declarations, which should be familiar by now, to your view control's header file:

```
#import <UIKit/UIKit.h>
#import <CoreMotion/CoreMotion.h>

@interface ViewController : UIViewController

@property (strong, nonatomic) CMMotionManager *motionManager;

- (void)startUpdates;
- (void)stopUpdates;

@end
```

Now switch to ViewController.m and implement the property using lazy initialization; add stubs for the startUpdate and stopUpdate methods. See the following code:

```
@implementation ViewController
@synthesize motionManager = _motionManager;

- (CMMotionManager *)motionManager
{
    // Lazy initialization
    if (_motionManager == nil)
    {
        _motionManger = [[CMMotionManager alloc] init];
    }
    return _motionManager;
}

- (void)startUpdates
{

}

- (void)stopUpdates
{

}

// ...

@end
```

As in the previous two recipes, your app should only support the portrait interface orientation, so make sure you make that change in the project settings.

Next, go to AppDelegate.m and add the code to start and stop the updates when the application goes in and out of the active state.

```
@implementation AppDelegate

// ...

- (void)applicationWillResignActive:(UIApplication *)application
{
    [self.viewController stopUpdates];
}

// ...

- (void)applicationDidBecomeActive:(UIApplication *)application
{
    [self.viewController startUpdates];
}

// ...

@end
```

Finally, in the main view, add a label and create an outlet for it so that you'll be able to change its position at runtime. Name the label's outlet myLabel. Your user interface should look something like the one in Figure 5-10.

Figure 5-10. *The user interface with the label you will move using gravity*

Your app is now ready for the next step, implementing gravity-caused movement of the label.

Moving the Label with Gravity

You're going to use a very simple algorithm for the initial version of your label moving feature. Later you'll spice it up with a little acceleration, but for now you will settle for a linear movement that is proportional to the angle in which you tilt the device.

As you can see, you have increased the update frequency to once per 20 milliseconds (1/50). This enhances the feeling and responsiveness of the app. The next thing to notice is that you use the CMAttitudeReferenceFrameXArbitraryCorrectedZVertical reference frame. This gives you a z-axis that's aligned with Earth's gravity force, which is what you want.

```
- (void)startUpdates
{
    if ([self.motionManager isDeviceMotionAvailable] &&
        ![self.motionManager isDeviceMotionActive])
    {
        [self.motionManager setDeviceMotionUpdateInterval:1.0/50.0];
        [self.motionManager startDeviceMotionUpdatesUsingReferenceFrame:
```

```objc
                            CMAttitudeReferenceFrameXArbitraryCorrectedZVertical
                            toQueue:[NSOperationQueue mainQueue]
                            withHandler:
        ^(CMDeviceMotion *motion, NSError *error)
        {
            CGRect labelRect = self.myLabel.frame;
            double scale = 5.0;

            // Calculate movement on the x-axis
            double dx = motion.gravity.x * scale;
            labelRect.origin.x += dx;

            // Don't move outside the view's x bounds
            if (labelRect.origin.x < 0)
            {
                labelRect.origin.x = 0;
            }
            else if (labelRect.origin.x + labelRect.size.width >
                    self.view.bounds.size.width)
            {
                labelRect.origin.x =
                    self.view.bounds.size.width - labelRect.size.width;
            }

            // Calculate movement on the y-axis
            double dy = motion.gravity.y * scale;
            labelRect.origin.y -= dy;

            // Don't move outside the view's y bounds
            if (labelRect.origin.y < 0)
            {
                labelRect.origin.y = 0;
            }
            else if (labelRect.origin.y + labelRect.size.height >
                    self.view.bounds.size.height)
            {
                labelRect.origin.y =
                    self.view.bounds.size.height - labelRect.size.height;
            }

            [self.myLabel setFrame:labelRect];
        }];
    }
}

- (void)stopUpdates
{
    if ([self.motionManager isDeviceMotionAvailable] &&
        [self.motionManager isDeviceMotionActive])
    {
        [self.motionManager stopDeviceMotionUpdates];
    }
}
```

The algorithm in the preceding code is the simplest possible. Use the `deviceMotion.gravity` property as a velocity value (although it's actually an acceleration) and calculate the delta movement from it. Because each value only reaches between –1.0 and 1.0 you use a scaling factor to adjust the general speed of the movement.

If you run the app now you should see the label moving in the direction you tilt your device; the bigger the tilt, the faster the movement. But the movement feels a bit unnatural. This is because it lacks an important component: acceleration. Acceleration is the topic of the next section.

Adding Acceleration

Now you'll adjust the `startUpdates` method to implement a simple acceleration algorithm. Change your code according to this listing:

```
- (void)startUpdates
{
    if ([self.motionManager isDeviceMotionAvailable] &&
        ![self.motionManager isDeviceMotionActive])
    {
        __block double accumulatedDx = 0;
        __block double accumulatedDy = 0;

        [self.motionManager setDeviceMotionUpdateInterval:1.0/50.0];
        [self.motionManager startDeviceMotionUpdatesUsingReferenceFrame:
                            CMAttitudeReferenceFrameXArbitraryCorrectedZVertical
                            toQueue:[NSOperationQueue mainQueue]
                            withHandler:
        ^(CMDeviceMotion *motion, NSError *error)
        {
            CGRect labelRect = self.myLabel.frame;
            double scale = 1.5;

            double dx = motion.gravity.x * scale;
            accumulatedDx += dx;
            labelRect.origin.x += accumulatedDx;

            if (labelRect.origin.x < 0)
            {
                labelRect.origin.x = 0;
                accumulatedDx = 0;
            }
            else if (labelRect.origin.x + labelRect.size.width >
                    self.view.bounds.size.width)
            {
                labelRect.origin.x =
                    self.view.bounds.size.width - labelRect.size.width;
                accumulatedDx = 0;
            }
```

```
        double dy = motion.gravity.y * scale;
        accumulatedDy += dy;
        labelRect.origin.y -= accumulatedDy;

        if (labelRect.origin.y < 0)
        {
            labelRect.origin.y = 0;
            accumulatedDy = 0;
        }
        else if (labelRect.origin.y + labelRect.size.height > self.view.bounds.size.height)
        {
            labelRect.origin.y = self.view.bounds.size.height - labelRect.size.height;
            accumulatedDy = 0;
        }
        [self.myLabel setFrame:labelRect];
    }];
    }
}
```

> **Note**   You may be wondering what the __block declarations in front of the accumulatedDx and accumulatedDy variables are. They are making the variables accessible from within a code block. What is more, they stay accessible even though the surrounding method has gone out of scope. This provides a clean and easy way for blocks to share variables, avoiding the need to create properties or global variables for local needs.

Notable, also, is that you have decreased the scaling factor. Now it's not a problem if the label moves slowly at first; it'll pick up pace soon enough thanks to the acceleration. You can play around with different values and find the one that you like best.

Last, but important, if the label reaches a border you reset the speed. Otherwise it'll keep on accumulating speed (in the accumulatedXX variables) even though the movement has stopped, making it less responsive when you tilt the device in the opposite direction again.

Summary

This chapter discusses specific detail about accessing the multiple different values and information that the Core Motion framework has to offer. You went from raw data to more calibrated, functional values that you could translate into a mildly useful (if not slightly entertaining) application. Core Motion, however, is not a framework that can simply be an entire application in itself. You can use it to acquire values about your device, but you must then have the creativity to put them to use. From a simple application to measure the rotation speed of a person flipping to incorporating the magnetometer into an augmented-reality application, Core Motion provides a basic framework for accessing information, which can then translate into some of the most powerful pieces of software in iOS.

Chapter 6

Map Recipes

The Map Kit framework is an incredibly powerful and useful toolkit that adds immense functionality to the location services that iOS devices offer. The framework's key focus is the ability to place a user-interactive map in an application, with countless other features expanding functionality, allowing for a nearly entirely customizable mapping interface.

With iOS 6, Apple made a fundamental change by replacing the Google Maps back-end with a map engine of its own. There are many improvements, including a new cartography that gives great looking maps at any zoom level, better zooming experience thanks to the seamless rendering, and of course the turn-by-turn navigation. Despite all the changes beneath, the Map Kit API has not changed, so code that worked on iOS 5 works without changes in iOS 6 as well.

Recipe 6-1: Showing a Map with the Current Location

The core foundation of any Map Kit application is the actual displaying of the world map. In this section, you will go over how to create an app with a map and allow the map to show the user's location.

Setting Up the Application

Create a new single-view application and add the Map Kit framework and the Core Location framework to the project. You should also provide a location usage description in the application property list. This is done by adding the `NSLocationUsageDescription` key in the application's `Info.plist` file. We've set its value to "Testing map views" and that description is used when the user is prompted and asked for permission to use location services. Figure 6-2 provides an example of this system alert box.

> **Note**   Descriptions on how to link frameworks and setting values in the application's property list file, can be found in Chapter 1.

When the frameworks have been added, you can start building the user interface. Select the view controller's `.xib` file from the navigation pane, and drag a map view from the object library to the work space. Make it fill the entire view.

Next, add a label for displaying the current latitude and longitude of the device. Place it on top of the map, close to the bottom of the screen. Set the label's text alignment to center justified. Also, to make the text easier to read on the map, set a background color (e.g., white). Your user interface should now look something like the one in Figure 6-1.

Figure 6-1. Main view controller with a map and a label

Create outlets for both the map view and the label. Name the outlets `mapView` and `userLocationLabel`, respectively. Because you haven't imported the Map Kit API yet you'll get an error indication next to the `mapView` property at this point. We'll take care of that next.

> **Note**   Chapter 1 provides detailed instructions on how to create outlets.

Your user interface is fully set up, so you can turn your attention to the view controller's interface file (ViewController.h). You need to make two additions to this class interface before moving to the implementation file. The first is to add the MapKit/MapKit.h framework library to the class with an import statement, and the second is to make the view controller a map view delegate by adding MKMapViewDelegate as a supported protocol.

Your ViewController.h should now look something like this, with the foregoing changes in bold:

```
//
//  ViewController.h
//  Recipe 6.1: Showing Current Location
//

#import <UIKit/UIKit.h>
#import <MapKit/MapKit.h>

@interface ViewController : UIViewController<MKMapViewDelegate>

@property (weak, nonatomic) IBOutlet MKMapView *mapView;
@property (weak, nonatomic) IBOutlet UILabel *userLocationLabel;

@end
```

Switch to the implementation file, ViewController.m, and the viewDidLoad method where you'll initialize the map view. We'll begin by explaining the steps and then show you the complete viewDidLoad method.

First, make the view controller be the map view's delegate.

```
self.mapView.delegate = self;
```

Next, set the region of the map view. The region is the portion of the map that is currently being displayed. It consists of a center coordinate and a distance in latitude and longitude to show surrounding the center coordinate.

If you are like most people, you don't think of distances in latitudinal and longitudinal degrees, so you can use the method MKCoordinateRegionMakeWithDistance to create a region using a center coordinate and meters surrounding the coordinate. In this recipe, you start with a region of 10 by 10 kilometers over Baltimore, Maryland, in the United States.

```
// Set initial region
CLLocationCoordinate2D baltimoreLocation = CLLocationCoordinate2DMake(39.303, -76.612);
self.mapView.region =
    MKCoordinateRegionMakeWithDistance(baltimoreLocation, 10000, 10000);
```

Two optional properties worth mentioning are zoomEnabled and scrollEnabled. These control whether a user can zoom or pan the map, respectively.

```
// Optional Controls
//    self.mapView.zoomEnabled = NO;
//    self.mapView.scrollEnabled = NO;
```

Finally, you define the map as showing the user's location. This is easily done by setting the showUserLocation property to YES. However, you should only set this property if location services are enabled on the device, like so:

```
//Control User Location on Map
if ([CLLocationManager locationServicesEnabled])
{
    self.mapView.showsUserLocation = YES;
}
```

Keep in mind that the feature to display the user's location in the map requires an authorization from the user, which is prompted and asked for permission the first time the app is run.

> **Note**   Just because showUserLocation is set to YES, the user's location is not automatically visible on the map. To determine whether the location is visible in the current region, use the property userLocationVisible.

When you have specified that you want the map to display the user's location, you can also make it track the user location by setting the userTrackingMode property or calling the setUserTrackingMode:animated: method.

The tracking mode can be one of three values:

- MKUserTrackingModeNone: Does not track the user's location; the map can be moved to a region that does not contain the user's location.

- MKUserTrackingModeFollow: Map is panned to keep the user's location at the center. The top of the map is north. If the user pans the map manually, tracking stops.

- MKUserTrackingModeFollowWithHeading: Map is panned to keep the user's location at the center, and the map rotated so that the user's heading is at the top of the map. If the user pans the map manually, tracking stops. This setting won't work in the iOS simulator.

Initially, you are going to set userTrackingMode to MKUserTrackingModeFollow, but later we will show you how to give users the ability to control the tracking mode themselves:

```
//Control User Location on Map
if ([CLLocationManager locationServicesEnabled])
{
    self.mapView.showsUserLocation = YES;
    [self.mapView setUserTrackingMode:MKUserTrackingModeFollow animated:YES];
}
```

Your `viewDidLoad` method should now resemble the following:

```
- (void)viewDidLoad
{
    [super viewDidLoad];

    self.mapView.delegate = self;

    // Set initial region
    CLLocationCoordinate2D baltimoreLocation =
        CLLocationCoordinate2DMake(39.303, -76.612);
    self.mapView.region =
        MKCoordinateRegionMakeWithDistance(baltimoreLocation, 10000, 10000);

    // Optional Controls
    //    self.mapView.zoomEnabled = NO;
    //    self.mapView.scrollEnabled = NO;

    // Control User Location on Map
    if ([CLLocationManager locationServicesEnabled])
    {
        self.mapView.showsUserLocation = YES;
        [self.mapView setUserTrackingMode:MKUserTrackingModeFollow animated:YES];
    }
}
```

Finally, respond to location updates and update the label with the new location data. This is done in the `mapView:didUpdateUserLocation:` delegate method which you add to your view controller. Your implementation of the method looks like the following:

```
-(void)mapView:(MKMapView *)mapView didUpdateUserLocation:(MKUserLocation *)userLocation
{
    self.userLocationLabel.text =
        [NSString stringWithFormat:@"Current Location: %.5f°, %.5f°",
            userLocation.coordinate.latitude, userLocation.coordinate.longitude];
}
```

You have enough of a start that you can now run your app on the simulator. When the app launches on the simulator, the user is prompted to allow the app access to his or her location. Figure 6-2 shows your application displaying this prompt. Note that the message includes the location usage description if you provided it in the `.plist` file.

Figure 6-2. The app's prompt to access location

If you tap OK and there is no sign of your location on the map, start one of the location debug services (e.g., Freeway Drive). On the simulator, go to the menu option Debug ➤ Location ➤ Freeway Drive, and this starts the location simulation services on the simulator. The map should pan to the new location (a drive recorded in California) and update the location label.

User-Controlled Tracking

If users try to pan the map manually, one of the problems they will encounter is that the user location tracking stops. Apple has provided a new `UIBarButtonItem` class named `MKUserTrackingBarButtonItem`. This button can be added to any `UIToolBar` or `UINavigationbar` and toggles the user tracking modes on the specified map view.

To set this up, you add a toolbar to your user interface. You should adjust the size of the map view and move the label so that the toolbar doesn't hide them. Then create an outlet named `mapToolbar` to reference the toolbar.

Delete the button that is added to the toolbar by default as you will not need it. You add a button programmatically in just a moment, but for now your user interface should resemble that in Figure 6-3.

Figure 6-3. *Adding a toolbar to the bottom of the* `.xib`

Now add your `MKUserTrackingBarButtonItem` in code. Switch to the view controller's implementation file and scroll to the `viewDidLoad` method. Add the following code at the bottom of the method:

```
// Add button for controlling user location tracking
MKUserTrackingBarButtonItem *trackingButton =
    [[MKUserTrackingBarButtonItem alloc] initWithMapView:self.mapView];
[self.mapToolbar setItems: [NSArray arrayWithObject: trackingButton] animated:YES];
```

With this new add-on, users can manually pan the map and then get back to tracking their location with the tap of this new bar button. Figure 6-4 demonstrates the user-tracking functionality you have implemented.

Figure 6-4. *Simulated application with panning and user tracking*

Recipe 6-2: Marking Locations with Pins

A common usage of maps is to mark not only your current location and destination but also various points of interest along the route. In iOS, these highlights of points within the map are called *annotations*. Annotations, by default, look like pins, and Recipe 6-2 shows you how to add them to your map.

Using Recipe 6-2, you'll build an application similar to the one in Recipe 6-1. Follow these steps to set up the application:

1.   Create a new single-view application project.

2.   Add the Map Kit framework to the project.

3.   Add the Core Location framework to the project. In this recipe you're not going to use the location services so there's no need to provide a location usage description. You still need to link in the framework though, or you'll get linker errors when building later.

4. Add a map view to the application's main view.

5. Create an outlet for referencing the map view. Name the outlet `mapView`.

6. Make your view controller class conform to the `MKMapViewDelegate` protocol.
    The view controller's header file should now look something like the
    following:

```
//
//  ViewController.h
//  Recipe 6.2: Pinning Locations
//

#import <UIKit/UIKit.h>
#import <MapKit/MapKit.h>

@interface ViewController : UIViewController<MKMapViewDelegate>

@property (weak, nonatomic) IBOutlet MKMapView *mapView;

@end
```

7. Finally, initialize the map view delegate property in the `viewDidLoad` method
    of the view controller.

```
- (void)viewDidLoad
{
    [super viewDidLoad];
        // Do any additional setup after loading the view, typically from a nib.
    self.mapView.delegate = self;
}
```

Your application is now set up and you should build and run it to make sure everything is okay
before moving on.

Adding Annotation Objects

Two objects are involved when you display an annotation on the map: the annotation object and
the annotation view. The job of the annotation view is to draw an annotation. The annotation view is
provided with a drawing context and an annotation object, which holds the data associated with the
annotation. In its simplest form, an annotation object contains a title and a coordinate.

To create an annotation object you can use the built-in `MKPointAnnotation` class that holds
properties for title, subtitle, and location. Then all you need to do is to add the annotations to the
map view with its `addAnnotation:` or `addAnnotations:` method.

Let's add a few annotations to the map view. Add the following code to the `viewDidLoad` method.

```
- (void)viewDidLoad
{
    [super viewDidLoad];
        // Do any additional setup after loading the view, typically from a nib.
    self.mapView.delegate = self;

    MKPointAnnotation *annotation1 = [[MKPointAnnotation alloc] init];
    annotation1.title = @"Miami";
    annotation1.subtitle = @"Annotation 1";
    annotation1.coordinate = CLLocationCoordinate2DMake(25.802, -80.132);

    MKPointAnnotation *annotation2 = [[MKPointAnnotation alloc] init];
    annotation2.title = @"Denver";
    annotation2.subtitle = @"Annotation 2";
    annotation2.coordinate = CLLocationCoordinate2DMake(39.733, -105.018);

    [self.mapView addAnnotation:annotation1];
    [self.mapView addAnnotation:annotation2];
}
```

We chose to make the pins drop in Miami and Denver, but any coordinates work just as well. If you run this app now, you should see your map with two pins stuck in, as in Figure 6-5. You may need to zoom out to see them; this can be done in the simulator by holding Alt (⌥), to simulate a pinch, and dragging.

Figure 6-5. Application with map and pins

In the beginning of this section, we spoke of two objects being necessary to display an annotation. You may be wondering what happened to the second object, the annotation view. We didn't create one, still the annotation objects show up on the map. The reason is that if you don't provide it, the framework will create instances of the MKPinAnnotationView class and use them as annotation views.

Changing the Pin Color

The default annotation view displays your annotation as a red pin on the map. Usually, the red color indicates a destination location. The other two possible pin colors of an MKPinAnnotationView are green (for starting points) and purple (for user-defined points). If you want a color other than red for your pin, you'll need to create the views yourself, which can be done in the mapView:viewForAnnotation: delegate method.

Let's change the pin color to purple for the annotations. Start by adding the mapView:viewForAnnotation: method to your view controller.

```
- (MKAnnotationView *)mapView:(MKMapView *)mapView viewForAnnotation:(id<MKAnnotation>)annotation
{
    // Returning nil will result in a default annotation view being used
    return nil;
}
```

The map view sends all annotations that are within its current range to the mapView:viewForAnnotation: method to retrieve the annotation view it uses to do the drawing. The user location, which is a special kind of annotation, also is sent to this method, so you need to make sure the provided annotation is of the type you expect.

```
- (MKAnnotationView *)mapView:(MKMapView *)mapView viewForAnnotation:(id<MKAnnotation>)annotation
{
    // Don't create annotation views for the user location annotation
    if ([annotation isKindOfClass:[MKPointAnnotation class]])
    {
        // Create and return our own annotation view here
    }

    // Returning nil will result in a default annotation view being used
    return nil;
}
```

To minimize the number of annotation views needed, map views provide a way to reuse annotation views by caching them. The code to cache the views looks a lot like the one used to create cells for table views.

```
- (MKAnnotationView *)mapView:(MKMapView *)mapView viewForAnnotation:(id<MKAnnotation>)annotation
{
    // Don't create annotation views for the user location annotation
    if ([annotation isKindOfClass:[MKPointAnnotation class]])
    {
        static NSString *userPinAnnotationId = @"userPinAnnotation";

        // Create an annotation view, but reuse a cached one if available
        MKPinAnnotationView *annotationView =
            (MKPinAnnotationView *)[self.mapView
            dequeueReusableAnnotationViewWithIdentifier:userPinAnnotationId];
        if(annotationView)
        {
            // Cached view found. It'll have the pin color set but not annotation.
            annotationView.annotation = annotation;
        }
        else
        {
            // No cached view were available, create a new one
            annotationView = [[MKPinAnnotationView alloc] initWithAnnotation:annotation
                            reuseIdentifier:userPinAnnotationId];
```

```
        // Purple indicates user defined pin
        annotationView.pinColor = MKPinAnnotationColorPurple;
    }

    return annotationView;
    }
    return nil;
}
```

> **Note** The identifier string should be different for every type of annotation view you create. For example, an annotation view that draws red pins should have a different ID than one that draws purple pins; otherwise you may get unexpected behavior when you retrieve views from the cache.

If you build and run now you should see the same pins as those in Figure 6-5, but they'll be purple instead of red. Besides changing pin color, a lot more can be done to customize annotations. This is the topic of Recipe 6-3.

Recipe 6-3: Creating Custom Annotations

While the majority of the time the default `MKPinAnnotationView` objects are incredibly useful, you may at some point decide you want a different image instead of the pin to represent an annotation on your map. Likewise, you may want to display more usable and pleasing looking callouts when the user taps your annotations. To create a custom annotation view, you will be subclassing the `MKAnnotationView` class. Using Recipe 6-3, you also create a custom annotation object to hold additional data, as well as a detailed view, which is displayed when the user taps your callouts.

Setting Up the Application

To set up the application, you must first create your project the same way you did in the previous recipes. Follow these steps to get your app skeleton set up:

1. Create a new single-view application project.

2. Add the Map Kit framework to the project.

3. Add the Core Location framework to the project. In Recipe 6-3 you're not going to use the location services so there's no need to provide a location usage description. You still need to link in the framework though or you'll get linker errors when building later.

4. Add a map view to the application's main view.

5. Create an outlet for referencing the map view. Name the outlet `mapView`.

6.   Import the Map Kit API in `ViewController.h`.

7.   Make your view controller class conform to the `MKMapViewDelegate` protocol. The view controller's header file should now look something like the following:

```
//
// ViewController.h
// Recipe 6.3: Customizing Annotations
//

#import <UIKit/UIKit.h>
#import <MapKit/MapKit.h>

@interface ViewController : UIViewController<MKMapViewDelegate>

@property (weak, nonatomic) IBOutlet MKMapView *mapView;

@end
```

8.   Finally, initialize the map view delegate property in the `viewDidLoad` method of the view controller.

```
- (void)viewDidLoad
{
    [super viewDidLoad];
        // Do any additional setup after loading the view, typically from a nib.
    self.mapView.delegate = self;
}
```

Before going any further, you must add an image to be used instead of a pin. For Recipe 6-3 we have chosen a small image, `overlay.png`, shown here in Figure 6-6. You may, of course, pick any image you like.

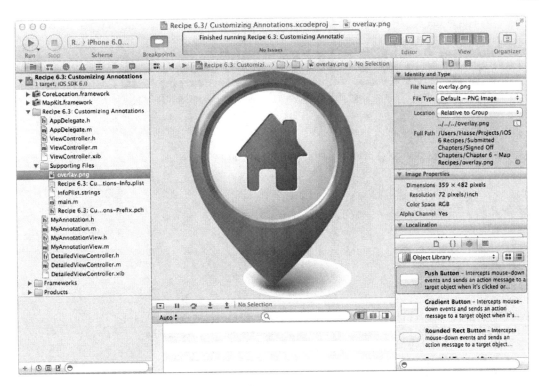

Figure 6-6. *The custom annotation image added to the project*

The image is a bit large to use on a map, so you will be scaling it down later. However, in a real scenario you would scale down the image to the size of your annotation before adding it to the project. This way you save some space and clock cycles because the application won't have to do the scaling at runtime.

Creating a Custom Annotation Class

The next step is to create your custom annotation class. Use the built-in `Objective-C` class template to create a new subclass of `MKPointAnnotation`. Name the new class `MyAnnotation`.

The `MKPointAnnotation` already contains properties for the title and the subtitle so you don't have to declare them in your class. However, to show you how to attach custom data to your annotation objects, you'll extend the class with an additional property to keep contact information. You'll also add a designated initialization method to contain all the annotation setup code.

Go ahead and make the following changes to `MyAnnotation.h`.

```
//
//  MyAnnotation.h
//  Recipe 6.3: Customizing Annotations
//

#import <MapKit/MapKit.h>
```

```
@interface MyAnnotation : MKPointAnnotation

@property (nonatomic, strong) NSString *contactInformation;

-(id)initWithCoordinate:(CLLocationCoordinate2D)coord title:(NSString *)title
subtitle:(NSString *)subtitle contactInformation:(NSString *)contactInfo;

@end
```

The following are corresponding changes to MyAnnotation.m:

```
//
//  MyAnnotation.m
//  Recipe 6.3: Customizing Annotations
//

#import "MyAnnotation.h"

@implementation MyAnnotation

-(id)initWithCoordinate:(CLLocationCoordinate2D)coord title:(NSString *)title
subtitle:(NSString *)subtitle contactInformation:(NSString *)contactInfo
{
    self = [super init];
    if (self)
    {
        self.coordinate = coord;
        self.title = title;
        self.subtitle = subtitle;
        self.contactInformation = contactInfo;
    }
    return self;
}

@end
```

> **Note**   As you may have realized we didn't include a @synthesize declaration for the contactInformation property. Starting in Xcode 4.5 this is no longer necessary because the compiler synthesizes any nondeclared getters and setters automatically.

Creating a Custom Annotation View

Now you can proceed to create your custom annotation view. As before, create a new Objective-C class, this time with the name MyAnnotationView and MKAnnotationView as the parent class.

The only thing you do in the custom annotation view class is to override the initWithAnnotation: resuseIdentifier: method. There's where all the customization takes place. But before we go ahead and do that, let's take a quick look at the code that's been generated for you in MyAnnotationView.m.

```
// ...

@implementation MyViewAnnotation

- (id)initWithFrame:(CGRect)frame
{
    // ...
}

/*
// Only override drawRect: if you perform custom drawing.
// An empty implementation adversely affects performance during animation.
- (void)drawRect:(CGRect)rect
{
    // Drawing code
}
*/

@end
```

Xcode has added an initWithFrame: method to your class. You will not need it so feel free to remove it. For your convenience, Xcode has also added the drawRect: method but commented it out. drawRect: is interesting because it provides a way to completely control the drawing of your annotation. We will not use it in this recipe so you can remove it as well.

Instead, add the following:

```
//
//  MyAnnotationView.m
//  Recipe 6.3: Customizing Annotations
//

#import "MyAnnotationView.h"

@implementation MyAnnotationView

- (id)initWithAnnotation:(id <MKAnnotation>)annotation
reuseIdentifier:(NSString *)reuseIdentifier
{
    self = [super initWithAnnotation:annotation reuseIdentifier:reuseIdentifier];
    if (self)
    {
        UIImage *myImage = [UIImage imageNamed:@"overlay.png"];
        self.image = myImage;
        self.frame = CGRectMake(0, 0, 40, 40);
        // Use contentMode to ensure best scaling of image
        self.contentMode = UIViewContentModeScaleAspectFill;
        // Use centerOffset to adjust the position of the image
```

```
        self.centerOffset = CGPointMake(1, 1);
    }
    return self;
}

@end
```

The preceding code creates the custom annotation image to be used instead of the pin. Also, the frame of the annotation view is adjusted to 40 by 40 pixels that the image is scaled down to.

If necessary, you can also adjust the position of the image relative to the coordinates by using the centerOffset property. This is especially useful if the image you are using has a particular point, such as a pin or arrow, that you would like to have at the exact coordinates.

Now that your custom classes are all set up, you can return to your view controller to implement your map's delegate method. You'll probably recognize a lot of it from the previous recipes. The main difference is that you don't create instances from MKPinAnnotationView, but from the custom MyAnnotationView class.

```
//
//  ViewController.m
//  Recipe 6.3: Customizing Annotations
//

#import "ViewController.h"
#import "MyAnnotation.h"
#import "MyAnnotationView.h"

// ...

@implementation ViewController

// ...

- (MKAnnotationView *)mapView:(MKMapView *)mapView viewForAnnotation:(id<MKAnnotation>)annotation
{
    // Don't create annotation views for the user location annotation
    if ([annotation isKindOfClass:[MyAnnotation class]])
    {
        static NSString *myAnnotationId = @"myAnnotation";

        // Create an annotation view, but reuse a cached one if available
        MyAnnotationView *annotationView =
            (MyAnnotationView *)[self.mapView
            dequeueReusableAnnotationViewWithIdentifier:myAnnotationId];
        if(annotationView)
        {
            // Cached view found, associate it with the annotation
            annotationView.annotation = annotation;
        }
```

```
        else
        {
            // No cached view were available, create a new one
            annotationView = [[MyAnnotationView alloc] initWithAnnotation:annotation
                                reuseIdentifier:myAnnotationId];
        }

        return annotationView;
    }

    // Use a default annotation view for the user location annotation
    return nil;
}

@end
```

Finally, all you need to run this is some test data. In the `viewDidLoad` method, add the following lines to create a couple of annotations and add them to your map:

```
@implementation ViewController

// ...

- (void)viewDidLoad
{
    [super viewDidLoad];
        // Do any additional setup after loading the view, typically from a nib.
    self.mapView.delegate = self;

    MyAnnotation *ann1 = [[MyAnnotation alloc]
        initWithCoordinate: CLLocationCoordinate2DMake(37.68, -97.33)
        title: @"Company 1"
        subtitle: @"Something Catchy"
        contactInformation: @"Call 555-123456"];

    MyAnnotation *ann2 = [[MyAnnotation alloc]
        initWithCoordinate:CLLocationCoordinate2DMake(41.500, -81.695)
        title:@"Company 2"
        subtitle:@"Even More Catchy"
        contactInformation:@"Call 555-654321"];

    NSArray *annotations = [NSArray arrayWithObjects: ann1, ann2, nil];
    [self.mapView addAnnotations:annotations];
}

// ...

@end
```

At this point, when you run the app, you should see your two annotations appear on the map with your image (shrunk down to a reasonable size) over Wichita, Kansas and Cleveland, Ohio. Figure 6-7 provides a simulation of this app.

Figure 6-7. Application with map and custom annotations

Customizing the Callouts

Now you will add a few extra lines of code to customize your callouts.

First, you will place an image to the left of the annotation's title and subtitle. This is done through the use of the annotationView's property leftCalloutAccessoryView. You will also add an accessory button to the right-hand side of the callout. You'll use it later to display a detailed view of the annotation.

Go back to MyAnnotationView.m and extend the initWithAnnotation:reuseidentifier: method with the following code:

```
- (id)initWithAnnotation:(id <MKAnnotation>)annotation
reuseIdentifier:(NSString *)reuseIdentifier
{
    self = [super initWithAnnotation:annotation reuseIdentifier:reuseIdentifier];
```

```
    if (self)
    {
        UIImage *myImage = [UIImage imageNamed:@"overlay.png"];
        self.image = myImage;
        self.frame = CGRectMake(0, 0, 40, 40);
        //Use contentMode to ensure best scaling of image
        self.contentMode = UIViewContentModeScaleAspectFill;
        //Use centerOffset to adjust the position of the image
        self.centerOffset = CGPointMake(1, 1);

        self.canShowCallout = YES;

        // Left callout accessory view
        UIImageView *leftAccessoryView = [[UIImageView alloc] initWithImage:myImage];
        leftAccessoryView.frame = CGRectMake(0, 0, 20, 20);
        leftAccessoryView.contentMode = UIViewContentModeScaleAspectFill;
        self.leftCalloutAccessoryView = leftAccessoryView;

        // Right callout accessory view
        self.rightCalloutAccessoryView =
            [UIButton buttonWithType:UIButtonTypeDetailDisclosure];
    }
    return self;
}
```

As you can see, we're reusing the annotation image but wrapping it into a image view to scale it down, this time to 20 by 20 pixels.

If you build and run your application now, your annotations will present callouts like the one in Figure 6-8.

Figure 6-8. Map with custom annotations, one of which is showing a callout

Adding a Detailed View

At this point, your callouts are all set up visually, but there's a massive amount of potential in having those buttons inside the callouts that you haven't tapped into yet. Most map-based apps that use buttons on their callouts usually use the button to push another view controller onto the screen. An application focused on displaying the locations of a specific business on the map might allow the user to view all the details or pictures from a specific location.

To increase your functionality, you will implement another one of your map's delegate methods, -mapView:annotationView:calloutAccessoryControlTapped:, and have it present a modal view controller. For the purpose of this recipe, you will have it display only your particular annotation's title, subtitle, and contact information texts.

Start by creating the new view controller. Name it DetailedViewController and make sure it's a subclass of UIViewController, and that you have the "With XIB for user interface" option checked.

Up next, go into your DetailedViewController's .xib file, and add three labels. Place them near the bottom of the view, as in Figure 6-9.

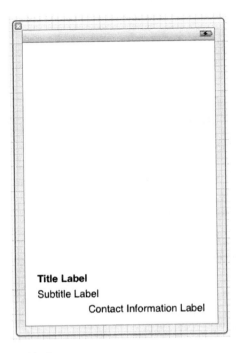

Figure 6-9. `DetailedViewController.xib` *view*

Now, create outlets for the three labels. Name them `titleLabel`, `subtitleLabel`, and `contactInformationLabel`, respectively. Also, make the following additions to the header file:

```
//
//  DetailedViewController.h
//  Recipe 6.3: Customizing Annotations
//

#import <UIKit/UIKit.h>
#import "MyAnnotation.h"

@interface DetailedViewController : UIViewController

@property (weak, nonatomic) IBOutlet UILabel *titleLabel;
@property (weak, nonatomic) IBOutlet UILabel *subtitleLabel;
@property (weak, nonatomic) IBOutlet UILabel *contactInfoLabel;

@property (strong, nonatomic) MyAnnotation *annotation;

-(id)initWithAnnotation:(MyAnnotation *)annotation;

@end
```

In `DetailedViewController.m`, start by removing the `initWithNibName:bundle:` method that Xcode added to your class. In its place, implement the `initWithAnnotation:` method you declared earlier.

```
//
//  DetailedViewController.m
//  Recipe 6.3: Customizing Annotations
//

// ...

@implementation DetailedViewController

// ...

-(id)initWithAnnotation:(MyAnnotation *)annotation
{
    self = [super init];
    if (self)
    {
        self.annotation = annotation;
    }
    return self;
}

// ...

@end
```

Now, in the `viewDidLoad` method of the detailed view controller, add code to initialize the labels with texts from the stored annotation object.

```
- (void)viewDidLoad
{
    [super viewDidLoad];
    // Do any additional setup after loading the view from its nib.
    self.titleLabel.text = self.annotation.title;
    self.subtitleLabel.text = self.annotation.subtitle;
    self.contactInfoLabel.text = self.annotation.contactInformation;
}
```

Finally, you are ready to implement your map's delegate method back in your main view controller. In this method, you create and present your `DetailedViewController`. For Recipe 6-3 chose the partial curl transition, which is a pretty cool effect. Here's how you set it up.

```
-(void)mapView:(MKMapView *)mapView annotationView:(MKAnnotationView *)view
calloutAccessoryControlTapped:(UIControl *)control
{
    DetailedViewController *dvc = [[DetailedViewController alloc]
        initWithAnnotation:view.annotation];
    dvc.modalTransitionStyle = UIModalTransitionStylePartialCurl;
    [self presentViewController:dvc animated:YES completion:^{}];
}
```

Now you're done with Recipe 6-3. Your application should resemble Figure 6-10 when you tap a detail disclosure button in one of your customized callouts.

Figure 6-10. Application responding to the tapping of callouts

Recipe 6-4: Dragging a Pin

Using this recipe you'll make a little tool that allows you to drag a pin on a map and read its location from the console.

Start by creating a new map-based application, just as you did in the previous recipes. Here are the steps again:

1. Create a new single-view application project.

2. Add the Map Kit framework to the project.

3. Add the Core Location framework to the project.

4. Add a map view to the application's main view.

5. Create an outlet for referencing the map view. Name the outlet mapView.

6. Make your view controller class conform to the `MKMapViewDelegate` protocol. The view controller's header file should now look something like the following:

```
//
//  ViewController.h
//  Recipe 6.3: Customizing Annotations
//

#import <UIKit/UIKit.h>
#import <MapKit/MapKit.h>

@interface ViewController : UIViewController<MKMapViewDelegate>

@property (weak, nonatomic) IBOutlet MKMapView *mapView;

@end
```

7. Finally, initialize the map view delegate property in the `viewDidLoad` method of the view controller.

```
- (void)viewDidLoad
{
    [super viewDidLoad];
        // Do any additional setup after loading the view, typically from a nib.
    self.mapView.delegate = self;
}
```

Adding a Draggable Pin

You're going to make a really simple tool with a single pin on the map that the user can drag around. Let's start by placing the pin on the map when the application has loaded the main view.

```
- (void)viewDidLoad
{
    [super viewDidLoad];
        // Do any additional setup after loading the view, typically from a nib.
    self.mapView.delegate = self;

    MKPointAnnotation *annotation = [[MKPointAnnotation alloc] init];
    annotation.coordinate = CLLocationCoordinate2DMake(39.303, -76.612);
    [self.mapView addAnnotation:annotation];
}
```

We've put the pin in Baltimore, but soon you'll be able to replace it with coordinates of your own using this tool. But first you need to make the pin draggable. To do that you need to customize the annotation view that displays your pin. The code is nearly identical to the one used in Recipes 6.2 and 6.3, except that you now set the `draggable` property.

```
- (MKAnnotationView *)mapView:(MKMapView *)mapView view
ForAnnotation:(id<MKAnnotation>)annotation
```

```
{
    // Don't create annotation views for the user location annotation
    if ([annotation isKindOfClass:[MKPointAnnotation class]])
    {
        static NSString *draggableAnnotationId = @"draggableAnnotation";

        // Create an annotation view, but reuse a cached one if available
        MKPinAnnotationView *annotationView =
        (MKPinAnnotationView *)[self.mapView
            dequeueReusableAnnotationViewWithIdentifier:draggableAnnotationId];
        if(annotationView)
        {
            // Cached view found, associate it with the annotation
            annotationView.annotation = annotation;
        }
        else
        {
            // No cached view were available, create a new one
            annotationView = [[MKPinAnnotationView alloc]
            initWithAnnotation:annotation
                reuseIdentifier:draggableAnnotationId];
            annotationView.pinColor = MKPinAnnotationColorPurple;
            annotationView.draggable = YES;
        }

        return annotationView;
    }

    // Use a default annotation view for the user location annotation
    return nil;
}
```

If you run the application now you can drag the pin from Baltimore to any other place of your choice. However, let's turn this albeit cool but somewhat useless app into a tool. You are going to intercept when the user drops the pin and output the new location to the console. To do this you will make use of another delegate method, the long but explanatory named
mapView:annotationView:didChangeDragState:fromOldState:.

```
-(void)mapView:(MKMapView *)mapView annotationView:(MKAnnotationView *)view
didChangeDragState:(MKAnnotationViewDragState)newState
fromOldState:(MKAnnotationViewDragState)oldState
{
    if (newState == MKAnnotationViewDragStateEnding)
    {
        MKPointAnnotation *annotation = view.annotation;
        NSLog(@"\nPin Location: %f, %f (Lat, Long)",
            annotation.coordinate.latitude, view.annotation.coordinate.longitude);
    }
}
```

Run the application in the simulator and drag the pin to a new location. The console now shows the world coordinate of the pin, as in Figure 6-11. The tool could be quite useful if you want to create some location test data of your own.

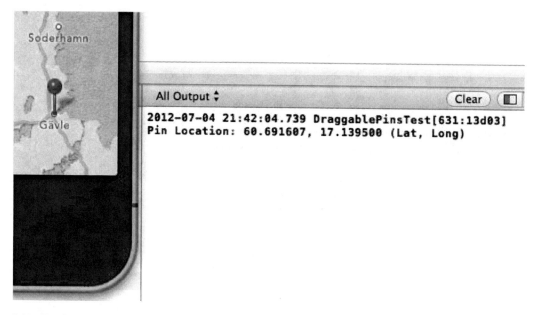

Figure 6-11. *The tool prints new pin locations to the console*

Not bad for a handful of lines of code.

Recipe 6-5: Adding Overlays to a Map

An annotation, as you've seen in the previous recipes, is a marking on a map. Because annotations are associated with a single coordinate they stay the same size at all times, even when the user zooms in or out in the map.

This recipe looks at another type of map marking, so-called *overlays*. These are shapes such as circles or polygons, and unlike annotations, they scale when the map zoom changes.

You will be adding three kinds of overlays to your MapView: circle, polygon, and line overlays. The process to add these is very similar to that of adding annotations, but this time you will not create a custom class for the overlays like you did with annotations in Recipe 6-3.

Again, start by setting up a new map-based application. We trust you know the steps by now, but you could always look back at the previous recipes for guidance.

Creating the Overlays

Again you will create your test data in the viewDidLoad method of your view controller. First out is a circle overlay over big parts of Mexico.

```
CLLocationCoordinate2D mexicoCityLocation = CLLocationCoordinate2DMake(19.808, -98.965);
MKCircle *circleOverlay = [MKCircle circleWithCenterCoordinate:mexicoCityLocation
                    radius:500000];
```

Then, a polygon overlay. Note that a polygon must always start and end in the same location.

```
CLLocationCoordinate2D polyCoords[5] =
{
    CLLocationCoordinate2DMake(39.9, -76.6),
    CLLocationCoordinate2DMake(36.7, -84.0),
    CLLocationCoordinate2DMake(33.1, -89.4),
    CLLocationCoordinate2DMake(27.3, -80.8),
    CLLocationCoordinate2DMake(39.9, -76.6)
};
MKPolygon *polygonOverlay = [MKPolygon polygonWithCoordinates:polyCoords count:5];
```

And a line overlay.

```
CLLocationCoordinate2D pathCoords[2] =
{
    CLLocationCoordinate2DMake(46.8, -100.8),
    CLLocationCoordinate2DMake(43.7, -70.4)
};
MKPolyline *pathOverlay = [MKPolyline polylineWithCoordinates:pathCoords count:2];
```

Finally, add the three overlays to the map.

```
[self.mapView addOverlays:
    [NSArray arrayWithObjects: circleOverlay, polygonOverlay, pathOverlay, nil]
];
```

If you build and run your application at this point, you'll see a map but none of the overlays you've created and added. This is because you haven't provided the overlay view objects. This is done in the mapView:viewForOverlay: delegate method, which you'll add to your view controller:

```
-(MKOverlayView *)mapView:(MKMapView *)mapView viewForOverlay:(id )overlay
{
    if([overlay isKindOfClass:[MKCircle class]])
    {
        MKCircleView *view = [[MKCircleView alloc] initWithOverlay:overlay];

        //Display settings
        view.lineWidth = 1;
        view.strokeColor = [UIColor blueColor];
        view.fillColor = [[UIColor blueColor] colorWithAlphaComponent:0.5];
        return view;
    }
    if([overlay isKindOfClass:[MKPolygon class]])
    {
        MKPolygonView *view = [[MKPolygonView alloc] initWithOverlay:overlay];

        //Display settings
        view.lineWidth=1;
        view.strokeColor=[UIColor blueColor];
        view.fillColor=[[UIColor blueColor] colorWithAlphaComponent:0.5];
        return view;
    }
```

```
    else if ([overlay isKindOfClass:[MKPolyline class]])
    {
        MKPolylineView *view = [[MKPolylineView alloc] initWithOverlay:overlay];

        //Display settings
        view.lineWidth = 3;
        view.strokeColor = [UIColor blueColor];
        return view;
    }

    return nil;
}
```

As you can see from the preceding code, each overlay shape type has a corresponding overlay view type that you use to instantiate the view objects. Each view class has similar properties for customizing the appearance of the overlay, such as colors and transparency (alpha component).

You're finished with this recipe. When you build and run it you should see a screen resembling the one in Figure 6-12.

Figure 6-12. An app with a circle, a polygon, and a line overlay

Recipe 6-6: Grouping Annotations Dynamically

When it comes to using annotations on a map view, a common problem is the possibility of having many annotations appear very close to each other, cluttering up the screen and making the application difficult to use. One solution is to group annotations based on the location and the size of the visible map. Using Recipe 6-6, you employ a simple algorithm that, when the visible region changes, compares the location of the annotations and temporarily removes those that are too close to others.

First, you need to create a new map-based application project. Refer to Recipe 6-1 for details on how to do this.

A Forest of Pins

Let's start by creating the test data, 1,000 pins randomly distributed within a relatively small area on the map. First you need a couple of instance variables, one to keep track of your current zoom level and a mutable array to hold your annotations. Make the following changes to your `ViewController.h` file:

```
//
//  ViewController.h
//  Recipe 6.6: Grouping Annotations Dynamically
//

#import <UIKit/UIKit.h>
#import <MapKit/MapKit.h>

@interface ViewController : UIViewController<MKMapViewDelegate>
{
    CLLocationDegrees _zoomLevel;
    NSMutableArray *_annotations;
}

@property (weak, nonatomic) IBOutlet MKMapView *mapView;

@end
```

Now switch to the implementation file and add the following code to instantiate the _annotations array. Give the array an initial capacity of 1,000 objects because you'll be making that many annotations soon.

```
- (void)viewDidLoad
{
    [super viewDidLoad];
    // Do any additional setup after loading the view, typically from a nib.
    self.mapView.delegate = self;

    _annotations = [[NSMutableArray alloc] initWithCapacity:1000];
}
```

Next create a custom annotation class. As usual, use the `Objective-C` class template to add the files to your project. Make sure to use NSObject as the parent class, and name the new class Hotspot.

To make the new class an annotation class, make it conform to the MKAnnotation protocol. Also, to make it easy to instantiate annotations with your new class, add an initializing method that takes a coordinate, a title, and a subtitle. The header file should now look like the following:

```
//
// Hotspot.h
// Recipe 6.6: Grouping Annotations Dynamically
//

#import <MapKit/MapKit.h>

@interface Hotspot : NSObject<MKAnnotation>
{
    CLLocationCoordinate2D _coordinate;
    NSString *_title;
    NSString *_subtitle;
}

@property (nonatomic) CLLocationCoordinate2D coordinate;
@property (nonatomic, readonly, copy) NSString *title;
@property (nonatomic, readonly, copy) NSString *subtitle;

-(id)initWithCoordinate:(CLLocationCoordinate2D)coordinate title:(NSString *)title
subtitle:(NSString *)subtitle;

@end
```

And the corresponding implementation:

```
//
// Hotspot.m
// Recipe 6.6: Grouping Annotations Dynamically
//

#import "Hotspot.h"

@implementation Hotspot

-(id)initWithCoordinate:(CLLocationCoordinate2D)coordinate
title:(NSString *)title subtitle:(NSString *)subtitle
{
    self = [super init];
    if (self) {
        self.coordinate = coordinate;
        self.title = title;
        self.subtitle = subtitle;
    }
```

```objc
    return self;
}

-(CLLocationCoordinate2D)coordinate
{
    return _coordinate;
}

-(void)setCoordinate:(CLLocationCoordinate2D)coordinate
{
    _coordinate = coordinate;
}

-(NSString *)title
{
    return _title;
}

-(void)setTitle:(NSString *)title
{
    _title = title;
}

-(NSString *)subtitle
{
    return _subtitle;
}

-(void)setSubtitle:(NSString *)subtitle
{
    _subtitle = subtitle;
}

@end
```

You'll also define a few constants that set up your starting coordinates and grouping parameters. These are also used to help generate some random locations for demonstration purposes. Place the following statements before your import statements in the Hotspot.m file:

```objc
#define centerLat 39.2953
#define centerLong -76.614
#define spanDeltaLat 4.9
#define spanDeltaLong 5.8
#define scaleLat 9.0
#define scaleLong 11.0
```

Next, you need some testing data. Begin by importing Hotspot.h in at the top of your ViewController.m file.

```objc
#import "Hotspot.h"
```

The following two methods generate some 1,000 hotspots for you to use, all within fairly close proximity to each other so that you can see what kind of issue you are working with:

```
-(float)randomFloatFrom:(float)a to:(float)b
{
    float random = ((float) rand()) / (float) RAND_MAX;
    float diff = b - a;
    float r = random * diff;
    return a + r;
}

-(void)generateAnnotations
{
    srand((unsigned)time(0));

    for (int i=0; i<1000; i++)
    {
        CLLocationCoordinate2D randomLocation =
            CLLocationCoordinate2DMake(
                [self randomFloatFrom:37.0 to:42.0],
                [self randomFloatFrom:-72.0 to:-79.0]
            );

        Hotspot *place = [
            [Hotspot alloc]
            initWithCoordinate:randomLocation
            title: [NSString stringWithFormat:@"Place %d title", i]
            subtitle: [NSString stringWithFormat:@"Place %d subtitle", i]
        ];
        [_annotations addObject:place];
    }
}
```

Now that you have your method for generating testing data, you'll make sure to invoke it in your viewDidLoad method, then add the annotations to the map and adjust its region to display them all. Here's the code to do that.

```
- (void)viewDidLoad
{
    [super viewDidLoad];
        // Do any additional setup after loading the view, typically from a nib.
    self.mapView.delegate = self;

    _annotations = [[NSMutableArray alloc] initWithCapacity:1000];

    [self generateAnnotations];
    // The line below is for setup purposes only. It will be unnecessary
    // when grouping is implemented.
    [self.mapView addAnnotations:_annotations];

    CLLocationCoordinate2D centerPoint = {centerLat, centerLong};
    MKCoordinateSpan coordinateSpan = MKCoordinateSpanMake(spanDeltaLat, spanDeltaLong);
```

```
MKCoordinateRegion coordinateRegion =
    MKCoordinateRegionMake(centerPoint, coordinateSpan);

[self.mapView setRegion:coordinateRegion];
[self.mapView regionThatFits:coordinateRegion];
}
```

Finally, you need to implement your map's viewForAnnotation method so that you can correctly display your pins. This code is similar to the one used in the previous recipes, as shown here:

```
- (MKAnnotationView *)mapView:(MKMapView *)mapView viewForAnnotation:(id <MKAnnotation>)annotation
{
    // if it's the user location, just return nil.
    if ([annotation isKindOfClass:[MKUserLocation class]])
        return nil;
        else
    {
        static NSString *startPinId = @"StartPinIdentifier";
        MKPinAnnotationView *startPin =
            (id)[mapView dequeueReusableAnnotationViewWithIdentifier:startPinId];
                if (startPin == nil)
        {
            startPin = [[MKPinAnnotationView alloc]
                        initWithAnnotation:annotation
                        reuseIdentifier:startPinId];
            startPin.canShowCallout = YES;
            startPin.animatesDrop = YES;
        }
        return startPin;
    }
}
```

> **Note**   When adding the mapView:viewForAnnotation: delegate method, you may get a compiler warning saying Local declaration of 'mapView' hides instance variable. This is because the parameter of the method and the mapView property share the same name. While the name clash in this case is not a real problem, you should always try to resolve warnings.
>
> There are two ways to make the warning go away. The easiest is to rename the parameter, but the better way is to rename the property's instance variable. This can be done by explicitly naming it in the @synthesize declaration.
>
> @synthesize mapView = _mapView;
>
> The property is still named mapView, but the underlying instance variable has the conventional underscore prefix and thus no longer is conflicting with delegate parameters.

At this point, if you run the application you should see a view resembling Figure 6-13, a nice illustration of the problem you are trying to solve.

Figure 6-13. *A map with far too many annotations*

Implementing a Solution

To properly iterate through your annotations and group them, you will be going through each pin and determining how it should be placed. If it is close to another pin that has already been dropped, it will be considered "found," and it will be removed from the map. If not, you will add it to the list of those already in the map, and add it to the map itself as an annotation. The following method provides an efficient implementation and should be placed in your view controller's `.m` file:

```
-(void)group:(NSArray *)annotations
{
    float latDelta = self.mapView.region.span.latitudeDelta / scaleLat;
    float longDelta = self.mapView.region.span.longitudeDelta / scaleLong;
    NSMutableArray *visibleAnnotations = [[NSMutableArray alloc] initWithCapacity:0];
```

```
for (Hotspot *current in annotations)
{
    CLLocationDegrees lat = current.coordinate.latitude;
    CLLocationDegrees longi = current.coordinate.longitude;

    bool found = FALSE;
    for (Hotspot *temp in visibleAnnotations)
    {
        if(fabs(temp.coordinate.latitude - lat) < latDelta &&
            fabs(temp.coordinate.longitude - longi) < longDelta)
        {
            [self.mapView removeAnnotation:current];
            found = TRUE;
            break;
        }
    }
    if (!found)
    {
        [visibleAnnotations addObject:current];
        [self.mapView addAnnotation:current];
    }
}
}
```

> **Note**   In this method, you use the `fabs` function. This is different from the `abs` function in that it is specifically used for floats. Using the `abs` function here would result in grouping only at the integer level of coordinates, and your app would not work correctly.

Next, you need to deal with your application's regrouping the points every time the visible section of the map is changed. This is fairly easy to do by implementing the following delegate method:

```
-(void)mapView:(MKMapView *)mapView regionDidChangeAnimated:(BOOL)animated
{
    if (_zoomLevel != mapView.region.span.longitudeDelta)
    {
        [self group:_annotations];
        _zoomLevel = mapView.region.span.longitudeDelta;
    }
}
```

> **Note**   When implementing these methods, make sure that any methods that use the `-group:` method are implemented after it, otherwise the compiler will complain. Another way to solve this problem is to simply declare the `(void)group(NSArray *)annotations` method in your header file or in a private `@interface` section.

Now you can remove the following line from the viewDidLoad method, as its function will be performed by your group: method.

```
[self.mapView addAnnotations:_annotations];
```

You don't need to call the group: method at the end of your viewDidLoad method, because when the map is first displayed, your delegate method -mapView: regionDidChangeAnimated: is called and does the initial grouping automatically.

Upon running the app now, you should see your map populated with significantly fewer annotations, somewhat regularly distributed as in Figure 6-14. When zooming in or out, you can see annotations appear or disappear, respectively, as the map changes.

Figure 6-14. Grouped annotations by location

Adding Color Coding

While your annotations are correctly grouping at this point, you have a new issue. You cannot easily tell whether a single annotation is standing on its own or whether it is encapsulating multiple hotspots. To correct this problem, you can add in functionality to allow hotspots to keep track of the number of other hotspots they represent.

First, you need to go to your Hotspot class and add in a mutable array property, places. You also add a few method definitions that you can use shortly to help manage this array. The following lines need to be added to Hotspot.h:

```
//
//  Hotspot.h
//  Recipe 6.6: Grouping Annotations Dynamically
//

#import <MapKit/MapKit.h>

@interface Hotspot : NSObject<MKAnnotation>
{
    CLLocationCoordinate2D _coordinate;
    NSString * _title;
    NSString * _subtitle;
}

@property (nonatomic) CLLocationCoordinate2D coordinate;
@property (nonatomic, copy) NSString *title;
@property (nonatomic, copy) NSString *subtitle;

@property (nonatomic, strong) NSMutableArray *places;

-(void)addPlace:(Hotspot *)hotspot;
-(int)placesCount;

-(id)initWithCoordinate:(CLLocationCoordinate2D)coordinate title:(NSString *)title
subtitle:(NSString *)subtitle;

@end
```

Not only do you need to implement these methods, but you also need to change your –initWithCoordinate:title:subtitle: method to ensure that your places array is correctly created. You also have to change the title property's getter, so that the callout title shows the number of hotspots represented. Your implementation file now looks like the following (some unchanged getters and setters have been removed for brevity):

```
//
//  Hotspot.m
//  Recipe 6.6: Grouping Annotations Dynamically
//
```

```objc
#import "Hotspot.h"

@implementation Hotspot

-(id)initWithCoordinate:(CLLocationCoordinate2D)coordinate title:(NSString *)title
subtitle:(NSString *)subtitle
{
    self = [super init];
    if (self) {
        self.coordinate = coordinate;
        self.title = title;
        self.subtitle = subtitle;
        self.places = [[NSMutableArray alloc] initWithCapacity:0];
    }
    return self;
}

// ...

-(NSString *)title
{
    if ([self placesCount] == 1)
    {
        return _title;
    }
    else
        return [NSString stringWithFormat:@"%i Places", [self.places count]];
}

-(void)addPlace:(Hotspot *)hotspot
{
    [self.places addObject:hotspot];
}

-(int)placesCount
{
    return [self.places count];
}

-(void)cleanPlaces
{
    [self.places removeAllObjects];
    [self.places addObject:self];
}

@end
```

The foregoing placesCount method is not necessary; it just makes accessing the number of places represented by a single hotspot slightly easier. Your cleanPlaces method is used simply to reset the places array whenever you regroup your annotations. All you have to do now is to add the following two lines to the group: method:

```
-(void)group:(NSArray *)annotations
{
    float latDelta = self.mapView.region.span.latitudeDelta / scaleLat;
    float longDelta = self.mapView.region.span.longitudeDelta / scaleLong;
    [_annotations makeObjectsPerformSelector:@selector(cleanPlaces)];
    NSMutableArray *visibleAnnotations = [[NSMutableArray alloc] initWithCapacity:0];

    for (Hotspot *current in annotations)
    {
        CLLocationDegrees lat = current.coordinate.latitude;
        CLLocationDegrees longi = current.coordinate.longitude;

        bool found = FALSE;
        for (Hotspot *temp in visibleAnnotations)
        {
            if(fabs(temp.coordinate.latitude - lat) < latDelta &&
                fabs(temp.coordinate.longitude - longi) < longDelta)
            {
                [self.mapView removeAnnotation:current];
                found = TRUE;
                [temp addPlace:current];
                break;
            }
        }
        if (!found)
        {
            [visibleAnnotations addObject:current];
            [self.mapView addAnnotation:current];
        }
    }
}
```

Now you have a fairly easy way to determine whether any given hotspot is representing any other hotspot, but only by selecting that specific hotspot. It would be much better if you could easily see which hotspots are groups and which are individuals. To do this, give each hotspot a pointer to its own MKPinAnnotationView. This allows you to control how an annotation is presented based on the number of places it represents. In this case you use this reference to display a red pin for an individual and a green pin for a grouped hotspot.

First, you will add the following property to your Hotspot.h file:

```
@property (nonatomic, strong) MKPinAnnotationView *annotationView;
```

Next you need to tell your map's delegate how to display the pins correctly, as shown in the new version of your viewForAnnotation: method here.

```
- (MKAnnotationView *)mapView:(MKMapView *)mapView viewForAnnotation:(id <MKAnnotation>)annotation
{
    // if it's the user location, just return nil.
    if ([annotation isKindOfClass:[MKUserLocation class]])
        return nil;
        else
    {
        static NSString *startPinId = @"StartPinIdentifier";
        MKPinAnnotationView *startPin =
            (id)[mapView dequeueReusableAnnotationViewWithIdentifier:startPinId];
                if (startPin == nil)
        {
            startPin = [[MKPinAnnotationView alloc]
                        initWithAnnotation:annotation reuseIdentifier:startPinId];
            startPin.canShowCallout = YES;
            startPin.animatesDrop = YES;

            Hotspot *place = annotation;
            place.annotationView = startPin;
            if ([place placesCount] > 1)
            {
                startPin.pinColor = MKPinAnnotationColorGreen;
            }
            else if ([place placesCount] == 1)
            {
                startPin.pinColor = MKPinAnnotationColorRed;
            }
        }

        return startPin;
    }
}
```

This makes all your annotations correctly appear as either green or red, depending on whether they are groups or individualized. However, if you zoom in on a specific green annotation, it will not correctly change color as it goes from a group to an individual. As your final step, to correct this problem, you add code to the mapView:regionDidChangeAnimated: method to change the pin color based on the number of places represented, as shown here:

```
-(void)mapView:(MKMapView *)mapView regionDidChangeAnimated:(BOOL)animated
{
    if (_zoomLevel != mapView.region.span.longitudeDelta)
    {
        [self group:_annotations];
        _zoomLevel = mapView.region.span.longitudeDelta;

        NSSet *visibleAnnotations =
            [mapView annotationsInMapRect:mapView.visibleMapRect];
        for (Hotspot *place in visibleAnnotations)
        {
            if ([place placesCount] > 1)
                place.annotationView.pinColor = MKPinAnnotationColorGreen;
```

```
        else
            place.annotationView.pinColor = MKPinAnnotationColorRed;
    }

  }
}
```

Now, any pins that represent groups of hotspots are green, while individual ones are red, as demonstrated in Figure 6-15.

Figure 6-15. *Grouped annotations with number-specific colors*

Recipe 6-7: Starting Maps from Your App

In iOS 6, a new API called MKMapItem is available that makes it easy to interact with the built-in Maps app. Instead of building your own half-baked map features you can now, with only a couple of lines of code, turn your users over to the one app that specializes in providing maps and directions. For many apps, this makes perfect sense. After all, map support is a nice feature but not the main focus for most apps.

Although it was possible to launch Maps from within your app before iOS 6, doing so required somewhat ugly URL (uniform resource locator) hacking. The new API is native Objective-C and it allows you to do more than what was possible before. Recipe 6-7 shows you the main ingredients.

Let's build a really simple application with three buttons that start Maps in different ways. Start by creating a new single-view application and link the Map Kit and the Core Location frameworks to it. Then add three buttons with the titles "Start Maps With One Placemark," "Start Maps With Multiple Placemarks," and "Start Maps in Directions Mode," respectively, to the view controller's user interface. Your user interface should resemble the one in Figure 6-16.

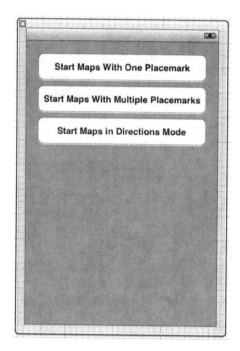

Figure 6-16. User interface for starting Maps in three ways

Now create actions for each of the three buttons. Name the actions startWithOnePlacemark, startWithMultiplePlacemarks, and startInDirectionsMode, respectively.

Adding Map Items

We'll start with the simplest case, launching Maps with a single map item. We'll show you the steps first and then the complete implementation of the startWithOnePlacemark: action method.

First, create a new map item for the location of the famous Big Ben in London. A map item encapsulates a placemark that in turn represents a location coordinate, so start by defining the coordinate.

```
CLLocationCoordinate2D bigBenLocation = CLLocationCoordinate2DMake(51.50065200, -0.12483300);
```

Then we create the placemark.

```
MKPlacemark *bigBenPlacemark =
[[MKPlacemark alloc] initWithCoordinate:bigBenLocation addressDictionary:nil];
```

The address dictionary can be used to provide address information for the placemark to the Maps app. Keep it simple though and send in nil. With the placemark you are ready to create the map item that you will send to the Maps app later.

```
MKMapItem *bigBenItem = [[MKMapItem alloc] initWithPlacemark:bigBenPlacemark];
bigBenItem.name = @"Big Ben";
```

Besides the address dictionary of the placemark object, MKMapItem has properties for providing three additional pieces of information associated with the map item: name, phone, and URL. For Recipe 6-7, name is sufficient.

> **Note**   Often, you'll be dealing with placemarks that you receive from the Core Location framework. These placemarks have a different class (CLPlacemark), than the one in the Map Kit framework (MKPlacemark). However, you can use the initWithPlacemark: method to initialize a Map Kit placemark with one from core location.

Finally, ask Maps to launch with your map item using the openInMapsWithLaunchOptions: method.

```
[bigBenItem openInMapsWithLaunchOptions:nil];
```

With all the pieces together, the complete action method looks like the following:

```
- (IBAction)startWithOnePlacemark:(id)sender
{
    CLLocationCoordinate2D bigBenLocation = CLLocationCoordinate2DMake(51.50065200, -0.12483300);
    MKPlacemark *bigBenPlacemark = [[MKPlacemark alloc]
    initWithCoordinate:bigBenLocation addressDictionary:nil];
    MKMapItem *bigBenItem = [[MKMapItem alloc] initWithPlacemark:bigBenPlacemark];
    bigBenItem.name = @"Big Ben";

    [bigBenItem openInMapsWithLaunchOptions:nil];
}
```

If you build and run now you can press the first button and launch Maps with a pin showing the location of the famous clock tower of London, as in Figure 6-17.

Figure 6-17. Maps launched showing Big Ben

When launching Maps with multiple map items you'll need to use the openMapsWithItems:launch Options: class method of MKMapItem. It takes an array with map items, but the rest is the same.

Go to the next action method, startWithMultiplePlacemarks, and implement the following:

```
- (IBAction)startWithMultiplePlacemarks:(id)sender
{
    CLLocationCoordinate2D bigBenLocation = CLLocationCoordinate2DMake(51.50065200, -0.12483300);
    MKPlacemark *bigBenPlacemark = [[MKPlacemark alloc]
initWithCoordinate:bigBenLocation addressDictionary:nil];
    MKMapItem *bigBenItem = [[MKMapItem alloc] initWithPlacemark:bigBenPlacemark];
    bigBenItem.name = @"Big Ben";

    CLLocationCoordinate2D westminsterLocation =
CLLocationCoordinate2DMake(51.50054300, -0.13570200);
    MKPlacemark *westminsterPlacemark = [[MKPlacemark alloc]
initWithCoordinate:westminsterLocation addressDictionary:nil];
    MKMapItem *westminsterItem = [[MKMapItem alloc]
initWithPlacemark:westminsterPlacemark];
    westminsterItem.name = @"Westminster Abbey";
```

```
    NSArray *items = [[NSArray alloc] initWithObjects:bigBenItem, westminsterItem, nil];
    [MKMapItem openMapsWithItems:items launchOptions:nil];
}
```

If you build and run now you can see two pins, one for Big Ben and one for Westminster Abbey, as in Figure 6-18.

Figure 6-18. Maps launched with two map items

Launching in Directions Mode

A brand-new feature of iOS 6 is providing the user with turn-by-turn directions in the Maps app. From there, the user can select any placemark and ask Maps how to get there by car or by foot. It is possible for your app to employ this great feature to provide value to your users in a more direct way by launching Maps in directions mode. Let's go ahead and do that in the last action.

To start Maps in directions mode, all you need to do is to provide an options dictionary with the MKLaunchOptionsDirectionsModeKey set to either MKLaunchOptionsDirectionsModeWalking or MKLaunchOptionsDirectionsModeDriving. The following code launches Maps in directions mode, showing the walking path between Westminster Abbey and Big Ben, as in Figure 6-19. Add it to the startInDirectionsMode action method so that it gets triggered when the user hits the third button in your app.

Figure 6-19. *Maps launched in directions mode*

```
- (IBAction)startInDirectionsMode:(id)sender
{
    CLLocationCoordinate2D bigBenLocation =
        CLLocationCoordinate2DMake(51.50065200, -0.12483300);
    MKPlacemark *bigBenPlacemark = [[MKPlacemark alloc]
        initWithCoordinate:bigBenLocation addressDictionary:nil];
    MKMapItem *bigBenItem = [[MKMapItem alloc] initWithPlacemark:bigBenPlacemark];
    bigBenItem.name = @"Big Ben";

    CLLocationCoordinate2D westminsterLocation =
        CLLocationCoordinate2DMake(51.50054300, -0.13570200);
    MKPlacemark *westminsterPlacemark = [[MKPlacemark alloc]
        initWithCoordinate:westminsterLocation addressDictionary:nil];
```

```
MKMapItem *westminsterItem = [[MKMapItem alloc]
    initWithPlacemark:westminsterPlacemark];
westminsterItem.name = @"Westminster Abbey";

NSArray *items = [[NSArray alloc] initWithObjects:bigBenItem, westminsterItem, nil];
NSDictionary *options =
    @{MKLaunchOptionsDirectionsModeKey: MKLaunchOptionsDirectionsModeWalking};
[MKMapItem openMapsWithItems:items launchOptions:options];
}
```

When launching in directions mode, Maps takes the first item in the array as the starting point and the last as the destination. However, if the array contains only one placemark, Maps will consider that to be the destination, and the device's current location as the starting point.

But what if you want to find the route *from* a point *to* your current location? That's possible too. MKMapItem provides a way to create a symbolic map item that points out the current location. All you have to do is to add that map to the end of the array of map items. Here's an example that asks Maps for directions from Big Ben to the current location:

```
NSArray *items = [[NSArray alloc]
    initWithObjects:bigBenItem, [MKMapItem mapItemForCurrentLocation], nil];
[MKMapItem openMapsWithItems:items launchOptions:nil];
```

Before finishing this recipe we want to point out that there are more options that can control how Maps will launch—for example, in satellite map mode, or with a specific region. Please refer to Apple's documentation for details about these and other Maps launch options.

Recipe 6-8: Registering a Routing App

The previous recipe used a brand-new API to launch Maps directly from your app. Another new feature of iOS 6 is that it's possible to go the other way around; if your app is a registered Routing app, it may be launched from within Maps.

As an example of how this may work, consider a user who has localized Big Ben as a point of interest in Maps. She now wants to know how to get there by bus, so she presses the directions button and selects the routing mode. She then browses through available Routing apps and discovers one that seems to fit her needs. She selects it and the Routing app is launched by Maps.

Recipe 6-8 shows you how you can register your app as a Routing app.

Declaring a Routing App

For Recipe 6-8 we'll just create a simple dummy app that does nothing more than display the starting point and destination point provided by Maps upon launch. So start by creating a new single-view application and link Map Kit and Core Location frameworks to it.

Next, add a label to the user interface. Make it big enough to contain at least five rows of text. Your main view should look something like the one in Figure 6-20. Also, create an outlet named routingLabel that's connected to the label.

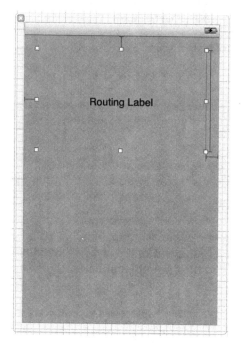

Figure 6-20. *A dummy Routing app with a single label*

To allow your app to be launchable from Maps you need to declare it as a Routing app. This is done in the application's `property list` file, but there's a convenient user interface for it in Xcode.

Select the root node in the Project navigator, select the Summary tab, and scroll down to the Maps section. Now check the Enable Directions control, and because this app doesn't support any of the available transportation types, select Other. (See Figure 6-21.)

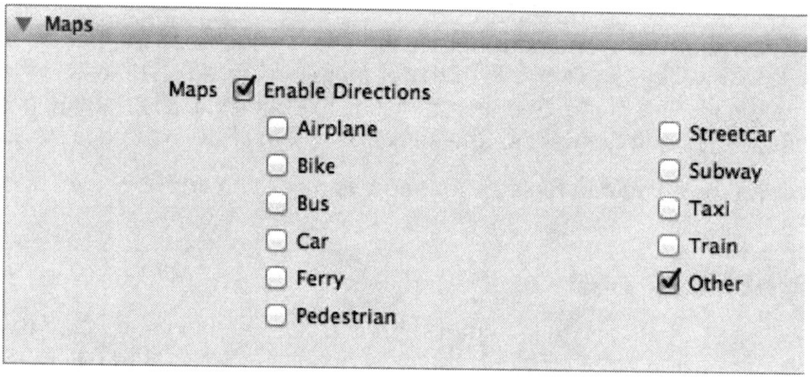

Figure 6-21. *Declaring a Routing app*

Handling Launches

Now that your app is registered as a Routing app, Maps may integrate with it through URL requests. To respond to such a request, add the application:openURL:sourceApplication:annotation: delegate method to your app delegate. Make sure the request is a directions request by using the isDirectionsRequestURL: convenience method of the MKDirectionsRequest class, like so:

```
- (BOOL)application:(UIApplication *)application openURL:(NSURL *)url
sourceApplication:(NSString *)sourceApplication annotation:(id)annotation
{
    if ([MKDirectionsRequest isDirectionsRequestURL:url])
    {
        // Code to handle request goes here

        return YES;
    }

    return NO;
}
```

The request contains a starting point and an end point that your app can use to adjust to the user's needs. You extract the request from the URL using the initWithContentsOfURL: method.

```
- (BOOL)application:(UIApplication *)application openURL:(NSURL *)url
sourceApplication:(NSString *)sourceApplication annotation:(id)annotation
{
    if ([MKDirectionsRequest isDirectionsRequestURL:url])
    {
        MKDirectionsRequest *request = [[MKDirectionsRequest alloc]
            initWithContentsOfURL:url];

        MKMapItem *source = [request source];
        MKMapItem *destination = [request destination];

        return YES;
    }
    return NO;
}
```

For the purpose of Recipe 6-8 we'll simply display these points in the routing label of our application. One important aspect is that any of the provided map items may be the symbolic Current Location item, which won't have an actual placemark attached. You can use the isCurrentLocation property to detect whether that is the case and take appropriate action. In this case you'll just display the text "Current Location."

Here's the final launch response:

```objc
- (BOOL)application:(UIApplication *)application openURL:(NSURL *)url
sourceApplication:(NSString *)sourceApplication annotation:(id)annotation
{
    if ([MKDirectionsRequest isDirectionsRequestURL:url])
    {
        MKDirectionsRequest *request = [[MKDirectionsRequest alloc]
            initWithContentsOfURL:url];

        MKMapItem *source = [request source];
        MKMapItem *destination = [request destination];

        NSString *sourceString;
        NSString *destinationString;

        if (source.isCurrentLocation)
            sourceString = @"Current Location";
        else
            sourceString = [NSString stringWithFormat:@"%f, %f",
                            source.placemark.location.coordinate.latitude,
                            source.placemark.location.coordinate.longitude];

        if (destination.isCurrentLocation)
            sourceString = @"Current Location";
        else
            destinationString = [NSString stringWithFormat:@"%f, %f",
                            destination.placemark.location.coordinate.latitude,
                            destination.placemark.location.coordinate.longitude];

        self.viewController.routingLabel.text =
            [NSString stringWithFormat:@"Start at: %@\nStop at: %@",
             sourceString, destinationString];

        return YES;
    }
    return NO;
}
```

Testing the Routing App

It's time to take your app on a test run. Build and run it in the simulator. When your app launches, click on the home button to close the app. You are going to test a routing between Westminster Abbey and Big Ben in London, so start by setting the current location of the simulator to the coordinates of Westminster Abbey. This can be done in the main menu of the simulator, under Debug ➤ Location ➤ Custom Location..., Enter **51.500543** for Latitude and **-0.135702** for Longitude in the dialog (see Figure 6-22).

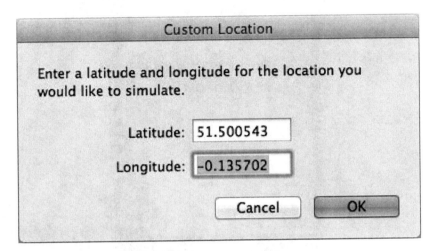

Figure 6-22. Setting a custom location for the simulator

When the custom location has been set, locate and launch the Maps app on the simulator. Enter "Big Ben, London" in the search field and let the Maps app find it. You should eventually see a screen like the one in Figure 6-23 (you'll need to pan a little to the left to get Westminster Abbey within the visible region).

Figure 6-23. The simulator with Big Ben point of interest selected and current location dot at Westminster Abbey

With the Big Ben placemark selected, click the Directions button located to the left of the search field at the top of the Maps app screen, as shown in Figure 6-24.

Figure 6-24. The Directions button of Maps

In the Directions screen, select the Routing apps mode. This is the button that looks like a bus, next to the walking mode button (see Figure 6-25). With the Routing apps mode selected, click the Routing button on the top right-hand side of the screen.

Figure 6-25. Maps Directions screen with the Routing app mode selected

You're now presented with a screen of available Routing apps. If everything is set up correctly, your app should be in the list with a Route button next to it, as in Figure 6-26.

Figure 6-26. Your app as a routing option in Maps

Now, if you tap the Route button, your app will be launched and if you've implemented the `application:openURL:sourceApplication:annotation:` method correctly, your app should look like the one in Figure 6-27.

Figure 6-27. *Your Routing app launched from within Maps*

Specifying Coverage Area

Even though your Routing app successfully integrates with the Maps app, there's actually one essential piece missing; you need to tell Maps in which region your app provides the routing service. This is done using a special file, a GeoJSON file, to declare the geographic coverage area. Maps uses the information to filter among the available Routing apps so that the user won't be flooded with irrelevant choices.

The reason it worked for you without the GeoJSON file is that for testing purposes, all Routing apps installed on the simulator are available and considered valid. However, an app cannot be approved for the App Store without submitting a valid GeoJSON file.

Now create a GeoJSON file for your app. Add a file to the Supporting Files folder in the Project Navigator. Pick the GeoJSON template under the Resource section (see Figure 6-28). Name the file London.geojson. You don't need to add it to the target because it should be submitted with your app and not as part of its bundle.

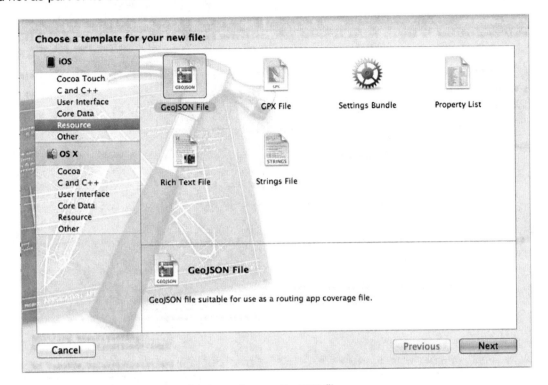

Figure 6-28. You can use the GeoJSON template to create a new GeoJSON file

Make the content of the new file as follows:

```
{
    "type": "MultiPolygon",
    "coordinates": [
                [[[52.257770, -0.989542],
                  [51.001232, -0.943830],
                  [51.050521, 0.303471],
                  [51.848169, 0.362244],
                  [52.257770, -0.989542]]]
                ]
}
```

The numbers in the file represent world coordinates and together they make a closed polygon. Because the polygon must be closed, the first and the last coordinate must also be the same.

You can test your GeoJSON file by pointing it out in your Xcode Scheme for the project. Go to Product ➤ Edit Scheme… in the menu. In the Options page there's a setting for Routing App Coverage file. Click on it and select your GeoJSON file. (See Figure 6-29.)

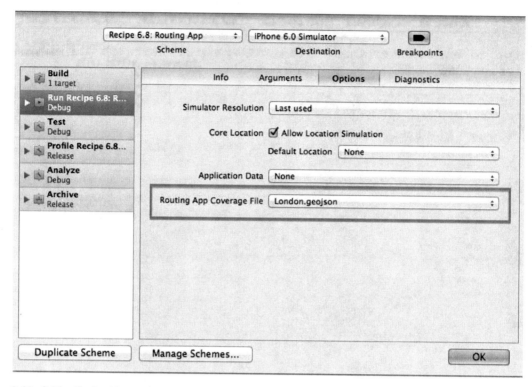

Figure 6-29. Setting the Routing App Coverage file for testing purposes

You now can test whether your file works by selecting points of interests in or out of the coverage area. Be sure to have both the starting and the ending points within the coverage area if you want to test whether your app shows up in the list of available Routing apps.

Note If your app doesn't show up as a choice for routing, as you expect it to, then there might be an error in your GeoJSON file. Check the Console because Maps reports any errors with the GeoJSON file there.

A final note before closing this recipe. When you design your own GeoJSON file, we recommend that you keep it simple. Apple suggests no more than 20 polygons containing at most 20 points each. There is no need to be exact, so a simple bounding rectangle will do in most cases.

Summary

The Map Kit framework is probably one of the most popularly used frameworks, purely for its powerful yet incredibly flexible ability to provide a fully customizable yet simplistic map interface. In this chapter, you have seen the major capabilities of Map Kit, from locating the user to adding annotations and overlays to the new interaction possibilities with Maps. However, you have only scratched the surface of the capabilities of Map Kit, especially in the areas of map-based problem solving. A quick look at the Map Kit documentation[1] reveals the various other commands, methods, and properties you did not cover, which range from isolating particular sections of a map to entirely customizing how touch events are handled by the map. The effectiveness of these countless capabilities is limited only by the developer's imagination.

---

[1]http://developer.apple.com/library/ios/#documentation/MapKit/Reference/MapKit_Framework_Reference.

Chapter 7

Social Network Recipes

Social networking is perhaps the strongest trend on the Internet right now. People with an online presence are sharing and consuming content on one or more of the many sites that offer such services. Because forming communities is part of our nature and the Internet platform makes it so easy, we can be sure the trend will last and get stronger as more and more services join this pattern.

In iOS 6, Apple has introduced the Social Framework, making it easy to integrate your apps with social networks. The framework currently offers support for Facebook, Twitter, and the China-based Weibo networks, but the general nature of the API reveals that more is likely to come in future releases.

> **Note** The Twitter Framework that was introduced in iOS 5 is now deprecated and has been superseded by the Social Framework.

In this chapter we will show you how you can share the content in your app with social networking applications using the convenient UIActivityViewController. We'll also show you how you can implement more advanced integration with Twitter and Facebook using the new Social Framework.

Recipe 7-1: Sharing Content with the Activity View

Most apps are not in the social networking business. However, many that are not do have content that their users would benefit from sharing. Fortunately, Apple has introduced an API that makes this easy. The UIActivityViewController takes the content you provide and presents the user with relevant "activities," such as posting to Facebook or Twitter. In this recipe we'll show you how to set up the UIActivityViewController to share a snippet of text and an URL.

Start by creating a new single-view application. Add a text view, a text field, and a navigation bar to the main view and arrange them so that the main view resembles Figure 7-1. To create the button with the activity icon you see in the upper-right corner of Figure 7-1, drag a bar button to the navigation bar. Then in the Attribute inspector, set the button's Identifier attribute to "Action."

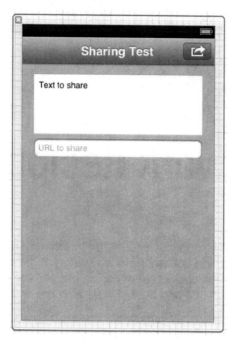

Figure 7-1. A simple user interface for sharing some text and a URL

The text field is used to input URL links, so set its Placeholder attribute to read "URL to share." You may also want to change its Keyboard attribute to "URL" to better match the data that'll be entered there.

As usual you need to reference the edit controls from your code, so create outlets named messageTextView and urlTextField for the text view and the text field, respectively. You also need to create an action for when the user taps the activity button in the navigation bar. Name the action shareContent.

Setting Up an Activity View Controller

Now that you have the user interface set up you can go to ViewController.m to implement the shareContent action method. Add the following code to initialize and present a UIActivityViewController to share the text and the URL:

```objc
- (IBAction)shareContent:(id)sender
{
    NSString *text = self.messageTextView.text;
    NSURL *url = [NSURL URLWithString:self.urlTextField.text];
    NSArray *items = @[text, url];

    UIActivityViewController *vc = [[UIActivityViewController alloc]
        initWithActivityItems:items applicationActivities:nil];
    [self presentViewController:vc animated:YES completion:nil];
}
```

> **Note**   Apple has introduced a new convenient syntax for creating arrays, which we have used in the preceding code. You can now write @[object1, object2] instead of [NSArray arrayWithObjects:object1, object2, nil] as you had to do before Xcode 4.5.

That's it! That's all the code you need for sharing the content on Facebook, Twitter, or any of the other ways Apple provides. You can now build and run the application, enter some text and a URL, and then tap the activity button to bring up the Activity View as shown in Figure 7-2.

Figure 7-2. The built-in Activity View for sharing the content

Once the Activity View is presented you have turned the control of the sharing over to iOS. It uses the accounts that have been set up on the device or asks the user for login details if the accounts haven't been configured. Users new to Facebook, Twitter, or Weibo can even create new accounts and get a seamless experience. And all of this you get with only about five lines of code.

Figure 7-3 shows an example of when a user of this app has selected to share the content to Twitter. The user is allowed to change the text before sending it to the service. She can also change the account (if more than one is available) from which the tweet will be sent. The Facebook integration has a similar sheet in which the user can lay the final touch. However, due to the nature of Facebook, only one account is allowed on any single device.

Figure 7-3. The Tweet sheet in which the user can lay the last touch to the content before it's shared

Excluding Activity View Items

When the Activity View is shown, iOS looks at the content and tries to make an educated guess and only show relevant options. For example, the Weibo service only shows if you have a Chinese keyboard installed.

> **Note**   The number of options also depends on the availability of the services, for example, sending text messages isn't available if you run your app in the iOS Simulator so it won't show up as an option.

In addition to the system limiting options, there may be situations when you want to cut down on the number of options even more yourself. For example, if you know that your users will never email the content, it makes no sense to have that option.

Fortunately, there is a way to exclude items from the Activity View; by using the excludeActivityTypes property of the UIActivityViewController. For instance, if you want to exclude the Mail and the Copy to Pasteboard services, add the following line of code to the shareContent: method:

```
- (IBAction)shareContent:(id)sender
{
    NSString *text = self.messageTextView.text;
    NSURL *url = [NSURL URLWithString:self.urlTextField.text];
    NSArray *items = @[text, url];

    UIActivityViewController *vc = [[UIActivityViewController alloc]
        initWithActivityItems:items applicationActivities:nil];
    vc.excludedActivityTypes = @[UIActivityTypeMail, UIActivityTypeCopyToPasteboard];
    [self presentViewController:vc animated:YES completion:nil];
}
```

If you make the preceding change, and build and run the app again, you'll see (as shown in Figure 7-4) that both Mail and Copy are no longer visible in the Activity View.

Figure 7-4. *The Activity View without Mail and Copy options*

A complete set of valid Activity Types and the type of objects you can send to them as data, can be found in Table 7-1.

Table 7-1. *Activity Types*

Constant	Valid Data Items
UIActivityTypePostToFacebook	NSString, NSAttributedString, UIImage, AVAsset, NSURL
UIActivityTypePostToTwitter	NSString, NSAttributedString, UIImage, AVAsset, NSURL
UIActivityTypePostToWeibo	NSString, NSAttributedString, UIImage, AVAsset, NSURL
UIActivityTypeMessage	NSString, NSAttributedString, NSURL (with the sms: scheme)
UIActivityTypeMail	NSString, UIImage, NSURL (local files, or using the mailto: scheme)
UIActivityTypePrint	UIImage, NSData, NSURL (local files only), UIPrintPageRenderer, UIPrintFormatter, UIPrintInfo
UIActivityTypeCopyToPasteboard	NSString, UIImage, NSURL, UIColor, NSDictionary
UIActivityTypeAssignToContact	UIImage
UIActivityTypeSaveToCameraRoll	UIImage, NSURL (for video)

Including Activity View Items

Excluding items from the Activity View was easy; the contrary, including activities not currently supported in iOS is also possible but requires a little more work on your behalf. What you need to do is to create a subclass of UIActivity to implement the service you want to provide.

To see how that is done we're going to implement a simple logging service that accepts text and URL objects and sends them to stdout (the Standard Output Stream). Start by creating a new subclass of UIActivity with the name MyLogActivity (by going to File ➤ New ➤ File ... and selecting Objective-C class).

In the MyLogActivity.h, add the following property to hold the text message that should be sent to stdout:

```
//
//  MyLogActivity.h
//  Sharing Text
//

#import <UIKit/UIKit.h>

@interface MyLogActivity : UIActivity

@property (strong, nonatomic)NSString *logMessage;

@end
```

You need to add an image to your project to use as the icon for your activity. For best results, use a 72 × 72 PNG image with only white color in combination with the alpha channel to produce a white icon. (Apple doesn't allow multi-color icons for custom activities yet.) You *can* provide an image with no transparency, which is what we did in this example; however, you then get a plain all-white icon (this is shown later in Figure 7-5).

With an icon file imported to your project, you can turn your attention to the implementation of the MyLogActivity class. A UIActivity subclass must provide the following pieces of information:

- *Activity Type:* A unique identifier for the activity, which is not shown to the user. Table 7-1 contains constants for the identifiers of the built-in services.

- *Activity Title:* The title displayed to the user in the Activity View.

- *Activity Image:* The icon displayed along with the title in the Activity View.

- *Can Perform on Activity Items:* Whether the activity can handle the provided data objects.

To provide the preceding information, add the following code to the MyLogActivity.m file:

```
//
//  MyLogActivity.m
//  Sharing Test
//

#import "MyLogActivity.h"

@implementation MyLogActivity

-(NSString *)activityType
{
    return @"MyLogActivity";
}

-(NSString *)activityTitle
{
    return @"Log";
}

-(UIImage *)activityImage
{
    // Replace the file name with the one of the file you imported into your project
    return [UIImage imageNamed:@"log_icon.png"];
}

-(BOOL)canPerformWithActivityItems:(NSArray *)activityItems
{
    for (NSObject *item in activityItems)
    {
        if (![item isKindOfClass:[NSString class]] && ![item isKindOfClass:[NSURL class]])
        {
            return NO;
        }
    }
```

```
    return YES;
}
```

```
@end
```

Then, if your activity has been displayed and the user taps its button, the custom activity class will be sent a prepareWithActivityItems: message. In this case we simply append the content for each item and store the result in the logMessage property. Add the method with the following implementation to the MyLogActivity.m file:

```
-(void)prepareWithActivityItems:(NSArray *)activityItems
{
    self.logMessage = @"";
    for (NSObject *item in activityItems)
    {
        self.logMessage = [NSString stringWithFormat:@"%@\n%@",
                        self.logMessage, item];
    }
}
```

Finally, the activity is asked to perform whatever it's supposed to do. If your custom activity wants to display an additional user interface, like the Twitter activity does with its Tweet sheet, the custom activity should override the activityViewController method of UIActivity.

However, because we're not interested in displaying a user interface for our logging service, we instead override the performActivity method, like so:

```
-(void)performActivity
{
    NSLog(@"%@", self.logMessage);
    [self activityDidFinish:YES];
}
```

Your custom log service is finished and you can now go back to the shareContent: action method in ViewController.m to setup the View Controller to include the new activity. Make the following changes:

```
//
//  ViewController.m
//  Sharing Text
//

#import "ViewController.h"
#import "MyLogActivity.h"

@implementation ViewController

// ...

- (IBAction)shareContent:(id)sender
{
    NSString *text = self.messageTextView.text;
```

```
    NSURL *url = [NSURL URLWithString:self.urlTextField.text];
    NSArray *items = @[text, url];
    MyLogActivity *myLogService = [[MyLogActivity alloc] init];
    NSArray *customServices = @[myLogService];

    UIActivityViewController *vc = [[UIActivityViewController alloc]
        initWithActivityItems:items applicationActivities:customServices];
    vc.excludedActivityTypes = @[UIActivityTypeMail, UIActivityTypeCopyToPasteboard];
    [self presentViewController:vc animated:YES completion:nil];
}

@end
```

If you run the code now and tap the activity button, you'll see, as Figure 7-5 shows, that your Log activity is among the valid options.

Figure 7-5. The Activity View with a custom activity for logging the content on the standard output stream

If you tap the Log icon, you'll see that your content is sent to the standard output stream, as Figure 7-6 shows.

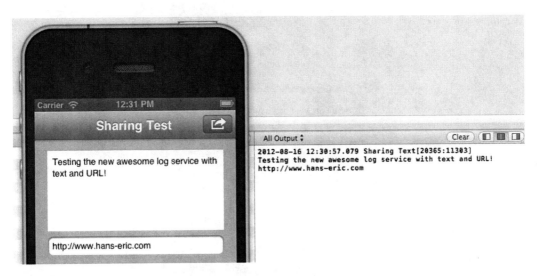

Figure 7-6. The sharing test app after it's sent its content to the custom log activity item

Recipe 7-2: Sharing Content Using a Compose View

The Activity View, as you saw in the previous recipe, provides a standardized way to share content through several different channels. In most cases, this is what you want; the user recognizes the user interface from other apps and can choose to share the content in all the ways that makes sense to her. However, there may be situations when you want your app to provide a more direct sharing experience, without forcing the user to select the service you know she'll pick anyway. For these situations you can use the SLComposeViewController.

The SLComposeViewController currently has support for posting to Facebook, Twitter, and Weibo. In this recipe you build on what you did in Recipe 7-1 and add a button that uses SLComposeViewController to display a compose view populated with the content, and from which the user can post directly to Facebook.

SLComposeViewController resides in the Social Framework, so start by adding it to your project. Then add to the main view a button titled "Post to Facebook." Make the new user interface look something like Figure 7-7.

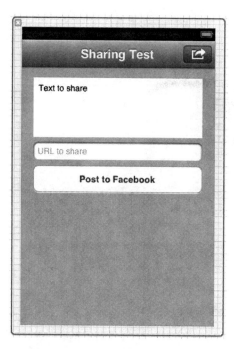

Figure 7-7. A user interface with a button for direct targeting of Facebook sharing

Now, for the Touch up inside event of the new button, create an action named shareOnFacebook. Also, import the Social Framework API in your view controller's header file. It should now look like this:

```
//
//  ViewController.h
//  Sharing Test
//

#import <UIKit/UIKit.h>
#import <Social/Social.h>

@interface ViewController : UIViewController

@property (weak, nonatomic) IBOutlet UITextView *messageTextView;
@property (weak, nonatomic) IBOutlet UITextField *urlTextField;

- (IBAction)shareContent:(id)sender;
- (IBAction)shareOnFacebook:(id)sender;

@end
```

Finally, implement the shareOnFacebook: action method. Here's the code to do that:

```
//
//  ViewController.m
//  Sharing Text
//

#import "ViewController.h"
#import "MyLogActivity.h"

@implementation ViewController

// ...

- (IBAction)shareOnFacebook:(id)sender
{
    NSString *text = self.messageTextView.text;
    NSURL *url = [NSURL URLWithString:self.urlTextField.text];

    SLComposeViewController *cv =
        [SLComposeViewController composeViewControllerForServiceType:SLServiceTypeFacebook];
    [cv setInitialText:text];
    [cv addURL:url];

    [self presentViewController:cv animated:YES completion:nil];
}

@end
```

> **Note** Besides URL objects, the Compose View also supports the adding of image objects via the addImage: method.

As you can see, you initialize the Compose View with the text from the text view and the URL from the text field. If you build and run the project now and tap the Post to Facebook button, you'll be presented with a Facebook Compose sheet from which you can post the content to your Facebook account. Like with the Activity View, you get all the built-in integration for free, so if a user doesn't have an account installed she's asked whether she wants to set one up. Figure 7-8 shows an example of this.

Figure 7-8. If the user has no account for the selected service, iOS asks whether one should be setup

In this example you initialized the Compose View to target Facebook. The code for setting up Twitter or Weibo is nearly identical. The only thing you need to do is to replace the SLServiceTypeFacebook constant with SLServiceTypeTwitter or SLServiceTypeWeibo, respectively, for example:

```
SLComposeViewController *cv =
    [SLComposeViewController composeViewControllerForServiceType:SLServiceTypeTwitter];
```

Recipe 7-3: Sharing Content Using SLRequest

In Recipes 7-1 and 7-2 you've learned how to use the built-in user interfaces for sharing content. For some apps, however, it makes sense to build a completely customized user interface; for example if you're planning to build the best Twitter or Facebook app ever, or maybe your users aren't interested in the last touch editing possibility that the built-in Compose views are offering, maybe they would benefit from a more automatic posting experience.

These apps want to use the native API of the respective Social Network service. Fortunately, iOS 6 offers a great help in the SLRequest API. It takes care of the complicated authentication handling for you, making your job a lot easier.

In this recipe we'll show you how to send a tweet using SLRequest. You'll need a new single-view application project. You're also going to use two external frameworks, the Social Framework and the Accounts Framework, which are used by the Social Framework to handle authorizations. Make sure you link their binaries to your project before you go on.

Setting Up the Main View

Start by setting up the user interface so that it resembles Figure 7-9. You'll need a text view, a button, and a label.

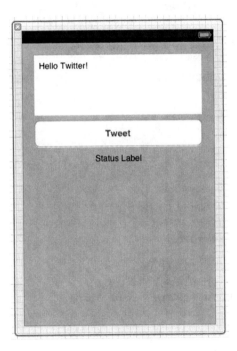

Figure 7-9. A simple user interface for posting to Twitter

Create outlets named textView and statusLabel for the text view and the label, respectively. Also, create an action named shareOnTwitter for the button. Finally, import the Social and the Accounts Framework APIs. Your ViewController.h should now look like this code:

```
//
//  ViewController.h
//  Twitter Integration
//
```

```
#import <UIKit/UIKit.h>
#import <Social/Social.h>
#import <Accounts/Accounts.h>

@interface ViewController : UIViewController

@property (weak, nonatomic) IBOutlet UITextView *textView;
@property (weak, nonatomic) IBOutlet UILabel *statusLabel;

- (IBAction)shareOnTwitter:(id)sender;

@end
```

Requesting Access to Twitter Accounts

The first thing you'll need to do when preparing an SLRequest object is to request access to the account type in question. For this you need an ACAccountStore instance. What's important with this instance is that it needs to stay alive through the whole process of sending requests. The easiest way to do that is to assign it to a property where it'll be retained.

Add the following property declaration to your ViewController.h file:

```
//
//  ViewController.h
//  Twitter Integration
//

#import <UIKit/UIKit.h>
#import <Social/Social.h>
#import <Accounts/Accounts.h>

@interface ViewController : UIViewController

@property (weak, nonatomic) IBOutlet UITextView *textView;
@property (weak, nonatomic) IBOutlet UILabel *statusLabel;
@property (strong, nonatomic) ACAccountStore *accountStore;

- (IBAction)shareOnTwitter:(id)sender;

@end
```

Now you can start implementing shareOnTwitter: action method in ViewController.m. Begin by adding the following code to request access to the Twitter accounts registered on the device:

```
- (IBAction)shareOnTwitter:(id)sender
{
    self.accountStore = [[ACAccountStore alloc] init];

    ACAccountType *accountType =
        [self.accountStore accountTypeWithAccountTypeIdentifier:ACAccountTypeIdentifierTwitter];

    [self.accountStore requestAccessToAccountsWithType:accountType options:nil
```

```
    completion:^(BOOL granted, NSError *error)
    {
        if (granted)
        {
            //TODO: Get Twitter account and send tweet to it
        }
        else
        {
            //TODO: Handle not granted
        }
    }
];
}
```

What's interesting here is the `requestAccessToAccountsWithType:options:completion:` method. It's asynchronous so you provide a block which will be invoked when the method is finished. You then know whether the request was granted by checking the argument with the same name.

If access to the Twitter accounts was denied, just update the status label. However, the fact that you are in a code block complicates things a bit. The problem is that the completion block may be invoked on any arbitrary thread, but you shouldn't update user interface from anything but the main thread.

So, to handle that, use the `dispatch_async` function, which also takes a code block argument, to perform the updating of the status label from the main thread:

```
[self.accountStore requestAccessToAccountsWithType:accountType options:nil
completion:^(BOOL granted, NSError *error)
{
    __block NSString *statusText = @"";

    if (granted)
    {
        //TODO: Get Twitter account and send tweet to it
    }
    else
    {
        statusText = @"Access to Twitter accounts was not granted";
    }

    dispatch_async(dispatch_get_main_queue(), ^(void)
    {
        self.statusLabel.text = statusText;
    });
}
```

If access were granted, though, you can use the `accountsWithAccountType` method of the Account Store to get an array of available accounts. A user may have several Twitter accounts installed on the device and later you will add code that allows her to choose which one to use, but for now you are going to make it simple and grab the first in the list:

```
- (IBAction)shareOnTwitter:(id)sender
{
    self.accountStore = [[ACAccountStore alloc] init];
```

```
ACAccountType *accountType =
    [self.accountStore accountTypeWithAccountTypeIdentifier:ACAccountTypeIdentifierTwitter];

[self.accountStore requestAccessToAccountsWithType:accountType options:nil
 completion:^(BOOL granted, NSError *error)
 {
     __block NSString *statusText = @"";

     if (granted)
     {
         NSArray *availableTwitterAccounts =
             [self.accountStore accountsWithAccountType:accountType];

         if (availableTwitterAccounts.count == 0)
         {
             statusText = @"No Twitter accounts available";
         }
         else
         {
             ACAccount *account = [availableTwitterAccounts objectAtIndex:0];
             [self sendText:self.textView.text toTwitterAccount:account];
         }
     }
     else
     {
         statusText = @"Access to Twitter accounts was not granted";
     }

     dispatch_async(dispatch_get_main_queue(), ^(void)
     {
         self.statusLabel.text = statusText;
     });
 }];
}
```

The actual posting to Twitter is performed by the sendText:toTwitterAccount: helper method. It's actually the core of this recipe so we'll explain its parts.

First, it builds an SLRequest object for the operation. In this case you are going to ask Twitter to update the status text:

```
- (void)sendText:(NSString *)text toTwitterAccount:(ACAccount *)twitterAccount
{
    NSURL *requestURL = [NSURL URLWithString:@"http://api.twitter.com/1/statuses/update.json"];
    SLRequest *tweetRequest = [SLRequest requestForServiceType:SLServiceTypeTwitter
        requestMethod:SLRequestMethodPOST URL:requestURL
        parameters:[NSDictionary dictionaryWithObject:text forKey:@"status"]];

    // ...
}
```

Next, it assigns the account to the request. This step is really important because it's what allows the Service Framework to handle all the authentication communication with Twitter.

```
- (void)sendText:(NSString *)text toTwitterAccount:(ACAccount *)twitterAccount
{
    NSURL *requestURL = [NSURL URLWithString:@"http://api.twitter.com/1/statuses/update.json"];
    SLRequest *tweetRequest = [SLRequest requestForServiceType:SLServiceTypeTwitter
        requestMethod:SLRequestMethodPOST URL:requestURL
        parameters:[NSDictionary dictionaryWithObject:text forKey:@"status"]];

    [tweetRequest setAccount:twitterAccount];

    // ...
}
```

Then it sends the request asynchronously and provides a code block that will be invoked on completion. As you can see, this block uses the same technique for updating the status label as you saw previously.

```
- (void)sendText:(NSString *)text toTwitterAccount:(ACAccount *)twitterAccount
{
    NSURL *requestURL = [NSURL URLWithString:@"http://api.twitter.com/1/statuses/update.json"];
    SLRequest *tweetRequest = [SLRequest requestForServiceType:SLServiceTypeTwitter
        requestMethod:SLRequestMethodPOST URL:requestURL
        parameters:[NSDictionary dictionaryWithObject:text forKey:@"status"]];

    [tweetRequest setAccount:twitterAccount];

    [tweetRequest performRequestWithHandler:
     ^(NSData *responseData, NSHTTPURLResponse *urlResponse, NSError *error)
     {
         __block NSString *status;

         if ([urlResponse statusCode] == 200)
         {
             status = [NSString stringWithFormat:@"Tweeted successfully to %@",
                 twitterAccount.accountDescription];
         }
         else
         {
             status = @"Error occurred!";
             NSLog(@"%@", error);
         }

         dispatch_async(dispatch_get_main_queue(), ^(void)
         {
             self.statusLabel.text = status;
         });
     }];
}
```

> **Note**   As shown in the preceding method, you can evaluate the results of a SLRequest by checking
> the statusCode of the urlResponse. If this value is 200, the request was successfully completed.
> Otherwise, there was some sort of error. Refer to the Twitter API at
> https://dev.twitter.com/docs/error-codes-responses for specific details on all the
> various error codes.

If you build and run now (and have at least one Twitter account set up on the device) you should, as
Figure 7-10 shows, be able to tweet from your app.

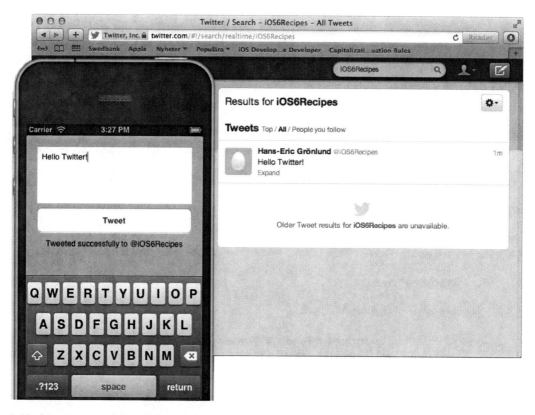

Figure 7-10. A tweet successfully sent from the app

Handling Multiple Accounts

What if the user has more than one Twitter account setup on the device? Currently this app uses the
first in the list, but you are going to add a feature to it that allows the user to actually choose which
to use.

You are going to use an Alert View to present the available accounts from which the user will pick
one. So the first thing you need to do is to promote the availableTwitterAccounts array, which is

currently a local variable in the shareOnTwitter: method, into an instance variable. You'll need to reference that array from the delegate method of the Alert View. You'll also need to make the view controller an Alert View Delegate by adding the UIAlertViewDelegate protocol to your view controller class. To do these things, add the following code to your ViewController.h file:

```
//
//  ViewController.h
//  Twitter Integration
//

#import <UIKit/UIKit.h>
#import <Social/Social.h>
#import <Accounts/Accounts.h>

@interface ViewController : UIViewController<UIAlertViewDelegate>
{
    @private
    NSArray *availableTwitterAccounts;
}

@property (weak, nonatomic) IBOutlet UITextView *textView;
@property (weak, nonatomic) IBOutlet UILabel *statusLabel;
@property (strong, nonatomic) ACAccountStore *accountStore;

- (IBAction)shareOnTwitter:(id)sender;

@end
```

And in the shareOnTwitter: method in ViewController.m, make the following changes:

```
- (IBAction)shareOnTwitter:(id)sender
{
    self.accountStore = [[ACAccountStore alloc] init];

    ACAccountType *accountType =
        [self.accountStore accountTypeWithAccountTypeIdentifier:ACAccountTypeIdentifierTwitter];

    [self.accountStore requestAccessToAccountsWithType:accountType options:nil
     completion:^(BOOL granted, NSError *error)
     {
         __block NSString *statusText = @"";

         if (granted)
         {
             availableTwitterAccounts = [self.accountStore accountsWithAccountType:accountType];

             if (availableTwitterAccounts.count == 0)
             {
                 statusText = @"No Twitter accounts available";
             }
```

```
                    if (availableTwitterAccounts.count == 1)
                    {
                        ACAccount *account = [availableTwitterAccounts objectAtIndex:0];
                        [self sendText:self.textView.text toTwitterAccount:account];
                    }
                    else if (availableTwitterAccounts.count > 1)
                    {
                        dispatch_async(dispatch_get_main_queue(), ^(void)
                        {
                            UIAlertView *alert =
                                [[UIAlertView alloc] initWithTitle:@"Select Twitter Account"
                                    message:@"Select the Twitter account you want to use."
                                    delegate:self
                                    cancelButtonTitle:@"Cancel"
                                    otherButtonTitles:nil];

                            for (ACAccount *twitterAccount in availableTwitterAccounts)
                            {
                                [alert addButtonWithTitle:twitterAccount.accountDescription];
                            }

                            [alert show];
                        });
                    }
                }
                else
                {
                    statusText = @"Access to Twitter accounts was not granted";
                }

                dispatch_async(dispatch_get_main_queue(), ^(void)
                {
                    self.statusLabel.text = statusText;
                });
        }];
}
```

Note that you are wrapping the Alert View in the same dispatch_async() call as you did with the updating of the status label. The reason is the same, Alert Views must run on the main thread or you may experience problems.

The only thing left now is to respond to when the user selects one of the accounts in the Alert View. Do that by adding the following delegate method:

```
-(void)alertView:(UIAlertView *)alertView clickedButtonAtIndex:(NSInteger)buttonIndex
{
    if (buttonIndex == 0)
    {
        // User Canceled
        return;
    }
```

```
    NSInteger indexInAvailableTwitterAccountsArray = buttonIndex - 1;
    ACAccount *selectedAccount = [availableTwitterAccounts
                                    objectAtIndex:indexInAvailableTwitterAccountsArray];
    [self sendText:self.textView.text toTwitterAccount:selectedAccount];
}
```

Before you build and run your app again, make sure you have more than one Twitter account set up on the device (or the iOS Simulator). Then the next time you tap the Tweet button, you'll get to choose which of your accounts to send the tweet to. Figure 7-11 shows an example of the Alert View.

Figure 7-11. *An Alert View that allows the user to pick the Twitter account to post to*

Recipe 7-4: Retrieving Tweets

Now that you have covered several different methods with which you can post updates to Twitter, you can apply the concepts used in the previous recipe, revolving around the SLRequest class, to build an application that can acquire and display tweets.

You build a simple Twitter reader app that allows the user to view the recent tweets from the public Twitter timeline, or from the Twitter accounts she has installed on the device. You set up an application consisting of a Navigation Controller in combination with Table View Controllers for the basic tweet navigation.

Setting Up a Navigation-Based Application

Start by setting up the new project from scratch. This time use the Empty Application template. You can name the project "My Tweet Reader."

As in the previous recipe you use both the Social and the Accounts Framework so go ahead and link those to your project.

Next, you're going to create the main view controller. It displays a list of Twitter Feeds, so create a new UITableViewController class with the name MainTableViewController. You do not need a .xib file to design any user interface, so be sure the option "With XIB for user interface" is unchecked.

Before you go on to implement the new view controller, you're going to go to the App Delegate to hook it up with a Navigation Controller. Open the AppDelegate.h file and add a property for the Navigation Controller:

```
//
//  AppDelegate.h
//  My Tweet Reader
//

#import <UIKit/UIKit.h>

@interface AppDelegate : UIResponder <UIApplicationDelegate>

@property (strong, nonatomic) UIWindow *window;
@property (strong, nonatomic) UINavigationController *navigationController;

@end
```

Then, in AppDelegate.m make the following changes:

```
//
//  AppDelegate.m
//  My Tweet Reader
//

#import "AppDelegate.h"
#import "MainTableViewController.h"

@implementation AppDelegate

- (BOOL)application:(UIApplication *)application didFinishLaunchingWithOptions:(NSDictionary *)launchOptions
```

```
{
    self.window = [[UIWindow alloc] initWithFrame:[[UIScreen mainScreen] bounds]];
    // Override point for customization after application launch.
    UITableViewController *mainViewController =
        [[MainTableViewController alloc] initWithStyle:UITableViewStyleGrouped];
    self.navigationController =
        [[UINavigationController alloc] initWithRootViewController:mainViewController];
    self.window.rootViewController = self.navigationController;
    [self.window makeKeyAndVisible];
    return YES;
}

// ...

@end
```

Displaying Available Feeds

Now, with the Navigation Controller and the Main Table View Controller hooked up, you can start implementing the Table View. It displays a number of Twitter feeds that the user may choose to view. In this recipe, you add the public Twitter feed and the feeds of the currently installed Twitter accounts.

To retrieve the installed accounts, you need an Account Store and an array to store the available accounts. Go to MainTableViewController.h and add the following declarations:

```
//
//  MainTableViewController.h
//  My Tweet Reader
//

#import <UIKit/UIKit.h>
#import <Accounts/Accounts.h>

@interface MainTableViewController : UITableViewController

@property (strong, nonatomic) ACAccountStore *accountStore;
@property (strong, nonatomic) NSArray *twitterAccounts;

@end
```

Now, go to MainTableViewController.m and add the following code to the viewDidLoad method:

```
- (void)viewDidLoad
{
    [super viewDidLoad];

    self.navigationItem.title = @"My Twitter Reader";
    self.accountStore = [[ACAccountStore alloc] init];
    [self retrieveAccounts];
}
```

In the `retrieveAccounts` helper method we're going to ask for permissions to access the Twitter accounts. Here's the implementation, which you might recognize from the previous recipe:

```
- (void)retrieveAccounts
{
    ACAccountType *accountType =
        [self.accountStore accountTypeWithAccountTypeIdentifier:ACAccountTypeIdentifierTwitter];

    [self.accountStore requestAccessToAccountsWithType:accountType options:nil
                                        completion:^(BOOL granted, NSError *error)
    {
        if (granted)
        {
            self.twitterAccounts = [self.accountStore accountsWithAccountType:accountType];
            dispatch_async(dispatch_get_main_queue(), ^(void)
                {
                    [self.tableView reloadData];
                });
        }
    }];
}
```

Next, implement the following Table View Data Source delegate methods that let the Table View know how many cells it should display. You are use only one section in which you display the public feed plus the available Twitter accounts:

```
- (NSInteger)numberOfSectionsInTableView:(UITableView *)tableView
{
    // Return the number of sections.
    return 1;
}

- (NSInteger)tableView:(UITableView *)tableView numberOfRowsInSection:(NSInteger)section
{
    // Return the number of rows in the section.
    return 1 + self.twitterAccounts.count;
}
```

Next, you're going to create a Table View Cell class that displays the items in the Table View. Create a new UITableViewCell class and name it `TwitterFeedCell`. Then open the header file of the new class and add the following code:

```
//
//  TwitterFeedCell.h
//  My Tweet Reader
//

#import <UIKit/UIKit.h>
#import <Accounts/Accounts.h>

extern NSString * const TwitterFeedCellId;
```

```
@interface TwitterFeedCell : UITableViewCell

@property (strong, nonatomic)ACAccount *twitterAccount;

@end
```

You're going to set up a very simple cell with the default look. However, you're going to add a disclosure indicator that signals to the user that there's a detailed view waiting if she taps the cell. Open the TwitterFeedCell.m file and make the following change to the initWithStyle:reuseIdentifier: method that Xcode generated for you:

```
- (id)initWithStyle:(UITableViewCellStyle)style reuseIdentifier:(NSString *)reuseIdentifier
{
    self = [super initWithStyle:style reuseIdentifier:reuseIdentifier];
    if (self) {
        // Initialization code
        self.accessoryType = UITableViewCellAccessoryDisclosureIndicator;
    }
    return self;
}
```

You'll also set up the reuse constant that you'll use later to "dequeue" cells from the cell cache of the Table View. Add the following lines of code:

```
//
//  TwitterFeedCell.m
//  My Tweet Reader
//

#import "TwitterFeedCell.h"

NSString * const TwitterFeedCellId = @"TwitterFeedCell";

@implementation TwitterFeedCell

// ...

@end
```

Finally, you'll add a custom setter method for the twitterAccount property. The setter sets the property, but also updates the label text of the cell. If the account property is nil, you are going to assume that the cell is representing the public Twitter feed. Here's the implementation of the setter:

```
- (void)setTwitterAccount:(ACAccount *)account
{
    _twitterAccount = account;
    if (_twitterAccount)
    {
        self.textLabel.text = _twitterAccount.accountDescription;
    }
```

```
    else
    {
        self.textLabel.text = @"Public";
    }
}
```

With the cell class finished you can go back to the Main Table View Controller to finish the implementation. First, you'll need to register the TwitterFeedCell class with the Table View. You can do that in the viewDidLoad method, like so:

```
//
//  MainTableViewController.m
//  My Tweet Reader
//

#import "MainTableViewController.h"
#import "TwitterFeedCell.h"

@implementation MainTableViewController

// ...

- (void)viewDidLoad
{
    [super viewDidLoad];

    [self.tableView registerClass:TwitterFeedCell.class
        forCellReuseIdentifier:TwitterFeedCellId];

    self.navigationItem.title = @"Twitter Feeds";
    self.accountStore = [[ACAccountStore alloc] init];
    [self retrieveAccounts];
}

// ...

@end
```

Now, you can implement the creation of the cells in the tableView:cellForRowAtIndexPath: delegate method:

```
- (UITableViewCell *)tableView:(UITableView *)tableView
cellForRowAtIndexPath:(NSIndexPath *)indexPath
{
    TwitterFeedCell *cell =
        [tableView dequeueReusableCellWithIdentifier:TwitterFeedCellId forIndexPath:indexPath];
    // Configure the cell...
    if (indexPath.row == 0)
    {
        // Public Feed
        cell.twitterAccount = nil;
    }
```

```
    else
    {
        cell.twitterAccount = [self.twitterAccounts objectAtIndex:indexPath.row - 1];
    }

    return cell;
}
```

If you build and run your app now, you should see a screen similar to the one in Figure 7-12.

Figure 7-12. A simple Twitter Reader displaying three available Twitter Feeds

Displaying Tweets

With the main view in place and working you can move on to add another view to display the selected timeline. You also implement this view with a Table View, so begin by creating a new UITableViewController class; this time with the name TweetTableViewController. Again you do not need an .xib file for the user interface, so leave that option unselected.

The new view takes a Twitter account and displays its timeline in the Table View. You'll start by setting up the header file. Add the following to TweetTableViewController.h:

```
//
//  TweetTableViewController.h
//  My Tweet Reader
//

#import <UIKit/UIKit.h>
#import <Accounts/Accounts.h>
#import <Social/Social.h>

@interface TweetTableViewController : UITableViewController

@property (strong, nonatomic) ACAccount *twitterAccount;
@property (strong, nonatomic) NSMutableArray *tweets;

-(id)initWithTwitterAccount:(ACAccount *)account;

@end
```

In the implementation file you'll start by implementing the initialization methods:

```
- (id)initWithStyle:(UITableViewStyle)style
{
    self = [super initWithStyle:style];
    if (self) {
        // Custom initialization
        self.tweets = [[NSMutableArray alloc] initWithCapacity:50];
    }
    return self;
}

-(id)initWithTwitterAccount:(ACAccount *)account
{
    self = [self initWithStyle:UITableViewStylePlain];
    if (self) {
        self.twitterAccount = account;
    }
    return self;
}
```

As you'll see later, you use the initWithTwitterAccount: method to set up the view controller. However, by separating the initialization in two methods, you make sure the view controller works in a default setup scenario as well (using the initWithStyle: method).

Now, in the viewDidLoad method you update the title of the Navigation Bar and order a retrieving of the timeline.

```
- (void)viewDidLoad
{
    [super viewDidLoad];

    if (self.twitterAccount)
    {
        self.navigationItem.title = self.twitterAccount.accountDescription;
    }
    else
    {
        self.navigationItem.title = @"Public Tweets";
    }
    [self retrieveTweets];
}
```

The retrieveTweets method holds the essence of this recipe. It's the one that retrieves the tweets from the given Twitter feed. The Twitter feed can be either the home timeline of a Twitter account, or the public timeline of Twitter. Here is the method's implementation:

```
-(void)retrieveTweets
{
    [self.tweets removeAllObjects];

    SLRequest *request;

    if (self.twitterAccount)
    {
        // Get home timeline of the Twitter account
        NSURL *requestURL =
            [NSURL URLWithString:@"http://api.twitter.com/1/statuses/home_timeline.json"];
        request = [SLRequest requestForServiceType:SLServiceTypeTwitter
            requestMethod:SLRequestMethodGET URL:requestURL parameters:nil];
        [request setAccount:self.twitterAccount];
    }
    else
    {
        // Get the public timeline of Twitter
        NSURL *requestURL =
            [NSURL URLWithString:@"http://api.twitter.com/1/statuses/public_timeline.json"];
        request = [SLRequest requestForServiceType:SLServiceTypeTwitter
            requestMethod:SLRequestMethodGET URL:requestURL parameters:nil];
    }

    [request performRequestWithHandler:
    ^(NSData *responseData, NSHTTPURLResponse *urlResponse, NSError *error)
     {
        if ([urlResponse statusCode] == 200)
        {
            NSError *jsonParsingError;
            self.tweets = [NSJSONSerialization JSONObjectWithData:responseData
                options:0 error:&jsonParsingError];
        }
```

```
            else
            {
                NSLog(@"HTTP response status: %i\n", [urlResponse statusCode]);
            }
            dispatch_async(dispatch_get_main_queue(), ^(void)
                        {
                            [self.tableView reloadData];
                        });
    }];
}
```

Note that the response from Twitter comes in a JSON format, which you decode using the NSJSONSerialization class. The result is an array of dictionaries, one for each tweet.

Note If you are unsure of the format of your JSON data retrieved from Twitter, you can simply take the URL used to make your request and enter it in your web browser. You will receive a text view of the exact same data your code would have gotten. It can be a little difficult to read due to a lack of space formatting, but you can look for the necessary layers of content needed to build your application.

With the data in place you can start implementing the Table View to display it. As in the main Table View, you are going to have only one section. It contains the recent tweets, so make the following changes to the numberOfSectionsInTableView: and the tableView:numberOfRowsInSection: methods:

```
- (NSInteger)numberOfSectionsInTableView:(UITableView *)tableView
{
    // Return the number of sections.
    return 1;
}
```

```
- (NSInteger)tableView:(UITableView *)tableView numberOfRowsInSection:(NSInteger)section
{
    // Return the number of rows in the section.
    return self.tweets.count;
}
```

Because the cells in this Table View have a slightly different look and content than the ones in the main Table View, you need to create a new UITableViewCell subclass. This time, name the class TweetCell.

Open TweetCell.h and make the following changes:

```
//
//  TweetCell.h
//  My Tweet Reader
//
```

```
#import <UIKit/UIKit.h>

NSString * const TweetCellId = @"TweetCell";

@interface TweetCell : UITableViewCell

@property (strong, nonatomic)NSDictionary *tweetData;

@end
```

This cell type uses the standard look with a subtitle and a disclosure indicator. Make these changes to the initWithStyle:reuseIdentifier: method (in the TweetCell.m file):

```
- (id)initWithStyle:(UITableViewCellStyle)style reuseIdentifier:(NSString *)reuseIdentifier
{
    self = [super initWithStyle:UITableViewCellStyleSubtitle reuseIdentifier:reuseIdentifier];
    if (self)
    {
        // Initialization code
        self.accessoryType = UITableViewCellAccessoryDisclosureIndicator;
    }
    return self;
}
```

The cell updates its labels when it receives new tweet data. To accomplish that you'll add a custom setter method for the tweetData property, like so:

```
-(void)setTweetData:(NSDictionary *)tweetData
{
    _tweetData = tweetData;
    // Update cell
    NSDictionary *userData = [_tweetData objectForKey:@"user"];
    self.textLabel.text = [userData objectForKey:@"name"];
    self.detailTextLabel.text = [_tweetData objectForKey:@"text"];
}
```

Now, let's complete the implementation of the Table View. Go back to TweetTableViewController.m and make the following changes:

```
//
//  TweetTableViewController.m
//  My Tweet Reader
//

#import "TweetTableViewController.h"
#import "TweetCell.h"

@implementation TweetTableViewController
```

```
- (void)viewDidLoad
{
    [super viewDidLoad];

    [self.tableView registerClass:TweetCell.class forCellReuseIdentifier:TweetCellId];

    if (self.twitterAccount)
    {
        self.navigationItem.title = self.twitterAccount.accountDescription;
    }
    else
    {
        self.navigationItem.title = @"Public Tweets";
    }
    [self retrieveTweets];
}

// ...

- (UITableViewCell *)tableView:(UITableView *)tableView cellForRowAtIndexPath:(NSIndexPath *)
indexPath
{
    TweetCell *cell = [tableView dequeueReusableCellWithIdentifier:TweetCellId
forIndexPath:indexPath];
    // Configure the cell...
    cell.tweetData = [self.tweets objectAtIndex:indexPath.row];

    return cell;
}

// ...

@end
```

You're done for now with the Tweet Table View, let's go back to the main Table View and implement the code that displays the new view controller. Open MainTableViewController.m and make the following changes to the tableView:didSelectRowAtIndexPath: delegate method:

```
- (void)tableView:(UITableView *)tableView didSelectRowAtIndexPath:(NSIndexPath *)indexPath
{
    // Navigation logic may go here. Create and push another view controller.
    ACAccount *account = nil;
    if (indexPath.row > 0)
    {
        account = [self.twitterAccounts objectAtIndex:indexPath.row - 1];
    }
    TweetTableViewController *detailViewController =
        [[TweetTableViewController alloc] initWithTwitterAccount:account];

    // Pass the selected object to the new view controller.
    [self.navigationController pushViewController:detailViewController animated:YES];
}
```

Don't forget to import the `TweetTableViewController.h` file:

```
#import "TweetTableViewController.h"
```

It's time again to build and run your app. This time you should be able to select one of the timelines and get a list of the most recent tweets. Figure 7-13 shows an example of this new Table View.

Figure 7-13. A simple tweet reader app displaying the public tweets feed of Twitter

Showing Individual Tweets

When the user taps a tweet cell, you want to display a detailed view of that tweet. This will be a simple view controller, so create a new `UIViewController` subclass with the name `TweetViewController`. This time, however, you'll build its user interface in Interface Builder so make sure to select the "With XIB for user interface" option.

Open the new `TweetViewController.xib` file to bring up Interface Builder. The first thing you're going to do is to make sure you design the user interface with the Navigation Bar in mind. Select the view and go to the Attribute inspector. In the Simulated Metrics section, change the value of the Top Bar attribute from "None" to "Navigation Bar" (see Figure 7-14). This displays a Navigation Bar in the view, which is helpful when you're creating your layout.

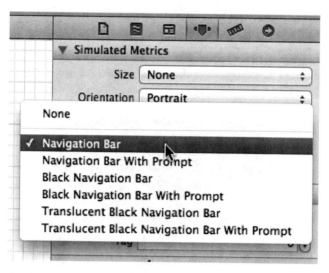

Figure 7-14. Simulating a Navigation Bar to help in user interface design

While you're still in the Attribute inspector for the view, go to the View section and change the background color to Light Grey. It makes a better contrast against the text view that you'll add in a minute.

You're going to create a user interface like the one in Figure 7-15. You'll need an image view, four labels, and a text view to display the actual tweet.

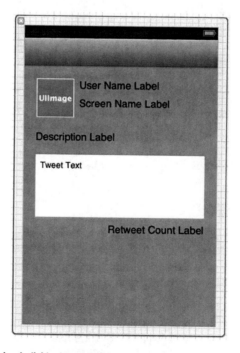

Figure 7-15. A user interface for showing individual tweets

When you're done with the layout of the user interface, create outlets for all the components. Give the outlets the following names:

- userImageView
- userNameLabel
- userScreenNameLabel
- userDescriptionLabel
- tweetTextView
- retweetCountLabel

Now, add the following declarations to the header file of the new class:

```
//
//  TweetViewController.h
//  Testing Retrieving Tweets
//

#import <UIKit/UIKit.h>

@interface TweetViewController : UIViewController

@property (weak, nonatomic) IBOutlet UIImageView *userImageView;
@property (weak, nonatomic) IBOutlet UILabel *userNameLabel;
@property (weak, nonatomic) IBOutlet UILabel *userScreenNameLabel;
@property (weak, nonatomic) IBOutlet UILabel *userDescriptionLabel;
@property (weak, nonatomic) IBOutlet UITextView *tweetTextView;
@property (weak, nonatomic) IBOutlet UILabel *retweetCountLabel;

@property (strong, nonatomic) NSDictionary *tweetData;

-(id)initWithTweetData:(NSDictionary *)tweetData;

@end
```

The implementation of the initializer is pretty straightforward:

```
//
//  TweetViewController.m
//  Testing Retrieving Tweets
//

#import "TweetViewController.h"

@implementation TweetViewController

-(id)initWithTweetData:(NSDictionary *)tweetData
{
    self = [super initWithNibName:nil bundle:nil];
```

```
    if (self) {
        _tweetData = tweetData;
    }
    return self;
}

// ...

@end
```

If someone changes the tweetData property, you need to update the view with the new data. Therefore, add a custom setter with the following implementation:

```
-(void)setTweetData:(NSDictionary *)tweetData
{
    _tweetData = tweetData;
    [self updateView];
}
```

The updateView helper method takes the tweet data and updates the controls in the view, including the image view:

```
-(void)updateView
{
    NSDictionary *userData = [self.tweetData objectForKey:@"user"];

    NSString *imageURLString = [userData objectForKey:@"profile_image_url"];
    NSURL *imageURL = [NSURL URLWithString:imageURLString];
    NSData *imageData = [NSData dataWithContentsOfURL:imageURL];
    self.userImageView.image = [UIImage imageWithData:imageData];

    self.userNameLabel.text = [userData objectForKey:@"name"];
    self.userScreenNameLabel.text = [userData objectForKey:@"screen_name"];
    self.userDescriptionLabel.text = [userData objectForKey:@"description"];

    self.tweetTextView.text = [self.tweetData objectForKey:@"text"];
    self.retweetCountLabel.text = [NSString stringWithFormat:@"Retweet Count: %@",
        [self.tweetData objectForKey:@"retweet_count"]];
}
```

Finally, in the viewDidLoad method, set the title of the Navigation Bar and update the other controls with the tweet data:

```
- (void)viewDidLoad
{
    [super viewDidLoad];
    // Do any additional setup after loading the view from its nib.
    self.navigationItem.title = @"Tweet";
    [self updateView];
}
```

Your Tweet View Controller is now ready to use. Let's implement the code that will display it. Go back to TweetTableViewController.m and add the following implementation of the tableView:didSelectRowAtIndexPath: method

```
- (void)tableView:(UITableView *)tableView didSelectRowAtIndexPath:(NSIndexPath *)indexPath
{
    // Navigation logic may go here. Create and push another view controller.
    NSDictionary *tweetData = [self.tweets objectAtIndex:indexPath.row];
    TweetViewController *detailViewController =
        [[TweetViewController alloc] initWithTweetData:tweetData];
    // ...
    // Pass the selected object to the new view controller.
    [self.navigationController pushViewController:detailViewController animated:YES];
}
```

Finally, all you have left to complete this recipe is to import the Tweet View Controller:

```
#import "TweetViewController.h"
```

With the individual tweet view, your app is finished. You can now select a feed, then a tweet, and see its detail as shown in Figure 7-16.

Figure 7-16. A view displaying a tweet

Summary

In this chapter you have gone through the three major ways in which you can implement Social Networking features in iOS 6; you've seen `UIActivityViewController`, which is the easiest way to share your app's content, you've looked at a more direct way to target Twitter, Facebook, or Weibo using the `SLComposeViewController`, and finally you've seen how you can use `SLRequest` to utilize every aspect of the native APIs of these social networks. Social networking is a thing of the past, the present, as well as the future, and iOS 6 has the tools you need to help your users keep sharing and connecting, even when they're using your apps.

Chapter 8

Camera Recipes

A great number of mobile applications can interact with your device's camera, including apps that take pictures, record videos, and provide overlays (e.g. augmented-reality applications). iOS developers have a great deal of control in how they can interact with any given device's hardware. In this chapter, you will go over multiple ways to access and use these functionalities, from simple, predefined interfaces to incredibly flexible, custom implementations.

> **Note** The iOS simulator does not support camera hardware. To test most recipes in this chapter, you must run them on a physical device.

Recipe 8-1: Taking Pictures

iOS has an incredibly handy and simple interface to your device's camera. With this interface you can allow users to take pictures and record video from inside an app. Here, you learn the basics of starting the camera interface to capture a still image.

You create a simple project that allows you to pull up your camera, take a picture, and then display the most recently taken image on your screen. Start by creating a new single-view application project. You don't need to import any extra frameworks into your project to access your camera in the predefined way you use here.

Setting Up the User Interface

Start by setting up a simple user interface containing an image view and a button. Switch over to your view controller's .xib file. Then drag an image view from the object library and make it fill the entire view. Next, drag out a UIButton into your view. The button accesses the camera, so set its text to "Take Picture." Your view should now resemble the view in Figure 8-1.

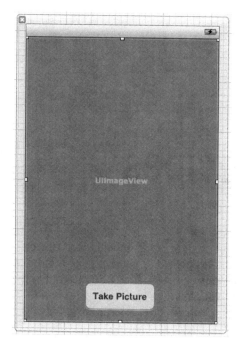

Figure 8-1. A simple user interface for taking pictures

Create outlets for your image view and your button, name them `imageView` and `cameraButton`, respectively. Also, create an action with the name `takePicture` for your button.

Your `ViewController.h` file should now resemble the following code:

```
//
//  ViewController.h
//  Recipe 8.1: Taking Pictures
//

#import <UIKit/UIKit.h>

@interface ViewController : UIViewController

@property (weak, nonatomic) IBOutlet UIImageView *imageView;
@property (weak, nonatomic) IBOutlet UIButton *cameraButton;

- (IBAction)takePicture:(id)sender;

@end
```

Accessing the Camera

Use an instance of the `UIImagePickerController` class to access your camera. Whenever dealing with the camera hardware on iOS, it is essential that, as a developer, you include a function to have your app check for hardware availability. This is done through the `isSourceTypeAvailable:` class method of UIImagePickerController. The method takes one of the following predefined constants as an argument:

- UIImagePickerControllerSourceTypeCamera.

- UIImagePickerControllerSourceTypePhotoLibrary.

- UIImagePickerControllerSourceTypeSavedPhotosAlbum.

For this recipe you'll use the first choice, UIImagePickerControllerSourceTypeCamera. UIImagePickerControllerPhotoLibrary is used to access all the stored photos on the device, while UIImagePickerControllerSavedPhotosAlbum is used to access only the Camera Roll album.

Now, switch to the ViewController.m file and locate the stubbed out takePicture: action method. There, you'll begin by checking whether the Camera source type is available, and if not, display a UIAlertView saying so.

```objc
- (IBAction)takePicture:(id)sender
{
        // Make sure camera is available
    if ([UIImagePickerController
            isSourceTypeAvailable:UIImagePickerControllerSourceTypeCamera] == NO)
    {
        UIAlertView *alert = [[UIAlertView alloc] initWithTitle:@"Error"
                                                    message:@"Camera Unavailable"
                                                    delegate:self
                                              cancelButtonTitle:@"Cancel"
                                              otherButtonTitles:nil, nil];

        [alert show];
        return;
    }
}
```

The iOS Simulator does not have camera functionality. Therefore you'll only see the error message, demonstrated in Figure 8-2, when you run your app there. To fully test this application you need to run it on a physical device.

Figure 8-2. The simulator does not have camera support so you need to test your app on a real device

Now before you expand the takePicture: method with the case in which the camera is in fact available, you need to make a couple of changes in ViewController.h. The first is to add a property to hold the image picker instance through which interface you'll access the camera. The second change is to prepare the view controller for receiving events from the image picker. Such a delegate needs to conform to both UIImagePickerControllerDelegate and UINavigationControllerDelegate protocols. Following is the header file with those changes marked in bold:

```
//
//  ViewController.h
//  Recipe 8.1: Taking Pictures
//

#import <UIKit/UIKit.h>

@interface ViewController : UIViewController<UIImagePickerControllerDelegate,
                                    UINavigationControllerDelegate>
```

```
@property (weak, nonatomic) IBOutlet UIImageView *imageView;
@property (weak, nonatomic) IBOutlet UIButton *cameraButton;
@property (strong, nonatomic) UIImagePickerController *imagePicker;

- (IBAction)takePicture:(id)sender;

@end
```

Now you can add the following code to your takePicture: action method in ViewController.m. It creates and initializes the image picker instance—if it hasn't already done so—and presents it to handle the camera device.

```
- (IBAction)takePicture:(id)sender
{
        // Make sure camera is available
    if ([UIImagePickerController
         isSourceTypeAvailable:UIImagePickerControllerSourceTypeCamera] == NO)
    {
        UIAlertView *alert = [[UIAlertView alloc] initWithTitle:@"Error"
                                                message:@"Camera Unavailable"
                                               delegate:self
                                      cancelButtonTitle:@"Cancel"
                                      otherButtonTitles:nil, nil];

        [alert show];
        return;
    }
    if (self.imagePicker == nil)
    {
        self.imagePicker = [[UIImagePickerController alloc] init];
        self.imagePicker.delegate = self;
        self.imagePicker.sourceType = UIImagePickerControllerSourceTypeCamera;

    }
    [self presentViewController:self.imagePicker animated:YES completion:NULL];
}
```

If you run your app now (on a real device) and tap the button, you should be presented with a simple camera interface that allows you to take a picture and select it for the purpose of your app (or retake it if you're not satisfied). Figure 8-3 shows the user interface of UIImagePickerController.

Figure 8-3. *The user interface of an* UIImagePickerViewController

Retrieving a Picture

Now that you have set up your view controller to successfully present your
UIImagePickerController, you need to handle how your view controller reacts to the completion of
the UIImagePickerController's selection, when a picture has been taken and selected for use. You
do this by using the delegate method imagePickerController:didFinishPickingMediaWithInfo:. You
retrieve the picture, update the image view, and finally dismiss the image picker, as follows:

```
-(void)imagePickerController:(UIImagePickerController *)picker
didFinishPickingMediaWithInfo:(NSDictionary *)info
{
    UIImage *image = [info objectForKey:UIImagePickerControllerOriginalImage];
    self.imageView.image = image;
    self.imageView.contentMode = UIViewContentModeScaleAspectFill;
    [self dismissViewControllerAnimated:YES completion:NULL];
}
```

> **Note**   By setting the content mode property of the image view to
> UIViewContentModeScaleAspectFill, we ensure that the picture will fill the entire view while
> still maintaining its aspect ratio. This usually results in the picture's being cropped instead of looking
> stretched. Alternatively, you could use UIViewContentModeScaleAspectFit, which displays the
> whole picture with retained aspect ratio but not necessarily fill the entire view.

You also implement another `UIImagePickerController` delegate method to handle the cancellation of an image selection. The only thing you need to do there is to dismiss the image picker view.

```
- (void) imagePickerControllerDidCancel: (UIImagePickerController *) picker
{
    [self dismissViewControllerAnimated:YES completion:NULL];
}
```

Your app can now access the camera, take a picture, and set it as the background of the app, as Figure 8-4 illustrates.

Figure 8-4. Your app with a photo set as the background

> **Note** The `UIImagePickerController` class does not support landscape orientation for taking pictures. Although you *can* take pictures that way, the view does not adjust according to the landscape orientation, which results in a rather weird user experience.

Implement Basic Editing

As an optional setting, you could allow your camera interface to be editable, enabling the user to crop and frame the picture she or he has taken. To do this, you simply have to set the `UIImagePickerController`'s allowsEditing property to YES.

```objc
- (IBAction)takePicture:(id)sender
{
    // ...

    if (self.imagePicker == nil)
    {
        self.imagePicker = [[UIImagePickerController alloc] init];
        self.imagePicker.delegate = self;
        self.imagePicker.sourceType = UIImagePickerControllerSourceTypeCamera;
        self.imagePicker.allowsEditing = YES;

    }
    [self presentViewController:self.imagePicker animated:YES completion:NULL];
}
```

Then, to acquire the edited image, you also need to make the following change in the imagePickerController:didFinishPickingMediaWithInfo: method:

```objc
-(void)imagePickerController:(UIImagePickerController *)picker
didFinishPickingMediaWithInfo:(NSDictionary *)info
{
    UIImage *image = [info objectForKey:UIImagePickerControllerEditedImage];
    self.imageView.image = image;
    self.imageView.contentMode = UIViewContentModeScaleAspectFill;
    [self dismissViewControllerAnimated:YES completion:NULL];
}
```

Saving Picture to Photos Album

You might want to save the pictures you take to the device's saved photos album. This is easily done with the UIImageWriteToSavedPhotosAlbum() function. Add the following line to your imagePickerViewController:didFinishPickingMediaWithInfo: method:

```objc
-(void)imagePickerController:(UIImagePickerController *)picker
didFinishPickingMediaWithInfo:(NSDictionary *)info
{
    UIImage *image = (UIImage *)[info objectForKey:UIImagePickerControllerEditedImage];
    UIImageWriteToSavedPhotosAlbum (image, nil, nil , nil);
    self.imageView.image = image;
    self.imageView.contentMode = UIViewContentModeScaleAspectFill;
    [self dismissViewControllerAnimated:YES completion:NULL];
}
```

However, in iOS 6 privacy restrictions have been applied to the saved photos album; an app that wants to access it now needs an explicit authorization from the user. Therefore, you should also provide an explanation as to why your app requests access to the saved photos library. This is done in the application's Info.plist file (found in the Supporting Files folder in the Project Navigator) and the key NSPhotoLibraryUsageDescription (or "Privacy—Photo Library Usage Description" as it's displayed in the property list).

You can enter any text you want for the usage description; we chose "Testing the camera." The important thing to know is that the text will be displayed to the user when he or she is prompted for authorizing the app access to the photos album, as in Figure 8-5.

Figure 8-5. Saving the picture to the photos library will need an authorization from the user

Recipe 8-2: Recording Video

Your UIImagePickerController is actually a lot more flexible than you've seen so far, especially because you've been using it exclusively for still images. Here you'll go through how to set up your UIImagePickerController to handle both still images and video.

For this recipe, you build off the code from the Recipe 8-1 as it already includes the setup you need. You add to its functionality by implementing the option to record and save videos.

Start by setting the image picker's allowed media types to all available types for the camera. This can be done using the availableMediaTypesForSourceType: class method of the UIImagePickerController, as follows:

```
- (IBAction)takePicture:(id)sender
{
        // Make sure camera is available
    if ([UIImagePickerController
        isSourceTypeAvailable:UIImagePickerControllerSourceTypeCamera] == NO)
    {
        UIAlertView *alert = [[UIAlertView alloc] initWithTitle:@"Error"
                                                    message:@"Camera Unavailable"
                                                    delegate:self
                                            cancelButtonTitle:@"Cancel"
                                            otherButtonTitles:nil, nil];
        [alert show];
        return;
    }
    if (self.imagePicker == nil)
    {
        self.imagePicker = [[UIImagePickerController alloc] init];
        self.imagePicker.delegate = self;
        self.imagePicker.sourceType = UIImagePickerControllerSourceTypeCamera;
        self.imagePicker.mediaTypes = [UIImagePickerController
availableMediaTypesForSourceType:UIImagePickerControllerSourceTypeCamera];
        self.imagePicker.allowsEditing = YES;
    }
    [self presentViewController:self.imagePicker animated:YES completion:NULL];
}
```

Next, you need to instruct your application on how to handle when the user records and uses a video. To do this, first you need to link the Mobile Core Services framework to your project, then you need to import its API in your view controller's header file:

```
//
//  ViewController.h
//  Recipe 8.2: Recording Videos
//


#import <UIKit/UIKit.h>
#import <MobileCoreServices/MobileCoreServices.h>

@interface ViewController : UIViewController<UIImagePickerControllerDelegate,
UINavigationControllerDelegate>

@property (weak, nonatomic) IBOutlet UIImageView *imageView;
@property (weak, nonatomic) IBOutlet UIButton *cameraButton;
@property (strong, nonatomic) UIImagePickerController *imagePicker;

- (IBAction)takePicture:(id)sender;

@end
```

Now add the following code to your UIImagePickerController's delegate method:

```
-(void)imagePickerController:(UIImagePickerController *)picker
didFinishPickingMediaWithInfo:(NSDictionary *)info
{
    NSString *mediaType = [info objectForKey: UIImagePickerControllerMediaType];

    if (CFStringCompare((__bridge CFStringRef) mediaType, kUTTypeMovie, 0) ==
        kCFCompareEqualTo)
    {
        // Movie Captured
        NSString *moviePath =
            [[info objectForKey: UIImagePickerControllerMediaURL] path];

        if (UIVideoAtPathIsCompatibleWithSavedPhotosAlbum (moviePath))
        {
            UISaveVideoAtPathToSavedPhotosAlbum (moviePath, nil, nil, nil);
        }
    }
    else
    {
        // Picture Taken
        UIImage *image =
            (UIImage *)[info objectForKey:UIImagePickerControllerEditedImage];
        UIImageWriteToSavedPhotosAlbum (image, nil, nil , nil);
        self.imageView.image = image;
        self.imageView.contentMode = UIViewContentModeScaleAspectFill;
    }
    [self dismissViewControllerAnimated:YES completion:NULL];
}
```

Essentially, what you are doing here is comparing the media type of the saved file. The main issue comes into play when you attempt to compare mediaType, an NSString, with kUTTypeMovie, which is of the type CFStringRef. You accomplish this by casting your NSString down to a CFStringRef. In iOS 5 this process became slightly more complicated with the introduction of Automatic Reference Counting (ARC), because ARC deals with Objective-C object types such as NSString, but not with C types like CFStringRef. You create a bridged casting by placing __bridge before your CFStringRef, as shown earlier, in order to instruct ARC not to deal with this object.

If all has gone well your app should now be able to record video by selecting the video mode in the image picker view, as shown in Figure 8-6. The video is then saved (if allowed by the user) to the private photos library.

Figure 8-6. *The image picker view with a switch control between photo and video modes*

Recipe 8-3: Editing Videos

Although your UIImagePickerController offers a convenient way to record and save video files, it does nothing to allow you to edit them. Fortunately, iOS has another built-in controller called UIVideoEditorController, which you can use to edit your recorded videos.

You can build this fairly simple recipe off your second project, in which you added video functionality to your UIImagePickerController.

Start by adding a second button with the title "Edit Video" to your view controller's interface file. Arrange the two buttons as in Figure 8-7.

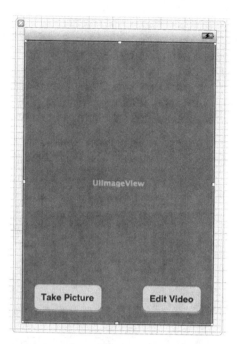

Figure 8-7. New user interface with button for editing the video

Next, create an action named `editVideo` for when the user taps the Edit Video button.

You'll also need a property to store the path to the video that the user records. Define it in the view controller's header file:

```
//
//  ViewController.h
//  Recipe 8.3: Editing Videos
//

#import <UIKit/UIKit.h>
#import <MobileCoreServices/MobileCoreServices.h>

@interface ViewController : UIViewController<UIImagePickerControllerDelegate,
UINavigationControllerDelegate>

@property (weak, nonatomic) IBOutlet UIImageView *imageView;
@property (weak, nonatomic) IBOutlet UIButton *cameraButton;
@property (strong, nonatomic) UIImagePickerController *imagePicker;
@property (strong, nonatomic) NSString *pathToRecordedVideo;

- (IBAction)takePicture:(id)sender;
- (IBAction)editVideo:(id)sender;

@end
```

Now, in the imagePickerController:didFinishPickingMediaWithInfo: method, make sure the pathToRecordedVideo property gets updated with the path to the newly recorded video.

```
-(void)imagePickerController:(UIImagePickerController *)picker
didFinishPickingMediaWithInfo:(NSDictionary *)info
{
    NSString *mediaType = [info objectForKey: UIImagePickerControllerMediaType];

    if (CFStringCompare((__bridge CFStringRef) mediaType, kUTTypeMovie, 0) ==
        kCFCompareEqualTo)
    {
        NSString *moviePath =
            [[info objectForKey: UIImagePickerControllerMediaURL] path];
        self.pathToRecordedVideo = moviePath;

        if (UIVideoAtPathIsCompatibleWithSavedPhotosAlbum (moviePath))
        {
            UISaveVideoAtPathToSavedPhotosAlbum (moviePath, nil, nil, nil);
        }
    }
    else
    {
        //...
    }
}
```

With the pathToRecordedVideo property in place, you can turn the focus to your editVideo action. It opens the last recorded video for editing in a video editor controller, or displays an error if no video was recorded.

```
- (IBAction)editVideo:(id)sender
{
    if (self.pathToRecordedVideo)
    {
        UIVideoEditorController *editor = [[UIVideoEditorController alloc] init];
        editor.videoPath = self.pathToRecordedVideo;
        editor.delegate = self;
        [self presentViewController:editor animated:YES completion:NULL];
    }
    else
    {
        UIAlertView *alert = [[UIAlertView alloc] initWithTitle:@"Error"
            message:@"No Video Recorded Yet"
            delegate:self
            cancelButtonTitle:@"Cancel"
            otherButtonTitles:nil, nil];
        [alert show];
    }
}
```

Because the video editor's receiving delegate is your view controller, you need to make sure it conforms to the UIVideoEditorControllerDelegate protocol.

```
// ...
```

```
@interface ViewController : UIViewController<UIImagePickerControllerDelegate,
                                             UINavigationControllerDelegate,
                                             UIVideoEditorControllerDelegate>
```

```
// ...
```

```
@end
```

Finally, you need to implement a few delegate methods for your `UIVideoEditorController`. First, a delegate method to handle a successful editing/trimming of the video follows:

```
-(void)videoEditorController:(UIVideoEditorController *)editor
didSaveEditedVideoToPath:(NSString *)editedVideoPath
{
    self.pathToRecordedVideo = editedVideoPath;
    if (UIVideoAtPathIsCompatibleWithSavedPhotosAlbum (editedVideoPath))
    {
        UISaveVideoAtPathToSavedPhotosAlbum (editedVideoPath, nil, nil, nil);
    }
    [self dismissViewControllerAnimated:YES completion:NULL];
}
```

As you can see, your application sets the newly edited video as your next video to be edited, so that you can create increasingly trimmed clips. It also saves each edited version to your photos album if possible.

You need one more delegate method to handle the cancellation of your `UIVideoEditorController`:

```
-(void)videoEditorControllerDidCancel:(UIVideoEditorController *)editor
{
    [self dismissViewControllerAnimated:YES completion:NULL];
}
```

Upon testing on a physical device, your application should now successfully allow you to edit your videos. Figure 8-8 shows a view of your application giving you the option to edit a recorded video.

Figure 8-8. Editing (trimming) a video using `UIVideoEditorController`

Recipe 8-4: Using Custom Camera Overlays

There is a variety of applications that implement the camera interface but also implement a custom overlay—for example, to display constellations on the sky or simply to implement their own custom camera controls. In this recipe you'll continue building on the project from the previous recipes and implement a very basic custom camera screen overlay. Specifically, you'll be replacing the default button controls with your own versions of them. Although simple, the example should give you an idea of how to create your own, more useful overlay functionalities.

You build your custom overlay view directly in code, in a method that you'll name `customViewForImagePicker:`. It creates an overlay view and populates it with three buttons: one for taking the picture, one for turning flash on and off, and one to toggle between the front and rear cameras. Here's the code, which you add to `ViewController.m` in the code from Recipe 8-3:

```
-(UIView *)customViewForImagePicker:(UIImagePickerController *)imagePicker;
{
    UIView *view = [[UIView alloc] initWithFrame:CGRectMake(0, 0, 280, 480)];
    view.backgroundColor = [UIColor clearColor];

    UIButton *flashButton =
        [[UIButton alloc] initWithFrame:CGRectMake(10, 10, 120, 44)];
    flashButton.backgroundColor = [UIColor colorWithRed:.5 green:.5 blue:.5 alpha:.5];
    [flashButton setTitle:@"Flash Auto" forState:UIControlStateNormal];
    [flashButton setTitleColor:[UIColor whiteColor] forState:UIControlStateNormal];
    flashButton.layer.cornerRadius = 10.0;
```

```
    UIButton *changeCameraButton =
        [[UIButton alloc] initWithFrame:CGRectMake(190, 10, 120, 44)];
    changeCameraButton.backgroundColor =
        [UIColor colorWithRed:.5 green:.5 blue:.5 alpha:.5];
    [changeCameraButton setTitle:@"Rear Camera" forState:UIControlStateNormal];
    [changeCameraButton setTitleColor:[UIColor whiteColor]
        forState:UIControlStateNormal];
    changeCameraButton.layer.cornerRadius = 10.0;

    UIButton *takePictureButton =
        [[UIButton alloc] initWithFrame:CGRectMake(100, 432, 120, 44)];
    takePictureButton.backgroundColor =
        [UIColor colorWithRed:.5 green:.5 blue:.5 alpha:.5];
    [takePictureButton setTitle:@"Click!" forState:UIControlStateNormal];
    [takePictureButton setTitleColor:[UIColor whiteColor]
        forState:UIControlStateNormal];
    takePictureButton.layer.cornerRadius = 10.0;

    [flashButton addTarget:self action:@selector(toggleFlash:)
        forControlEvents:UIControlEventTouchUpInside];
    [changeCameraButton addTarget:self action:@selector(toggleCamera:)
        forControlEvents:UIControlEventTouchUpInside];
    [takePictureButton addTarget:imagePicker action:@selector(takePicture)
        forControlEvents:UIControlEventTouchUpInside];

    [view addSubview:flashButton];
    [view addSubview:changeCameraButton];
    [view addSubview:takePictureButton];

    return view;
}
```

Here, you have defined your UIView, as well as your buttons to be put in it; given them their actions to perform and added them into the view; set the title of each button to be either its starting value or its purpose; and also set their cornerRadius so that the buttons will have rounded corners. One of the most important details here is that you set your buttons to be semitransparent, as they are placed over your camera's display. You do not want to cover up any of your picture, so the buttons have to be at least partially see-through.

As you may have noticed, the action for the takePictureButton is directly connected to the takePicture method on the image picker. The other two buttons, on the other hand, are connected to methods (toggleFlash and toggleCamera, respectively) on your view controller. At this point, those two methods don't exist so you need to implement them next.

```
-(void)toggleFlash:(UIButton *)sender
{
    if (self.imagePicker.cameraFlashMode == UIImagePickerControllerCameraFlashModeOff)
    {
        self.imagePicker.cameraFlashMode = UIImagePickerControllerCameraFlashModeOn;
        [sender setTitle:@"Flash On" forState:UIControlStateNormal];
    }
    else
```

```
    {
        self.imagePicker.cameraFlashMode = UIImagePickerControllerCameraFlashModeOff;
        [sender setTitle:@"Flash Off" forState:UIControlStateNormal];
    }
}

-(void)toggleCamera:(UIButton *)sender
{
    if (self.imagePicker.cameraDevice == UIImagePickerControllerCameraDeviceRear)
    {
        self.imagePicker.cameraDevice = UIImagePickerControllerCameraDeviceFront;
        [sender setTitle:@"Front Camera" forState:UIControlStateNormal];
    }
    else
    {
        self.imagePicker.cameraDevice = UIImagePickerControllerCameraDeviceRear;
        [sender setTitle:@"Rear Camera" forState:UIControlStateNormal];
    }
}
```

Next, you hide the default camera buttons and provide the image picker with your custom overlay view. Add the following two lines of code to your takePicture: method. You can also comment out the setting of the allowsEditing property because the new way of taking pictures doesn't support that.

```
- (IBAction)takePicture:(id)sender
{
        // Make sure camera is available
    if ([UIImagePickerController
        isSourceTypeAvailable:UIImagePickerControllerSourceTypeCamera] == NO)
    {
        UIAlertView *alert = [[UIAlertView alloc] initWithTitle:@"Error"
                                                        message:@"Camera Unavailable"
                                                       delegate:self
                                              cancelButtonTitle:@"Cancel"
                                              otherButtonTitles:nil, nil];
        [alert show];
        return;
    }
    if (self.imagePicker == nil)
    {
        self.imagePicker = [[UIImagePickerController alloc] init];
        self.imagePicker.delegate = self;
        self.imagePicker.sourceType = UIImagePickerControllerSourceTypeCamera;
        self.imagePicker.mediaTypes = [UIImagePickerController
availableMediaTypesForSourceType:UIImagePickerControllerSourceTypeCamera];
        // self.imagePicker.allowsEditing = YES;
        self.imagePicker.showsCameraControls = NO;
        self.imagePicker.cameraOverlayView =
            [self customViewForImagePicker:self.imagePicker];
    }
    [self presentViewController:self.imagePicker animated:YES completion:NULL];
}
```

Finally, you need to make a small change to the
imagePickerController:didFinishPickingMediaWithInfo: method. As mentioned earlier, the
takePicture method of the image picker doesn't support editing. This means that you have to
retrieve your picture from the info dictionary using the UIImagePickerControllerOriginalImage key
instead of UIImagePickerControllerEditedImage, as shown in the code that follows:

```
-(void)imagePickerController:(UIImagePickerController *)picker
didFinishPickingMediaWithInfo:(NSDictionary *)info
{
    NSString *mediaType = [info objectForKey: UIImagePickerControllerMediaType];

    if (CFStringCompare((__bridge CFStringRef) mediaType, kUTTypeMovie, 0) ==
        kCFCompareEqualTo)
    {
        NSString *moviePath =
            [[info objectForKey: UIImagePickerControllerMediaURL] path];
        self.pathToRecordedVideo = moviePath;

        if (UIVideoAtPathIsCompatibleWithSavedPhotosAlbum (moviePath))
        {
            UISaveVideoAtPathToSavedPhotosAlbum (moviePath, nil, nil, nil);
        }
    }
    else
    {
        UIImage *image =
            (UIImage *)[info objectForKey:UIImagePickerControllerOriginalImage];
        UIImageWriteToSavedPhotosAlbum(image, nil, nil , nil);
        self.imageView.image = image;
        self.imageView.contentMode = UIViewContentModeScaleAspectFill;
    }
    [self dismissViewControllerAnimated:YES completion:NULL];
}
```

If you run your app now, your camera should, as shown in Figure 8-9, display your three buttons in
an overlay.

Figure 8-9. *An image picker controller with a custom overlay view replacing the standard buttons*

From here you can create your own custom overlays and easily change their functions to fit nearly any situation. The following recipes leave the image picker controller and instead look into the Audiovisual (AV) Foundation framework for capturing your pictures and videos.

Recipe 8-5: Displaying Camera Preview with AVCaptureSession

While the UIImagePickerController and UIVideoEditorController interfaces are incredibly useful, they certainly aren't as customizable as they could be. With the AV framework, however, you can create your camera interfaces from scratch, making them just the way you want.

In this recipe and the ones that follow, you use the AVCaptureSession API to essentially create your own version of the camera. You'll do this in steps, starting with the displaying of a camera preview.

Begin by creating a new single-view project. You'll be using the same project for the rest of this chapter so name it accordingly (e.g., MyCamera). Also make sure to add the AVFoundation framework to your project or you'll run into linker errors later.

Now, add a property to your view controller to hold your AVCaptureSession instance, and one to hold the video input instance, by making the following changes to your ViewController.h file:

```
//
// ViewController.h
// Recipe 8.5: Displaying Camera Preview With AVCaptureSession
//
```

```
#import <UIKit/UIKit.h>
#import <AVFoundation/AVFoundation.h>

@interface ViewController : UIViewController

@property (strong, nonatomic) AVCaptureSession *captureSession;
@property (strong, nonatomic) AVCaptureDeviceInput *videoInput;

@end
```

Next, switch over to the ViewController.m file and locate the viewDidLoad method. There you set up the capture session to receive input from the camera. We'll show you step by step now and later present you with the complete viewDidLoad implementation.

First, you create your AVCaptureSession. Optionally, you may also want to change the resolution preset, which is set to AVCaptureSessionPresetHigh by default.

```
self.captureSession = [[AVCaptureSession alloc] init];
//Optional: self.captureSession.sessionPreset = AVCaptureSessionPresetMedium;
```

Next specify your input device, which is your rear camera (assuming one is accessible). You specify this through the use of the AVCaptureDevice class method +defaultDeviceWithMediaType:, which can take a variety of different arguments, depending on the type of media desired, the most prominent of which are AVMediaTypeVideo and AVMediaTypeAudio.

```
AVCaptureDevice *device = [AVCaptureDevice defaultDeviceWithMediaType:AVMediaTypeVideo];
```

Next, you need to set up the instance of AVCaptureDeviceInput to specify your chosen device as an input for your capture session. Also include a check to make sure the input has been correctly created before adding it to your session.

```
NSError *error = nil;
self.videoInput = [AVCaptureDeviceInput deviceInputWithDevice:device error:&error];
if (self.videoInput)
{
    [self.captureSession addInput:self.videoInput];
}
else
{
    NSLog(@"Input Error: %@", error);
}
```

The last part of your viewDidLoad is the creation of a preview layer, with which you can see what your camera is viewing. Set your preview layer to be the layer of your main view, but with a slightly altered height, so as not to block a button that you'll set up in the next recipe.

```
AVCaptureVideoPreviewLayer *previewLayer =
    [AVCaptureVideoPreviewLayer layerWithSession:self.captureSession];
UIView *aView = self.view;
previewLayer.frame =
    CGRectMake(0, 0, self.view.frame.size.width, self.view.frame.size.height-70);
[aView.layer addSublayer:previewLayer];
```

Here's the complete viewDidLoad method:

```
- (void)viewDidLoad
{
    [super viewDidLoad];
    // Do any additional setup after loading the view, typically from a nib.

    self.captureSession = [[AVCaptureSession alloc] init];
    //Optional: self.captureSession.sessionPreset = AVCaptureSessionPresetMedium;

    AVCaptureDevice *device =
        [AVCaptureDevice defaultDeviceWithMediaType:AVMediaTypeVideo];

    NSError *error = nil;
    self.videoInput = [AVCaptureDeviceInput deviceInputWithDevice:device error:&error];
    if (self.videoInput)
    {
        [self.captureSession addInput:self.videoInput];
    }
    else
    {
        NSLog(@"Input Error: %@", error);
    }

    AVCaptureVideoPreviewLayer *previewLayer =
        [AVCaptureVideoPreviewLayer layerWithSession:self.captureSession];
    UIView *aView = self.view;
    previewLayer.frame =
        CGRectMake(0, 0, self.view.frame.size.width,
            self.view.frame.size.height-70);
    [aView.layer addSublayer:previewLayer];
}
```

> **Note**   Just like any other CALayer, an AVCaptureVideoPreviewLayer can be repositioned,
> rotated, and resized. With it, you are no longer bound to using the entire screen to record video as
> you are with the UIImagePicker, meaning you could have your preview layer in one part of the
> screen and other information for the user in another. As with almost every part of iOS development, the
> possibilities of use are limited only by the developer's imagination.

Now, the only thing that remains is to start and stop your capture session. In this app you'll display
the camera preview upon application launch, so a good place to put the start code is in the
viewWillAppear: method:

```
- (void)viewWillAppear:(BOOL)animated
{
    [super viewWillAppear:animated];
    [self.captureSession startRunning];
}
```

And the corresponding stopping of the capture session:

```
- (void)viewWillDisappear:(BOOL)animated
{
    [super viewWillDisappear:animated];
    [self.captureSession stopRunning];
}
```

If you build and run your application now, it should display a live camera preview as in Figure 8-10.

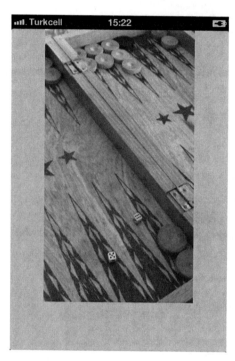

Figure 8-10. Displaying a camera preview with `AVCaptureSession`

Recipe 8-6: Capturing Still Images with AVCaptureSession

In the previous recipe you learned how to set up an `AVCaptureSession` with input from the camera. You also saw how you can connect an `AVCaptureVideoPreviewLayer` to display a live camera preview in your app. Now you will expand the project by connecting a `AVCaptureStillImageOutput` object to take still images and save them to the saved photos library on the device.

Before digging in to the coding, you need to make a couple of changes to the project. The first is to link `AssetsLibrary.framework` to your project. You use functionality from that framework to write the photos to the photos library.

The second thing you need to do, because you access the shared photos library of the device, is provide a usage description in the application's `Info.plist` file. Go ahead and add the `NSPhotoLibraryUsageDescription` key (displayed as "Privacy—Photo Library Usage Description" in the property editor) with a brief text containing the reason why your app seeks the access (e.g., "Testing AVCaptureSession").

Adding a Capture Button

You need a way to trigger a still image capture. Start by adding a button with the title "Capture" to your view controller's .xib file, as in Figure 8-11. Also make sure to create an action named capture for the button.

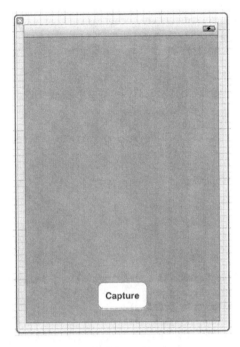

Figure 8-11. A user interface with a button to capture a video frame

Now, switch to your ViewController.h file and import the AssetsLibrary API. Also, add a property to hold your still image output instance, as follows:

```
//
// ViewController.h
// Recipe 8.6: Taking Still Images With AVCaptureSession
//

#import <UIKit/UIKit.h>
#import <AVFoundation/AVFoundation.h>
#import <AssetsLibrary/AssetsLibrary.h>

@interface ViewController : UIViewController

@property (strong, nonatomic) AVCaptureSession *captureSession;
@property (strong, nonatomic) AVCaptureDeviceInput *videoInput;
@property (strong, nonatomic) AVCaptureStillImageOutput *stillImageOutput;
```

```
- (IBAction)capture:(id)sender;
```

```
@end
```

In ViewController.m, add the following code to the viewDidLoad method. The new code (marked in bold) allocates and initializes your still image output object and connects it to the capture session.

```
- (void)viewDidLoad
{
    [super viewDidLoad];
        // Do any additional setup after loading the view, typically from a nib.
    self.captureSession = [[AVCaptureSession alloc] init];
    //Optional: self.captureSession.sessionPreset = AVCaptureSessionPresetMedium;

    AVCaptureDevice *device =
        [AVCaptureDevice defaultDeviceWithMediaType:AVMediaTypeVideo];

    NSError *error = nil;
    self.videoInput = [AVCaptureDeviceInput deviceInputWithDevice:device error:&error];
    if (self.videoInput)
    {
        [self.captureSession addInput:self.videoInput];
    }
    else
    {
        NSLog(@"Input Error: %@", error);
    }

    self.stillImageOutput = [[AVCaptureStillImageOutput alloc] init];
    NSDictionary *stillImageOutputSettings =
        [[NSDictionary alloc] initWithObjectsAndKeys:
            AVVideoCodecJPEG, AVVideoCodecKey, nil];
    [self.stillImageOutput setOutputSettings:stillImageOutputSettings];
    [self.captureSession addOutput:self.stillImageOutput];

    AVCaptureVideoPreviewLayer *previewLayer =
        [AVCaptureVideoPreviewLayer layerWithSession:self.captureSession];
    UIView *aView = self.view;
    previewLayer.frame =
        CGRectMake(0, 0, self.view.frame.size.width, self.view.frame.size.height-70);
    [aView.layer addSublayer:previewLayer];
}
```

> **Note**   Besides AVCaptureStillImageOutput, you can use a number of other output formats—for example, the AVCaptureMovieFileOutput, which you use in the next recipe, the AVCaptureVideoDataOutput with which you can access the raw video output frame by frame, AVCaptureAudioFileOutput for saving audio files, and AVCaptureAudioDataOutput for processing audio data.

Now it's time to implement the action method. All it should do is trigger the capturing of a still image. We chose to extract the capturing code into a helper method for the sake of making changes that will come in the next recipe easier.

```objc
- (IBAction)capture:(id)sender
{
    [self captureStillImage];
}
```

The implementation of `captureStillImage` can seem daunting at first so we'll take it in steps and then show you the complete method.
First you acquire the capture connection and make sure it uses the portrait orientation to capture the image.

```objc
- (void) captureStillImage
{
    AVCaptureConnection *stillImageConnection =
        [self.stillImageOutput.connections objectAtIndex:0];
    if ([stillImageConnection isVideoOrientationSupported])
        [stillImageConnection setVideoOrientation:AVCaptureVideoOrientationPortrait];

    // ...
}
```

Then you run the `captureStillImageAsynchronouslyFromConnection` method and provide a code block that is invoked when the still image capture has been completed.

```objc
[self.stillImageOutput
    captureStillImageAsynchronouslyFromConnection:stillImageConnection
    completionHandler:^(CMSampleBufferRef imageDataSampleBuffer, NSError *error)
    {
        // ...
    }
];
```

When the capture has completed, first check to see whether it was successful; otherwise log the error.

```objc
[self.stillImageOutput
    captureStillImageAsynchronouslyFromConnection:stillImageConnection
    completionHandler:^(CMSampleBufferRef imageDataSampleBuffer, NSError *error)
    {
        if (imageDataSampleBuffer != NULL)
        {
            // ...
        }
        else
        {
            NSLog(@"Error capturing still image: %@", error);
        }
    }
];
```

If the capturing was successful, extract the image from the buffer.

```
if (imageDataSampleBuffer != NULL)
{
    NSData *imageData = [AVCaptureStillImageOutput
        jpegStillImageNSDataRepresentation:imageDataSampleBuffer];
    UIImage *image = [[UIImage alloc] initWithData:imageData];

    // ...
}
```

Then save the image to the photos library. This is also an asynchronous task so provide a block for when it completes. Whether the task completed successfully or with an error (e.g., if the user didn't allow access to the photos library,) display an alert to notify the user.

```
ALAssetsLibrary *library = [[ALAssetsLibrary alloc] init];
[library writeImageToSavedPhotosAlbum:[image CGImage]
    orientation:(ALAssetOrientation)[image imageOrientation]
    completionBlock:^(NSURL *assetURL, NSError *error)
    {
        UIAlertView *alert;
        if (!error)
        {
            alert = [[UIAlertView alloc] initWithTitle:@"Photo Saved"
                message:@"The photo was successfully saved to your photos library"
                delegate:nil
                cancelButtonTitle:@"OK"
                otherButtonTitles:nil, nil];
        }
        else
        {
            alert = [[UIAlertView alloc] initWithTitle:@"Error Saving Photo"
                message:@"The photo was not saved to you photos library"
                delegate:nil
                cancelButtonTitle:@"OK"
                otherButtonTitles:nil, nil];
        }

        [alert show];
    }
];
```

Here's the captureStillImage method in it's entirety:

```
- (void) captureStillImage
{
    AVCaptureConnection *stillImageConnection =
        [self.stillImageOutput.connections objectAtIndex:0];
    if ([stillImageConnection isVideoOrientationSupported])
        [stillImageConnection setVideoOrientation:AVCaptureVideoOrientationPortrait];
    [self.stillImageOutput
```

```
    captureStillImageAsynchronouslyFromConnection:stillImageConnection
    completionHandler:^(CMSampleBufferRef imageDataSampleBuffer, NSError *error)
    {
        if (imageDataSampleBuffer != NULL)
        {
            NSData *imageData = [AVCaptureStillImageOutput
                jpegStillImageNSDataRepresentation:imageDataSampleBuffer];
            ALAssetsLibrary *library = [[ALAssetsLibrary alloc] init];
            UIImage *image = [[UIImage alloc] initWithData:imageData];
            [library writeImageToSavedPhotosAlbum:[image CGImage]
                orientation:(ALAssetOrientation)[image imageOrientation]
                completionBlock:^(NSURL *assetURL, NSError *error)
                {
                    UIAlertView *alert;
                    if (!error)
                    {
                        alert = [[UIAlertView alloc] initWithTitle:@"Photo Saved"
                            message:@"The photo was successfully saved to your photos library"
delegate:nil
cancelButtonTitle:@"OK"
                            otherButtonTitles:nil, nil];
                    }
                    else
                    {
                        alert = [[UIAlertView alloc] initWithTitle:@"Error Saving Photo"
                            message:@"The photo was not saved to you photos library"
                            delegate:nil
                            cancelButtonTitle:@"OK"
                            otherButtonTitles:nil, nil];
                    }

                    [alert show];
                }
            ];
        }
        else
        {
            NSLog(@"Error capturing still image: %@", error);
        }
    }
];
}
```

That completes Recipe 8-6. You now can run your app and tap the Capture button to take a picture that's saved in your photos library, as in Figure 8-12.

Figure 8-12. A still image captured and saved to the photos library

While you haven't included any fancy animations to make it look like a camera, this is quite useful as far as a basic camera goes. Recipe 8-7 takes it to the next level and shows you how to record a video using AVCaptureSession.

Recipe 8-7: Capturing Video with AVCaptureSession

Now that you have covered some of the basics of using AVFoundation, you will use it to implement a slightly more complicated project. This time, you'll extend your app to include a mode control that allows the user to switch between taking pictures and recording videos. You'll build on the same project that you have been working on since Recipe 8-5.

Adding a Video Recording Mode

You're going to add a new component to your user interface that lets the user switch between still image and video recording modes. A simple segmented control works for the purpose of this recipe, so go ahead and add one from the object library. Make it have two options, "Take Photo" and "Record Video," and place it so that your view resembles the one in Figure 8-13.

Figure 8-13. A simple user interface that allows the user to switch modes between photo and video capturing

You're going to access both the segmented control and the button from your code, so add outlets for them. Use the names `modeControl` and `captureButton`, respectively. You're also going to need to respond when the segment control's value change, so create an action for that event. Name the action `updateMode`.

Now switch over to your `ViewController.h` file. You're going to add a couple of properties that are for the video recording setup of your capture session, one for audio input and one for the movie file output. Also, to prepare the view controller for being an output delegate for the movie file recording, you're going to add `AVCaptureFileOutputRecordingDelegate` protocol to the header. Following is the code with the changes, which are marked in bold:

```objc
//
// ViewController.h
// Recipe 8.7: Recording Video With AVCaptureSession
//

#import <UIKit/UIKit.h>
#import <AVFoundation/AVFoundation.h>
#import <AssetsLibrary/AssetsLibrary.h>

@interface ViewController : UIViewController<AVCaptureFileOutputRecordingDelegate>

@property (strong, nonatomic) AVCaptureSession *captureSession;
@property (strong, nonatomic) AVCaptureDeviceInput *videoInput;
@property (strong, nonatomic) AVCaptureDeviceInput *audioInput;
@property (strong, nonatomic) AVCaptureStillImageOutput *stillImageOutput;
@property (strong, nonatomic) AVCaptureMovieFileOutput *movieOutput;
```

```
@property (weak, nonatomic) IBOutlet UIButton *captureButton;
@property (weak, nonatomic) IBOutlet UISegmentedControl *modeControl;

- (IBAction)capture:(id)sender;
- (IBAction)updateMode:(id)sender;

@end
```

Now that your header file is all set up, switch over to your implementation file. To start, you're going to make several changes to the viewDidLoad method. The first is to set up an audio input object to capture sound from the device's microphone while recording video.

```
- (void)viewDidLoad
{
    [super viewDidLoad];
    self.captureSession = [[AVCaptureSession alloc] init];
    //Optional: self.captureSession.sessionPreset = AVCaptureSessionPresetMedium;

    AVCaptureDevice *videoDevice =
        [AVCaptureDevice defaultDeviceWithMediaType:AVMediaTypeVideo];
    AVCaptureDevice *audioDevice =
        [AVCaptureDevice defaultDeviceWithMediaType:AVMediaTypeAudio];

    self.videoInput =
        [AVCaptureDeviceInput deviceInputWithDevice:videoDevice error:nil];
    self.audioInput =
        [[AVCaptureDeviceInput alloc] initWithDevice:audioDevice error:nil];

    // ...
}
```

Next, you're going to set up an output object that records the data from the input objects and produces a movie file.

```
- (void)viewDidLoad
{
    // ...

    self.stillImageOutput = [[AVCaptureStillImageOutput alloc] init];
    NSDictionary *stillImageOutputSettings = [[NSDictionary alloc]
        initWithObjectsAndKeys:AVVideoCodecJPEG, AVVideoCodecKey, nil];
    [self.stillImageOutput setOutputSettings:stillImageOutputSettings];

    self.movieOutput = [[AVCaptureMovieFileOutput alloc] init];

    // ...
}
```

Finally, you're going to set up the capture session in the picture-taking mode and adjust the size of the preview layer so that it won't cover the new segment control.

```
- (void)viewDidLoad
{
    // ...

    // Setup capture session for taking pictures
    [self.captureSession addInput:self.videoInput];
    [self.captureSession addOutput:self.stillImageOutput];

    AVCaptureVideoPreviewLayer *previewLayer =
        [AVCaptureVideoPreviewLayer layerWithSession:self.captureSession];
    UIView *aView = self.view;
    previewLayer.frame =
        CGRectMake(0, 70, self.view.frame.size.width,
self.view.frame.size.height-140);
    [aView.layer addSublayer:previewLayer];
}
```

With all these changes, your viewDidLoad method should resemble the code that follows:

```
- (void)viewDidLoad
{
    [super viewDidLoad];
    self.captureSession = [[AVCaptureSession alloc] init];
    //Optional: self.captureSession.sessionPreset = AVCaptureSessionPresetMedium;

    AVCaptureDevice *videoDevice =
        [AVCaptureDevice defaultDeviceWithMediaType:AVMediaTypeVideo];
    AVCaptureDevice *audioDevice =
        [AVCaptureDevice defaultDeviceWithMediaType:AVMediaTypeAudio];

    self.videoInput =
        [AVCaptureDeviceInput deviceInputWithDevice:videoDevice error:nil];
    self.audioInput =
        [[AVCaptureDeviceInput alloc] initWithDevice:audioDevice error:nil];

    self.stillImageOutput = [[AVCaptureStillImageOutput alloc] init];
    NSDictionary *stillImageOutputSettings = [[NSDictionary alloc]
        initWithObjectsAndKeys:AVVideoCodecJPEG, AVVideoCodecKey, nil];
    [self.stillImageOutput setOutputSettings:stillImageOutputSettings];

    self.movieOutput = [[AVCaptureMovieFileOutput alloc] init];

    // Setup capture session for taking pictures
    [self.captureSession addInput:self.videoInput];
    [self.captureSession addOutput:self.stillImageOutput];

    AVCaptureVideoPreviewLayer *previewLayer =
        [AVCaptureVideoPreviewLayer layerWithSession:self.captureSession];
    UIView *aView = self.view;
    previewLayer.frame =
        CGRectMake(0, 70, self.view.frame.size.width, self.view.frame.size.height-140);
    [aView.layer addSublayer:previewLayer];
}
```

Note that you're not adding audioInput and movieOutput objects to the capture session. Later you'll add and remove input objects, depending on which mode the user selects, but for now it's assumed to be the "Take Photo" mode. Therefore, only input and output objects associated with that particular mode are added in the viewDidLoad method. (For the same reason, it's also important that the segment control has the correct selected index value set.)

Now, update the capture action method. It should now check what mode the application is in and if in "Take Photo" mode, do what it used to do, namely, capture a still image.

```
- (IBAction)capture:(id)sender
{
    if (self.modeControl.selectedSegmentIndex == 0)
    {
        // Picture Mode
        [self captureStillImage];
    }
    else
    {
        // Video Mode
    }
}
```

If in video recording mode, however, it should toggle between a start and stop recording mode, depending on whether or not a movie is currently being recorded, as shown in the following code.

```
- (IBAction)capture:(id)sender
{
    if (self.modeControl.selectedSegmentIndex == 0)
    {
        // Picture Mode
        [self captureStillImage];
    }
    else
    {
        // Video Mode
        if (self.movieOutput.isRecording == YES)
        {
            [self.captureButton setTitle:@"Capture" forState:UIControlStateNormal];
            [self.movieOutput stopRecording];
        }
        else
        {
            [self.captureButton setTitle:@"Stop" forState:UIControlStateNormal];
            [self.movieOutput startRecordingToOutputFileURL:[self tempFileURL]
                recordingDelegate:self];
        }
    }
}
```

You have probably noticed that you called the method tempFileURL to set up your AVCaptureOutput earlier. This method, in short, returns a path for your recorded video to be temporarily saved on your device. If there is already a file saved at the location, it will delete that file. (This way, you never use more than one video's worth of disk space.) Here's its implementation.

```
- (NSURL *) tempFileURL
{
    NSString *outputPath = [[NSString alloc] initWithFormat:@"%@%@",
        NSTemporaryDirectory(), @"output.mov"];
    NSURL *outputURL = [[NSURL alloc] initFileURLWithPath:outputPath];
    NSFileManager *manager = [[NSFileManager alloc] init];
    if ([manager fileExistsAtPath:outputPath])
    {
        [manager removeItemAtPath:outputPath error:nil];
    }
    return outputURL;
}
```

The next step is to set up your AVCaptureMovieFileOutput's delegate method to be invoked when an AVCaptureSession has finished recording a movie. The method starts by checking whether there were any errors in recording the video to a file, and then saves your video file into your Asset Library. The process of writing a video to the photos album is nearly the same as with photos, so you'll probably recognize a lot of that code from the previous recipe:

```
- (void)captureOutput:(AVCaptureFileOutput *)captureOutput
didFinishRecordingToOutputFileAtURL:(NSURL *)outputFileURL
        fromConnections:(NSArray *)connections
                  error:(NSError *)error
{
    BOOL recordedSuccessfully = YES;
    if ([error code] != noErr)
    {
        // A problem occurred: Find out if the recording was successful.
        id value = [[error userInfo]
            objectForKey:AVErrorRecordingSuccessfullyFinishedKey];
        if (value)
            recordedSuccessfully = [value boolValue];
        // Logging the problem anyway:
        NSLog(@"A problem occurred while recording: %@", error);
    }
    if (recordedSuccessfully)
    {
        ALAssetsLibrary *library = [[ALAssetsLibrary alloc] init];

        [library writeVideoAtPathToSavedPhotosAlbum:outputFileURL
            completionBlock:^(NSURL *assetURL, NSError *error)
            {
                UIAlertView *alert;
                if (!error)
                {
                    alert = [[UIAlertView alloc] initWithTitle:@"Video Saved"
                        message:@"The movie was successfully saved to you photos library"
                        delegate:nil
                        cancelButtonTitle:@"OK"
                        otherButtonTitles:nil, nil];
                }
```

```
        else
        {
            alert = [[UIAlertView alloc] initWithTitle:@"Error Saving Video"
                message:@"The movie was not saved to you photos library"
                delegate:nil
                cancelButtonTitle:@"OK"
                otherButtonTitles:nil, nil];
        }
        [alert show];
    }
];
    }
}
```

Finally, you'll implement the action method that's invoked when the user switches between the two modes. Here is its implementation:

```
- (IBAction)updateMode:(id)sender
{
    [self.captureSession stopRunning];
    if (self.modeControl.selectedSegmentIndex == 0)
    {
        // Still Image Mode
        if (self.movieOutput.isRecording == YES)
        {
            [self.movieOutput stopRecording];
        }
        [self.captureSession removeInput:self.audioInput];
        [self.captureSession removeOutput:self.movieOutput];
        [self.captureSession addOutput:self.stillImageOutput];
    }
    else
    {
        // Video Mode
        [self.captureSession removeOutput:self.stillImageOutput];
        [self.captureSession addInput:self.audioInput];
        [self.captureSession addOutput:self.movieOutput];

        // Set orientation of capture connections to portrait
        NSArray *array = [[self.captureSession.outputs objectAtIndex:0] connections];
        for (AVCaptureConnection *connection in array)
        {
            connection.videoOrientation = AVCaptureVideoOrientationPortrait;
        }
    }
    [self.captureButton setTitle:@"Capture" forState:UIControlStateNormal];

    [self.captureSession startRunning];
}
```

This method updates the capture session with the correct input and output objects that are associated with the corresponding mode. It also sets the orientation mode for the video mode output objects. (This is already taken care of for the still image mode; see Recipe 8-6 for details.) Finally, it resets the title of the capture button.

Now you are ready to build and run your app. You should be able to switch between taking photos and recording videos and the results should be stored in the photos library of your device. Figure 8-14 shows the app in action.

Figure 8-14. An app that can take photos and record videos

Recipe 8-8: Capturing Video Frames

For many applications that utilize videos, a thumbnail image is a useful way to "represent" a given video. In this recipe you expand your previous recipe and generate and display a thumbnail image when a video has been recorded.

Start by adding the CoreMedia framework to your project. You use it to generate the thumbnail.

Next, add an image view to the lower-left corner of your main view's user interface so that it resembles Figure 8-15.

Figure 8-15. The user interface with a thumbnail image view in the lower-left corner

Also, add an outlet for the image view so that you can reference it later from your code. Name it thumbnailImageView.

Now, let's get to the core of this recipe, the method that extracts an image from the halfway point of the movie and updates the thumbnail image view. Add the method to your view controller:

```
-(void)createThumbnailForVideoURL:(NSURL *)videoURL
{
    AVURLAsset *myAsset = [[AVURLAsset alloc] initWithURL:videoURL
options:[NSDictionary dictionaryWithObject:@"YES"
forKey:AVURLAssetPreferPreciseDurationAndTimingKey]];

    AVAssetImageGenerator *imageGenerator =
        [AVAssetImageGenerator assetImageGeneratorWithAsset:myAsset];
    //Make sure images are correctly rotated.
    imageGenerator.appliesPreferredTrackTransform = YES;
    Float64 durationSeconds = CMTimeGetSeconds([myAsset duration]);
    CMTime half = CMTimeMakeWithSeconds(durationSeconds/2.0, 600);
    NSArray *times = [NSArray arrayWithObjects: [NSValue valueWithCMTime:half], nil];

    [imageGenerator generateCGImagesAsynchronouslyForTimes:times
        completionHandler:^(CMTime requestedTime, CGImageRef image, CMTime actualTime,
                            AVAssetImageGeneratorResult result, NSError *error)
        {
            if (result == AVAssetImageGeneratorSucceeded)
            {
                self.thumbnailImageView.image = [UIImage imageWithCGImage:image];
            }
```

```
        else if (result == AVAssetImageGeneratorFailed)
        {
            NSLog(@"Failed with error: %@", [error localizedDescription]);
        }
    }
    };
}
```

Now, all that's left is to call the method when a video has been recorded. Add the following line to your captureOutput:didFinishRecordingToOutputFileAtURL: method:

```
- (void)captureOutput:(AVCaptureFileOutput *)captureOutput
didFinishRecordingToOutputFileAtURL:(NSURL *)outputFileURL
     fromConnections:(NSArray *)connections
                error:(NSError *)error
{
    BOOL recordedSuccessfully = YES;
    if ([error code] != noErr)
    {
        // A problem occurred: Find out if the recording was successful.
        id value =
            [[error userInfo] objectForKey:AVErrorRecordingSuccessfullyFinishedKey];
        if (value)
            recordedSuccessfully = [value boolValue];
        // Logging the problem anyway:
        NSLog(@"A problem occurred while recording: %@", error);
    }
    if (recordedSuccessfully)
    {
        [self createThumbnailForVideoURL:outputFileURL];
        ALAssetsLibrary *library = [[ALAssetsLibrary alloc] init];

        [library writeVideoAtPathToSavedPhotosAlbum:outputFileURL
            completionBlock:^(NSURL *assetURL, NSError *error)
            {
                UIAlertView *alert;
                if (!error)
                {
                    alert = [[UIAlertView alloc] initWithTitle:@"Video Saved"
                        message:@"The movie was successfully saved to you photos library"
                        delegate:nil
                        cancelButtonTitle:@"OK"
                        otherButtonTitles:nil, nil];
                }
                else
                {
                    alert = [[UIAlertView alloc] initWithTitle:@"Error Saving Video"
                        message:@"The movie was not saved to you photos library"
                        delegate:nil
                        cancelButtonTitle:@"OK"
                        otherButtonTitles:nil, nil];
                }
```

```
                [alert show];

            }
        ];
    }
}
```

Now build and run your application and switch to the Record Video mode when it has launched. Record a video by pressing the Capture button twice (once for start and again for stop). A few seconds later a thumbnail from halfway into your movie is now displayed in the lower-left corner, as Figure 8-16 shows.

Figure 8-16. Your app displaying a movie thumbnail in the lower-left corner

Note　As you may have noticed, the method used in Recipe 8-8 is rather slow, and it usually takes a couple of seconds to extract the image. There are other ways you may want to try—for example, adding a AVCaptureStillImageOutput to your capture session (it's possible to have several output objects connected) and taking a snapshot when the recording starts. You can use what you learned in Recipe 8-6. Another way is to use the AVCaptureVideoDataOutput mentioned earlier. With that method you can grab any frame you like during recording and extract an image.

Summary

As a developer, you have a great deal of choice when it comes to dealing with your device's camera. The predefined interfaces such as `UIImagePickerController` and `UIVideoEditorController` are incredibly useful and well designed, but Apple's implementation of the AV Foundation framework allows for more possibilities. Everything from dealing with video, audio, and still images is possible. Even a quick glance at the full documentation reveals countless other functionalities not discussed here, including everything from device capabilities (such as the video camera's LED "torch") to the implementation of your own "Touch-To-Focus" functionality. We live in a world where images, audio, and video fly around the world in a matter of seconds, and as developers we must be able to design and create innovative solutions that fit in with our media-based community.

Chapter 9

Multimedia Recipes

In the words of Aldous Huxley, "After silence, that which comes nearest to expressing the inexpressible is music." We live in a world where we are surrounded by sound and music. From the most subtle background tune in an advertisement, to the immense blast of the electric guitar at a rock concert, sound has a tremendous impact and plays an integral part in our lives. It is our responsibility as developers to translate this force into our applications and bring the most complete and ideal experience to users.

Throughout this chapter, a variety of recipes make use of accessing the music library. Therefore, in order to fully test these recipes, you should ensure that there are at least a few songs in your device's music library.

Recipe 9-1: Playing Audio

If you ask almost any random person what they think of when they hear the words "iPhone" and "audio," they will probably be thinking along the lines of their iPod and the thousands of songs they have downloaded. What most users tend to overlook, despite its immense importance, is the concept of background audio and sound effects. These sound clips and tunes may go completely unnoticed by the user in normal use, but in terms of app functionality and design they can tremendously improve the quality of an app. It may be the little "shutter click" when you take a picture, or some background music that gets stuck in your head after you play a game for too long; regardless of whether the user notices it, sound can make a world of difference. The iOS AV Foundation framework provides a simple way to access, play, and manipulate sound files using the AVAudioPlayer. Here you create a sample project that allows you to play an audio file, as well as allows the user to manipulate the clip's playback.

Setting Up the Application

Start by creating a new single-view application project. In this recipe you utilize two frameworks that aren't linked by default so you need to add them to your project. These are AVFoundation.framework, which includes the AVAudioPlayer class, and AudioToolbox.framework, which you'll use to vibrate the device.

Next, to import the APIs for these frameworks, switch over to your view controller's header file and add the following statements:

```
//
//  ViewController.h
//  Recipe 9.1: Playing Audio
//

#import <UIKit/UIKit.h>
#import <AVFoundation/AVFoundation.h>
#import <AudioToolbox/AudioToolbox.h>

@interface ViewController : UIViewController

@end
```

Now build your view in the view controller's XIB file. Add three sliders for rate, pan, and volume. Also add three buttons; one for playing the device vibration, one for starting the player, and one for pausing it. Finally, you monitor the audio player's channel levels via labels at the top of the view. Set up your view so it looks like Figure 9-1. (Note that the "0.0" labels are separate from the "Average" and the "Peak" labels.)

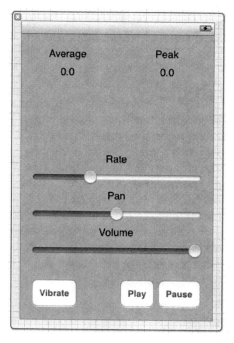

Figure 9-1. *A user interface to control an AVAudioPlayer*

You need your slider's values to match the possible values of the properties they control. Using the Attribute inspector, adjust the minimum and maximum values of your "Rate" slider to **0.5** and **2.0** (corresponding to half speed and 2x speed.) Also, set its current value set to **0**. The values for the "Pan" slider should be **-1** and **1** (correspond to left pan and right pan) with 0 as the current value. The "Volume" slider's default values should already be fine, as the volume property goes from 0 to 1. Just set its current value to **1** (maximum volume).

As you have done in the past recipes, you create outlets for the controls that are referenced from your code, and actions for the events that you need to respond to. Create the following outlets:

- `rateSlider`, `panSlider`, and `volumeSlider` for the sliders
- `averageLabel` and `peakLabel` for your two level-monitoring labels (the ones with the texts "0.0" in Figure 9-1)

And the following actions:

- `updateRate`, `updatePan`, and `updateVolume` for the Value Changed events of the respective sliders
- `playVibrateSound`, `startPlayer`, and `pausePlayer` for the Touch Up Inside events of the buttons

Also add a property to your header file to keep track of your AVAudioPlayer:

```
@property (strong, nonatomic) AVAudioPlayer *player;
```

The last step in your header file is to make your view controller conform to the AVAudioPlayerDelegate protocol. Your ViewController.h file should now resemble this code:

```
//
//  ViewController.h
//  Recipe 9.1: Playing Audio
//

#import <UIKit/UIKit.h>
#import <AVFoundation/AVFoundation.h>
#import <AudioToolbox/AudioToolbox.h>

@interface ViewController : UIViewController<AVAudioPlayerDelegate>

@property (weak, nonatomic) IBOutlet UILabel *averageLabel;
@property (weak, nonatomic) IBOutlet UILabel *peakLabel;
@property (weak, nonatomic) IBOutlet UISlider *rateSlider;
@property (weak, nonatomic) IBOutlet UISlider *panSlider;
@property (weak, nonatomic) IBOutlet UISlider *volumeSlider;
@property (strong, nonatomic) AVAudioPlayer *player;

- (IBAction)updateRate:(id)sender;
- (IBAction)updatePan:(id)sender;
- (IBAction)updateVolume:(id)sender;
- (IBAction)playVibrateSound:(id)sender;
```

```
- (IBAction)startPlayer:(id)sender;
- (IBAction)pausePlayer:(id)sender;

@end
```

Before you proceed, you need to select and import the sound file that your application will be playing. The file we use is called `midnight-ride.mp3`, and the code reflects this file name. You need to change any filename or file type according to the file that you choose. You should consult Apple's documentation[1] on which file types are appropriate, but it is fairly safe to assume that most commonly used file types such as `.wav` or `.mp3` will work.

> **Tip**   We downloaded our sound file from Sound Jay, which offers sound and music files free of charge. Be sure to read the terms of use (`http://www.soundjay.com/tos.html`) for how you may use Sound Jay's files in your projects.

Add the sound file to your project by dragging and dropping it into the Supported Files Folder. For more detailed information on adding resource files refer to Chapter 1, Recipe 1-8.

Setting Up the Audio Player

Now, switch over to ViewController.m and locate the `viewDidLoad` method. Add the following code to set up the AVAudioPlayer:

```
- (void)viewDidLoad
{
    [super viewDidLoad];
    // Do any additional setup after loading the view, typically from a nib.
    NSString *fileName = @"midnight-ride"; // Change this to your own file
    NSString *fileType = @"mp3";
    NSString *soundFilePath =
        [[NSBundle mainBundle] pathForResource:fileName ofType:fileType];
    NSURL *soundFileURL = [NSURL fileURLWithPath:soundFilePath];

    NSError *error;
    self.player =
        [[AVAudioPlayer alloc] initWithContentsOfURL:soundFileURL error:&error];
    if (error)
    {
        NSLog(@"Error creating the audio player: %@", error);
    }
    self.player.enableRate = YES; //Allows us to change the playback rate.
    self.player.meteringEnabled = YES; //Allows us to monitor levels
    self.player.delegate = self;
    self.volumeSlider.value = self.player.volume;
```

---

[1]https://developer.apple.com/library/ios/documentation/AudioVideo/Conceptual/MultimediaPG/MultimediaProgrammingGuide.pdf

```
    self.rateSlider.value = self.player.rate;
    self.panSlider.value = self.player.pan;

    [self.player prepareToPlay]; //Preload audio to decrease lag

    [NSTimer scheduledTimerWithTimeInterval:0.1
         target:self selector:@selector(updateLabels) userInfo:nil repeats:YES];
}
```

As you can see, you've gotten the URL for your sound file and initialized your AVAudioPlayer with it; You set up the enableRate property to allow you to change the playback rate, and set the meteringEnabled property to allow you to monitor the player's levels; You called the optional prepareToPlay on your player to pre-load the sound file, hopefully making your application slightly faster; you created a timer at the end, which performs your updateLabels method ten times a second. This way you can have your labels updating at a nearly constant rate.

Let's put in a simple implementation of the updateLabels method.

```
-(void)updateLabels
{
    [self.player updateMeters];
    self.averageLabel.text =
        [NSString stringWithFormat:@"%f", [self.player averagePowerForChannel:0]];
    self.peakLabel.text =
        [NSString stringWithFormat:@"%f", [self.player peakPowerForChannel:0]];
}
```

You need to call updateMeters anytime that you use the averagePowerForChannel or peakPowerForChannel methods to get up-to-date values. Both methods take an NSUInteger argument that specifies the channel for which to retrieve information. By giving it the value of 0, you specify the left channel for a stereo track, or the single channel for a mono track. Given that you are dealing with only a basic use of the functionality, channel 0 is a good default.

Next, implement your action methods for your sliders. These actions are called every time the respective slider's value is changed.

```
- (IBAction)updateRate:(id)sender
{
    self.player.rate = self.rateSlider.value;
}

- (IBAction)updatePan:(id)sender
{
    self.player.pan = self.panSlider.value;
}

- (IBAction)updateVolume:(id)sender
{
    self.player.volume = self.volumeSlider.value;
}
```

Now, implement your button action methods, which are also quite simple.

```
- (IBAction)playVibrateSound:(id)sender
{
    AudioServicesPlaySystemSound(kSystemSoundID_Vibrate);
}

- (IBAction)startPlayer:(id)sender
{
    [self.player play];
}

- (IBAction)pausePlayer:(id)sender
{
    [self.player pause];
}
```

> **Note** Although most of the AV Foundation functionalities that you are currently working with will work on the simulator (using your computer's microphone and speakers), the foregoing vibrate sound will not. You need a physical device to test this functionality.

Handling Errors and Interruptions

At this point, your app can successfully play and pause your music, and you can adjust your playback rate, pan, and volume, and monitor your output levels. However, it lacks some basic error handling and interruption handling.

To catch any errors in playing files, you can implement the following method from the AVAudioPlayerDelegate protocol:

```
-(void)audioPlayerDecodeErrorDidOccur:(AVAudioPlayer *)player error:(NSError *)error
{
    NSLog(@"Error playing file: %@", [error localizedDescription]);
}
```

Whenever you are dealing with an app that has sound or music involved, there is always a concern that your app may be interrupted by a phone call or text message, and you should always include functionality to deal with these concerns. This can be done through a couple of AVAudioPlayer delegate methods. The audioPlayerBeginInterruption: method is called when an audio player has been interrupted while playing. For most cases, you don't have to provide an implementation for that method because your player is automatically paused by the system. However, if you want your player to resume playing after such an interruption, you need to implement audioPlayerEndInterruption:. In this recipe you want the audio player to resume, so add the following code to your view controller:

```
- (void)audioPlayerEndInterruption:(AVAudioPlayer *)player withOptions:(NSUInteger)flags
{
    if (flags == AVAudioSessionInterruptionOptionShouldResume)
    {
        [player play];
    }
}
```

You can now see the flexibility with which you can use the AVAudioPlayer, despite its simplistic use. By using multiple instances of AVAudioPlayer, you can implement complex audio designs using multiple sounds at the same time. One could possibly have a background music track running in one AVAudioPlayer, and have one or two others to handle event-based sound effects. The power, simplicity, and flexibility of the AVAudioPlayer class are what make it so popular among iOS developers.

Recipe 9-2: Recording Audio

Now that you have dealt with the key concept of playing audio, you can familiarize yourself with the reverse: recording audio. This process is very similar in both structure and implementation to playing audio. You use the AVAudioRecorder class to do your recording in conjunction with an AVAudioPlayer to handle the playback of your recording. We also make this project slightly more complicated by setting up two multi-functional buttons; one for starting and stopping a recording, and one for playing and pausing a recording.

Start by creating a new single view application project. You need to link and import the AVFoundation framework into your project again, as you did in the previous recipe. Unlike the previous recipe, however, you do not need the Audio Toolbox framework.

Now, set up the user interface so that it looks like Figure 9-2.

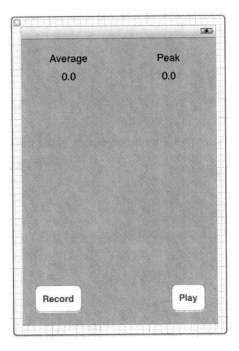

Figure 9-2. User interface for recording and playing audio

Create the following outlets:

- averageLabel and peakLabel for the level-monitoring labels
- recordButton and playButton for the buttons

Create the following actions:

- toggleRecording for the Change Value event of the Record button
- togglePlaying for the Change Value event of the Play button

Before you proceed to your implementation file, you'll make some additional changes to the ViewController.h file. The first is to prepare the view controller for being a delegate for both the audio player and audio recorder by conforming to the AVAudioPlayerDelegate and the AVAudioRecorderDelegate protocols.

```
@interface ViewController : UIViewController<AVAudioPlayerDelegate,
                                             AVAudioRecorderDelegate>
```

Next, add an instance variable to flag when a new recording is available:

```
@interface ViewController : UIViewController<AVAudioPlayerDelegate,
                                             AVAudioRecorderDelegate>
{
    @private
    BOOL _newRecordingAvailable;
}

// ...

@end
```

Finally, add three properties for holding the instance of the audio player, the audio recorder, and the file path to the recorded file. With these and the previous changes, your ViewController.h file should resemble this code, changes in bold:

```
//
//  ViewController.h
//  Recipe 9.2: Recording Audio
//

#import <UIKit/UIKit.h>
#import <AVFoundation/AVFoundation.h>

@interface ViewController : UIViewController<AVAudioPlayerDelegate, AVAudioRecorderDelegate>
{
    BOOL _newRecordingAvailable;
}

@property (weak, nonatomic) IBOutlet UILabel *averageLabel;
@property (weak, nonatomic) IBOutlet UILabel *peakLabel;
@property (weak, nonatomic) IBOutlet UIButton *recordButton;
```

```
@property (weak, nonatomic) IBOutlet UIButton *playButton;
@property (strong, nonatomic) AVAudioPlayer *player;
@property (strong, nonatomic) AVAudioRecorder *recorder;
@property (strong, nonatomic) NSString *recordedFilePath;

- (IBAction)toggleRecording:(id)sender;
- (IBAction)togglePlaying:(id)sender;

@end
```

Setting Up an Audio Recorder

Now, it's time to implement the viewDidLoad method in the ViewController.m file. First, you'll define a file path for the recording:

```
self.recordedFilePath = [[NSString alloc] initWithFormat:@"%@%@",
    NSTemporaryDirectory(), @"recording.wav"];
```

Next, you'll initialize the audio recorder with the file path converted to a URL.

```
NSURL *url = [[NSURL alloc] initFileURLWithPath:self.recordedFilePath];
NSError *error;
self.recorder = [[AVAudioRecorder alloc] initWithURL:url settings:nil error:&error];
if (error)
{
    NSLog(@"Error initializing recorder: %@", error);
}
self.recorder.meteringEnabled = YES;
self.recorder.delegate = self;
[self.recorder prepareToRecord];
```

The call to prepareToRecord assures that when the user taps the Record button later, the recording will start immediately.

Finally, as in Recipe 9-1, start a timer that triggers updating of the level-monitoring labels. The viewDidLoad method should now look like the following code:

```
- (void)viewDidLoad
{
    [super viewDidLoad];
        // Do any additional setup after loading the view, typically from a nib.
    self.recordedFilePath = [[NSString alloc] initWithFormat:@"%@%@",
        NSTemporaryDirectory(), @"recording.wav"];
    NSURL *url = [[NSURL alloc] initFileURLWithPath:self.recordedFilePath];
    NSError *error;
    self.recorder = [[AVAudioRecorder alloc] initWithURL:url settings:nil error:&error];
    if (error)
    {
        NSLog(@"Error initializing recorder: %@", error);
    }
```

```
    self.recorder.meteringEnabled = YES;
    self.recorder.delegate = self;
    [self.recorder prepareToRecord];

    [NSTimer scheduledTimerWithTimeInterval:0.01 target:self
        selector:@selector(updateLabels) userInfo:nil repeats:YES];
}
```

You may be wondering why you aren't also initializing the audio player in the viewDidLoad method. The reason is that the player's initializer requires a URL that points to an audio file, but at the time of the view loading, there are no audio files recorded. Therefore, as you'll see later, you create the player when the user taps the Play button.

Your updateLabels method resembles the one in Recipe 9-1 with the exception that now it's the audio recorder that's being monitored and not the audio player.

```
-(void)updateLabels
{
    [self.recorder updateMeters];
    self.averageLabel.text =
        [NSString stringWithFormat:@"%f", [self.recorder averagePowerForChannel:0]];
    self.peakLabel.text =
        [NSString stringWithFormat:@"%f", [self.recorder peakPowerForChannel:0]];
}
```

Now, let's turn to the action methods. Start with the simplest one, toggleRecording:. It has just two cases. If the recorder is currently active, it should stop the recording and reset the title of the Record button; if not, it should start recording and change the title of the Record button to "Stop", as shown here:

```
- (IBAction)toggleRecording:(id)sender
{
    if ([self.recorder isRecording])
    {
        [self.recorder stop];
        [self.recordButton setTitle:@"Record" forState:UIControlStateNormal];
    }
    else
    {
        [self.recorder record];
        [self.recordButton setTitle:@"Stop" forState:UIControlStateNormal];
    }
}
```

Also, implement the following method of the AVAudioRecorderDelegate protocol. It will be called when a recording has finished, with a flag that indicates whether the recording was completed successfully. Here's the implementation:

```
- (void)audioRecorderDidFinishRecording:(AVAudioRecorder *)recorder successfully:(BOOL)flag
{
    _newRecordingAvailable = flag;
    [self.recordButton setTitle:@"Record" forState:UIControlStateNormal];
}
```

As you can see, if the recording was successful you indicate that a new recording is available by setting an instance variable flag. You also reset the title of the button to read "Record" again.

Now to the slightly more complicated Play button. When the user taps it there are four possible states (we'll only need to consider three):

1. The audio player is active, in which case you pause it and reset the button's title to "Play."

2. A new recording is available, which forces you to re-create the audio player with the new file. Then start the player and set the button's title to "Pause."

3. A player has been created but is currently not active, which means it has been paused and should be restarted. Start the player and set the button title to "Pause."

4. No player has been created yet. This means that there is no valid recording available. Just ignore this case.

Here are the preceding points translated into code:

```
- (IBAction)togglePlaying:(id)sender
{
    if (self.player.playing)
    {
        [self.player pause];
        [self.playButton setTitle:@"Play" forState:UIControlStateNormal];
    }
    else if (_newRecordingAvailable)
    {
        NSURL *url = [[NSURL alloc] initFileURLWithPath:self.recordedFilePath];
        NSError *error;
        self.player = [[AVAudioPlayer alloc] initWithContentsOfURL:url error:&error];
        if (!error)
        {
            self.player.delegate = self;
            [self.player play];
        }
        else
        {
            NSLog(@"Error initializing player: %@", error);
        }
        [self.playButton setTitle:@"Pause" forState:UIControlStateNormal];
        _newRecordingAvailable = NO;
    }
    else if (self.player)
    {
        [self.player play];
        [self.playButton setTitle:@"Pause" forState:UIControlStateNormal];
    }
}
```

When the player has finished playing the button's title should be reset. The following delegate method takes care of that:

```
-(void)audioPlayerDidFinishPlaying:(AVAudioPlayer *)player successfully:(BOOL)flag
{
    [self.playButton setTitle:@"Play" forState:UIControlStateNormal];
}
```

Handling Interruptions

At this point, your application successfully records and plays a sound. As with the previous recipe, you should implement the delegate methods to handle interruptions such as phone calls or text messages. Here are the methods for handling interruptions for both the audio and the recorder:

```
- (void)audioPlayerEndInterruption:(AVAudioPlayer *)player withOptions:(NSUInteger)flags
{
    if (flags == AVAudioSessionInterruptionOptionShouldResume)
    {
        [player play];
    }
}

- (void)audioRecorderEndInterruption:(AVAudioRecorder *)recorder withOptions:(NSUInteger)flags
{
    if (flags == AVAudioSessionInterruptionOptionShouldResume)
    {
        [recorder record];
    }
}
```

Now you have a fully functional app to record and play sounds from your device. As you can see, the AVAudioRecorder and AVAudioPlayer work well together to provide a complete yet simple audio interface for the user.

Recipe 9-3: Accessing the Music Library

So far you have been able to deal with playing and manipulating sound files that you have included in your project, but there is an easy way to access a significantly larger supply of sound files: by accessing the user's music library.

Here you make another new project. This time you need to link it with the Media Player framework, and as usual add an import statement for it to your view controller.

Setting Up a Basic Music Player

You set up your view to work as a basic music player, so it looks like Figure 9-3.

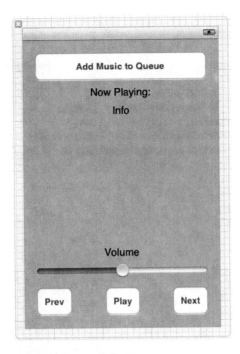

Figure 9-3. User interface for queuing music from the music library

Create the following outlets for the controls which are referenced from your code:

- infoLabel
- volumeSlider
- playButton

And the following actions:

- addItems, for the Touch Up Inside event of the Add Music to Queue button
- prevTapped, playTapped, and nextTapped, respectively, for the three buttons at the bottom side.
- updateVolume, for the Value Changed event of the volume slider

You also define two properties in your header file, one of type MPMusicPlayerController called player, which you use to play music, and one of type MPMediaItemCollection called myCollection, which helps you keep track of your chosen tracks to play. Finally, you make your view controller the delegate for a class called MPMediaPickerController, which allows your user to select music to play. Overall, your header file should now look like so:

```
//
// ViewController.h
// Recipe 9.3: Accessing Music Library
//
```

```
#import <UIKit/UIKit.h>
#import <MediaPlayer/MediaPlayer.h>

@interface ViewController : UIViewController<MPMediaPickerControllerDelegate>

@property (weak, nonatomic) IBOutlet UILabel *infoLabel;
@property (weak, nonatomic) IBOutlet UISlider *volumeSlider;
@property (weak, nonatomic) IBOutlet UIButton *playButton;
@property (strong, nonatomic) MPMediaItemCollection *myCollection;
@property (strong, nonatomic) MPMusicPlayerController *player;

- (IBAction)addItems:(id)sender;
- (IBAction)prevTapped:(id)sender;
- (IBAction)playTapped:(id)sender;
- (IBAction)nextTapped:(id)sender;
- (IBAction)updateVolume:(id)sender;

@end
```

Now, you can set up your viewDidLoad method.

```
- (void)viewDidLoad
{
    [super viewDidLoad];
        // Do any additional setup after loading the view, typically from a nib.
    self.infoLabel.text = @"...";

    self.player = [MPMusicPlayerController applicationMusicPlayer];

    [self setNotifications];

    [self.player beginGeneratingPlaybackNotifications];

    [self.player setShuffleMode:MPMusicShuffleModeOff];
    self.player.repeatMode = MPMusicRepeatModeNone;

    self.volumeSlider.value = self.player.volume;
}
```

> **Note** The MPMusicPlayerController class has two important class methods that allow you to access an instance of the class. The one you used previously, applicationMusicPlayer, returns an application-specific music player. This option can be useful for keeping your music separate from the device's music player, but has the downside of being unable to play once the app enters the background. Alternatively, you can use the iPodMusicPlayer, which allows for continuous play despite being in the background. The main thing to keep in mind in this case, however, is that your player may already have a nowPlayingItem from the actual iPod that you should be able to handle.

Handling Notifications

Whenever you use an instance of `MPMusicPlayerController`, it is recommended to register for notifications for whenever the playback state changes, or whenever the currently playing song changes. We have extracted this code into a helper method named `setNotifications`. Here is its implementation:

```
-(void)setNotifications
{
    NSNotificationCenter *notificationCenter = [NSNotificationCenter defaultCenter];

    [notificationCenter
     addObserver: self
     selector:    @selector(handleNowPlayingItemChanged:)
     name:        MPMusicPlayerControllerNowPlayingItemDidChangeNotification
     object:      self.player];

    [notificationCenter
     addObserver: self
     selector:    @selector(handlePlaybackStateChanged:)
     name:        MPMusicPlayerControllerPlaybackStateDidChangeNotification
     object:      self.player];

    [notificationCenter
     addObserver: self
     selector:    @selector(handleVolumeChangedFromHardware:)
     name:        @"AVSystemController_SystemVolumeDidChangeNotification"
     object:      nil];
}
```

Except for the music player notifications, you have included a third notification registration in order to make sure you know any time the user adjusts the device volume using the device's side buttons. This way, your application can update its slider control to reflect these changes.

Now implement the method that responds to the volume changed notification. It simply updates the slider (animated) with the new level:

```
-(void)handleVolumeChangedFromHardware:(id)sender
{
    [self.volumeSlider setValue:self.player.volume animated:YES];
}
```

Next, the method to handle the playback state change notification simply updates the title of the play button to reflect the new state, like so:

```
- (void) handlePlaybackStateChanged: (id) notification
{
    MPMusicPlaybackState playbackState = [self.player playbackState];
```

```
    if (playbackState == MPMusicPlaybackStateStopped)
    {
        [self.playButton setTitle:@"Play" forState:UIControlStateNormal];
    }
    else if (playbackState == MPMusicPlaybackStatePaused)
    {
        [self.playButton setTitle:@"Play" forState:UIControlStateNormal];
    }
    else if (playbackState == MPMusicPlaybackStatePlaying)
    {
        [self.playButton setTitle:@"Pause" forState:UIControlStateNormal];
    }
}
```

Finally, whenever the currently playing song is changed, the info label should be updated. The following method handles that:

```
- (void) handleNowPlayingItemChanged: (id) notification
{
    MPMediaItem *currentItemPlaying = [self.player nowPlayingItem];
    if (currentItemPlaying)
    {
        NSString *info = [NSString stringWithFormat:@"%@ - %@",
            [currentItemPlaying valueForProperty:MPMediaItemPropertyTitle],
            [currentItemPlaying valueForProperty:MPMediaItemPropertyArtist]];
        self.infoLabel.text = info;
    }
    else
    {
        self.infoLabel.text = @"...";
    }
}
```

Picking Media to Play

To add music to your list of tunes use the MPMediaPickerController class. It provides, as shown in Figure 9-4, a standardized way to make a music selection. Add the following code to the addItems action method to set up and display a media picker:

```
- (IBAction)addItems:(id)sender
{
    MPMediaPickerController *picker =
        [[MPMediaPickerController alloc] initWithMediaTypes:MPMediaTypeMusic];
    picker.delegate = self;
    picker.allowsPickingMultipleItems = YES;
    picker.prompt = NSLocalizedString (@"Add songs to play",
        "Prompt in media item picker");
    [self presentViewController:picker animated:YES completion:NULL];
}
```

Figure 9-4. The user interface of the MPMediaPickerController to select songs

The media picker communicates with your view controller through the `MPMediaPickerControllerDelegate` protocol that you added to the header earlier. You implement the following two delegate methods to handle both cancellation and successful selection of media:

```
-(void)mediaPickerDidCancel:(MPMediaPickerController *)mediaPicker
{
    [self dismissViewControllerAnimated:YES completion:NULL];
}

-(void)mediaPicker:(MPMediaPickerController *)mediaPicker
didPickMediaItems:(MPMediaItemCollection *)mediaItemCollection
{
    [self updateQueueWithMediaItemCollection:mediaItemCollection];
    [self dismissViewControllerAnimated:YES completion:NULL];
}
```

An `MPMediaItemCollection` is the group of media items that were selected by the user. You use it to update the media player's queue in the `updateQueueWithMediaItemCollection:` method, like so:

```
-(void)updateQueueWithMediaItemCollection:(MPMediaItemCollection *)collection
{
    if (collection)
    {
        if (self.myCollection == nil)
```

```
        {
            self.myCollection = collection;
            [self.player setQueueWithItemCollection: self.myCollection];
            [self.player play];
        }
        else
        {
            BOOL wasPlaying = NO;
            if (self.player.playbackState == MPMusicPlaybackStatePlaying)
            {
                wasPlaying = YES;
            }

            MPMediaItem *nowPlayingItem        = self.player.nowPlayingItem;
            NSTimeInterval currentPlaybackTime = self.player.currentPlaybackTime;

            NSMutableArray *combinedMediaItems =
                [[self.myCollection items] mutableCopy];
            NSArray *newMediaItems = [collection items];
            [combinedMediaItems addObjectsFromArray: newMediaItems];

            self.myCollection =
                [MPMediaItemCollection collectionWithItems:combinedMediaItems];

            [self.player setQueueWithItemCollection:self.myCollection];

            self.player.nowPlayingItem        = nowPlayingItem;
            self.player.currentPlaybackTime = currentPlaybackTime;

            if (wasPlaying)
            {
                [self.player play];
            }
        }
    }
}
```

This method may seem complex, but it is actually a fairly linear progression. First, after checking to make sure that the collection of newly selected items is not nil, you check to see whether there is a previous queue set up. If not, you simply set your player's queue to this collection. On the other hand, if a collection does exist, you combine the two, set your player's queue as the result, and then restore your playback to where it previously was.

The remaining action methods' implementations are pretty straightforward. Here's the one that responds to user tapping the Prev button:

```
- (IBAction)prevTapped:(id)sender
{
    if ([self.player currentPlaybackTime] > 5.0)
    {
        [self.player skipToBeginning];
    }
```

```
    else
    {
        [self.player skipToPreviousItem];
    }
}
```

As you can see, in this example we've given the Prev button two functionalities; if the media player is at the beginning of the current song, tapping the button will skip to the previous song; however, if the playback is more than five seconds into the current song, tapping the button will skip to the beginning of the current song.

The next button is even simpler. It just skips to the next song:

```
- (IBAction)nextTapped:(id)sender
{
    [self.player skipToNextItem];
}
```

The Play button toggles between Play and Pause and updates the button title accordingly, like so:

```
- (IBAction)playTapped:(id)sender
{
    if ((self.myCollection != nil) &&
        (self.player.playbackState != MPMusicPlaybackStatePlaying))
    {
        [self.player play];
        [self.playButton setTitle:@"Pause" forState:UIControlStateNormal];
    }
    else if (self.player.playbackState == MPMusicPlaybackStatePlaying)
    {
        [self.player pause];
        [self.playButton setTitle:@"Play" forState:UIControlStateNormal];
    }
}
```

And finally, the action method for when the user drags the volume slider. It simply updates the player volume with the slider's value:

```
- (IBAction)updateVolume:(id)sender
{
    self.player.volume = self.volumeSlider.value;
}
```

Your application is now ready to build and run. One thing to note when you run this application is that until you start playing music, you cannot adjust your AVAudioPlayer's volume by using the external volume buttons, as these still control the ringer volume, as opposed to the playback volume. After you select a song to play, you receive full control over the playback volume through these buttons.

You'll now go on by adding the possibility to search the music library for media to add to the playback queue.

Querying Media

The media player comes with a powerful querying capability with which you can search the music library. To give you an idea of its possibilities we're going to add a new feature to the application. The feature allows the user to query the music library for items containing a certain text, and have them added to the media player's queue.

First, you add a UIButton as well as a UITextField to your XIB, so that your view now looks like Figure 9-5.

Figure 9-5. User interface with a feature for querying music by artist

Create an outlet with the name artistTextField for referencing the text field, and an action, named queueMusicByArtist, for the button.

The first thing you do with your new UITextField is to set its delegate to your view controller by adding the following lines to the viewDidLoad method:

```
- (void)viewDidLoad
{
    // ...

    self.artistTextField.delegate = self;
    self.artistTextField.enablesReturnKeyAutomatically = YES;
}
```

Make sure to adjust your header file to declare that your view controller conforms to the UITextFieldDelegate protocol.

```
@interface ViewController : UIViewController<MPMediaPickerControllerDelegate,
                                UITextFieldDelegate>

// ...

@end
```

Next, implement the following delegate method to have your text field dismiss the keyboard and automatically perform the query when the user taps the return key:

```
-(BOOL)textFieldShouldReturn:(UITextField *)textField
{
    [textField resignFirstResponder];
    [self queueMusicByArtist:self];
    return NO;
}
```

Finally, the queueMusicByArtist: method.

```
- (IBAction)queueMusicByArtist:(id)sender
{
    NSString *artist = self.artistTextField.text;
    if (artist != nil && artist != @"")
    {
        MPMediaPropertyPredicate *artistPredicate =
            [MPMediaPropertyPredicate
                predicateWithValue:artist
                forProperty:MPMediaItemPropertyArtist
                comparisonType:MPMediaPredicateComparisonContains];
        MPMediaQuery *query = [[MPMediaQuery alloc] init];
        [query addFilterPredicate:artistPredicate];

        NSArray *result = [query items];
        if ([result count] > 0)
        {
            [self updateQueueWithMediaItemCollection:
                [MPMediaItemCollection collectionWithItems:result]];
        }
        else
            self.infoLabel.text = @"Artist Not Found.";
    }
}
```

You can now run and test the new feature. Enter a search string in the artist text field, press Return (or tap the Queue Music By button) and the media player should start playing all songs from artists whose names contain the provided text.

As you can see, querying the media library is a fairly simple process, which at its bare minimum requires only an instance of the MPMediaQuery class. You can then add MPMediaPropertyPredicates to a query to make it more specific.

Using `MPMediaPropertyPredicates` requires a decent knowledge of the different `MPMediaItemProperties`, so that you can know exactly what kind of information you can acquire. Not all `MPMediaItemProperties` are filterable, and the filterable properties are also different if you are dealing specifically with a podcast. You should refer to the Apple documentation on `MPMediaItem` for a full list of properties, but following is a list of the most commonly used ones:

- `MPMediaItemPropertyMediaType`

- `MPMediaItemPropertyTitle`

- `MPMediaItemPropertyAlbumTitle`

- `MPMediaItemPropertyArtist`

- `MPMediaItemPropertyArtwork`

Tip   Whenever you use the `MPMediaItemPropertyArtwork`, you can use the `imageWithSize:` method defined in `MPMediaItemPropertyArtwork` to create a `UIImage` from the artwork.

We have barely scratched the surface of media item queries, but here comes a few points to keep in mind when dealing with them:

1. Whenever multiple filter predicates specifying different properties are added to a query, the predicates are evaluated using the `AND` operator, meaning that if you specify an artist name and an album name, you will receive only songs by that artist `AND` from that specific album.

2. Do not add two filter predicates of the same property to a query because the resulting behavior is not defined. If you wish to query a database for multiple specific values of the same property, such as filtering for all songs by two different artists, the better method is to simply create two queries, and then combine their results afterward.

3. The comparisonType property of an `MPMediaPropertyPredicate` helps specify how exact you want your predicate to be. A value of `MPMediaPredicateComparisonEqualTo` returns only items with the string exactly equal to the given one, while a value of `MPMediaPredicateComparisonContains`, as shown earlier, returns items that contain the given string, which is a less specific search.

`MPMediaQuery` instances can also be given a "grouping property", so that they automatically group their results. You could, for example, filter a query by a specific artist, but group according to the album name:

```
[query setGroupingType: MPMediaGroupingAlbum];
```

In this way, you can retrieve all the songs by a specific artist but iterate through them as if they were in albums, as demonstrated by the following code:

```
NSArray *albums = [query collections];
for (MPMediaItemCollection *album in albums)
{
    MPMediaItem *representativeItem = [album representativeItem];
    NSString *albumName =
        [representativeItem valueForProperty: MPMediaItemPropertyAlbumTitle];
    NSLog (@"%@", albumName);
}
```

You can also set a grouping type by using MPMediaQuery class methods, such as albumsQuery, which creates your query instance with a pre-set grouping property.

Even though we haven't dug deep into the media player framework, you can probably see the power of it; accessing the user's own library opens up a whole new level of audio customization for your applications, possibilities like selecting music to wake up to, or allowing the user to specify her own background music for your game. You're probably coming up with several other usages yourself right now. Why not go ahead and implement them?

Recipe 9-4: Playing Background Audio

In this recipe you'll build a basic music player app that can keep on playing even in background mode. Additionally, you'll use the MPNowPlayingInfoCenter to allow your app to be controlled from the multitasking bar and to display information about the current tune on the lock screen.

Start by creating a new single view application project. You'll need the following frameworks so make sure you link their binaries to your project.

- AVFoundation.framework, to play your audio files.

- MediaPlayer.framework, to access your library of media files.

- CoreMedia.framework, you won't use any classes from this framework but you will need some of the CMTime functions to help deal with your audio player.

Also, add the following import statements to your view controller's header file. You do not need one for the Core Media framework in this project:

```
#import <MediaPlayer/MediaPlayer.h>
#import <AVFoundation/AVFoundation.h>
```

Setting Up the User Interface

It's usually a good idea to start with the design of the user interface. You'll build a simple media player with the following features:

- Adding items from the music library to the playlist

- Starting and pausing playback

- Navigate backward and forward in the playlist

- Clear the playlist

- Information about the current song and album

Create the user interface as shown in Figure 9-6, using a label, an image view, and buttons.

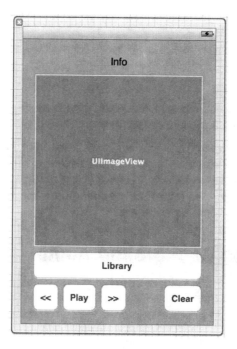

Figure 9-6. A user interface for a simple media player with background playback

Add outlets for the play button, info label, and the image view, name them playButton, infoLabel, and artworkImageView, respectively. Also, create actions for the buttons. Use the names queueFromLibrary, goToPrevTrack, togglePlay, goToNextTrack and clearPlaylist.

Declaring Background Mode Playback

Now set up your app to continue playing music after it has entered the background of the device. The first thing you need to do is declare a property of type AVAudioSession, called session.

```
@property (nonatomic, strong) AVAudioSession *session;
```

Next, add the following code to your viewDidLoad method:

```
- (void)viewDidLoad
{
    [super viewDidLoad];
    self.session = [AVAudioSession sharedInstance];
    NSError *error;
    [self.session setCategory:AVAudioSessionCategoryPlayback error:&error];
```

```
    if (error)
    {
        NSLog(@"Error setting audio session category: %@", error);
    }
    [self.session setActive:YES error:&error];
    if (error)
    {
        NSLog(@"Error activating audio session: %@", error);
    }
}
```

By specifying that your session's category is of type AVAudioSessionCategoryPlayback, you are telling your device that your application's main focus is playing music, and should therefore be allowed to continue playing audio while the application is in the background.

Now that you have configured your AVAudioSession, you need to edit your application's .plist file to specify that your application, when in the background mode, must be allowed to run audio. You do that by adding audio as a required background mode in the properties list, as shown in Figure 9-7.

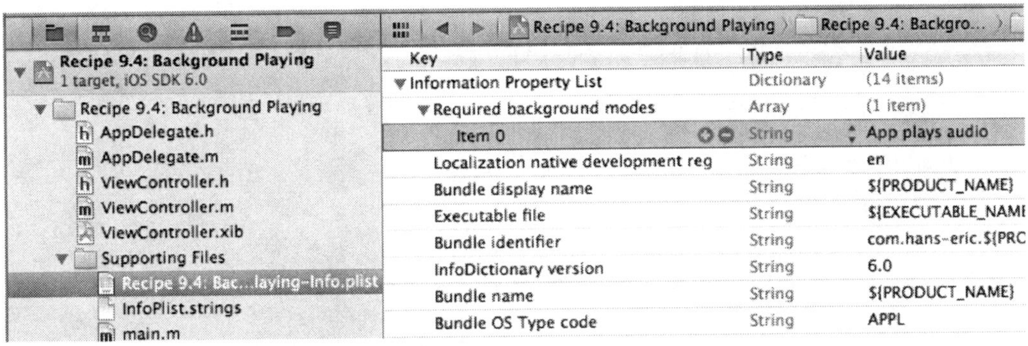

Figure 9-7. Setting audio as a required background mode

To allow the user to control your media player remotely, either from the buttons of her earphones or from the activity bar, you need to respond to remote control events. For these events to work, your view controller needs to be the first responder so start by allowing this by overriding the canBecomeFirstResponder method:

```
-(BOOL)canBecomeFirstResponder
{
    return YES;
}
```

Now, implement the `viewDidAppear:` and `viewWillDisappear:` methods to set the first responder status, as well as registering for the remote control events, like so:

```
- (void)viewDidAppear:(BOOL)animated
{
    [super viewDidAppear:animated];
    [[UIApplication sharedApplication] beginReceivingRemoteControlEvents];
    [self becomeFirstResponder];
}

- (void)viewWillDisappear:(BOOL)animated
{
    [[UIApplication sharedApplication] endReceivingRemoteControlEvents];
    [self resignFirstResponder];
    [super viewWillDisappear:animated];
}
```

Now, to receive and respond to remote control events, implement the following method:

```
- (void)remoteControlReceivedWithEvent: (UIEvent *) receivedEvent
{
    if (receivedEvent.type == UIEventTypeRemoteControl)
    {
        switch (receivedEvent.subtype)
        {
            case UIEventSubtypeRemoteControlTogglePlayPause:
                [self togglePlay:self];
                break;

            case UIEventSubtypeRemoteControlPreviousTrack:
                [self goToPrevTrack:self];
                break;

            case UIEventSubtypeRemoteControlNextTrack:
                [self goToNextTrack:self];
                break;

            default:
                break;
        }
    }
}
```

As you can see, you only redirect the events by invoking the respective action method which you'll implement shortly.

Implementing the Player

You use an `AVPlayer` to do the playback. It differs from the `MPMusicPlayerController` you saw in the previous recipe in that it can continue playing in background mode. However, it doesn't work directly with items from your music library which requires a little more coding than with MPMusicPlayerController.

Add the following properties to your view controller:

```
@property (nonatomic, strong) AVPlayer *player;
@property (nonatomic, strong) NSMutableArray *playlist;
@property (nonatomic)NSInteger currentIndex;
```

The playlist property holds an array of items from the music library, and the currentIndex holds the index of the current track within the playlist. Go back to the viewDidLoad and add the following code to initialize the player and the playlist:

```
- (void)viewDidLoad
{
    [super viewDidLoad];

    // ...

    self.playlist = [[NSMutableArray alloc] init];
    self.player = [[AVPlayer alloc] init];
}
```

Now let's start by implementing the Library button. It should present a media picker controller and append the selected items to the playlist. Here's the implementation:

```
- (IBAction)queueFromLibrary:(id)sender
{
    MPMediaPickerController *picker =
        [[MPMediaPickerController alloc] initWithMediaTypes:MPMediaTypeMusic];
    picker.delegate = self;
    picker.allowsPickingMultipleItems = YES;
    picker.prompt = @"Choose Some Music!";
    [self presentViewController:picker animated:YES completion:NULL];
}
```

You also need to add the MPMediaPickerControllerDelegate protocol to your view controller:

```
@interface ViewController : UIViewController<MPMediaPickerControllerDelegate>
```

Now implement the delegate methods that receive the selected items. It should append them to the list and dismiss the media picker. Also, if these are the first items added, playback should be started:

```
-(void)mediaPicker:(MPMediaPickerController *)mediaPicker
didPickMediaItems:(MPMediaItemCollection *)mediaItemCollection
{
    BOOL shallStartPlayer = self.playlist.count == 0;

    [self.playlist addObjectsFromArray:mediaItemCollection.items];
```

```
    if (shallStartPlayer)
        [self startPlaybackWithItem:[self.playlist objectAtIndex:0]];

    [self dismissViewControllerAnimated:YES completion:NULL];
}
```

Which leads us to the startPlaybackWithItem: method. It replaces the currently played item (if any), resets the current playback position (in case the item has been played before), and starts the playback.

```
-(void)startPlaybackWithItem:(MPMediaItem *)mpItem
{
    [self.player replaceCurrentItemWithPlayerItem:[self avItemFromMPItem:mpItem]];
    [self.player seekToTime:kCMTimeZero];
    [self startPlayback];
}
```

Because the AVPlayer is working with AVPlayerItems and not MPMediaItems, you need to create one. This is the job of the avItemFromMPItem: method:

```
-(AVPlayerItem *)avItemFromMPItem:(MPMediaItem *)mpItem
{
    NSURL *url = [mpItem valueForProperty:MPMediaItemPropertyAssetURL];

    AVPlayerItem *item = [AVPlayerItem playerItemWithURL:url];

    [[NSNotificationCenter defaultCenter]
     addObserver:self
     selector:@selector(playerItemDidReachEnd:)
     name:AVPlayerItemDidPlayToEndTimeNotification
     object:item];

    return item;
}
```

What's interesting here is that you not only create the AVPlayerItem, but also register a method to receive a notification when the song has reached its end. This is so that you can go on to the next tune in the playlist:

```
- (void)playerItemDidReachEnd:(NSNotification *)notification
{
    [self goToNextTrack:self];
}
```

The next stop is the startPlayback method. It starts the player, changes the title of the play button to "Pause," and calls updateNowPlaying.

```
-(void)startPlayback
{
    [self.player play];
    [self.playButton setTitle:@"Pause" forState:UIControlStateNormal];
    [self updateNowPlaying];
}
```

Finally, the last method to implement in this chain of calls is updateNowPlaying. The method, aside from updating your user interface to display the current song information, also uses the MPNowPlayingInfoCenter. This class allows the developer to place information on the device's lock screen (see Figure 9-8 for an example), or on other devices when the application is displaying info through AirPlay. You can pass information to it by setting the nowPlayingInfo property of the defaultCenter to a dictionary of values and properties that you created.

```
-(void)updateNowPlaying
{
    if (self.player.currentItem != nil)
    {
        MPMediaItem *currentMPItem = [self.playlist objectAtIndex:self.currentIndex];

        self.infoLabel.text =
            [NSString stringWithFormat:@"%@ - %@",
                [currentMPItem valueForProperty:MPMediaItemPropertyTitle],
                [currentMPItem valueForProperty:MPMediaItemPropertyArtist]];

        UIImage *artwork = [[currentMPItem valueForProperty:MPMediaItemPropertyArtwork]
                imageWithSize:self.artworkImageView.frame.size];
        self.artworkImageView.image = artwork;

        NSString *title = [currentMPItem valueForProperty:MPMediaItemPropertyTitle];
        NSString *artist =
            [currentMPItem valueForProperty:MPMediaItemPropertyArtist];
        NSString *album =
            [currentMPItem valueForProperty:MPMediaItemPropertyAlbumTitle];

        NSDictionary *mediaInfo =
            [NSDictionary dictionaryWithObjectsAndKeys:
                artist, MPMediaItemPropertyArtist,
                title, MPMediaItemPropertyTitle,
                album, MPMediaItemPropertyAlbumTitle,
                [currentMPItem valueForProperty:MPMediaItemPropertyArtwork],
                    MPMediaItemPropertyArtwork,
                nil];
        [MPNowPlayingInfoCenter defaultCenter].nowPlayingInfo = mediaInfo;
    }
    else
    {
        self.infoLabel.text = @"...";
        [self.playButton setTitle:@"Play" forState:UIControlStateNormal];
        self.artworkImageView.image = nil;
    }
}
```

Figure 9-8. Information on the lock screen about the current track

The next action method is togglePlay, which should toggle between play and pause modes. An edge case here is that if the player has not yet been initialized you need to initialize it with the first item in your playlist.

```
- (IBAction)togglePlay:(id)sender
{
    if (self.playlist.count > 0)
    {
        if (self.player.currentItem == nil)
        {
            [self startPlaybackWithItem:[self.playlist objectAtIndex:0]];
        }
        else
        {
            // Player has an item, pause or resume playing it
            BOOL isPlaying = self.player.currentItem && self.player.rate != 0;
            if (isPlaying)
            {
                [self pausePlayback];
            }
            else
            {
                [self startPlayback];
            }
        }
    }
}
```

From the preceding code, there's only the pausePlayback method that you haven't yet implemented. That's easily fixed. All it needs to do is to pause the player and update the play button title:

```
-(void)pausePlayback
{
    [self.player pause];
    [self.playButton setTitle:@"Play" forState:UIControlStateNormal];
}
```

Next up is the goToPrevTrack: and goToNextTrack: action methods. They are pretty straightforward. What's worth noting though, is that if playback is more than five seconds into the song, the back button will rewind the current song and not skip to the previous item in the playlist:

```
- (IBAction)goToPrevTrack:(id)sender
{
    if (self.playlist.count == 0)
        return;

    if (CMTimeCompare(self.player.currentTime, CMTimeMake(5.0, 1)) > 0)
    {
        [self.player seekToTime:kCMTimeZero];
    }
    else
    {
        if (self.currentIndex == 0)
        {
            self.currentIndex = self.playlist.count - 1;
        }
        else
        {
            self.currentIndex -= 1;
        }
        MPMediaItem *previousItem = [self.playlist objectAtIndex:self.currentIndex];
        [self startPlaybackWithItem:previousItem];
    }
}

- (IBAction)goToNextTrack:(id)sender
{
    if (self.playlist.count == 0)
        return;

    if (self.currentIndex == self.playlist.count - 1)
    {
        self.currentIndex = 0;
    }
```

```
    else
    {
        self.currentIndex += 1;
    }
    MPMediaItem *nextItem = [self.playlist objectAtIndex:self.currentIndex];
    [self startPlaybackWithItem: nextItem];
}
```

The CMTimeMake() function that you just used is a very flexible function that takes two inputs. The first represents the number of time units you want, and the second represents the timescale, where 1 represents a second, 2 represents half a second, and so on. A call of CMTimeMake(100, 10) would make 100 units of (1/10) seconds each, resulting in 10 seconds.

There's only one feature remaining unimplemented: clearing the playlist. Here is its implementation:

```
- (IBAction)clearPlaylist:(id)sender
{
    [self.player replaceCurrentItemWithPlayerItem:nil];
    [self.playlist removeAllObjects];
    [self updateNowPlaying];
    [self.playButton setTitle:@"Play" forState:UIControlStateNormal];
}
```

Finally, your app is now ready to build and run. When you test the app, it should continue to play music even after the application has entered the background. Figure 9-9 shows the multitasking bar with which you can control your media player even when another app is active.

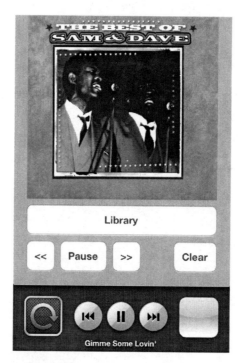

Figure 9-9. *The "remote" controls in the multitasking bar that can control an app playing audio in the background*

Tip   This recipe used AVPlayer to do the playback. It can only handle one item at a time, which is why we had to implement an external playlist. However, there is an alternative player that you can use to play queued items. The AVQueuePlayer is suitable for applications that need to play a sequence of items, but don't need complex navigation within the playlist.

Summary

The complete multimedia experience is one that goes beyond a simple matter of listening to music. Sound, as a product, is about the tiny details that make things just a little bit better. From recording music, to filtering media items, to creating volume ramps, every little detail that you, as a developer, take care to include will eventually result in more powerful and enjoyable tools. In iOS development, Apple has provided us with an incredibly powerful set of multimedia-based functionalities. We should not let it go to waste.

Chapter 10

Image Recipes

Often times a developer is faced with an all-too common problem: Too much information to display with not enough space to show it. For this, you turn to images. Pictures and graphics allow you to convey a variety of information far beyond simple text, combining emotion, information, and style. In iOS, you have several different methods with which to create, utilize, manipulate, and display images. A fairly new feature applies filters to images, allowing for drastic alteration of display with very little code. By understanding these inherent functionalities and techniques in iOS, you can more easily implement stronger, more powerful, and more informative applications.

Recipe 10-1: Drawing Simple Shapes

From the youngest age, every person is taught the most basic of images, dealing with shapes, colors, and pictures. In iOS too, you can start off with the basics of drawing simple shapes in a view. Many concepts dealt with in these first implementations will end up returning in more complex image-based recipes.

Start by creating a new single-view application project.

Before building the user interface, you will create a custom view that will implement some simple drawing code. So, create a new subclass of UIView called MyView and add the following code to its drawRect: method:

```
//
//  MyView.m
//  Recipe 10-1: Drawing Simple Shapes
//

#import "MyView.h"

@implementation MyView

// ...
```

```
// Only override drawRect: if you perform custom drawing.
// An empty implementation adversely affects performance during animation.
- (void)drawRect:(CGRect)rect
{
    CGContextRef context = UIGraphicsGetCurrentContext();
    // Draw rectangle
    CGRect drawingRect = CGRectMake(0.0, 20.0f, 100.0f, 180.0f);
    const CGFloat *rectColorComponents =
        CGColorGetComponents([[UIColor greenColor] CGColor]);
    CGContextSetFillColor(context, rectColorComponents);
    CGContextFillRect(context, drawingRect);
    // Draw ellipse
    CGRect ellipseRect = CGRectMake(140.0f, 200.0f, 75.0f, 50.0f);
    const CGFloat *ellipseColorComponents =
        CGColorGetComponents([[UIColor blueColor] CGColor]);
    CGContextSetFillColor(context, ellipseColorComponents);
    CGContextFillEllipseInRect(context, ellipseRect);
}

@end
```

This method uses the following steps to draw basic shapes:

1. Obtain a reference to the current "context," represented by a CGContextRef.

2. Define a CGRect in which to draw.

3. Acquire color components for the desired color to fill each shape with.

4. Set the Fill Color.

5. Fill the specified shape using the CGContextFillRect() and CGContextFillEllipseInRect() functions.

To actually display this in your preconfigured view, you must add an instance of this class to your user interface. This is done programmatically or through Interface Builder, the latter of which we demonstrate.

In the view controller's .xib file, drag out a UIView from the Object library in the Utilities pane into your view. Place it with the default spacing on each edge, so that the view looks like Figure 10-1.

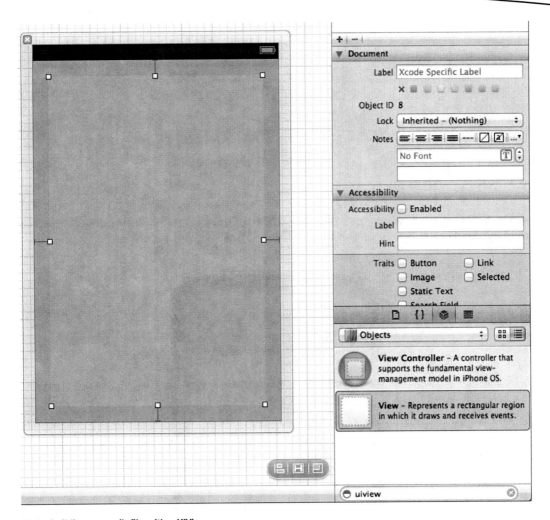

Figure 10-1. Building your .xib file with a UIView

While your UIView is selected, go to the Identity inspector in the right panel. Under the Custom Class section, change the Class field from "UIView" to "MyView", as shown in Figure 10-2. This connects the view you added in Interface Builder with the custom class you created earlier.

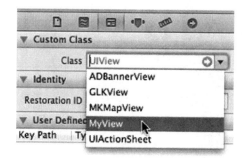

Figure 10-2. *Connecting a custom class to a UIView*

When running this application, you see the output of your drawing commands converted into a visual display, resulting in the simulated view in Figure 10-3.

Figure 10-3. *A custom view drawing a green rectangle and a blue ellipse*

Thankfully, you are not limited to drawing only rectangles and ellipses. There are a few other functions. You can draw custom shapes by creating "paths" of points connected by lines or curves. As an example, add the following code to the drawRect: method to draw a gray semitransparent parallelogram:

```
- (void)drawRect:(CGRect)rect
{
    CGContextRef context = UIGraphicsGetCurrentContext();

    // Draw rectangle
    CGRect drawingRect = CGRectMake(0.0, 20.0f, 100.0f, 180.0f);
    const CGFloat *rectColorComponents =
        CGColorGetComponents([[UIColor greenColor] CGColor]);
    CGContextSetFillColor(context, rectColorComponents);
    CGContextFillRect(context, drawingRect);

    // Draw ellipse
    CGRect ellipseRect = CGRectMake(140.0f, 200.0f, 75.0f, 50.0f);
    const CGFloat *ellipseColorComponents =
        CGColorGetComponents([[UIColor blueColor] CGColor]);
    CGContextSetFillColor(context, ellipseColorComponents);
    CGContextFillEllipseInRect(context, ellipseRect);

    // Draw parallelogram
    CGContextBeginPath(context);
    CGContextMoveToPoint(context, 0.0f, 0.0f);
    CGContextAddLineToPoint(context, 100.0f, 0.0f);
    CGContextAddLineToPoint(context, 140.0f, 100.0f);
    CGContextAddLineToPoint(context, 40.0f, 100.0f);
    CGContextClosePath(context);
    CGContextSetGrayFillColor(context, 0.4f, 0.85f);
    CGContextSetGrayStrokeColor(context, 0.0, 0.0);
    CGContextFillPath(context);
}
```

> **Note** When creating these paths, you do not have to add a final line back to your last point. By calling the CGContextClosePath() function, your shape is automatically closed between its ending point and starting point.

When you run your application now, you will see your view with a new parallelogram created from your path, as in Figure 10-4.

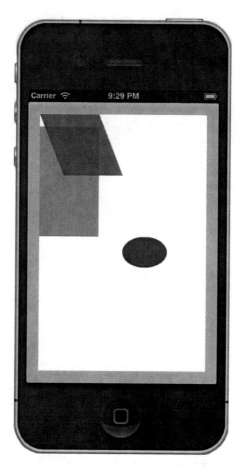

Figure 10-4. A custom UIView drawing three different shapes

Recipe 10-2: Programming Screenshots

Just as you can put things into a CGContext, you also can easily take them out. By making use of the UIGraphicsGetImageFromCurrentImageContext() function, you can extract an image from whatever is currently drawn.

You're going to build on the previous recipe and the app you created there. You add to it a feature that takes a snapshot of the current view whenever the user shakes the device. It displays the snapshot in the lower-right corner of the screen, causing a nice symmetric effect on subsequent shakes.

Start by adding a property to the MyView class to hold the latest snapshot. Open MyView.h and add the following declaration:

```
//
//  MyView.h
//  Recipe 10-1: Drawing Simple Shapes
//
```

```
#import <UIKit/UIKit.h>

@interface MyView : UIView

@property (strong, nonatomic)UIImage *image;

@end
```

Next, select ViewController.xib to bring up Interface Builder. Open the Assistant editor and create an outlet for the custom view by Ctrl-dragging a blue line from it onto the ViewController.h file. Name the outlet myView. For the outlet declaration to compile you'll need to import MyView.h:

```
//
//  ViewController.h
//  Recipe 10-1: Drawing Simple Shapes
//

#import <UIKit/UIKit.h>
#import "MyView.h"

@interface ViewController : UIViewController

@property (weak, nonatomic) IBOutlet MyView *myView;

@end
```

Now, add the code that will draw the snapshot: to the drawRect: method in MyView.m:

```
- (void)drawRect:(CGRect)rect
{
    // ...

    if (self.image)
    {
        CGFloat imageWidth = self.frame.size.width / 2;
        CGFloat imageHeight = self.frame.size.height / 2;
        CGRect imageRect = CGRectMake(imageWidth, imageHeight, imageWidth, imageHeight);
        [self.image drawInRect:imageRect];
    }
}

@end
```

As the next step, add the following methods to the view controller. The code implements shake recognition that triggers the screenshot:

```
//
//  ViewController.m
//  Recipe 10-1: Drawing Simple Shapes
//
```

```
#import "ViewController.h"

@implementation ViewController

// ...

- (BOOL) canBecomeFirstResponder
{
    return YES;
}

- (void) viewWillAppear: (BOOL)animated
{
    [self.view becomeFirstResponder];
    [super viewWillAppear:animated];
}

- (void) viewWillDisappear: (BOOL)animated
{
    [self.view resignFirstResponder];
    [super viewWillDisappear:animated];
}

- (void) motionEnded: (UIEventSubtype)motion withEvent: (UIEvent *)event
{
    if (event.subtype == UIEventSubtypeMotionShake)
    {
        // Device was shaken

        // TODO: Take a screenshot
    }
}

@end
```

Finally, you implement the code for taking a snapshot and hand it over to the custom view for displaying. But before that, you will need to import the QuartzCore API. Failing to do so causes a compiler error later when you access a layer on the view to draw the screenshot. So, open ViewController.h again and add the following lines of code:

```
//
//  ViewController.h
//  Recipe 10-1: Drawing Simple Shapes
//

#import <UIKit/UIKit.h>
#import <QuartzCore/QuartzCore.h>
#import "MyView.h"
```

```
@interface ViewController : UIViewController

@property (weak, nonatomic) IBOutlet MyView *myView;

@end
```

Now you're ready to finish the implementation of the shake event in ViewController.m:

```
- (void) motionEnded: (UIEventSubtype)motion withEvent: (UIEvent *)event
{
    if (event.subtype == UIEventSubtypeMotionShake)
    {
        // Device was shaken

        // Acquire image of current layer
        UIGraphicsBeginImageContext(self.view.bounds.size);
        CGContextRef context = UIGraphicsGetCurrentContext();
        [self.view.layer renderInContext:context];
        UIImage *image = UIGraphicsGetImageFromCurrentImageContext();
        UIGraphicsEndImageContext();

        self.myView.image = image;
        [self.myView setNeedsDisplay];
    }
}
```

The setNeedsDisplay method in the UIView class instructs it to re-call its drawRect: method to incorporate any recent changes.

Now, after testing the application again, when shaking the device a couple of times, you should see a screen similar to Figure 10-5.

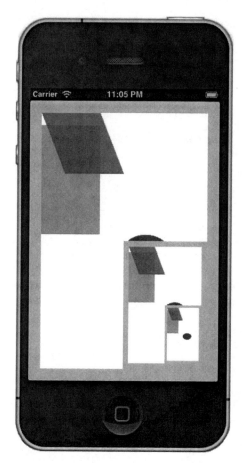

Figure 10-5. An application showing a screenshot of a screen that was displaying a screenshot already

Note If you run the app in iOS Simulator you can simulate a shake by pressing Ctrl + Cmd + Z.

Recipe 10-3: Using Image Views

The easiest way to display an image in your application is to use the `UIImageView` class. In this recipe you create a simple app that displays an image chosen by the user. Later on you'll build on top of it to take full advantage of the image processing power of iOS.

To enhance the functionality of your application, you will specifically design it for the iPad, and then make use of the `UISplitViewController`. Create a new project, and select the Master-Detail Application template. On the next screen, after entering the project name **Image Recipes**, be sure the application's device-family is set to **iPad**, as shown in Figure 10-6.

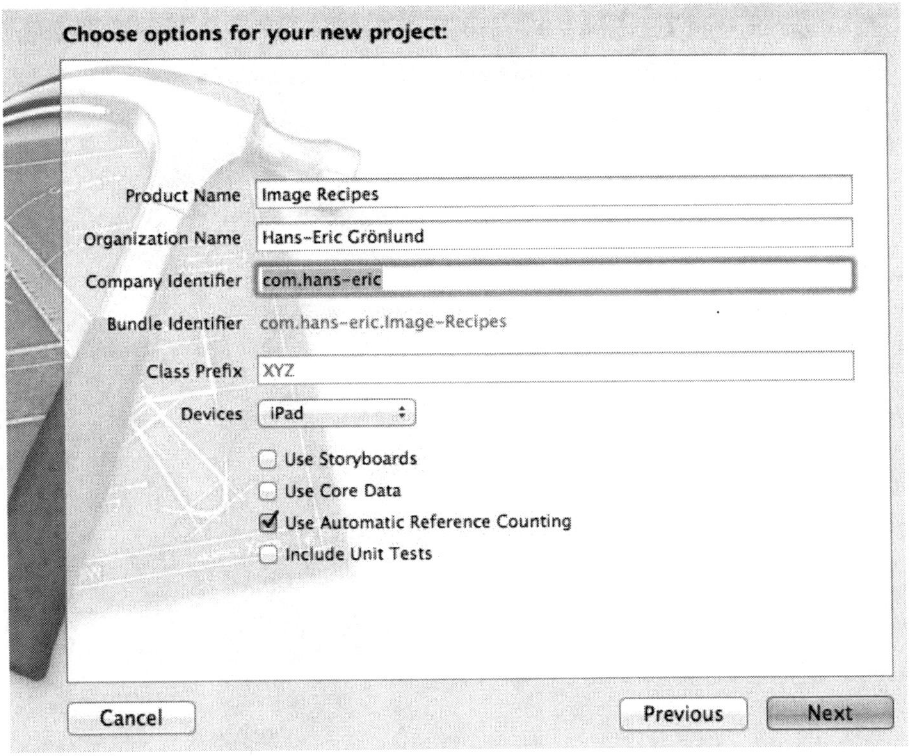

Choose options for your new project:

Product Name	Image Recipes
Organization Name	Hans-Eric Grönlund
Company Identifier	com.hans-eric
Bundle Identifier	com.hans-eric.Image-Recipes
Class Prefix	XYZ
Devices	iPad

☐ Use Storyboards
☐ Use Core Data
☑ Use Automatic Reference Counting
☐ Include Unit Tests

Cancel   Previous   Next

Figure 10-6. Configuring an iPad project

Upon creating your application, Xcode generates a project with a `UISplitViewController` set up with master and detail view controllers. If your simulator or device is in portrait mode, you will see only the view of the detail view controller, but if you rotate to landscape, then you will get a nice mix of both views. You do not see both views when working in Interface Builder, but if you simulate the app, the generic view will resemble Figure 10-7.

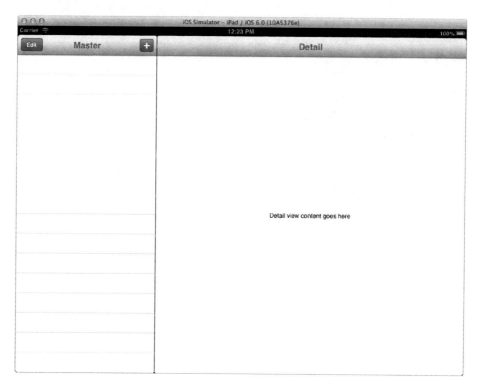

Figure 10-7. An empty UISplitViewController

Now, you configure the detail view controller to include some content. Select the
DetailViewController.xib file and use Interface Builder to create the user interface. Add a label (or
reuse the one created by default by the template,) an image view and two buttons and arrange them
as in Figure 10-8. Note that we've changed the background color of the image view to black (set in
the Attributes inspector, Background field).

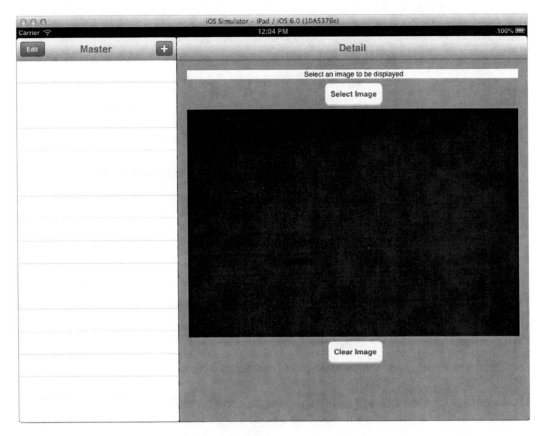

Figure 10-8. A simulated view of your configured user interface

Select the image view and open the Attributes inspector. In the View section, change the Mode attribute from Scale to Fill to Aspect Fill. This makes the image view scale its content so that it fills the image view's bounds while preserving the proportions of the image. This usually means that a part of the image is drawn outside the frame of the image view. To prevent this you should also check the Drawing option Clip Subviews. Figure 10-9 shows these settings.

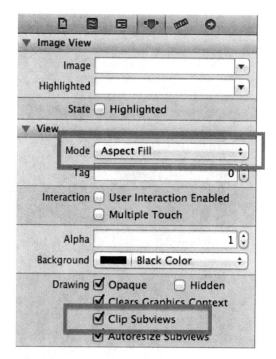

Figure 10-9. Configuring an image view to fill with maintained proportions and clip to its bounds

Next, create outlets for the label and the image view, use the names detailDesctriptionLabel and imageView, respectively. Also, create the actions selectImage: and clearImage: for the respective buttons.

Configure your application to display a UIPopoverController containing a UIImagePickerController to allow users to select an image from their phone. To do this, you need your detail view controller to conform to several extra protocols: UIImagePickerControllerDelegate, UINavigationControllerDelegate and UIPopoverControllerDelegate. You also need two properties, one for storing the selected image, and one to reference the UIPopoverController. To incorporate these changes, add the following to the DetailViewController.h file:

```
//
//  DetailViewController.h
//  Image Recipes
//

#import <UIKit/UIKit.h>

@interface DetailViewController : UIViewController <UISplitViewControllerDelegate,
    UIImagePickerControllerDelegate,UINavigationControllerDelegate,
    UIPopoverControllerDelegate>

@property (strong, nonatomic) id detailItem;
```

```objc
@property (weak, nonatomic) IBOutlet UILabel *detailDescriptionLabel;
@property (weak, nonatomic) IBOutlet UIImageView *imageView;

@property (strong, nonatomic) UIPopoverController *pop;

- (IBAction)selectImage:(id)sender;
- (IBAction)clearImage:(id)sender;

@end
```

Now you can implement the selectImage: method to present an interface to select an image to display.

```objc
-(void)selectImage:(UIButton *)sender
{
    UIImagePickerController *picker = [[UIImagePickerController alloc] init];
    if ([UIImagePickerController
            isSourceTypeAvailable:UIImagePickerControllerSourceTypePhotoLibrary])
    {
        picker.sourceType = UIImagePickerControllerSourceTypePhotoLibrary;
        picker.delegate = self;

        self.pop = [[UIPopoverController alloc] initWithContentViewController:picker];
        self.pop.delegate = self;
        [self.pop presentPopoverFromRect:sender.frame inView:self.view
            permittedArrowDirections:UIPopoverArrowDirectionAny animated:YES];
    }
}
```

You can then implement your UIImagePickerController delegate methods to properly handle the selection of an image or cancellation.

```objc
-(void)imagePickerControllerDidCancel:(UIImagePickerController *)picker
{
    [self.pop dismissPopoverAnimated:YES];
}

-(void)imagePickerController:(UIImagePickerController *)picker
didFinishPickingMediaWithInfo:(NSDictionary *)info
{
    UIImage *image = [info valueForKey:@"UIImagePickerControllerOriginalImage"];
    self.imageView.image = image;

    [self.pop dismissPopoverAnimated:YES];
}
```

As you can see, you configure the image view to display the selected image by using the image property. You also set the contentMode property to UIViewContentModeScaleAspectFill to ensure that the bounds of your UIImageView are always filled by at least most of the image. To prevent the image view from drawing outside its bounds, you also set the clipsToBounds property to YES.

Finally, you can implement the `clearImage:` action method to allow your view to be reset:

```
- (IBAction)clearImage:(id)sender
{
    self.imageView.image = nil;
}
```

At this point, you can run your application, select an image, and display it in a `UIImageView`, as shown in Figure 10-10.

Figure 10-10. Your application displaying an image in a UIImageView

Tip If you are testing the application on the iOS simulator, you will need to have some images to display. The easiest way to save images to the simulator's photos library is to drag and drop them onto the simulator window. This brings up Safari, where you can click and hold the mouse on the image. You then are given an option to save the image, and after this you can use it in your application.

Recipe 10-4: Scaling Images

Often the images that your applications deal with come from a variety of sources, and usually do not fit your specific view's display perfectly. To adjust for this, you can implement methods to scale and resize your images.

With an image view, scaling and resizing is easy. For example, in the previous recipe you used Aspect Fill in combination with Clip subviews to scale proportionally and still fill the entire image view. This results in a clipped but nice looking image. Another option is to use the Aspect Fit mode, which also scales the image with retained aspect but makes sure the entire image is displayed. This, of course, may cause some parts of the image view not being filled by the image. If you don't care about image aspect you can use the default mode Scale to Fill. You can use these and other options by simply changing the Mode attribute of the image view.

However, sometimes you'd like to scale the actual image programmatically, for example if you want to save the resulting image or just optimize the display by providing an already scaled image. In this recipe we'll show you how to scale an image using code. You're going to implement two different methods corresponding to the Scale to Fill and the Aspect Fit modes of an image view.

You build on the previous recipe but now use the master view's table view that contains the three functions: Select Image, Resize Image, and Scale Image. Because these functions operate directly on a UIImage, you need to turn off the inherent scaling function of the image view. Do that by changing its Mode attribute to Center instead of Aspect Fill.

Now, start by creating a method to configure the user interface of your detail view controller. For this you'll need to add a couple of outlets more to reference the two buttons. Go ahead and create the outlets selectImageButton and clearImageButton, respectively.

Now add the following method declaration to your DetailViewController.h file:

```
//
//  DetailViewController.h
//  Image Recipes
//

#import <UIKit/UIKit.h>

@interface DetailViewController : UIViewController <UISplitViewControllerDelegate,
                                                    UIImagePickerControllerDelegate,
                                                    UINavigationControllerDelegate,
                                                    UIPopoverControllerDelegate>

@property (strong, nonatomic) id detailItem;

@property (weak, nonatomic) IBOutlet UILabel *detailDescriptionLabel;
@property (weak, nonatomic) IBOutlet UIImageView *imageView;
@property (weak, nonatomic) IBOutlet UIButton *selectImageButton;
@property (weak, nonatomic) IBOutlet UIButton *clearImageButton;

@property (strong, nonatomic) UIPopoverController *pop;
```

```
- (IBAction)selectImage:(id)sender;
- (IBAction)clearImage:(id)sender;

- (void)configureDetailsWithImage:(UIImage *)image label:(NSString *)label
showsButtons:(BOOL)showButton;

@end
```

You implement this method like so:

```
-(void)configureDetailsWithImage:(UIImage *)image label:(NSString *)label
showsButtons:(BOOL)showsButton
{
    self.imageView.image = image;
    self.detailDescriptionLabel.text = label;
    if (showsButton == NO)
    {
        self.selectImageButton.hidden = YES;
        self.clearImageButton.hidden = YES;
    }
    else if (showsButton == YES)
    {
        self.selectImageButton.hidden = NO;
        self.clearImageButton.hidden = NO;
    }
}
```

Next, add a reference to the master view controller in your detail view controller. This allows the image selected to be passed back to the master view controller. Add the following code to DetailViewController.h:

```
//
//  DetailViewController.h
//  Image Recipes
//

#import <UIKit/UIKit.h>
#import "MasterViewController.h"

@interface DetailViewController : UIViewController <UISplitViewControllerDelegate,
                                                    UIImagePickerControllerDelegate,
                                                    UINavigationControllerDelegate,
                                                    UIPopoverControllerDelegate>

// ...

@property (strong, nonatomic) MasterViewController *masterViewController;

@end
```

Now, add a property to your master view controller class to store the chosen image:

```
//
// MasterViewController.h
// Image Recipes
//

#import <UIKit/UIKit.h>

@class DetailViewController;

@interface MasterViewController : UITableViewController

@property (strong, nonatomic) DetailViewController *detailViewController;
@property (strong, nonatomic) UIImage *mainImage;

@end
```

Back in your detail view controller, you update the
imagePickerController:didFinishPickingMediaWithInfo: delegate method to update the image of
the master view controller:

```
-(void)imagePickerController:(UIImagePickerController *)picker
didFinishPickingMediaWithInfo:(NSDictionary *)info
{
    UIImage *image = [info valueForKey:@"UIImagePickerControllerOriginalImage"];
    self.masterViewController.mainImage = image;
    self.imageView.image = image;
    [self.pop dismissPopoverAnimated:YES];
}
```

You also adjust the implementation of the clearImage: action method accordingly:

```
- (IBAction)clearImage:(id)sender
{
    self.imageView.image = nil;
    self.masterViewController.mainImage = nil;
}
```

In your master view controller, you will later add code to use your images in the actual table, so
implement a custom setter method for the mainImage property to reload the UITableView's data:

```
-(void)setMainImage:(UIImage *)image
{
    _mainImage = image;
    NSIndexPath *currentIndexPath = self.tableView.indexPathForSelectedRow;
    [self.tableView reloadData];
    [self.tableView selectRowAtIndexPath:currentIndexPath animated:YES
        scrollPosition:UITableViewScrollPositionTop];
}
```

Next, create two different methods to resize an image. Add the following two class method declarations to your detail view controller's header file:

```
//
//  MasterViewController.h
//  Image Recipes
//

#import <UIKit/UIKit.h>

@class DetailViewController;

@interface MasterViewController : UITableViewController

@property (strong, nonatomic) DetailViewController *detailViewController;
@property (strong, nonatomic) UIImage *mainImage;

+ (UIImage *)scaleImage:(UIImage *)image toSize:(CGSize)size;
+ (UIImage *)aspectScaleImage:(UIImage *)image toSize:(CGSize)size;

@end
```

The first method simply re-creates the image within a specified size, ignoring the aspect ratio of the image. Here is the implementation:

```
+ (UIImage *)scaleImage:(UIImage *)image toSize:(CGSize)size
{
    UIGraphicsBeginImageContext(size);
    [image drawInRect:CGRectMake(0, 0, size.width, size.height)];
    UIImage *scaledImage = UIGraphicsGetImageFromCurrentImageContext();
    UIGraphicsEndImageContext();
    return scaledImage;
}
```

The second method, with a little calculation, determines the best way to resize the image to both preserve the aspect ratio and fit inside the given size:

```
+ (UIImage *)aspectScaleImage:(UIImage *)image toSize:(CGSize)size
{
    if (image.size.height < image.size.width)
    {
        float ratio = size.height / image.size.height;
        CGSize newSize = CGSizeMake(image.size.width * ratio, size.height);

        UIGraphicsBeginImageContext(newSize);
        [image drawInRect:CGRectMake(0, 0, newSize.width, newSize.height)];
    }
    else
    {
        float ratio = size.width / image.size.width;
        CGSize newSize = CGSizeMake(size.width, image.size.height * ratio);
```

```
        UIGraphicsBeginImageContext(newSize);
        [image drawInRect:CGRectMake(0, 0, newSize.width, newSize.height)];
    }
    UIImage *aspectScaledImage = UIGraphicsGetImageFromCurrentImageContext();
    UIGraphicsEndImageContext();
    return aspectScaledImage;
}
```

To make sure your view controllers are properly interacting, connect the two on application launch. Go to the `application:didFinishLaunchingWithOptions:` method in the `AppDelegate.m` file and add the following line:

```
//
//  AppDelegate.m
//  Image Recipes
//

#import "AppDelegate.h"
#import "MasterViewController.h"
#import "DetailViewController.h"

@implementation AppDelegate

- (BOOL)application:(UIApplication *)application didFinishLaunchingWithOptions:(NSDictionary *)
launchOptions
{
    self.window = [[UIWindow alloc] initWithFrame:[[UIScreen mainScreen] bounds]];
    // Override point for customization after application launch.

    MasterViewController *masterViewController = [[MasterViewController alloc]
initWithNibName:@"MasterViewController" bundle:nil];
    UINavigationController *masterNavigationController = [[UINavigationController alloc]
initWithRootViewController:masterViewController];

    DetailViewController *detailViewController = [[DetailViewController alloc]
initWithNibName:@"DetailViewController" bundle:nil];
    UINavigationController *detailNavigationController = [[UINavigationController alloc]
initWithRootViewController:detailViewController];

    masterViewController.detailViewController = detailViewController;
    detailViewController.masterViewController = masterViewController;

    self.splitViewController = [[UISplitViewController alloc] init];
    self.splitViewController.delegate = detailViewController;
    self.splitViewController.viewControllers = @[masterNavigationController,
detailNavigationController];
    self.window.rootViewController = self.splitViewController;
```

```
    [self.window makeKeyAndVisible];
    return YES;
}

// ...

@end
```

Now, to finish configuring the behavior of the master view controller, modify the following delegate methods:

```
- (NSInteger)tableView:(UITableView *)tableView numberOfRowsInSection:(NSInteger)section
{
    if (self.mainImage == nil)
        return 1;
    else
        return 3;
}

// ...

- (UITableViewCell *)tableView:(UITableView *)tableView cellForRowAtIndexPath:
(NSIndexPath *)indexPath
{
    static NSString *CellIdentifier = @"Cell";

    UITableViewCell *cell = [tableView dequeueReusableCellWithIdentifier:CellIdentifier];
    if (cell == nil) {
        cell = [[UITableViewCell alloc] initWithStyle:UITableViewCellStyleDefault
reuseIdentifier:CellIdentifier];
    }

    if (indexPath.row == 0)
        cell.textLabel.text = NSLocalizedString(@"Selected Image", @"Detail");
    else if (indexPath.row == 1)
        cell.textLabel.text = NSLocalizedString(@"Resized Image", @"Detail");
    else if (indexPath.row == 2)
        cell.textLabel.text = NSLocalizedString(@"Scaled Image", @"Detail");
    return cell;
}

// ...

- (void)tableView:(UITableView *)tableView didSelectRowAtIndexPath:(NSIndexPath *)indexPath
{
    if (self.mainImage != nil)
    {
        UIImage *image;
        NSString *label;
        BOOL showsButtons = NO;
        if (indexPath.row == 0)
```

```
    {
        image = self.mainImage;
        label = @"Select an Image to Display";
        showsButtons = YES;
    }
    else if (indexPath.row == 1)
    {
        image = [MasterViewController scaleImage:self.mainImage
            toSize:self.detailViewController.imageView.frame.size];
        label = @"Chosen Image Resized";
    }
    else if (indexPath.row == 2)
    {
        image = [MasterViewController aspectScaleImage:self.mainImage
            toSize:self.detailViewController.imageView.frame.size];
        label = @"Chosen Image Scaled";
    }
    [self.detailViewController configureDetailsWithImage:image label:label
        showsButtons:showsButtons];
    }
}
```

You're done and can now build and run the application. This time, when you select an image you'll see that it doesn't scale and (assuming the image is larger than the image view) will be clipped like the one in Figure 10-11.

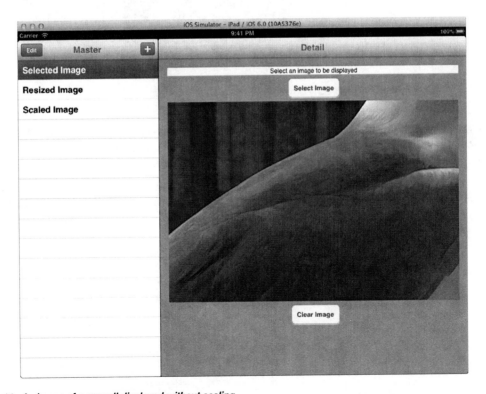

Figure 10-11. An image of a seagull displayed without scaling

Now, if you select the Resized Image cell in the master view you see the same picture, this time run through the `scaleImage:toSize:` method you created. The image has been scaled, without considering its original proportions, to the same size as the image view. Figure 10-12 shows an example of this.

Figure 10-12. An image scaled without keeping its proportions

The issue with this option, however, is that the picture has become slightly deformed. This may not be quite obvious with this particular image, but when dealing with images of people, the distortion of physical features is quite obvious and unsightly. To solve this, use the Aspect-Scaled image.

When you select the Scaled Image cell you'll see the effect of your `aspectScaleImage:toSize:` method. This method has created a UIImage of a size that fits within the image view but with maintained original proportions. This results in an image without any size distortions but instead it doesn't fill the entire image view, as shown in Figure 10-13.

Figure 10-13. An alternative method of scaling to remove distortion, resulting in empty spaces on the sides

In Review

You have covered two simple methods for resizing a UIImage, each with their own advantages and issues.

1. Your first method simply resized the image to a given size, regardless of aspect ratio. While this kept your image from obstructing any other elements, it ended up giving you a fair bit of distortion.

2. By using a little math, you scaled down your image to a size while manually maintaining the aspect ratio. Because this leaves a blank space around the image, you can apply a black background. This is a useful technique to use when displaying large images in an application that has no control over the original image size. It allows for any image to be comfortably fit in a given space, yet it maintains a visually appealing black background no matter the case.

Recipe 10-5: Manipulating Images with Filters

The Core Image framework, a group of classes that was introduced in iOS 5.0, allows you to creatively apply a great variety of "filters" to images. In this recipe you'll apply two kinds of filters to an image, the Hue filter and the Straightening filter. The former changes the hue of the image, while the latter rotates an image to straighten it out.

Again you build on the project you created in Recipes 10-3 and 10-4, adding functions to apply these filters.

Start by linking the CoreImage.framework library to your project (see Chapter 1 for a description on how to do this), and then import its API in the MasterViewController.h file. You also need a mutable array property to hold the filtered images you will display. Here's the MasterViewController.h file with these changes marked in bold:

```
//
//   MasterViewController.h
//   Image Recipes
//

#import <UIKit/UIKit.h>
#import <CoreImage/CoreImage.h>

@class DetailViewController;

@interface MasterViewController : UITableViewController

@property (strong, nonatomic) DetailViewController *detailViewController;
@property (strong, nonatomic) UIImage *mainImage;
@property (strong, nonatomic) NSMutableArray *filteredImages;

+ (UIImage *)scaleImage:(UIImage *)image toSize:(CGSize)size;
+ (UIImage *)aspectScaleImage:(UIImage *)image toSize:(CGSize)size;

@end
```

Implement lazy initialization of the filteredImages property by adding the following custom getter to MasterViewController.m:

```
-(NSMutableArray *)filteredImages
{
    if (!_filteredImages)
    {
        _filteredImages = [[NSMutableArray alloc] initWithCapacity:3];
    }
    return _filteredImages;
}
```

Now, modify your setMainImage: method again to include handling of this array.

```
-(void)setMainImage:(UIImage *)image
{
    [self.filteredImages removeAllObjects];
    if (image != nil)
    {
        [self populateImageViewWithImage:image];
    }
```

```
    _mainImage = image;
    NSIndexPath *currentIndexPath = self.tableView.indexPathForSelectedRow;
    [self.tableView reloadData];
    [self.tableView selectRowAtIndexPath:currentIndexPath animated:YES
        scrollPosition:UITableViewScrollPositionTop];
}
```

The populateFilteredImagesWithImage: method, which contains most of your Core Image code, is implemented as follows:

```
-(void)populateImageViewWithImage:(UIImage *)image
{
    CIImage *main = [[CIImage alloc] initWithImage:image];

    CIFilter *hueAdjust = [CIFilter filterWithName:@"CIHueAdjust"];
    [hueAdjust setDefaults];
    [hueAdjust setValue:main forKey:@"inputImage"];
    [hueAdjust setValue:[NSNumber numberWithFloat: 3.14/2.0f]
                forKey:@"inputAngle"];
    CIImage *outputHueAdjust = [hueAdjust valueForKey:@"outputImage"];
    CIContext *context = [CIContext contextWithOptions:nil];
    CGImageRef cgImage1 = [context createCGImage:outputHueAdjust
        fromRect:outputHueAdjust.extent];
    UIImage *outputImage1 = [UIImage imageWithCGImage:cgImage1];
    CGImageRelease(cgImage1);
    [self.filteredImages addObject:outputImage1];

    CIFilter *strFilter = [CIFilter filterWithName:@"CIStraightenFilter"];
    [strFilter setDefaults];
    [strFilter setValue:main forKey:@"inputImage"];
    [strFilter setValue:[NSNumber numberWithFloat:3.14f] forKey:@"inputAngle"];
    CIImage *outputStr = [strFilter valueForKey:@"outputImage"];
    CGImageRef cgImage2 = [context createCGImage:outputStr fromRect:outputStr.extent];
    UIImage *outputImage2 = [UIImage imageWithCGImage:cgImage2];
    CGImageRelease(cgImage2);
    [self.filteredImages addObject:outputImage2];
}
```

As you can see from this method, creating a CIImage requires the following steps:

1. Obtain a CIImage of the intended input image.

2. Create a filter using a specific name key. The name defines which filter will be applied, as well as its various parameters that can be used.

3. Reset all parameters of the filter to defaults for good measure.

4. Set the input image to the filter using the "inputImage" key.

5. Set any additional values related to the filter to customize output.

6. Retrieve the output CIImage using the "outputImage" key.

7. Create a UIImage from the CIImage by use of a CIContext. Because the CIContext returns a CGImage, which memory is not managed by ARC, you also need to release it using CGImageRelease().

Note   There is a large number of filters that can be applied to images, all with their own specific parameters and keys. To find details for a specific filter, use the Apple documentation at `http://developer.apple.com/library/ios/#DOCUMENTATION/GraphicsImaging/Reference/CoreImageFilterReference/Reference/reference.html`.

The next thing you'll do is to add the filter functions to the table view. Start by making the following small change to the tableView:numberOfRowsInSection: delegate method:

```
- (NSInteger)tableView:(UITableView *)tableView numberOfRowsInSection:(NSInteger)section
{
    if (self.mainImage == nil)
        return 1;
    else
        return 5;
}
```

Also update tableView:cellForRowAtIndexPath: to configure the cells for the new rows:

```
- (UITableViewCell *)tableView:(UITableView *)tableView cellForRowAtIndexPath:(NSIndexPath *)
indexPath
{
    static NSString *CellIdentifier = @"Cell";

    UITableViewCell *cell =
        [tableView dequeueReusableCellWithIdentifier:CellIdentifier];
    if (cell == nil)
    {
        cell = [[UITableViewCell alloc] initWithStyle:UITableViewCellStyleDefault
            reuseIdentifier:CellIdentifier];
    }

    if (indexPath.row == 0)
        cell.textLabel.text = NSLocalizedString(@"Selected Image", @"Detail");
    else if (indexPath.row == 1)
        cell.textLabel.text = NSLocalizedString(@"Resized Image", @"Detail");
    else if (indexPath.row == 2)
        cell.textLabel.text = NSLocalizedString(@"Scaled Image", @"Detail");
    else if (indexPath.row == 3)
        cell.textLabel.text = NSLocalizedString(@"Hue Adjust", @"Detail");
```

```
    else if (indexPath.row == 4)
        cell.textLabel.text = NSLocalizedString(@"Straighten Filter", @"Detail");
    return cell;
}
```

Also modify the tableView:didSelectRowAtIndexPath: method:

```
- (void)tableView:(UITableView *)tableView didSelectRowAtIndexPath:(NSIndexPath *)indexPath
{
    if (self.mainImage != nil)
    {
        UIImage *image;
        NSString *label;
        BOOL showsButtons = NO;
        if (indexPath.row == 0)
        {
            image = self.mainImage;
            label = @"Select an Image to Display";
            showsButtons = YES;
        }
        else if (indexPath.row == 1)
        {
            image = [MasterViewController scaleImage:self.mainImage
                toSize:self.detailViewController.imageView.frame.size];
            label = @"Chosen Image Resized";
        }
        else if (indexPath.row == 2)
        {
            image = [MasterViewController aspectScaleImage:self.mainImage
                toSize:self.detailViewController.imageView.frame.size];
            label = @"Chosen Image Scaled";
        }
        else if (indexPath.row == 3)
        {
            image = [self.filteredImages objectAtIndex:0];
            CGSize contentSize = self.detailViewController.imageView.frame.size;
            image = [MasterViewController aspectScaleImage:image toSize:contentSize];
            label = @"Hue Adjustment";
        }
        else if (indexPath.row == 4)
        {
            image = [self.filteredImages objectAtIndex:1];
            CGSize contentSize = self.detailViewController.imageView.frame.size;
            image = [MasterViewController aspectScaleImage:image toSize:contentSize];
            label = @"Straightening Filter";
        }
        [self.detailViewController configureDetailsWithImage:image label:label
            showsButtons:showsButtons];
    }
}
```

As you can see, you're reusing the `aspectScaleImage:toSize:` method you created in the previous recipe to scale the filtered images so that they will fit nicely within the image view.

When running your application now, you can see the outputs of the two types of filters. Shown in Figure 10-14 is an example of the straighten filter. As you may remember from the code, it specified an angle of pi (3.14) which means a 180 degree rotation and an upside down image.

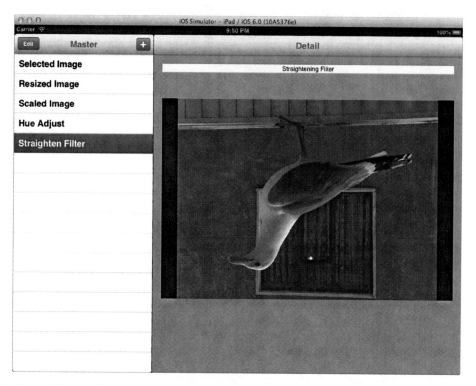

Figure 10-14. *The straightening filter has rotated an image 180 degrees*

Combining Filters

It's easy to apply multiple filters to an image. You just combine them in a series by specifying the output image of one filter as the input image of another. As an example, you'll add a function that applies both the hue filter and the straightening filter to the selected image.

Add the following code to the `populateImagesWithImage:` method to create a combination filter:

```
-(void)populateImageViewWithImage:(UIImage *)image
{
    // ...

    CIFilter *seriesFilter = [CIFilter filterWithName:@"CIStraightenFilter"];
    [seriesFilter setDefaults];
    [seriesFilter setValue:outputHueAdjust forKey:@"inputImage"];
    [seriesFilter setValue:[NSNumber numberWithFloat:3.14/2.0f] forKey:@"inputAngle"];
```

```
        CIImage *outputSeries = [seriesFilter valueForKey:@"outputImage"];
        CGImageRef cgImage3 = [context createCGImage:outputSeries
            fromRect:outputSeries.extent];
        UIImage *outputImage3 = [UIImage imageWithCGImage:cgImage3];
        [self.filteredImages addObject:outputImage3];
}
```

Update the `tableView:numberOfRowsInSection:` method to show a sixth cell:

```
- (NSInteger)tableView:(UITableView *)tableView numberOfRowsInSection:(NSInteger)section
{
    if (self.mainImage == nil)
        return 1;
    else
        return 6;
}
```

Likewise, add a sixth case to your `tableView:cellForRowAtIndexPath:` method to display the name of this fourth cell.

```
- (UITableViewCell *)tableView:(UITableView *)tableView cellForRowAtIndexPath:(NSIndexPath *)
indexPath
{
    // ...

    if (indexPath.row == 0)
        cell.textLabel.text = NSLocalizedString(@"Selected Image", @"Detail");
    else if (indexPath.row == 1)
        cell.textLabel.text = NSLocalizedString(@"Resized Image", @"Detail");
    else if (indexPath.row == 2)
        cell.textLabel.text = NSLocalizedString(@"Scaled Image", @"Detail");
    else if (indexPath.row == 3)
        cell.textLabel.text = NSLocalizedString(@"Hue Adjust", @"Detail");
    else if (indexPath.row == 4)
        cell.textLabel.text = NSLocalizedString(@"Straighten Filter", @"Detail");
    else if (indexPath.row == 5)
        cell.textLabel.text = NSLocalizedString(@"Series Filter", @"Detail");
    return cell;
}
```

Finally, add another case to the `tableView:didSelectRowAtIndexPath:` to initialize the detail view controller with the combined filter image.

```
- (void)tableView:(UITableView *)tableView didSelectRowAtIndexPath:(NSIndexPath *)indexPath
{
    if (self.mainImage != nil)
    {
        UIImage *image;
        NSString *label;
        BOOL showsButtons = NO;
        if (indexPath.row == 0)
```

```
        {
            image = self.mainImage;
            label = @"Select an Image to Display";
            showsButtons = YES;
        }

// ...

        else if (indexPath.row == 5)
        {
            image = [self.filteredImages objectAtIndex:2];
            CGSize contentSize = self.detailViewController.imageView.frame.size;
            image = [MasterViewController aspectScaleImage:image toSize:contentSize];
            label = @"Series Filter";
        }
        [self.detailViewController configureDetailsWithImage:image label:label
showsButtons:showsButtons];
    }
}
```

Now, on testing the application, your new double-filter combines the effects of your previous two, resulting in a hue-adjusted and rotated image; this time with a 90 degree rotation, as shown in Figure 10-15.

Figure 10-15. An image with both a hue filter and a 90-degree straightening filter applied

> **Note**   The majority of the processing work, when dealing with the Core Image framework, comes from when the `UIImage` is created from the `CIImage` using the `CIContext`. The creation of a `CIImage` itself is a very fast operation. In this application, we have chosen to create all the filtered images at once to allow for quick navigation between each display. This is why, on selecting an image, your simulator may take a couple seconds to actually display the image and refresh. If you were building this application for release, you would want to convey in some way to the user that work is being done through a `UIActivityIndicatorView` or `UIProgressView`.

Creating Thumbnail Images for the Table View

As a final touch we're going to return to the resizing topic of the previous recipe. You'll implement another aspect-scaling method that does what the Aspect Fill mode of an image view does, that is, scales with maintained proportions but ensures that the entire area is being covered. This method is more suitable for the creation of thumbnail images, which you're now going to implement for the filter functions in the table view.

Start by adding the new scaling method to the master view controller:

```
+ (UIImage *)aspectFillImage:(UIImage *)image toSize:(CGSize)size
{
    UIGraphicsBeginImageContext(size);
    if (image.size.height< image.size.width)
    {
        float ratio = size.height/image.size.height;
        [image drawInRect:CGRectMake(0, 0, image.size.width*ratio, size.height)];
    }
    else
    {
        float ratio = size.width/image.size.width;
        [image drawInRect:CGRectMake(0, 0, size.width, image.size.height*ratio)];
    }
    UIImage *aspectScaledImage = UIGraphicsGetImageFromCurrentImageContext();
    UIGraphicsEndImageContext();
    return aspectScaledImage;
}
```

Now you just need to modify the `tableView:cellForRowAtIndexPath:` again to include the selection of an image for the cell's imageView:

```
- (UITableViewCell *)tableView:(UITableView *)tableView cellForRowAtIndexPath:(NSIndexPath *)
indexPath
{
    static NSString *CellIdentifier = @"Cell";

    UITableViewCell *cell =
        [tableView dequeueReusableCellWithIdentifier:CellIdentifier];
```

```
    if (cell == nil) {
        cell = [[UITableViewCell alloc] initWithStyle:UITableViewCellStyleDefault
            reuseIdentifier:CellIdentifier];
    }

    if (indexPath.row == 0)
        cell.textLabel.text = NSLocalizedString(@"Selected Image", @"Detail");
    else if (indexPath.row == 1)
        cell.textLabel.text = NSLocalizedString(@"Resized Image", @"Detail");
    else if (indexPath.row == 2)
        cell.textLabel.text = NSLocalizedString(@"Scaled Image", @"Detail");
    else if (indexPath.row == 3)
    {
        CGSize thumbnailSize = CGSizeMake(120, 75);
        UIImage *displayImage = [self.filteredImages objectAtIndex:0];
        UIImage *thumbnailImage = [MasterViewController aspectFillImage:displayImage
            toSize:thumbnailSize];
        cell.imageView.image = thumbnailImage;
        cell.textLabel.text = NSLocalizedString(@"Hue Adjust", @"Detail");
    }
    else if (indexPath.row == 4)
    {
        CGSize thumbnailSize = CGSizeMake(120, 75);
        UIImage *displayImage = [self.filteredImages objectAtIndex:1];
        UIImage *thumbnailImage = [MasterViewController aspectFillImage:displayImage
            toSize:thumbnailSize];
        cell.imageView.image = thumbnailImage;
        cell.textLabel.text = NSLocalizedString(@"Straighten Filter", @"Detail");
    }
    else if (indexPath.row == 5)
    {
        CGSize thumbnailSize = CGSizeMake(120, 75);
        UIImage *displayImage = [self.filteredImages objectAtIndex:2];
        UIImage *thumbnailImage = [MasterViewController aspectFillImage:displayImage
            toSize:thumbnailSize];
        cell.imageView.image = thumbnailImage;
        cell.textLabel.text = NSLocalizedString(@"Series Filter", @"Detail");
    }
    return cell;
}
```

When you test your application now, the cells for the hue, straightening, and series filters have a scaled thumbnail version of the larger image they refer to. Figure 10-16 shows an example of this.

Figure 10-16. An application with thumbnails in its table view

Recipe 10-6: Detecting Features

Along with the flexible use of filters, the Core Image framework has also brought the possibility of feature detection. With it, you can "search" images for key components such as faces.

In this recipe you implement a facial detection application. Create a new single-view project for the iPhone device family. Once your project is created, add the Core Image framework to your project, just as in the previous recipe.

Set the background color of the main view to black and add two image views and a button, so that the user interface resembles Figure 10-17.

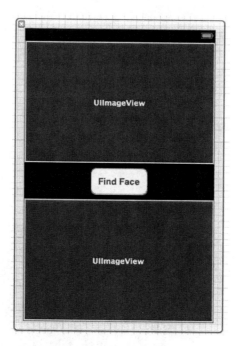

Figure 10-17. A simple user interface for face recognition

Create outlets for each of the three elements, use the property names `mainImageView`, `findFaceButton`, and `faceImageView`, respectively. Also, create an action with the name `findFace` for the button.

Next, find an image to be displayed in your application and add it to your project. You can do this by dragging the file from the Finder onto Project Navigator. To properly test this application, try to find an image with an easily visible face.

Now, you can build your `viewDidLoad` method to configure the image views, as well as set the initial image to your main image view. Be sure to change the name of the image (`testimage.jpg` in the following code) to your own filename.

```
- (void)viewDidLoad
{
    [super viewDidLoad];
    // Do any additional setup after loading the view, typically from a nib.
    self.mainImageView.contentMode = UIViewContentModeScaleAspectFit;
    self.faceImageView.contentMode = UIViewContentModeScaleAspectFit;

    UIImage *image = [UIImage imageNamed:@"testimage.jpg"];
    if (image != nil)
    {
        self.mainImageView.image = image;
    }
    else
```

```
    {
        [self.findFaceButton setTitle:@"No Image" forState:UIControlStateNormal];
        self.findFaceButton.enabled = NO;
        self.findFaceButton.alpha = 0.6;
    }
}
```

Now you can implement the findFace: action method to do the feature detection. You can use this method to determine the location of any faces in the given image, create a UIImage from the last face found, and then display it in the face image view.

```
- (IBAction)findFace:(id)sender
{
    UIImage *image = self.mainImageView.image;
    CIImage *coreImage = [[CIImage alloc] initWithImage:image];
    CIContext *context = [CIContext contextWithOptions:nil];
    CIDetector *detector =
        [CIDetector detectorOfType:@"CIDetectorTypeFace"context:context
            options:[NSDictionary dictionaryWithObjectsAndKeys:
                @"CIDetectorAccuracyHigh", @"CIDetectorAccuracy", nil]]];
    NSArray *features = [detector featuresInImage:coreImage];

    if ([features count] >0)
    {
        CIImage *faceImage =
            [coreImage imageByCroppingToRect:[[features lastObject] bounds]];
        UIImage *face = [UIImage imageWithCGImage:[context createCGImage:faceImage
            fromRect:faceImage.extent]];
        self.faceImageView.image = face;

        [self.findFaceButton setTitle:[NSString stringWithFormat:@"%i Face(s) Found",
            [features count]] forState:UIControlStateNormal];
        self.findFaceButton.enabled = NO;
        self.findFaceButton.alpha = 0.6;
    }
    else
    {
        [self.findFaceButton setTitle:@"No Faces Found"forState:UIControlStateNormal];
        self.findFaceButton.enabled = NO;
        self.findFaceButton.alpha = 0.6;
    }
}
```

This method contains the following steps:

1. Acquire a CIImage object from your initial UIImage.

2. Create a CIContext with which to analyze images.

3. Create an instance of CIDetector with type and options parameters.

   The type parameter specifies the specific feature to identify. Currently, the only possible value for this is CIDetectorTypeFace, which allows you to specifically look for faces.

   The options parameter allows you to specify the accuracy with which you want to look for features. Low accuracy will be faster, but high accuracy will be more precise.

4. Create an array of all the features found in your image. Because you specified the CIDetectorTypeFace type, these objects will all be instances of the CIFaceFeature class.

5. Create a CIImage using the imageByCroppingToRect: method with the original image, as well as the bounds specified by the last CIFaceFeature found in the image. These bounds specify the CGRect in which the face exists.

6. Create a UIImage out of your CIImage (done exactly as in the previous recipe), and then display it in your UIImageView.

When running your application, you can detect any faces inside your image, which will be displayed in your lower UIImageView, as in Figure 10-18.

Figure 10-18. An application detecting and cropping a face from an image

Summary

Images create our world. From the simplest of picture books that children love to read to the massive amounts of visual data transmitted around the Internet, pictures and images have certainly become one of the key foundations of modern culture. iOS offers great tools to create, handle, manipulate, and display images in your applications. With these simple APIs you can create more interesting and useful apps in less time.

In this chapter you have seen how to draw simple shapes; create screenshot images, using image views; resize images with maintained proportions; use filters to manipulate images and detect faces in a photo. We hope this has given you the head start you need to take full advantage of the powerful graphics features of iOS.

11

User Data Recipes

No two people are alike, and, in the same way, no two iOS devices are alike, as the information that one device stores is dependent on the person who uses it. We populate our devices with our lives, including our photos, calendars, notes, contacts, and music. As developers, it is important to be able to access all of this information regardless of the device, so that we may incorporate it into our applications and provide a more unique, user-specific interface. In this chapter, we will cover a variety of methods for dealing with user-based data, dealing first with the calendar, and then with the address book.

Recipe 11-1: Working with NSCalendar and NSDate

Many different applications are often used for time- and date-based calculations. This could be anything from converting calendars, to sorting to-do lists, to telling the user how much time remains before an alarm will go off. To use the more intricate event-based user interface, you must have a solid understanding of the simpler NSDate-focused APIs. Here, you implement a simple application to illustrate the use of the NSDate, NSCalendar, and NSDateComponents classes by converting dates from the Gregorian calendar to the Hebrew calendar.

Create a new single-view application project. Switch over to the view controller's .xib file and build a user interface that resembles Figure 11-1.

Figure 11-1. User interface for calendar conversion

You need to set up properties to represent each UITextField. Create the following outlets:

- gMonthTextField
- gDayTextField
- gYearTextField
- hMonthTextField
- hDayTextField
- hYearTextField

> **Note**   The "G" and "H" in these property names refer to whether the given UITextField is on the Gregorian or Hebrew side of the application.

You do not need outlets for the buttons, but create the following actions for when the user taps them:

- convertToHebrew
- convertToGregorian

To control the UITextFields programmatically, you need to make your view controller the delegate for them. First, add <UITextFieldDelegate> to your controller's header line, so that it now looks like so:

```
//
//  ViewController.h
//  Recipe 11.1: Working With NSCalendar and NSDate
//

#import <UIKit/UIKit.h>

@interface ViewController : UIViewController<UITextFieldDelegate>

@property (weak, nonatomic) IBOutlet UITextField *gMonthTextField;
@property (weak, nonatomic) IBOutlet UITextField *gDayTextField;
@property (weak, nonatomic) IBOutlet UITextField *gYearTextField;
@property (weak, nonatomic) IBOutlet UITextField *hMonthTextField;
@property (weak, nonatomic) IBOutlet UITextField *hDayTextField;
@property (weak, nonatomic) IBOutlet UITextField *hYearTextField;

- (IBAction)convertToHebrew:(id)sender;
- (IBAction)convertToGregorian:(id)sender;

@end
```

Next, set all the UITextField delegates to your view controller by adding the following code to the viewDidLoad method:

```
- (void)viewDidLoad
{
    [super viewDidLoad];

    self.gMonthTextField.delegate = self;
    self.gDayTextField.delegate = self;
    self.gYearTextField.delegate = self;
    self.hMonthTextField.delegate = self;
    self.hDayTextField.delegate = self;
    self.hYearTextField.delegate = self;
}
```

Next, define the UITextFieldDelegate method textFieldShouldReturn: to properly dismiss the keyboard.

```
-(BOOL)textFieldShouldReturn:(UITextField *)textField
{
    [textField resignFirstResponder];
    return NO;
}
```

The first new class that you see here is the NSCalendar class. This is essentially used to set a standard for the dates that you will later refer to. The NSCalendar method also allows you to perform several useful functions dealing with a calendar, such as changing which day a week starts on, or changing the time zone used. The NSCalendar class also acts as a bridge between the NSDate and NSDateComponents classes that you will see later.

You use two instances of the NSCalendar class to translate dates between the Gregorian calendar and the Hebrew calendar. Add these properties of your class:

```
@property (nonatomic, strong) NSCalendar *gregorianCalendar;
@property (nonatomic, strong) NSCalendar *hebrewCalendar;
```

You use lazy initialization for these properties, so add the following custom getter implementations:

```
-(NSCalendar *)gregorianCalendar
{
    if (!_gregorianCalendar)
    {
        _gregorianCalendar =
            [[NSCalendar alloc] initWithCalendarIdentifier:NSGregorianCalendar];
    }
    return _gregorianCalendar;
}

-(NSCalendar *)hebrewCalendar
{
    if (!_hebrewCalendar)
    {
        _hebrewCalendar =
            [[NSCalendar alloc] initWithCalendarIdentifier:NSHebrewCalendar];
    }
    return _hebrewCalendar;
}
```

These method overrides are necessary to make sure that your calendars are initialized with their correct calendar types. Alternatively, you could simply initialize your calendars in the viewDidLoad method to be created when the app launches.

> **Note**   There are a large variety of different calendar types that are available for use with the NSCalendar class, including NSBuddhistCalendar, NSIslamicCalendar and NSJapaneseCalendar.
>
> Given the immense multicultural nature of today's technological world, you may find it quite necessary to make use of some of these calendars! Consult the Apple documentation for a full list of possible calendar types.

Now that your setup is done, you can implement your conversion method, starting with the conversion from Gregorian to Hebrew.

```
- (IBAction)convertToGregorian:(id)sender
{
    NSDateComponents *hComponents = [[NSDateComponents alloc] init];
    [hComponents setDay:[self.hDayTextField.text integerValue]];
    [hComponents setMonth:[self.hMonthTextField.text integerValue]];
    [hComponents setYear:[self.hYearTextField.text integerValue]];
```

```
    NSDate *hebrewDate = [self.hebrewCalendar dateFromComponents:hComponents];

    NSUInteger unitFlags =
        NSDayCalendarUnit | NSMonthCalendarUnit | NSYearCalendarUnit;

    NSDateComponents *hebrewDateComponents =
        [self.gregorianCalendar components:unitFlags fromDate:hebrewDate];

    self.gDayTextField.text =
        [[NSNumber numberWithInteger:hebrewDateComponents.day] stringValue];
    self.gMonthTextField.text =
        [[NSNumber numberWithInteger:hebrewDateComponents.month] stringValue];
    self.gYearTextField.text =
        [[NSNumber numberWithInteger:hebrewDateComponents.year] stringValue];
}
```

As you can see, you are using a combination of NSDateComponents, NSDate, and NSCalendar to perform this conversion.

The NSDateComponents class is used to define the details that make up an NSDate, such as the day, month, year, time, and so on. Here, only the month, day, and year are being used.

As mentioned earlier, you use an instance of the NSCalendar to create an instance of NSDate out of the components that you have defined.

One of the more confusing parts of the above method may be the use of the NSUInteger unitFlags, which is formatted quite unusually. Whenever you specify creating an instance of NSDateComponents out of an NSDate, you need to specify exactly which components to include from the date. You can specify these flags, called NSCalendarUnits, through the use of the NSUInteger, as shown.

Other types of NSCalendarUnits include the following, among many others:

- ▓ NSSecondCalendarUnit
- ▓ NSWeekOfYearCalendarUnit
- ▓ NSEraCalendarUnit
- ▓ NSTimeZoneCalendarUnit

As you can see, the specificity with which you can create instances of NSDate is highly customizable, allowing you to perform unique calculations and comparisons. For a full list of NSCalendarUnit values, refer to the NSCalendar class reference in Apple's developer API.

Because the values of NSDateComponents are of type NSInteger, you must first convert them to instances of NSNumber, and then take their stringValue before you set them into your text fields.

Once you have defined your conversion from one calendar to the other, the reverse is simple, as you just need to change which text fields and calendar you use.

```
- (IBAction)convertToHebrew:(id)sender
{
    NSDateComponents *gComponents = [[NSDateComponents alloc] init];
    [gComponents setDay:[self.gDayTextField.text integerValue]];
    [gComponents setMonth:[self.gMonthTextField.text integerValue]];
```

```
    [gComponents setYear:[self.gYearTextField.text integerValue]];

    NSDate *gregorianDate = [self.gregorianCalendar dateFromComponents:gComponents];

    NSUInteger unitFlags =
        NSDayCalendarUnit | NSMonthCalendarUnit | NSYearCalendarUnit;

    NSDateComponents *hebrewDateComponents =
        [self.hebrewCalendar components:unitFlags fromDate:gregorianDate];

    self.hDayTextField.text =
        [[NSNumber numberWithInteger:hebrewDateComponents.day] stringValue];
    self.hMonthTextField.text =
        [[NSNumber numberWithInteger:hebrewDateComponents.month] stringValue];
    self.hYearTextField.text =
        [[NSNumber numberWithInteger:hebrewDateComponents.year] stringValue];
}
```

Your application can now correctly convert instances of NSDate between calendars, as shown in Figure 11-2. Try experimenting with different dates or even different calendars to see what kinds of powerful date conversions you can do.

Figure 11-2. An app that converts between Gregorian and Hebrew dates

Recipe 11-2: Fetching Calendar Events

Now that you have covered how to deal with basic date conversions and calculations, you can go into details on dealing with events and calendars, interacting with the user's own events and schedule. The next few recipes all compound to create a complete utilization of the Event Kit framework.

First, create a new single-view application project with the name "My Events App." This time you use the Event Kit framework, so go ahead and link `EventKit.framework` to your newly created project.

Because this app is going to access the device's calendars, you should provide a usage description in the project's `Info.plist` file. Add the "Privacy – Calendars Usage Description" key to the Information Property List and enter the text **Testing Calendar Events**, as Figure 11-3 shows.

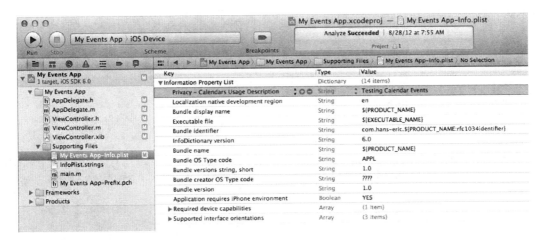

Figure 11-3. An app providing a calendar usage description in the Information Property List

Whenever you're dealing with the Event Kit framework, the main element you work with is an `EKEventStore`. This class allows you to access, delete, and save events in your calendars. An `EKEventStore` takes a relatively long time to initialize, so you should do it only once and store it in a property. Add the following declarations to the `ViewController.h` file:

```
//
//  ViewController.h
//  My Events App
//

#import <UIKit/UIKit.h>
#import <EventKit/EventKit.h>

@interface ViewController : UIViewController

@property (strong, nonatomic) EKEventStore *eventStore;

@end
```

The implementation for this first recipe is a simple logging of all calendar events within 48 hours from now. You're not going to build a user interface at this point, instead all the relevant code will reside in the viewDidLoad method. We'll go through the steps first and then show you the complete implementation.

The first thing you need to do when you want to access the device's calendar entries is to ask the user for permission to do so. dodo this using the requestAccessToEntityType:completion: method of EKEventStore, passing a code block that will be invoked when the asynchronous process is done:

```
self.eventStore = [[EKEventStore alloc] init];

[self.eventStore requestAccessToEntityType:EKEntityTypeEvent
completion:^(BOOL granted, NSError *error)
{
    if (granted)
    {
        //...
    }
    else
    {
        NSLog(@"Access not granted: %@", error);
    }
}];
```

If access was indeed granted, you can go ahead and retrieve the information you want. In this case you'll fetch all the calendar events from between now and 48 hours from now. First, create the two dates:

```
NSDate *now = [NSDate date];

NSCalendar *calendar = [NSCalendar currentCalendar];
NSDateComponents *fortyEightHoursFromNowComponents = [[NSDateComponents alloc] init];
fortyEightHoursFromNowComponents.day = 2; // 48 hours forward
NSDate *fortyEightHoursFromNow =
    [calendar dateByAddingComponents:fortyEightHoursFromNowComponents toDate:now
        options:0];
```

> **Note**   As you can see, you use NSCalendar to help create the future date. This ensures a more accurate time than if you use NSDate's method dateWithTimeIntervalSinceNow:. The reason it's more accurate is that NSCalendar takes into account the fact that not all days in a year are exactly 24 hours long. Although the difference in this case is insignificant, it's considered good practice to use the dateByAddingComponents:toDate: method to construct relative dates.

Now that you have the start date and the end date, you can create a search predicate for finding the events within that interval by using the predicateForEventsWithStartDate:endDate:calendars: method on the event store. By passing a value of nil to the calendars parameter of this method, you specify that you want your predicate to be applied to all calendars.

```
NSPredicate *allEventsWithin48HoursPredicate =
    [self.eventStore predicateForEventsWithStartDate:now endDate:fortyEightHoursFromNow
        calendars:nil];
```

You then use the predicate to retrieve the actual events from the event store:

```
NSArray *events =
    [self.eventStore eventsMatchingPredicate:allEventsWithin48HoursPredicate];
```

Finally, you'll just iterate over the retrieved events and print their titles to the debug log:

```
for (EKEvent *event in events)
{
    NSLog(@"%@", event.title);
}
```

Here's the complete implementation of the viewDidLoad method:

```
- (void)viewDidLoad
{
    [super viewDidLoad];

    self.eventStore = [[EKEventStore alloc] init];

    [self.eventStore requestAccessToEntityType:EKEntityTypeEvent
     completion:^(BOOL granted, NSError *error)
     {
         if (granted)
         {
             NSDate *now = [NSDate date];

             NSCalendar *calendar = [NSCalendar currentCalendar];
             NSDateComponents *fortyEightHoursFromNowComponents =
                 [[NSDateComponents alloc] init];
             fortyEightHoursFromNowComponents.day = 2; // 48 hours forward
             NSDate *fortyEightHoursFromNow =
                 [calendar dateByAddingComponents:fortyEightHoursFromNowComponents
                     toDate:now options:0];

             NSPredicate *allEventsWithin48HoursPredicate =
                 [self.eventStore predicateForEventsWithStartDate:now
                     endDate:fortyEightHoursFromNow calendars:nil];
             NSArray *events = [self.eventStore
                 eventsMatchingPredicate:allEventsWithin48HoursPredicate];
             for (EKEvent *event in events)
             {
                 NSLog(@"%@", event.title);
             }
         }
```

```
        else
        {
            NSLog(@"Access not granted: %@", error);
        }
    }];
}
```

Because the iOS Simulator doesn't have calendar support, you need to test your app on a real device. Be sure that the device has events scheduled to serve as your test data. Because the only output you are creating here is in the log, you also need to run the application from Xcode, so as to capture the output. See Figure 11-4 for an example of such output.

All Output ⇕			Clear
2012-08-27 21:20:07.422 My Events App[6845:1103] Report to shareholders
2012-08-27 21:20:07.428 My Events App[6845:1103] Daily Scrum
2012-08-27 21:20:07.433 My Events App[6845:1103] Lunch with Soner
2012-08-27 21:20:07.436 My Events App[6845:1103] Floorball Practice
2012-08-27 21:20:07.439 My Events App[6845:1103] Requirements Meeting
2012-08-27 21:20:07.443 My Events App[6845:1103] Daily Scrum

Figure 11-4. Output log for the application, showing the names of nearby events

The first time you run this app you'll get an alert asking if your app should be allowed to access your calendar (see Figure 11-5). This is a part of the new privacy policy implemented in iOS 6. Because the calendar can contain private information that may sensitive, apps must now ask the user's explicit permission before accessing it.

"My Events App" Would Like to Access Your Calendar

Testing Calendar Events

Don't Allow   OK

Figure 11-5. An alert asking for the user's permission to access the calendar

The user is only asked once to grant an app access to the calendar. iOS remembers the user's answer on subsequent runs. If the user wants to change the current access setting, she can do that in the Settings app, under Privacy ➤ Calendars (see Figure 11-6).

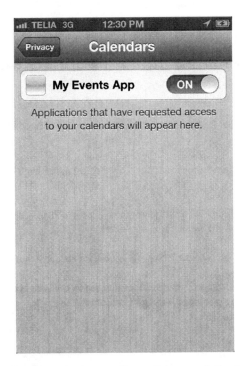

Figure 11-6. *The privacy settings showing an app that's currently granted access to the device's calendar*

Tip Sometimes as a developer of these restricted features, you want to reset the privacy settings to test the initial run scenario again. You can reset these settings in the Settings app, under General ➤ Reset using the Reset Location & Privacy option.

Recipe 11-3: Displaying Events in a Table View

Now that you can access your events, continue by creating a better interface with which to deal with them. In this recipe, you implement a grouped UITableView to display your events.

You start by turning the project into a navigation based application. Declare the UINavigationController property in the AppDelegate.h file:

```
//
//  AppDelegate.h
//  My Events App
//

#import <UIKit/UIKit.h>

@class ViewController;

@interface AppDelegate : UIResponder <UIApplicationDelegate>
```

```
@property (strong, nonatomic) UIWindow *window;

@property (strong, nonatomic) ViewController *viewController;
@property (strong, nonatomic) UINavigationController *navigationController;

@end
```

Now, make the following changes to the `application:didFinishLaunchingWithOptions:` method in the AppDelegate.m file:

```
- (BOOL)application:(UIApplication *)application didFinishLaunchingWithOptions:(NSDictionary *)
launchOptions
{
    self.window = [[UIWindow alloc] initWithFrame:[[UIScreen mainScreen] bounds]];
    // Override point for customization after application launch.
    self.viewController =
        [[ViewController alloc] initWithNibName:@"ViewController" bundle:nil];
    self.navigationController =
        [[UINavigationController alloc] initWithRootViewController:self.viewController];
    self.window.rootViewController = self.navigationController;
    [self.window makeKeyAndVisible];
    return YES;
}
```

Next, you set up the user interface consisting of a UITableView. Select the ViewController.xib file in the Project Navigator to bring up Interface Builder. To be sure you take into account the navigation bar when you design your user interface, you should set the corresponding Simulated Metrics attribute in the Attributes inspector. Select the main view and go to the Attributes inspector. There, in the Simulated Metrics section, change the value of the Top Bar attribute to Navigation Bar, as shown in Figure 11-7.

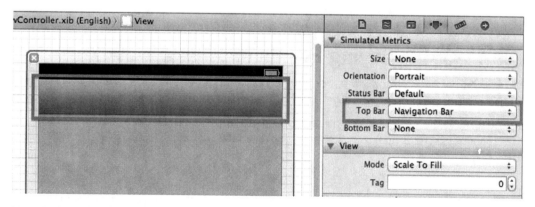

Figure 11-7. Setting the Top Bar simulated metrics to Navigation Bar

Now, you can add the table view and make it take up the remaining parts of the view. In the Attributes inspector for the table view, be sure that the Style attribute is set to Grouped. Your main view should now resemble Figure 11-8.

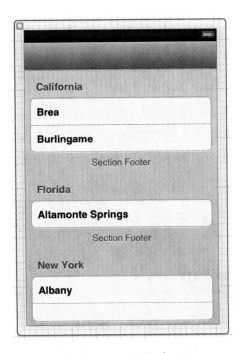

Figure 11-8. A user interface with a navigation bar and a grouped table view

Next, create an outlet for your UITableView. Name the outlet eventsTableView.

Before you switch over to your implementation file, you will need to make some additional changes to the header file. First, add the UITableViewDelegate and the UITableViewDataSource protocols to the class. Also define two new properties, an NSArray, which is used to hold references to all the calendars in the EKEventStore, and an NSMutableDictionary that is used to store all your events based on which calendar they belong to. The ViewController.h file should now resemble the following code:

```
//
//  ViewController.h
//  My Events App
//

#import <UIKit/UIKit.h>
#import <EventKit/EventKit.h>

@interface ViewController : UIViewController<UITableViewDelegate, UITableViewDataSource>

@property (strong, nonatomic) EKEventStore *eventStore;
@property (weak, nonatomic) IBOutlet UITableView *eventsTableView;
@property (nonatomic, strong) NSMutableDictionary *events;
@property (nonatomic, strong) NSArray *calendars;

@end
```

The next thing you need to do is to modify the viewDidLoad method. Specifically, you do these things:

- ▓ Set the title displayed in the navigation bar.
- ▓ Add a refresh button to the navigation bar.
- ▓ Set up the table view's two delegate methods.
- ▓ Populate the calendars array and the events dictionary.

To accomplish these things, make the following changes to the viewDidLoad method:

```
- (void)viewDidLoad
{
    [super viewDidLoad];

    self.title = @"Events";

    UIBarButtonItem *refreshButton = [[UIBarButtonItem alloc]
        initWithBarButtonSystemItem:UIBarButtonSystemItemRefresh target:self
        action:@selector(refresh:)];
    self.navigationItem.leftBarButtonItem = refreshButton;

    self.eventsTableView.delegate = self;
    self.eventsTableView.dataSource = self;

    self.eventStore = [[EKEventStore alloc] init];

    [self.eventStore requestAccessToEntityType:EKEntityTypeEvent
     completion:^(BOOL granted, NSError *error)
     {
         if (granted)
         {
             self.calendars =
                 [self.eventStore calendarsForEntityType:EKEntityTypeEvent];
             [self fetchEvents];
         }
         else
         {
             NSLog(@"Access not granted: %@", error);
         }
     }];
}
```

There are two methods that the preceding code uses that you haven't implemented yet. The first is the refresh: action method that will be invoked when the user taps the Refresh button on the navigation bar. Go ahead and add the following code to the view controller class:

```
- (void)refresh:(id)sender
{
    [self fetchEvents];
    [self.eventsTableView reloadData];
}
```

The second unimplemented method is fetchEvent, which contains the code to actually query the eventStore for the events. Because you sort your events by the calendar they belong to, you perform a different query for each calendar, rather than just one for all events:

```
- (void)fetchEvents
{
    self.events = [[NSMutableDictionary alloc] initWithCapacity:[self.calendars count]];

    NSDate *now = [NSDate date];

    NSCalendar *calendar = [NSCalendar currentCalendar];
    NSDateComponents *fortyEightHoursFromNowComponents =
        [[NSDateComponents alloc] init];
    fortyEightHoursFromNowComponents.day = 2; // 48 hours forward
    NSDate *fortyEightHoursFromNow =
        [calendar dateByAddingComponents:fortyEightHoursFromNowComponents toDate:now
            options:0];

    for (EKCalendar *calendar in self.calendars)
    {
        NSPredicate *allEventsWithin48HoursPredicate =
            [self.eventStore predicateForEventsWithStartDate:now
                endDate:fortyEightHoursFromNow calendars:@[calendar]];
        NSArray *eventsInThisCalendar =
            [self.eventStore eventsMatchingPredicate:allEventsWithin48HoursPredicate];
        if (eventsInThisCalendar != nil)
        {
            [self.events setObject:eventsInThisCalendar forKey:calendar.title];
        }
    }

    dispatch_async(dispatch_get_main_queue(),^{
        [self.eventsTableView reloadData];
    });
}
```

You should recognize most of the preceding code from the previous recipe. The main difference is that you now perform a search for each individual calendar and store the results in the events dictionary using the respective calendar names as keys.

Also, when all the fetching is done you're notifying the table view that its data has changed. However, because the fetchEvents is invoked on an arbitrary thread and any user interface–related code must be run on the main thread, you need to dispatch that particular piece of code to make it run in the main thread.

With the data model in place, you can move your attention over to the table view and its implementation. But before you do that you'll add a few helper methods. These methods are quite small and simple in nature, but they help make the code you'll add in a minute easier to read. So add the following code to the ViewController.m file:

```
- (EKCalendar *)calendarAtSection:(NSInteger)section
{
    return [self.calendars objectAtIndex:section];
}


- (EKEvent *)eventAtIndexPath:(NSIndexPath *)indexPath
{

    EKCalendar *calendar = [self calendarAtSection:indexPath.section];
    NSArray *calendarEvents = [self eventsForCalendar:calendar];
    return [calendarEvents objectAtIndex:indexPath.row];
}


- (NSArray *)eventsForCalendar:(EKCalendar *)calendar
{

    return [self.events objectForKey:calendar.title];
}
```

Now, implement a method to specify the number of sections it should display. You have one section per calendar so this method is nice and easy:

```
-(NSInteger)numberOfSectionsInTableView:(UITableView *)tableView
{
    return [self.calendars count];
}
```

You can also implement a method to specify your section titles:

```
-(NSString *)tableView:(UITableView *)tableView titleForHeaderInSection:(NSInteger)section
{
    return [self calendarAtSection:section].title;
}
```

You also need to implement a method to determine the number of rows in each group, as given by the count of the array returned by your dictionary for a given section:

```
-(NSInteger)tableView:(UITableView *)tableView numberOfRowsInSection:(NSInteger)section
{
    EKCalendar *calendar = [self calendarAtSection:section];
    return [self eventsForCalendar:calendar].count;
}
```

Finally, add the method that defines how your table's cells are created:

```
- (UITableViewCell *)tableView:(UITableView *)tableView cellForRowAtIndexPath:(NSIndexPath *)
indexPath
{
    static NSString *CellIdentifier = @"Cell";
```

```
UITableViewCell *cell =
    [tableView dequeueReusableCellWithIdentifier:CellIdentifier];
if (cell == nil)
{
    cell = [[UITableViewCell alloc] initWithStyle:UITableViewCellStyleValue1
        reuseIdentifier:CellIdentifier];
}

cell.accessoryType = UITableViewCellAccessoryDetailDisclosureButton;
cell.textLabel.backgroundColor = [UIColor clearColor];
cell.textLabel.font = [UIFont systemFontOfSize:19.0];

cell.textLabel.text = [self eventAtIndexPath:indexPath].title;

return cell;
}
```

As Figure 11-9 shows, your application can now display all calendar events that occur within 48 hours.

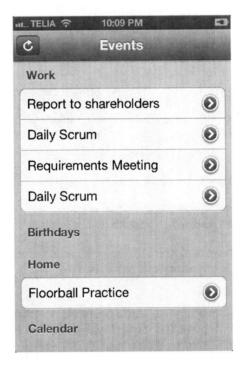

Figure 11-9. A simple app that displays calendar events within two days from now

Recipe 11-4: Viewing, Editing, and Deleting Events

The next step is to look into how to allow the user to view, edit, and delete events through pre-defined classes in the Event Kit UI framework.

You'll continue adding to the same project that you've been using since Recipe 11-2. This time you're going to make use of a couple of predefined user interfaces for viewing and editing calendar events. Specifically, you'll be utilizing the EKEventViewController and EKEventViewEditController classes. These are a part of the Event Kit UI framework, so go ahead and add EventKitUI.framework to the project.

You also need to import its API into the main view controller's header file:

```
//
//  ViewController.h
//  Calendar Events
//

#import <UIKit/UIKit.h>
#import <EventKit/EventKit.h>
#import <EventKitUI/EventKitUI.h>

@interface ViewController : UIViewController<UITableViewDelegate,
                                             UITableViewDataSource>

@property (strong, nonatomic) EKEventStore *eventStore;
@property (weak, nonatomic) IBOutlet UITableView *eventsTableView;
@property (nonatomic, strong) NSMutableDictionary *events;
@property (nonatomic, strong) NSArray *calendars;

@end
```

The next thing you do is to implement behavior for when a user selects a specific row in your table view. You use an instance of the EKEventViewController to display information on the selected event. To do this, add the following tableView:DidSelectRowAtIndexPath: data source method:

```
-(void)tableView:(UITableView *)tableView didSelectRowAtIndexPath:(NSIndexPath *)indexPath
{
    EKEventViewController *eventVC = [[EKEventViewController alloc] init];
    eventVC.event = [self eventAtIndexPath:indexPath];
    eventVC.allowsEditing = YES;
    [self.navigationController pushViewController:eventVC animated:YES];
    [tableView deselectRowAtIndexPath:indexPath animated:YES];
}
```

Now, if the user has edited or removed the selected event from within the event view controller, you'll need to update the table view somehow. The easiest way to do this is to refresh it in the main view controller's viewDidLoad method, like so:

```
- (void)viewWillAppear:(BOOL)animated
{
    [self refresh:self];
    [super viewWillAppear:animated];
}
```

For extra functionality, make your cell's detail disclosure buttons allow the user to proceed directly to editing mode through the use of the EKEventEditViewController. The EKEventEditViewController requires you to assign a delegate to handle its dismissal so start by adding the EKEventEditViewDelegate protocol to the main view controller's class declaration:

```
//
//  ViewController.h
//  Calendar Events
//

#import <UIKit/UIKit.h>
#import <EventKit/EventKit.h>
#import <EventKitUI/EventKitUI.h>

@interface ViewController : UIViewController<UITableViewDelegate, UITableViewDataSource,
    EKEventEditViewDelegate>

@property (strong, nonatomic) EKEventStore *eventStore;
@property (weak, nonatomic) IBOutlet UITableView *eventsTableView;
@property (nonatomic, strong) NSMutableDictionary *events;
@property (nonatomic, strong) NSArray *calendars;

@end
```

Then, implement a method to handle the tapping of the disclosure buttons:

```
-(void)tableView:(UITableView *)tableView accessoryButtonTappedForRowWithIndexPath:(NSIndexPath *)
indexPath
{
    EKEventEditViewController *eventEditVC = [[EKEventEditViewController alloc] init];
    eventEditVC.event = [self eventAtIndexPath:indexPath];
    eventEditVC.eventStore = self.eventStore;
    eventEditVC.editViewDelegate = self;
    [self presentViewController:eventEditVC animated:YES completion:nil];
}
```

Finally, implement the eventEditViewController:didCompleteWithAction: delegate method to dismiss the edit view controller:

```
-(void)eventEditViewController:(EKEventEditViewController *)controller didCompleteWithAction:
(EKEventEditViewAction)action
{
    [self dismissViewControllerAnimated:YES completion:nil];
}
```

Before you're done, you need to implement one last delegate method to specify the default calendar that will be used for the creation of new events. In this implementation, you simply return the default calendar of the device:

```
-(EKCalendar *)eventEditViewControllerDefaultCalendarForNewEvents:
(EKEventEditViewController *)controller
{
    return [self.eventStore defaultCalendarForNewEvents];
}
```

At this point, your application now allows the user to view and edit the details of an event in two different ways, through the use of either an EKEventViewController or an EKEventEditViewController. An example of the user interfaces of these view controllers can be seen in Figure 11-10.

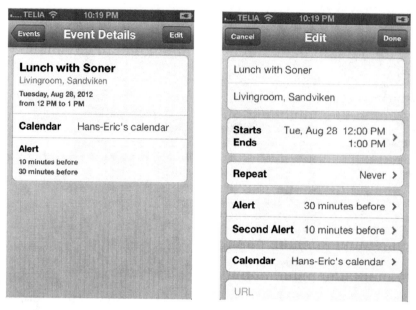

Figure 11-10. *The user interfaces of an EKEventViewController and an EKEventEditViewController, respectively*

Recipe 11-5: Creating Calendar Events

While it is fairly simple to allow users to create a calendar event by themselves, we, as developers, should always strive to simplify even the simple things. The less that users have to do on their own, the happier they tend to be with the final product. To this end, it is important to be able to create and edit events programmatically, at the tap of a button.

Again, you'll continue adding to the project you created in Recipe 11-2. The first thing is to add an Add button to the navigation bar. Go to the viewDidLoad method in ViewController.m and add the following code:

```
- (void)viewDidLoad
{
    [super viewDidLoad];

    self.title = @"Events";

    UIBarButtonItem *refreshButton = [[UIBarButtonItem alloc]
        initWithBarButtonSystemItem:UIBarButtonSystemItemRefresh target:self
        action:@selector(refresh:)];
    self.navigationItem.leftBarButtonItem = refreshButton;
```

```
UIBarButtonItem *addButton = [[UIBarButtonItem alloc]
    initWithBarButtonSystemItem:UIBarButtonSystemItemAdd target:self
    action:@selector(addEvent:)];
self.navigationItem.rightBarButtonItem = addButton;

// ...

}
```

When the user taps the Add button, the app will create a new event in the device's default calendar. To make things simple in this recipe, you ask the user to enter a title for the event using an alert view. To implement that, start by adding the UIAlertViewDelegate protocol to the main view controller's header declaration:

```
@interface ViewController : UIViewController<UITableViewDelegate, UITableViewDataSource,
    EKEventEditViewDelegate, UIAlertViewDelegate>
```

Then add the action method that presents the alert view:

```
- (void)addEvent:(id)sender
{
    UIAlertView * inputAlert = [[UIAlertView alloc] initWithTitle:@"New Event"
        message:@"Enter a title for the event" delegate:self cancelButtonTitle:@"Cancel"
        otherButtonTitles:@"OK", nil];
    inputAlert.alertViewStyle = UIAlertViewStylePlainTextInput;
    [inputAlert show];
}
```

Finally, add the delegate method that will be invoked when the user has tapped a button in the alert view:

```
- (void)alertView:(UIAlertView *)alertView clickedButtonAtIndex:(NSInteger)buttonIndex
{
    if (buttonIndex == 1)
    {
        // OK button tapped

        // Calculate the date exactly one day from now
        NSCalendar *calendar = [NSCalendar currentCalendar];
        NSDateComponents *aDayFromNowComponents = [[NSDateComponents alloc] init];
        aDayFromNowComponents.day = 1;
        NSDate *now = [NSDate date];
        NSDate *aDayFromNow = [calendar dateByAddingComponents:aDayFromNowComponents
            toDate:now options:0];

        // Create the event
        EKEvent *event = [EKEvent eventWithEventStore:self.eventStore];
        event.title = [alertView textFieldAtIndex:0].text;
        event.calendar = [self.eventStore defaultCalendarForNewEvents];
        event.startDate = aDayFromNow;
        event.endDate = [NSDate dateWithTimeInterval:60*60.0 sinceDate:event.startDate];
```

```
        // Save the event and update the table view
        [self.eventStore saveEvent:event span:EKSpanThisEvent error:nil];
        [self refresh:self];
    }
}
```

For the sake of demonstration we have chosen a very simple method for creating these new events (see Figure 11-11). They are all set up a day in advance and last an hour. Most likely in your application you would choose a more complex or user-input-based method for creating EKEvents.

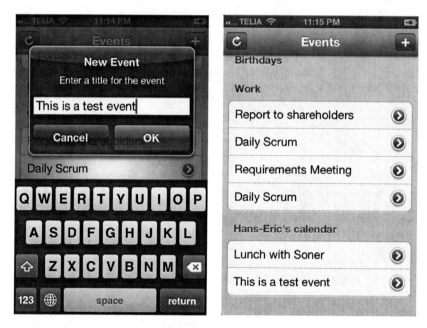

Figure 11-11. A simple user interface to add new calendar events

Creating Recurring Events

The Event Kit framework provides a powerful API for working with recurring events. To see how it works you're going to change the event that this app creates and make it recur. Let's add the code first and look at how it works later:

```
- (void)alertView:(UIAlertView *)alertView clickedButtonAtIndex:(NSInteger)buttonIndex
{
    if (buttonIndex == 1)
    {
        // OK button tapped

        // Calculate the date exactly one day from now
        NSCalendar *calendar = [NSCalendar currentCalendar];
        NSDateComponents *aDayFromNowComponents = [[NSDateComponents alloc] init];
        aDayFromNowComponents.day = 1;
        NSDate *now = [NSDate date];
```

```
NSDate *aDayFromNow = [calendar dateByAddingComponents:aDayFromNowComponents
    toDate:now options:0];

// Create the event
EKEvent *event = [EKEvent eventWithEventStore:self.eventStore];
event.title = [alertView textFieldAtIndex:0].text;
event.calendar = [self.eventStore defaultCalendarForNewEvents];
event.startDate = aDayFromNow;
event.endDate = [NSDate dateWithTimeInterval:60*60.0 sinceDate:event.startDate];

// Make it recur
EKRecurrenceRule *repeatEverySecondWednesdayRecurrenceRule =
[[EKRecurrenceRule alloc] initRecurrenceWithFrequency:EKRecurrenceFrequencyDaily
    interval:2
    daysOfTheWeek:@[[EKRecurrenceDayOfWeek dayOfWeek:4]]
    daysOfTheMonth:nil
    monthsOfTheYear:nil
    weeksOfTheYear:nil
    daysOfTheYear:nil
    setPositions:nil
    end:[EKRecurrenceEnd recurrenceEndWithOccurrenceCount:20]];

event.recurrenceRules = @[repeatEverySecondWednesdayRecurrenceRule];

// Save the event and update the table view
[self.eventStore saveEvent:event span:EKSpanThisEvent error:nil];
[self refresh:self];
    }
}
```

As you can see, you create an instance of the class EKRecurrenceRule to provide to your event. This class is an incredibly flexible method with which to programmatically implement recurrent events. With only one method, a developer can create nearly any combination of recurrences imaginable. The function of each parameter of this method is listed as follows. For any parameter, passing a value of nil indicates a lack of restriction.

- initRecurrenceWithFrequency: Specifies a basic level of how often the event repeats, whether on a daily, weekly, monthly, or annual basis.

- interval: Specifies the interval of repetition based on the frequency. A recurring event with a weekly frequency and an interval of 3 repeats every three weeks.

- daysOfTheWeek: Takes an NSArray of objects that must be accessed through the EKRecurrenceDayOfWeek dayOfWeek method, which takes an integer parameter representing the day of the week, starting with 1 referring to Sunday. By setting this parameter, a developer can create an event to repeat every few days, but only if the event falls on specified days of the week.

- daysOfTheMonth: Similar to daysOfTheWeek. Specifies which days in a month to restrict a recurring event to. It is only valid for events with monthly frequency.

- monthsOfTheYear: Similar to daysOfTheWeek and daysOfTheMonth, valid only for events with a yearly frequency.

▣ weeksOfTheYear: Just like monthsOfTheYear, this is restricted only to events with an annual frequency, but with specific weeks to restrict instead of months.

▣ daysOfTheYear: Another parameter restricted to annually recurring events, this allows you to specify only certain days, counting from either the beginning or the end of the year, to filter a specific event to.

▣ setPositions: This parameter is the ultimate filter, allowing you to entirely restrict the event you have created to only specific days of the year. In this way, an event that repeats daily could, for example, be restricted to occur only on the 28th, 102nd, and 364th days of the year for whatever reason a developer might choose.

▣ end: Requires a class call to the EKRecurrenceEnd class, and specifies when your event will no longer repeat. The two class methods to choose between are as follows:

▣ recurrenceEndWithEndDate: Allows the developer to specify a date after which the event will no longer repeat

▣ recurrenceEndWithOccurenceCount: Restricts an event's repetition to a limited number of occurrences

Based on all this, you can see that the recurring event you have created for demonstration will repeat every second Wednesday up to a limit of 20 occurrences.

This concludes the series of recipes that demonstrates the part of the Event Kit framework that handles calendar events. Next, you'll take a quick look at a related topic, namely reminders.

Recipe 11-6: Creating Reminders

In iOS 6, Apple released an API that allows you to add entries to the Reminders app that was introduced in iOS 5. With this new API, your apps can interact directly with this great utility and build features that automatically create reminders relevant to your users.

Setting Up the Application

In this recipe you build a simple user interface that allows you to create reminders with two different types of alarms: time-based and location-based. Start by creating a new single-view application project. You use both the Event Kit framework and the Core Location framework, so link the EventKit.framework and CoreLocation.framework binaries to the project.

This time you access two restricted services, Core Location and Reminders, which means you should provide Usage Descriptions for these in the project property list. Add the key Privacy – Location Usage Description with the text Testing Location-Based Reminders and the key Privacy – Reminders Usage Description with the text Testing Reminders, as shown in Figure 11-12.

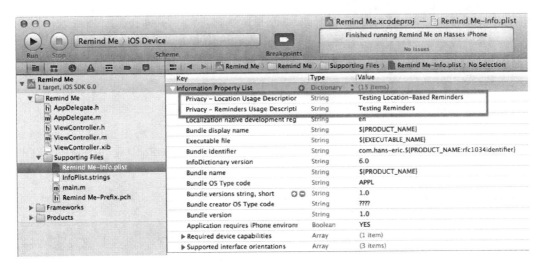

Figure 11-12. Setting usage descriptions for Location Services and Reminders

Next, you'll build a user interface that resembles Figure 11-13. So go to the `ViewController.xib` to bring up Interface Builder. Drag in and position the two buttons and the Activity Indicator. To make the Activity Indicator only appear when active, set its Hides When Stopped checkbox in the Attributes inspector. This will make it initially hidden as well, which is what you want.

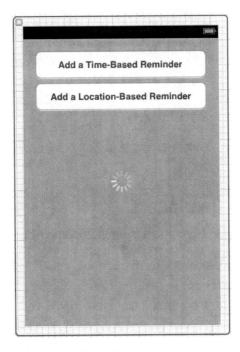

Figure 11-13. A user interface for creating two types of reminders

Create actions with the names addTimeBasedReminder and addLocationBasedReminder for the buttons, and an outlet named activityIndicator for the Acitivity Indicator.

Next, go to ViewController.h and import the additional APIs you'll be utilizing, and declare the usual eventStore property:

```
//
//  ViewController.h
//  Remind Me
//

#import <UIKit/UIKit.h>
#import <EventKit/EventKit.h>
#import <CoreLocation/CoreLocation.h>

@interface ViewController : UIViewController<CLLocationManagerDelegate>

@property (weak, nonatomic) IBOutlet UIActivityIndicatorView *activityIndicator;
@property (strong, nonatomic)EKEventStore *eventStore;

- (IBAction)addTimeBasedReminder:(id)sender;
- (IBAction)addLocationBasedReminder:(id)sender;

@end
```

You'll use lazy initialization for the eventStore property, so go to ViewController.m and add the following custom getter:

```
- (EKEventStore *)eventStore
{
    if (_eventStore == nil)
    {
        _eventStore = [[EKEventStore alloc] init];
    }
    return _eventStore;
}
```

Requesting Access to Reminders

As with Calendar Events, access to Reminders is restricted and requires explicit acceptance from the user. In this recipe you're going to implement a helper method that handles the requesting of Reminders access. Because this process is asynchronous, you use the block technique to inject code to run in case access was granted.

Start by declaring a block type and the method signature in ViewController.h:

```
//
//  ViewController.h
//  Remind Me
//
```

```objc
#import <UIKit/UIKit.h>
#import <EventKit/EventKit.h>
#import <CoreLocation/CoreLocation.h>

typedef void(^RestrictedEventStoreActionHandler)();

@interface ViewController : UIViewController<CLLocationManagerDelegate>

@property (weak, nonatomic) IBOutlet UIActivityIndicatorView *activityIndicator;
@property (strong, nonatomic)EKEventStore *eventStore;

- (IBAction)addTimeBasedReminder:(id)sender;
- (IBAction)addLocationBasedReminder:(id)sender;

- (void)handleReminderAction:(RestrictedEventStoreActionHandler)block;

@end
```

The mission of the handleReminderAction: helper method is to request access to Reminders and invoke the provided block of code if granted. If access was denied, it simply displays an alert to inform the user. Here's the implementation:

```objc
- (void)handleReminderAction:(RestrictedEventStoreActionHandler)block
{
    [self.eventStore requestAccessToEntityType:EKEntityTypeReminder
                                    completion:^(BOOL granted, NSError *error)
     {
         if (granted)
         {
             block();
         }
         else
         {
             UIAlertView *notGrantedAlert = [[UIAlertView alloc] initWithTitle:@"Access Denied"
                 message:@"Access to device's reminders has been denied for this app."
                 delegate:nil cancelButtonTitle:@"OK" otherButtonTitles:nil];

             dispatch_async(dispatch_get_main_queue(), ^{
                 [notGrantedAlert show];
             });
         }
     }];
}
```

An important thing to remember is that the completion block may be invoked on any arbitrary thread. So, if you want to perform an action that affects the user interface, for example displaying an alert view, you need to wrap it in a dispatch_async() function call to make it run on the main thread.

With the helper method in place, you can start implementing the action methods, starting with addTimeBasedReminder:. Here's the general structure:

```
- (IBAction)addTimeBasedReminder:(id)sender
{
    [self.activityIndicator startAnimating];

    [self handleReminderAction:^()
    {
        //TODO: Create and add Reminder

        dispatch_async(dispatch_get_main_queue(), ^{
            // TODO: Notify user if the reminder was successfully added or not
            [self.activityIndicator stopAnimating];
        });
    }];
}
```

Here you make use of the helper method you just created, providing a code block that will be invoked if access was granted by the user.

Now, let's look at how to implement the first of the two TODOs in the preceding code.

Creating Time-Based Reminders

We'll show you the steps first and then the complete implementation of the addTimeBasedReminder: method later. The first thing you'll do when granted access is to create a new reminder object and set its title, and the calendar (that is, Reminder List) in which it will be stored.

```
EKReminder *newReminder = [EKReminder reminderWithEventStore:self.eventStore];
newReminder.title = @"Simpsons is on";
newReminder.calendar = [self.eventStore defaultCalendarForNewReminders];
```

Next, you want to set a time for the reminder. In this example you set the actual time to tomorrow at 6 PM. First, you calculate the date for tomorrow by retrieving the current date and adding one day to it using NSDateComponents:

```
NSCalendar *calendar = [NSCalendar currentCalendar];
NSDateComponents *oneDayComponents = [[NSDateComponents alloc] init];
oneDayComponents.day = 1;
NSDate *nextDay =
    [calendar dateByAddingComponents:oneDayComponents toDate:[NSDate date] options:0];
```

Then, to set the specific time to 6 PM you'll extract the NSDateComponents object from nextDay, change its hour component to 18 (6 PM on a 24 hour clock) and create a new date from these adjusted components:

```
NSUInteger unitFlags = NSEraCalendarUnit | NSYearCalendarUnit | NSMonthCalendarUnit |
    NSDayCalendarUnit;
NSDateComponents *tomorrowAt6PMComponents =
    [calendar components:unitFlags fromDate:nextDay];
```

```
tomorrowAt6PMComponents.hour = 18;
tomorrowAt6PMComponents.minute = 0;
tomorrowAt6PMComponents.second = 0;
NSDate *nextDayAt6PM = [calendar dateFromComponents:tomorrowAt6PMComponents];
```

Next, you'll create an EKAlarm with the time and add it to the reminder. It's recommended that you also set the dueDateComponents property of the Reminder. This helps the Reminders app display more relevant information. Fortunately, you've already constructed the required NSDateComponents object when you previously constructed the alarm date.

```
EKAlarm *alarm = [EKAlarm alarmWithAbsoluteDate:nextDayAt6PM];
[newReminder addAlarm:alarm];
newReminder.dueDateComponents = tomorrowAt6PMComponents;
```

Finally, save and commit the new Reminder and inform the user whether the operation was successful. Because displaying a UIAlertView is affecting the user interface, this particular code too needs to be run on the main thread:

```
// ...

NSString *alertTitle;
NSString *alertMessage;
NSString *alertButtonTitle;
NSError *error;
[self.eventStore saveReminder:newReminder commit:YES error:&error];
if (error == nil)
{
    alertTitle = @"Information";
    alertMessage = [NSString stringWithFormat:@"\"%@\" was added to Reminders",
        newReminder.title];
    alertButtonTitle = @"OK";
}
else
{
    alertTitle = @"Error";
    alertMessage = [NSString stringWithFormat:@"Unable to save reminder: %@", error];
    alertButtonTitle = @"Dismiss";
}

dispatch_async(dispatch_get_main_queue(), ^{
    UIAlertView *alertView = [[UIAlertView alloc]initWithTitle:alertTitle
        message:alertMessage delegate:nil cancelButtonTitle:alertButtonTitle
        otherButtonTitles:nil];
    [alertView show];
    [self.activityIndicator stopAnimating];
});
```

Here's the complete implementation of the addTimeBasedReminder: action method:

```
- (IBAction)addTimeBasedReminder:(id)sender
{
    [self.activityIndicator startAnimating];
```

```objc
[self handleReminderAction:^()
{
    // Create Reminder
    EKReminder *newReminder = [EKReminder reminderWithEventStore:self.eventStore];
    newReminder.title = @"Simpsons is on";
    newReminder.calendar = [self.eventStore defaultCalendarForNewReminders];

    // Calculate the date exactly one day from now
    NSCalendar *calendar = [NSCalendar currentCalendar];
    NSDateComponents *oneDayComponents = [[NSDateComponents alloc] init];
    oneDayComponents.day = 1;
    NSDate *nextDay = [calendar dateByAddingComponents:oneDayComponents
        toDate:[NSDate date] options:0];

    NSUInteger unitFlags = NSEraCalendarUnit | NSYearCalendarUnit |
        NSMonthCalendarUnit | NSDayCalendarUnit;
    NSDateComponents *tomorrowAt6PMComponents = [calendar components:unitFlags
        fromDate:nextDay];
    tomorrowAt6PMComponents.hour = 18;
    tomorrowAt6PMComponents.minute = 0;
    tomorrowAt6PMComponents.second = 0;
    NSDate *nextDayAt6PM = [calendar dateFromComponents:tomorrowAt6PMComponents];

    // Create an Alarm
    EKAlarm *alarm = [EKAlarm alarmWithAbsoluteDate:nextDayAt6PM];
    [newReminder addAlarm:alarm];
    newReminder.dueDateComponents = tomorrowAt6PMComponents;

    // Save Reminder
    NSString *alertTitle;
    NSString *alertMessage;
    NSString *alertButtonTitle;
    NSError *error;
    [self.eventStore saveReminder:newReminder commit:YES error:&error];
    if (error == nil)
    {
        alertTitle = @"Information";
        alertMessage = [NSString stringWithFormat:@"\"%@\" was added to Reminders",
            newReminder.title];
        alertButtonTitle = @"OK";
    }
    else
    {
        alertTitle = @"Error";
        alertMessage = [NSString stringWithFormat:@"Unable to save reminder: %@",
            error];
        alertButtonTitle = @"Dismiss";
    }

    dispatch_async(dispatch_get_main_queue(), ^{
        UIAlertView *alertView = [[UIAlertView alloc]initWithTitle:alertTitle
            message:alertMessage delegate:nil cancelButtonTitle:alertButtonTitle
```

```
                otherButtonTitles:nil];
            [alertView show];
            [self.activityIndicator stopAnimating];
        });
    }];
}
```

You can now build and run the application and have it create a time-based reminder. The first time this app runs and you tap the button to create a time-based reminder, you'll be asked whether the app is allowed to access your Reminders. Figure 11-14 shows an example of this alert.

Figure 11-14. An app asking permission to access the user's Reminders, giving "Testing Reminders" as a reason

Creating Location-Based Reminders

We're now going to raise the bar a little and create a location-based reminder. What you're going to do is to implement the addLocationBasedReminder: action method and make it create a new Reminder with an alarm that's triggered when the user leaves the current location.

Again, you're going to use code blocks and make a helper method that handles the retrieving of the user's current location. As you'll soon realize, this will be a little more complicated because the API to get the device location is based on the delegate pattern and not on the usage of blocks. However, the complication will be hidden behind the nice little API that you'll set up to retrieve the location.

Add the following code to the ViewController.h file:

```
//
//  ViewController.h
//  Remind Me
//

#import <UIKit/UIKit.h>
#import <EventKit/EventKit.h>
#import <CoreLocation/CoreLocation.h>

typedef void(^RestrictedEventStoreActionHandler)();
```

```objc
typedef void(^RetrieveCurrentLocationHandler)(CLLocation *);

@interface ViewController : UIViewController<CLLocationManagerDelegate>
{
    @private
    CLLocationManager *_locationManager;
    RetrieveCurrentLocationHandler _retrieveCurrentLocationBlock;
    int _numberOfTries;
}

@property (weak, nonatomic) IBOutlet UIActivityIndicatorView *activityIndicator;
@property (strong, nonatomic)EKEventStore *eventStore;

- (IBAction)addTimeBasedReminder:(id)sender;
- (IBAction)addLocationBasedReminder:(id)sender;

- (void)handleReminderAction:(RestrictedEventStoreActionHandler)block;
- (void)retrieveCurrentLocation:(RetrieveCurrentLocationHandler)block;

@end
```

As you can see, the signature of the retrieveCurrentLocation: helper method resembles handleReminderAction: that you created in the previous section. The only difference is that its block argument has a CLLocation * parameter. You've also prepared the ViewController class to act as a Location Manager delegate by adding the CLLocationManagerDelegate protocol. Additionally, you've declared three private instance variables that you'll be using in the helper method later.

Now, implement the retrieveCurrentLocation: helper method like so:

```objc
- (void)retrieveCurrentLocation:(RetrieveCurrentLocationHandler)block
{
    if ([CLLocationManager locationServicesEnabled] == NO)
    {
        UIAlertView *locationServicesDisabledAlert = [[UIAlertView alloc]
            initWithTitle:@"Location Services Disabled" message:@"This feature requires
            location services. Enable it in the privacy settings on your device"
            delegate:nil cancelButtonTitle:@"Dismiss" otherButtonTitles:nil];
        [locationServicesDisabledAlert show];
        return;
    }

    if (_locationManager == nil)
    {
        _locationManager = [[CLLocationManager alloc] init];
        _locationManager.desiredAccuracy = kCLLocationAccuracyBest;
        _locationManager.distanceFilter = 1; // meter
        _locationManager.activityType = CLActivityTypeOther;
        _locationManager.delegate = self;
    }
    _numberOfTries = 0;
    _retrieveCurrentLocationBlock = block;
    [_locationManager startUpdatingLocation];
}
```

Refer to Chapter 4, Location Recipes, for the details of this method. Note that you're initializing the _numberOfTries and _retrieveCurrentLocationBlock instance methods before starting the location updates.

Next, implement the delegate method for getting the location:

```
- (void)locationManager:(CLLocationManager *)manager didUpdateLocations:(NSArray *)locations
{
    // Make sure this is a recent location event
    CLLocation *lastLocation = [locations lastObject];
    NSTimeInterval eventInterval = [lastLocation.timestamp timeIntervalSinceNow];
    if(abs(eventInterval) < 30.0)
    {
        // Make sure the event is accurate enough
        if (lastLocation.horizontalAccuracy >= 0 &&
            lastLocation.horizontalAccuracy < 20)
        {
            [_locationManager stopUpdatingLocation];
            _retrieveCurrentLocationBlock(lastLocation);
            return;
        }
    }
    if (_numberOfTries++ == 10)
    {
        [_locationManager stopUpdatingLocation];
        UIAlertView *unableToGetLocationAlert =
            [[UIAlertView alloc]initWithTitle:@"Error"
                message:@"Unable to get the current location." delegate:nil
                cancelButtonTitle:@"Dismiss" otherButtonTitles: nil];
        [unableToGetLocationAlert show];
    }
}
```

Again, refer to Chapter 4 for the details of retrieving locations. The important thing with the preceding implementation, though, is that:

1. You invoke the code block that's stored in the _retrieveCurrentLocationBlock instance variable, and…

2. If you, after ten tries, still not have gotten an accurate enough reading, you abandon it and inform the user.

Finally, you implement the addLocationBasedReminder: action method. It resembles a lot of the addTimeBasedReminder: method you implemented earlier, except that it makes use of both helper methods and of course sets up a location-based reminder. Here's the complete implementation with the differences to addTimeBasedReminder: method marked in bold:

```
- (IBAction)addLocationBasedReminder:(id)sender
{
    [self.activityIndicator startAnimating];

    [self retrieveCurrentLocation:
     ^(CLLocation *currentLocation)
```

```
{
    if (currentLocation != nil)
    {
        [self handleReminderAction:^()
        {
            // Create Reminder
            EKReminder *newReminder =
                [EKReminder reminderWithEventStore:self.eventStore];
            newReminder.title = @"Buy milk!";
            newReminder.calendar =
                [self.eventStore defaultCalendarForNewReminders];

            // Create Location-based Alarm
            EKStructuredLocation *currentStructuredLocation =
                [EKStructuredLocation locationWithTitle:@"Current Location"];
            currentStructuredLocation.geoLocation = currentLocation;

            EKAlarm *alarm = [[EKAlarm alloc] init];
            alarm.structuredLocation = currentStructuredLocation;
            alarm.proximity = EKAlarmProximityLeave;

            [newReminder addAlarm:alarm];

            // Save Reminder
            NSString *alertTitle;
            NSString *alertMessage;
            NSString *alertButtonTitle;
            NSError *error;
            [self.eventStore saveReminder:newReminder commit:YES error:&error];
            if (error == nil)
            {
                alertTitle = @"Information";
                alertMessage =
                    [NSString stringWithFormat:@"\"%@\" was added to Reminders",
                        newReminder.title];
                alertButtonTitle = @"OK";
            }
            else
            {
                alertTitle = @"Error";
                alertMessage =
                    [NSString stringWithFormat:@"Unable to save reminder: %@",
                        error];
                alertButtonTitle = @"Dismiss";
            }

            dispatch_async(dispatch_get_main_queue(), ^{
                UIAlertView *alertView =
                    [[UIAlertView alloc]initWithTitle:alertTitle
                        message:alertMessage delegate:nil
                        cancelButtonTitle:alertButtonTitle otherButtonTitles:nil];
                [alertView show];
```

```
                    [self.activityIndicator stopAnimating];
                });
            }];
        }
    }];
}
```

You can build and run the application again and this time create both a time-based and a location-based reminder. Figure 11-15 shows an example with the Reminders app displaying two different Reminders created using this app.

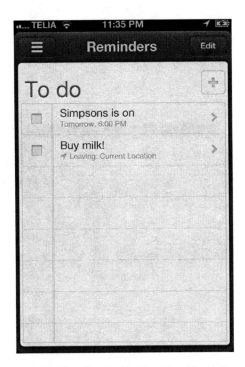

Figure 11-15. The Reminders app showing a time-based and a location-based Reminder

Caution   Although working, this app has one serious flaw. Because the creating of Reminders is running on a separate thread and may take a few seconds, the user can tap the buttons before the task has had the chance to finish. This starts a new process that, while accessing the same instance variables, may interfere with the ongoing task and cause unexpected behavior. The easy way to fix this issue is to disable the buttons while the creating of Reminders is ongoing. We leave this implementation to you, as an exercise.

Recipe 11-7: Accessing the Address Book

One of the most imperative functions of any modern device is storing contact information, and, as such, you should take care to develop applications that take advantage of this important data. In this recipe, you cover three basic functionalities for accessing and dealing with a device's contacts list.

First, create a new single-view application project called "My Pick Contact App."

For this recipe, you need to add two extra frameworks to your project: AddressBook.framework, and AddressBookUI.framework.

Because the Address Book, like the Calendar, is a restricted entity, you should provide a usage description in the application's property list. Add the Privacy – Contacts Usage Description key with the value Testing Address Book Access.

Next, switch over to your view controller's .xib file, and create a view that resembles the one in Figure 11-16.

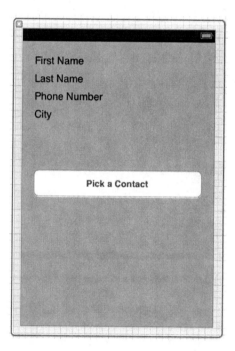

Figure 11-16. *User interface for accessing contact information*

Create these outlets to connect the elements to your code:

- firstNameLabel
- lastNameLabel
- phoneNumberLabel
- cityNameLabel

You do not need an outlet for the button, but create an action with the name `pickContact` for when the user taps it.

Now that your interface is set up, make some changes to the header file. First, add the following two import statements so that you can access the Address Book and Address Book UI frameworks.

```
#import <AddressBook/AddressBook.h>
#import <AddressBookUI/AddressBookUI.h>
```

You use an instance of the class `ABPeoplePickerNavigationController`, and setting its `peoplePickerDelegate` property to your view controller, so you need to add the `ABPeoplePickerNavigationControllerDelegate` protocol implementation to your header file.

The header file, in its entirety, should now look like this:

```
//
//  ViewController.h
//  My Pick Contact App
//

#import <UIKit/UIKit.h>
#import <AddressBook/AddressBook.h>
#import <AddressBookUI/AddressBookUI.h>

@interface ViewController : UIViewController<ABPeoplePickerNavigationControllerDelegate>

@property (weak, nonatomic) IBOutlet UILabel *firstNameLabel;
@property (weak, nonatomic) IBOutlet UILabel *lastNameLabel;
@property (weak, nonatomic) IBOutlet UILabel *phoneNumberLabel;
@property (weak, nonatomic) IBOutlet UILabel *cityNameLabel;

- (IBAction)pickContact:(id)sender;

@end
```

Switch over to the implementation file. You implement the `pickContact:` method to create an instance of `ABPeoplePickerNavigationController`, set its delegate, and then display it.

```
- (IBAction)pickContact:(id)sender
{
    ABPeoplePickerNavigationController *picker =
        [[ABPeoplePickerNavigationController alloc] init];
    picker.peoplePickerDelegate = self;
    [self presentViewController:picker animated:YES completion:nil];
}
```

Now you just need to create your delegate methods, of which there are three you are required to implement. The first, and simplest, is for when the picker controller is canceled.

```
-(void)peoplePickerNavigationControllerDidCancel:
(ABPeoplePickerNavigationController *)peoplePicker
{
    [self dismissViewControllerAnimated:YES completion:nil];
}
```

Next, define your main delegate method to handle the selection of a contact. Here is a step-by-step method implementation to discuss each part.

First, your method header looks like so:

```
-(BOOL)peoplePickerNavigationController:
(ABPeoplePickerNavigationController *)peoplePicker
shouldContinueAfterSelectingPerson:(ABRecordRef)person
```

The first odd thing you may notice about this header is that the variable person is of type ABRecordRef, which does not have a "*" after it. This essentially means that person is not a pointer, and thus will not be used to call methods. Instead, you will use predefined functions that utilize and access it. As you see, many parts of the Address Book framework use this "C-based" style.

Inside the method body, you first access the simplest properties, which are the first and last names of the chosen contact.

```
self.firstNameLabel.text =
    (__bridge_transfer NSString *)ABRecordCopyValue(person, kABPersonFirstNameProperty);
self.lastNameLabel.text =
    (__bridge_transfer NSString *)ABRecordCopyValue(person, kABPersonLastNameProperty);
```

The ABRecordCopyValue() function is your go-to call for any kind of accessing data in this section. It takes two parameters, the first is the ABRecordRef that you want to access, and the second is a predefined PropertyID that instructs the function on which piece of data to retrieve.

There are two types of values that can be dealt with by this function: single values and multi-values. For these first two calls, you are dealing only with single values, for which the ABRecordCopyValue() function returns a type of CFStringRef. You can cast this up to an NSString by adding the (__bridge_ transfer NSString *) code in front of the value.

> **Note** The __bridge_transfer command specifies that the memory management of the object is being transferred to ARC. You can find more information on this in Apple's documentation[1].

The next value you can access is the person's phone number, which is a multi-value. Multi-values are usually used for the properties of a person for which multiple entries can be given, such as address, phone number, or email. When you copy this, you will receive a variable of type ABMultiValueRef, which you can then use to access a specific value.

```
ABMultiValueRef phoneRecord = ABRecordCopyValue(person, kABPersonPhoneProperty);
CFStringRef phoneNumber = ABMultiValueCopyValueAtIndex(phoneRecord, 0);
self.phoneNumberLabel.text = (__bridge_transfer NSString *)phoneNumber;
CFRelease(phoneRecord);
```

By using the call ABMultiValueCopyValueAtIndex(phoneProperty, 0), you have specified that you want the first phone number stored for the given user. From there, you can set your label's text just as you did before.

---

[1]http://developer.apple.com/library/ios/#documentation/CoreFoundation/Conceptual/CFDesignConcepts/ Articles/tollFreeBridgedTypes.html

The next multi-value you deal with is the main address of the chosen contact. When dealing with the address, an extra step is required, as an address is stored as a CFDictionary. You retrieve this dictionary using the ABMultiValueCopyValueAtIndex() function again, and then query its values:

```
ABMultiValueRef addressRecord = ABRecordCopyValue(person, kABPersonAddressProperty);
if (ABMultiValueGetCount(addressRecord) > 0)
{
    CFDictionaryRef addressDictionary = ABMultiValueCopyValueAtIndex(addressRecord, 0);
    self.cityNameLabel.text =
        [NSString stringWithString:
            (__bridge NSString *)CFDictionaryGetValue(addressDictionary,
                kABPersonAddressCityKey)];
    CFRelease(addressDictionary);
}
else
{
    self.cityNameLabel.text = @"...";
}
CFRelease(addressRecord);
```

There are a couple of things with the preceding code that you may be wondering about. First, why do you need to release, for example, addressDictionary and addressRecord, but not the First Name and Last Name values that you retrieved earlier?

The reason is that in those cases, you transferred the ownership of the value over to the respective outlet by using the __bridge_transfer type specifier. But for the multi-value records, you didn't transfer ownership so they must be released or their memory will be leaked.

The second thing you might be wondering is what the following piece of code is about:

```
self.cityNameLabel.text =
    [NSString stringWithString:
        (__bridge NSString *)CFDictionaryGetValue(addressDictionary,
            kABPersonAddressCityKey)];
```

Why are you suddenly using __bridge and not __bridge_transfer here? And why construct a new string using the stringWithString class method? Here too, the answer is ownership. The CFDictionaryGetValue() function, as opposed to ABMultiValueCopyValueAtIndex(), retains ownership of the value it returns. Because you want to store the string in your cityNameLabel.text property, you need to copy it first. And because you don't want to transfer ownership of the original string value (which would lead to a memory leak), you use a plain __bridge cast.

To finalize the implementation of the peoplePickerNavigationController:shouldContinueAfterSelectingPerson: delegate method, you dismiss the modal view controller and return NO. As a whole, your method should look like so:

```
-(BOOL)peoplePickerNavigationController:
(ABPeoplePickerNavigationController *)peoplePicker
    shouldContinueAfterSelectingPerson:(ABRecordRef)person
{

    self.firstNameLabel.text =
        (__bridge_transfer NSString *)ABRecordCopyValue(person,
            kABPersonFirstNameProperty);
```

```
    self.lastNameLabel.text =
        (__bridge_transfer NSString *)ABRecordCopyValue(person,
            kABPersonLastNameProperty);

    ABMultiValueRef phoneRecord = ABRecordCopyValue(person, kABPersonPhoneProperty);
    CFStringRef phoneNumber = ABMultiValueCopyValueAtIndex(phoneRecord, 0);
    self.phoneNumberLabel.text = (__bridge_transfer NSString *)phoneNumber;
    CFRelease(phoneRecord);

    ABMultiValueRef addressRecord = ABRecordCopyValue(person, kABPersonAddressProperty);
    if (ABMultiValueGetCount(addressRecord) > 0)
    {
        CFDictionaryRef addressDictionary =
            ABMultiValueCopyValueAtIndex(addressRecord, 0);
        self.cityNameLabel.text =
            [NSString stringWithString:
                (__bridge NSString *)CFDictionaryGetValue(addressDictionary,
                    kABPersonAddressCityKey)];
        CFRelease(addressDictionary);
    }
    else
    {
        self.cityNameLabel.text = @"...";
    }
    CFRelease(addressRecord);

    [self dismissViewControllerAnimated:YES completion:nil];
    return NO;
}
```

There is a third delegate method you must implement in order to fully conform to the ABPeoplePickerNavigationControllerDelegate protocol. It handles the selection of a specific contact's property. However, because this recipe is simply returning after the selection of a contact, this method will not actually be called. To get rid of the compiler warning, add this method with a simple implementation similar to your cancellation method:

```
-(BOOL)peoplePickerNavigationController:(ABPeoplePickerNavigationController *)peoplePicker shouldCon
tinueAfterSelectingPerson:(ABRecordRef)person property:(ABPropertyID)property identifier:(ABMultiVal
ueIdentifier)identifier
{
    [self dismissViewControllerAnimated:YES completion:nil];
    return NO;
}
```

> **Caution** Whenever you are copying values from an ABRecordRef, include a check to be sure that a value exists, as you did with the address. The previous code assumed that the first name, last name, and phone number exist, but an empty query can result in your application throwing an exception.

Your application can now access the address book, select a user, and display the information for which you have queried. The first time the function is run you're asked to grant the app access to the device's Contacts. Figure 11-17 shows examples of the app in different modes.

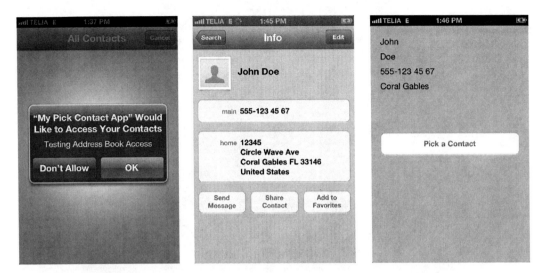

Figure 11-17. To the left, a request to access Contact information is required. In the middle, a contact in the user's Address Book. To the right, contact information retrieved from the Address Book and displayed in the app.

While you have not included code to access all the possible values for an `ABRecordRef`, you should be able to use any combination of the utilized functions to access whichever ones you need.

Recipe 11-8: Setting Contact Information

Just as important as being able to access values is being able to set them. To this end, you will implement two different methods for creating and setting values of a contact and adding it to your device's address book.

First, create a new single-view application project to which you link the Address Book and the Address Book UI frameworks. Also, like you did in the previous recipe, provide a usage description explaining why your app wants to access the device's Address Book. We chose "Testing creating contacts."

Set up a simple user interface that allows users to create a new contact themselves. In the view controller's `.xib` file, add a single `UIButton` titled "New Contact," like in Figure 11-18. Then create an action named `addNewContact`, for when the user taps the button.

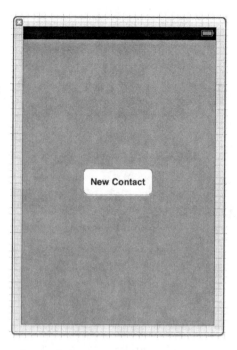

Figure 11-18. Simple user interface setup for creating contacts

Next, you need to import your frameworks into your header file and configure your view controller's protocol to conform to. Conform your view controller to the ABNewPersonViewControllerDelegate protocol, and then add the usual two import statements.

```
#import <AddressBook/AddressBook.h>
#import <AddressBookUI/AddressBookUI.h>
```

Now, create a very simple implementation, for which you have to define only two methods: the action to handle the selection of your button, and the delegate method for an ABNewPersonViewController.

The action method looks like so:

```
- (IBAction)addNewContact:(id)sender
{
    ABNewPersonViewController *view = [[ABNewPersonViewController alloc] init];
    view.newPersonViewDelegate = self;

    UINavigationController *newNavigationController =
        [[UINavigationController alloc] initWithRootViewController:view];
    [self presentViewController:newNavigationController animated:YES completion:nil];
}
```

Here is the delegate method:

```
-(void)newPersonViewController:(ABNewPersonViewController *)newPersonView didCompleteWithNewPerson:
(ABRecordRef)person
```

```
{
    if (person == NULL)
    {
        NSLog(@"User Cancelled Creation");
    }
    else
    {
        NSLog(@"Successfully Created New Person");
    }
    [self dismissViewControllerAnimated:YES completion:nil];
}
```

Unlike most modal view controllers that you deal with, the ABNewPersonViewController has only one delegate method that handles both success and cancellation, as opposed to others that have one method for each. As you can see, you differentiate between each result by checking to see if the ABRecordRef person parameter is not NULL. Because this parameter is not a pointer, you compare it to the NULL value instead of nil.

At this point, you should be able to allow your user to create a new contact to be added to the address book, as the simulated app in Figure 11-19 shows.

Figure 11-19. A blank ABNewPersonViewController

While you have provided users with a great deal of flexibility as to how they want their contacts to be set up, you have also provided them with a great deal of work to do, in that they have to type in every value that they want. You will next see how to programmatically create records and set their values. For the purpose of demonstration, we will make it simple and provide the ABNewPersonViewController with preset values that are hard-coded.

What you're going to do, is to populate the ABNewPersonViewController with preset values. Update the addNewContact: method, starting with the adding of hard-coded values:

```
- (IBAction)addNewContact:(id)sender
{
    NSString *firstName = @"John";
    NSString *lastName = @"Doe";
    NSString *mobileNumber = @"555-123-4567";
    NSString *street = @"12345 Circle Wave Ave";
    NSString *city = @"Coral Gables";
    NSString *state = @"FL";
    NSString *zip = @"33146";
    NSString *country = @"United States";

    // ...
}
```

Next, create a new contact record and add values for the first name, last name and phone contact information:

```
- (IBAction)addNewContact:(id)sender
{
    // ...

    ABRecordRef contactRecord = ABPersonCreate();

    // Setup first and last name records
    ABRecordSetValue(contactRecord, kABPersonFirstNameProperty,
        (__bridge_retained CFStringRef)firstName, nil);
    ABRecordSetValue(contactRecord, kABPersonLastNameProperty,
        (__bridge_retained CFStringRef)lastName, nil);

    // Setup phone record
    ABMutableMultiValueRef phoneRecord =
        ABMultiValueCreateMutable(kABMultiStringPropertyType);
    ABMultiValueAddValueAndLabel(phoneRecord,
        (__bridge_retained CFStringRef)mobileNumber, kABPersonPhoneMobileLabel, NULL);
    ABRecordSetValue(contactRecord, kABPersonPhoneProperty, phoneRecord, nil);
    CFRelease(phoneRecord);

    // ...
}
```

The __bridge_retained type specifier indicates that you want to transfer ownership from an ARC controlled object (NSString in this case) to a Core Foundation object (CFStringRef). This is necessary so these objects don't prematurely get released by ARC.

Now, the address record involves a bit more work to create the dictionary and add it to the contact record:

```
- (IBAction)addNewContact:(id)sender
{
    // ...

    // Setup address record
    ABMutableMultiValueRef addressRecord =
        ABMultiValueCreateMutable(kABDictionaryPropertyType);
    CFStringRef dictionaryKeys[5];
    CFStringRef dictionaryValues[5];
    dictionaryKeys[0] = kABPersonAddressStreetKey;
    dictionaryKeys[1] = kABPersonAddressCityKey;
    dictionaryKeys[2] = kABPersonAddressStateKey;
    dictionaryKeys[3] = kABPersonAddressZIPKey;
    dictionaryKeys[4] = kABPersonAddressCountryKey;
    dictionaryValues[0] = (__bridge_retained CFStringRef)street;
    dictionaryValues[1] = (__bridge_retained CFStringRef)city;
    dictionaryValues[2] = (__bridge_retained CFStringRef)state;
    dictionaryValues[3] = (__bridge_retained CFStringRef)zip;
    dictionaryValues[4] = (__bridge_retained CFStringRef)country;

    CFDictionaryRef addressDictionary = CFDictionaryCreate(kCFAllocatorDefault,
        (void *)dictionaryKeys, (void *)dictionaryValues, 5,
        &kCFCopyStringDictionaryKeyCallBacks, &kCFTypeDictionaryValueCallBacks);
    ABMultiValueAddValueAndLabel(addressRecord, addressDictionary, kABHomeLabel, NULL);
    CFRelease(addressDictionary);

    ABRecordSetValue(contactRecord, kABPersonAddressProperty, addressRecord, nil);
    CFRelease(addressRecord);

    // ...
}
```

Finally, you initialize and display the ABNewPersonerViewController with the new contact record, which you then release to avoid a memory leak:

```
- (IBAction)addNewContact:(id)sender
{
    // ...

    // Display View Controller
    ABNewPersonViewController *view = [[ABNewPersonViewController alloc] init];
    view.newPersonViewDelegate = self;
    view.displayedPerson = contactRecord;

    UINavigationController *newNavigationController =
        [[UINavigationController alloc] initWithRootViewController:view];
    [self presentViewController:newNavigationController animated:YES completion:nil];

    CFRelease(contactRecord);
}
```

If you build and run your application now, you should have the `ABNewPersonViewController` populated with the preset values, as shown in Figure 11-20.

Figure 11-20. The ABNewPersonViewController with preset values that have been added programmatically

Summary

As you can see, there are many methods and functionalities for interacting with any specific user's personal data. From recurring events, to multiple calendars, to the vast number of contacts and phone numbers that most users have—all this information can be used to personalize an application for each and every user. In terms of user experience, being able to access, display, and edit all this information allows us as developers to create more powerful, more unique, and more useful applications.

Chapter 12

Data Storage Recipes

When working in iOS, one of the most important topics to understand is the concept, use, and implementation of persistence. Implementation of persistence refers to the idea of having information saved and retrieved, or persist, through the closing or restarting of an application. Just as pages from books can be read and re-read, even after closing and re-opening them, you can make use of certain key concepts in iOS to allow your information—from the simplest of values to the most complex of data structures—to stay stored in your device for indefinite periods of time. We cover a variety of methods of persistence throughout this chapter with different advantages, disadvantages, general uses, and complexities, so that you can develop a full understanding of the best method of storage for any given situation.

Recipe 12-1: Persisting Data with NSUserDefaults

When developing applications, you often run into situations where you want to store simple values, for example user settings or some part of an app's state. While there are a variety of ways to store data, the easiest of these is NSUserDefaults, built specifically for such simple situations.

The NSUserDefaults class is a simple API used to store basic values, such as instances of NSString, NSNumber, BOOL, and so on. It can also be used to store more complex data structures, such as NSArray or NSDictionary, as long as they do not contain massive amounts of data; images, for example, should not be stored with NSUserDefaults.

In this recipe you'll build a simple app that has a state that'll persist using NSUserDefaults. Start off by creating a new single-view application project called "Stubborn" (because you want your information to stick around).

Set up the user interface of this app. Select the ViewController.xib file to bring up Interface Builder for the main view. Add two Text fields, a Switch and an Activity indicator and set them up so that the user interface resembles Figure 12-1.

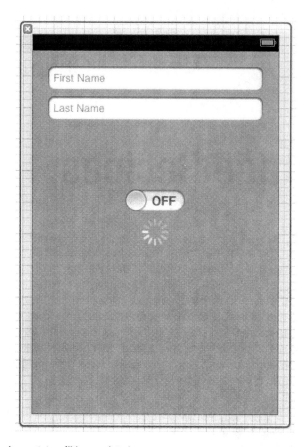

Figure 12-1. *A user interface whose state will be persisted*

As you can probably guess, the Switch starts and stops the Activity indicator. You also write code that persists the state of the Switch along with the text you've entered in the Text fields.

First you need a way to reference the controls from your code, so create the following outlets:

- firstNameTextField
- lastNameTextField
- activitySwitch
- activityIndicator

You also need to intercept when the user taps the Switch, so create an action named toggleActivity for its Value Changed event.

In the ViewController.h file, add the UITextFieldDelegate protocol to the ViewController class. You need this to control the keyboard later. In all, the ViewController.h file should now resemble the code that follows:

```
//
// ViewController.h
```

```
//   Stubborn
//

#import <UIKit/UIKit.h>

@interface ViewController : UIViewController<UITextFieldDelegate>

@property (weak, nonatomic) IBOutlet UITextField *firstNameTextField;
@property (weak, nonatomic) IBOutlet UITextField *lastNameTextField;
@property (weak, nonatomic) IBOutlet UISwitch *activitySwitch;
@property (weak, nonatomic) IBOutlet UIActivityIndicatorView *activityIndicator;

- (IBAction)toggleActivity:(id)sender;

@end
```

You now start implementing the basic functionality of the controls, starting with the text fields. Open to the ViewController.m file and add the following code to the viewDidLoad method:

```
- (void)viewDidLoad
{
    [super viewDidLoad];

    self.firstNameTextField.delegate = self;
    self.lastNameTextField.delegate = self;
}
```

Now, add the following delegate method. It makes sure the keyboard gets removed if the user taps the Return button:

```
-(BOOL)textFieldShouldReturn:(UITextField *)textField
{
    [textField resignFirstResponder];
    return NO;
}
```

Now it's time to implement the behavior of the Switch. Add the following implementation to the toggleActivity: action method:

```
- (IBAction)toggleActivity:(id)sender
{
    if (self.activitySwitch.on)
    {
        [self.activityIndicator startAnimating];
    }
    else
    {
        [self.activityIndicator stopAnimating];
    }
}
```

The simple user interface is now fully functioning and you should take it on a test spin. You should be able to enter text in the text fields and start and stop the activity indicator animation by tapping the switch. However, if you shut down the app and rerun it, the text will be gone and the switch will be back to its OFF state again. Let's implement some persistency, shall we?

As you know, there are two things you need to do to persist data; you need to save it, and you need to restore it—at appropriate times. There are basically two strategies for when to save persisted data. You could either store the data whenever it's changed, or you could save it right before the app terminates. In this recipe, you implement the second strategy and have the state saved when the app enters the background.

> **Note**   Normally, an app that's suspended is not killed but put to sleep and can be reactivated and brought back to the same state without the need for persisting its data. However, in case of low-memory conditions, an app can be terminated without warning. Because there is no way to know whether your app is being killed off, you should always be sure that your persisted data is saved when the app enters the background.

To know when the app enters the background mode you can use the Notification center and register an Observer of UIApplicationDidEnterBackgroundNotification. A good place to do this is when the view is loaded, so add the following code to viewDidLoad:

```
- (void)viewDidLoad
{
    [super viewDidLoad];
        // Do any additional setup after loading the view, typically from a nib.
    self.firstNameTextField.delegate = self;
    self.lastNameTextField.delegate = self;

    [[NSNotificationCenter defaultCenter] addObserver:self
        selector:@selector(savePersistentData:)
        name:UIApplicationDidEnterBackgroundNotification object:nil];
}
```

Now you can implement in the savePersistentData: method the actual storing of the persistent data, like so:

```
- (void)savePersistentData:(id)sender
{
    NSUserDefaults *userDefaults = [NSUserDefaults standardUserDefaults];

    //Set Objects/Values to Persist
    [userDefaults setObject:self.firstNameTextField.text forKey:@"firstName"];
    [userDefaults setObject:self.lastNameTextField.text forKey:@"lastName"];
    [userDefaults setBool:self.activitySwitch.on forKey:@"activityOn"];

    //Save Changes
    [userDefaults synchronize];
}
```

> **Tip** You can use NSUserDefault's `resetStandardUserDefaults` method to clear all data that's been previously stored. This can be a good way to reset your app to its standard settings.

What's left now is to load the data when the app launches. Start by adding the following method to perform the loading:

```
- (void)loadPersistentData:(id)sender
{
    NSUserDefaults *userDefaults = [NSUserDefaults standardUserDefaults];

    self.firstNameTextField.text = [userDefaults objectForKey:@"firstName"];
    self.lastNameTextField.text = [userDefaults objectForKey:@"lastName"];
    [self.activitySwitch setOn:[userDefaults boolForKey:@"activityOn"] animated:NO];

    if (self.activitySwitch.on)
    {
        [self.activityIndicator startAnimating];
    }
}
```

And finally, call the `loadPersistentData:` method from the `viewDidLoad` method:

```
- (void)viewDidLoad
{
    [super viewDidLoad];
        // Do any additional setup after loading the view, typically from a nib.
    self.firstNameTextField.delegate = self;
    self.lastNameTextField.delegate = self;

    [self loadPersistentData:self];

    [[NSNotificationCenter defaultCenter] addObserver:self
        selector:@selector(savePersistentData:)
        name:UIApplicationDidEnterBackgroundNotification object:nil];
}
```

You're now done implementing the persistencey of the app's state. Open the app, enter some text in the text fields and turn the activity switch to ON. Now press the Home button on the device to make the app enter the background mode. The data should now be saved to NSUserDefault, but to truly test whether that really happened, you need to kill the app before relaunching it. To do that you can either stop the app's execution from Xcode, or you can double-press the Home button, locate the "Stubborn" app in the list of suspended apps; if you tap and hold its icon until a wiggling "–" minus sign appears, which you tap to terminate the app.

Now, if you rerun the app you'll see that it appears just as you left it. Figure 12-2 shows an example of this app right after it has been relaunched.

Figure 12-2. An app that has restored its state from the previous run, using NSUserDefaults

Although you did not use a great variety of values to store with NSUserDefaults in this short recipe, there are in fact methods to store almost any type of lightweight value, including BOOL, Float, Integer, Double, and URL. For any kind of more complex object, such as an NSString, NSArray, or NSDictionary, you use the general setObject:forKey: method.

Remember, though, NSUserDefaults is meant for relatively small amounts of data. In the next recipe we'll show you how you can store somewhat bigger chunks, using files.

Recipe 12-2: Persisting Data Using Files

While the NSUserDefaults class is especially useful for doing quick persistence of light data, it is not nearly as efficient for dealing with large objects, such as documents, videos, music, or images. For these more complex items, you can make use of iOS's file management system.

In this recipe you'll create a simple app that allows you to enter a long text and save it to a file. Start by creating a new single-view application project. You can name it "My Text Document Editor."

Next, build a user interface that resembles Figure 12-3. You'll need a Label, a Text Field, a Text View, and three Round Rect Buttons.

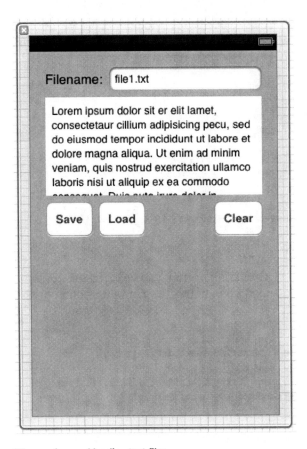

Figure 12-3. A simple app for editing, saving, and loading text files

Create the following outlets and actions for the respective components:

■ *Outlets:* filenameTextField and contentTextView

■ *Actions:* saveContent, loadContent, and clearContent

With the user interface in place you can start implementing its functionality. But first, create a helper method that transforms the relative filename into an absolute file path within the Documents directory of the device. Add the following method to the ViewController.m file:

```
- (NSString *)currentContentFilePath
{
    NSArray *documentDirectories =
        NSSearchPathForDirectoriesInDomains(NSDocumentDirectory, NSUserDomainMask, YES);
    NSString *documentsDirectory = [documentDirectories objectAtIndex:0];

    return [documentsDirectory
        stringByAppendingPathComponent:self.filenameTextField.text];
}
```

Now, when the user taps the Save button, you're going to save the content of the Text View to the file path provided by the helper method you just created. Add the following implementation to the saveContent: action method:

```
- (IBAction)saveContent:(id)sender
{
    NSString *filePath = [self currentContentFilePath];
    NSString *content = self.contentTextView.text;
    NSError *error;
    BOOL success = [content writeToFile:filePath atomically:YES
        encoding:NSUnicodeStringEncoding error:&error];
    if (!success)
    {
        NSLog(@"Unable to save file: %@\nError: %@", filePath, error);
    }
}
```

Conversely, when the user taps the Load button, you will load the content from the file and update the Text View. Here's the implementation of the loadContent: action method:

```
- (IBAction)loadContent:(id)sender
{
    NSString *filePath = [self currentContentFilePath];
    NSError *error;
    NSString *content = [NSString stringWithContentsOfFile:filePath
        encoding:NSUnicodeStringEncoding error:&error];
    if (error)
    {
        NSLog(@"Unable to load file: %@\nError: %@", filePath, error);
    }
    self.contentTextView.text = content;
}
```

Finally, the Clear button simply clears the Text View, like so:

```
- (IBAction)clearContent:(id)sender
{
    self.contentTextView.text = nil;
}
```

You now have a very rudimentary text file editor, now try it out. Build and run the app. Enter some text in the Text View, enter a filename in the Filename text input, and hit the Save button. The app then creates a file in the Documents directory on the device (or on your disk if you're running the app in the iOS Simulator). To verify that its been correctly saved, you can tap Clear to reset the Text View and then Load. The text you just wrote should now reappear in the Text View. You can also try to create different files by changing the contents of the Filename text field.

Although this app works, it has one serious problem which we'd like to address before leaving this recipe. If you save the content to an existing file, the app will silently overwrite its content, which may or may not be what the user wants. To make sure you catch the user's intention, you're going to check whether the file exists and ask for permissions to replace it if it does. You do this by changing the implementation of the saveContent: method. Start by extracting the actual saving into a helper method, called saveContentToFile:, like so:

```
- (void)saveContentToFile:(NSString *)filePath
{
    NSString *content = self.contentTextView.text;
    NSError *error;
    BOOL success = [content writeToFile:filePath atomically:YES
        encoding:NSUnicodeStringEncoding error:&error];
    if (!success)
    {
        NSLog(@"Unable to save file: %@\nError: %@", filePath, error);
    }
}
```

Next, make the following changes to the saveContent: method:

```
- (IBAction)saveContent:(id)sender
{
    NSString *filePath = [self currentContentFilePath];
    NSFileManager *fileManager = [NSFileManager defaultManager];
    if ([fileManager fileExistsAtPath:filePath])
    {
        UIAlertView *overwriteAlert = [[UIAlertView alloc] initWithTitle:@"File Exists"
            message:@"Do you want to replace the file?" delegate:self
            cancelButtonTitle:@"No" otherButtonTitles:@"Yes", nil];
        [overwriteAlert show];
    }
    else
        [self saveContentToFile:filePath];
}
```

Now, go to ViewController.h and add the UIAlertViewDelegate protocol so that the view controller can act as the Alert view's delegate and intercept when the user taps its buttons:

```
//
//  ViewController.h
//  My Text Document Editor
//

#import <UIKit/UIKit.h>

@interface ViewController : UIViewController<UIAlertViewDelegate>

@property (weak, nonatomic) IBOutlet UITextField *filenameTextField;
@property (weak, nonatomic) IBOutlet UITextView *contentTextView;

- (IBAction)saveContent:(id)sender;
- (IBAction)loadContent:(id)sender;
- (IBAction)clearContent:(id)sender;

@end
```

Finally, back in ViewController.m, add the following delegate method for when the user taps one of the Alert view's buttons:

```
- (void)alertView:(UIAlertView *)alertView clickedButtonAtIndex:(NSInteger)buttonIndex
{
    if (buttonIndex == 1)
    {
        // User tapped Yes button, overwrite the file
        NSString *filePath = [self currentContentFilePath];
        [self saveContentToFile:filePath];
    }
}
```

Now you're done and can run the app again. This time, if you try to save a file that already exists, you'll be asked if you want to replace it (see Figure 12-4).

Figure 12-4. *An app asking if the user's intention was to overwrite an existing file*

In this demo app, you've only worked with text data. However, other types of data are equally simple. NSImage, for example, has methods for saving and loading from files, as have most other common data types. And even if what you want to save doesn't have direct file support, you can always convert it to an NSData object, which has.

While files are great for storing documents and isolated pieces of data, they are not very handy when it comes to persisting multiple objects with internal relationships, which is the natural data model of many apps. For these applications, a better alternative is to use the Core Data framework, the topic of the next recipe.

Recipe 12-3: Using Core Data

So far you have dealt with the quick implementation of NSUserDefaults for lightweight values, as well as the file management system for larger amounts of data. While using the file management system is incredibly powerful for storing data, it can easily become quite cumbersome when dealing with complex data models of intertwined classes. For such cases, the best option becomes Core Data.

In this recipe you build a simple word list app that persists its data using Core Data. But before you start, let's quickly go through the basics of this framework.

Understanding Core Data

The Core Data framework is designed around the concept of relational data. However, it's not a relational database, but rather a layer of abstraction on top of some storage entity, usually SQLite. With Core Data you can focus on the structure of your data and leave the low-level relational database details for the framework to handle.

Put simply, Core Data, in conjunction with Xcode, allows a developer to perform three main tasks:

1. Create a data model

2. Persist information

3. Access data

First, it is important to understand exactly what a *data model* is. This term applies essentially to whatever structure any given application's data is built around. This could be something as simple as an NSString or an NSArray in a simple application, all the way up to a complex, interconnected system of object types, each with their own properties, methods, and pointers to other objects.

Core Data is one of the most powerful frameworks in iOS. Despite this, its API is surprisingly small, consisting of only a handful of classes for you to handle. Here are some brief descriptions of the few main classes that makes up Core Data:

- NSManagedObjectModel: This object is how iOS refers to your data model, but you will have little to do with this class yourself. When you create your project for the first recipe, you will see an instance of this type in your application delegate, and you will see it used in some pre-generated methods, but aside from that, you will have no reason to deal with this class programmatically.

- NSPersistentStoreCoordinator: This class, too, is one that you very rarely will need to deal with. It works mostly in the background of an application to "coordinate" between your application and the underlying database or "Persistent Store," but you will not need to send any actions to it. The most important part of this class that you need to know about is the "type" of persistent store that is being used. There are three types of persistent stores:

  - NSSQLiteStoreType

  - NSBinaryStoreType

  - NSInMemoryStoreType

  The default value is NSSQLiteStoreType, specifying that you are using a persistent store built around the SQLite foundation. You will continue to use this typefor the purpose of the Core Data recipes in this chapter.

- NSManagedObjectContext: This class, unlike the previous two, is one that you will be dealing with quite often. In the simplest terms, this class acts as a sort of "workspace" for your information. Any time you need to retrieve or store information, you will need a pointer to this class to perform the action. For this reason, a very common practice in Core Data–based applications is to "pass around" a pointer to this class between each part of the application by giving each view controller an NSManagedObjectContext property

- NSManagedObject: This class represents an instance of actual data in the data model.

- NSFetchedResultsController: This is the primary class for "fetching" results through the NSManagedObjectContext. It is not only very powerful, but also very easy to use, especially in conjunction with a UITableView. You will see plenty of examples of using this class in the recipes to come.

Now, let's start building the word list app.

Setting Up Core Data

The easiest way to setup Core Data for your app is to let Xcode generate the necessary code when you create the project. Create a new project called "My Vocabularies" using the Empty Application template, as shown in Figure 12-5.

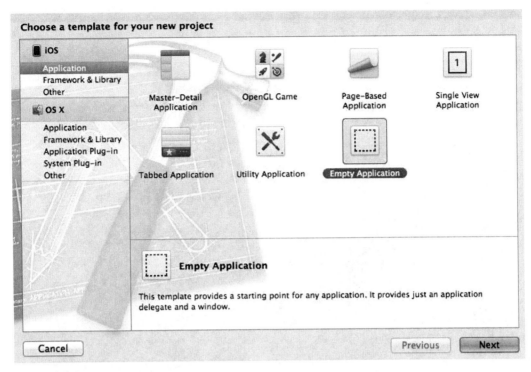

Figure 12-5. Creating an empty application to start from scratch using the Empty Application template

On the next screen, where you enter the project name, be sure to select the box labeled Use Core Data (see Figure 12-6).

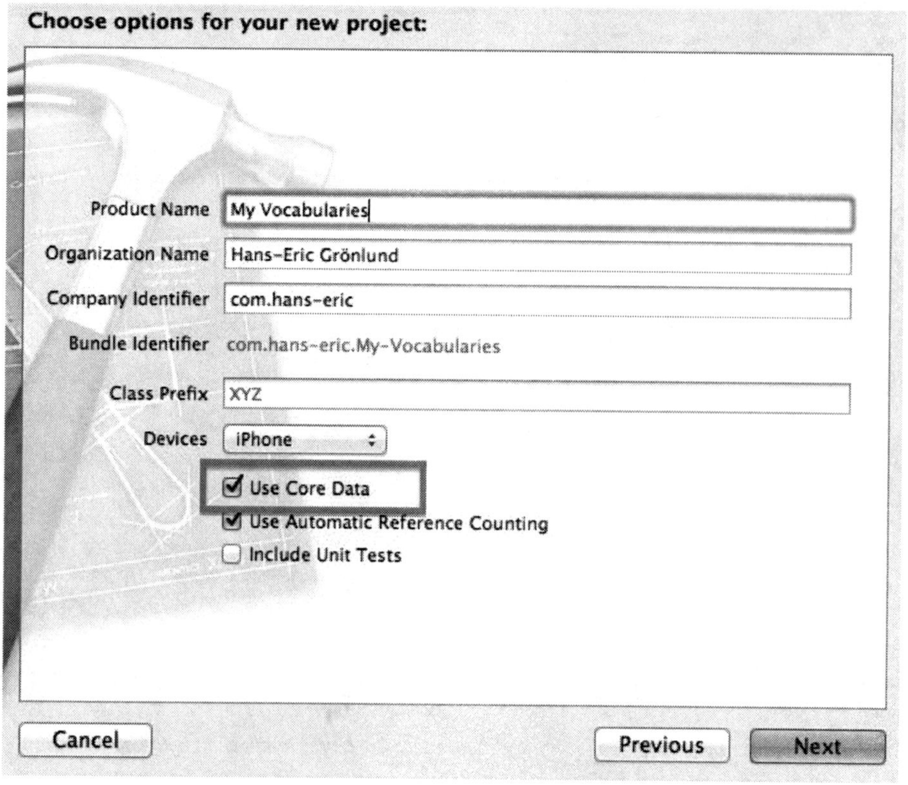

Figure 12-6. Checking the Use Core Data option makes Xcode set up Core Data for the application

After clicking Next, click Create on the next dialog box to finish the creation of your project as usual.

Now that you have set up your project to use Core Data, you have a lot of the work involved in using the Core Data framework already done for you, so you can move directly on to building your data model.

Designing the Data Model

For this app, you build a simple data model consisting of only Vocabularies and Words. However, before you proceed to do anything in Xcode, you need to plan out exactly how your model will work.

When working with a data model, the first kind of item you have to make is an "entity." An *entity* is essentially the Core Data equivalent of a class, representing a specific object type that will be stored in the model.

In the same way that objects (or NSObjects in Objective-C) have properties, entities have "attributes." These are the simpler pieces of data associated with any given entity, such as a name, age, or birthday, that do not require a pointer to any other entity.

Whenever you want one entity to have a pointer to another, you use a "relationship." A relationship can be either "to-one" or "to-many," referring to whether an entity has a pointer to one instance of another entity or multiple ones.

When dealing with the "to-many" relationship, you will notice that the entity has a pointer to a set of multiple other entities. Entities can easily have relationships that point to themselves, which might be the case of a Person entity having a relationship to another Person, in the form of a spouse. You can also set up "inverse relationships," which act as paths back and forth between entities. For example, a Teacher entity might have a "to-many" relationship to a Student entity called "students," and the Student's relationship to the Teacher, called "teachers," will be the inverse of this. Figure 12-7 shows a diagram of this two-way relationship.

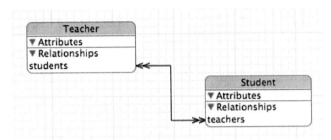

Figure 12-7. Two entities with a to-many relationship pointing to one another

So for your data model, you have two entities with their respective attributes and relationships as defined in Table 12-1.

Table 12-1. The Data Model of the "My Vocabularies" app

Entity	Attributes	Relationships
Vocabulary	name	words
Word	word, translation	vocabulary

Note   By convention, pluralized relationship names indicate a to-many relationship, while singular names is used for to-one relationships.

Now that you have the data model planned out, you can build this in Xcode. Switch over to view your data model file, which is named My_Vocabularies.xcdatamodeld in your project. Your view should now resemble Figure 12-8.

Figure 12-8. The Data model editor with an empty data model

Now, add the two entities of your data model. You can do this from either the Editor menu, or by using the Add Entity button located in the bottom-center area of the Xcode window. When you add an Entity, you immediately can change the name of the entity, so enter "Vocabulary" and hit Return. Repeat the process for the "Word" entity.

> **Note**   It's easier to create all your entities first before trying to configure them, otherwise you won't be able to set up the relationships.

After you've added the two entities, the list of Entities should resemble Figure 12-9.

ENTITIES

E Vocabulary

E Word

Figure 12-9. The two entities of the "My Vocabulary" app data model

Start by configuring the Vocabulary entity, so be sure the "Vocabulary" text is selected in the ENTITIES section. By using the + button in the Attributes section, add an attribute called `name` with the type `String` selected in the Type drop-down menu, as in Figure 12-10.

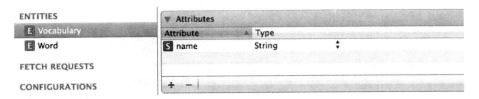

Figure 12-10. An entity, Vocabulary, with a single attribute, name

Now you define the relationship of the Vocabulary entity. Under the Relationships area, add a relationship using the + button in that section. Name the relationship words. As the relationship's Destination, assign the Word entity. Until you create the relationship in the other entity, you cannot set up the "Inverse" relationship, so leave it at "No Inverse." The relationships setup for the Vocabulary entity should at this point be as in Figure 12-11.

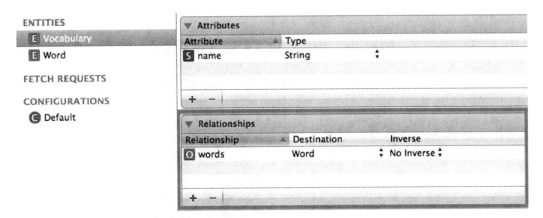

Figure 12-11. Configuring the Vocabulary entity's relationships

Now you're going to define this relationship as a to-many relationship. You do that by selecting one of the relationships and check the "To-Many Relationship" option in the Data Model inspector (which corresponds to the Attribute inspector for view elements), as shown in Figure 12-12.

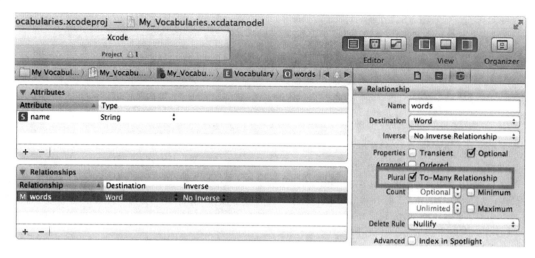

Figure 12-12. Defining a "to-many" relationship in the Data Model inspector

While you will most likely need not worry about most of the other values in this inspector (at least for the purposes of this recipe), one of the values of higher importance is the Delete Rule drop-down menu. This value specifies exactly how this relationship is handled when an instance of the given entity is deleted from the NSManagedObjectContext. It has four possible values:

- *No Action*: This is probably the most dangerous value, as it simply allows related objects to continue to attempt to access the deleted object.

- *Nullify*: The default value, this specifies that the relationship will be nullified upon deletion, and will thus return a nil value.

- *Cascade*: This value can be slightly dangerous to use, as it specifies that if one object is deleted, all the objects it is related to via this Delete Rule will also be deleted, so as to avoid having nil values. If you're not careful with this, you can delete unexpectedly large amounts of data, though it can also be very good for keeping your data clean. You may use this, for example, in the case of a "folder" with multiple objects. When a folder is deleted, you would want to delete all the contained objects as well.

- *Deny*: This prevents the object from being deleted as long as the relationship does not point to nil.

Keep the Delete Rule on "Nullify" for this recipe.

Now, the turn has come to configure the Word entity. In the same way you did for the Vocabulary entity, select the "Word" text in the ENTITIES section, then move to the Attributes section and add two attributes this time, named word and translation. Use the type "String" for both of these attributes as well.

Also, add a relationship named vocabulary with the Destination set to Vocabulary. You can now also set the "Inverse" relationship to words, as shown in Figure 12-13. This automatically sets up the inverse relationship for the words relationship as well (to vocabulary).

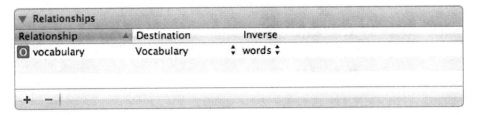

Figure 12-13. Configuring a relationship with an inverse

Note   Inverse relationships are not always required, though they tend to make the organization and flow of your application a little bit better, allowing you to more easily access any piece of data you need from any other piece of data.

Because the vocabulary relationship is a to-one relationship (a Word can only belong to one Vocabulary), you should not select the "to-many" option as you did with the words relationship.

As the final step in the process of creating the data model, you create Objective-C classes that map to the respective entity. Be sure the Vocabulary entity is selected, go to the Editor menu and choose **Create NSManagedObject Subclass…**, and then click the Create button. This adds a new class to the project named Vocabulary, which you use later to access Vocabulary data in the data model. Repeat the process for the Word entity to create a corresponding Word class.

This is actually all you need to do to create your data model. To get a graphic overview of the data model, change the Editor Style to Graph in the lower-right corner of the Data Model editor. The Graph Editor style uses a UML notation to display the entities, their attributes and relationships, where a single arrow represents a "to-one" relationship, and a double arrow represents a "to-many" relationship. The blocks may initially appear all stacked on top of each other, but if you drag them apart, your display should resemble Figure 12-14.

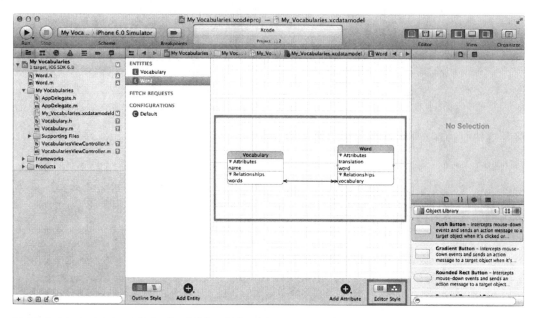

Figure 12-14. *A data model shown in the Graph Editor Style mode*

Now that you have your data model set up, you can start to build the user interface to display its data.

Setting Up the Vocabularies Table View

Next you set up a navigation-based app with a main table view displaying a list of Vocabularies.

To start implementing this, add a new class to the project. Name the class VocabulariesViewController and make it a subclass of UITableViewController. You do not need an .xib file so leave that option unchecked.

> **Note**   The UITableViewController class automatically sets up a table view and hooks up the necessary delegate properties. It's a convenient way to quickly set up a table view controller in an application.

Now, make the following changes to the VocabulariesViewController.h file:

```
//
//  VocabulariesViewController.h
//  My Vocabularies
//

#import <UIKit/UIKit.h>
#import "Vocabulary.h"
```

```
@interface VocabulariesViewController : UITableViewController<UIAlertViewDelegate>

@property (strong, nonatomic)NSManagedObjectContext *managedObjectContext;
@property (strong, nonatomic)NSFetchedResultsController *fetchedResultsController;

- (id)initWithManagedObjectContext:(NSManagedObjectContext *)context;

@end
```

What's worth mentioning from the preceding code is that the fetchedResultsController property keeps track of the fetched data and the managedObjectContext property allows you to make any necessary requests for data. You may also be wondering why you make the view controller conform to the UIAlertViewDelegate protocol. The reason is that you use an alert view as an input dialog for the Vocabulary name later.

Now, switch to the VocabulariesViewController.m file to start implementing the view controller. Begin with the implementation for the custom initializer method:

```
- (id)initWithManagedObjectContext:(NSManagedObjectContext *)context
{
    self = [super initWithStyle:UITableViewStylePlain];
    if (self)
    {
        self.managedObjectContext = context;
    }
    return self;
}
```

Next, add the following helper method, which fetches all Vocabularies in the data model and stores them in the fetchedResultsController property:

```
-(void)fetchVocabularies
{
    NSFetchRequest *fetchRequest =
        [NSFetchRequest fetchRequestWithEntityName:@"Vocabulary"];
    NSString *cacheName = [@"Vocabulary" stringByAppendingString:@"Cache"];

    NSSortDescriptor *sortDescriptor =
        [NSSortDescriptor sortDescriptorWithKey:@"name" ascending:YES];
    [fetchRequest setSortDescriptors:@[sortDescriptor]];

    self.fetchedResultsController = [[NSFetchedResultsController alloc]
        initWithFetchRequest:fetchRequest managedObjectContext:self.managedObjectContext
        sectionNameKeyPath:nil cacheName:cacheName];
    NSError *error;
    if (![self.fetchedResultsController performFetch:&error])
    {
        NSLog(@"Fetch failed: %@", error);
    }
}
```

In detail, the previous method does the following:

1. The first thing you need for fetching data is an instance of the NSFetchRequest class. Here, you have used a designated initializer to specify an NSEntityDescription, though you can also add it later using the -setEntity: method.

2. While not required, you have set up a "cache name" to be used with your fetch request, with a different cache for each entity. This allows you to slightly improve the speed of your application if you are making frequent fetch requests, as a local cache is first checked to see if the request has already been performed.

3. Every instance of NSFetchRequest is required to have at least one NSSortDescriptor associated with it. Here, you have specified a very simple alphabetic sort of the name property for each of your entities. After all your NSSortDescriptors have been created, they must be attached to the NSFetchRequest using the setSortDescriptors: method.

4. After the NSFetchRequest is fully configured, you can initialize the NSFetchedResultsController using the NSFetchRequest and the NSManagedObjectContext. The last two parameters are both optional, though you have specified a cacheName for optimization. You can set both of these to nil if you want to ignore them.

5. Finally, you must use the performFetch: method to complete the fetch request and retrieve the stored data. With this method, you can pass a pointer to an NSError, as shown previously, to keep track of and log any errors that occur with a fetch.

In the viewDidLoad method you initialize the view controller by setting its title and load the Vocabularies, like so:

```
- (void)viewDidLoad
{
    [super viewDidLoad];

    self.title = @"Vocabularies";

    [self fetchVocabularies];
}
```

To avoid presenting an empty list the first time the app is run, you'll preload the data model with a "Spanish" Vocabulary, but only if no Vocabularies exist. To do that, add the following code to the viewDidLoad method:

```
- (void)viewDidLoad
{
    [super viewDidLoad];
```

```
    self.title = @"Vocabularies";

    [self fetchVocabularies];
    // Preload with a "Spanish" Vocabulary if empty
    if (self.fetchedResultsController.fetchedObjects.count == 0)
    {
        NSEntityDescription *vocabularyEntityDescription =
            [NSEntityDescription entityForName:@"Vocabulary"
                inManagedObjectContext:self.managedObjectContext];
        Vocabulary *spanishVocabulary = (Vocabulary *)[[NSManagedObject alloc]
            initWithEntity:vocabularyEntityDescription
            insertIntoManagedObjectContext:self.managedObjectContext];
        spanishVocabulary.name = @"Spanish";
        NSError *error;
        if (![self.managedObjectContext save:&error])
        {
            NSLog(@"Error saving context: %@", error);
        }
        [self fetchVocabularies];
    }
}
```

Next, you need to implement the required delegate and data source methods for the table view. First, the methods to specify the number of sections and rows:

```
- (NSInteger)numberOfSectionsInTableView:(UITableView *)tableView
{
    return 1;
}

- (NSInteger)tableView:(UITableView *)tableView numberOfRowsInSection:(NSInteger)section
{
    return self.fetchedResultsController.fetchedObjects.count;
}
```

As shown, the NSFetchedResultsController class contains a method fetchedObjects, which returns an NSArray of the objects that were queried for.

Here is the method to configure the cells of the table view:

```
- (UITableViewCell *)tableView:(UITableView *)tableView cellForRowAtIndexPath:(NSIndexPath *)
indexPath
{
    static NSString *CellIdentifier = @"VocabularyCell";

    UITableViewCell *cell =
        [tableView dequeueReusableCellWithIdentifier:CellIdentifier];
    if (cell == nil)
    {
        cell = [[UITableViewCell alloc] initWithStyle:UITableViewCellStyleValue1
            reuseIdentifier:CellIdentifier];
        cell.accessoryType = UITableViewCellAccessoryDisclosureIndicator;
    }
```

```
Vocabulary *vocabulary = (Vocabulary *)[self.fetchedResultsController
    objectAtIndexPath:indexPath];
cell.textLabel.text = vocabulary.name;
cell.detailTextLabel.text =
    [NSString stringWithFormat:@"(%d)", vocabulary.words.count];

return cell;
}
```

The basic setup of the main view controller is now finished and the time has come to wire it up. Go to the AppDelegate.h file and add the following declarations:

```
//
//  AppDelegate.h
//  My Vocabularies
//

#import <UIKit/UIKit.h>
#import "VocabulariesViewController.h"

@interface AppDelegate : UIResponder <UIApplicationDelegate>

@property (strong, nonatomic) UIWindow *window;

@property (readonly, strong, nonatomic) NSManagedObjectContext *managedObjectContext;
@property (readonly, strong, nonatomic) NSManagedObjectModel *managedObjectModel;
@property (readonly, strong, nonatomic) NSPersistentStoreCoordinator
    *persistentStoreCoordinator;
@property (strong, nonatomic) UINavigationController *navigationController;
@property (strong, nonatomic) VocabulariesViewController *vocabulariesViewController;

- (void)saveContext;
- (NSURL *)applicationDocumentsDirectory;

@end
```

As you can see from the preceding code, the application is the place where Core Data has been set up for you. All you need to do is to distribute the managed object context to the parts of your app that deal with the data.

Now, in the application:didFinishLaunchingWithOptions: method in AppDelegate.m, add the following code to create and display the view controller in a navigation controller:

```
- (BOOL)application:(UIApplication *)application didFinishLaunchingWithOptions:(NSDictionary *)
launchOptions
{
    self.window = [[UIWindow alloc] initWithFrame:[[UIScreen mainScreen] bounds]];
    self.window.backgroundColor = [UIColor whiteColor];

    self.vocabulariesViewController = [[VocabulariesViewController alloc]
        initWithManagedObjectContext:self.managedObjectContext];
    self.navigationController = [[UINavigationController alloc]
```

```
        initWithRootViewController:self.vocabulariesViewController];
    self.window.rootViewController = self.navigationController;

    [self.window makeKeyAndVisible];
    return YES;
}
```

Now is a good time to build and run the app to make sure everything is set up correctly. If things went right, you should see a screen resembling Figure 12-15.

Figure 12-15. A word list app with a single Vocabulary

To allow the user to add some data in the form of new Vocabularies, put an Add button on the Navigation bar. Go back to the viewDidLoad method in VocabulariesViewController.m and add the following code:

```
- (void)viewDidLoad
{
    [super viewDidLoad];
```

```
    self.title = @"Vocabularies";

    UIBarButtonItem *addButton =
        [[UIBarButtonItem alloc] initWithBarButtonSystemItem:UIBarButtonSystemItemAdd
            target:self action:@selector(add)];
    self.navigationItem.rightBarButtonItem = addButton;

    [self fetchVocabularies];

    // ...
}
```

Now, implement the add action method. It brings up an alert view for the user to input a name of a new Vocabulary:

```
- (void)add
{
    UIAlertView * inputAlert = [[UIAlertView alloc] initWithTitle:@"New Vocabulary"
        message:@"Enter a name for the new vocabulary" delegate:self
        cancelButtonTitle:@"Cancel" otherButtonTitles:@"OK", nil];
    inputAlert.alertViewStyle = UIAlertViewStylePlainTextInput;
    [inputAlert show];
}
```

Finally, implement the alertView:clickedButtonAtIndex: delegate method to create the new Vocabulary if the user taps the OK button:

```
- (void)alertView:(UIAlertView *)alertView clickedButtonAtIndex:(NSInteger)buttonIndex
{
    if (buttonIndex == 1)
    {
        NSEntityDescription *vocabularyEntityDescription =
            [NSEntityDescription entityForName:@"Vocabulary"
                inManagedObjectContext:self.managedObjectContext];
        Vocabulary *newVocabulary = (Vocabulary *)[[NSManagedObject alloc]
            initWithEntity:vocabularyEntityDescription
            insertIntoManagedObjectContext:self.managedObjectContext];
        newVocabulary.name = [alertView textFieldAtIndex:0].text;
        NSError *error;
        if (![self.managedObjectContext save:&error])
        {
            NSLog(@"Error saving context: %@", error);
        }
        [self fetchVocabularies];
        [self.tableView reloadData];
    }
}
```

If you build and run the app again, you now can add new Vocabularies, as shown in Figure 12-16.

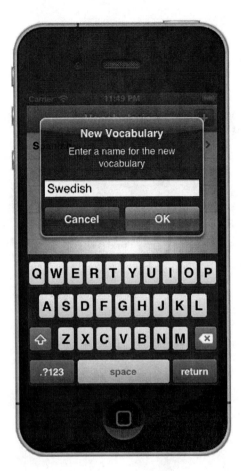

Figure 12-16. Adding a new Vocabulary

As a final feature of the Vocabularies view controller, you implement the possibility to delete items. Do that by implementing the tableView:commitEditingStyle:forRowAtIndexPath: delegate method, like so:

```
-(void)tableView:(UITableView *)tableView commitEditingStyle:(UITableViewCellEditingStyle)
editingStyle forRowAtIndexPath:(NSIndexPath *)indexPath
{
    if (editingStyle == UITableViewCellEditingStyleDelete)
    {
        NSManagedObject *deleted =
            [self.fetchedResultsController objectAtIndexPath:indexPath];
        [self.managedObjectContext deleteObject:deleted];
        NSError *error;
        BOOL success = [self.managedObjectContext save:&error];
        if (!success)
        {
            NSLog(@"Error saving context: %@", error);
        }
```

```
        [self fetchVocabularies];
        [self.tableView deleteRowsAtIndexPaths:@[indexPath]
            withRowAnimation:UITableViewRowAnimationRight];
    }
}
```

To test this feature, run the app again and swipe an item in the list. A red button then appears that allows you to delete the item in question. Figure 12-17 shows an example of this.

Figure 12-17. Deleting a Vocabulary

With the Vocabularies view all setup, it's time to create the view that handles the words.

Implementing the Words View Controller

When the user selects a cell in the Vocabularies table view, another table view is presented displaying the words of that Vocabulary.

Create a new UITableViewController subclass named WordsViewController, again without checking the "With XIB" option.

You initialize the Words view controller with a Vocabulary, so you need a property and a custom initializer for that. You also need to import the Vocabulary and Word classes. Go to WordsViewController.h and add the following declarations:

```
//
//  WordsViewController.h
//  My Vocabularies
//

#import <UIKit/UIKit.h>
#import "Vocabulary.h"
#import "Word.h"

@interface WordsViewController : UITableViewController

@property (strong, nonatomic)Vocabulary *vocabulary;

- (id)initWithVocabulary:(Vocabulary *)vocabulary;

@end
```

Now, switch to the WordsViewController.m. The initializer method simply assigns the vocabulary property and is pretty straightforward. Here are its implementations:

```
- (id)initWithVocabulary:(Vocabulary *)vocabulary
{
    self = [super initWithStyle:UITableViewStylePlain];
    if (self)
    {
        self.vocabulary = vocabulary;
    }
    return self;
}
```

The viewDidLoad method is even simpler (at this point), only setting the view controller's title:

```
- (void)viewDidLoad
{
    [super viewDidLoad];

    self.title = self.vocabulary.name;
}
```

Here are the data source delegate methods:

```
- (NSInteger)numberOfSectionsInTableView:(UITableView *)tableView
{
    return 1;
}
```

```
- (NSInteger)tableView:(UITableView *)tableView numberOfRowsInSection:(NSInteger)section
{
    return self.vocabulary.words.count;
}
```

Notice how you use the corresponding property of the Vocabulary entity's words relationship to get the number of words. This is where the power of Core Data starts to show; you can handle the data as normal objects and ignore the fact that its actually stored in a database.

Next, you'll design the table view cells to display both the word and its translation (as a subtitle.) You do that by adding the following implementation of the `tableView:cellForRowAtIndexPath:` delegate method:

```
- (UITableViewCell *)tableView:(UITableView *)tableView cellForRowAtIndexPath:(NSIndexPath *)
indexPath
{
    static NSString *CellIdentifier = @"WordCell";

    UITableViewCell *cell =
        [tableView dequeueReusableCellWithIdentifier:CellIdentifier];
    if (cell == nil)
    {
        cell = [[UITableViewCell alloc] initWithStyle:UITableViewCellStyleSubtitle
            reuseIdentifier:CellIdentifier];
        cell.accessoryType = UITableViewCellAccessoryDisclosureIndicator;
    }

    Word *word = [self.vocabulary.words.allObjects objectAtIndex:indexPath.row];
    cell.textLabel.text = word.word;
    cell.detailTextLabel.text = word.translation;

    return cell;
}
```

To connect the two view controllers with each other, go back to VocabulariesViewController.h and import the Words view controller header file:

```
//
//  VocabulariesViewController.h
//  My Vocabularies
//

#import <UIKit/UIKit.h>
#import "Vocabulary.h"
#import "WordsViewController.h"

@interface VocabulariesViewController : UITableViewController<UIAlertViewDelegate>

@property (strong, nonatomic)NSManagedObjectContext *managedObjectContext;
@property (strong, nonatomic) NSFetchedResultsController *fetchedResultsController;
```

```
- (id)initWithManagedObjectContext:(NSManagedObjectContext *)context;

@end
```

And finally, in the VocabulariesViewController.m file, add the following delegate method:

```
- (void)tableView:(UITableView *)tableView didSelectRowAtIndexPath:(NSIndexPath *)indexPath
{
    Vocabulary *vocabulary = (Vocabulary *)[self.fetchedResultsController
        objectAtIndexPath:indexPath];

    WordsViewController *detailViewController =
        [[WordsViewController alloc] initWithVocabulary:vocabulary];
    [self.navigationController pushViewController:detailViewController animated:YES];
}
```

Now is a good time to build and run to be sure everything is okay so far. You can now select a Vocabulary and see its word list view, although empty at this point, as in Figure 12-18.

Figure 12-18. A Vocabulary with no words in it

The next step is to implement a way for the user to add Words to the Vocabulary, again in the form of an Add button on the Navigation Bar. But before you add that button, create the view controller that handles the editing of the new Word object.

Adding a Word Edit View

Create a new subclass of UIViewController (not UITableViewController as before) with the name EditWordViewController. You'll build a user interface for it, so make sure the With XIB for user interface option is checked this time.

Open the EditWordViewController.xib file and build a user interface like the one in Figure 12-19.

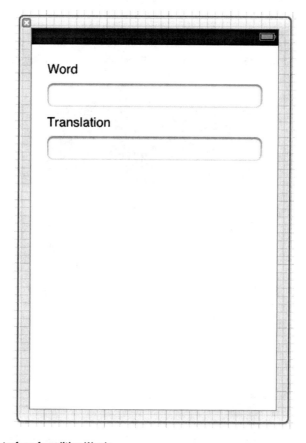

Figure 12-19. A simple user interface for editing Words

As usual, create outlets for the text fields. Name them wordTextField and translationTextField, respectively.

With the user interface in place, you can move on to define the programming interface of this view controller. You use Objective-C blocks to simplify the code on the calling side, which uses the following class method to present the edit view controller:

```
+ (void)editWord:(Word *)word
    inNavigationController:(UINavigationController *)navigationController
    completion:(EditWordViewControllerCompletionHandler)completionHandler;
```

The EditWordViewControllerCompletionHandler is a block type with two arguments, sender and canceled:

```
typedef void (^EditWordViewControllerCompletionHandler)
    (EditWordViewController *sender, BOOL canceled);
```

To implement this API you need a couple of instance variables and a custom initializer method, as well. In all, add the following code to the EditWordViewController.h file:

```
//
//  EditWordViewController.h
//  My Vocabularies
//

#import <UIKit/UIKit.h>
#import "Word.h"

@class EditWordViewController;

typedef void (^EditWordViewControllerCompletionHandler)(EditWordViewController *sender,
BOOL canceled);

@interface EditWordViewController : UIViewController
{
@private
    EditWordViewControllerCompletionHandler _completionHandler;
    Word *_word;
}

@property (weak, nonatomic) IBOutlet UITextField *wordTextField;
@property (weak, nonatomic) IBOutlet UITextField *translationTextField;

- (id)initWithWord:(Word *)word
    completion:(EditWordViewControllerCompletionHandler)completionHandler;

+ (void)editWord:(Word *)word
    inNavigationController:(UINavigationController *)navigationController
    completion:(EditWordViewControllerCompletionHandler)completionHandler;

@end
```

Now, go to EditWordViewController.m and add the following implementation of the class method. It simply instantiates the edit view controller and pushes it onto the provided Navigation controller, like so:

```
+ (void)editWord:(Word *)word
    inNavigationController:(UINavigationController *)navigationController
    completion:(EditWordViewControllerCompletionHandler)completionHandler
{
    EditWordViewController *editViewController =
        [[EditWordViewController alloc] initWithWord:word completion:completionHandler];
    [navigationController pushViewController:editViewController animated:YES];
}
```

The initializer method stores away the Word and the Completion handler in the respective instance variable. Here, the implementation:

```
- (id)initWithWord:(Word *)word completion:(EditWordViewControllerCompletionHandler)
completionHandler
{
    self = [super initWithNibName:nil bundle:nil];
    if (self)
    {
        _completionHandler = completionHandler;
        _word = word;
    }
    return self;
}
```

When the edit view controller loads, it updates the two text fields with data from the provided Word object. It also adds two buttons, Done and Cancel, to the Navigation Bar. To achieve that, add the following code to the viewDidLoad method:

```
- (void)viewDidLoad
{
    [super viewDidLoad];

    self.title = @"Edit Word";

    self.wordTextField.text = _word.word;
    self.translationTextField.text = _word.translation;

    self.navigationItem.rightBarButtonItem =
        [[UIBarButtonItem alloc] initWithBarButtonSystemItem:UIBarButtonSystemItemDone
            target:self action:@selector(done)];
    self.navigationItem.leftBarButtonItem =
        [[UIBarButtonItem alloc] initWithBarButtonSystemItem:UIBarButtonSystemItemCancel
            target:self action:@selector(cancel)];
}
```

As you can see from the code, two action methods have been hooked up to the buttons. Now implement those.

The first, done, updates the Word object with the data from the two text fields and then notifies the caller by invoking the completion handler block, sending NO for the cancel argument, like so:

```
- (void)done
{
    _word.word = self.wordTextField.text;
    _word.translation = self.translationTextField.text;
    _completionHandler(self, NO);
}
```

The cancel action method is even simpler. It'll only notify the caller if the user has canceled the edit:

```
- (void)cancel
{
    _completionHandler(self, YES);
}
```

You're now done with the edit view controller, so implement the code to display it. First, import the edit view controller in the WordsViewController.h file:

```
//
//  WordsViewController.h
//  My Vocabularies
//

#import <UIKit/UIKit.h>
#import "Vocabulary.h"
#import "Word.h"
#import "EditWordViewController.h"

@interface WordsViewController : UITableViewController

@property (strong, nonatomic)Vocabulary *vocabulary;

- (id)initWithVocabulary:(Vocabulary *)vocabulary;

@end
```

Then you add an Add button to the Navigation Bar of the Words view controller. Switch to WordsViewController.m and add the following lines to the viewDidLoad method:

```
- (void)viewDidLoad
{
    [super viewDidLoad];

    UIBarButtonItem *addButton =
        [[UIBarButtonItem alloc] initWithBarButtonSystemItem:UIBarButtonSystemItemAdd
            target:self action:@selector(add)];
    self.navigationItem.rightBarButtonItem = addButton;

    self.title = self.vocabulary.name;
}
```

Next, start implementing the action method of this button. It creates a new Word object, which it provides as an argument to the edit view controller:

```
- (void)add
{
    NSEntityDescription *wordEntityDescription =
        [NSEntityDescription entityForName:@"Word"
            inManagedObjectContext:self.vocabulary.managedObjectContext];
    Word *newWord = (Word *)[[NSManagedObject alloc]
        initWithEntity:wordEntityDescription
        insertIntoManagedObjectContext:self.vocabulary.managedObjectContext];

    [EditWordViewController editWord:newWord
     inNavigationController:self.navigationController completion:
     ^(EditWordViewController *sender, BOOL canceled)
     {
         // TODO: Handle edit finished
     }];
}
```

When the edit view controller finishes, you either delete the new Word object if the user canceled, or add it to the vocabulary and save it to the database. Either way, the edit view controller should be popped from the Navigation controller. The complete implementation of the add action method should be as follows:

```
- (void)add
{
    NSEntityDescription *wordEntityDescription =
        [NSEntityDescription entityForName:@"Word"
            inManagedObjectContext:self.vocabulary.managedObjectContext];
    Word *newWord = (Word *)[[NSManagedObject alloc]
        initWithEntity:wordEntityDescription
        insertIntoManagedObjectContext:self.vocabulary.managedObjectContext];
    [EditWordViewController editWord:newWord
     inNavigationController:self.navigationController completion:
     ^(EditWordViewController *sender, BOOL canceled)
     {
         if (canceled)
         {
             [self.vocabulary.managedObjectContext deleteObject:newWord];
         }
         else
         {
             [self.vocabulary addWordsObject:newWord];

             NSError *error;
             if (![self.vocabulary.managedObjectContext save:&error])
             {
                 NSLog(@"Error saving context: %@", error);
             }
```

```
        [self.tableView reloadData];
    }

    [self.navigationController popViewControllerAnimated:YES];
}];
}
```

If you build and run now, you can add words to your vocabularies using the Add button in the respective Words view. Figure 12-20 shows an example of this.

Figure 12-20. Adding Words to a Vocabulary

The user should of course be able to edit an existing word. You'll implement it so that when a user selects a cell, the edit view for that Word is displayed. To do that, add the following implementation in WordsViewController.m to the tableView:didSelectRowAtIndexPath: delegate method:

```
- (void)tableView:(UITableView *)tableView didSelectRowAtIndexPath:(NSIndexPath *)indexPath
{
    Word *word = [self.vocabulary.words.allObjects objectAtIndex:indexPath.row];
    [EditWordViewController editWord:word
```

```
    inNavigationController:self.navigationController completion:
    ^(EditWordViewController *sender, BOOL canceled)
    {
        NSError *error;
        if (![self.vocabulary.managedObjectContext save:&error])
        {
            NSLog(@"Error saving context: %@", error);
        }

        [self.tableView reloadData];
        [self.navigationController popViewControllerAnimated:YES];
    }];
}
```

To allow the user to delete Words, add the tableView:commitEditingStyle:forRowAtIndexPath:
delegate method with the following implementation:

```
-(void)tableView:(UITableView *)tableView
    commitEditingStyle:(UITableViewCellEditingStyle)editingStyle
    forRowAtIndexPath:(NSIndexPath *)indexPath
{
    if (editingStyle == UITableViewCellEditingStyleDelete)
    {
        Word *deleted = [self.vocabulary.words.allObjects objectAtIndex:indexPath.row];
        [self.vocabulary.managedObjectContext deleteObject:deleted];
        NSError *error;
        BOOL success = [self.vocabulary.managedObjectContext save:&error];
        if (!success)
        {
            NSLog(@"Error saving context: %@", error);
        }
        [self.tableView deleteRowsAtIndexPaths:@[indexPath]
            withRowAnimation:UITableViewRowAnimationRight];
    }
}
```

If you build and run now you can delete words by sweeping your finger (or mouse pointer if you run
in the iOS Simulator), as shown in Figure 12-21.

Figure 12-21. Deleting a word in a Spanish vocabulary list

You're almost finished with this simple word list app, but there is one small issue that we'd like you to fix before we close this recipe. You've probably noticed that if you add Words to a Vocabulary and return to the main view, the item count for the Vocabulary doesn't update. The easiest way to fix this is to reload the data whenever the view appears. To do that, add the following method to the VocabulariesViewController.m file:

```
- (void)viewWillAppear:(BOOL)animated
{
    [self fetchVocabularies];
    [self.tableView reloadData];
}
```

Now, if you try again you'll see that the number within the parentheses updates to reflect the new number of items in the Vocabulary (see Figure 12-22).

Figure 12-22. A word list app with two Vocabularies containing five and three words, respectively

In this recipe, we have covered the basics of Core Data, one of the most integral parts of iOS development. You have seen a glimpse of its power and simplicity of use when it comes to data modeling, persistence, and access. However, we have by no means detailed every facet in the Core Data framework, or even touched on many of the general subjects related to it. You can easily find entire books devoted to the subject of Core Data, and you probably should to get a more complete view of exactly how much ability you have in controlling how your data is stored. The overview here has demonstrated a basic use of the framework and explained the key concepts needed to get started working with Core Data, so that you can implement simple persistence in your applications without worrying about the more esoteric complexities. If you want to know more about this great framework, we recommend you start with Apple's documentation on this topic.[1]

---

[1]https://developer.apple.com/library/mac/#documentation/cocoa/conceptual/coredata/
cdprogrammingguide.html

Persisting Data on iCloud

iCloud is Apple's data storage service for iOS devices. If set up, iOS uses the service for things such as backups and synchronizing images between the user's different devices. iCloud comes with an extensive API so that your apps too can take advantage of its features, including persisting data, and sharing state and files between all the user's devices.

Basically, iCloud comes with three kinds of storage:

- *Key-value storage*, which can be used to store preferences, settings, and other small-sized data.
- *Document storage*, for file-based information such as images, text documents, files containing information about your app's state, etc.
- *Core Data storage*, which actually uses Document storage to persist and synchronize your app's Core Data.

In Recipe 12-4, we show you how you can implement Key-value storage in your apps. Recipe 12-5 shows you how you can create and store custom documents in iCloud. If you're interested in Core Data storage on iCloud, we recommend Apple's documentation.[2]

> **Note** Throughout this section, all recipes will require access to an iOS development program account, as well as a physical iOS device.

Recipe 12-4: Storing Key-Value Data in iCloud

In this recipe, you set up an app for storing key-value data in iCloud. You use the key-value store to persist a simple user preference governing the font size of a displayed text. You start with the basic functionality of the app and then implement the persisting to iCloud.

Create a new single-view app project with the name "Testing iCloud." Select the ViewController.xib file and start building a user interface resembling the one in Figure 12-23.

---

[2]https://developer.apple.com/library/ios/#documentation/General/Conceptual/iCloudDesignGuide/Chapters/DesignForCoreDataIniCloud.html#//apple_ref/doc/uid/TP40012094-CH3-SW1

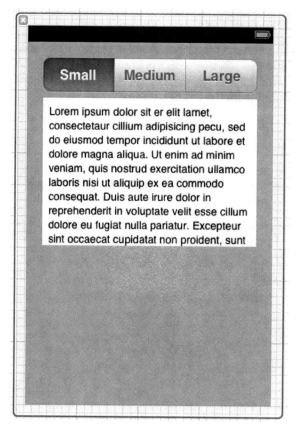

Figure 12-23. A simple user interface with a Text View and a Segmented Control

Create outlets for the controls and use the names fontSizeSegmentedControl and documentTextView, respectively. Also create an action named updateTextSize for the Segmented control.

As you've probably guessed, the user can change the size of the text in the Text View using the Segmented Control. To implement that, go to ViewController.m and add the following code to the updateTextSize action method:

```
- (IBAction)updateTextSize:(id)sender
{
    CGFloat newFontSize;
    switch (self.fontSizeSegmentedControl.selectedSegmentIndex)
    {
        case 1:
            newFontSize = 19;
            break;
        case 2:
            newFontSize = 24;
            break;
```

```
    default:
        newFontSize = 14;
        break;
    }
    self.documentTextView.font = [UIFont systemFontOfSize:newFontSize];
}
```

That's it! You can now run the app and change the text size from the Segment Control, as shown in Figure 12-24.

Figure 12-24. Changing the text size with a Segmented Control

Notice that if you change the text size to, say, Large and kill the app, the preference is not persisted and will be back to Small when you run the app again. You will implement persistence next, but instead of using NSUserDefaults you'll use iCloud's key-value store. This advantage of using iCloud over local storage, is that the preference can be persisted, not only between executions on your device, but also shared by all your devices running this app. Additionally, if you remove and reinstall the app for some reason, the preferences will not be erased.

Let's go ahead and implement this feature, but first you need to do some configuring tasks to set up your app with iCloud.

Setting Up iCloud For an App

First, you must configure "entitlements" for the project to allow for iCloud and its Key-Value store. Navigate to the project's Target settings and scroll down to the section called "Entitlements." Click the check boxes labeled "Entitlements," "Enable iCloud," and "Key-Value Store," as shown in Figure 12-25. Xcode then automatically generates an entitlements file with the correct settings.

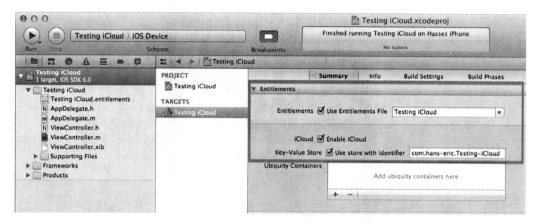

Figure 12-25. Enabling entitlements to allow communication with iCloud

Next, you need to generate a special "App ID" for this application. In your web browser, log into the iOS Developer's Member Center at `http://developer.apple.com/membercenter/`. Navigate to the iOS Provisioning Portal, and then move to the App IDs section. Click the button titled "New App ID."

The next screen you see prompts you to enter a description, as well as a bundle identifier. Set the description to "Testing iCloud." For the bundle identifier, you need to enter the exact same identifier that Xcode has given your app. This can be found at the top of the project's Targets settings, as shown in Figure 12-26. It will most likely have a format along the lines of "com.domainName. Testing-iCloud."

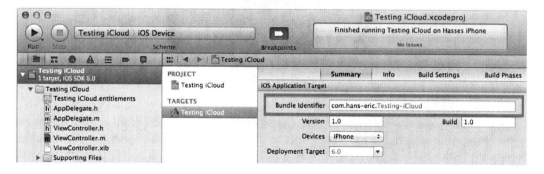

Figure 12-26. Finding an app's bundle identifier

In Figure 12-26, my identifier is "com.hans-eric.Testing-iCloud", so I enter this text in my browser. Figure 12-27 shows my Description and the bundle id configurations in Apple's iOS provisioning portal.

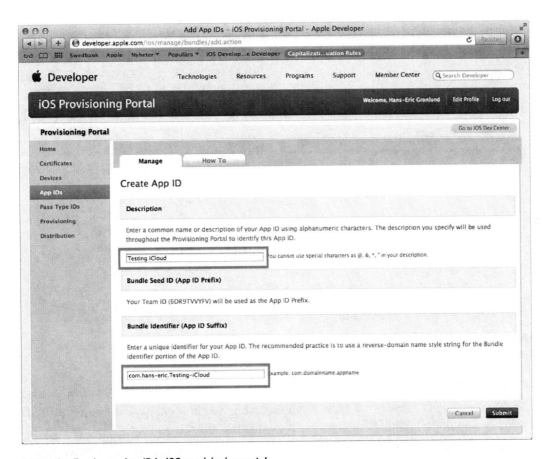

Figure 12-27. Configuring an App ID in iOS provisioning portal

On creating this new App ID, you are returned to your table of created App IDs. Find the one that you just created, and click the Configure link.

In this screen, all you need to do is check the box labeled Enable for iCloud, shown in Figure 12-28. If a dialog appears warning you of having to manually regenerate profiles, simply click OK.

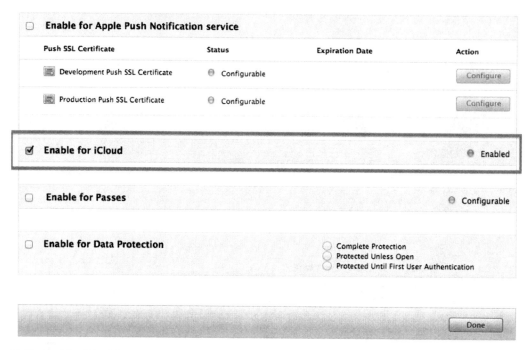

Figure 12-28. Enabling iCloud for your certificate

Click Done to finish configuring your App ID.

Next, click the Provisioning link in the table of contents on the left-hand side of the page. Then click the New Profile button to begin creating a new provisioning profile.

Name this new profile "Testing iCloud Profile." Select your certificate that you should already have as an iOS developer. Set the App ID field to your recently made "Testing iCloud" App ID, and be sure to check the boxes next to whichever devices on which you want to test this application. Figure 12-29 shows my configuration screen, which yours should resemble with your own information.

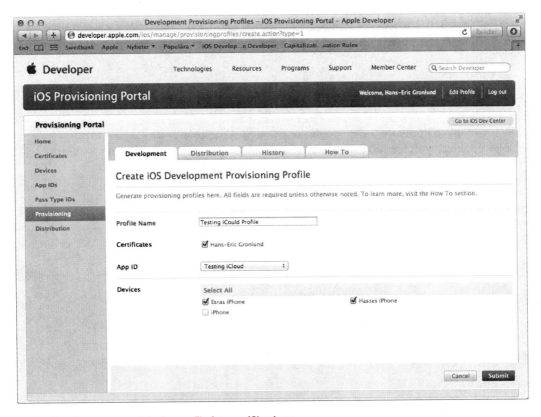

Figure 12-29. *Creating a new provisioning profile for your iCloud app*

Click Submit to return to your list of provisioning profiles. You should see your new profile listed. If its status is listed as "Pending," simply refresh the page until it says "Active."

Next, click the Download button next to your newly created profile to download it to your computer.

After your file has finished downloading (it shouldn't take long), drag the file from the Finder to the Xcode icon in your dock to import it into Xcode. This should bring up the Organizer window as well, which lists all your provisioning profiles.

Finally, in the Organizer, while your device is connected to your computer, drag the new profile from the displayed list to the Provisioning Profiles section under your device, shown in Figure 12-30.

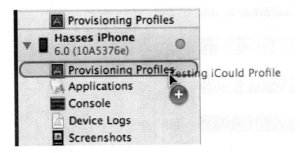

Figure 12-30. *Copying your new profile by dragging it into the Provisioning Profiles section of your device*

At this point, your device is fully configured to run the project you have created. Because both your application and your device are configured to work with iCloud, you can continue to build your actual application.

Persisting Data in iCloud Key-Value Store

You'll now move on to implement the storing of the text size preference in the iCloud Key-Value store. First, you'll need a property to store a reference to the Key-Value store. Go to ViewController.h and add the following declaration:

```
//
//  ViewController.h
//  Testing iCloud
//

#import <UIKit/UIKit.h>

@interface ViewController : UIViewController

@property (weak, nonatomic) IBOutlet UISegmentedControl *fontSizeSegmentedControl;
@property (weak, nonatomic) IBOutlet UITextView *documentTextView;
@property (strong, nonatomic) NSUbiquitousKeyValueStore *iCloudKeyValueStore;

- (IBAction)updateTextSize:(id)sender;

@end
```

Now, switch to ViewController.m and add the following code to the viewDidLoad method:

```
- (void)viewDidLoad
{
    [super viewDidLoad];
    self.iCloudKeyValueStore = [NSUbiquitousKeyValueStore defaultStore];

    [[NSNotificationCenter defaultCenter] addObserver:self
        selector:@selector(handleStoreChange:)
        name:NSUbiquitousKeyValueStoreDidChangeExternallyNotification
        object:self.iCloudKeyValueStore];

    [self.iCloudKeyValueStore synchronize];
    [self updateUserInterfaceWithPreferences];
}
```

What the above code does is

1. Get a reference to the Key-Value store

2. Sign up for notifications when the data in the Key-Value store is changed by an external source (NSUbiquitousKeyValueStoreDidChangeExternallyNotification)

3. Make sure the Key-Value store cache is up-to-date by calling synchronize

4. Update the user interface with the values from the Key-Value store

> **Note**   Here, you're setting up the iCloud access directly in the main view controller, which is fine for the
> purpose of this recipe. However, in an app with several view controllers that access the Key-Value store,
> you should set it up in the App delegate instead, and distribute the reference to the regarded parties.

Next, implement the notification handler for when the iCloud data is changed by an external source.
For the sake of this recipe, you'll simply update the user interface with the new values:

```
- (void)handleStoreChange:(NSNotification *)notification
{
    [self updateUserInterfaceWithPreferences];
}
```

The updateUserInterfaceWithPreference helper method extracts the text size value from the
Key-Value store and sets the selected index of the Segment Control:

```
- (void)updateUserInterfaceWithPreferences
{
    NSInteger selectedSize = [self.iCloudKeyValueStore doubleForKey:@"TextSize"];
    self.sizeSegmentedControl.selectedSegmentIndex = selectedSize;
    [self updateTextSize:self];
}
```

Finally, when the user changes the text size using the Segment Control, you should write
the new value to the Key-Value store for persistency in iCloud. Add the following code to the
updateTextSize: action method:

```
- (IBAction)updateTextSize:(id)sender
{
    CGFloat newFontSize;
    switch (self.fontSizeSegmentedControl.selectedSegmentIndex)
    {
        case 1:
            newFontSize = 19;
            break;
        case 2:
            newFontSize = 24;
            break;

        default:
            newFontSize = 14;
            break;
    }
    self.documentTextView.font = [UIFont systemFontOfSize:newFontSize];
```

```
    // Update Preferences
    NSInteger selectedSize = self.fontSizeSegmentedControl.selectedSegmentIndex;
    [self.iCloudKeyValueStore setDouble:selectedSize forKey:@"TextSize"];
}
```

> **Note**   You're using the setDouble:forKey: method to store an Integer value here, but you can store any kind of Key-Value compliant data, e.g. NSStrings, BOOLs, NSData objects, or even NSArrays and NSDictionary objects.

That's all you need to do to store the preference value in iCloud. But before you can test your application, you must make sure that your test device is properly configured to work with iCloud. In the Settings app on your device, navigate to the iCloud section. For this application to properly store data, your iCloud account must be properly configured and verified. This requires you to have verified your email address and registered it as your Apple ID. The item marked "Documents & Data" should also be set to "ON", as in Figure 12-31. You can, of course, easily configure this once your account is verified.

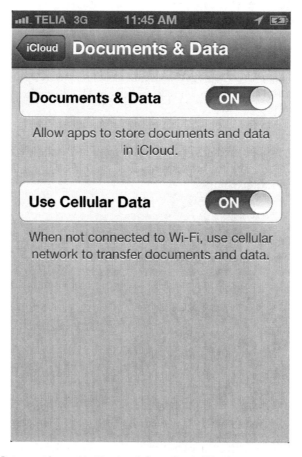

Figure 12-31. Documents and Data must be enabled to store information in iCloud

With iCloud setup on your device, you can build and run the app to test its new persistency feature. You should now be able to do the following:

- Set the text size preference to Medium or Large, kill the app and restart it; it should now automatically set the preference to the value you chose.

- Set the text size preference to Medium or Large, uninstall the app from the device and then reinstall it; in a second or two, it should automatically set the preference to the value it had before uninstalling.

- Run the app on two different devices, change the preference on one device and see it automatically reflected in the other (it may take some time before the change takes place).

This is all well and good; however, there is a problem with this implementation. It will not work if iCloud is turned off or unavailable. You can easily test this by running the app in the iOS simulator (which doesn't have support for iCloud). You'll see there, that the persistency doesn't work and the app is reset to the Small text size on every launch.

For these reasons, it's recommended that you in addition to the iCloud Key-Value store, save the values in a local NSUserDefaults cache as well. This makes your app more robust and resilient to problems stemming from iCloud access problems. Fortunately, this is an easy fix as the next section shows.

Caching iCloud Data Locally Using NSUserDefaults

Start by adding an NSUserDefaults property in the ViewController.h file:

```
//
//  ViewController.h
//  Testing iCloud
//

#import <UIKit/UIKit.h>

@interface ViewController : UIViewController

@property (weak, nonatomic) IBOutlet UISegmentedControl *fontSizeSegmentedControl;
@property (weak, nonatomic) IBOutlet UITextView *documentTextView;
@property (strong, nonatomic) NSUbiquitousKeyValueStore *iCloudKeyValueStore;
@property (strong, nonatomic) NSUserDefaults *userDefaults;

- (IBAction)updateTextSize:(id)sender;

@end
```

There's only a few changes needed for setting up the local cache. First, in viewDidLoad you'll initialize the property:

```
- (void)viewDidLoad
{
    [super viewDidLoad];
    self.iCloudKeyValueStore = [NSUbiquitousKeyValueStore defaultStore];
    self.userDefaults = [NSUserDefaults standardUserDefaults];

    // ...
}
```

Next, when the preference value is written to iCloud, you'll write the same value to the NSUserDefaults as well. To do this, add the following line to the updateTextSize: method:

```
- (IBAction)updateTextSize:(id)sender
{
    // ...

    // Update Preferences
    NSInteger selectedSize = self.sizeSegmentedControl.selectedSegmentIndex;
    [self.userDefaults setDouble:selectedSize forKey:@"TextSize"];
    [self.userDefaults synchronize];
    [self.iCloudKeyValueStore setDouble:selectedSize forKey:@"TextSize"];
}
```

Finally, when updating user interface with the preferences, instead of just blindly taking the value from the iCloud Key-Value store, you'll first check and see if it exists. If it doesn't, you'll use the value from the local cache instead. Here is the new implementation of the updateUserInterfaceWithPreferences method:

```
- (void)updateUserInterfaceWithPreferences
{
    NSInteger selectedSize;

    if ([self.iCloudKeyValueStore objectForKey:@"TextSize"] != nil)
    {
        // iCloud value exists
        selectedSize = [self.iCloudKeyValueStore doubleForKey:@"TextSize"];
        // Make sure local cache is synced
        [self.userDefaults setDouble:selectedSize forKey:@"TextSize"];
        [self.userDefaults synchronize];
    }
    else
    {
        // iCloud unavailable, use value from local cache
        selectedSize = [self.userDefaults doubleForKey:@"TextSize"];
    }

    self. fontSizeSegmentedControl.selectedSegmentIndex = selectedSize;
    [self updateTextSize:self];
}
```

Now the app should work and persist its size text preference, both with iCloud and without it.

As you can see, working with iCloud Key-Value store is extremely simple. There's but one problem: you cannot store big chunks of data. There is a limit of 1MB per application and you can use no more than 1,024 keys to store the data. This makes it a poor candidate for application data model storage. For that, you can use the Documents store, which is what the next recipe will be about.

Recipe 12-5: Storing UIDocuments in iCloud

Besides the Key-Value store, an iCloud account may consist of one or more so called *ubiquity* containers. A ubiquity container is like a file folder on your device that is automatically synced with a corresponding file folder in iCloud. Using the UIDocument API, you can create custom documents and store them in such a ubiquity container.

In this recipe, you'll build on the project from Recipe 12-4 and allow the user to store the text as a document in iCloud. You'll start by adding a ubiquity container to the app's "Entitlements." Navigate to the Target settings and its "Entitlements" section. Click on the + button beneath the Ubiquity Containers box. This adds the default container, with the same name as the project's Bundle identifier, as shown in Figure 12-32.

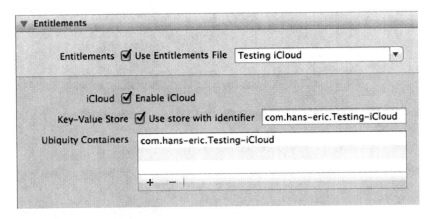

Figure 12-32. Adding a ubiquity container to the project

Next, you'll make a small change to the user interface. Open the `ViewController.xib` file and add a button as shown in Figure 12-33. Notice that we've decreased the height of the text view so that the Save button won't be concealed by the keyboard when the user enters text.

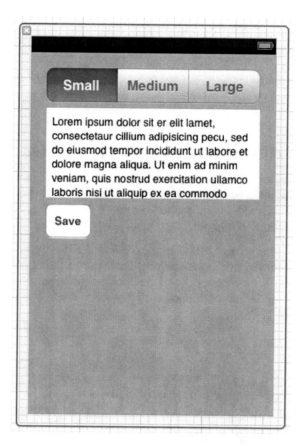

Figure 12-33. The user interface with an added Save button for storing the text document in iCloud

Also, create an action with the name saveDocument for the Save button.

Next, you'll create a UIDocument subclass to handle the saving and loading of the text. Name the new class "MyDocument."

The document has two properties, one for the text and one for a delegate used to notify the view controller that the remote text document has changed. Open MyDocument.h and add the following code:

```
//
//  MyDocument.h
//  Testing iCloud
//

#import <UIKit/UIKit.h>

@class MyDocument;

@protocol MyDocumentDelegate <NSObject>
- (void)documentDidChange:(MyDocument*)document;
@end
```

```
@interface MyDocument : UIDocument

@property (strong, nonatomic) NSString *text;
@property (weak, nonatomic) id<MyDocumentDelegate> delegate;

@end
```

The UIDocument class requires you to implement two methods. The first is contentsForType:error:, which is used to encode the data into its storing format. In this case, you save the string with an UTF8 encoding:

```
- (id)contentsForType:(NSString *)typeName error:(NSError *__autoreleasing *)outError
{
    if (!self.text)
        self.text = @"";
    return [self.text dataUsingEncoding:NSUTF8StringEncoding];
}
```

The other method, loadFromContents:ofType:error:, does the reverse, building an NSString out of raw data and setting it to your property. In this implementation, this method also invokes the delegate to notify the view controller of the content change:

```
-(BOOL) loadFromContents:(id)contents ofType:(NSString *)typeName error:(NSError *__autoreleasing *)
outError
{
    if ([contents length] > 0)
    {
        self.text = [[NSString alloc] initWithBytes:[contents bytes] length:[contents length]
encoding:NSUTF8StringEncoding];
    }
    else
    {
        self.text = @"";
    }

    [self.delegate documentDidChange:self];

    return YES;
}
```

Now that your data model is configured (yes, it is that simple!), you can move on to implement the persisting of the document. Go to the ViewController.h file and add two property declarations, one for referencing the document and one for the document's URL. Also, add the MyDocumentDelegate protocol to prepare the view controller for being the document's delegate. The ViewController.h file should now look like this:

```
//
//  ViewController.h
//  Testing iCloud
//
```

```
#import <UIKit/UIKit.h>
#import "MyDocument.h"

@interface ViewController : UIViewController<MyDocumentDelegate>

@property (weak, nonatomic) IBOutlet UISegmentedControl *fontSizeSegmentedControl;
@property (weak, nonatomic) IBOutlet UITextView *documentTextView;
@property (strong, nonatomic) NSUbiquitousKeyValueStore *iCloudKeyValueStore;
@property (strong, nonatomic) NSUserDefaults *userDefaults;
@property (strong, nonatomic) MyDocument *document;
@property (strong, nonatomic) NSURL *documentURL;

- (IBAction)updateTextSize:(id)sender;
- (IBAction)saveDocument:(id)sender;

@end
```

Now, go to ViewController.m. In the viewDidLoad, add the following line to initiate an update of the Text View with the persisted text, if existent:

```
- (void)viewDidLoad
{
    [super viewDidLoad];
    self.iCloudKeyValueStore = [NSUbiquitousKeyValueStore defaultStore];
    self.userDefaults = [NSUserDefaults standardUserDefaults];

    [[NSNotificationCenter defaultCenter] addObserver:self
        selector:@selector(handleStoreChange:)
        name:NSUbiquitousKeyValueStoreDidChangeExternallyNotification
        object:self.iCloudKeyValueStore];

    [self.iCloudKeyValueStore synchronize];
    [self updateUserInterfaceWithPreferences];

    [self updateDocument];
}
```

The updateDocument first checks to see whether iCloud is available:

```
- (void)updateDocument
{
    NSFileManager *fileManager = [NSFileManager defaultManager];
    id iCloudToken = [fileManager ubiquityIdentityToken];
    if (iCloudToken)
    {
        // iCloud available

        // Register to notifications for changes in availability
        [[NSNotificationCenter defaultCenter] addObserver:self
            selector:@selector(handleICloudDidChangeIdentity:)
            name:NSUbiquityIdentityDidChangeNotification object:nil];
```

```
        //TODO: Open existing document or create new
    }
    else
    {
        // No iCloud access
        self.documentURL = nil;
        self.document = nil;
        self.documentTextView.text = @"<NO iCloud Access>";
    }
}
```

If iCloud is available, updateDocument will create an instance of MyDocument and either open it if it exists in the ubiquity container, or save it to upload it. To avoid freezing the user interface during this time, it'll perform these actions on a different thread:

```
- (void)updateDocument
{
    NSFileManager *fileManager = [NSFileManager defaultManager];
    id iCloudToken = [fileManager ubiquityIdentityToken];
    if (iCloudToken)
    {
        // iCloud available

        // Register to notifications for changes in availability
        [[NSNotificationCenter defaultCenter] addObserver:self
            selector:@selector(handleICloudDidChangeIdentity:)
            name:NSUbiquityIdentityDidChangeNotification object:nil];

        dispatch_async(dispatch_get_global_queue(DISPATCH_QUEUE_PRIORITY_DEFAULT, 0),
        ^{
            NSURL *documentContainer = [[fileManager URLForUbiquityContainerIdentifier:nil]
                URLByAppendingPathComponent:@"Documents"];

            if (documentContainer != nil)
            {
                self.documentURL =
                    [documentContainer URLByAppendingPathComponent:@"mydocument.txt"];
                self.document =
                    [[MyDocument alloc] initWithFileURL:self.documentURL];
                self.document.delegate = self;
                // If the file exists, open it; otherwise, create it.
                if ([fileManager fileExistsAtPath:self.documentURL.path])
                    [self.document openWithCompletionHandler:nil];
                else
                    [self.document saveToURL:self.documentURL
                        forSaveOperation:UIDocumentSaveForCreating
                        completionHandler:nil];
            }
        });
    }
```

```
    else
    {
        // No iCloud access
        self.documentURL = nil;
        self.document = nil;
        self.documentTextView.text = @"<NO iCloud Access>";
    }
}
```

To handle if the user logs out of iCloud, or changes to a different account, add the following implementation of the handleICloudDidChangeIdentity: notification method. It simply calls the updateDocument helper method:

```
- (void)handleICloudDidChangeIdentity: (NSNotification *)notification
{
    NSLog(@"ID changed");
    [self updateDocument];
}
```

When the document content changes, the app should update the Text View. This is done in the documentDidChange: delegate method. Because it may be called on an arbitrary thread, you need to make sure the updating is run on the main thread, like so:

```
- (void)documentDidChange:(MyDocument *)document
{
    dispatch_async(dispatch_get_main_queue(),
    ^{
        self.documentTextView.text = document.text;
    });
}
```

Finally, when the user taps the Save button, the document shall be updated with the new text and saved to iCloud. To do that, add the following implementation of the saveDocument: action method:

```
- (IBAction)saveDocument:(id)sender
{
    if (self.document)
    {
        self.document.text = self.documentTextView.text;
        [self.document saveToURL:self.documentURL
            forSaveOperation:UIDocumentSaveForOverwriting completionHandler:
        ^(BOOL success)
        {
            if (success)
            {
                NSLog(@"Written to iCloud");
            }
```

```
        else
        {
            NSLog(@"Error writing to iCloud");
        }
    }];
    }
}
```

That's it! Assuming your device is correctly configured, your simple application can store the document using the user's iCloud account, allowing you to easily persist data across multiple devices, application shutdowns, and even through system resets, as shown by Figure 12-34.

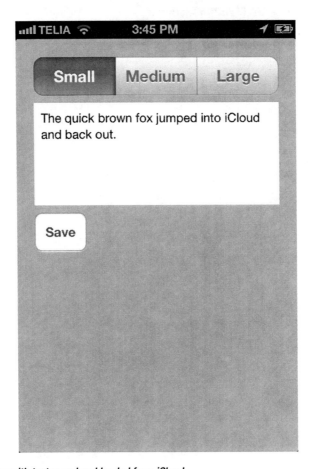

Figure 12-34. Your application with text saved and loaded from iCloud

Summary

Data persistence is one of the most important considerations in developing an application. Developers must consider the type of data they want to store, how much of it, how it connects, and whether their application might even stretch across multiple devices. From there, the choice must be made on which approach to use to store data, whether it is the simple `NSUserDefaults` method, the file management system, or the intricate Core Data framework. On top of this, the relatively new addition of iCloud service has revolutionized the way that applications can store data, allowing persistence of data in near real time across devices running the same application. As memory, storage, and mobile applications continue to grow in size, importance, and relevance in the technological world, these topics will become significantly more relevant. By firmly understanding the most up-to-date concepts of data persistence in iOS, you can always keep your users updated with the fastest, most efficient, and most powerful methods of storing data possible.

Data Transmission Recipes

As time has progressed and technology has developed, one of the clearest trends to be noticed is the growth in user-generated content. With the improvement of design technologies, Internet connection speeds, and network availability, the amount of data generated electronically per year has increased at a nearly unbelievable rate. The heart of this matter is based around the idea of allowing users to easily take in and re-distribute information. You can incorporate these same concepts into your development through a variety of built-in classes in order to improve the functionality and usefulness of your applications.

In this chapter, you will need only a physical device to implement texting functionality, which you will build in your first recipe. All your other functionalities can simulated.

Recipe 13-1: Composing Text Messages

Text messaging is still one of the most popular methods of transmitting data between individuals. It's quick, easy, and powerful, and is used across nearly all age groups. In iOS you can incorporate text messaging into your applications and provide the simple cross-application functionality that can so easily improve the overall quality of an application.

Start off by creating a new project called "Send It Out," which you use throughout this chapter. As usual, use the Single View Application template to create the project.

To fully demonstrate a few of the functionalities of this topic, specifically choose to develop your application for the iPad, rather than the iPhone. Be sure the Device Family is set accordingly in the next screen after entering the project's name. Because some of the functionalities you will test require a physical device to be fully capable, you can make this application for the iPhone as well, and simply adjust the view elements as you wish.

After clicking through to create your project, switch over to your view controller's .xib file. In the Utilities pane, set the orientation (under the Simulated Metrics section, under the Attributes inspector tab) to landscape, and be sure that the background color is set to light gray, as shown in Figure 13-1.

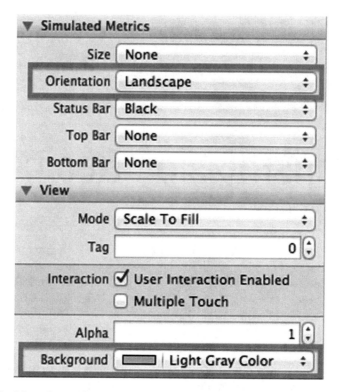

Figure 13-1. Configuring the Orientation and Background color of the iPad app

Start off by adding a UITextView, with the default Lorem Ipsum text, to the top half of your view, as well as a UIButton, with the label Text Message, to the bottom. Connect these to your view controller as outlets with property names inputTextView and textMessageButton. Also, create an action named textMessage for the button.

Before you proceed, go ahead and round the corners of your UITextView to improve your application's visual quality. Add the following import statement to your view controller's header file:

```
//
//  ViewController.h
//  Send It Out
//

#import <UIKit/UIKit.h>
#import <QuartzCore/QuartzCore.h>

@interface ViewController : UIViewController

@property (weak, nonatomic) IBOutlet UITextView *inputTextView;
@property (weak, nonatomic) IBOutlet UIButton *textMessageButton;

- (IBAction)textMessage:(id)sender;

@end
```

Next add the following line to the end of your `viewDidLoad` method:

```
- (void)viewDidLoad
{
    [super viewDidLoad];
    self.inputTextView.layer.cornerRadius = 15.0;
}
```

If you test your app in the iPad simulator, your view should now resemble that simulated in Figure 13-2 once you rotate the simulator. This can be done through either the Rotate Left (Cmd (⌘) + left arrow key) or Rotate Right (Cmd (⌘) + right arrow key) commands found in the Hardware menu of the iOS simulator.

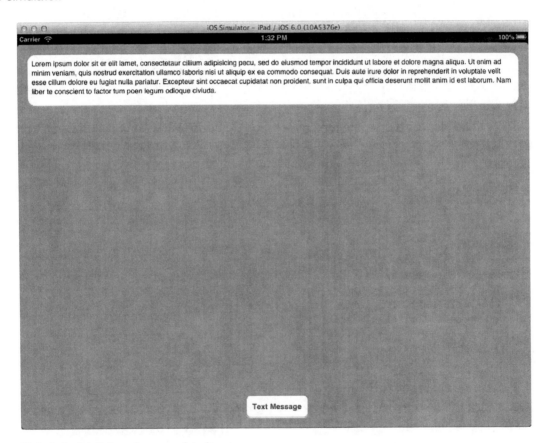

Figure 13-2. A simulated view of your user interface

You will also configure your view controller as the delegate for your `UITextView`. Add the `UITextViewDelegate` protocol to the view controller's `@interface` declaration:

```
//
// ViewController.h
// Send It Out
//
```

```
// ...

@interface ViewController : UIViewController<UITextViewDelegate>

// ...

@end
```

And, assign the Text View's delegate property in the `viewDidLoad` method in `ViewController.m`:

```
- (void)viewDidLoad
{
    [super viewDidLoad];
    self.inputTextView.layer.cornerRadius = 15.0;
    self.inputTextView.delegate = self;
}
```

Next, add the `MessageUI` framework to your project. Do this under the Build Phases tab of your project (see Recipe 1-2, Linking a Framework, for details). Also, add the required import statement to your view controller's header file.

Your view controller acts as a delegate for the Message Compose View Controller that you'll create later, so add the `MFMessageComposeViewControllerDelegate` protocol to `ViewController.h` as well:

```
//
//  ViewController.h
//  Send It Out
//

#import <UIKit/UIKit.h>
#import <QuartzCore/QuartzCore.h>
#import <MessageUI/MessageUI.h>

@interface ViewController : UIViewController<UITextViewDelegate,
    MFMessageComposeViewControllerDelegate>

// ...

@end
```

Now switch back to `ViewController.m`, where you implement one of your `UITextView`'s delegate methods to ensure that your keyboard is properly dismissed when the user taps the Enter key.

```
- (BOOL)textView:(UITextView *)textView shouldChangeTextInRange:(NSRange)range
 replacementText:(NSString *)text
{
if ([text isEqualToString:@"\n"])
    {
        [textView resignFirstResponder];
        return NO;
    }
    return YES;
}
```

Now you can implement your -textMessage: action method such that the text of your UITextView is transposed into a text message. You simply set the recipient to a fake number.

```
-(IBAction)textMessage:(id)sender
{
    if ([MFMessageComposeViewController canSendText])
    {
        MFMessageComposeViewController *messageVC =
            [[MFMessageComposeViewController alloc] init];
        messageVC.messageComposeDelegate = self;
        messageVC.recipients = @[@"3015555309"];
        messageVC.body = self.inputTextView.text;
        [self presentViewController:messageVC animated:YES completion:nil];
    }
    else
    {
        NSLog(@"Text Messaging Unavailable");
    }
}
```

The implementation of this method should appear fairly straightforward. After using the canSendText method to check for texting availability, you create an instance of the MFMessageComposeViewController class, and then configure it with your fake recipient, as well as the intended text. Finally, you simply present the controller to allow your user to review the text message before sending it.

The MFMessageComposeViewController and its counterpart, the MFMailComposeViewController, which you will encounter later, are both classes that allow you to set their initial conditions and present them, but they do not allow you any control of the class once it has been shown. This is to ensure that the user has the final say in whether a message or mail sends, rather than any application sending it without informing the user.

You can implement your MFMessageComposeViewController's messageComposeDelegate method to handle the completion of the message like so:

```
-(void)messageComposeViewController:(MFMessageComposeViewController *)controller
didFinishWithResult:(MessageComposeResult)result
{
    if (result == MessageComposeResultSent)
    {
        self.inputTextView.text = @"Message sent.";
    }
    else if (result == MessageComposeResultFailed)
    {
        NSLog(@"Failed to send message!");
    }
    [self dismissViewControllerAnimated:YES completion:nil];
}
```

Along with the two possible values of MessageComposeResults demonstrated in the previous code, there is a third result, MessageComposeResultCancelled, which indicates that the user cancelled the sending of the text message.

A new functionality in iOS 5.0 was the ability to receive notifications about the changing of the availability of text messaging. You can register for such notifications by adding the following line to the -viewDidLoad method in ViewController.m:

```
- (void)viewDidLoad
{
    [super viewDidLoad];
    self.inputTextView.layer.cornerRadius = 15.0;
    self.inputTextView.delegate = self;
    [[NSNotificationCenter defaultCenter] addObserver:self
        selector:@selector(textMessagingAvailabilityChanged:)
        name:MFMessageComposeViewControllerTextMessageAvailabilityDidChangeNotification
        object:nil];
}
```

The selector specified here can easily be defined to simply inform you of the change. In a full application, you might likely make use of a UIAlert to notify the user of this change as well, but you will avoid this process for demonstration purposes.

```
-(void)textMessagingAvailabilityChange:(id)sender
{
    if ([MFMessageComposeViewController canSendText])
    {
        NSLog(@"Text Messaging Available");
    }
    else
    {
        NSLog(@"Text Messaging Unavailable");
    }
}
```

Your app can now copy the body of your UITextView into a text message to be sent off to your fake recipient. If you test this, however, keep in mind that the text messaging functionality will not be available on the iOS simulator. You have to test this on your physical device with 3G capabilities. To test this application as it is exactly, you need a 3G-capable iPad, but you could edit the project to work for an iPhone instead.

Recipe 13-2: Composing Email

Just as you could create and configure text messages to be sent from your application, you can also use the MessageUI framework to configure mail messages using the counterpart to the MFMessageComposeViewController class, which is MFMailComposeViewController.

Building on the application from Recipe 13-1, add an option to email the message. Start by adding another button with the label "Mail Message". Create an outlet named mailMessageButton and an action called mailMessage for the button.

Similar to what you did in Recipe 13-1 with the MFMessageComposeViewController, you'll prepare the main view controller to be a delegate of the MFMailComposeViewController:

```objc
//
//  ViewController.h
//  Send It Out
//

#import <UIKit/UIKit.h>
#import <QuartzCore/QuartzCore.h>
#import <MessageUI/MessageUI.h>

@interface ViewController : UIViewController<UITextViewDelegate,
    MFMessageComposeViewControllerDelegate, MFMailComposeViewControllerDelegate>

@property (weak, nonatomic) IBOutlet UITextView *inputTextView;
@property (weak, nonatomic) IBOutlet UIButton *textMessageButton;
@property (weak, nonatomic) IBOutlet UIButton *mailMessageButton;

- (IBAction)textMessage:(id)sender;
- (IBAction)mailMessage:(id)sender;

@end
```

The setup for your mailMessage: method is also very similar to your previous textMessage: method. You create your composing view controller, configure it, and then present it. Here is the implementation:

```objc
- (IBAction)mailMessage:(id)sender
{
    if ([MFMailComposeViewController canSendMail])
    {
        MFMailComposeViewController *mailVC =
            [[MFMailComposeViewController alloc] init];
        [mailVC setSubject:@"Send It Out"];
        [mailVC setToRecipients:@[@"test@example.com"]];
        [mailVC setMessageBody:self.inputTextView.text isHTML:NO];
        mailVC.mailComposeDelegate = self;
        [self presentViewController:mailVC animated:YES completion:nil];
    }
    else
    {
        NSLog(@"E-mailing Unavailable");
    }
}
```

As you can see, the MFMailComposeViewController has a few extra properties compared to the MFMessageComposeViewController to specifically configure a more complex email.

The MFMailComposeViewControllerDelegate protocol defines only one method, which you are required to implement to properly handle the completed use of the view controller by the user. You give this a simple implementation to log the result.

```
-(void)mailComposeController:(MFMailComposeViewController *)controller
didFinishWithResult:(MFMailComposeResult)result error:(NSError *)error
{
    if (result == MFMailComposeResultSent)
        self.inputTextView.text = @"Mail sent.";
    else if (result == MFMailComposeResultCancelled)
        NSLog(@"Mail Cancelled");
    else if (result == MFMailComposeResultFailed)
        NSLog(@"Error, Mail Send Failed");
    else if (result == MFMailComposeResultSaved)
        NSLog(@"Mail Saved");
    [self dismissViewControllerAnimated:YES completion:nil];
}
```

Now, your new application can present a view controller for sending mail, as shown in Figure 13-3. Unlike the MFMessageViewController, however, you can actually test this functionality in the iOS Simulator.

Figure 13-3. Composing an email using the MFMailMailComposeViewController

Quite conveniently, you can easily test all the functionalities of the `MFMailComposeViewController` using the simulator without any fear of sending out multiple emails to any addresses, real or fake. The simulator does not actually send out your test messages over the Internet, so you can easily test your `mailComposeDelegate` method's handling of the `MailComposeResults`.

Attaching Data to Mail

The `MFMailComposeViewController` includes functionality for you to attach data to your email from your application through the use of the `addAttachmentData:mimeType:fileName:` method. This method takes three parameters:

1. `attachment`: This instance of `NSData` refers to the actual data of the object that you want to send. This means for any object you want to attach, you will need to acquire the `NSData` for it.

2. `mimeType`: This property is an `NSString` that the controller uses to define the data type of the attachment. These values are not specific to iOS, and so are not defined in the Apple documentation. They can, however, be easily found online. Wikipedia offers a very comprehensive article on possible values at `http://en.wikipedia.org/wiki/Internet_media_type`. The MIME type of a JPEG image, for example, is `image/jpeg`.

3. `fileName`: Use this `NSString` property to set the preferred name for the file sent in the email.

You now add functionality to your application to access the user's image library, select an image, and then attach that image to your email.

Start off by adding a `UIImageView` underneath your `UITextView`, along with a `UIButton` with the label "Get Image." To make the Image View visible when no image is currently selected, change the Background color attribute to white. Additionally, to avoid drawing outside the image view's frame, check its Clip Subviews attribute in the Attributes inspector. Your view now resembles that simulated in Figure 13-4.

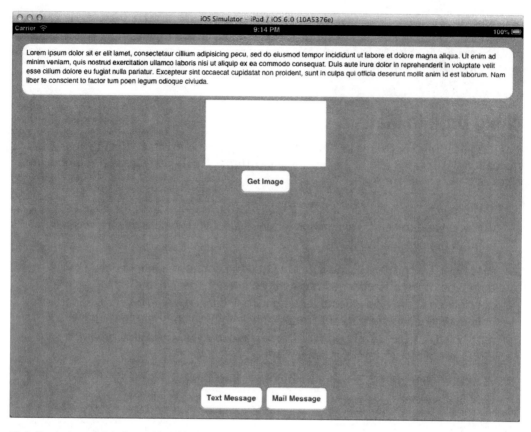

Figure 13-4. Your new user interface with ability to select an image

Create outlets for the two elements and name them `imageView` and `getImageButton` respectively. Also, create the action `getImage` for the button.

Whenever you want to access the photo library of an iPad, you need to use a `UIImagePickerController` set inside of a `UIPopoverController`. Declare a `UIPopoverController` property called popover in the main view controller's header file. You also need to instruct the view controller to conform to the `UIImagePickerControllerDelegate`, `UIPopoverControllerDelegate` and `UINavigationControllerDelegate` protocols. Overall your header file should now resemble the following:

```
//
//  ViewController.h
//  Send It Out
//

#import <UIKit/UIKit.h>
#import <QuartzCore/QuartzCore.h>
#import <MessageUI/MessageUI.h>
```

```
@interface ViewController : UIViewController<UITextViewDelegate,
    MFMessageComposeViewControllerDelegate, MFMailComposeViewControllerDelegate,
    UIImagePickerControllerDelegate, UIPopoverControllerDelegate,
    UINavigationControllerDelegate>

@property (weak, nonatomic) IBOutlet UITextView *inputTextView;
@property (weak, nonatomic) IBOutlet UIButton *textMessageButton;
@property (weak, nonatomic) IBOutlet UIButton *mailMessageButton;
@property (weak, nonatomic) IBOutlet UIImageView *imageView;
@property (weak, nonatomic) IBOutlet UIButton *getImageButton;
@property (strong, nonatomic) UIPopoverController *popover;

- (IBAction)textMessage:(id)sender;
- (IBAction)mailMessage:(id)sender;
- (IBAction)getImage:(id)sender;

@end
```

Now, you can write your getImage: method to present your popover controller with access to the photo library:

```
- (IBAction)getImage:(id)sender
{
    UIImagePickerController *picker = [[UIImagePickerController alloc] init];
    if ([UIImagePickerController
        isSourceTypeAvailable:UIImagePickerControllerSourceTypePhotoLibrary])
    {
        picker.sourceType = UIImagePickerControllerSourceTypePhotoLibrary;
        picker.delegate = self;

        self.popover =
            [[UIPopoverController alloc] initWithContentViewController:picker];
        self.popover.delegate = self;
        [self.popover presentPopoverFromRect:self.getImageButton.frame inView:self.view
            permittedArrowDirections:UIPopoverArrowDirectionAny animated:YES];
    }
}
```

Now you just need to implement your UIImagePickerControllerDelegate protocol methods.

```
-(void)imagePickerControllerDidCancel:(UIImagePickerController *)picker
{
    [self.popover dismissPopoverAnimated:YES];
}

-(void)imagePickerController:(UIImagePickerController *)picker
didFinishPickingMediaWithInfo:(NSDictionary *)info
{
    self.imageView.image = [info valueForKey:@"UIImagePickerControllerOriginalImage"];
    self.imageView.contentMode = UIViewContentModeScaleAspectFill;

    [self.popover dismissPopoverAnimated:YES];
}
```

At this point, your application can select an image and set it in your `UIImageView`. If you are testing this application in the simulator, you will need to acquire at least one image to put in your simulator's photo library. You can do this by dragging an image onto the iOS Simulator window, which launches the Safari app. Click and hold the image to save it to the library. In Figure 13-5, your app is shown with an image already selected.

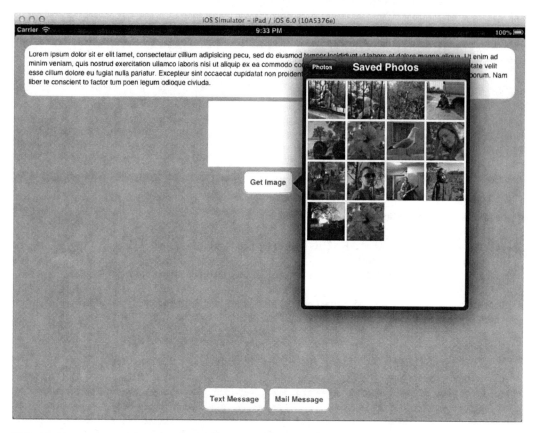

Figure 13-5. Running your app and tapping the Get Image button to attach an image to the email

Now you can continue to add the chosen image into your email. Modify your `mailPressed:` method to attach the image if one has been selected.

```
- (IBAction)mailMessage:(id)sender
{
    if ([MFMailComposeViewController canSendMail])
    {
        MFMailComposeViewController *mailVC =
            [[MFMailComposeViewController alloc] init];
        [mailVC setSubject:@"Send It Out"];
        [mailVC setToRecipients:@[@"test@example.com"]];
        [mailVC setMessageBody:self.inputTextView.text isHTML:NO];
        mailVC.mailComposeDelegate = self;
```

```
        if (self.imageView.image != nil)
        {
            NSData *imageData = UIImageJPEGRepresentation(self.imageView.image, 1.0);
            [mailVC addAttachmentData:imageData mimeType:@"image/jpeg"
                fileName:@"SelectedImage"];
        }

        [self presentViewController:mailVC animated:YES completion:nil];
    }
    else
    {
        NSLog(@"Emailing Unavailable");
    }
}
```

Finally, you can modify your MFMailComposeViewController's delegate method to reset the app if the email has been successfully sent:

```
-(void)mailComposeController:(MFMailComposeViewController *)controller
didFinishWithResult:(MFMailComposeResult)result error:(NSError *)error
{
    if (result == MFMailComposeResultSent)
    {
        self.inputTextView.text = @"Mail sent.";
        self.imageView.image = nil;
    }
    else if (result == MFMailComposeResultCancelled)
        NSLog(@"Mail Cancelled");
    else if (result == MFMailComposeResultFailed)
        NSLog(@"Error, Mail Send Failed");
    else if (result == MFMailComposeResultSaved)
        NSLog(@"Mail Saved");
    [self dismissViewControllerAnimated:YES completion:nil];
}
```

If you test the application in the simulator now and you attempt to send an email after selecting an image, you should see the chosen image placed into your message, as in Figure 13-6.

Figure 13-6. Your application composing email with an attached image

Recipe 13-3: Printing an Image

Now that you have your application set up to handle both text and images, you can continue to enhance your functionality by adding the ability to print.

Before you specifically work on printing, you will reconfigure your application's user interface a bit to include your view controller inside of a `UINavigationController` so that you can get a nice toolbar across the top. To do this, first declare a `UINavigationController` property in `AppDelegate.h`:

```
//
//  AppDelegate.h
//  Send It Out
//

#import <UIKit/UIKit.h>

@class ViewController;

@interface AppDelegate : UIResponder <UIApplicationDelegate>

@property (strong, nonatomic) UIWindow *window;
```

```
@property (strong, nonatomic) ViewController *viewController;
@property (strong, nonatomic) UINavigationController *navigationController;

@end
```

And, in AppDelegate.m, make the following changes to the application:didFinishLaunchingWithOptions method:

```
- (BOOL)application:(UIApplication *)application didFinishLaunchingWithOptions:(NSDictionary *)
launchOptions
{
    self.window = [[UIWindow alloc] initWithFrame:[[UIScreen mainScreen] bounds]];
    // Override point for customization after application launch.
    self.viewController = [[ViewController alloc] initWithNibName:@"ViewController"
        bundle:nil];
    self.navigationController = [[UINavigationController alloc]
        initWithRootViewController:self.viewController];
    self.window.rootViewController = self.navigationController;
    [self.window makeKeyAndVisible];
    return YES;
}
```

You also need to adjust the user interface to account for the Navigation bar; for example, the lower buttons in your view may be pushed off-screen. To see what changes are necessary, set the main view's .xib file "Top Bar" attribute to "Navigation Bar" in the "Simulated Metrics" section of the Attributes inspector. Go ahead and correct the layout by dragging and resizing the affected elements if necessary.

Next, add the following lines to the end of your viewDidLoad method to configure your navigation bar and add a Print button to the Navigation bar if printing is available:

```
- (void)viewDidLoad
{
    [super viewDidLoad];
    self.inputTextView.layer.cornerRadius = 15.0;
    self.inputTextView.delegate = self;
    [[NSNotificationCenter defaultCenter] addObserver:self
        selector:@selector(textMessagingAvailabilityChanged:)
        name:MFMessageComposeViewControllerTextMessageAvailabilityDidChangeNotification
        object:nil];

    self.title = @"Send It Out!";

    if ([UIPrintInteractionController isPrintingAvailable])
    {
        UIBarButtonItem *printButton = [[UIBarButtonItem alloc] initWithTitle:@"Print"
            style:UIBarButtonItemStyleBordered target:self
            action:@selector(print:)];

        self.navigationItem.rightBarButtonItem = printButton;
    }
}
```

Now, you can add the action method `print:` method in order to add your printing functionality, primarily through the use of the `UIPrintInteractionController` class. This class is your "hub" of activity when it comes to configuring print jobs. We discuss the steps to set up this class individually before seeing the method as a whole.

Whenever you want to access an instance of a `UIPrintInteractionController`, you simply call for a reference to the shared instance through the `sharedPrintController` class method.

```
UIPrintInteractionController *pic = [UIPrintInteractionController sharedPrintController];
```

Up next, you must configure the `printInfo` property of your controller, which specifies the settings for the print job.

```
UIPrintInfo *printInfo = [UIPrintInfo printInfo];
printInfo.outputType = UIPrintInfoOutputPhoto;
printInfo.jobName = self.title;
printInfo.duplex = UIPrintInfoDuplexLongEdge;
```

As you can see, you have set the `outputType` to specify an image. The three possible values for this property are as follows:

- `UIPrintInfoOutputPhoto`: Used specifically for photos to be printed
- `UIPrintInfoOutputGrayscale`: Used when dealing only with black text so as to improve performance
- `UIPrintInfoOutputGeneral`: Used for any mix of graphics and text, with or without color

You did not yet set this `printInfo` object as the `printInfo` of your controller because you will do a little bit more configuration of it shortly.

Next, you have to do an interesting specification for your `UIPrintInteractionController`. I say interesting because you absolutely have to do one, and only one, of four possible tasks:

1. Set a single item to be printed.
2. Set multiple items to be printed.
3. Specify an instance of `UIPrintFormatter` to the controller to configure the layout of your page.
4. Specify an instance of `UIPrintPageRenderer`, which can then have multiple instances of `UIPrintFormatter` assigned to it to gain full customization of your content layout over multiple pages.

Start off with the simplest option of setting a single item to be printed. This item must be either an image or a PDF file to use these simpler options, so choose to simply print your `selectedImage`.

```
UIImage *image = self.imageView.image;
pic.printingItem = image;
```

Now that you know what you want to print, you can check the orientation of the image and configure your `printInfo` accordingly.

```
if (!pic.printingItem && image.size.width > image.size.height)
    printInfo.orientation = UIPrintInfoOrientationLandscape;

pic.printInfo = printInfo;
pic.showsPageRange = YES;
```

Finally, present your `UIPrintInteractionController`. This class is equipped with three different methods for presenting itself, depending on your specific implementation:

- `presentFromBarButtonItem:animated:completionHandler::` If you are writing for an iPad, this method is designed for use when the application's Print button is placed in a toolbar, such as in this recipe.

- `presentFromRect:inView:animated:completionHandler::` This method is also only for use with the iPad, but allows you to present the controller from any part of the view. Usually, the rect specified will be the frame of your Print button, wherever it is located.

- `presentAnimated:completionHandler::` This method should be used whenever implementing printing on an iPhone due to the smaller screen.

With this final method call, your `print:` method in its entirety will look like so:

```
-(void)print:(id)sender
{
    if ([UIPrintInteractionController isPrintingAvailable]
        && (self.imageView.image != nil))
    {
        UIPrintInteractionController *pic =
            [UIPrintInteractionController sharedPrintController];

        UIPrintInfo *printInfo = [UIPrintInfo printInfo];
        printInfo.outputType = UIPrintInfoOutputPhoto;
        printInfo.jobName = self.title;
        printInfo.duplex = UIPrintInfoDuplexLongEdge;

        UIImage *image = self.imageView.image;
        pic.printingItem = image;

        if (!pic.printingItem && image.size.width> image.size.height)
            printInfo.orientation = UIPrintInfoOrientationLandscape;

        pic.printInfo = printInfo;
        pic.showsPageRange = YES;

        [pic presentFromBarButtonItem:sender animated:YES completionHandler:
         ^(UIPrintInteractionController *printInteractionController, BOOL completed,
             NSError *error)
         {
             if (!completed && (error != nil))
             {
                 NSLog(@"Error Printing: %@", error);
             }
```

```
        else
        {
            NSLog(@"Cancelled Printing");
        }
    }];
  }
}
```

Now when you run your application and select an image, you can print the image by tapping the Print button. This presents a small controller from which you can select a printer and further configure your specific print job. Unfortunately, if you're testing this in your simulator or don't have any wireless printers set up, you won't see any available printers to use, as shown in Figure 13-7.

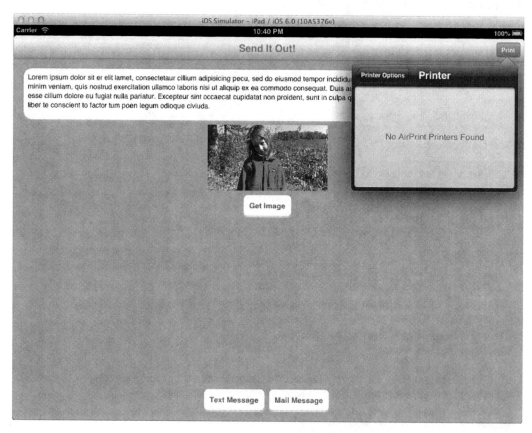

Figure 13-7. Your app with a new Print button, unable to find any AirPrint printers

Luckily, Xcode comes with a fantastic application called Printer Simulator. With this program, you can fully simulate print jobs from your app. It even gives you a PDF file of your simulated output, so you can see exactly how your image would have turned out without wasting any paper!

To run this program, open the Application folder (or the folder in which Xcode resides on your computer) in a Finder window; Ctrl-click Xcode and choose Show Package Contents as Figure 13-8 shows. Then, navigate to Contents/Applications and click the Printer Simulator.app file.

Figure 13-8. Showing the packaged content of the Xcode bundle

On running the Printer Simulator application, a variety of printer types are automatically registered for use. The simulator looks similar to Figure 13-9.

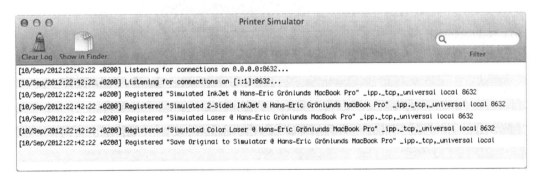

Figure 13-9. Printer Simulator registering multiple types of printers to simulate

Now, on testing your application, you should see different types of simulated printers with which to test your application. You can now choose one of the simulated printers from your app, as in Figure 13-10.

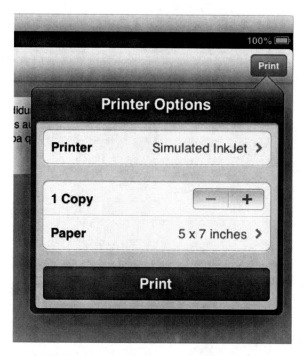

Figure 13-10. *Selecting a simulated inkjet printer from your app*

After you have selected a printer, you can print multiple copies as well as change the paper type before you print. After you tap the Print button, you should start seeing activity in your Printer Simulator, and shortly afterward, a PDF file opens with your final printout, resembling that shown in Figure 13-11.

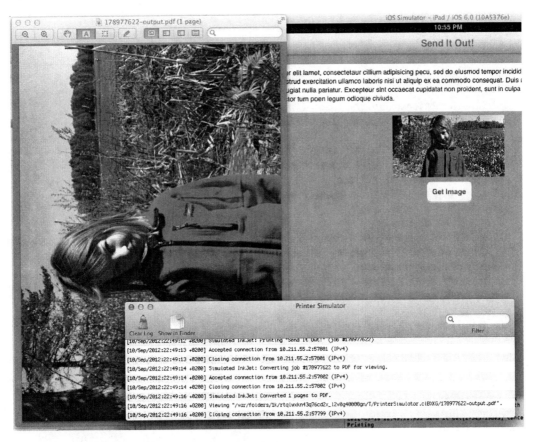

Figure 13-11. Output of printing an image from a simulated printer

Recipe 13-4: Printing Plain Text

Expanding on your previous recipe, you will add functionality to make use of a print formatter to allow you to print simple text.

First, modify your `viewDidLoad` method to add an extra button to print the text in your `UITextView`. Change the condition statement in the method to look like so:

```
if ([UIPrintInteractionController isPrintingAvailable])
{
    UIBarButtonItem *printButton =
        [[UIBarButtonItem alloc] initWithTitle:@"Print Image"
            style:UIBarButtonItemStyleBordered target:self action:@selector(print:)];
    UIBarButtonItem *printTextButton =
        [[UIBarButtonItem alloc] initWithTitle:@"Print Text"
            style:UIBarButtonItemStyleBordered target:self
            action:@selector(printText:)];

    self.navigationItem.rightBarButtonItems = @[printButton, printTextButton];
}
```

The new selector to print your text is then implemented as follows:

```
-(void)printText:(id)sender
{
    if ([UIPrintInteractionController isPrintingAvailable])
    {
        UIPrintInteractionController *pic =
            [UIPrintInteractionController sharedPrintController];

        UIPrintInfo *printInfo = [UIPrintInfo printInfo];
        printInfo.outputType = UIPrintInfoOutputGeneral;
        printInfo.jobName = self.title;
        printInfo.duplex = UIPrintInfoDuplexLongEdge;
        pic.printInfo = printInfo;

        UISimpleTextPrintFormatter *simpleTextPF =
            [[UISimpleTextPrintFormatter alloc] initWithText:self.inputTextView.text];
        simpleTextPF.startPage = 0;
        simpleTextPF.contentInsets = UIEdgeInsetsMake(72.0, 72.0, 72.0, 72.0);
        simpleTextPF.maximumContentWidth = 6*72.0;

        pic.printFormatter = simpleTextPF;

        pic.showsPageRange = YES;

        [pic presentFromBarButtonItem:sender animated:YES
            completionHandler:
        ^(UIPrintInteractionController *printInteractionController, BOOL completed,
            NSError *error)
        {
            if (!completed && (error != nil))
            {
                NSLog(@"Error Printing: %@", error);
            }
            else
            {
                NSLog(@"Printing Cancelled");
            }
        }];
    }
}
```

There are two main differences between this method and its predecessor:

1. The outputType property in your UIPrintInfo is modified to the
   UIPrintInfoOutputGeneral value, because you are no longer printing photos.

2. Instead of setting a UIImage to the printingItem property, you set an
   instance of UISimpleTextPrintFormatter to the printFormatter property.
   This object is initialized with the desired text, and then configured through its
   properties.

a. Values of 72.0 as insets translate to 1 inch, so you have given your output 1-inch insets, and specified a 6-inch width for your content.

b. The `startPage` property is used more at a later point, but allows you to specify the page in your job for your formatter to be applied to.

> **Tip**   When printing simple text, it is also quite easy to apply the preceding method to printing HTML-formatted text. To do this, simply make use of a `UIMarkupTextPrintFormatter` instead of a `UISimpleTextPrintFormatter`.

Just as before, by using the Printer Simulator, you can generate your test output. Because you set your text view's text as the content of your print formatter, you simply get a document with some Lorem Ipsum text in it, as in Figure 13-12.

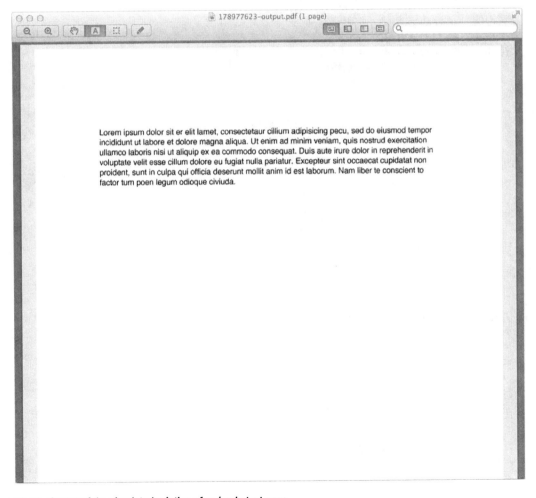

Figure 13-12. Output of the simulated printing of a simple text page

Recipe 13-5: Printing a View

This recipe builds on Recipe 13-4.

Just as you can print text using a UISimpleTextPrintFormatter, you can print the contents of a view using another subclass of UIPrintFormatter: UIViewPrintFormatter.

Start by modifying your viewDidLoad's (in ViewController.m) conditional setup to now appear like so:

```
if ([UIPrintInteractionController isPrintingAvailable])
{
    UIBarButtonItem *printButton =
        [[UIBarButtonItem alloc] initWithTitle:@"Print Image"
        style:UIBarButtonItemStyleBordered target:self action:@selector(print:)];

    UIBarButtonItem *printTextButton =
        [[UIBarButtonItem alloc] initWithTitle:@"Print Text"
            style:UIBarButtonItemStyleBordered target:self
            action:@selector(printText:)];

    UIBarButtonItem *printViewButton =
        [[UIBarButtonItem alloc] initWithTitle:@"Print View"
            style:UIBarButtonItemStyleBordered target:self
            action:@selector(printViewPressed:)];

    self.navigationItem.rightBarButtonItems =
        @[printButton, printTextButton, printViewButton];
}
```

Your newest printing method, printView:, closely resembles your previous one, with the key change of using a UIViewPrintFormatter.

```
-(void)printViewPressed:(id)sender
{
    if ([UIPrintInteractionController isPrintingAvailable])
    {
        UIPrintInteractionController *pic =
            [UIPrintInteractionController sharedPrintController];

        UIPrintInfo *printInfo = [UIPrintInfo printInfo];
        printInfo.outputType = UIPrintInfoOutputGeneral;
        printInfo.jobName = self.title;
        printInfo.duplex = UIPrintInfoDuplexLongEdge;
        printInfo.orientation = UIPrintInfoOrientationLandscape;
        pic.printInfo = printInfo;

        UIViewPrintFormatter *viewPF = [self.inputTextView viewPrintFormatter];

        pic.printFormatter = viewPF;
        pic.showsPageRange = YES;

        [pic presentFromBarButtonItem:sender animated:YES
            completionHandler:
```

```
    ^(UIPrintInteractionController *printInteractionController, BOOL completed,
       NSError *error)
    {
        if (!completed && (error != nil))
        {
            NSLog(@"Error Printing View: %@", error);
        }
        else
        {
            NSLog(@"Printing Cancelled");
        }
    }];
    }
}
```

Unfortunately, the UIViewPrintFormatter is, at the moment, currently configured only to provide printing views of three system views: UITextView, UIWebView, and MKMapView. Because your application makes use of only one of these, you simply have it print your UITextView's view, resulting in an output like that in Figure 13-13.

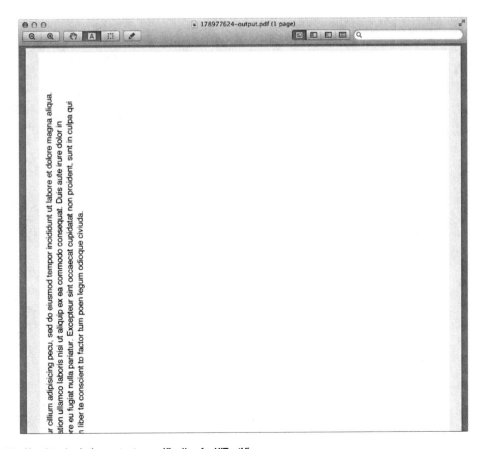

Figure 13-13. *Simulated printing output, specifically of a UITextView*

Despite the `UIViewPrintFormatter`'s limitations, it can provide an easy way to print the contents of any text, map, or web page.

Recipe 13-6: Formatted Printing with Page Renderers

A *page renderer* is essentially what allows you to fully customize the content of any print job. It allows you to not only format multiple pages with different print formatters, but also draw custom content in the header, body, and footer of any page.

To use a page renderer, you must create a custom subclass of the `UIPrintPageRenderer` class, from which you can override methods to customize the content of your printing job.

Create a new file, using the Objective-C class template. When you enter your filename of `SendItOutPageRenderer`, be sure that the file is a subclass of `UIPrintPageRenderer`, as in Figure 13-14.

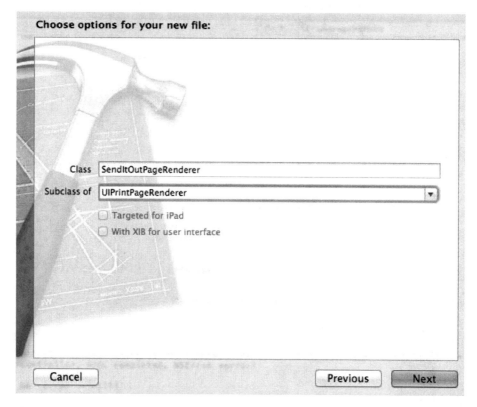

Figure 13-14. Creating a UIPrintPageRenderer subclass

Click through to create your new file.

Next, define two NSString properties, title and author, in the header of your renderer.

```
//
// SendItOutPageRenderer.h
// Send It Out
//

#import <UIKit/UIKit.h>

@interface SendItOutPageRenderer : UIPrintPageRenderer

@property (nonatomic, strong) NSString *title;
@property (nonatomic, strong) NSString *author;

@end
```

To customize the layout of your specific page renderer, you can override methods inherited from the UIPrintPageRenderer class. The way that this class is set up is that the drawPageAtIndex:inRect: method then calls four other methods:

- drawHeaderForPageAtIndex:inRect:: Used to specify header content; if the headerHeight property of the renderer is zero, this method will not be called.

- drawContentForPageAtIndex:inRect:: Draws custom content within the page's content rectangle.

- drawFooterForPageAtIndex:inRect:: Specifies footer content; this method will also not be called if the renderer's footerHeight property is zero.

- drawPrintFormatter:forPageAtIndex:: Uses a combination of print formatters and custom content to overlay or fill in a view.

You can override any of these five methods (including drawPageAtIndex:inRect:) to customize your printing content. In your case, you override the header, footer, and print-formatter methods.

You have your header print the document's author on the left, and the title on the right. Your method then looks like so:

```
- (void)drawHeaderForPageAtIndex:(NSInteger)pageIndex  inRect:(CGRect)headerRect
{
if (pageIndex != 0)
    {
        UIFont *font = [UIFont fontWithName:@"Helvetica" size:12.0];
        CGSize titleSize = [self.title sizeWithFont:font];

        CGFloat drawXTitle = CGRectGetMaxX(headerRect) - titleSize.width;
        CGFloat drawXAuthor = CGRectGetMinX(headerRect);
        CGFloat drawY = CGRectGetMinY(headerRect);
        CGPoint drawPointAuthor = CGPointMake(drawXAuthor, drawY);
        CGPoint drawPointTitle = CGPointMake(drawXTitle, drawY);
```

```
        [self.title drawAtPoint:drawPointTitle withFont:font];
        [self.author drawAtPoint:drawPointAuthor withFont:font];
    }
}
```

Your footer-implementation method looks similar, and prints a centered page number. Because the page indexes start with 0, you must remember to increment all your values by 1.

```
- (void)drawFooterForPageAtIndex:(NSInteger)pageIndex inRect:(CGRect)footerRect
{
    UIFont *font = [UIFont fontWithName:@"Helvetica" size:12.0];
    NSString *pageNumber = [NSString stringWithFormat:@"%d.", pageIndex+1];

    CGSize pageNumSize = [pageNumber sizeWithFont:font];
    CGFloat drawX = CGRectGetMaxX(footerRect)/2.0 - pageNumSize.width - 1.0;
    CGFloat drawY = CGRectGetMaxY(footerRect) - pageNumSize.height;
    CGPoint drawPoint = CGPointMake(drawX, drawY);
    [pageNumber drawAtPoint:drawPoint withFont:font];
}
```

Finally, to deal with interlaced print formatters, you implement the drawPrintFormatter:forPageAtIndex: method to overlay a simple text over your view. This could easily be used to place some kind of "Proprietary Content" label over images or documents in a more targeted application.

```
-(void)drawPrintFormatter:(UIPrintFormatter *)printFormatter forPageAtIndex:(NSInteger)pageIndex
{
    CGRect contentRect = CGRectMake(self.printableRect.origin.x,
        self.printableRect.origin.y+self.headerHeight, self.printableRect.size.width,
        self.printableRect.size.height-self.headerHeight-self.footerHeight);
    [printFormatter drawInRect:contentRect forPageAtIndex:pageIndex];

    NSString *overlayText = @"Overlay Text";
    UIFont *font = [UIFont fontWithName:@"Helvetica"size:26.0];
    CGSize overlaySize = [overlayText sizeWithFont:font];

    CGFloat xCenter = CGRectGetMaxX(self.printableRect)/2.0 - overlaySize.width/2.0;
    CGFloat yCenter = CGRectGetMaxY(self.printableRect)/2.0 - overlaySize.height/2.0;
    CGPoint overlayPoint = CGPointMake(xCenter, yCenter);

    [overlayText drawAtPoint:overlayPoint withFont:font];
}
```

In this method, it is important to note that you must draw the content of each printFormatter manually using its own drawInRect:forPageAtIndex: method. To avoid covering your header or footer, you specified a drawing area restricted by the headerHeight and footerHeight.

Now, back in your main view controller, be sure to import the newly created SendItOutPageRenderer.h file.

```
#import "SendItOutPageRenderer.h"
```

Add a final extra `UIBarButtonItem` to present a Print Custom option to your user. Including all functions from your previous recipes, your `viewDidLoad` method should now read like so:

```objc
- (void)viewDidLoad
{
    [super viewDidLoad];
    self.inputTextView.layer.cornerRadius = 15.0;
    self.inputTextView.delegate = self;
    [[NSNotificationCenter defaultCenter] addObserver:self
        selector:@selector(textMessagingAvailabilityChanged:)
        name:MFMessageComposeViewControllerTextMessageAvailabilityDidChangeNotification
        object:nil];

    self.title = @"Send It Out!";

    if ([UIPrintInteractionController isPrintingAvailable])
    {
        UIBarButtonItem *printButton =
            [[UIBarButtonItem alloc] initWithTitle:@"Print Image"
                style:UIBarButtonItemStyleBordered target:self
                action:@selector(print:)];

        UIBarButtonItem *printTextButton =
            [[UIBarButtonItem alloc] initWithTitle:@"Print Text"
                style:UIBarButtonItemStyleBordered target:self
                action:@selector(printText:)];

        UIBarButtonItem *printViewButton =
            [[UIBarButtonItem alloc] initWithTitle:@"Print View"
                style:UIBarButtonItemStyleBordered target:self
                action:@selector(printViewPressed:)];

        UIBarButtonItem *printCustomButton =
            [[UIBarButtonItem alloc] initWithTitle:@"Print Custom"
                style:UIBarButtonItemStyleBordered target:self
                action:@selector(printCustom:)];

        self.navigationItem.rightBarButtonItems = @[printButton, printTextButton,
            printViewButton, printCustomButton];
    }
}
```

Finally, you can implement your `printCustom:` action method:

```objc
-(void)printCustom:(id)sender
{
    if ([UIPrintInteractionController isPrintingAvailable])
    {
        UIPrintInteractionController *pic =
            [UIPrintInteractionController sharedPrintController];

        UIPrintInfo *printInfo = [UIPrintInfo printInfo];
        printInfo.outputType = UIPrintInfoOutputGeneral;
```

```
    printInfo.jobName = self.title;
    printInfo.duplex = UIPrintInfoDuplexLongEdge;
    printInfo.orientation = UIPrintInfoOrientationPortrait;
    pic.printInfo = printInfo;

    UISimpleTextPrintFormatter *simplePF =
        [[UISimpleTextPrintFormatter alloc] initWithText:[self.inputTextView.text
            stringByAppendingString:@"THIS TEXT IS MY FIRST PAGE"]];
    UIViewPrintFormatter *viewPF = [self.inputTextView viewPrintFormatter];

    SendItOutPageRenderer *sendPR = [[SendItOutPageRenderer alloc] init];
    sendPR.title = @"My Print Job Title";
    sendPR.author = @"Document Author";
    sendPR.headerHeight = 72.0/2;
    sendPR.footerHeight = 72.0/2;
    [sendPR addPrintFormatter:simplePF startingAtPageAtIndex:0];
    [sendPR addPrintFormatter:viewPF startingAtPageAtIndex:1];

    pic.printPageRenderer = sendPR;

    pic.showsPageRange = YES;

    [pic presentFromBarButtonItem:sender animated:YES
        completionHandler:
    ^(UIPrintInteractionController *printInteractionController, BOOL completed,
        NSError *error)
    {
        if (!completed && (error != nil))
        {
            NSLog(@"Error Printing: %@", error);
        }
        else
        {
            NSLog(@"Printing Cancelled");
        }
    }];
    }
}
```

This method includes the following extra steps from your previous recipe:

1. Create multiple print formatters to be given to different pages. Because you do not have a UIWebView or MKMapView in this application, you have simply chosen to print your UITextView's text, as well as its overall view.

2. Create an instance of your SendItOutPageRenderer class, and configure it with a title, author, headerHeight, and footerHeight. If you did not specify the last two of these, your header and footer customization methods would not be called.

3. Add your print formatters to your page renderer, and assign this renderer to your UIPrintInteractionController.

On testing this new functionality, your output is a two-page text document, complete with simple headers, footers, and even a text overlay, as shown in Figure 13-15.

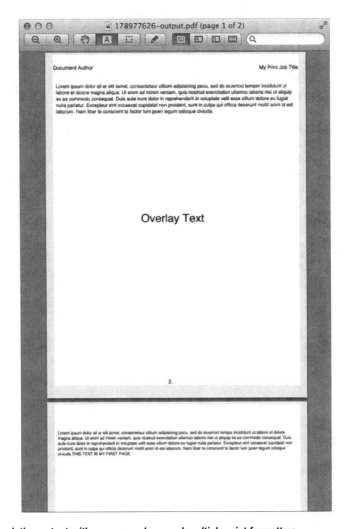

Figure 13-15. Simulated printing output with a page renderer and multiple print formatters

Due to the simplicity of your application, the screenshot in Figure 13-14 may not look like much, but considering your application of custom headers, footers, overlay content, and page formatters, it actually gives a very good representation of the power of making use of a page renderer for printing when striving for ideal customizations.

Summary

When creating your applications, you are responsible to always have the user in mind. Every single aspect of your application should be designed to both allow and help the user to accomplish a goal, and each aspect should then be optimized to expedite these goals. Functionalities to transmit data, such as sending text messages, constructing emails, or creating printouts, tend to be overlooked as unnecessary in this process, and most often erroneously. Developers must always be careful to think from the user's standpoint, and imagine what a user could do with any given feature. The simple possibility of printing content for later use, or being able to easily email an interesting image to a friend, could be the dividing line between what makes a customer buy your app over someone else's. By understanding and utilizing these "extra" functionalities, you can drastically improve the functionality of your applications to better serve your end users.

Chapter 14

Game Kit Recipes

Game Center is an iOS service that increases the "replay factor" of your games. It provides an easy way to implement features such as leaderboards, game achievements tracking and multiplayer gameplay, which can greatly enhance the social aspect of the games you make.

In this chapter, we'll go through some of the basics of the Game Kit framework, which is what you use to make your games Game Center aware.

Recipe 14-1: Making Your App Game Center Aware

In this recipe you create a very simple game and connect it to Game Center. The game consists of four buttons. When the player taps a button, one of two things may happen: It's either a "safe" button in which case the player's score is increased by one and he or she is allowed to continue the game; or, it's a "killer" button, which ends the game. Because the player has no way to know which button is which, there's no skill involved and thus not much of a game. However, it's easy to implement and therefore a good platform to show some of the basic features of Game Center.

> **Note** When creating a Game Center–aware game, it's always a good idea to implement the game first and be sure it works properly before involving Game Center.

Implementing the Game

Start by creating a new single-view app project with the name "Lucky."

The game has three difficulty levels: Easy game, where only one of the four buttons is a "killer" button; Normal game with two "killer" buttons; and Hard game, with three of the buttons being "killers."

You set up the main view of the app to be a menu page with options to start a game with one of those levels. Open the `ViewController.xib` file and build a user interface that resembles the one in Figure 14-1.

Figure 14-1. The main menu view of the Lucky game

Create an outlet named welcomeLabel for the label, and actions named playEasyGame, playNormalGame, and playHardGame for when the user taps the respective button.

Now, before you move on to add and implement a view controller for the actual game, you'll make this a navigation-based app with a Navigation bar. Start by adding the following property declaration to the AppDelegate.h file:

```
//
//  AppDelegate.h
//  Testing Game Center
//

#import <UIKit/UIKit.h>

@class ViewController;

@interface AppDelegate : UIResponder <UIApplicationDelegate>

@property (strong, nonatomic) UIWindow *window;

@property (strong, nonatomic) ViewController *viewController;
@property (strong, nonatomic) UINavigationController *navigationController;

@end
```

Then go to AppDelegate.m and make the following changes to the application:didFinishLaunchingWithOptions: method:

```
- (BOOL)application:(UIApplication *)application didFinishLaunchingWithOptions:(NSDictionary
*)launchOptions
{
    self.window = [[UIWindow alloc] initWithFrame:[[UIScreen mainScreen] bounds]];
    // Override point for customization after application launch.
    self.viewController =
        [[ViewController alloc] initWithNibName:@"ViewController" bundle:nil];
    self.navigationController =
        [[UINavigationController alloc] initWithRootViewController:self.viewController];
    self.window.rootViewController = self.navigationController;
    [self.window makeKeyAndVisible];
    return YES;
}
```

Finally, set the title of the main view controller to "Lucky," and change the text of the Welcome label. Go to ViewController.m and add the following code to the viewDidLoad method:

```
- (void)viewDidLoad
{
    [super viewDidLoad];

    self.title = @"Lucky";
    self.welcomeLabel.text = @"Welcome Anonymous Player";
}
```

Build and run the app to be sure everything is okay so far; you should see a screen resembling the one in Figure 14-2.

Figure 14-2. The Lucky game has three levels

Now you're going to add the view controller in which the actual gameplay will take place. Create a new UIViewController subclass with the name GameViewController and make sure the "With XIB for user interface" option is checked.

Go ahead and create a user interface that resembles Figure 14-3 for the new view controller.

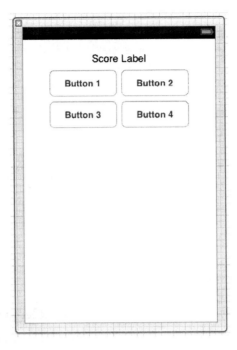

Figure 14-3. The user interface of the Lucky game

Create the following outlets for the added user interface elements:

- scoreLabel

- button1

- button2

- button3

- button4

For the buttons, also create an action that is shared by all the buttons and invoked when the user taps any one of them. To do that, start by creating an action named gameButtonSelected for Button 1. Be sure you use the specific type of UIButton for the method argument, as shown in Figure 14-4.

Figure 14-4. Creating an action with a specific type parameter

Now, connect the remaining buttons to the same action that you created for Button 1. You do this by Ctrl-clicking the button to be connected, and dragging the blue line onto the `gameButtonSelected` action declaration. When a Connect Action sign appears, as in Figure 14-5, you can release the mouse button and the action will become connected to the button.

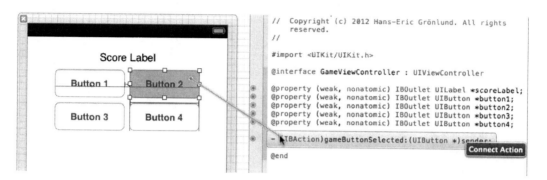

Figure 14-5. *Connecting a button to an existing IBAction*

Be sure to connect all the remaining buttons to the `gameButtonSelected` action.

With the user interface elements properly connected to the code, you can move on to add some necessary declarations to the game view controller's header file. You need an initializer method, a couple of private instance variables, and you need the view controller to conform to the `UIAlertViewDelegate` protocol. So go to `GameViewController.h` and add the following code:

```
//
//  GameViewController.h
//  Lucky
//

#import <UIKit/UIKit.h>
#import <GameKit/GameKit.h>

@interface GameViewController : UIViewController<UIAlertViewDelegate>
{
    @private
    int _score;
    int _level;
}

@property (weak, nonatomic) IBOutlet UILabel *scoreLabel;
@property (weak, nonatomic) IBOutlet UIButton *button1;
@property (weak, nonatomic) IBOutlet UIButton *button2;
@property (weak, nonatomic) IBOutlet UIButton *button3;
@property (weak, nonatomic) IBOutlet UIButton *button4;
```

```
- (IBAction)gameButtonSelected:(UIButton *)sender;

- (id)initWithLevel:(int)level;

@end
```

Now, go to GameViewController.m to start implementing the initializing code. First, add the following implementation of the initializer method:

```
- (id)initWithLevel:(int)level
{
    self = [super initWithNibName:nil bundle:nil];
    if (self)
    {
        _level = level;
        _score = 0;
    }
    return self;
}
```

Next, add the following helper method for updating the score label:

```
- (void)updateScoreLabel
{
    self.scoreLabel.text = [NSString stringWithFormat:@"Score: %i", _score];
}
```

Finally, add the following code to the viewDidLoad method to set up the title and update the score label on game launch:

```
- (void)viewDidLoad
{
    [super viewDidLoad];

    switch (_level)
    {
        case 0:
            self.title = @"Easy Game";
            break;
        case 1:
            self.title = @"Normal Game";
            break;
        case 2:
            self.title = @"Hard Game";
            break;

        default:
            break;
    }

    [self updateScoreLabel];
}
```

Now pause the implementation of the game controller and go back to the main menu controller to connect the two view controllers. Start by adding the following import statement to the ViewController.h file:

```
//
//   ViewController.h
//   Lucky
//

#import <UIKit/UIKit.h>
#import "GameViewController.h"

@interface ViewController : UIViewController

@property (weak, nonatomic) IBOutlet UILabel *welcomeLabel;

- (IBAction)playEasyGame:(id)sender;
- (IBAction)playNormalGame:(id)sender;
- (IBAction)playHardGame:(id)sender;

@end
```

Now switch to ViewController.m. To avoid some code duplication, add the following helper method that will take a level argument and instantiate and display a game view controller:

```
- (void)playGameWithLevel:(int)level
{
    GameViewController *gameViewController =
        [[GameViewController alloc] initWithLevel:level];
    [self.navigationController pushViewController:gameViewController animated:YES];
}
```

You can now use this helper method to invoke a game of the respective level from the three action methods, like so:

```
- (IBAction)playEasyGame:(id)sender
{
    [self playGameWithLevel:0];
}

- (IBAction)playNormalGame:(id)sender
{
    [self playGameWithLevel:1];
}

- (IBAction)playHardGame:(id)sender
{
    [self playGameWithLevel:2];
}
```

Now is a good time to again build and run your app. If you've followed the steps correctly, you should be able to tap any of the three buttons in the menu view and have the game view presented, as in Figure 14-6.

Figure 14-6. The screen of an easy level of the Lucky game

With the main architecture of the app all set up, you can move on to implement the gameplay functionality. Start by initializing the buttons to be either "killer" or "safe" buttons. Go back to GameViewController.m and add the following line to the viewDidLoad method:

```
- (void)viewDidLoad
{
    [super viewDidLoad];

    // ...

    [self updateScoreLabel];
    [self setupButtons];
}
```

Note that you implement this piece of code top-down meaning you add code that invokes helper methods that do not yet exist. Don't worry about the compiler errors, as they clear out as you add the missing methods. Now, implement the setupButtons helper method. It simply delegates the job to three specific methods, one for each level, like so:

```
- (void)setupButtons
{
    switch (_level) {
        case 0:
            [self setupButtonsForEasyGame];
            break;
        case 1:
            [self setupButtonsForNormalGame];
            break;
        case 2:
            [self setupButtonsForHardGame];
            break;

        default:
            break;
    }
}
```

Next, implement the setup method for an Easy level game. An easy game sets up only one of the four buttons to be a "killer." To indicate a "killer" button, use the tag property; a zero (0) means "safe" while a one (1) indicates "killer." Here is the implementation:

```
- (void)setupButtonsForEasyGame
{
    [self resetButtonTags];
    int killerButtonIndex = rand() % 4;
    [self buttonForIndex:killerButtonIndex].tag = 1;
}
```

As you can see, this method resets the button's tag property and picks a random button to make a "killer." It makes use of two helper methods that have not yet been created, resetButtonTags and buttonForIndex:. Let's start with resetButtonTags. It iterates over the four buttons and sets their tag property to 0:

```
- (void)resetButtonTags
{
    for (int i = 0; i < 4; i++)
    {
        UIButton *button = [self buttonForIndex:i];
        button.tag = 0;
    }
}
```

This method also makes use of the `buttonForIndex:` helper method. So go ahead and add it with the following implementation:

```
- (UIButton *)buttonForIndex:(int)index
{
    switch (index)
    {
        case 0:
            return self.button1;
        case 1:
            return self.button2;
        case 2:
            return self.button3;
        case 3:
            return self.button4;
        default:
            return nil;
    }
}
```

Now, let's turn to setting up a Normal game. It's like an Easy game except that it selects two "killer" buttons; implementation as follows:

```
- (void)setupButtonsForNormalGame
{
    [self resetButtonTags];
    int killerButtonIndex1 = rand() % 4;
    int killerButtonIndex2;
    do {
        killerButtonIndex2 = rand() % 4;
    } while (killerButtonIndex1 == killerButtonIndex2);

    [self buttonForIndex:killerButtonIndex1].tag = 1;
    [self buttonForIndex:killerButtonIndex2].tag = 1;
}
```

Finally, the set up method for a Hard game, where all but one button are "killers."

```
- (void)setupButtonsForHardGame
{
    int safeButtonIndex = rand() % 4;
    for (int i=0; i < 4; i++) {
        if (i == safeButtonIndex) {
            [self buttonForIndex:i].tag = 0;
        }
        else
        {
            [self buttonForIndex:i].tag = 1;
        }
    }
}
```

What's left now is to implement the gameButtonSelected: action method. It checks the tag property of the sending button to see whether it is a "killer" or a "safe" button. If it's "safe", the score will be increased and new "killers" will be picked. On the other hand, if it's a "killer" the game is finished and an alert will be displayed showing the final score. Here is the complete implementation:

```
- (IBAction)gameButtonSelected:(UIButton *)sender
{
    if (sender.tag == 0)
    {
        // Safe, continue game
        _score += 1;
        [self updatfeScoreLabel];
        [self setupButtons];
    }
    else
    {
        // Game Over
        NSString *message = [NSString stringWithFormat:@"Your score was %i.", _score];
        UIAlertView *gameOverAlert = [[UIAlertView alloc] initWithTitle:@"Game Over"
            message:message delegate:self cancelButtonTitle:@"OK"
            otherButtonTitles:nil];
        [gameOverAlert show];
    }
}
```

The only thing remaining now until the basics of the game are complete, is to take the user back to the menu screen when the game is over and the user has dismissed the alert view. Do this by adding the following delegate method:

```
- (void)alertView:(UIAlertView *)alertView didDismissWithButtonIndex:(NSInteger)buttonIndex
{
    [self.navigationController popViewControllerAnimated:YES];
}
```

The game is now finished, so go ahead and test it. You should be able to choose between an Easy, Normal, and Hard game and play until you hit a "killer" button. Figure 14-7 shows an Easy level finished game.

Figure 14-7. A player has hit a "killer" button in a game of Lucky

With the game in place and working, you can turn your focus to making it Game Center aware.

Registering with iTunes Connect

Normally when you develop an iOS app, registering with iTunes Connect is the last step before publishing to the App Store. With Game Center aware apps, this is a bit different. With a Game Center aware app, you must register the app as soon as you are ready to start developing the Game Center–specific functions.

Once you've registered, and marked the app as Game Center aware, iTunes Connect sets up a Game Center sandbox for your app. The *Game Center sandbox* is a development area where you can test the Game Center integration without impacting production scores or achievements.

The first step to enabling Game Center integration is to create a bundle identifier in the iOS Provisioning Portal. The *bundle identifier* is used to identify all the related data for an app. For instance, if you have a free and a paid version of your game and you want them to use the same high score tables, you would give them the same bundle identifier.

Start by logging in to the iOS Dev Center portal (developer.apple.com/devcenter/ios) and click on the iOS Provisioning Portal link. In there, go to the App IDs page and click the New App ID button. For the description, enter **Lucky** and as Bundle Identifier, use your project's bundle identifier, which can be found on the Summary page in the Target settings editor. Figure 14-8 shows the configuration. (Your bundle identifier will of course be different.)

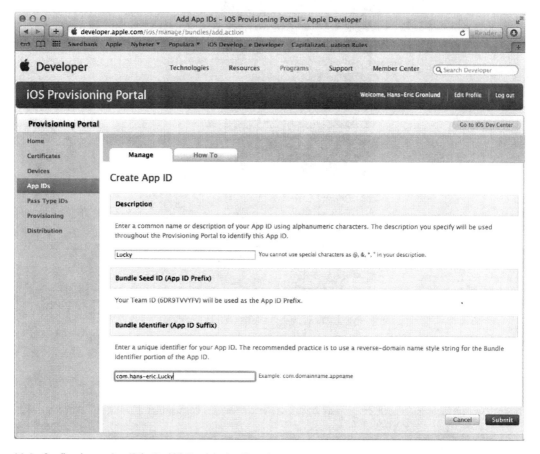

Figure 14-8. Configuring an App ID in the iOS Provisioning Portal

Now that you have registered the app with the iOS Provisioning Portal, you can move on to make a corresponding registration with iTunes Connect. Go to itunesconnect.apple.com and log in using your Developer ID. Now, click the Manage Your Applications link and then the Add New App button. Follow the instructions, and when you reach the page titled App Information, enter the information in Figure 14-9, except for the app name, which needs to be unique and not used by any other developer. You could try using your initials as a prefix, as we did in the figure.

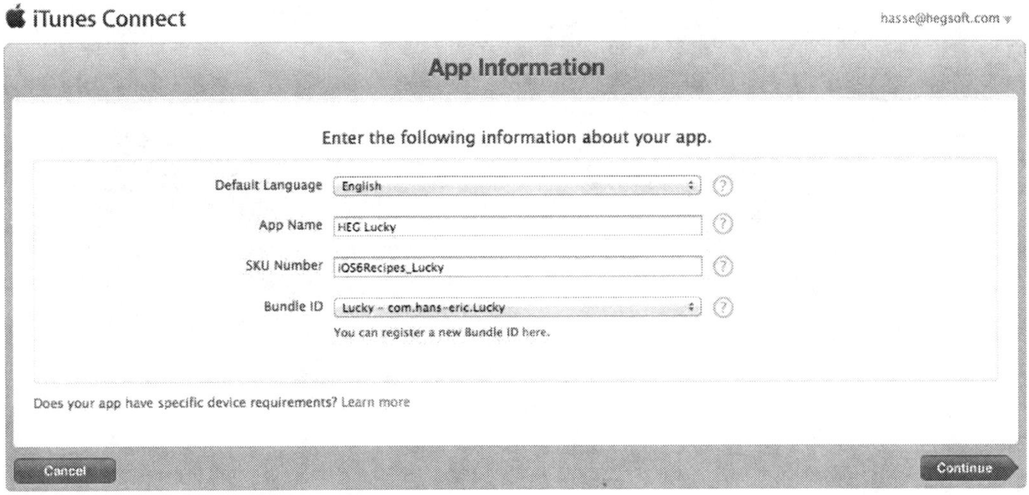

Figure 14-9. Entering application information in iTunes Connect

Continue to fill out the required metadata information about your app. You also need to upload a screenshot and a large app icon. To save time, you can download the images from Source Code/ Downloads on this book's page at www.apress.com. The required files are

- `Lucky Large App Icon.jpg`
- `Lucky Screenshot.png`
- `Lucky Screenshot (iPhone 5).png`

When you're done filling out the required information, click Save. At this point you'll see a page resembling the one in Figure 14-10.

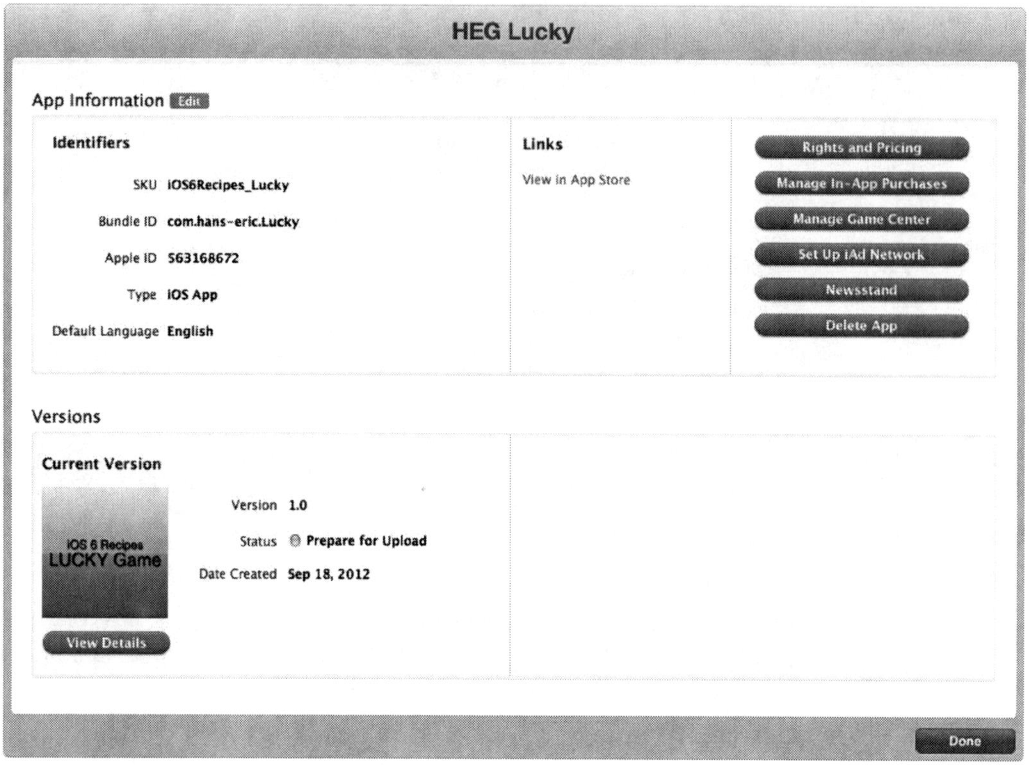

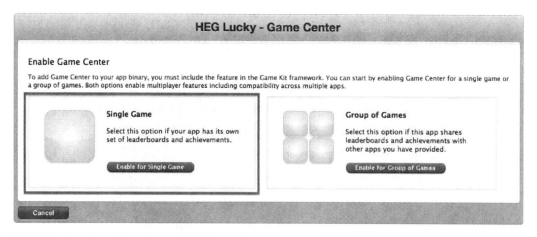

Figure 14-10. An app registered with iTunes Connect

Now, click the Manage Game Center button on the right side of the page. In the Enable Game Center page, click the Enable for Single Game button, as shown in Figure 14-11.

Figure 14-11. Enabling Game Center for an app in iTunes Connect

You're now done with the registration. Later you get back to iTunes Connect to configure leaderboards and achievements, but for now return to your Xcode project to set up the basic Game Center support.

Authenticating Local Player

With the Game Center sandbox enabled, you can go back to Xcode to implement Game Center support in the app. Your app checks whether Game Center is available and allows the user to sign in if she hasn't already done so.

Start by adding the Game Kit framework to your project. Because you want the game to work without Game Center support, make this link optional, as shown in Figure 14-12.

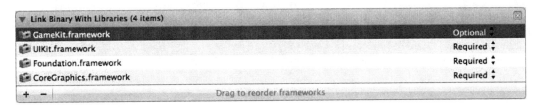

Figure 14-12. *Configuring the Game Kit framework to be optional*

> **Note**   If you develop a game that requires Game Center, you need to mark the GameKit.framework link as "Required," but also add "gamekit" to the Required device capabilities array in the project's .plist file, as shown in Figure 14-13.

Supporting Files		
▼ 📁 Supporting Files	Bundle name	$|PRODUCT_NAM
Lucky-Info.plist ⓜ	Bundle OS Type code	APPL
InfoPlist.strings	Bundle versions string, short	1.0
m main.m	Bundle creator OS Type code ⊕⊖	????
h Lucky-Prefix.pch	Bundle version	1.0
🖼 Default.png	Application requires iPhone environ	YES
🖼 Default@2x.png	▼ Required device capabilities	(2 items)
🖼 Default-568h@2x.png	Item 0 ⊕⊖	gamekit
h GameViewController.h ❓	Item 1	armv7

Figure 14-13. *Making Game Kit a required device capability*

Your users need to be logged in to Game Center to take advantage of its features. It's usually a good idea to authenticate the player at application launch so that he or she can start receiving challenges and other Game Center notifications right away. Go to ViewController.h, import the Game Kit API, and add the following property to keep track of the logged in player:

```
//
//  ViewController.h
//  Lucky
//

#import <UIKit/UIKit.h>
#import "GameViewController.h"
#import <GameKit/GameKit.h>

@interface ViewController : UIViewController

@property (weak, nonatomic) IBOutlet UILabel *welcomeLabel;
@property (strong, nonatomic) GKLocalPlayer *player;

- (IBAction)playEasyGame:(id)sender;
- (IBAction)playNormalGame:(id)sender;
- (IBAction)playHardGame:(id)sender;

@end
```

Add a custom setter for the property to update the Welcome label when the authenticated player changes. Go to ViewController.m and add the following method:

```
- (void)setPlayer:(GKLocalPlayer *)player
{
    _player = player;
    NSString *playerName;
    if (_player)
    {
        playerName = _player.alias;
    }
    else
    {
        playerName = @"Anonymous Player";
    }
    self.welcomeLabel.text = [NSString stringWithFormat:@"Welcome %@", playerName];
}
```

The Game Kit framework handles the authentication process for you. All you have to do is provide an authentication handler block to the localPlayer shared instance. Add the following helper method, which assigns such a block:

```
- (void)authenticatePlayer
{
    GKLocalPlayer *localPlayer = [GKLocalPlayer localPlayer];
    localPlayer.authenticateHandler =
    ^(UIViewController *authenticateViewController, NSError *error)
```

```
    {
        if (authenticateViewController != nil)
        {
            [self presentViewController:authenticateViewController animated:YES
                completion:nil];
        }
        else if (localPlayer.isAuthenticated)
        {
            self.player = localPlayer;
        }
        else
        {
            // Disable Game Center
            self.player = nil;
        }
    };
}
```

After an authentication handler is assigned, Game Kit tries to authenticate the local player. The outcome can be one of three possible scenarios:

1. If the user is not signed into Game Center, the authentication handler will be invoked with a login view controller provided by Game Kit. All your app needs to do then is to present the view controller at an appropriate time. Whether the user signs in, or cancels the view controller, your authentication handler will be invoked again with the new state.

2. If the user is currently signed in, no view controller is provided, and the isAuthenticated property of localPlayer returns YES. Your app can then enable its Game Center features. In this case, that means assigning the player property.

3. If the user is not signed in, or if Game Center is unavailable for some reason, no view controller is provided and the isAuthenticated property returns NO. Your app should then disable its Game Center features or stop the execution, whichever makes the most sense. In this case, because you allow anonymous playing, you simply set the player property to nil.

Finally, to start the authentication process after the main view has finished loading, make the following changes to the viewDidLoad method:

```
- (void)viewDidLoad
{
    [super viewDidLoad];

    self.title = @"Lucky";
    self.player = nil;
    [self authenticatePlayer];
}
```

That's pretty much all there is to authenticating a user. When you run your app, it will prompt you to log in or create a new account, as in Figure 14-14. Authenticated users can be passed between apps, so if you or a user have authenticated to Game Center in another app, this can be passed to your app without prompting you to log in again.

Figure 14-14. The Lucky app prompting for a Game Center account and then displaying a welcoming message on the menu screen

As a final touch before moving on to implement Game Center features, you add a button to the menu screen allowing the user to go to Game Center without leaving your app.

Displaying Game Center From Your App

Open the ViewController.xib file again and add a button so that the user interface resembles Figure 14-15.

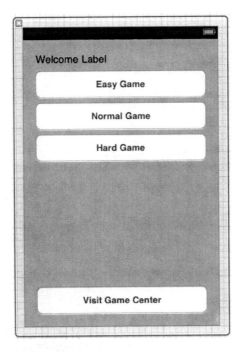

Figure 14-15. *The menu screen with a Visit Game Center button*

Create an action with the name showGameCenter: for when the user taps the new button.

Next, go to ViewController.h and add the GKGameCenterControllerDelegate protocol:

```
//
//  ViewController.h
//  Lucky
//

#import <UIKit/UIKit.h>
#import "GameViewController.h"
#import <GameKit/GameKit.h>

@interface ViewController : UIViewController<GKGameCenterControllerDelegate>

@property (weak, nonatomic) IBOutlet UILabel *welcomeLabel;
@property (strong, nonatomic) GKLocalPlayer *player;

- (IBAction)playEasyGame:(id)sender;
- (IBAction)playNormalGame:(id)sender;
- (IBAction)playHardGame:(id)sender;
- (IBAction)showGameCenter:(id)sender;

@end
```

Now, go to ViewController.m and add the following implementation to the showGameCenter: action method:

```
- (IBAction)showGameCenter:(id)sender
{
    GKGameCenterViewController *gameCenterController =
        [[GKGameCenterViewController alloc] init];
    if (gameCenterController != nil)
    {
        gameCenterController.gameCenterDelegate = self;
        [self presentViewController:gameCenterController animated:YES completion:nil];
    }
}
```

Finally, add the following delegate method to dismiss the Game Center view controller when the user is finished with it:

```
- (void)gameCenterViewControllerDidFinish:(GKGameCenterViewController *)gameCenterViewController
{
    [self dismissViewControllerAnimated:YES completion:nil];
}
```

Now that you have a basic Game Center aware app all set up, it's time to start implementing some of the Game Center features, starting with Leaderboards.

Recipe 14-2: Implementing Leaderboards

Competing against others is an essential ingredient in gaming. The possibility for players to compare highscores and compete is an effective way to increase the replay factor of any game. With Game Center, this feature is easily implemented using Leaderboards. In this recipe you build on the project from Recipe 14-1 and implement Leaderboard support.

The first thing you need to do is to define in iTunes Connect the Leaderboards you'll be using.

Defining the Leaderboards

Set up three different Leaderboards for your app, one for each difficulty level.

Log in to itunesconnect.apple.com and click the Manage Your Applications link. Select the Lucky app that you registered in Recipe 14-1 and then click the Manage Game Center button.

In the Leaderboards section, click the Add Leaderboard button. Now, in the Add Leaderboard page (see Figure 14-16), choose to create a Single Leaderboard.

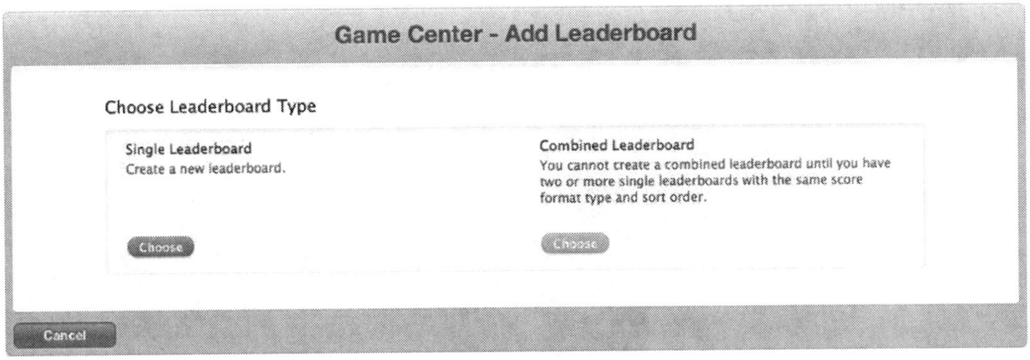

Figure 14-16. Creating a Single Leaderboard

Note   Once a leaderboard has gone live for an app, it cannot be deleted, so create leaderboards with some thought. You can have up to 25 leaderboards per app. This allows you to create multiple leaderboards for different difficulties or even one for each level of your game, whatever makes the most sense.

Fill in a name and an identifier for the leaderboard. The name is an internal name for tracking purposes and will not be displayed to the player. (The display name is configured in the next step when adding a language.) Now select the score format type; in this case, you're going to use a simple integer, but you also can use time-based, floats, and currency. Select the sort order for your leaderboard. If you want high scores at the top (typical), then sort "High to Low"; if you want your low scores at the top (for instance in a golf game), then sort "Low to High."

You also need to set up at least one language for the leaderboard. To do that, click the Add Language button. Select the language and then enter a display name for the leaderboard; this is the name that is visible to the player in the game. You can set the formatting of the score and what unit to call them (singular and plural); in this case, they are "Point" and "Points."

Figure 14-17 shows the configurations you'll be using for this Leaderboard.

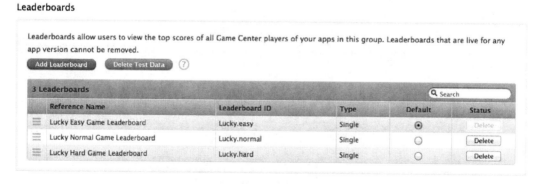

Figure 14-17. *Configuring a Leaderboard for Lucky easy game high scores*

Once complete, click Save to store the Leaderboard.

Repeat the process for the remaining two Leaderboards, this time using Lucky.normal and Lucky.hard as Leaderboard IDs. The resulting Leaderboards section should now resemble Figure 14-18.

Leaderboards

Leaderboards allow users to view the top scores of all Game Center players of your apps in this group. Leaderboards that are live for any app version cannot be removed.

Add Leaderboard   Delete Test Data   ⑦

3 Leaderboards				Q Search
Reference Name	Leaderboard ID	Type	Default	Status
Lucky Easy Game Leaderboard	Lucky.easy	Single	⦿	Delete
Lucky Normal Game Leaderboard	Lucky.normal	Single	○	Delete
Lucky Hard Game Leaderboard	Lucky.hard	Single	○	Delete

Figure 14-18. *Three Leaderboards registered for the Lucky game in iTunes Connect*

Now, let's dive in to some code.

Reporting Scores to Game Center

To report a score to Game Center, use the GKScore class. Go to the GameViewController.m file and add the following helper method:

```objc
- (void)reportScore:(int64_t)score forLeaderboard: (NSString*)leaderboardID
{
    GKScore *gameCenterScore = [[GKScore alloc] initWithCategory:leaderboardID];
    gameCenterScore.value = score;
    gameCenterScore.context = 0;

    [gameCenterScore reportScoreWithCompletionHandler:^(NSError *error)
     {
         if (error)
         {
             NSLog(@"Error reporting score: %@", error);
         }
     }];
}
```

The preceding method creates and initiates a new GKScore object, which it then reports to Game Center providing a completion handler.

> **Note**   If a score could not be reported due to connection problems, Game Kit stores the request and tries to resend the score later, making any kind of retry handling unnecessary in the preceding completion handler.

You can now use the reportScore:forLeaderboard: helper method to report the score to Game Center when a game has finished. In this app, you do this right after the user has dismissed the Game Over alert view. Add the following code to the alertView:didDismissWithButtonIndex: delegate method:

```objc
- (void)alertView:(UIAlertView *)alertView didDismissWithButtonIndex:(NSInteger)buttonIndex
{
    [self.navigationController popViewControllerAnimated:YES];
    if ([GKLocalPlayer localPlayer].isAuthenticated)
    {
        [self reportScore:_score forLeaderboard:[self leaderboardID]];
    }
}
```

The `leaderboardID` helper method returns the ID that corresponds to the current game level. Here is its implementation:

```
- (NSString *)leaderboardID
{
    switch (_level) {
        case 0:
            return @"Lucky.easy";
        case 1:
            return @"Lucky.normal";
        case 2:
            return @"Lucky.hard";
        default:
            return @"";
    }
}
```

You can now build and run the app, play a game, and your score is automatically reported to Game Center. You can use the Visit Game Center button to view the resulting Leaderboard, as shown in Figure 14-19.

Figure 14-19. A Game Center Leaderboard with one score

Recipe 14-3: Implementing Achievements

Achievements in games are similar to badges and other unlockables in other apps and games. Using Game Center Achievements you can provide your players with a notification when they reach certain milestones. Achievements make most sense in games with natural milestones, but to show you how they work you'll set one up for the Lucky game project that you've built on in Recipes 14-1 and 14-2.

Specifically, you reward the player with an Achievement if he or she has managed to use all four buttons in a game. As with Leaderboards, you'll start by registering the Achievements in iTunes Connect.

Defining Achievements in iTunes Connect

Again, log in to `itunesconnect.apple.com`. Click Manage Your Applications, click the app you have set up for Game Center, and then the Manage Game Center button.

You'll define three achievements, one for each level of difficulty. Start by clicking the Add Achievement button in the Manage Game Center page. Enter a name, ID, and point value as shown in Figure 14-20. Also, set the Hidden and the Achievable More Than Once options to No.

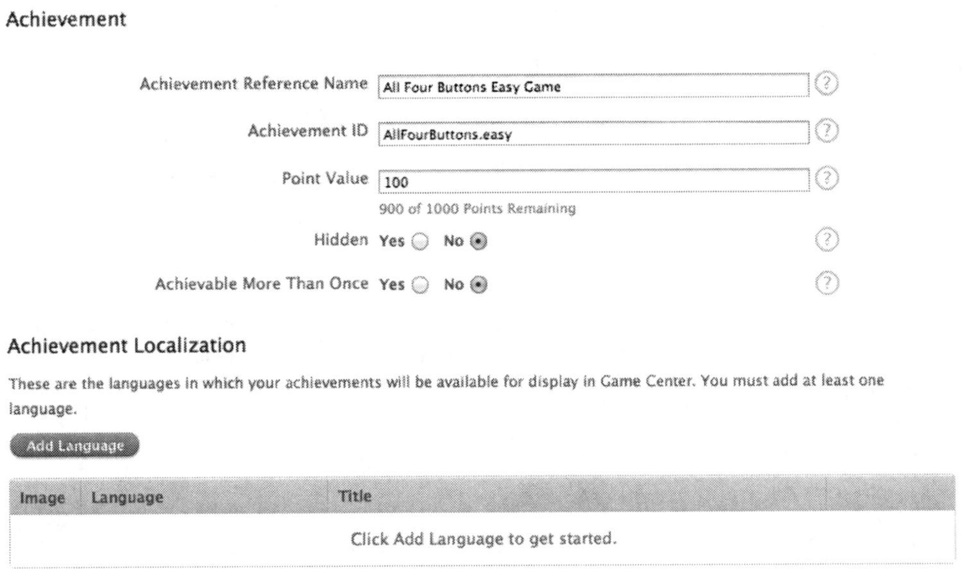

Figure 14-20. *Configuring a Game Center Achievement in iTunes Connect*

Each game can have up to 1,000 achievement points. These points can be assigned to different achievements as you see fit, but each achievement can have a max of only 100 achievement points, which is what you used here.

As with Leaderboards, you can't save an achievement until you add at least one language to it. To do that, click Add Language button. The resulting view resembles Figure 14-21 (after filling out the fields). Here, you can set the achievement title as well as the "pre-earned" description. The pre-earned description should detail how the achievement is earned. There is also an earned description, which is the description shown after the achievement is earned.

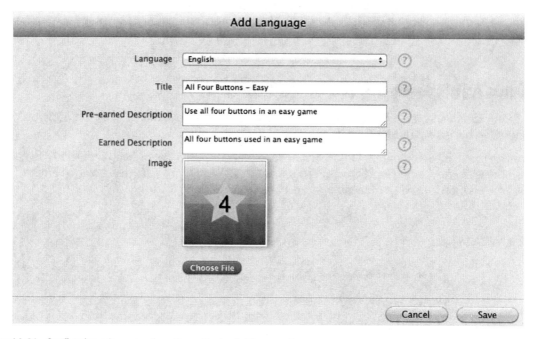

Figure 14-21. Configuring a language for a Game Center Achievement

Note that you need an image to depict the Achievement in the Game Center app. You can download premade images for the three Achievements from the web page of this book:

- `All Four Buttons Achievement Easy.png`
- `All Four Buttons Achievement Normal.png`
- `All Four Buttons Achievement Hard.png`

Save the language and then the Achievement. You can now repeat the process for the other two Achievements, using the IDs `AllFourButtons.normal` and `AllFourButtons.hard`, respectively.

Your list of Achievements should now resemble Figure 14-22.

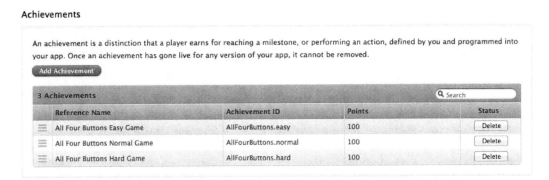

Figure 14-22. Three Achievements defined in iTunes Connect

You are now finished with the configuration of the achievements. Code writing is next.

Reporting the Achievements

This app keeps track of which buttons have been tapped. You do this using a simple
NSMutableArray. Start by going to GameViewController.h and add the following instance variable:

```
//
//  GameViewController.h
//  Lucky
//

#import <UIKit/UIKit.h>
#import <GameKit/GameKit.h>

@interface GameViewController : UIViewController<UIAlertViewDelegate>
{
    @private
    int _score;
    int _level;
    NSMutableArray *_selectedButtons;
}

// ...

@end
```

Next, go to ViewController.m and add code to instantiate the array in the initWithLevel: method:

```
- (id)initWithLevel:(int)level
{
    self = [super initWithNibName:nil bundle:nil];
    if (self)
```

```
    {
        _level = level;
        _score = 0;
        _selectedButtons = [[NSMutableArray alloc] initWithCapacity:4];
    }
    return self;
}
```

Finally, in the gameButtonSelected: action method, add the following code:

```
- (IBAction)gameButtonSelected:(UIButton *)sender
{
    if (sender.tag == 0)
    {
        // Safe, continue game
        _score += 1;
        [self updateScoreLabel];
        [self setupButtons];
        if (![_selectedButtons containsObject:sender])
        {
            [_selectedButtons addObject:sender];
            if (_selectedButtons.count == 4)
            {
                [self reportAllFourButtonsAchievementCompleted];
            }
        }
    }
    else
    {
        // Game Over
        // ...
    }
}
```

The code adds the selected button to the array if it hasn't already been added. Then, if all four buttons have been tapped, it reports the achievement to Game Center using the helper method you implement next.

Reporting an achievement is very similar to the way you report Leaderboard scores, except you use the class GKAchievement instead of GKScore. Here is the implementation of the reportAllFourButtonsAchievementCompleted helper method:

```
- (void)reportAllFourButtonsAchievementCompleted
{
    NSString *achievementID = [self achievementID];
    GKAchievement *achievement = [[GKAchievement alloc] initWithIdentifier:achievementID];
    if (achievement != nil)
    {
        achievement.percentComplete = 100;
        achievement.showsCompletionBanner = NO;
```

```
    [achievement reportAchievementWithCompletionHandler:^(NSError *error)
    {
        if (error != nil)
        {
            NSLog(@"Error when reporting achievement: %@", error);
        }
        else
        {
            [GKNotificationBanner showBannerWithTitle:@"Achievement Completed"
                message:@"You have used all four buttons and earned 100 points!"
                completionHandler:nil];
        }
    }];
    }
}
```

> **Note** For achievements that have a way to track sub milestones, you can use the percentComplete
> property to report partial progress. For the purpose of this Recipe, you directly set the
> percentComplete property to 100, which means the achievement is fully completed.

Finally, implement the achievementID helper method, which returns the achievement ID based on the current game level:

```
- (NSString *)achievementID
{
    switch (_level) {
        case 0:
            return @"AllFourButtons.easy";
        case 1:
            return @"AllFourButtons.normal";
        case 2:
            return @"AllFourButtons.hard";
        default:
            return @"";
    }
}
```

You can now build and run the app again. Start a game and try to use all four buttons. If you're lucky and don't hit a "killer," you'll be awarded an achievement. Figure 14-23 shows the Game Center view controller displaying a player who has been awarded all three available achievements.

Figure 14-23. A player who has completed three achievements in the game

With the current implementation, an achievement will be reported even though the player already has completed it. Let's fix that. What you'll do is to cache the achievements of the current player so that you can check whether an achievement has been completed before reporting it to Game Center.

Start by adding an NSMutableDictionary property to hold the achievements. Go to ViewController.h and add the following declaration:

```
//
//  ViewController.h
//  Lucky
//

#import <UIKit/UIKit.h>
#import "GameViewController.h"
#import <GameKit/GameKit.h>

@interface ViewController : UIViewController<GKGameCenterControllerDelegate>
```

```
@property (weak, nonatomic) IBOutlet UILabel *welcomeLabel;
@property (strong, nonatomic) GKLocalPlayer *player;
@property (strong, nonatomic) NSMutableDictionary *achievements;

// ...

@end
```

Next, go to ViewController.m and add the following line to the viewDidLoad method:

```
- (void)viewDidLoad
{
    [super viewDidLoad];

    self.achievements = [[NSMutableDictionary alloc] init];
    self.title = @"Lucky";
    self.player = nil;
    [self authenticatePlayer];
}
```

In the setter method of the player property, add the following lines to initiate the achievements dictionary:

```
- (void)setPlayer:(GKLocalPlayer *)player
{
    if (_player == player)
        return;
    [self.achievements removeAllObjects];

    _player = player;

    NSString *playerName;
    if (_player)
    {
        playerName = _player.alias;
        [self loadAchievements];
    }
    else
    {
        playerName = @"Anonymous Player";
    }
    self.welcomeLabel.text = [NSString stringWithFormat:@"Welcome %@", playerName];
}
```

The loadAchievements helper method loads the achievements for the current player and populates the dictionary, like so:

```
- (void)loadAchievements
{
    [GKAchievement loadAchievementsWithCompletionHandler:
    ^(NSArray *achievements, NSError *error)
```

```
    {
        if (error == nil)
        {
            for (GKAchievement* achievement in achievements)
                [self.achievements setObject: achievement
                    forKey: achievement.identifier];
        }
        else
        {
            NSLog(@"Error loading achievements: %@", error);
        }
    }];
}
```

Now initiate the game view controller with the achievements dictionary. First, go to
GameViewController.h and make the following changes:

```
//
//  GameViewController.h
//  Lucky
//

#import <UIKit/UIKit.h>
#import <GameKit/GameKit.h>

@interface GameViewController : UIViewController<UIAlertViewDelegate>
{
    @private
    int _score;
    int _level;
    NSMutableArray *_selectedButtons;
}

@property (weak, nonatomic) IBOutlet UILabel *scoreLabel;
@property (weak, nonatomic) IBOutlet UIButton *button1;
@property (weak, nonatomic) IBOutlet UIButton *button2;
@property (weak, nonatomic) IBOutlet UIButton *button3;
@property (weak, nonatomic) IBOutlet UIButton *button4;
@property (strong, nonatomic) NSMutableDictionary *achievements;

- (IBAction)gameButtonSelected:(UIButton *)sender;

- (id)initWithLevel:(int)level achievements:(NSMutableDictionary *)achievements;

@end
```

In GameViewController.m, make the corresponding changes the initWithLevel: method:

```
- (id)initWithLevel:(int)level achievements:(NSMutableDictionary *)achievements
{
    self = [super initWithNibName:nil bundle:nil];
    if (self)
```

```
    {
        _level = level;
        _score = 0;
        _selectedButtons = [[NSMutableArray alloc] initWithCapacity:4];
        self.achievements = achievements;
    }
    return self;
}
```

Next, define a helper method to get the current achievement by fetching it from the cache or create a new GKAchievement object if it doesn't exist:

```
- (GKAchievement *)getAchievement
{
    NSString *achievementID = [self achievementID];
    GKAchievement *achievement = [self.achievements objectForKey:achievementID];
    if (achievement == nil)
    {
        achievement = [[GKAchievement alloc] initWithIdentifier:achievementID];
        [self.achievements setObject:achievement forKey:achievement.identifier];
    }
    return achievement;
}
```

Finally, change the reportAllFourButtonsAchievement method to use the new helper method:

```
- (void)reportAllFourButtonsAchievementCompleted
{
    GKAchievement *achievement = [self getAchievement];
    if (achievement != nil && !achievement.completed)
    {
        achievement.percentComplete = 100;
        achievement.showsCompletionBanner = NO;
        [achievement reportAchievementWithCompletionHandler:^(NSError *error)
         {
             if (error != nil)
             {
                 NSLog(@"Error when reporting achievement: %@", error);
             }
             else
             {
                 [GKNotificationBanner showBannerWithTitle:@"Achievement Completed"
                     message:@"You have used all four buttons and earned 100 points!"
                     completionHandler:nil];
             }
         }];
    }
}
```

That's it. The app now only reports real progress and therefore does not unnecessarily use up network activity for reports that don't change the state of the Game Center.

Recipe 14-4: Creating a Simple Turn-Based Multiplayer Game

Gaming at its essence, is a social activity. While playing against a computer can be fun, playing with or against other humans puts a whole new dimension to the gaming experience. Game Kit has great support for multiplayer games, both real-time and turn-based. In this chapter you'll build a simple Tic Tac Toe multiplayer game that uses Game Center for matchmaking and the low-level network implementation.

As usual when building a Game Center aware app, start with the basic game functionality before adding any Game Center support.

Building the Tic Tac Toe Game

Create a new single-view project called "Tic Tac Toe."

Start by making this a Navigation-based app. Go to AppDelegate.h and add a UINavigationController property:

```
//
//  AppDelegate.h
//  Tic Tac Toe
//

#import <UIKit/UIKit.h>

@class ViewController;

@interface AppDelegate : UIResponder <UIApplicationDelegate>

@property (strong, nonatomic) UIWindow *window;

@property (strong, nonatomic) ViewController *viewController;
@property (strong, nonatomic) UINavigationController *navigationController;

@end
```

Switch to AppDelegate.m and make the following changes to the application:didFinishLaunchingWithOptions: method:

```
- (BOOL)application:(UIApplication *)application didFinishLaunchingWithOptions:(NSDictionary *)launchOptions
{
    self.window = [[UIWindow alloc] initWithFrame:[[UIScreen mainScreen] bounds]];
    // Override point for customization after application launch.
    self.viewController =
        [[ViewController alloc] initWithNibName:@"ViewController" bundle:nil];
    self.navigationController =
        [[UINavigationController alloc] initWithRootViewController:self.viewController];
    self.window.rootViewController = self.navigationController;
    [self.window makeKeyAndVisible];
    return YES;
}
```

Next, build the basic user interface of the game. Open the `ViewController.xib` file. To help you account for the Navigation bar when laying out your user interface elements later, go to the Attributes inspector and set Top Bar attribute in the Simulated Metrics section to "Navigation Bar."

Now, add a label and nine buttons to the view so that it resembles Figure 14-24.

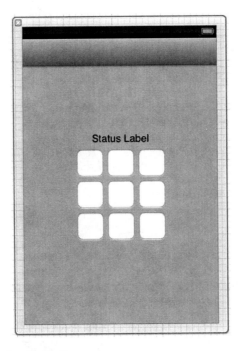

Figure 14-24. A simple user interface for a Tic Tac Toe game

Create outlets with the following names for the respective element:

- `statusLabel`
- `row1Col1Button, row1Col2Button, row1Col3Button`
- `row2Col1Button, row2Col2Button, row2Col3Button`
- `row3Col1Button, row3Col2Button, row3Col3Button`

Also, create an action with the name `selectButton` with the parameter type `UIButton`. Connect all the nine buttons to that action.

Next, go to `ViewController.h` and add the following private instance variable:

```
//
//  ViewController.h
//  Tic Tac Toe
//
```

```
#import <UIKit/UIKit.h>

@interface ViewController : UIViewController
{
    @private
    NSString *_currentMark;
}

@property (weak, nonatomic) IBOutlet UILabel *statusLabel;
@property (weak, nonatomic) IBOutlet UIButton *row1Col1Button;
@property (weak, nonatomic) IBOutlet UIButton *row1Col2Button;
@property (weak, nonatomic) IBOutlet UIButton *row1Col3Button;
@property (weak, nonatomic) IBOutlet UIButton *row2Col1Button;
@property (weak, nonatomic) IBOutlet UIButton *row2Col2Button;
@property (weak, nonatomic) IBOutlet UIButton *row2Col3Button;
@property (weak, nonatomic) IBOutlet UIButton *row3Col1Button;
@property (weak, nonatomic) IBOutlet UIButton *row3Col2Button;
@property (weak, nonatomic) IBOutlet UIButton *row3Col3Button;

- (IBAction)selectButton:(UIButton *)sender;

@end
```

Because it's not the essential part of this recipe, we skip the details of the basic game implementation and instead ask you go to the web page of this book (at www.apress.com), download the file ViewController.m and add it to your project. However, be sure you go through the code carefully so that you understand how it works before moving on.

If you've added the code correctly, you should be able to run the app now and play a game of Tic Tac Toe against yourself. Figure 14-25 shows an example of a game that's half-way complete.

Figure 14-25. An ongoing game of Tic Tac Toe

With the basic game functionality in place, you can move on to implement Game Center support. As you know by now, that starts with registering your app.

Preparing the Game for Game Center

First, you need to create a new App ID for your game in the iOS Provisioning Portal. For details on how to do this, refer to Recipe 14-1. Enter **iOS 6 Recipes Tic Tac Toe** as the App ID description and be sure you enter the bundle identifier of your project.

After you've submitted the new App ID in the Provisioning Portal, the next step is to register your app with iTunes Connect. Again, refer to Recipe 14-1 for details. To save time, use the following art files from this book's web page, for the Large App Icon and iPhone Screenshot files that you must upload as a part of the registration.

- ▓ Tic Tac Toe Large App Icon.png
- ▓ Tic Tac Toe Screenshot.png
- ▓ Tic Tac Toe Screenshot (iPhone 5).png

Also, don't forget to enable Game Center (for Single Game) in the Manage Game Center page. Enabling Game Center is all you need to do for the sake of this Recipe; there's no need to define any Leaderboards or Achievements for the Tic Tac Toe game.

When you've registered the app with iTunes Connect, you can start preparing it for Game Center. Go back to Xcode and link the Game Kit framework to your project. Then open up ViewController.h and add the following property declaration to hold a reference to the local player:

```
//
//  ViewController.h
//  Tic Tac Toe
//

#import <UIKit/UIKit.h>
#import <GameKit/GameKit.h>

@interface ViewController : UIViewController
{
@private
    NSString *_currentMark;
}

@property (weak, nonatomic) IBOutlet UILabel *statusLabel;
@property (weak, nonatomic) IBOutlet UIButton *row1Col1Button;
@property (weak, nonatomic) IBOutlet UIButton *row1Col2Button;
@property (weak, nonatomic) IBOutlet UIButton *row1Col3Button;
@property (weak, nonatomic) IBOutlet UIButton *row2Col1Button;
@property (weak, nonatomic) IBOutlet UIButton *row2Col2Button;
@property (weak, nonatomic) IBOutlet UIButton *row2Col3Button;
@property (weak, nonatomic) IBOutlet UIButton *row3Col1Button;
@property (weak, nonatomic) IBOutlet UIButton *row3Col2Button;
@property (weak, nonatomic) IBOutlet UIButton *row3Col3Button;

@property (strong, nonatomic) GKLocalPlayer *localPlayer;

- (IBAction)selectButton:(UIButton *)sender;

@end
```

The method to authenticate the local player is identical to what you did in Recipe 14-1. Go to ViewController.m and add the authenticateLocalPlayer helper method:

```
- (void)authenticateLocalPlayer
{
    GKLocalPlayer *localPlayer = [GKLocalPlayer localPlayer];
    localPlayer.authenticateHandler =
    ^(UIViewController *authenticateViewController, NSError *error)
    {
        if (authenticateViewController != nil)
        {
            [self presentViewController:authenticateViewController animated:YES
                completion:nil];
        }
```

```
        else if (localPlayer.isAuthenticated)
        {
            self.localPlayer = localPlayer;
        }
        else
        {
            // Disable Game Center
            self.localPlayer = nil;
        }
    };
}
```

As in Recipe 14-1, you try to authenticate the local player directly on app launch. Add the following line to the viewDidLoad method:

```
- (void)viewDidLoad
{
    [super viewDidLoad];
    UIBarButtonItem *playButton = [[UIBarButtonItem alloc] initWithTitle:@"Play"
        style:UIBarButtonItemStyleBordered target:self action:@selector(playGame:)];
    self.navigationItem.rightBarButtonItem = playButton;
    [self enableSquareButtons:NO];
    self.title = @"Tic Tac Toe";
    self.statusLabel.text = @"Press Play to start a game";
    [self authenticateLocalPlayer];
}
```

Finally, add a couple of elements to the user interface for displaying the two Game Center players currently participating in the match. Open ViewController.xib, add four labels, and arrange them so that the user interface resembles Figure 14-26. Note that "Playing X:" and "<Player 1 Label>," as well as "Playing O:" and "<Player 2 Label>" are separate labels.

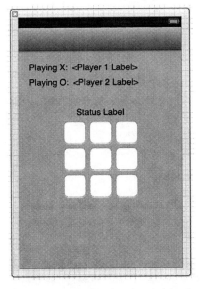

Figure 14-26. A simple Tic Tac Toe user interface with labels showing the participating players

Create outlets called `player1Label` and `player2Label` for the corresponding labels.

Now that you have the basic Game Center authentication in place, you can go on to implement the next step, which is the matchmaking feature.

Implementing Matchmaking

For this recipe, you use the standard view controller provided by the Game Kit framework, to allow the user to find other players to play your Tic Tac Toe game with, and to keep track of the games he or she is currently involved in. Using the standard view controller saves you a lot of trouble implementing these matchmaking features.

Specifically, you're going to use the `GKTurnBasedMatchmakerViewController` to handle the matchmaking. You'll start by making the main view controller conform to the `GKTurnBasedMatchmakerViewControllerDelegate` protocol. You also need to hold a reference to a `GKTurnBasedMatch` object, as well as two `GKPlayer` instances. So, go to `ViewController.h` and add the following code:

```
//
//  ViewController.h
//  Tic Tac Toe
//

// ...

@interface ViewController : UIViewController<GKTurnBasedMatchmakerViewControllerDelegate>

// ...

@property (strong, nonatomic) GKLocalPlayer *localPlayer;
@property (strong, nonatomic) GKTurnBasedMatch *match;
@property (strong, nonatomic) GKPlayer *player1;
@property (strong, nonatomic) GKPlayer *player2;

- (IBAction)selectButton:(UIButton *)sender;

@end
```

Now, return to `ViewController.m` and replace the current implementation of the `playGame:` action method with the following code:

```
- (void)playGame:(id)sender
{
    if (self.localPlayer.isAuthenticated)
    {
        GKMatchRequest *request = [[GKMatchRequest alloc] init];
        request.minPlayers = 2;
        request.maxPlayers = 2;

        GKTurnBasedMatchmakerViewController *matchMakerViewController =
            [[GKTurnBasedMatchmakerViewController alloc] initWithMatchRequest:request];
```

```
        matchMakerViewController.turnBasedMatchmakerDelegate = self;
        [self presentViewController:matchMakerViewController animated:YES
            completion:nil];
    }
    else
    {
        UIAlertView *notLoggedInAlert = [[UIAlertView alloc] initWithTitle:@"Error"
            message:@"You must be logged into Game Center to play this game!"
            delegate:nil cancelButtonTitle:@"Dismiss" otherButtonTitles:nil];
        [notLoggedInAlert show];
    }
}
```

What the preceding code does, is to check whether the user has signed in with Game Center; if not, an error message is displayed; otherwise the method proceeds to create a match request and present a matchmaker view controller.

The matchmaker view controller requires you to implement a few delegate methods to handle the result of the user's decisions. The first is if the user cancels the dialog, in which case you should simply dismiss the matchmaker view controller:

```
- (void)turnBasedMatchmakerViewControllerWasCancelled:
(GKTurnBasedMatchmakerViewController *)viewController
{
    [self dismissViewControllerAnimated:YES completion:nil];
}
```

The next scenario is if the view controller fails for some reason. Apart from dismissing the view, you also log the error:

```
- (void)turnBasedMatchmakerViewController:
(GKTurnBasedMatchmakerViewController *)viewController didFailWithError:(NSError *)error
{
    [self dismissViewControllerAnimated:YES completion:nil];
    NSLog(@"Error while matchmaking: %@", error);
}
```

Finally, if the matchmaker produced a match, the viewController:didFindMatch: delegate method is invoked with a GKTurnBasedMatch object. For now, you just store a reference to the match object, like so:

```
- (void)turnBasedMatchmakerViewController:
(GKTurnBasedMatchmakerViewController *)viewController didFindMatch:(GKTurnBasedMatch *)match
{
    [self dismissViewControllerAnimated:YES completion:nil];

    self.match = match;
}
```

Receiving the match object from Game Center is a key event when implementing a turn-based game. At that point, the app should load the game data and set up the user interface to reflect the current state of the game.

To handle these things, add a custom setter method for the `match` property. It loads the participating players and the match data, using two currently nonexistent helper methods that you'll implement in a minute:

```
- (void)setMatch:(GKTurnBasedMatch *)match
{
    _match = match;

    [self loadPlayers];
    [self loadMatchData];
}
```

Let's start with the `loadPlayers` method. Roughly what you want to do, is to identify the players participating in the match and load information about them from the Game Center. The match object contains an array of `GKTurnBasedParticipant` objects, which you can use to get the `playerIDs` you need to load the information. Because you know that a game of Tic Tac Toe contains exactly two players, which is what you defined in the matchmaking request earlier, you can extract the participant objects like so:

```
- (void)loadPlayers
{
    GKTurnBasedParticipant *participant1 = [self.match.participants objectAtIndex:0];
    GKTurnBasedParticipant *participant2 = [self.match.participants objectAtIndex:1];

    // TODO: Load player info
}
```

> **Note** The participants array of the match object is arranged in the order of how the players take turns. You can therefore assume that the first object is player 1, and the second object is player 2 of the game.

A turn-based match can start without all seats being filled. This way, a player who starts a new match can make the first move without having to wait for the other player. Because of this, the playerID of the opponent's participant object may be `nil` at this point. For that reason, you need to design your code with care so that you don't send undefined playerIDs to the `loadPlayersForIdentifiers:withCompletionHandler:` method. Add the following code to the `loadPlayers` method to handle that:

```
- (void)loadPlayers
{
    GKTurnBasedParticipant *participant1 = [self.match.participants objectAtIndex:0];
    GKTurnBasedParticipant *participant2 = [self.match.participants objectAtIndex:1];

    NSMutableArray *playerIDs = [[NSMutableArray alloc] initWithCapacity:2];
    if (participant1.playerID &&
        ![participant1.playerID isEqualToString:self.player1.playerID])
    {
        [playerIDs addObject:participant1.playerID];
    }
```

```
    if (participant2.playerID  &&
        ![participant2.playerID isEqualToString:self.player2.playerID])
    {
        [playerIDs addObject:participant2.playerID];
    }

    if (playerIDs.count == 0)
        return; // No players to load

    [GKPlayer loadPlayersForIdentifiers:playerIDs withCompletionHandler:
     ^(NSArray *players, NSError *error)
     {
         // TODO: Handle Result
     }];
}
```

Finally, when the players' objects have been loaded, you need to figure out which is which by checking their playerIDs. Here's the complete loadPlayers method:

```
- (void)loadPlayers
{
    GKTurnBasedParticipant *participant1 = [self.match.participants objectAtIndex:0];
    GKTurnBasedParticipant *participant2 = [self.match.participants objectAtIndex:1];

    NSMutableArray *playerIDs = [[NSMutableArray alloc] initWithCapacity:2];
    if (participant1.playerID && ![participant1.playerID isEqualToString:self.player1.playerID])
    {
        [playerIDs addObject:participant1.playerID];
    }
    if (participant2.playerID  && ![participant2.playerID isEqualToString:self.player2.playerID])
    {
        [playerIDs addObject:participant2.playerID];
    }

    if (playerIDs.count == 0)
        return; // No players to load

    [GKPlayer loadPlayersForIdentifiers:playerIDs withCompletionHandler:^(NSArray *players, NSError
*error)
        {
            if (players)
            {
                GKPlayer *player1;
                GKPlayer *player2;
                for (GKPlayer *player in players)
                {
                    if ([player.playerID isEqualToString:participant1.playerID])
                    {
                        player1 = player;
                    }
                    else if ([player.playerID isEqualToString:participant2.playerID])
```

```
                    {
                        player2 = player;
                    }
                }
            dispatch_async(dispatch_get_main_queue(),^{
                self.player1 = player1;
                self.player2 = player2;
            });
        }
        if (error)
        {
            NSLog(@"Error loading players: %@", error);
        }
    }];
}
```

The reason you wrap the assigning of the player1 and player2 properties within a dispatch_async call in the preceding code, is because these assignments trigger an update of the user interface, so that piece of code needs to run on the main thread.

When the player1 and player2 properties are set, the respective label should be updated. To accomplish this, add the following custom setter methods:

```
- (void)setPlayer1:(GKPlayer *)player1
{
    _player1 = player1;
    if (_player1)
    {
        self.player1Label.text = _player1.displayName;
    }
    else
    {
        self.player1Label.text = @"<vacant>";
    }
}


- (void)setPlayer2:(GKPlayer *)player2
{
    _player2 = player2;
    if (_player2)
    {
        self.player2Label.text = _player2.displayName;
    }
    else
    {
        self.player2Label.text = @"<vacant>";
    }
}
```

Now, to initiate the player labels on app launch, you simply need set the player1 and player2 properties to nil in viewDidLoad, like so:

```
- (void)viewDidLoad
{
    [super viewDidLoad];
    UIBarButtonItem *playButton = [[UIBarButtonItem alloc] initWithTitle:@"Play"
        style:UIBarButtonItemStyleBordered target:self action:@selector(playGame:)];
    self.navigationItem.rightBarButtonItem = playButton;
    [self enableSquareButtons:NO];
    self.title = @"Tic Tac Toe";
    self.statusLabel.text = @"Press Play to start a game";
    self.player1 = nil;
    self.player2 = nil;
    [self authenticateLocalPlayer];
}
```

Next, you'll turn your focus to the loadMatchData helper method. But before you start implementing that, let's add a couple of helper methods to encode and decode such data.

Encoding and Decoding Match Data

It's completely up to you to encode and decode the data you need to store the state of the game in Game Center. The only restriction is that you keep the size of the data within 64k. For the sake of this recipe, keep it simple and store the current state in a simple array, which you then transform to a NSData object using the NSKeyedArchiver class. Here is the implementation:

```
- (NSData *)encodeMatchData
{
    NSArray *stateArray = @[@1 /* version */,
    self.row1Col1Button.currentTitle, self.row1Col2Button.currentTitle,
        self.row1Col3Button.currentTitle,
    self.row2Col1Button.currentTitle, self.row2Col2Button.currentTitle,
        self.row2Col3Button.currentTitle,
    self.row3Col1Button.currentTitle, self.row3Col2Button.currentTitle,
        self.row3Col3Button.currentTitle
    ];
    return [NSKeyedArchiver archivedDataWithRootObject:stateArray];
}
```

It's generally a good idea to store a version number with the data in case you need to change the storage format in future upgrades of your app. This is why we added a number (1) as the first object of the array.

The corresponding decode helper method does the reverse and extracts the current state from the provided NSData object, like so:

```
- (void)decodeMatchData:(NSData *)matchData
{
    NSArray *stateArray = [NSKeyedUnarchiver unarchiveObjectWithData:matchData];
```

```
    [self.row1Col1Button setTitle:[stateArray objectAtIndex:1]
        forState:UIControlStateNormal];
    [self.row1Col2Button setTitle:[stateArray objectAtIndex:2]
        forState:UIControlStateNormal];
    [self.row1Col3Button setTitle:[stateArray objectAtIndex:3]
        forState:UIControlStateNormal];
    [self.row2Col1Button setTitle:[stateArray objectAtIndex:4]
        forState:UIControlStateNormal];
    [self.row2Col2Button setTitle:[stateArray objectAtIndex:5]
        forState:UIControlStateNormal];
    [self.row2Col3Button setTitle:[stateArray objectAtIndex:6]
        forState:UIControlStateNormal];
    [self.row3Col1Button setTitle:[stateArray objectAtIndex:7]
        forState:UIControlStateNormal];
    [self.row3Col2Button setTitle:[stateArray objectAtIndex:8]
        forState:UIControlStateNormal];
    [self.row3Col3Button setTitle:[stateArray objectAtIndex:9]
        forState:UIControlStateNormal];
}
```

The loadMatchData method retrieves the stored data from Game Center and decodes it using the decodeMatchData method you just added. However, if the match contains no data yet, the method will instead reset the user interface to set the state for a new game. Here is the implementation:

```
- (void)loadMatchData
{
    [_match loadMatchDataWithCompletionHandler:^(NSData *matchData, NSError *error)
    {
        dispatch_async(dispatch_get_main_queue(),^{
            if (matchData.length > 0)
            {
                [self decodeMatchData:matchData];
            }
            else
            {
                [self resetButtonTitles];
            }
            NSString *currentMark;
            if ([self localPlayerIsCurrentPlayer])
            {
                [self enableSquareButtons:YES];
                currentMark = [self localPlayerMark];
            }
            else
            {
                [self enableSquareButtons:NO];
                currentMark = [self opponentMark];
            }
            self.statusLabel.text =
                [NSString stringWithFormat:@"%@'s turn", currentMark];
        });
    }];
}
```

The preceding piece of code makes use of three helper methods that you've not yet defined. The localPlayerIsCurrentPlayer checks the currentParticipant property of the match object and compares it with the identity of the local player:

```
- (BOOL)localPlayerIsCurrentPlayer
{
    return [self.localPlayer.playerID
        isEqualToString:self.match.currentParticipant.playerID];
}
```

The localPlayerMark returns "X" or "O" depending on whether the local player is player 1 or player 2.

```
- (NSString *)localPlayerMark
{
    if ([self.localPlayer.playerID isEqualToString:self.player1.playerID])
    {
        return @"X";
    }
    else
    {
        return @"O";
    }
}
```

And the opponentMark simply returns the opposite of localPlayerMark:

```
- (NSString *)opponentMark
{
    if ([[self localPlayerMark] isEqualToString:@"X"])
    {
        return @"O";
    }
    else
    {
        return @"X";
    }
}
```

Now that you have code to load match data all set up, let's look at the methods where your app saves the data. One place where you're expected to store an updated state to Game Center is when the local player has made a move and hands over the turn to the opponent.

But before we look at updating the advanceTurn method, let's make a necessary change to the selectButton: action method. You no longer rely on the _currentMark instance variable when setting the mark of a selected square button. In fact, when you've finished implementing the Game Center support, you can completely remove the _currentMark instance variable. Instead, you can safely assume that it's the local player who is making the moves (which is right because the opponent makes his or her moves remotely from another instance of the app). So, make the following change to the existing code:

```
- (IBAction)selectButton:(UIButton *)sender
{
    if (sender.currentTitle.length != 0)
    {
        UIAlertView *squareOccupiedAlert =
            [[UIAlertView alloc] initWithTitle:@"Invalid Move"
                message:@"You can only pick empty squares" delegate:nil
                cancelButtonTitle:@"OK" otherButtonTitles:nil];
        [squareOccupiedAlert show];
        return;
    }

    [sender setTitle:[self localPlayerMark] forState:UIControlStateNormal];
    [self checkCurrentState];
}
```

Now, the new implementation of the advanceTurn method saves the current state to Game Center, disables the square buttons and hands over the turn to the opponent. Here is the new code doing this:

```
- (void)advanceTurn
{
    [self enableSquareButtons:NO];
    self.statusLabel.text =
        [NSString stringWithFormat:@"%@'s turn", [self opponentMark]];
    self.match.message = self.statusLabel.text;
    NSData *matchData = [self encodeMatchData];
    [self.match endTurnWithNextParticipants:@[[self opponentParticipant]]
        turnTimeout:GKTurnTimeoutDefault matchData:matchData completionHandler:
     ^(NSError *error)
     {
         if (error)
         {
             NSLog(@"Error advancing turn: %@", error);
         }
     }];
}
```

The preceding code hands over the turn using a helper method to identify the opponent's participant object. Here is the implementation for that method:

```
- (GKTurnBasedParticipant *)opponentParticipant
{
    GKTurnBasedParticipant *candidate = [self.match.participants objectAtIndex:0];
    if ([self.localPlayer.playerID isEqualToString:candidate.playerID])
    {
        return [self.match.participants objectAtIndex:1];
    }
```

```
    else
    {
        return candidate;
    }
}
```

Another place you should store the game state is when the game has ended. There are two reasons why this is necessary. First, this is how the opponent will know the final state of the game. Second, the players can open a game that's ended to view the final state again.

In addition to saving the final state, when a game ends your app needs to set the matchOutcome property of the participant objects. To do these things, make the following changes to the gameEndedWithWinner: method:

```
- (void)gameEndedWithWinner:(NSString *)mark
{
    NSString *message = [NSString stringWithFormat:@"%@ won!", mark];
    UIAlertView *gameOverAlert = [[UIAlertView alloc] initWithTitle:@"Game Over"
        message:message delegate:nil cancelButtonTitle:@"OK" otherButtonTitles:nil];
    [gameOverAlert show];

    self.statusLabel.text = message;
    self.match.message = self.statusLabel.text;

    GKTurnBasedParticipant *participant1 = [self.match.participants objectAtIndex:0];
    GKTurnBasedParticipant *participant2 = [self.match.participants objectAtIndex:1];
    participant1.matchOutcome = GKTurnBasedMatchOutcomeTied;
    participant2.matchOutcome = GKTurnBasedMatchOutcomeTied;

    if ([participant1.playerID isEqualToString:self.localPlayer.playerID])
    {
        participant1.matchOutcome = GKTurnBasedMatchOutcomeWon;
        participant2.matchOutcome = GKTurnBasedMatchOutcomeLost;
    }
    else
    {
        participant2.matchOutcome = GKTurnBasedMatchOutcomeWon;
        participant1.matchOutcome = GKTurnBasedMatchOutcomeLost;
    }

    NSData *matchData = [self encodeMatchData];
    [self.match endMatchInTurnWithMatchData:matchData completionHandler:
    ^(NSError *error)
    {
        if (error)
        {
            NSLog(@"Error ending match: %@", error);
        }
        //
    }];

    [self enableSquareButtons:NO];
}
```

The corresponding change to the gameEndedInTie method:

```
- (void)gameEndedInTie
{
    NSString *message = @"Game ended in a tie!";
    UIAlertView *gameOverAlert = [[UIAlertView alloc] initWithTitle:@"Game Over"
        message:message delegate:nil cancelButtonTitle:@"OK" otherButtonTitles:nil];
    [gameOverAlert show];

    self.statusLabel.text = message;
    self.match.message = self.statusLabel.text;
    NSData *matchData = [self encodeMatchData];
    GKTurnBasedParticipant *participant1 = [self.match.participants objectAtIndex:0];
    GKTurnBasedParticipant *participant2 = [self.match.participants objectAtIndex:1];
    participant1.matchOutcome = GKTurnBasedMatchOutcomeTied;
    participant2.matchOutcome = GKTurnBasedMatchOutcomeTied;
    [self.match endMatchInTurnWithMatchData:matchData completionHandler:
    ^(NSError *error)
    {
        if (error)
        {
            NSLog(@"Error ending match: %@", error);
        }
        //
    }];
    [self enableSquareButtons:NO];
}
```

If the opponent quits the game prematurely, which can be done from the matchmaking view controller, the app needs to respond to this and declare the local player as the winner. Add the following delegate method to deal with that scenario:

```
- (void)turnBasedMatchmakerViewController:(GKTurnBasedMatchmakerViewController *)viewController
playerQuitForMatch:(GKTurnBasedMatch *)match
{
    if ([self.match.matchID isEqualToString:match.matchID])
    {
        [self gameEndedWithWinner:[self localPlayerMark]];
    }
}
```

You're nearly finished with this rather extensive recipe. The only thing that's left is to handle the events triggered by the actions of the opponent.

Handling Turn-Based Events

To respond to the actions from the remote players, your app needs to assign a Turn-Based event handler. The first step to that, is to conform to the GKTurnBasedEventHandlerDelegate protocol. Go to ViewController.h and add it to the list of protocols:

```
//
//  ViewController.h
```

```
// Testing Turn-Based Game
//

// ...

@interface ViewController : UIViewController<GKTurnBasedMatchmakerViewControllerDelegate,
    GKTurnBasedEventHandlerDelegate>

// ...

@end
```

A good time to assign the event handler, is right after the local player has been authenticated. Therefore, add the following custom setter for the localPlayer property:

```
- (void)setLocalPlayer:(GKLocalPlayer *)localPlayer
{
    _localPlayer = localPlayer;
    if (_localPlayer)
    {
        [GKTurnBasedEventHandler sharedTurnBasedEventHandler].delegate = self;
    }
    else
    {
        [GKTurnBasedEventHandler sharedTurnBasedEventHandler].delegate = nil;
    }
}
```

There are two turn-based events that you need to handle. The first is when the turn has returned to the local player. Thanks to the code we've written, the only thing you need to do is to assign the match property. This sets up the game with the new state, and with the local player's turn to act:

```
- (void)handleTurnEventForMatch:(GKTurnBasedMatch *)match didBecomeActive:(BOOL)didBecomeActive
{
    self.match = match;
}
```

The second event is match ended remotely. What you need to do then is to load the match data using your decodeMatchData: helper method. This too, puts the game in a correct state:

```
- (void)handleMatchEnded:(GKTurnBasedMatch *)match
{
    if ([self.match.matchID isEqualToString:match.matchID])
    {
        [self.match loadMatchDataWithCompletionHandler:
         ^(NSData *matchData, NSError *error)
         {
             dispatch_async(dispatch_get_main_queue(),^{
                 if (matchData.length > 0)
```

```
        {
            [self decodeMatchData:matchData];
        }
        self.statusLabel.text = match.message;
    });
    }];
    }
}
```

You're now done! To test this app you need two or more Game Center accounts. It's recommended that you don't use your own account when testing Game Center features, so be sure you register a couple of test accounts.

You also need two devices to run the app simultaneously and get the real multiplayer feeling. You can however test it in the iOS Simulator, but then you need to sign out the current player and sign in the opponent between the moves.

Figure 14-27 shows the turn-based matchmaking view controller and an ongoing multiplayer game of Tic Tac Toe.

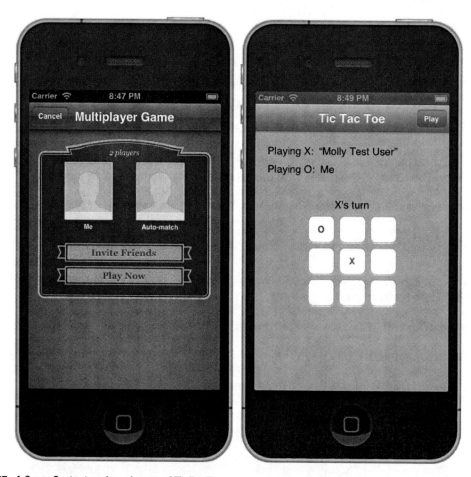

Figure 14-27. A Game Center turn-based game of Tic Tac Toe

Summary

In this chapter, you've learned how to extend your game with Game Center and Game Kit. You can include high scores in your games to encourage competition among players and establish bragging rights. You also can implement achievements that give your players a feeling of accomplishment during long levels or even easily provide mini-games within a game. Finally, you implemented basic multiplayer functionality in the form of a turn-based game to encourage even more social game play against live opponents.

Developing iOS applications is a multifarious process: a combination of visual design and programmatic functionality that requires a versatile skillset, as well as significant dedication. Thankfully, Apple provides an excellent development toolset and programming language to work with, both of which are constantly updated and improved on. With such a flexible language, tasks ranging from organizing massive data stores, to complex web requests, to image filtering can be simplified, designed, and implemented for some of the most widely used and powerful devices of our generation. Whether you use this book as a simple reference or a full guide, we hope that you can use these recipes to build stronger applications to help improve and contribute to the world of iOS technology.

Index

▓ V, W, X, Y, Z

CPSIA information can be obtained at www.ICGtesting.com
Printed in the USA
LVOW11s0028020114

367623LV00024B/1387/P